THE MISCELLANEOUS WORKS OF JOHN BUNYAN

General Editor: Roger Sharrock

VOLUME IV

A DEFENCE OF THE DOCTRINE OF JUSTIFICATION, BY FAITH

A CONFESSION OF MY FAITH, AND A REASON OF MY PRACTICE

DIFFERENCES IN JUDGMENT ABOUT WATER-BAPTISM, NO BAR TO COMMUNION

PEACEABLE PRINCIPLES AND TRUE

A CASE OF CONSCIENCE RESOLVED

QUESTIONS ABOUT THE NATURE AND PERPETUITY OF THE SEVENTH-DAY-SABBATH

A DEFENCE

OF THE

Doctrine of Iustification,

BY

FAITH IN JESUS CHRIST.

SHEWING,

True Gospel-Holiness flows from Thence.

OR,

Mr. *FOWLER'S* Pretended Design of *CHRISTIANITY*, Proved to be nothing more then to trample under Foot the Blood of the Son of God, and the Idolizing of Man's own Righteousness.

AS ALSO,

How while he pretends to be a Minister of the Church of *England*, he overthroweth the wholesom Doctrine contain'd in the 10*th.* 11*th.* and 13*th.* of the Thirty Nine Articles of the same, and that he falleth in with the Quaker, and Romarist, against them.

By *JOHN BUNYAN.*

Disalowed indeed of men, but chosen of God, and precious, 1 Pet. 2. 4.

Printed for *Francis Smith* , at the Elephant and Castle, without Temple-Bar. 1 6 7 2.

Title-page of *A Defence of the Doctrine of Justification, by Faith* (1672)

JOHN BUNYAN

*A Defence of the Doctrine of
Justification, by Faith*

*A Confession of my Faith, and A
Reason of my Practice*

*Differences in Judgment About
Water-Baptism, No Bar to
Communion*

Peaceable Principles and True

A Case of Conscience Resolved

*Questions About the Nature and
Perpetuity of the Seventh-Day-
Sabbath*

EDITED BY
T. L. UNDERWOOD

CLARENDON PRESS · OXFORD

1989

Oxford University Press, Walton Street, Oxford OX2 6DP

Oxford New York Toronto
Delhi Bombay Calcutta Madras Karachi
Petaling Jaya Singapore Hong Kong Tokyo
Nairobi Dar es Salaam Cape Town
Melbourne Auckland
and associated companies in
Berlin Ibadan

Oxford is a trade mark of Oxford University Press

Published in the United States
by Oxford University Press, New York

British Library Cataloguing in Publication Data
Bunyan, John, 1628–1688
John Bunyan.
1. Puritanism. Christian doctrine
I. Title
230'.59
ISBN 0–19–812732–4

Library of Congress Cataloging in Publication Data
Bunyan, John, 1628–1688.
[Selections. 1989]
A defence of the doctrine of justification by faith; A confession
of my faith, and a reason of my practice; Differences in judgment
about water-baptism, no bar to communion; Peaceable principles and
true; A case of conscience resolved; Questions about the nature
and perpetuity of the seventh-day Sabbath / John Bunyan; edited by
T. L. Underwood.
p. cm.—(The Miscellaneous works of John Bunyan; v. 4)
1. Theology—Early works to 1800. I. Underwood, T. L. (Ted L.)
II. Title. III. Series: Bunyan, John, 1628–1688. Selections. 1976; v.4.
BR75.B73 1976 vol. 4   230'.58 s—dc20   [230'.58] 89–9260
ISBN 0–19–812732–4

Set by Hope Services, Abingdon
Printed and bound in
Great Britain by Biddles Ltd,
Guildford and King's Lynn

To
Tamara Lyn Underwood
and
Mark Andrew Underwood

GENERAL EDITOR'S PREFACE

SINCE the middle of the nineteenth century, there has been no complete edition of Bunyan's works. The author who is known to the world for *The Pilgrim's Progress* was a prolific preacher and writer. As his first editor and friend, Charles Doe, the comb-maker of Southwark, said: 'Here are Sixty Pieces of his Labours and he was Sixty Years of Age.' Apart from his spiritual autobiography, *Grace Abounding to the Chief of Sinners*, and the three allegorical fictions, *The Pilgrim's Progress*, *The Life and Death of Mr Badman*, and *The Holy War*, these include sermons, theological treatises, biblical commentaries, and controversial works directed against the Quakers, the Latitudinarians (in the person of Edward Fowler), and the strict-communion Baptists; all these works are cast in the form of the popular sermon, with analysis of the text, abundant quotation from Scripture, a frequent employment of numbered heads and a meeting of objections by a series of questions and answers, and 'uses' or applications of the doctrine extracted from the text (these last usually conclude the work).

The purpose of this edition is to present all that Bunyan wrote in a text based on the earliest available editions, but incorporating those additions and revisions in later editions published during the author's lifetime which may reasonably be judged to have been made by Bunyan or to have received his approval. In fact, the method is that observed in the Oxford editions of *Grace Abounding*, and *The Pilgrim's Progress*. As in those editions, colloquial forms and irregular grammar (such as plural subjects with singular verbs) have been retained. The punctuation, capitalization, and italicization are those of the originals, though here the editors have corrected obvious printers' errors and inconsistencies, and anything in the accidentals which might be merely confusing to the reader. A short textual introduction with title-page transcriptions precedes each work; it includes information on the printers, a list of seventeenth-century editions, and a mention of later reprints that are of any importance.

The reader of Bunyan's *Miscellaneous Works* is more likely to be a social or ecclesiastical historian, a theologian or a psychologist, than a literary student. The introductions to the various works thus aim to give an adequate account of the background of Nonconformist life in the period, as well as of Bunyan's own life and career as minister of the Bedford separatist church and visitor to its associated churches in the eastern counties and in London. Explanatory notes have been kept to a minimum. However, a good measure of individual freedom has been left to editors in respect of the introductions and notes; it seemed, for instance, that *The Doctrine of the Law and Grace Unfolded*, Bunyan's chief theological treatise, required a fairly full consideration of his particular version of the theology of the two covenants, a dialectical system which may be said to provide the basic structure informing every work in these volumes, and indeed underlying the drama of salvation and damnation in *The Pilgrim's Progress* and other allegories.

The first attempt at a complete edition was that of Charles Doe in the Folio of 1692. This was announced in an advertisement in *Mercurius Reformatus* for 11 June 1690:

Mr. *John Bunyan*, author of *The Pilgrim's Progress*, and many other excellent Books, that have found great acceptance, hath left behind him Ten Manuscripts prepared by himself for the Press before his Death: His Widow is desired to print them (with some other of his Works, which have been already printed but are at present not to be had), which will make together a book for 10s. in sheets, in Fol. All persons who desire so great and good a work should be performed with speed, are desired to send in 5s. for their first payment to Dorman Newman, at the King's Arms in the *Poultrey*, London: Who is empower'd to give receipts for the same.

A year later, Doe issued a pamphlet, *The Struggler* (1691), telling of his efforts to bring out a collected edition of his friend's works. But when the Folio finally appeared, it contained only ten works apart from the previously unpublished ones obtained from Bunyan's widow and her son John. These were, in the order in which they appeared: *Saved by Grace, Christian Behaviour, I Will Pray with the Spirit, The Strait Gate, Gospel-Truths Opened, A Vindication of some Gospel-Truths Opened, Light for Them that Sit in Darkness, Instruction for the Ignorant, The Holy City: Or, The New Jerusalem, The Resurrection of the Dead*. It seems likely that Doe ran into trouble over copyrights, and was therefore not able to bring out the second volume that he had planned. It is noteworthy that none of Bunyan's best-selling books is represented in the Folio; it is difficult to imagine Nathaniel Ponder, another publisher in the Poultry, surrendering his control over that valuable property *The Pilgrim's Progress*; and it is significant that the Folio was finally published by William Marshall, and not by Dorman Newman, who had issued both editions of *The Holy War*. The Folio was published by subscription, and the many copies extant suggest that the subscription-list was a long one.

A second edition of the Folio was issued in 1736–7, and this included the second volume with those writings which Doe had been unable to assemble. The edition was edited by Ebenezer Chandler and Samuel Wilson (the son of Bunyan's friend John Wilson) and published by E. Gardner and John Marshall (the son of William Marshall). Three books were still not included, but these are found in the third edition of the collected works which appeared in two volumes in 1767, and was thus the first truly complete edition. There is a preface by George Whitefield. Another collected edition in six volumes by Alexander Hogg appeared in 1780.

In 1853 the complete works were re-edited by the devoted Bunyan scholar, George Offor. In the twentieth century this has continued to be the only collected edition available to the scholar. It contains an amount of painstaking if amateurish bibliographical information, and a verbose and often melodramatic evangelical commentary; as John Brown (Bunyan's biographer and minister of Bunyan Meeting, Bedford, 1854–1903) said: 'His notes . . . are occasionally a little superfluous, sometimes indeed raising a smile by their very simplicity.' Offor's edition was revised and reissued in three volumes (Edinburgh and London, 1860–2). There was also an edition in four volumes by Henry Stebbing (1859).

The great disaster of Bunyan studies was the fire which destroyed a great part of the Offor collection when it was to be auctioned at Sotheby's in 1865 (Tuesday, 29 June). Many of the surviving volumes came into the possession of Sir Leicester Harmsworth, and at the sale of the Harmondsworth Collection at Sotheby's in February 1947 passed into various public libraries. Some remained in the family or were bought back by it, and at the death of Richard Offor, George Offor's grandson and former Librarian of the University of Leeds, were presented to Elstow Moot Hall in Bunyan's birthplace. Several of the copies consulted by the present editors are badly charred books from the Offor collection.

Coleridge once drew a distinction between the Bunyan of genius and the Bunyan of the conventicle. If we accept this, the bulk of the works in this new edition represent the Bunyan of the conventicle; but Coleridge's romantic premisses, which we have in part inherited, draw a far sharper line between genius and the man rooted in his historical accidents than accuracy will admit. There is much strong, plain,

effective exhortation in the awakening sermons; many of the poems in
A Book for Boys and Girls are real poems; more important, the
Miscellaneous Works bring us up against the raw material, the subsoil,
on which the spirit of English Puritanism, which we meet in *The
Pilgrim's Progress* and experience in its historical succession, is
founded.

ROGER SHARROCK

CONTENTS

ILLUSTRATIONS

REFERENCES AND ABBREVIATIONS

[The place of publication, unless otherwise stated, is London]

BUNYAN'S WORKS

The Works of That Eminent Servant of Christ, Mr. John Bunyan, ed. Charles Doe (1692)	*1692 Folio*
The Works of John Bunyan, ed. George Offor (3 vols., Glasgow, Edinburgh, London, 1860–2)	Offor
The Miscellaneous Works of John Bunyan, general editor Roger Sharrock (Oxford, 1976–)	Oxford Bunyan
Grace Abounding to the Chief of Sinners, ed. Roger Sharrock (Oxford, 1962)	*G.A.*
The Pilgrim's Progress from This World to That Which is to Come, ed. J. B. Wharcy, rcv. Roger Sharrock (Oxford, 1960)	*P.P.*

OTHER WORKS

Biographical Dictionary of British Radicals in the Seventeenth Century, ed. Richard L. Greaves and Robert Zaller (Brighton, 1982–4)	*B.D.B.R.*
John Brown, *John Bunyan: His Life, Times, and Work*, rev. ed. Frank Mott Harrison (1928)	Brown
Dictionary of National Biography	*D.N.B.*
The Minutes of the First Independent Church (now Bunyan Meeting) at Bedford 1656–1766, ed. H. G. Tibbutt (Bedfordshire Historical Record Society Publication 55, Bedford, 1976)	*Minutes*
Oxford Dictionary of English Proverbs, third rev. ed. F. P. Wilson (Oxford, 1970)	*O.D.E.P.*
Oxford English Dictionary	*O.E.D.*
H. R. Plomer, *A Dictionary of the Printers and Booksellers . . . from 1668 to 1723* (Oxford, 1922)	Plomer

M. P. Tilley, *Dictionary of Sixteenth and Seventeenth Century Proverbs and Proverbial Phrases* (Ann Arbor, Mich. 1950)   Tilley

William York Tindall, *John Bunyan, Mechanick Preacher* (New York, 1934)   Tindall

Donald Wing, *Short-Title Catalogue of Books Printed in England . . . 1641–1700*, (3 vols., New York, 1972, 1982, 1951)   Wing

INTRODUCTION

A. THE CONTROVERSY OVER JUSTIFICATION*

(1) *Bunyan in the Post-imprisonment Years*

THE restoration of the monarchy in 1660 brought with it the restoration of Episcopacy, and subsequently those who refused to conform in matters of religion sometimes found themselves the objects of prosecution. Thus, in the years 1660–72, Bunyan suffered imprisonment for unlawful preaching, having violated the Elizabethan conventicle act. He refused to give assurances that he would cease public preaching, and attempts by other means to obtain his release were unsuccessful. But the laws against Nonconformity were selectively enforced, and in Bunyan's case the strictness of his confinement in the county gaol in Bedford varied a good deal so that at times he was able to carry on his ministerial activities. Thus he wrote and published a number of works including *Grace Abounding* (1666), he counselled and admonished church members, and he even journeyed to London to consult with other Nonconformists. The 1672 Declaration of Indulgence provided a special opportunity for imprisoned religious dissenters to seek their freedom. Ironically, Bunyan's release was obtained through the addition of his name to a petition already drawn up for nearly 500 Quakers whose doctrines he so vigorously attacked on numerous occasions.[1]

Even before Bunyan's official release from prison, however, he was called as pastor of the Bedford congregation. The *Minutes* record that at a full assembly on 21 January 1672, the congregation did 'call forth

* The editor gratefully acknowledges the support of his work by the Bush Foundation Sabbatical Fellowship Program and by a grant from the University of Minnesota Graduate School. He is also indebted to the librarians and staffs of the libraries listed in the Notes on the Texts and the footnotes, and to the following: Bancroft Library, University of California, Berkeley; Briggs and Wilson Libraries, University of Minnesota; Library of the Religious Society of Friends, London; John Rylands Library, Manchester. Copy-texts and title-page illustrations are reproduced through the courtesy of the libraries cited. The editor is also grateful to Richard L. Greaves, Geoffrey F. Nuttall, and Roger Sharrock who criticized a draft of the introduction, and to the following persons for their generous assistance: Oscar Burdick, John J. Morrison, Virginia Lundby, David W. Riley, Tamara L. Underwood, Pamela Veeder, Elizabeth Tarara Warfield, and Thomas M. Wilson.

[1] *Minutes*, pp. 56–71; Brown, pp. 151–180; Oxford Bunyan, i. xxi–xxxv.

and appoint our brother John Bunyan to the pastorall office or eldership. And he accepting thereof gave up himself to serve Christ and his church in that charge, and received of the elders the right hand of fellowship.[2] It was not long until he was able to undertake fully the responsibilities of this office. But his ministerial connections went well beyond Bedford, for while in prison he and several other Nonconformists drew up a plan for providing preachers and teachers for congregations in Bedford, Cranfield, Keysoe, and Stevington, for Newport Pagnell in Buckinghamshire, and for their satellite meetings as well. The May 1672 application for licenses for meeting places and to preach, which Bunyan himself may have written, lists twenty-seven men (including Bunyan) in twenty-six towns and villages in six counties. Thus Bunyan's post-imprisonment activities were pursued not only in northern Bedfordshire, but also in the region south and east of Bedford extending as far as London, and even beyond.[3]

One hope for this organizational plan was that it would enable the churches to withstand future persecution, and such persecution was not long in coming. The Declaration of Indulgence was cancelled in 1673, and the licenses issued in connection with it were revoked in 1675. Bunyan found himself imprisoned again for several months in 1676–7. Further complicating the lives of Nonconformists in the late 1670s and early 1680s was the growing fear of Catholic conspiracies and the increasing likelihood that the avowedly Roman Catholic Duke of York would become King James II. Bunyan described the times as 'days of trouble, especially since the discovery of the Popish Plot, for then we began to fear cutting of Throats, of being burned in our beds, and of seeing our Children dashed in pieces before our Faces.'[4] It was against a background of such fear that he urged rededication to spiritual values in *A Treatise of the Fear of God* (1679). And when the failure of the Whigs in the Exclusion Crisis was followed by renewed persecution of Nonconformists, Bunyan offered encouragement to the persecuted in his *Seasonable Counsel* (1684). He also professed loyalty to the king and in the reign of James II urged cautious co-operation

---

[2] *Minutes*, p. 71. for the other pastors of the congregation, see Brown, pp. 396–7.
[3] Richard L. Greaves, 'The Organizational Response of Nonconformity to Repression and Indulgence: The Case of Bedfordshire', *Church History*, 44 (1975), 472–84; id., 'John Bunyan and Nonconformity in the Midlands and East Anglia', *J. of the United Reformed Church History Society*, 1 (1976), 186–96. Brown, pp. 215–17. Christopher Hill, *A Turbulent Seditious and Factious People: John Bunyan and His Church* (Oxford, 1988).
[4] *Israel's Hope Encouraged*, in *1692 Folio*, p. 199. Cf. John Kenyon, *The Popish Plot* (1972), pp. 32–44.

with government efforts to effect greater religious toleration. The prospect of liberty for Nonconformists was not to be discounted, even when offered for his own purposes by a Catholic king.[5]

One of Bunyan's ministerial responsibilities in the post-imprisonment years was that of maintaining discipline in the congregation. The *Minutes* record numbers of church meetings which took up alleged misbehaviour of individual members and sometimes admonished or even excommunicated them. Among the offences are absence from church, Sabbath-breaking, card-playing, lying, debt, fraud, railing, brawling, and wife-beating. There are also such sexual offences as immodesty, 'light and wanton carriage', and fornication. The last discipline case recorded before Bunyan's death, for example, includes a letter of admonition witnessed by Bunyan and fifteen others and directed to John Wildman who has 'bin withdrawn from by the Church, for lying, railing, and scandalizing'.[6] Bunyan's successor at Bedford, Ebenezer Chandler, reported that one of Bunyan's useful characteristics as pastor was the '*Accuracy of his Knowledge in Church-discipline, and readiness to put that in practice in the Church (as occasion offered) which he saw was agreeable to the Word of God, whether Admonition, or Excommunication. . . .*'[7]

Another of Bunyan's responsibilities was preaching, an activity in which he had engaged within a year or two after joining the Bedford congregation. By 1657, he was so busily involved in this activity that he had to be relieved of his work as a deacon.[8] In the post-imprisonment years, he again took up this aspect of his ministry, preaching not only in Bedfordshire but in other areas as well, including London. In the latter, according to Charles Doe, he drew as many as 1,200 listeners on a weekday morning and 3,000 on a Sunday.[9] No doubt his growing fame as a writer helped to bring in many listeners, but his preaching itself must also have been a very strong attraction. Dr John Owen, Vice-Chancellor of Oxford University and Dean of Christ Church during the Commonwealth, and also a friend of Bunyan in London,

[5] Oxford Bunyan, ix, Introduction; xi. xv–xix.

[6] *Minutes*, pp. 76, 81, 76, 86, 83, 63, 76, 81, 84, 88 (quoted), 98–90. Wildman apparently showed some interest in being reconciled with the congregation, but the dispute was not resolved (pp. 121–2). Cf. Evelyn Curtis, *Crime in Bedfordshire, 1660–1688* (Elstow Moot Hall Leaflet 4, 1957).

[7] John Wilson and Ebenezer Chandler's preface to the reader, in *1692 Folio*, p. [2]. For Wilson and Chandler, see Brown, pp. 432, 397.

[8] *G.A.*, paras. 265–73, 282–5, pp. 82–5, 87–8. *Minutes*, p. 29.

[9] Charles Doe, 'The Struggler', in *1692 Folio*, p. [2].

reportedly declared to King Charles II, 'May it please your majesty, had I the tinker's abilities for preaching, I would most gladly relinquish all my learning.'[10] Bunyan published a number of his sermons, sometimes in considerably expanded form.[11] They included the popular *Come, & Welcome to Jesus Christ* (1678), which came out in six editions in his lifetime, and *The Greatness of the Soul* (1682), which he preached at Pinners' Hall in London. Apparently thanks to a listener, even an abstract of Bunyan's last sermon, which he preached in London less than a fortnight before his death, was published in the following year.[12]

Bunyan's fame as a writer, of course, rests primarily on his allegorical works, of which *The Pilgrim's Progress* (1678) is best known. But there is a genre, less well known, which flowed from yet another of his ministerial activities, 'contending for the faith'. 'It pleased me much', he declared in his spiritual autobiography, 'to contend with great earnestness for the Word of Faith, and the remission of sins by the Death and Sufferings of Jesus. . . .'[13] In fact, his dispute with the Quakers in the mid-1650s led to his first two published works, *Some Gospel-truths Opened* (1656) and *A Vindication of the Book Called, Some Gospel-Truths Opened* (1657), both of which received Quaker replies. Such 'tract warfare' over religious differences was not unusual, of course. In addition to heat, smoke, and light, it created a considerable body of printed polemical materials. In Bunyan's ministry, it produced, in addition to these two anti-Quaker tracts, the six controversial works which are included in this volume.[14] In the six, he contends not only for 'the remission of sins by the Death and Sufferings of Jesus', but also against requiring believers' baptism for church membership, against women worshipping separately from men, and against the seventh day Sabbath.

(2) *A Defence of the Doctrine of Justification, by Faith*

Bunyan's printed contention for 'the remission of sins by the Death and Sufferings of Jesus' was carried on primarily against the Quakers

[10] Joseph Ivimey, *A History of the English Baptists* (1811–30), ii. 41. Cf. William Orme, *Memoirs of the Life . . . of John Owen*, (1820), p. 399.

[11] Oxford Bunyan, i. xv–xvii; v, Introduction; xi. xx–xxi.

[12] Brown, p. 372, Offor, ii. 755–8.

[13] *G.A.*, para. 284. p. 87. See also N. H. Keeble, *The Literary Culture of Nonconformity in Seventeenth-Century England* (Leicester, 1987).

[14] Oxford Bunyan, i. xxi–xxxv; T. L. Underwood, ' "It pleased me much to contend": John Bunyan as Controversialist', *Church History*, 57 (1988), 456–69.

and Edward Fowler. Fowler (1632–1714) was educated at both Oxford and Cambridge and became Presbyterian chaplain to the dowager countess of Kent. As a result of her influence he was made rector of Northill, Bedfordshire in 1656. Following the Restoration, he conformed in religion, unlike his father and brother, who were ejected from their livings. In 1670, he published *The Principles and Practices of Certain Moderate Divines of the Church of England*, defending the Latitudinarian men whom he admired. But he never became part of their inner circle. Fowler was made rector of Allhallows, Bread Street, London in 1673, and in 1676 became a prebendary of Gloucester Cathedral, where he was installed as bishop in 1691.[15] Bunyan ignored neither his change from Presbyterianism to Episcopacy nor his promotion in the Church of England. More importantly, the Bedford preacher found much that was objectionable in Latitudinarianism, including its emphases on human reason and good works.

While still at Northill, Fowler published *The Design of Christianity* (1671) describing that design as the establishment of real righteousness and holiness in the world. '*The Business that brought the Blessed Jesus . . . down from Heaven . . . was the destroying of Sin in us, the Renewing of our depraved Natures, the Ennobling our Souls with Virtuous Qualities . . . ,*' he declares. Such holiness is not something merely applied externally but is 'Originally seated in the *Soul and Spirit*', and he further claims that imputed righteousness 'consists in dealing with *sincerely* righteous persons, as if they were *perfectly* so, for the sake and upon the account of Christ's Righteousness.' He warns against the dangerous error of Antinomianism and criticizes those ministers and preachers who emphasize free grace and 'never scarcely insist upon any *Duties*' and who speak of 'the Irrespectiveness of God's Decrees, the Absoluteness of his Promises, the utter disability and perfect impotence of Natural men to do any thing towards their own conversion'. He assures his readers that the design of Christianity will be accomplished in them 'if we make *our Saviour's most Excellent Life . . .* the *Pattern of our Lives*', and ends his treatise, '*Let us hear the Conclusion of the whole matter; Fear God, and keep his Commandments* (from a Principle of Love to him and them;) *for this is the whole of* (the Christian) *Man.*'[16] All of this, of course, ran contrary to Bunyan's beliefs and evoked his strong response in *A Defence of the Doctrine of Justification, by Faith* (1672).

---

[15] *D.N.B.* s.v.

[16] Edward Fowler, *The Design of Christianity* (1671), pp. 3, 5, 225–6, 261–2, 296, 308.

Theologically the Bedford tinker was a strict Calvinist who at times evinced antinomian tendencies. In addition, his concept of God was influenced by the emphasis on the wrath–grace dichotomy of Luther, whose spiritual struggle was similar to his own. His first doctrinal treatise, *The Doctrine of the Law and Grace Unfolded* (1659), and his subsequent works demonstrate the consistency of his basic views over the years. To Bunyan, God's honour and justice required satisfaction and atonement for the sin of fallen humankind, which only Christ, the God-Man, could provide. The justification which resulted from Christ's atonement was imputed to the elect, and faith was divinely bestowed as the instrument enabling them to embrace the justifying righteousness of Christ. In all of this, Bunyan emphasized the inability of fallen human beings to affect their own salvation in any degree. Election, justification, the imputation of righteousness, and the bestowing of faith were in no measure conditional or dependent upon an act of the human creature. To Bunyan, good works, human choice, co-operation with the divine will, and the like did not play a part in salvation.[17] It is no wonder then that he dated his preface in *Defence* just six weeks after he obtained a copy of Fowler's *Design* and while he was still in prison.

In his *Defence*, Bunyan gives attention first to his basic disagreement with Fowler over the nature of holiness, and then goes on to refute *The Design of Christianity* chapter by chapter. He perceives Fowler's position as being in the spirit of the Old Covenant, holding the design of Christ's work to be the restoring of the righteousness of Adam before the fall, and emphasizing the importance of the Old Testament law, human nature and reason, and righteousness and good works as contributors to justification. All such principles of Fowler he denounces as 'Diametrically opposite to the simplicity of the Gospel of Christ'.[18] Bunyan, as the avowed advocate of that Gospel, writes of the New Covenant, the Covenant of Grace. He describes Christ as the God-Man who perfectly fulfils the law and justice of God and whose

---

[17] Richard L. Greaves, *John Bunyan* (Studies in Reformation Theology 2, Abingdon, 1969), chs. 1–4; id., 'John Bunyan: Tercentenary Reflections', *American Baptist Quarterly*, 7 (1988), 496–508. Richard Baxter considered Fowler incautious in *How far Holiness is the Design of Christianity* (1671), and later criticized Bunyan's Antinomianism in *The Scripture Gospel Defended* (1690). See also Baxter's *Reliquiae Baxterianae*, ed. Matthew Sylvester (1696) Part 3, p. 85.

[18] Below p. 11. Cf. Dewey D. Wallace, jun., *Puritans and Predestination* (Chapel Hill NC, 1982), pp. 158–90. See also Alister E. McGrath, *IUSTITIA DEI: A History of the Doctrine of Justification*, i (1986), ii (forthcoming).

righteousness is therefore greater than that of Adam before the fall. He argues that Christ's righteousness is imputed to the ungodly while they are still ungodly, and they are thereby justified. He discusses the importance of acts of Christian holiness, but contrasts Fowler's natural human righteousness with the true Gospel righteousness, which involves faith in Christ, the work of the Holy Ghost, and a new heart and spirit in the Christian.

Bunyan includes several images from common life in this work. He describes, for example, the moral acts of natural man as doing things in the human sphere, 'as the Beast, the Hog or Horse doth things in his'. In contrasting human with divine righteousness, he declares that the Old Testament law and its perfection is swallowed up 'even as the light of a Candle, or Star is swallowed up by the light of the Sun'. But his most powerful language is reserved for more direct attacks on Fowler and his principles, which he likens to those of the Socinians and the Quakers. For example, Fowler is said to 'spit your intended venome at Christ', perhaps to be among those priests who 'have for the Love of filthy Lucre . . . made Shipwrack of their former Faith,' to be a 'Latitudinarian, that can, as to Religion, turn and twist like an Eel on the Angle; or rather like the Weather-cock that stands on the Steeple,' to be among those who prefer 'the Snivel of their own brains', to have a 'Devilish design to promote Paganism', and to need to change his views 'or at the last stick in the jaws of Death and everlasting Desperation'. Bunyan concludes, 'Your Book Sir is begun in Ignorance, mannaged with Errour, and ended in Blasphemy.'[19] Bunyan then ends his own book with short sections pointing out Fowler's disagreement with certain doctrines of the Church of England, and illustrating the similarity of his views to those of the Jesuit Edmund Campion (1540–81) and the Quaker William Penn (1644–1718). Latitudinarians, Socinians, Roman Catholics, and Quakers were all alike in their grievous error concerning justification and good works. And Fowler was guilty of the same error.

The dispute did not end with Bunyan's treatise, however. In the same year there appeared *Dirt Wip't Off* (1672), published anonymously in answer to Bunyan's 'Vile Pamphlet'. The work summarizes Fowler's *Design*, which Bunyan is accused of misrepresenting, and rebuts some of the Bedford tinker's views, but sheds little additional light on the basic issues. The author's vituperative exclamations are frequent as he

[19] Below pp. 16, 24, 39, 82, 102, 103, 106, 25, 123.

denounces Bunyan as a *'Ranting Antinomian'* who is guilty of 'gross ignorance' and of having an 'unchristian Spirit', and who urges 'wofully silly arguments'. The author also declares that Christ's *imputed* righteousness has in Bunyan's case only produced 'the most outrageous Fury, the most turbulent Spirit, the most reviling and defaming Pen and Tongue, and consequently the most malicious Soul'.[20]

In spite of *Dirt Wip't Off*, Bunyan did not direct any additional works against Fowler by name. However, his *Light for Them That Sit in Darkness* (1675) seems aimed at some of the views of Fowler and of the Quakers, and inveighs against those who *'adhere to a few of the Rags of their own Fleshly Righteousness*, and so become pure in their own Eyes, yet are not purged by Blood, from their Filthiness'.[21] *The Strait Gate* (1676) includes a list of false professors, among whom is the *'temporizing Latitudinarian'* as well as the Socinian and the Quaker.[22] In addition, Bunyan may have had Fowler in mind when he created the characters of Ignorance and By-ends for *The Pilgrim's Progress*. The former reflects Fowler's doctrinal position. 'I shall be justified before God . . . through his gracious acceptance of my obedience to his Law,' Ignorance asserts in his verbal exchange with Christian, explaining in another place that 'I have been a good Liver, I pay every man his own; I Pray, Fast, pay Tithes, and give Alms.'[23] Thus, as Bunyan in *Defence* calls Fowler a thief for trying to come to God by a wrong way, so Christian calls Ignorance a thief and robber for trying to enter the Celestial City by a crooked lane.[24]

By-ends represents Fowler's character and personality. In *A Few Sighs from Hell* (1658), Bunyan warned the person 'that for by-ends dost carry on an hypocrites profession' about the 'extreme torment, and anguish so soon as ever thou dost depart this world'. As he later constructed the person and name of By-ends for *The Pilgrim's Progress*, he may also have been cognizant of Fowler's derogatory reference to those who thought holiness as a design of Christianity 'was at best but a *Bye-one'*.[25] In any case, By-ends is described as a gentleman who has

[20] *Dirt Wip't Off* (1672), pp. 40, 27, 46. Brown (p. 218) suggests the work may have been a joint effort by Fowler and his curate.
[21] Oxford Bunyan, viii. xxxvii–xliv, 50 (quoted).
[22] Oxford Bunyan, v. 125–7.   [23] *P.P.*, pp. 147, 123–4.
[24] Below p. 37. *P.P.*, p. 162. Some of Fowler's views may also be reflected in Wordly-Wiseman, a gentleman who lives in the town of Carnal-Policy, attends church in the town of Morality, and sends Christian to see Legality and his Son Civility to find relief from his burden. *P.P.*, pp. 16–25.

family and friends among the great and the wealthy, and who is interested in advancement and willing to alter his religion for that end. By-ends admits to Christian and Hopeful. "'Tis true, we somewhat differ in Religion from those of the stricter sort, yet but in two small points: First, we never strive against Wind and Tide. Secondly we are always most zealous when Religion goes in his Silver Slippers; we love much to walk with him in the Street if the Sun shines and the people applaud it.' As Bunyan criticizes Fowler's acquisitive and weathercock qualities in *Defence*, so Christian condemns such qualities in *The Pilgrim's Progress* as he declares to By-ends '*If you will go with us you must go against Wind and Tide, the which I perceive is against your opinion: You must also own Religion in his Rags, as well as when in his Silver Slippers, and stand by him too when bound in Irons, as well as when he walketh the Streets with applause.*' Ignorance—like the Jesuit, the Quaker, the Socinian, and the Latitudinarian—trusts in human works rather than in divine grace, a major error leading to disastrous consequences. By-ends's error is of a different order, but with similar potential, for on the way to the Celestial City he and his companions stop at Demas's silver mine and then are never seen again.[26]

B. THE OPEN MEMBERSHIP CONTROVERSY

(1) *Bunyan and the Baptists*

Although the New Testament provides no explicit references to the administration of baptism to infants as the means of entrance into the Christian community, from the third century such practice was virtually universal. However, at the time of the Reformation, Anabaptists on the Continent, and later Baptists in England, rejected paedobaptism in favour of 'believers' baptism' on the grounds of New Testament authority and practice.[27] For some English Baptists, there arose the

[25] Oxford Bunyan, i. 301. Fowler, *Design*, p. 2; Tindall, p. 60.

[26] *P.P.*, pp. 98–108 (pp. 99–100 quoted). Cf. Oxford Bunyan, i. xxxviii–lvi; Tindall, pp. 60–3. For further analysis of the latitudinarianism which Fowler embraced and Bunyan rejected, see Isabel Rivers, 'Grace, Holiness, and the Pursuit of Happiness: Bunyan and Restoration Latitudinarianism', in N. H. Keeble (ed.), *John Bunyan: Conventicle and Parnassus: Tercentenary Essays* (1988), pp. 45–69.

[27] Oscar Cullmann, *Baptism in the New Testament* (Studies in Biblical Theology No. 1, Chicago, 1950), trans. by J. K. S. Reid. Johannes Warns, *Baptism* (Grand Rapids, Mich. 1958), trans. G. H. Lang. J. D. C. Fisher, *Christian Initiation: Baptism in the Medieval West* (Alcuin Club Collections, 47, 1965); *Christian Initiation: The Reformation Period*

further question of whether persons baptized as infants had to be rebaptized as believers in order to be church members. Or could paedobaptists and antipaedobaptists enjoy membership together in the same congregation? It was this issue which was the focus of the second controversy Bunyan entered in 1672. It resulted in the publication of *A Confession of my Faith, and A Reason of my Practice* (1672), *Differences in Judgment About Water-Baptism, No Bar to Communion* (1673), and *Peaceable Principles and True* (1674), and brought him into conflict with certain of the Baptists.

Whether in such controversy Bunyan was contending against *fellow* Baptists, however, has itself been a subject of controversy. Some writers, for example, have concluded that Bunyan was more likely a Congregationalist than a Baptist, citing as evidence the fact that in these three works he argued against the requirement of believers' baptism for church membership and communion, that parish registers recorded the baptisms of an infant daughter Elizabeth at Elstow in 1654 and an infant son Joseph at St Cuthbert's, Bedford in 1672, and that Bunyan applied for preaching licences in 1672 for himself and others as 'Congregationall'. Other writers, however, have maintained that the Elstow register recorded Elizabeth's birth, not her baptism, that the Joseph baptized in 1672 was actually Bunyan's grandson, that the Congregational designation was used indifferently to describe both Independents and Baptists, and have concluded that Bunyan was indeed a Baptist but of the 'open membership' variety. Bunyan's biographer, John Brown, described him as 'a Baptist of a very mild type'.[28]

The debate over Bunyan's denominational inclinations warns of the dangers of insufficiently recognizing the fluidity of thought and practice of the times and of drawing lines of division between seventeenth-century sects more sharply than they themselves might

(Alcuin Club Collections, 51, 1970). A. C. Underwood, *A History of the English Baptists* (1947), pp. 15–62. T. L. Underwood, 'Child Dedication Services Among British Baptists in the Seventeenth Century', *Baptist Quarterly*, 23 (1969), 165–69.

[28] Thomas Armitage, *A History of the Baptists* (New York, 1890), pp. 474–539; William Urwick, *Bible Truths & Church Errors, Including a Lecture upon John Bunyan Not a Baptist* (1888), pp. 75–104, 259–60; Brown, pp. 219–25, 236–8, W. T. Whitley, 'The Bunyan Christening, 1672', *Transactions of the Baptist Historical Society*, 2 (1911), 255–63; J. Hobson Thomas, 'Bunyan the Baptist', *The Baptist Quarterly*, 4 (1928), 97–103; Joseph D. Ban, 'Was John Bunyan a Baptist?', *The Baptist Quarterly*, 30 (1984), 367–76; James F. Forrest and Richard L. Greaves (ed.), *John Bunyan: A Reference Guide* (Boston, Mass., 1982), pp. 121–5.

have done.[29] Bunyan's two earliest biographers claimed that he was
baptized as a believer, and in one of his own printed works Bunyan
referred to himself as an Anabaptist.[30] Indeed, the argument which he
had with Baptists in these three works was not over the relative merits
of paedobaptism and believers' baptism, for he agreed with his
opponents on both the object and mode of baptism, and he described
those persons who did not hold to this position as 'wanting light'.
Where he differed with his adversaries was at the point of requiring
this baptism for church membership and communion. Bunyan erected
no such 'bar to communion'.

The Bedford pastor ws not alone in adhering to this open
membership approach. Henry Jessey, who was rebaptized in 1645,
followed the practice in his London congregation where he was pastor
from 1637 until his death in 1663. The Broadmead church in Bristol,
which was in communication with Jessey's congregation, also practised
open membership, treating 'saints as saints'. In the Bedford church,
which also had contacts with Jessey, Bunyan was carrying on the
practice of his predecessors.[31] According to the account of John
Gifford (d. 1655), the congregation's first pastor, the basis for
admission to the church's fellowship from the beginning was 'faith in
Christ and holiness of life, without respect to this or that circumstance
or opinion in outward and circumstantiall things'. Further, concerned
about the danger of members separating from the church over
'circumstantials', Gifford charged his flock 'that none of you be found
guilty of this great evill, which whiles some have committed and that
through a zeale for God, yet not according to knowledge, they have
erred from the lawe of the love of Christ, and have made a rent from
the true Church which is but one'. In an understanding reached with
the congregation in 1691, its pastor Ebenezer Chandler was to be
allowed liberty in baptizing infants but without promoting the practice,
and church members were to have similar freedom in following

[29] Christopher Hill, 'History and Denominational History', The Baptist Quarterly, 22 (1967), 65–71.
[30] G.A., p. 171; 1692 Folio, p. [873]; Oxford Bunyan, v. 153.
[31] Minutes, pp. 28, 31, 34, 77, 79. For other open membership congregations see A. C. Underwood, op. cit., n. 27 above, p. 69; G. F. Nuttall, Visible Saints: The Congregational Way 1640–1660 (Oxford, 1957), pp. 119–20; E. P. Winter, 'The Lord's Supper: Admission and Exclusion Among the Baptists of the Seventeenth Century', The Baptist Quarterly, 17 (1958), 273. Following his death, Jessey's congregation adopted the closed membership principle thanks partly to the influence of William Kiffin (Tindall, p. 240; Minutes, pp. 79–80).

believers' baptism but were to forbear 'discourse and debates on it that may have a tendency to break the peace of the church'.[32]

Although the open membership practice of the Bedford church was not unique, neither was it common. General Baptists and most Particular Baptists held to the opposite position.[33] The *1644 Confession*, the first printed by the Particular Baptists in England, gave a significant place to the doctrine of baptism, claiming that it was to be administered to persons professing faith, by means of dipping or plunging which signified the cleansing of the soul as well as death, burial, and resurrection with Christ. Perhaps it was only implied that the church was composed solely of visible saints thus baptized who together partook of the Lord's supper, but in the 1646 revision of the *1644 Confession* the restriction of such participation was made explicit.[34] In the same year, apparently to clarify this and certain other points, the London Particular Baptist Benjamin Coxe published *An Appendix, to a Confession of Faith* in which he argued that 'every beleever ought to desire Baptism, and to yeeld himself to be baptized . . . ,' that 'a company of baptized beleevers so agreeing and joining together, are a church or congregation of Christ . . .,' and that we 'doe not admit any to the use of the Supper . . . but disciples baptized. . . .'[35] Although the Bedford pastor obviously had more in common theologically with Particular than with General Baptists, he was clearly out of step with both groups on this issue.

(2) *A Confession of my Faith, and A Reason of my Practice*

Bunyan's writing of *A Confession* while still 'in bonds' served three purposes. First, it constituted a plea for freedom. As he explains in the preface, people think his long imprisonment is strange, so that he here presents his principles and practice, which he held when first imprisoned and which he has since examined and reaffirmed. Thus readers can judge for themselves if his position is characterized by heresy, rebellion, or anything deserving nearly twelve years of

---

[32] *Minutes*, pp. 17, 19, 93–4.
[33] B. R. White, *The English Baptists of the 17th Century* (1983), pp. 9–10.
[34] Article XXXIII, *1644 Confession*, in *Baptist Confessions of Faith*, ed. William L. Lumpkin (Philadelphia, 1959), p. 165; Article XXXIX, *1646 Confession*, in *Confessions of Faith* (Hanserd Knollys Society Publication 10, 1854), ed. Edward Bean Underhill, p. 41. See also B. R. White, 'The Doctrine of the Church in the Particular Baptist Confession of 1644', *J. of Theological Studies*, NS 19 (1968), 570–90.
[35] Benjamin Coxe, *An Appendix, to a Confession of Faith* (1646), pp. 9–11.

imprisonment. Second, the work fulfilled something of a pastoral responsibility in making his faith and practice clear at the beginning of his pastorate in Bedford.[36] Finally, as would be revealed in his next printed work on the subject, it served to counter some eighteen years of attempts to divide the Bedford congregation and others in the region over the open membership issue.

Bunyan begins *A Confession* with an overview of certain basic doctrines, then proceeds to give more detailed attention to the doctrines of imputed righteousness, election, calling, the scriptures, and magistracy. In discussing the last, he claims that many mercies are received from well-qualified magistrates, but poignantly adds that if any are otherwise inclined, *'let us shew our christianity in a patient suffering for well doing, what it shall please God to inflict by them'*.[37]

Most of this work, however, is devoted to a defence of Bunyan's practice of 'Communion' or the 'Communion of Saints', which he defines as fellowship in the things of the Kingdom of Christ. Such communion encompasses both church membership and the right of participation in the Lord's Supper. Bunyan's arguments include several major points. First, he admits that in Old Testament times circumcision was an initiating ordinance, without which none were to be admitted to the Old Testament church. Even then, he points out, Moses and Joshua admitted hundreds of thousands of the un-circumcised. In contrast to Old Testament circumcision, however, New Testament baptism is not an initiating ordinance, for it does not make persons members of any particular visible church. Admitting to the church and baptizing are distinct acts in the New Testament. The visible church is a community of visible saints, and because persons are believers and visible saints *before* baptism, it is therefore such sainthood, not baptism, which is the basis for church communion.

As a practical matter, then, how can it be determined *who* are visible saints and worthy of church communion? Visible saints are known by their faith and holiness of life, and this is discovered by their own testimony and if necessary by other witnesses, Bunyan argues. As believers, they experience a spiritual circumcision which becomes visible when confessed outwardly by word and life. Water baptism serves to strengthen persons' own faith by signifying their death, burial, and resurrection with Christ. Further, distinguishing between inward baptism of the spirit and outward baptism by water, Bunyan

[36] *Minutes*, pp. 70–1.   [37] Below, p. 153.

declares that the unbaptized believer 'hath the heart, power and doctrine of Baptism: all then that he wanteth, is but the sign, the shadow, or the outward circumstance thereof . . .' and that the 'best of Baptisms he hath; he is Baptized by that one spirit; he hath the heart of Water-baptism, he wanteth only the outward shew, which if he had would not prove him a truly visible Saint . . .'[38] He concludes that such visible saints who, for want of light, have not submitted to outward baptism should be received as saints, not excluded from church communion as if they were openly profane. Such a reception of visible saints is correlative with the spirit of love, edification, and unity. Finally, Bunyan professes his esteem for the two 'shaddowish' or 'figurative' ordinances which Christ has given to the church, but warns against ascribing more to them than was first ordered, for ''tis possible to commit Idolatry, even with Gods own appointments'.[39]

In his preface to the reader, Bunyan claims that he has not in this work '*abusively presented my Reader, with other doctrine or practices, then what I held*'. But he does describe something of his opponents' position, occasionally in a dialogue. And he does, in fact, include provocative statements, as when he declares that 'your dulness and deadness, and imperfections also reproach the holyness of God,' that 'thou errest in a substance,' that '*Carnall Christians with outward circumstances, will if they be let alone, make sad work in the Churches of Christ*,' and that his adversaries' action 'is a Prop to Antichrist'. He even suggests that their divisive practice is responsible for bringing down 'these judgments, which at present we feel and groan under'.[40]

(3) *Differences in Judgment About Water-Baptism, No Bar to Communion*

Given such provocations, it is not surprising that printed responses were forthcoming from certain Baptists. John Denne published *Truth Outweighing Error* (1673), and Thomas Paul wrote *Some Serious Reflections* (1673) for which William Kiffin provided a preface. Denne (fl. 1645–99), a General Baptist, was the son of the Baptist leader Henry Denne, who earlier defended Bunyan's right to preach. In 1645, the younger Denne was baptized and joined the Fenstanton, Huntingdonshire, congregation. He became influential among Baptist churches in that county and in Cambridgeshire. Little is known about

---

[38] Below, p. 172.
[40] Below, pp. 135, 173, 180, 183.

Thomas Paul (fl. 1673–4), whose writing is the least articulate of the three. He was probably a member of the particular Baptist church in London which Kiffin served for much of his life. Paul also participated in a controversy against the Quakers. Kiffin is the best known of these respondents. Over his long lifetime (1616–1701) he became a prosperous London merchant, served as an MP for Middlesex during the Interregnum, and following the Restoration used his influence in political circles to relieve the sufferings of Nonconformists. Formerly a member of an Independent congregation, he adopted Baptist views in 1642, was a signatory of the *1644 Confession*, served as pastor of the Devonshire Square church in London, and was a leader among Particular Baptists.[41]

In the counter-attack mounted by these writers, appeals to biblical authority are focused upon the great commission and the practice of the New Testament church. Thomas Paul, for example, declares that according to Christ's commission, 'ministers are, first to Disciple, and then Baptize them, so made Disciples; and afterward teach them to observe all that Christ had commanded, as to other ordinances of Worship'. Denne points out that following the conversions of Paul and Cornelius, both men were devout and holy like Bunyan's unbaptized believers, but both were still required to be baptized. Bunyan's opponents reject his arguments about love, edification, and unity and claim that the holiness of visible saints involves obedience to Christ's ordinances, and that true charity and friendship require one to tell the unbaptized of their duty to obey. According to Kiffin, Christians are 'not for Communion sake to leap over the Order Jesus Christ hath Prescribed in his Word . . .'.[42] The counter-attack also includes salvos of indignation and condemnation. Bunyan is accused of disparaging Gospel truths, of acting like 'one of *Machevel's* [Machiavelli's] Schollers', of vilifying the ordinance of baptism, and of being a person whose words are 'like the Oracles of the Devils' and who with his doctrine 'ought to be exploded, as a detected Gangrene'. Perhaps for Bunyan the most maligning statement was one that associated him with

---

[41] *B.D.B.R.*, s.vv.; Henry Denne, *The Quaker No Papist* (1659); T. L. Underwood, 'The Baptist Henry Denne and the Quaker Doctrine of the Inner Light', *Quaker History*, 56 (1967), 34–5. Brown, p. 223, wrongly attributes *Truth Outweighing Error* to 'Penn'. As a General Baptist, John Denne also gave some attention to the doctrinal statements in Bunyan's *Confession*, objecting to his strongly Calvinistic view of divine election.

[42] Thomas Paul, *Some Serious Reflections* (1673), pp. [7]–[8], 26–9, 46–7; John Denne, *Truth Outweighing Error* (1673), pp. 44–6, 53–4, 59, 62. Their biblical references include Matt. 28, Acts 2: 28 and 22: 16.

his old enemies the Quakers by pointing out that he 'hath often cryed out against others for saying, *The Light within is the Rule for Christians to walk by*; but now he himself confidently affirms it'.[43]

Bunyan's response, *Differences in Judgment About Water-Baptism, No Bar to Communion* (1673), is directed only against Paul and Kiffin. Less provocative and more moderate in tone than *A Confession*, it reveals more of the dispute's background. For example, Bunyan claims that closed communion Baptists had attempted to divide his congregation and others in the region over this issue for some eighteen years— about as long as Bunyan has been a member of the Bedford church. 'Yea, my self they have sent for, and endeavoured to perswade me to break Communion with my Brethren,' he declares. The *Minutes* record few explicit references to baptism, but some divisiveness and withdrawals are noted, and Gifford's previously cited admonition corroborates the presence of such a problem early in the life of the congregation. Bunyan's charge that 'the Persons which then they prevailed upon, are now a stink, and reproach to Religion' may refer to the case of John Child, his former colleague, who withdrew from the congregation in 1658, perhaps influencing others to do the same. Following the Restoration, Child turned further away from his earlier religious position, criticizing in print those who dissented from the Church of England. In *A Moderate Message for Quakers, Seekers, and Socinians* (1676), he threw out a challenge to Bunyan to debate whether in the church order established by Christ, 'Baptism by water is not to go before the celebration of the Lords supper . . .'. Later, Child became despondent for having turned against his former religious associates and in 1684, he commited suicide.[44]

Bunyan also reveals in *Differences* that *A Confession* was printed before he spoke with any of his opponents 'or knew whether I might be accepted of you', but that following its publication he received a letter from them inviting him to meet for a discussion. Bunyan apparently advised them *not* to defer their answer to *A Confession* until they spoke with him, and although he was actually in London, proceeded to leave without meeting them. I 'counted not my self, being a dull-headed man, able to engage so many of the chief of you, as I was then informed

[43] Paul, *Some Serious Reflections*, pp. 18, 42; Denne, *Truth Outweighing Error*, pp. [2], 17, 124, 78.
[44] Below p. 197. *Minutes*, pp. 22–3, 31–3; John Child, *A Moderate Message for Quakers, Seekers, and Socinians* (1676), p. 75. As a colleague of Bunyan, Child participated with him in a debate against Quakers, and with others signed a note to the reader in Bunyan's second printed work (see Oxford Bunyan, i. xxiv–xxvi).

intended to meet me,' he explains. He also feared being misrepresented and being involved in personal, contentious disputes.[45] In his next printed work on the subject, Bunyan also claims that John Owen agreed to write an epistle for *Differences* but that Bunyan's adversaries dissuaded him from doing so. But if he lost Owen's help, he gained assistance from another source, for he appends '*the Opinion of Mr. Henry Jesse, in the Case, which providentially I met with, as I was coming to* London *to put my Papers to the Press, and that it was his Judgment is Asserted to me, known many years since to some of the Baptists, to whom it was sent, but never yet Answered . . .'*.[46]

Bunyan's *Differences* is for the most part a rather plodding refutation of selected criticisms raised by Paul and Kiffin. However, there are occasional sparks of energy and forcefulness, and there are attempts, not always successful, to provide elaboration and clarification of his views. Thus in response to Paul's New Testament examples of church members being baptized, Bunyan contends that even if all New Testament church members were baptized, this does not mean that baptism is essential unless it is specifically required. Referring to such a supposed requirement and the resulting exclusion of unbaptized visible saints from church communion, he declares, '*There is not in all the Bible one syllable for such a Practice . . .*'. 'Is it not a wicked thing to make *bars* to Communion, where *God* hath made *none?*', he asks. He further argues that not only are churches not forbidden to receive unbaptized visible saints into communion, but they are in fact commanded to do it, for God and Christ have done so.[47] Thus Bunyan concludes that such persons who for want of light have not been outwardly baptized by water, should not be barred from communion. He pleads forcefully for 'a bearing with our Brother, that *cannot* do it for *want* of *Light*,' and refuses to let 'Water-baptism be the Rule, the Door, the Bolt, the Bar, the Wall of Division between the Righteous, & the Righteous'.[48]

(4) *Peaceable Principles and True*

Two responses to Bunyan's *Differences* were forthcoming. One, by Thomas Paul, has apparently been lost, but in *Peaceable Principles*

[45] Below pp. 247–8.
[46] Below pp. 272, 193.
[47] Below pp. 238, 235, 233, 243. His reference is to Rom. 14 and 15.
[48] Below pp. 216, 220.

Bunyan cites it. Paul's was a short reply which, according to Bunyan, devoted its first five pages to proving that Bunyan was either proud or a liar.[49] The other response, also brief, was included in Henry Danvers's *A Treatise of Baptism: . . . And, a brief Answer to Mr. Bunyan about Communion with Persons Unbaptized* (1673). Danvers (*c.* 1622–87), who was educated at Oxford, adopted Particular Baptist views in 1650–1, and Fifth Monarchist principles in 1653. He was a member of the parliamentary army and sat for Leicester in the Nominated Parliament. Following the Restoration he was involved in several anti-government plots.[50] His *Treatise of Baptism* devotes more than 300 pages to extolling believers' baptism and condemning paedobaptism. In the small section attacking Bunyan, he argues, like Thomas Paul, that baptism is believed to be the 'entering ordinance' of the church by both Catholics and Protestants, and he cites Richard Baxter for support. Bunyan's opposition is thus 'contrary to all men', he asserts. Like Bunyan's other adversaries, he also appeals to the great commission and to New Testament examples of baptism. Indeed, Danvers adds little that is new to the controversy, but he does introduce the analogy of marriage (perhaps also alluded to in Paul's lost work) in which 'that publick *Declaration* of consent is the *Marriage* and solemn *Contract* made betwixt Christ and the Believer in Baptisme, as before at large. And if it be *preposterous* and *wicked* for a Man and Woman to cohabit together, and to enjoy the Priviledges of a *Marriage-state*, without the passing of that publick *solemnity*; So it is no less, *disorderly* upon a *Spiritual* account, for any to claim the priviledges of a Church, or be admitted to the same till the passing of this *Solemnity* by them.'[51]

---

[49] Below pp. 270–5, 286–7.

[50] For Danvers, see Richard L. Greaves, *Saints and Rebels* (Macon, Ga., 1985), pp. 157–77. See also Richard L. Greaves, *Deliver Us From Evil: The Radical Underground in Britain, 1660–63* (New York and Oxford, 1986).

[51] Henry Danvers, *A Treatise of Baptism* (1673), pp. 44–8, 52–3 (second pagination). Richard Baxter, who debated the issue of paedobaptism with Baptists on more than one occasion, admitted that they '*differ from us in a point so difficult, that many of the Papists and Prelatists have maintained, that it is not determined in Scripture, but Dependeth on the tradition of the Church.*' (*A Defence of the Principles of Love* [1671], p. 7). Later Baxter responded to the major thrust of Danvers' work and observed that 'there are two sorts of men called Anabaptists amongst us: the one sort are sober Godly Christians, who when they are rebaptized to satisfie their Consciences, live among us in Christian Love and peace: and I shall be ashamed if I Love not them as heartily, and own them not as peaceably, as any of them shall do either me or better men than I that differ from them. The other sort hold it unlawful to hold Communion with such as are not of their mind and way, and are schismatically troublesome and unquiet, in labouring to increase their Party. These are they that offend me, and other lovers of peace.' (*More Proofs of Infants Church-Membership* [1675], Preface p. [3].)

Although his *Confession* had provoked the pamphlet war, Bunyan by this time may have felt besieged and even weary. He writes in *Peaceable Principles* that when he published *A Confession*, 'Mr. *Will. K.*, Mr. *Thomas Paul*, and Mr. *Henry D'anvers*, and Mr. *Den*, fell with might and main upon me; some comparing me to the Devil, others to a Bedlam, others to a sot and the like, for my seeking Peace and Truth among the Godly.' His valediction is, '*I am thine to serve thee, Christian, so long as I can look out at those Eyes, that have had so much dirt thrown at them by many.*'[52] Furthermore, no one was coming to his defence.[53] But perhaps such statements are just another attempt of the controversialist to gain the reader's sympathy and support. Whatever the case, in *Peaceable Principles* Bunyan responds selectively to the attacks of all four writers. He accuses Paul of seeming to retract his earlier denial of baptism as the initiating ordinance, perhaps because of Danvers's influence. He also questions Denne's morals. There is considerable repetition from his earlier works, as when he reiterates much of his argument about love. And he perfunctorily brushes aside Danvers's analogy of marriage by supposing that his opponents are making a preposterous and wicked charge against Christ and many of the saints. At this point in the controversy there was apparently little new light to be shed on the status of visible saints unbaptized for want of light. But Bunyan does insist that the names Anabaptist, Independent, and Presbyterian are 'Factious Titles', and he declares, 'since you would know by what Name I would be distinguished from others; I tell you, I would be, and hope I am, *a Christian*; and chuse, if God shall count me worthy, *to be called a Christian, a Believer*'.[54]

There were at least two more printed attacks on Bunyan's position in his lifetime. John Denne's *Hypocrisie Detected, or Peaceable and True Principles as so Pretended by John Bunyan, tryed and found False and Unsound* was published in 1674, but no known copy exists. William Kiffin's *A Sober discourse of Right to Church-Communion* appeared in 1681. Although it does not name Bunyan, it is clearly aimed at him and others of the open membership persuasion. It is the most articulate presentation of the closed membership position in this pamphlet war. Kiffin explains that the unbaptized Christians in question are excluded

[52] Below pp. 286, 289.

[53] There are references for June and Aug. of 1672 in the *Minutes* (pp. 73–4) to work being done on a confession of faith, which perhaps was an effort undertaken in Bunyan's defence.

[54] Below pp. 273, 285, 279–80, 284–5, 270.

only 'from our immediate Communion at the Lords Table, though not
from our Love and Affection, for we hope they walk according to their
Light, and the Error being not so fundamental as to endanger their
Eternal state, we esteem them Christian Brethren and Saints, for
whose further illumination we dayly put up our Prayers.'[55]

Although Bunyan did not devote additional tracts to the subject, he
did have more to say about it. For example, in *Saved by Grace* (1675),
he pleads for stooping, condescending, and having pity, love, and
compassion for others. In *The Strait Gate* (1676), he warns those
'whose religion lies in some circumstantials' that they might not be able
to enter the kingdom of God, and in *A Holy Life* (1684), he laments
that iniquity mixed with good opinions prevents Presbyterians,
Independents, and Baptists from having communion with each other.
He makes additional allusions to the controversy in *Of the House of the
Forest of Lebanon* (1692) and *A Discourse of the Building, Nature,
Excellency, and Government of the House of God* (1688). Moreover, in *The
Heavenly Foot-man* (1698), he warns readers not to 'have too much
Company with some *Anabaptists*, though I go under that name my
self'.[56]

A moderate and subtle, yet dramatic, expression of Bunyan's
position on this issue is found in the second part of *The Pilgrim's
Progress*. Here, Christiana and others submit to a cleansing in the
garden bath at Interpreter's house because they 'must orderly go from
hence' on their pilgrimage. Later Mr Feeble-mind, who is '*so weak a
Man, as to be offended with that which others have a liberty to do*', Mr
Ready-to-halt, and others who have not gone through the bath are
added to the company. Great-heart, in welcoming Feeble-mind,
assures him that the group will refrain from engaging in opinionated
and doubtful disputations. Still later, the shepherds welcome the entire
group to the Delectable Mountains, declaring that 'This is a
comfortable Company, you are welcome to us, for we have for the
Feeble, as for the *Strong*; our Prince has an Eye to what is done to the
least of these.' Arriving at the palace, 'the Feeble and the Weak went
in, and Mr. *Great-heart*, and the rest did follow'.[57]

[55] William Kiffin, *A Sober Discourse* (1681), p. 6.
[56] Oxford Bunyan, viii. 225–6; v. 125 (quoted); ix. 326–8. Offor, iii, 524–5. Oxford
Bunyan, vi. 310–11; v. 153 (quoted).
[57] *P.P.*, pp. 207–8, 270–1, 284, 285.

C. THE CONTROVERSY REGARDING THE STATUS OF WOMEN

(1) *Women and the Church*

The place of women in early Christianity was commensurate with their general position in society. From the belief that 'Adam was formed first, then Eve, and Adam was not deceived, but the woman was deceived and became a transgressor,' there followed the Pauline notions that the husband was head of the wife as Christ was the head of the church, that wives were to obey their husbands, and that women in the church were not to teach or have authority over men but were to learn in silence and submissiveness. These views were echoed in subsequent centuries. The development of monasticism in the Middle Ages, however, provided a special religious role for some women to play. With the coming of the Reformation that role was diminished, but another role, that of the minister's wife, became important and was played quite vigorously by many. Of course, women contributed to the Reformation movement in other ways as well.[58]

In seventeenth-century England, women's place in society was clearly secondary, but was also perceived as deteriorating in some respects. The roles of midwife, partner in family farming, and skilled artisan, among others, were lessening. And within the upper class, the useful function of women on family estates was declining. With respect to women's general role in marriage, the difficulties suffered by wives and mothers were recognized by Richard Baxter, who wrote that '*Women* especially must expect so much suffering in a married life, that if God had not put into them a natural inclination to it, and so strong a love to their children, as maketh them patient under the most annoying troubles, the world would ere this have been at end, through their refusal of so calamitous a life.' Yet he did not advocate change. There

---

[58] 1 Tim. 2: 8–15; Eph. 5: 22–4; Col. 3: 18. Georgia Harkness, *Women in Church and Society* (Nashville, 1972). Roland Bainton, *Women of the Reformation in Germany and Italy* (Minneapolis, 1971); *Women of the Reformation in France and England* (Minneapolis, 1973); *Women of the Reformation, from Spain to Scandinavia* (Minneapolis, 1977). Patrick Collinson, 'The Role of Women in the English Reformation Illustrated by the Life and Friendship of Anne Locke', in G. J. Cumming (ed.), *Studies in Church History*, ii (1965), pp. 258–72. However, for late medieval, pre-Reformation 'holy women who were wives and mothers', see Clarissa W. Atkinson, *Mystic and Pilgrim: The Book and the World of Margery Kempe* (1983), pp. 157–94, 219 (quoted).

were feminist writers, however, who objected to the secondary role of women in marriage and society in general as well as to the decline in certain specific positions, and who perceived social change as necessary for the restoration of appropriate opportunities for women.[59]

In a century which witnessed political and religious upheaval, one might expect to find revolutionary ideas about the role of women, especially among the 'revolutionaries'. Indeed, although advocates of an improved position for women were not limited to a single band of the political, social, or religious spectra, the more innovative practices were in greater evidence among radical religious types such as the Quakers. But even within a more conservative separatist group such as the Independents, 'prophesying' by women (as distinguished from regular preaching) occurred with some frequency, sometimes in separation from men but also occasionally among men in a mixed congregation.[60]

In general, the more favourable view of women's role among such religious groups was linked with their heightened consciousness of the individual's direct relationship with God. For example, the Quakers, who because of their comparative radicalism were described by a contemporary as the 'fag-end of Reformation', placed strong emphasis on the immediate, inward, and spiritual qualities of religious experience (with the potential of perfectibility) and appealed to the Light of Christ within each person as their authority in faith and practice.[61] That light was within women as well as men, and thus whereas among the more

---

[59] Richard Baxter, *A Christian Directory*, (2nd edn., 1678), p. 8. Hilda L. Smith, *Reason's Disciples: Seventeenth-Century Feminists* (1982), pp. 3–17, 75–114. See also Suzanne W. Hull, *Chaste Silent & Obedient* (San Marino, Calif., 1982); Wallace Notestein, 'The English Woman, 1580–1650', in J. H. Plumb (ed.), *Studies in Social History* (1955), pp. 69–107; Antonia Fraser, *The Weaker Vessel* (New York, 1984); Lawrence Stone, *The Family, Sex and Marriage in England, 1500–1800* (New York, 1977); Lois G. Schwoerer, 'Seventeenth-Century English Women, Engraved in Stone?', *Albion*, 16 (1984), pp. 375–403.

[60] Geoffrey F. Nuttall, 'The Early Congregational Conception of the Ministry and the Place of Women Within It', *The Congregational Quarterly*, 26 (1948), 153–61. See also Richard L. Greaves, 'The Role of women in Early English Nonconformity', *Church History*, 52 (1983), pp. 299–311. According to Christopher Hill, 'The only people in the seventeenth century who came anywhere near making women equal with men were Diggers, Ranters and Quakers, who believed that men and women were perfectible on earth, [and] could get back behind the Fall.' *Milton and the English Revolution* (New York, 1978), p. 118.

[61] R. H., *The Character of a Quaker* (1671), p. 1. See also Oxford Bunyan, i. xvi–xxi; Geoffrey F. Nuttall, *The Holy Spirit in Puritan Faith and Experience* (Oxford, 1946), pp. 1–19; Keith Thomas, 'Women and the Civil War Sects', in Trevor Aston (ed.), *Crisis in Europe, 1560–1660* (1965), pp. 317–40.

doctrinally conservative Independents women were restricted to
'prophesying', among the Quakers they were allowed to preach like the
men. One of George Fox's first converts was the Baptist Elizabeth
Hooton, whose name among the Quakers 'heads the noble roll of
women-ministers'. In addition, not only did some Quaker male
ministers go naked 'as a sign' in the professed tradition of certain Old
Testament prophets, but some Quaker women did so as well. Also of
interest was the development, encouraged by Fox but opposed by
some, of certain separate women's meetings, primarily for poor relief
and discipline matters, which gave women some share in church
government. Often worship was also a part of such meetings.[62]

Notable among Quaker women in this period was Margaret Fell
(1614–1702), wife of Judge Thomas Fell of Swarthmore Hall in
Lancashire, who was converted to Quakerism by Fox in 1652. With
the consent of her husband (who did not convert), Fell made
Swarthmore Hall the nerve centre of the movement. In 1669, more
than a decade after the judge's death, she married George Fox. Her
numerous activities as a Quaker included raising funds to support
travelling ministers, seeking the release of Quakers from prison (she
was sometimes a prisoner herself), and travelling, corresponding, and
writing tracts in support of the movement. Among her printed works is
Womens Speaking Justified (1666), which provides a defence of Quaker
practice. Like Fox, Fell argues that God created both male and female
in his image and that Christ confirmed that unity (Matt. 19). She also
points to the important contributions of women in the New Testament.
Indeed, throughout the Bible, 'it is evident that God made no
difference, but gave his good Spirit as it pleased him, both to Man and
Woman'. Finally, she interprets the Pauline injunction against
women's speaking in 1. Cor. 14, as a statement directed against
specific confused women in the Corinthian church, not Christian
women in general.[63] But Fell's emphasis is upon an enhanced *religious*

[62] William C. Braithwaite, *The Second Period of Quakerism* (Cambridge, 2nd edn.,
1955), pp. 269–350 (p. 271 quoted). Irene L. Edwards, 'The Women Friends of
London', *J. of the Friends' Historical Society*, 47 (1955), pp. 3–21. For the practice of
going naked as a sign, see Norman Penney (ed.), *The First Publishers of Truth*, (1907),
pp., 364–9; Kenneth L. Carroll, 'Early Quakers and "Going Naked as a Sign"', *Quaker
History*, 67 (1978), pp. 69–87. For additional information on Hooton see *B.D.B.R.*, s.v.

[63] Margaret Fell, *Womens Speaking Justified* (1666), pp. 8–9, 11 (quoted). Christopher
Hill (*Milton*, pp. 117–18) has mistaken George Fox's early position as more traditional
than it was, by taking the Quaker's statements too literally and apart from context. In *The
Woman Learning in Silence* (1656), Fox states the Pauline position about women being
silent and submissive and learning from their husbands at home (p. 1) which Hill

role for women, and although she is a strong advocate and model of this role, she nevertheless gives assent to the secondary position of women in family and society in general. It should also be remembered that in the political sphere, even the Levellers, who supported the radical extension of the franchise, did not argue that it should be extended to women. Movements supporting the full equality of the sexes were still to come.[64]

In this issue, as in others, the Baptists were less radical than the Quakers. Although one heresiographer of the period noted that in comparison to the Independents, among the Baptists 'many more of their women do venture to preach', the practice was not widespread in Bunyan's time. The biblical literalism of the Baptists bound them closely to the traditional Pauline view. Thus the General Baptist Thomas Grantham argued against women's preaching, and the Particular Baptist *1656 Confession* exhorted women to learn in silence.[65] In 1654, messengers of the association of Particular Baptist churches in the West Country declared that 'a woman is not permitted at all to speak in the church, neither by way of praying, prophecying nor enquiring'. In 1658, messengers of the Particular Baptist Abingdon Association gave more detailed directions that women were not to speak publicly in the church as teachers or rulers. Neither were they to speak in passing sentence on doctrines or church cases, or as 'the mouth of the church' in prayer. Women could, however, confess

quotes. But Fox goes on to describe this as the law from which Christians are freed by Christ who 'in the Male, and in the Female is one' (p. 1), to identify the *unlearned* as those who are to 'learn of their husband at home, Christ, who makes free from the Law . . .' (p. 2), and to appeal to the fulfilment of Joel's prophecy Joel 2: 28, Acts 2: 17–18) that God would pour out his spirit upon all flesh and that sons and daughters would prophesy (p. 2). See also Fox's *Concerning the Living God of Truth* (1680), p. 11), his *A Testimony for God's Truth* (1688), pp. 11–12, and T. L. Underwood, 'Early Quaker Eschatology', in Peter Toon (ed.), *Puritans, the Millennium and the Future of Israel: Puritan Eschatology 1600 to 1660* (1970), pp. 91–103.

[64] Margaret Fell, *Womens Speaking Justified*, p. 9. See also Hilda Smith, *Reason's Disciples*, pp. 95–7. Women did engage in 'political activities', however. As Lois G. Schwoerer has shown, at the time of the Glorious Revolution, despite 'countervailing influences and restrictions, women of all classes did play a part in politics'. 'Women and the Glorious Revolution', *Albion*, 18 (1986), p. 200. See also Dorothy P. Ludlow, 'Shaking Patriarchy's Foundations: Sectarian Women in England, 1641–1700', in Richard L. Greaves (ed.), *Triumph Over Silence: Women in Protestant History* (1985), pp. 95–108.

[65] Robert Baillie, *A Dissuasive From the Errours of the Time* (1645), p. 111; Baillie *Anabaptism* (1647), p. 53 (quoted). Thomas Grantham, *Christianismus Primitivus*, Pt. 3, p. 45. Article xxv, *1656 Confession*, in *Confessions of Faith* (Hanserd Knollys Society Publication 10, 1854), ed. Edward Bean Underhill, p. 91.

their faith in requesting membership, and speak as witnesses or in acts of repentance. But with respect to another church activity, the Particular Baptist Henry Danvers argued for the orderly appointment of baptismal administrators, fearing that 'otherwise Women, Apostates, or any, as some hold, may do it'.[66]

There is evidence, however, that obedience to husbands was not required by Baptists under all circumstances. In 1668, the General Assembly of the General Baptist Churches declared that in the marriage of a believer and an unbeliever, 'for those so married yet to live together as man and wife when repented of, is a sin'.[67] The General Baptist church at Fenstanton expelled Jane Adams in 1658 for not attending its meetings even though she explained that her husband denied her this right. The congregation decided that unless she were restrained by force, threats by her husband were not an excuse for her absence.[68] And in 1657, messengers of the Particular Baptist West Country Association decided that it was lawful for the wife of an unbelieving husband to dispose of the outward substance of his estate for the church without his knowledge or consent because 'women as well as men are created in Christ Jesus unto good works'.[69]

(2) *A Case of Conscience Resolved*

It is disappointing that so little is known about Bunyan's personal life and his relationship with women. Even the Christian name of his wife has been forgotten. It is known, however, that she brought to their marriage two influential religious books (see below) but apparently little else, and as a married couple they were so poor, Bunyan claimed, that they had not 'so much household-stuff as a Dish or Spoon betwixt us both'.[70] She bore him two sons and two daughters including the blind Mary. Bunyan's wife died in 1658, and in the following year he

[66] *Association Records of the Particular Baptists of England, Wales and Ireland to 1660*, ed. B. R. White, ii (1973), 55; iii (1974), 185. Danvers, *Treatise of Baptism*, p. 52 (second pagination).

[67] William T. Whitley (ed.), *Minutes of the General Assembly of the General Baptist Churches in England* (1909), i. 23.

[68] *Records of the Churches of Christ Gathered at Fenstanton, Warboys, and Hexham, 1644–1720* ed. Edward Bean Underhill (1854), p. 242.

[69] B. R. White, op. cit. n. 66 above, ii. 67. See also J. F. McGregor, 'The Baptists: Fount of All Heresy', in J. F. McGregor and Barry Reay (ed.), *Radical Religion in the English Revolution* (1984), pp. 23–63.

[70] *G.A.*, para. 15, p. 8.

married Elizabeth. She bore him another son and daughter. Elizabeth, along with all of Bunyan's children except Mary, outlived him.

The various references to women in Bunyan's spiritual autobiography include several early encounters with members of the Bedford congregation. While still living in Elstow, 'upon a day, the good providence of God did cast me to *Bedford*, to work on my calling: and in one of the streets of that town, I came where there was three or four poor women sitting at a door in the Sun, and talking about the things of God . . .'. Bunyan was attracted by what he heard, continued his contacts with 'these poor people at *Bedford*', and was eventually introduced to John Gifford.[71] That Bunyan's earliest encounter was with women members of the congregation is not surprising, since the *Minutes* indicate that during this time women outnumbered men by about two to one.[72] Also evident is the fact that women were active in congregational life, especially in the work of visitation. Like women in other dissenting congregations, they were no doubt relied on even more heavily during times of severe persecution when male members were imprisoned.[73] Women were also involved in various disciplinary cases, sometimes as victims of sexual abuse or physical violence.[74]

In 1674, Bunyan had a different type of encounter with a female member of the Bedford congregation, Agnes Beaumont. At the urging of her brother, Bunyan allowed the young woman to ride behind him on horseback to a religious gathering. The two were seen travelling in this manner and later were accused of scandalous behaviour by a Bedford minister. She was temporarily estranged from her father over the incident, and shortly after their reconciliation he mysteriously died. She was accused of murdering him with poison Bunyan furnished, but was found innocent. Bunyan maintained his own innocence and in the fifth edition (1680) of *Grace Abounding* condemned scandalous reports that 'I had my *Misses*, my *Whores*, my *Bastards*, yea *two wives at once*, and the like.'[75]

A Case of Conscience Resolved (1683) is a curious piece among Bunyan's many printed works. It addresses the question of whether

[71] *G.A.*, paras. 37 (quoted), 39, 53, 77, pp. 14–15, 19, 25.
[72] *Minutes*, pp. 17, 214–16.
[73] Ludlow, op. cit. n. 64 above, pp. 108–17.   [74] *Minutes*, pp. 83–4.
[75] *G.A.*, Appendix C, pp. 178–80; para. 309, p. 93 (quoted). See also Brown, pp. 225–30; *The Narrative of the Persecution of Agnes Beaumont in 1674* (1929), ed. G. B. Harrison. On an earlier occasion, Quakers accused Bunyan of circulating a tract (not extant) about a report of witchcraft performed by a Quaker widow (Oxford Bunyan, i. xxviii–xxix).

women should ordinarily meet separately from men to engage in certain acts of worship such as prayer. Bunyan explains that he had previously persuaded female members of the congregation to cease such practice. The women were 'so willing to let go' of this activity because '*Womens meetings*, wanted for their support, a bottom in the Word.' When 'Mr. K.' learned of it he wrote in support of such meetings, and his paper (perhaps multiple copies in manuscript) was sent to the Bedford area.[76] 'Mr. K.' may have been William Kiffin, for the paper was apparently sent from London, and in the open membership controversy Kiffin and others reflected an interest in the affairs of congregations in the Bedford area. In the same controversy Bunyan was chastised for writing Kiffin's name at length, hence in *Peaceable Principles* he referred to him simply as 'Mr. K.' In any case, a copy of the paper reached Bunyan with a request that he reply.

Bunyan's basic argument against women's meetings is that the practice is not mentioned in Scripture. Appealing to the traditional Pauline notions, he makes exception for the 'extraordinary' women of the Bible, laments the fact that Mr K. is 'so *Nunnish* in such a day as this', and declares, 'I do not believe they should Minister to God in Prayer before the whole Church, for then I should be a Ranter or a Quaker.'[77] Underlying these arguments is Bunyan's belief in the fundamental weakness and inferiority of women. He writes, 'When our first Mother, who was not attended with those weaknesses, either Sinful, or Natural, as our Women now are, stept out of her place but to speak a good Word for Worship, you see how she was baffled, and befooled therein; she utterly failed in the performance, tho she briskly attempted the thing. Yea she so failed there-about, that at one clap she over-threw, not only (as to that) the reputation of Women for ever, but her Soul, her Husband, and the whole World besides . . .' (Gen. 3: 1–7). Thus, since the cause of their condition was internal, women should be content to wear the badge of inferiority and be 'an Ornament in the Church of God on Earth'. These views are confirmed in *An Exposition on the First Ten Chapters of Genesis* in which Bunyan concludes that 'Women therefore, when-ever they would perk it and Lord it over their husbands, ought to remember, that both by Creation and Transgression they are made to be in Subjection to their own Husbands.' They are also expressed in his manual of conduct, *Christian Behaviour* (1663), in which he declares, 'It is an unseemly thing to see a *woman* so much as

[76] Below, p. 297.   [77] Below, pp. 326, 307, 305.

once in all her life-time, to offer to over-top her husband; she ought in every thing to be in subjection to him, and to do all she doth, as having her warrant, licence and authority from him.'[78]

At the end of *A Case of Conscience Resolved*, Bunyan suggests that when he has opportunity he may give his judgements on additional matters concerning women. He apparently never did, although the second part of *The Pilgrim's Progress* published in the following year reflects some of his views. The allegory describes the journey toward the Celestial City of Christiana and her children, whom Christian abandoned at his conversion, leaving with his fingers in his ears to shut out their cries for his return. Her journey has its lessons and its virtues, but it lacks the high drama of Part One and sometimes appears to be like a conducted tour of the historic sites of her husband's more adventurous pilgrimage before her.[79] At one point Christiana and others submit to the leadership of Interpreter's man-servant Great-heart, and later when he is about to take his leave of them, her friend Mercy exclaims, 'How can such poor Women as we, hold out in a way so full of Troubles as this way is, without a Friend, and Defender?'[80]

In another place, however, Bunyan provides some kindly words about women in the speech of Gaius: 'I will now speak on the behalf of Women, to take away their Reproach. For as Death and the Curse came into the World by a Woman, so also did Life and Health; *God sent forth his Son, made of a Woman*.' Having reminded his listeners of some of the positive exploits of New Testament women, Gaius concludes, 'Women therefore are highly favoured, and shew by these things that they are sharers with us in the Grace of Life.'[81] Later when Christiana is ready to cross the river to the Celestial City we are told that 'the road was full of people to see her take her journey,' and that her last words were '*I come Lord, to be with thee and bless thee.*' Finally, 'She went, and called, and entered in the Gate with all the Ceremonies of Joy that her Husband *Christian* had done before her.'[82] In allegory, as in biblical exposition, manual of conduct, and polemic, women, though sometimes honoured, were described by Bunyan clearly, but with varying intensity, as having secondary status.

---

[78] Below, pp. 306, 325. Bunyan, *An Exposition on the First Ten Chapters of Genesis*, in *1692 Folio*, p. 21. Oxford Bunyan, iii. 33; Cf. pp. xxx–xxxii, 26–8, 32–6.

[79] *P.P.* p. 26. Roger Sharrock, *John Bunyan* (1968), ch. 7; id., 'Women and Children', in id. (ed.) *Bunyan, The Pilgrim's Progress: A Casebook*' (1976), pp. 174–86. N. H. Keeble, 'Christiana's Key: The Unity of *The Pilgrim's Progress*', in Vincent Newey (ed.), *The Pilgrim's Progress: Critical and Historical Views* (Liverpool, 1980), pp. 1–20.

[80] *P.P.*, p. 220.   [81] *P.P.*, 261.   [82] *P.P.*, p. 306.

D. THE SEVENTH DAY SABBATH CONTROVERSY

(1) *The Sabbath and Sabbatarianism*

As early as New Testament times the Jewish Sabbath was beginning to be replaced among Christians by the observance of Sunday. The fourth century witnessed both church and civil legislation sanctioning Sunday as a day of rest and religious service.[83] In Elizabethan England, some ecclesiastical figures took special interest in the 'Christian Sabbath'. For example, Lancelot Andrewes, who would later become Bishop of Chichester, was in his Puritan phase in the 1580s when he delivered a series of lectures on the Ten Commandments at Pembroke Hall, Cambridge. His lecture on the fourth commandment stressed its status as part of the moral code and advocated a strict observance of Sunday, 'separating ourselves from all that is commodious or pleasant to the senses: from all commodities and delights of this life'.[84]

Others also took up this emphasis, which was given its fullest treatment in the works of the Puritans Richard Greenham and Nicolas Bownde. These advocates of Sabbatarianism argued that Sabbath observance was neither an obsolete Jewish ceremony nor only an ecclesiastical tradition in Christianity. Rather it was a perpetual moral law, grounded in God's own rest as described in the creation account, and clearly defined in the fourth commandment. As such, it was binding on all Christians. Furthermore, proper Sabbath observance required Christians to devote the day entirely to religious exercise and to avoid engaging in recreation, idleness, or the work of their calling. Some Sabbatarians went so far as to equate the violation of the Sabbath with such crimes as adultery and homicide! But in addition to the moral necessity of strict obedience to a divine commandment, Sabbatarians recognized the advantage of spiritual rejuvenation that came from observing this holy day. The Sabbath, wrote Greenham, is 'the schoole day, the faire day, the market day, the feeding day of the

---

[83] Willy Rordorf, *Sunday: The History of the Day of Rest and Worship in the Earliest Centuries of the Christian Church* (1968), trans. A. A. K. Graham; Horace G. Cowan, *The Sabbath in Scripture and History* (Kansas City, 1948); W. B. Whitaker, *Sunday in Tudor and Stuart Times* (1933); Kenneth L. Parker, *The English Sabbath: A Study of Doctrine and Practice from the Reformation to the Civil War* (1986).

[84] Lancelot Andrewes, *The Morall Law Expounded* (1642), pp. 329–31, 355. The 1642 edn. is the most complete and accurate for this particular lecture, according to Paul Welsby, *Lancelot Andrewes 1555–1626* (1958), p. 23.

soule, when men . . . arme themselves against sin to come, grow in knowledge, increase in faith'.[85]

Sabbatarianism in England was not a wholly insular development, for it was influenced by the work of second generation Reformed theologians on the continent. Nor should it be considered a phenomenon that sharply divided Puritans and their adversaries from the beginning, for members of both groups often shared a common concern for serious Sunday observance.[86] But by the time the Elizabethan era was drawing to a close, the issue was indeed a very strongly contested point of division. Bownde's *Doctrine of the Sabbath*, published in 1595, called upon the state to enforce his own strict and legalistic notions about appropriate Sabbath activities. Others responded by attempting to repress the circulation and further publication of his treatise. The controversy was further inflamed in the seventeenth century by James I's *Declaration of Sports* (1618; reissued by Charles I in 1633) supporting the legitimacy and desirability of recreation on the Sabbath, by Archbishop Laud's attempts to enforce conformity to his religious model, and by the numerous treatises published on the subject.[87]

Bunyan was, of course, affected by all this. When he married for the first time, his wife brought to the marriage two books left to her by her father, Lewis Bayly's *The Practise of Pietie* and Arthur Dent's *The Plaine Mans Path-way to Heaven*.[88] Husband and wife sometimes read together from these works, which 'did beget within me some desires to Religion', Bunyan later testified.[89] Bayly's book devoted more than one hundred pages to the subject of the Sabbath. His points were standard Puritan fare: God rested on the Sabbath, the fourth commandment is moral and perpetual, the observance of the Sabbath

[85] Richard Greenham, *The Works . . . Richard Greenham* (1599), p. 301; Richard L. Greaves, *Society and Religion in Elizabethan England* (Minneapolis, 1981), pp. 395–408. For Greenham (1535?–94?) and Bownde (d. 1613), see *D.N.B.*, s.vv.

[86] Patrick Collinson, 'The Beginnings of English Sabbatarianism', in C. W. Dugmore and Charles Duggan (eds.), *Studies in Church History* i (1964), pp. 207–21; Kenneth L. Parker, 'Thomas Rogers and the English Sabbath: The Case for Reappraisal', *Church History*, 53 (1984), 332–47.

[87] James T. Dennison, jun., *The Market Day of the Soul: The Puritan Doctrine of the Sabbath in England, 1532–1700* (Lanham, Md., 1983), pp. 43–116.

[88] For Bayly (d. 1631) and Dent (d. 1607), see *D.N.B.*, s.vv. Both works were popular. Although the original publication date of Bayly's book is unknown, a 3rd edn. was printed in 1613 and by 1735 it was in its 59th edn. Dent's book, first published in 1601, was in its 40th edn. in 1704 (see Maurice Hussey, 'Arthur Dent's *Plaine Mans Path-way to Heaven*', *Modern Language Review*, 44 [1949] 26).

[89] *G.A.*, para. 16, p. 89.

is not just ceremonial, and Christians are to devote the day entirely to religious exercise.[90]

Dent gave less attention to the issue, but denounced those who on the Sabbath 'sit Idle in the streetes', are 'at Cardes and Tables in their houses', 'run after whores and harlots', 'sit in their shops', or 'run to daunsings, and Beare-baitings'. 'O miserable wretches, o cursed caitiffes, o monstrous hel-hounds, which so grossely and openly contemne the Gospell of Christ,' he declared of those persons who hear a sermon in the morning and thus 'serve God in the forenoone', only to violate the Sabbath and serve 'the divell in the afternoone'.[91] Bunyan confessed that in spite of a troublesome conscience, he did just that before his conversion. On one occasion while still at Elstow, he was moved by a sermon preached against the evil of breaking the Sabbath by 'labour, sports, or otherwise', but later in the day he 'shook the Sermon out of my mind, and to my old custom of sports and gaming I returned with great delight'. Still later the same day he was playing a game of 'cat' when 'a voice did suddenly dart from Heaven into my Soul, which said, *Wilt thou leave thy sins, and go to Heaven? or have thy sins, and go to Hell?*' Bunyan's vacillation continued, but eventually he abandoned his sports.[92]

(2) *The Seventh Day Baptists*

Given the nature of the Sabbatarians' arguments for Sabbath observance, it is not surprising that some persons also concluded that it was to be observed on the seventh day of the week. Did not God rest on the seventh day? Did not God command the Jews to rest as He had on the seventh day? And was not that command for the seventh day moral and perpetual and therefore not a tradition subject to ecclesiastical alteration? Lancelot Andrewes, who as we have seen advocated Sabbatarianism in the 1580s, delivered a speech in 1618 at John Traske's trial before Star Chamber in which he denounced Traske's adherence to Jewish food laws and to the seventh day Sabbath.[93] Traske was sentenced to be branded with a 'J' (for Jew) and to life imprisonment, but he was eventually released.

[90] Lewis Bayly, *The Practise of Pietie* (3rd edn., 1613), pp. 481–624.
[91] Arthur Dent, *The Plaine Mans Path-way to Heaven* (1601), pp. 138–9.
[92] *G.A.*, para. 20–4, pp. 9–11.
[93] Lancelot Andrewes, *A Speech Delivered in the Starr-Chamber Against Two Judaicall Opinions of Mr. Traske*, in *Opuscula Quaedam Posthuma* (1629), ii. 63–75 (second pagination). For Traske (1558–1636), see *B.D.B.R.*, s.v.

There were others in the early seventeenth century who held Sabbath views like those of Traske. Returne Hebdon and Theophilus Brabourne (b. 1590), for example, were advocates of Saturday observance. However, it was not until mid-century that a continuous movement was in evidence. Most adherents were of Baptist persuasion and some also held Fifth Monarchist views. Notable among these Seventh Day Baptists were Peter Chamberlen, Thomas Tillam, Edward Stennett, and Francis Bampfield. Chamberlen (1601–83), a royal physician to the first three Stuart monarchs, advocated various economic, social, and legal reforms, and also adhered to Fifth Monarchist principles. He adopted Baptist views in 1648, and the seventh day position some three years later. Chamberlen was a member of the Lothbury Square Baptist church in London. He later joined the Seventh Day Baptist congregation which eventually settled at Mill Yard and still later joined the one meeting in Bell Lane. It was he who administered the laying on of hands to Thomas Tillam (fl. 1637–68). The latter was a member of the Particular Baptist church in Swan Alley, Coleman Street, London, when he was dispatched in 1651 as an evangelist to Hexham, Northumberland, where he established a Baptist church. He moved to Colchester, Essex in 1655, and having adopted seventh day views, gathered a Seventh Day Baptist congregation. He was also a Fifth Monarchist. In the 1660s he advocated emigration to the Palatinate, went abroad himself, and was eventually disowned by Edward Stennett and others who accused him and his associates of sharing a community of goods (and perhaps wives as well), and of adopting circumcision and other Jewish practices. Stennett (d. 1705) was a member of the Particular Baptist church in Abingdon, Berkshire in the 1650s, and perhaps was a Fifth Monarchist also. By 1658, he adhered to the seventh day principle and in the early 1670s moved to Wallingford, Berkshire where he practised medicine and ministered to a congregation of Seventh Day Baptists. In 1686, he reorganized the London congregation of the late Francis Bampfield. Educated at Oxford, Bampfield (c.1615–84) was ejected from his living at Sherborne, Dorset in 1662, and was later imprisoned for several years. Convinced of seventh day tenets about 1665, he organized a Seventh Day Baptist congregation at Bethnal Green, London in 1674, and eventually moved its meeting place to Pinners' Hall, Broad Street. Arrested once again in 1683, he spent the last months of his life in Newgate prison.[94]

[94] See *B.D.B.R.*, s.vv., and the following sources. The Tillam faction included

These and other leaders among the Seventh Day Baptists organized and ministered to congregations, and sometimes expounded their views in public debate as well as in print. Up to a point, many of their views reflected those held by Sabbatarians in general. For example, they believed that the Sabbath was established by God's rest from creation. Thus the Sabbath rule 'was given before the Law was proclaimed at *Sinai*', Bampfield declared, and was 'given to *Adam* in respect of his Humane nature, and in him to all the World of humane creatures'.[95] But they also stressed the fact that this rest took place literally on the seventh day. God, wrote Tillam, 'did both sanctifie and celebrate the seventh day Sabbath'. Seeking to counter arguments against its perpetuity, he added. 'and that before sin, and consequently before any need of a Saviour, or ceremony shadowing him'.[96] Also, like Sabbatarians in general, Seventh Day Baptists argued that the fourth commandment was not ceremonial but moral and perpetual, and that Sabbath observance was therefore a matter of moral obedience. Here again they held that the seventh day was the one commanded to be observed. Bampfield declared that the Ten Commandments are the unchangeable rule of life and that in the fourth commandment it is the seventh day which 'is alone that particular, peculiar day in every week, which is the weekly Sabbath day'.[97] 'The seventh-day and the Sabbath are one,' Stennett wrote, 'and the same God hath inseparably made them so by Creation and Institution.'[98] Tillam concluded, 'That the seventh day was the Lords holy Sabbath, from the Worlds foundation to our Saviours Passion is undeniable.' Furthermore, Christ observed the seventh day as the Sabbath, as did the Apostle Paul, he argued. Indeed, it was 'onely the apostasizing Church of Rome (with some few other adherents) did communicate upon the sunday, so called'.[99]

Christopher Pooley (b. *c.*1620), *B.D.B.R.*, s.v., and see Edward Browne, *An Account of Several Travels Through a Great Part of Germany* (1677), p. 56. At some point the Baptist Henry Jessey (1601–63) accepted seventh day views but was not active in the movement (*B.D.B.R.*, s.v.). For additional information on Bampfield, see Richard L. Greaves, *Saints and Rebels*, pp. 179–210. See also Oscar Burdick's very useful 'Seventh Day Baptist Origins in England, 1650–1683: A Bibliography', Graduate Theological Union Library, Berkeley, Calif., 1984. Among other advocates of the seventh day were James Ockford (fl. 1650s), William Saller (d. 1680?), and John Spittlehouse (fl. 1643–56) (see *D.N.B.*, *B.D.B.R.*, and Burdick, op. cit.)

[95] Francis Bampfield, *The Judgment of Mr. Francis Bampfield* (1672), pp. 6–6a.
[96] Thomas Tillam, *The Seventh-day Sabbath* (1657) p. 11.
[97] Bampfield, *The Judgment of Mr. Francis Bampfield*, p. 4a.
[98] Edward Stennett, *The Insnared Taken* (1677), p. 158.
[99] Tillam, *The Seventh-day Sabbath*, pp. 36, 98, 108. His biblical references include Luke 4: 16 and Acts 17: 2.

The implications of these biblical injunctions and practices for contemporary Christians were clear to Seventh Day Baptists. Emphasizing the importance of the fourth commandment within the law, Stennett declared, 'The same law that was writ in *Adams* heart, was writ in Tables of stone; the same law that was writ in Tables of stone, was writ in the heart of Christ the second *Adam*; the same Law that was writ in the heart of Christ, is writ in the heart of every true believer in Christ.'[100] Indeed, Christ was obedient 'unto this *fourth Word*, in observing in his life time the Seventh day as a Weekly Sabbath-day, which is the last day of the Week in the weekly returns of it,' Bampfield argued, and every believer 'is to conform unto Christ in all the acts of his Obedience to the Ten Words'.[101] 'THE SEVENTH DAY IS THE SABBATH OF THE LORD,' Chamberlen exclaimed, and lamenting the church's numerous departures from biblical practices, he asked whether it was better to continue in these departures or 'be forsworn to keep the COMMANDMENTS of *God* and the FAITH of *Jesus*'.[102]

Mingled with these views of the Seventh Day Baptists in some cases were millenarian and Fifth Monarchist concerns. For at least some there was also a special interest in Hebraic tradition. Stennett, for example, explored Jewish law in *The Royal Law Contended For* (second edition, 1667). Bampfield, a Hebraist, advocated the adoption of Hebrew as the universal language. Chamberlen visited synagogues in Italy, Germany, and the Low Countries, and an unnamed source, reported by Tillam, claimed that some Jews in London 'do frequent our meeting places every Sabbath', and that 'I am well aquainted with their Rabbi.'[103]

Although Seventh Day Baptists never constituted a large element among the sectaries, groups of them were to be found in a number of counties. As we have seen, certain leaders were active in establishing and ministering to churches in various places, and in one instance Francis Bampfield undertook a special preaching foray into several counties.[104] As a result of such activity, a list compiled in 1690

---

[100] Edward Stennett, *The Seventh Day is the Sabbath* (1664), p. 27.

[101] Bampfield, *The Judgment of Mr. Francis Bampfield*, pp. 6a–7.

[102] Peter Chamberlen, *Englands Choice* (1682), pp. 3–4.

[103] Peter Chamberlen, *The Sons of the East* (1682), broadside; Tillam, *The Seventh-day Sabbath*, pp. 50–51. See also R. G. Clouse, 'The Rebirth of Millenarianism', and Peter Toon, 'The Question of Jewish Immigration', in Peter Toon (ed.), *Puritans*, pp. 42–65, 115–25. B. S. Capp, *The Fifth Monarchy Men* (1972), p. 224, notes that at least three Seventh Day Baptists, including Chamberlen, 'seem to have adopted the Seventh Day Sabbath as an addition to their Fifth Monarchy beliefs, not as a replacement.'

[104] Bampfield, *A Name* (1681), p. 7.

identified three congregations in London, and other congregations (or
in some cases 'remnants') in Lincolnshire, Norfolk, Suffolk, Essex,
Surrey, Berkshire, Buckinghamshire, Oxfordshire, Gloucestershire,
Wiltshire, and Dorset. By the late 1660s, Seventh Day Baptists were
also present in Newport, Rhode Island and were in correspondence
with their associates in London.[105]

Among the writers who opposed the views of Seventh Day Baptists
were Richard Baxter and John Owen.[106] In 1671, both published works
critical of the seventh day position but conciliatory toward those who
held it. The two were in general agreement in defining the
fundamental Sabbath principle laid down in the creation account and
in the fourth commandment as a requirement to observe 'one day in
seven', rather than to observe a particular day. They argued that
although the Jews did, in fact, observe the seventh day, Christ's
resurrection provided the foundation for first day observance. This
Lord's Day, or Christian Sabbath, was appointed for holy worship by
the apostles, who were assigned by Christ to teach and guide the
primitive church. Thus Baxter and Owen concluded that the particular
day of the Sabbath observance was changed, but the fundamental
Sabbath principle of 'one day in seven' was upheld and continued.[107]

[105] Ernest A. Payne, 'More About the Sabbatarian Baptists', *The Baptist Quarterly*, 14
(1951–2), 161–6; W. T. Whitley, 'Seventh Day Baptists in England', *The Baptist
Quarterly*, 12 (1947), 252–8; Seventh Day Baptist General Conference, *Seventh Day
Baptists in Europe and America* (Plainfield, N.J., 1910), i. 51, 94–5, 122–6 (occasional
inaccuracies require this work to be used with caution). Something of the seventeenth-
century congregational life of the Pinners' Hall and Mill Yard churches in London may
be read in 'An Historical Record of . . . the Church . . . Formerly Gathered by Mr.
Francis Bampfield', pp. 'e', 1–77, and 'Mill-Yard Minutes . . . 1673–1840', pp. 1–100,
at the Seventh Day Baptist Historical Society, Janesville, Wis.; photocopies at Dr
Williams's Library, London. The autobiography and other materials relating to the life
of Joseph Davis, sen. (1627–1707), a member of the Mill Yard congregation who was
released from prison in 1672 under the same petition as John Bunyan, may be read in
William Henry Black (ed.), *The Last Legacy . . . of Joseph Davis, Senior* (1869), Mill Yard
Publications No. 1.

[106] There were internal disagreements as well. In addition to the Tillam dispute, John
Cowell left the group after thirteen years of membership and criticized his former
associates in *The Snare Broken* (1677), pp. 1–2, 102–52. Edward Stennett replied with
The Insnared Taken (1677). Long before discarding the seventh day principle, however,
Cowell had criticized the Tillam faction in *Divine Oracles* (1664), pp. 38–40. For Cowell,
see Seventh Day Baptist General Conference, op. cit., n. 105, p. 74.

[107] Richard Baxter, *The Divine Appointment of the Lord's Day* (1671), pp. 12, 73–5, 84–
9, 204–12; John Owen, *Exercitations Concerning the Name, Original Nature, Use, and
Continuance of a Day of Sacred Rest* (1671), pp. 45–70, 95–104, 132–5, 147–8, 181–3,
384–406. Their conciliatory approach was in keeping with their concern over healing
some of the divisions among Nonconformists. See Richard Baxter, *Reliquiae Baxterianae*,
ed. Matthew Sylvester (1696), Part 3, pp. 61–9; Geoffrey F. Nuttall, *Richard Baxter*

Baptists were also among the critics. In January and February 1659, Jeremiah Ives engaged in four public debates in London with Chamberlen, Tillam, and Matthew Coppinger, and subsequently published an account. Thomas Grantham of Lincolnshire wrote *The Seventh-Day Sabbath Ceased* (1667) and later included in his *Christianismus Primitivus* (1678) a section rejecting seventh day claims. The arguments of these General Baptist ministers were similar to those of Baxter and Owen, but differed in some respects (as will be shown below).[108] George Fox, employing the Quakers' spiritualizing and internalizing emphases, brought a considerably different perspective into the controversy, denying that the disciples celebrated the first day as a Sabbath, rejecting the Jewish Sabbath as a 'shadow', and describing Christ as the substance who puts an end to shadows and gives an inward rest from the spiritual burden to which people are bound.[109]

(3) *Questions About the Nature and Perpetuity of the Seventh-Day-Sabbath*

Perhaps Bunyan became aware of Seventh Day Baptist views in the 1650s when he may have had millenarian and possibly Fifth Monarchist sympathies. Or, perhaps he became aware of them in the 1670s through his ministerial network which extended into Buckinghamshire, Essex, Suffolk, and London, where Seventh Day Baptists were present. Whatever the case, among his London connections was Pinners' Hall. Here in 1682, he preached his *Greatness of the Soul* to the congregation of Independents and Baptists ministered to by Richard Wavel. The hall, which had been used for several years by this group, was also hired by the Seventh Day Baptist congregation of Francis Bampfield which had grown sufficiently large

(1965), pp. 64–84. Cowell, *The Snare Broken*, p. 53, found Owen's work 'of greatest use' in weighing arguments about the seventh day.

[108] Ives, *Saturday No Sabbath* (1659), title-page and pp. 3, 36, 93, 159, 211–37; Grantham, *The Seventh-Day Sabbath Ceased* (1667), pp. 2–4, 9–12, and *Christianismus Primitivus* (1678), Book 2, Part 2, pp. 156–77. For Ives (fl. 1653–74) and Grantham (1634–92), see *D.N.B.*, s.vv. For Coppinger, see Seventh Day Baptist General Conference, op. cit. n.405, p. 73. For additional evidence of Baptist concern about the issue, see *The Church Books of Ford or Cuddington and Amersham*, ed. W. T. Whitley (1912), p. 210; *Association Records of the Particular Baptists of England, Wales and Ireland to 1660*, ed. B. R. White, iii (1974), 158, 190–5, 209–14.

[109] George Fox, *An Answer to Thomas Tillams Book Called The Seventh-Day Sabbath* (1659), pp. 3–5, 9, 12–15, 21–2, 28.

to warrant moving its Saturday meetings there in 1681. It was perhaps this contact which prompted Bunyan to write against the seventh day Sabbath in 1685.[110] In any case, he recognizes in the preface to this work that much has already been written on the subject, but justifies his own publication by claiming that, among other things, its small size and cost may be best for the 'mean and poorest sort' of people.

As the title suggests, Bunyan groups his material around five questions: whether the seventh day Sabbath is of the law and light of nature; whether it was imposed by positive precept before the time of Moses; whether when given in the wilderness it concerned the Gentiles; whether it ended with the rest of the Jewish rites and ceremonies; and what time is fixed for New Testament saints to worship together. His answers to the first three questions are negative, to the fourth question positive, and to the last, of course, the first day of the week. He argues that the law of nature shows that a time, but not a specific day, must be allowed for worship, and that following creation, the seventh day was sanctified for God's rest, but not imposed as a holy Sabbath until the fourth commandment was given to Moses. Even then, the seventh day was not concerned with the Gentiles, and although the nature of the law was moral, the administration and circumstances were not. Finally, he argues that Christ's resurrection brought into the world the first day observance, which, as practised by the apostles, is the model for New Testament saints. Thus Bunyan's position is similar to that of the writers cited above. But unlike Baxter and Owen, and like Ives and Grantham, he rejects the notion of a Sabbath day established for human observation before the time of Moses. Also, instead of the 'one day in seven' Sabbath principle of Baxter and Owen, Bunyan uses, like Ives and Grantham, the less specific notion of 'a time' set aside for worship.[111]

Of course Bunyan's discussion lacks, among other things, the appeals to church councils and church fathers of Lancelot Andrewes and the meticulous analysis and use of biblical languages of John Owen. But there is an attractive plainness and directness about it, and there is at least one explicit similitude as well as an occasional

---

[110] Richard L. Greaves, 'John Bunyan and the Fifth Monarchists', *Albion*, 13 (1981), 83–95; Oxford Bunyan, iii. xxxii–xlv; Richard L. Greaves, 'John Bunyan's *Holy War* and London Nonconformity', *Baptist Quarterly*, 26 (1975), 163–4; Richard L. Greaves, 'John Bunyan and Nonconformity in the Midlands and East Anglia', *J. of the United Reformed Church History Society*, 1 (1976), 186–96. For Wavel (1633–1705), see *B.D.B.R.*, s.v. Two forms of an elegy for Bampfield were published in 1684 (Wing S53 and T66).

[111] Below, p. 350.

homiletical cadence, as when he declares that 'the *first day*, the *first day*, the *first day*, is now all the cry in the Churches by the Apostles'. There is also a much less rancorous tone than in the early anti-Quaker tracts, although in one place he does describe all other days than the first one as 'buried, in everlasting oblivion', and asks 'Shall we not take that notice thereof as to follow the Lord Jesus and the Churches herein? oh stupidity!' He also condemns the excesses of the Tillam group and suggests that there are some persons who want to reintroduce Jewish sacrifices. Furthermore, he carries the Jewish–Christian dichotomy so far as to describe the Jews as 'Christs deadliest Enemies' and Christian believers as 'his best Friends', in marked contrast to the more amicable attitude of Seventh Day Baptists toward the Jews and their traditions. Finally, although devoting some 150 duodecimo pages to the subject, Bunyan apologizes for his brevity and suggests that he may write a second part later on. He never did. Nor did his adversaries reply. In 1909, however, Bunyan's treatise was attacked in print by an author who concluded that 'one of the chief causes' of the Christian church's abandonment of the traditional Sabbath day was 'a Satanic kind of hatred towards the Jews'.[112]

'I never cared to meddle with things controverted, and in dispute amongst the Saints,' Bunyan wrote in his spiritual autobiography, 'because I saw they engendered strife, and because I saw they neither, in doing nor in leaving undone, did commend us to God to be his.' But, as we have seen, he did become involved in such disputes, and in major doctrinal matters he did 'contend with great earnestness for the Word of Faith'.[113] Indeed, such conflicts launched him into print and continued to appear in varying degrees in many of his subsequent publications. All of this furthers our understanding of the world of the mechanick preacher. It was a world in which controversy played a considerable role, for it was required for the protection of the flock, the defence of the preacher's legitimacy, and the preservation of the true faith—ministerial obligations which Bunyan took very seriously. The acrimonious denunciations of opponents as the agents of the Devil, and the professions of innocence and claims of being victimized by unprovoked attack, were part of the rough and tumble nature of religious controversy. Dirt was thrown, dirt struck, and dirt was wiped off. In part two of Bunyan's greatest allegory is to be found the man

[112] Below, pp. 374, 380–1, 386, 388, 386. Walter Lancelot Holland, *Bunyan's Sabbatic Blunders* (1909), p. 134.
[113] *G.A.*, para. 284, p. 87.

clothed in white upon whom dirt is continually cast. 'This man is
named *Godly-man*, and this Garment is to show the Innocency of his
Life,' the shepherds explain. 'Whoever they be that would make such
men dirty, they labour all in vain: for God . . . will cause that their
Innocence shall break forth as the Light, and their Righteousness as the
Noon day.'[114] Although not intended by the Bedford preacher, Godly-
man may judiciously be seen to represent both Bunyan and his
opponents.

[114] *P.P.*, p. 286.

A DEFENCE OF THE DOCTRINE
OF JUSTIFICATION, BY FAITH

A DEFENCE OF THE DOCTRINE OF JUSTIFICATION, BY FAITH

Note on the Text

One edition (in two issues) of this work was published in Bunyan's lifetime, and at least fourteen copies survive. The issues are identical except for the date on the title-page. Ten copies bear the date 1672, three have 1673, and one has the bottom of the title-page cropped and the date thus missing. The work is listed in the Term Catalogues for Michaelmas Term, 1672 (licensed 21 November).[1] The publisher was Francis Smith, who was known as 'Elephant Smith' because of his imprint 'at the Elephant and Castle, without Temple-Bar'. His political and religious views and his work as a printer of Nonconformist books sometimes made him the centre of controversy. He suffered attacks by mobs on his person and property, had numbers of books confiscated, and was imprisoned several times. Smith first served as Bunyan's publisher for *Profitable Meditations* (1661), and continued to be associated with him for some 25 years. Altogether, he may have printed as many as fifteen Bunyan works.[2]

Title-page: A | DEFENCE | OF THE | Doctrine of Iustification, | BY | FAITH IN JESUS CHRIST: | SHEWING, | True Gospel-Holiness flows from Thence. | OR, | Mr. *FOWLER'S* Pretended Design of | *CHRISTIANITY,* | Proved to be nothing more then to trample | under Foot the Blood of the Son of God; | and the Idolizing of Man's own Righte-|ousness. | AS ALSO, | How while he pretends to be a Minister of the Church of | *England,* he overthroweth the wholesom Doctrine contained | in the 10*th.* 11*th.* and 13*th.* of the Thirty Nine Articles of the | same, and that he falleth in with the Quaker, and Romanist, | against them. | [rule] | By *JOHN BUNYAN.* | [rule] | *Disalowed indeed of men, but chosen of God, and precious,* 1 Pet. 2. 4, | [rule] | Printed for *Francis Smith,* at the Elephant and Castle, without | *Temple-Bar.* 1672.

Collation: 4⁰; A¹–A², B–Q⁴; pp. [i–iv]+ 118 (+2) = 124. Page number 48 is misprinted 46; page numbers 66 and 67 are interchanged, as are 114 and 115; page numbers 33 to the end are in larger type; page number 32 has the larger type for 3 but a much smaller type for 2

[1] *The Term Catalogues, 1668–1709,* ed. E. Arber (1903), i. 116.
[2] Oxford Bunyan, i. 233, viii. 3. Plomer, 273–4.

which also is raised. The first printed page number is 1. Signature 'A1 is not printed, B3 is printed, otherwise signatures are printed on the first two leaves (e.g., C, C2). Q4 is missing from the Bedfordshire County Library copy. Signature L2 is misprinted F2 in the 1672 issues at the Bedfordshire County Library, the Rosenbach Museum and Library, Yale University, and probably the Bodleian (the page in this copy is cropped at the bottom leaving only the top half of the signature), and in the 1673 issues at the British Library and the Rosenbach Museum and Library.

Contents: A1ʳ title-page; A1ᵛ–A2ᵛ premonition to the reader, B1ʳ–Q3ᵛ text, Q3ᵛ errata, Q4ʳ–Q4ᵛ *Books Printed for* Francis Smith *at the* Elephant *and* Castle *near* Temple-Bar' [missing from the Bedfordshire County Library copy] which lists Bunyan's *Confession.* A2ᵛ is signed 'J. Bunyan.' A row of ornaments on B1ʳ is followed by 'A DEFENCE | Of the Doctrine of | JUSTIFICATION | By Faith in Jesus Christ; | Proving, | That Gospel-Holiness flows from thence, &c.' The conclusion of the text on Q3ᵛ is followed by '*The End*', a single rule, and the errata. A single rule on Q4ʳ precedes '*Books Printed for* Francis Smith *at the* Elephant *and* Castle *near* Temple-Bar.' The conclusion of the list of books is followed by 'FINIS.' A slip with three additional corrections (errata B) beginning 'In the Premonition' is pasted on Q3ᵛ below '*The End*' and covers in varying degrees the single rule and four-line introductory statement to the errata, in the 1672 issues at the British Library, Bedfordshire County Library, and Huntington Library, and in both the 1672 and 1673 issues at the Rosenbach Museum and Library.

Running Titles: To the Reader: 'A Premonition to the Reader.' Text: '*A Defence of the Doctrine of Justification | by Faith in Jesus Christ.*' None on B1ʳ, B1ᵛ has '*A Defence of the Doctrine of Justification, &c.*', B2ʳ has the first part, B2ᵛ–B3ʳ and B3ᵛ–B4ʳ have the parts reversed, B4ᵛ and C1ʳ both have the second part. A larger type fount is used from F1ʳ to the end. F2ᵛ, F3ᵛ, F4ᵛ have '*Dostrine*' for *Doctrine*. The 'J' is printed in lower case on 1ᵛ of I, K, L, M, N, and P; 2ᵛ of C, D, E, F, G, H, O, and Q; 3ᵛ of I, K, L, M, N, and P; 4ᵛ of F, G, H, and O. The 'J' is omitted from 4ᵛ of L, M, N, and P, and from O3ᵛ.

Catchwords (selected): A1ᵛ *and*, C1ᵛ different, H1ᵛ By, L2ᵛ more, O1ᵛ *exceed*, Q1ᵛ *especially*.

Copies collated, 1672 issue: Bedfordshire County Library; Bodleian, Oxford (the copy is cropped at the bottom and the date is thus missing from the title-page); British Library; Christ Church, Oxford; Harvard University; Huntington Library; University of Leicester; J. Pierpont Morgan Library; Rosenbach Museum and Library, Philadelphia; William Andrews Clark Memorial Library, Los Angeles; Yale University.

Copies collated, 1673 issue: British Library; Rosenbach Museum and Library, Philadelphia; William Andrews Clark Memorial Libvrary, Los Angeles.

The following text is based on the British Library copy of the 1672 issue.

A Premonition to the Reader.

Gentle Reader,

That thou mayest not be tired with longing to know what Errors, and Doctrines *Destructive* to Christianity, Mr. *Fowler*, in his *Feigned* design of Christianity, hath presented the World withal; and that thou mayest even in the *Entry*, see that which more fully is shewn in the House: Namely, of the Contradiction that is in his Book, to the wholesome Doctrine of the Church of *England*, while he stands a Minister of the same. I have thought convenient, instead of an Epistle, to present thee with those Doctrines contained in his; and that are refuted by the Book that thou hast in thy hand. The which also, I hope, will be a sufficient Apologie for this my undertaking.

His Doctrines are these.

1. *THat the* First *Principles of Morrals*, those *First Written in Mens hearts, are the Essentials, The Indispensible, and Fundamental Points or Doctrines of the Gospel*, Pag. 8, 281, 282. 2. *That these First Principles, are to be followed, Principally, as they are made known to us, by the Dictates of Humane Nature; and that this obedience, is the first, and best sort of obedience, we Christians can perform*, Pag. 8, 9, 10. 3. *That there is* such *a thing as a soundness of Soul, and the purity of Humane Nature in the World*, Pag. 6. 4. *That the* Law, *in the first Principles of it, is far beyond, and more obliging on the hearts of Christians, then is*, That of coming to God by Christ, Pag. 7, 8, 9, 10. 5. *That the Precept of coming to God by Christ, &c. is in its own Nature, a thing* indifferent, *and absolutely considered* neither good nor evil, Pag. 7, 8, 9. 6. *That Christ's great Errand, in coming into the World, was to put us again in Possession of the Holiness* we had lost, P. 12. 7. *That* John *the* Baptist, *the* Angel *that was sent to* Zecharias, *and* Mary, *Preached this Doctrine; and so also did* Malachy *the Prophet*, Pag. 13. 8. *That Christ by Saving us from Sin, is meant, not first, his saving us from the* punishment, *but from the* Filth, *and from the punishment, as a*

Consequence *of that*, Pag. 14, 15. 9. *That Christ's Work, when he was come, was to establish ONLY an inward Real Righteousness*, Pag. 16. 10. *That Christ's fufilling the Law FOR US, was giving more perfect, and lighter instances of Morral Duties, then were before expressly given*, Pag. 17. 11. *That Christ's* Doctrine, Life, Actions, Miracles, Death, Resurrection, Ascension, *and* coming again to Judgement, *is all Preached to establish us in this Righteousness*, Chap. 2, 3, 4, 5, 6, 7, 8. 12. *That is not* possible *a Wicked man should have God's* Pardon, Pag. 119. 13. *That it is impossible Christ's Righteousness should be imputed to an Unrighteous Man*, Pag. 120. 14. *And that if it were, he boldly affirms, it would signifie as little to his happiness, while he continueth so, as would a Gorgious and Splendid Garment, to one that is almost starved*, Pag. 120. 15. *For God to justifie a Wicked man, &c. would far more disparage his Justice and Holiness, then advance his Grace and Kindness*, Pag. 130. 16. *He saith, Men are not Capable of God's pardoning Grace, till they have truly repented of all their Sins*, Pag. 130. 17. *The Devils, saith he, have a large measure of these Attributes of God; as his Power, Knowledge, &c.* Pag. 124. 18. *That Christ did himself perform, as our example, what ever he required of us to do; Yea, That he trod, himself EVERY step of our Way to Heaven*, Pag. 148. 19. *The Salvation of Christ*, First, *Consists in curing our* Wounds, (our Filth.) *And* Secondarily, *In freeing us from the* Smart, Pag. 216. 20. *That pardon doth not so much Consist in Remission, as in healing; to wit, our filth*, Pag. 216. 21. *Faith justifieth, AS it includeth true Holiness in the Nature of it; it justifieth AS it doth SO*, Pag. 221. 22. *That Faith which Intitles a Sinner to so high a Priviledge as that of Justification, must* needs *be* such *as complyeth* with *ALL the purposes of Christ's coming into the World, &c. And it is no* no less *necessary that it should Justifie AS it doth THIS*, Pag. 222. 23. *He wonders that any Worldly man should be so difficultly perswaded, to imbrace THIS account of justifying Faith*, Pag. 222. 24. *There can be no pretence for a man, to think that Faith should be the condition or instrument of Justification, as it complyeth with, only the Precept of relying on Christ's Merits for the obtaining of it*, Pag. 223. 25. *It is, saith he, As clear as the Sun at Noon-day, that obedience to the other Precepts must go before obedience to this*, Pag. 223. 26. *He shall be his Apollo, that can give him a sufficient reason, why Justifying Faith should consist in Recombancy and Relyance on Christ's merits for the pardon of Sin*, Pag. 224.

27. *He will take the boldness to tell those who are displeased with this account of Justifying Faith, that in his opinion it is impossible they should ONCE think of another,* Pag. 225. 28. *The Imputation of Christ's Righteousness, Consisteth in dealing with sincerely Righteous*
5 *Persons, as if they were perfectly so, &c.* Pag. 225. 29. *The grand intent of the Gospel, is, to make us pertakers of inward real Righteousness; and it is but Secondary, that we should be accepted as before,* Pag. 226. 30. *It is not possible (he saith) that any other notion of this Doctrine should have truth in it,* Pag. 226. 31. *Whatsoever is*
10 *commended by the customes of the place we live in, or commanded by Superiours, or made by ANY circumstance convenient to be done, our Christian liberty consisteth in that we have leave to do them,* Pag. 242, 32. *For our refusing to comply with these, can hardly proceed from any thing, then a proud affection of singularity, or at best from*
15 *Supersticious Scrupulosity,* Pag. 242. 33. *Those Ministers hinder the design of Christianity, that Preach up free Grace, and Christian Priviledges OTHER WAYS then as Motives to obedience, and that scarce ever insist upon any other Duties then those of believing, laying hold of Christ's Righteousness, applying the Promifes, &c.* Pag. 262.
20 34. *But to make the Christian Duties to consist either wholly or MOSTLY in THESE, &c. is the way effectually to harden Hypocrites,* Pag. 262. 35. *Those Ministers do nothing less then Promote the design of Christianity, that are never in their Element but when they are talking of the irrespectiveness of God's Decrees, the absolute*
25 *promises, the utter Disability, and perfect Impotency of Natural men, to do any thing towards their own Conversion,* Pag. 262. 36. *He is the* only *Child of* Abraham, *who in the purity of his heart obeyeth those substantial Laws, that are by God imposed upon him,* Pag. 283. 37. *There is NO Duty more affectionately commanded in the Gospel,*
30 *then that of Alms-giving,* Pag. 284. 38. *It is impossible we should not have the design of Christianity accomplished in us, &c. if we make our Saviours most excellent life the Pattern of our lives,* Pag. 296. 39. *To do well is better then* believing, Pag. 299. 40. *To be imitators of Christ's Righteousness even of the Righteousness we shoud rely on, is*
35 *counted by Mr.* Fowler, *more* noble, *then to rely thereon, or trust thereto,* Pag. 300.

1 *displeased*] *dispeased*   5 *grand*] *rand*   39 *commended*] *errata B*;
commanded   13 *refusing*] *errata* B; *resuffering*

Reader,

I Have given thee here but a taste of these things; and by my
Book but a brief reply to the Errors that he by his hath
devulged to the World: Ai, though many more are by me
reflected then the 40 thou art here presented with.   5

God give thee eyes to see, and an heart to shun and escape all
these things that may yet come to pass, for hurt, and to stand
before the Son of Man.

Thus hoping that this short taste may make Mr. *Fowler*
ashamed, and thee receive satisfaction, touching the truth and   10
state of this Man's Spirit and Principles; I rest,

                    Thine to serve thee in the Gospel of Christ.
From Prison, the 27. of the
   12 *Month.* 1671.

                                        J. Bunyan.   15

A

DEFENCE

Of the Doctrine of

JUSTIFICATION

By Faith in Jesus Christ;

Proving,
That Gospel-Holiness flows from thence, &c.

SIR,

Having heard of your Book, Entituled, *The Design of Christianity*; and that in it was contained such Principles, as gave just offence to Christian ears; I was desirous of a view thereof, that from my sight of things I might be the better able to judge. But I could not obtain it till the 13*th* of this 11*th* Month, which was too soon for you Sir, a pretended Minister of the Word, so *vileley* to expose to publick view, the rottenness of your heart in Principles Diametrically opposite to the simplicity of the Gospel of Christ. And had it not been for this consideration, that it is not too late to oppose open Blasphemy, (such as endangereth the Souls of thousands.) I had cast by this answer, as a thing out of season.

Two things are the Design of your Book.

1. *To assert, and justify a thing which you call inward, reall righteousness, and Holiness.*
2. To prove, *That the whole, the grand, the only, and ultimate design of the Gospel of Christ, is to begin, and perfect this righteousness.*

Into the *truth*, or *untruth*, or both *these*, as briefly as I may; I shall at *this* time inquire.

First, Therefore, a little to examine the nature of your

3 that in it] *errata*; in that

Holiness and Righteousness, as your self hath described the same.

It is (say you) *so sound a complexion of Soul, as maintains in life &*
vigour, whatsoever is essential to it, & suffereth not any thing
unnatural to mix with that which is SO: By the force and power 5
whereof, a man is enabled to behave himself as a Creature indued with
a principle of reason; keeps his supreme faculty in its throne,
brings into due subjection all his inferiour ones; his sensual
imagination, his passions and brutish affections.

You adde farther,   10

It is the purity of the humane nature, ingaging those in whom it
resides, to demean themselves suitably in that state in which God hath
placed them; and not to act disbecomingly in any condition,
circumstance or relation. You say moreover,

It is a Divine, or God-like nature, causing an hearty approbation of, 15
and an affectionate complyance with the eternal laws of righteousness;
and a behaviour agreeable to the essential, and immutable differences of
good and evil. page 6.

Farther, *You call it a principle or habit of Soul; originally dictates*
of humane nature. page 8.   20

A disposition and temper of the inward man, as powerfully incline it
to regard, and attend to; affectionately to imbrace and adhere to; to be
actuated by, and under the government of, all those practical principles,
that are made known either by revelation, nature or the use of reason.
page 11. Which in conclusion you call *that* holiness which 25
already we have *lost.* page 12.

Thus Sir is your holiness, *by you* described, which holiness you
aver is that, which is the *great* and *onely* design of Christ to
promote both by his life and glorious Gospel.

To take therefore your description in pieces, if happily there 30
may be found *ought,* but *naught* therein.

It is (say you) *an healthful complexion of Soul, the purity of the*
humane Nature, &c.

Rom. 7. 24.   *Answ.* These are but words; there is no such thing as the
purity of our Nature, *abstract* and *distinct* from the *sinful* pollution 35
that dwelleth in us. 'Tis true, a man may talk of, and by
Argument distinguish between Nature and sin; but that there is
such a Principle in man (since *Adams* fall) a Principle by which

22 *adhere to*] adhere too

he may act, or that Christs whole Gospel-design is, *the helping forward such a Principle*, is altogether without Scripture or reason. There is no man by *Nature*, that hath any soundness in him, no, neither in Soul or Body; his understanding *is* darkened, his
5 Mind and Conscience *is* defiled, his Wills perverted and obstinate: *There is no judgment in his goings.* Where now is the sound and healthful complexion of Soul? Let the best come to the best, when we have mustered up all the excellencies of the Soul of man, as man, shall nought we find there, *but the* lame, the
10 blind, the defiled, the obstinate and misled faculties thereof. And never think to evade me by saying, the Graces of the Spirit of God are pure: for with *them* you have *nothing* to do; your Doctrine is *of the sound Complexion of Soul, the purity of the humane Nature, a habit of Soul, and the holiness we lost in* Adam, things a
15 great way off from the Spirit of Grace, or the gracious workings of the Spirit. You talk indeed of a *Divine* or *Godlike* Nature, but this is still the *same* with your pure *humane Nature*, or with your *sound* Complexion, or *habit* of Soul; and so must either respect man, as he was Created in the Image or likeness of God, or else
20 you have palpable contradiction in this your description. But it must be concluded, that the Divine Nature *you* talk of, is that, and no other *then the dictates of the humane Nature*, or your feigned *purity* thereof; because you make it by your words the self same; *it is the purity of the humane Nature, it is a Divine or*
25 *Godlike Nature.*

2. But you proceed to tell us of a Degree; *it is so* sound and healthful a complexion or temperature of the faculties, qualities or vertues of Soul, *as maintains in life and vigour, whatsoever is essential to it, and suffereth not any thing unnatural to mix with that*
30 *which is so.*

Answer. If, as was said before, there is no *soundness* of Soul in man, as man, and no such thing as a *purity* of our Nature, *abstract* from that which is sin; then where shall we find *so* healthful a complexion, or temperature of Soul, as to maintain in
35 life and vigour whatsoever is essential to it, and that suffereth not any thing unnatural to mix with that which is *so*?

But let us take *Pauls* definition of a man; *There is none righteous,* Rom. 3. *no not one, there is none that understandeth, there is none that seeketh*

3 that] that that

Isa 1. 6.
Tit. 1. 15.
Ephes. 4. 18.
Isa.59. 6, 7, 8, 9, 10.

after God, they are all gone out of the way, they are together become unprofitable, there is none that doth good, no not one. Their threat is an open Sepulchre, with their Tongues they have used deceit, the poison of Asps is under their lips, whose Mouth is full of Cursing and Bitterness; their feet are swift to shed Blood, destruction and misery are in their 5 *ways, and the way of Peace they have not known, there is no fear of God before their Eyes.* I the rather give you this of *Paul,* then any of my own; because it is the *soundest* complexion of Soul, that the Holy Ghost himself *could* draw. Here is now no purity of the humane Nature, nor such sound complexion of Soul as can keep 10 it self from mixing with that which is contrary to it self. And note, that this is the state of all men, and that as they stand in themselves before God; Wherefore *together,* even *altogether,* all the men in the World, take them in their most pure naturals, or with all the purity of humanity, which they can make, and 15 *together,* they *still* will be *unprofitable,* and so must come short of doing good, *that every mouth might be stopped, and all the World become guilty before God,* ver. 19.

3. But proceeding, you say, that this complexion *is so forcible as to keep his supreme faculty* (I suppose you mean the Conscience) *in* 20 *its Throne, and that brings into due subjection all his inferior ones as namely his sensual imagination, bruitish passions and affections.*

Answ. These words suppose that it is within the power of a mans own Soul, always to keep sin out of it self, and so guilt out of the Conscience; albeit the Scripture saith, that both the mind 25 and it are defiled with the filth of sin, in all whoever do not

Tit. 1. 15.   believe the Gospel, with which belief this description medleth not.

2. They suppose that *this* Conscience is perfectly clear and light, when the Scriptures say they have the understanding 30 darkened; yea and farther, in despite of these your sayings of the sound complexion of Soul, of the purity of humane Nature, and
Eph. 4. 18, 19. of this supreme faculty, the Scriptures teach, *that man in his best*
Thes. 5.   *estate is altogether vanity,* that they are *darkness* and *night,* &c.
Psal. 39. 5.

Yea, say you, *this sound complexion brings into due subjection all* 35 *his inferior ones.*

Asnw. Here seems to be a contradiction to the former part of this description, yea, to the Nature of the Soul it self; for you say; before it suffereth not any thing unnatural to mix it self therewith, when yet here you seem to suggest that part, I say, 40 even *part of it self* is disobedient and rebellious; *It brings into subjection all his inferiour ones.*

It brings into *due* subjection.

Answ. Due subjection is such as is everlasting, universal, perfect
5 in Nature, kind and manner, such as the most righteous, perfect, comprehensive Law, or Commandment cannot object against, or find fault therewith. Here's a Soul! here's a pure humane Nature! here are pure dictates of a brutish beastly man, that neither knows himself nor one tittle of the Word of God. *But*
10 *there is a Generation that are pure in their own Eyes, yet are not washed from their filthiness.*　　　Pro. 30. 12.

It is the purity of the humane Nature, ingaging those in whom it resides, &c.

Answ. That is, *verily* in none at all; for there is no such thing in
15 any man in this world, as a *purity of humane Nature: we are all an unclean thing, and who can bring a clean thing out of an unclean? not*　Isa. 64. 6.
one. Again, *what is man that he should be clean? or he that is born of a*　Job 15. 14.
Woman, that he should be holy? These are therefore expressions without the Testimony of the Word, arising from your own
20 phantasie.

It is a Divine or Godlike Nature.

Answ. Thus you seem allso to fetch from the similitude or likeness of God that was in us at our first Creation, before we sinned; but that similitude being at best but Created, and since
25 most unspeakably defiled, defaced and polluted with sin; there is now, no not in the best of men, as men, any sinless, likeness and similitude of God to be found, no such *petty* Divine or Godlike Nature to be found, as you imagine.

But having thus stated your holiness in its Nature and essence,
30 you come in the next place to tell us, under what considerations it moveth a person to act, also by what Rules and Laws it squareth its acts and doings.

First by or under what considerations it acts, and these you scatter here and there in this your description of holiness, under
35 these heads.

First, *To act as becomes a Creature indued with a principle of reason,* eyeing the state of place in which God hath set him; approving of, affecting and complying with the Eternal Laws of

26 Sinless] *errata*; smiles　　　28 imagine] magine

righteousness, *Page* 6. which eternal Laws in *Page* 8. you call the Divine moral Laws, *those that were first written in the hearts of men, and originally the dictates of humane Nature*, &c.

Secondly, To do these, *from truly generous Motives and Principles*, *Page* 7. such as these.

1. *Because it is most highly becoming all reasonable Creatures* (you might also have added, and those unreasonable) *to obey God in every thing* (within their Spheres) *and as much unbecoming them to disobey him, Page* 8.

2. *Because it is a base thing to do unjustly*, Page 11.

Now a little to touch upon all these, and then to proceed to what is behind.

First, To act and do the things of the moral Law, but as *Creatures indued with a Principle of Reason*, is but to do things in our Sphere as Men, as the Beast, the Hog or Horse doth things in his, as a Beast which is at best, if it could be attained, to act but . as pure naturals, which state of man is of an infinite distance from that, in which it is by God expected, the man must act, that doth ought that is pleasing in his sight. For

First, The qualification and consideration by you propounded, is that which is in *all* men, in men simply as men, they being reasonable Creatures, and somewhat, though but somewhat capable of acting as such.

Secondly, This qualification is not only *in*, but *of* men; *reason* is of the Man *himself*, even that which is as *essential* to him, as is *that* of his being Created or made.

Thirdly, The Law also, which *you* call *Divine*, Moral and Eternal is that which is *naturally* seated in the Heart, and as you your self express it, *is originally the Dictates of human Nature*, or that which Mankind *doth naturally assent to*, Page 11.

Now I say, that a man cannot by these Principles, and these qualifications, please the God of heaven, is apparent.

1. Because *none* of *these* are *Faith, but without Faith it is impossible to please him.* Heb. 11. 6.

2. Because none of these is the *Holy Ghost*, but there is nothing accepted of God, under a New Testament consideration, but those which are the fruits of the Spirit, *Gal.* 5. 22.

3. The *Man* and *Principles* you have stated, may be such as are

22 but] *errata*; qut

utterly Ignorant of Jesus Christ, and of all his New Testament things as *such*: *But the Natural man receiveth not the things of the Spirit of God* (the things of his New Testament) *for they are foolishness to him, neither can he know them, because they are*
5 *Spiritually discerned,* 1 Cor. 2. 24.

4. Your qualifications and considerations, know nothing at all of the *adoption of Sons*, and of our *acting* and *doing* our *Duty*, as *such*. You only content your self to rest within the confines of the humane Nature, acts of reason, as men or Creatures only, or in
10 their supposed *pure, natural Principles*.

And Sir, a little by way of digression; I will tell you also of our truly Christian righteousness, both as to its *original* or *first* Principle, and also *how*, or under *what capacity* it puts the Person that is acted by it.

15 First, The Principle which is laid within us, it is not the purity   1 Cor. 6. 19.
of the humane Nature, *but of the Holy Ghost it self*, which we have of God received, by believing in the Son of God, a principle as far above yours of Humanity, as is the Heavens above the Earth; yours being but like those of the first *Adam*, but ours truly those
20 of the second. *As is the Earthly, such are those that are Earthly; and*   1 Cor. 15.
as is the Heavenly, such are those that are Heavenly.

Now whosoever hath not this Principle, although he be a Creature, and also have *the Dictates* of the humane Nature, yea, and also follows them, yet he is not Christs: *If any man have not*
25 *the Spirit of Christ, he is none of his.* Thus therefore is the Christian   Rom. 8. 9.
Principle, another from, and far above your Heathenish Pagan one. By this Spirit is the Christian qualified with Principles, not Natural, but Spiritual, such as Faith, Hope, Joy, Peace, *&c.* all which are the fruits of the Revelation of the forgiveness of sins,
30 freely by Grace, *through the Redemption that is in Jesus Christ*. In this Spirit and Faith we walk, by this Spirit we are led, even into the Joy and Peace of the New Testament of our Lord; wherefore   Gal. 5. 25.
our Holy Actions are the fruits of Righteousness, *that is by Jesus*   Rom. 8. 14.
Christ, not by our humane Nature, or the purity of it in us; yea,
35 they are the fruits of the Spirit of God, the qualifications that attend the new Covenant, and those that by the work of regeneration are brought within the bounds and Priviledges thereof. Wherefore.

25 *marg.* Rom. 8. 9.] Rev. 8, 9.

Secondly, The capacity that we are in, who act and do from the Heavenly Principle; it is *that of Sons*, the Sons of God *by adoption*, as the Apostle said; *Because ye are Sons, God hath sent forth the Spirit of his Son into your Hearts, crying, Abba Father*. And again, *As many as are led by the Spirit of God they are the Sons of* 5 *God*. This is a far other then is your humane description of acting as a Creature, indued with a Principle of Reason; for here is a man acts as a Son, indued with the Holy Spirit of God, who hath before the World, predestinated him *to this Estate, by Jesus Christ to himself*, As a Son therefore, the Christian acts and does, 10 because he is indued with that high and heavenly Principle, mentioned before, by which Principle this man hath received a *new* Heart, a *new* Spirit, a *new* understanding, a *good* Conscience, so made by *Faith in the blood of the Lord Jesus*: Thus being made again anew, and *another* man; he acts from a *new*, and another 15 Principle then yours; a Principle as far beyond, and above you, as is a *Man* above a *Bruit*, and as is Grace above Nature.

Thirdly, As the Christian acts & does from a better Principle, and under a better capacity or consideration then that you have described; so (to allude to your own notion) the first Principles 20 by which they receive this Spirit and Adoption, are not those Principles of Morals, or those originally dictates of humane Nature; but it is through the *hearing of Faith, Gal.* 3. 1, 2, 3. by which we understand, that the Son of God became a Man, dyed for our sins, hath saved us from the curse of God, and accounted 25 us to be the righteousness of God *in him*; this being *heard* with the Gospel, and a new-Testament-*hearing*, the Holy Ghost forthwith possesseth us, by the glorious working whereof we are helped through the Son, to call the God of Heaven, *our Father*.

Now thus being made *free* from sin, by the only Faith of Jesus 30 Christ, *we have our fruit unto holiness, and the end everlasting life*.

And here come in those reasonable conclusions, which you would make the very radicals of Christianity, they being only remote, and after conclusions, drawn from the forementioned Mercy of God, *viz*. from predestination, Calling, Adoption, and 35 Justification by Christs Blood, *while we in our selves, are sinners*. I say these are the things which *Paul* endeavored to provoke the *Romans, Philippians* and *Colossians* to an Holy Conversation by.

Gal. 4.
Rom. 8.

Eph. 1. 4; 4. 6.

Heb. 10.
2 Cor. 5. 14, 15, 16.

Rom. 6.22, 23.

8 Spirit] Spirir   9 predestinated] *errata*; was predestinated

1. To the *Romans, I beseech you therefore*, saith he, *by the Mercies of God*; (What Mercies? Why those of Election, Redemption, Calling, Justification, and Adoption mentioned in the foregoing Chapters) *that you present your Bodies a living Sacrifice, Holy,*
5 *acceptable to God, which is your reasonable service*, Rom. 12. 1.

2. To the *Philippians, If there be therefore any consolation in Christ, if any Comfort of Love, if any fellowship of the Spirit, of any Bowels and Mercies, fulfill ye my joy, that ye be like minded*, Phil. 2. 1.

3. To the *Colossians, If you then be risen with Christ, seek those*
10 *things that are above, where Christ sitteth on the right hand of God; set your affections on things above, not on things of the Earth; for you are dead, and your life is hid with Christ in God, when Christ who is our life shall appear, then shall ye also appear with him in Glory*. Now mark; mortifie therefore, therefore! wherefore? why, because
15 they were risen with Christ; because they should appear at the end of this World with Christ himself in Glory; therefore mortifie the deeds of the Body, or our Members that are upon the Earth, *Col.* 3. 1, 2, 3, 4, 5.

These Sir are the Motives by which we Christians act;
20 because we are *forgiven*, because we are *Sons*, and if Sons, then Heirs, and so we act; but to speak to this more anon.

Perhaps you will say I deal not fairly with you, because you treat, as of moral, so of Gospel or New Testament Laws.

But to that I will answer at present, that in this description of
25 your Holy Principle, which is the Foundation of your Book, whether the Laws be Natural or Spiritual, moral or of Grace, the Principle by which you do them, is no other then the Principle of Nature, *the dictates of the humane Nature*; and so such as can by no means reach the Doctrines of the Gospel any farther then to
30 make a Judgment of them, by that wisdom which is *enmity with God*, as will farther be seen in my progress through your Book.

Indeed you make mention of Divine Laws, and that under two Heads.

1. *Such as are of an indispensible and Eternal Obligation, as those*
35 *purely moral.*

2. *Such which you call positive precepts, in themselves of an indifferent Nature, and absolutely considered are neither good nor evil.* Of those of this kind that we have under the Gospel, you say you

know but three, *viz, That of coming to God by Christ, and the Institutions of Baptism and the Lords Supper.* Page 7 and Page 9.

So then, although you talk of Gospel positive Laws, and particularly that *of coming to God by Christ*; yet those which you call first Principles of Morals, are of higher concern with you, and more indispensible by far then this, this being a thing of an indifferent Nature, and in it self absolutely considered, is neither good nor evil; but the other is the life of the matter. But a little to gather you up.

The Morals, say you, are indispensible, and good in themselves; *but that of coming to God by Christ, a thing indifferent, and in it self neither good nor evil.* Wherefore though in this your description, you talk of confirming to all those good and practical Principles, that are made known either by Revelation, Nature, or the use of Reason, yet in this your obedience you reckon *coming to God by Christ*, but an act of a very indifferent Nature, a thing if done *not good in it self*, neither evil in it self, should a man leave it undone; and so consequently a man may have in him the ground and essentials of Christianity without; it may be saved, and go to Heaven without it: for this I say, whatsoever is of an indifferent Nature in it self, is not essential to the Christian Religion; but may or may not be done without the hazard of Eternal Salvation; but say you, this of coming to God by Christ, is one of the positive precepts, *Page* 9. which are in themselves things indifferent, and neither good nor evil: therefore not of the substance of Christianity.

But Sir, *where learned you this new Doctrine*, as to reckon coming to God by Christ, a thing of so indifferent a Nature, a thing not good in it self, but with *respect to certain Circumstances*, Page 7? Had you said this of Baptism and the Supper of the Lord; I could with some allowance have born your words, but to count coming to God by Christ a thing indifferent in it self, is a blasphemy that may not be born by Christians; it being too high a contempt of the Blood, and too great a disgrace to the Person of the Lord, the King of Glory, of which more hereafter, but to return.

The intent of this your description is to set before us these two things.

1. What are the essentials of the Rule of that Holiness, which by the Gospel we are immediately obliged to, if we would be justified in the sight of God.

5

10

15

20

25

30

35

40

2. What are the principles by which we act, when we do these
works aright.

For the first you tell us, *they are the first Principles of Morals,*
such as are self evident, and therefore not capable of being properly
5 *demonstrated; as being no less knowable, and easily assented to, then*
any proposition that may be brought for the proof of them, Page 8.
Such as are self-evident or evident of themselves; to what? To us
as men that know the Principles of Reason, and that are as easily
assented to as any proposition; why said you not such as may be
10 as easily known, as we know there is a day or night, Winter and
Summer, or any other thing that may be brought for the proof of
them. This Law therefore is none other, then that mentioned in
Rom. 2. 14, 15. which is the *Law* of *our* Nature, or *that* which was
implanted in us in the day of our *Creation*, and therefore is said to
15 be *our selves*, even *Nature it self*, 1 Cor. 11. 14.

Secondly, the Principle, say you, by which we act, and in the
strength of which we do this Law, it is the Principle of Reason,
or a reasonable compliance with this Law written in our Hearts,
and originally dictates of humane Nature, *&c.* which certain
20 Principle, say you, is this, *To count it most highly becoming all*
reasonable Creatures, to obey God in every thing and as much
disbecoming them, in any thing to disobey him, Page 8.

The sum is; this your Holiness both in root and act is no other
then what is common to all the men on Earth; I mean so
25 common as that for the first, is more in *their* Nature, as the
second is also part of *themselves*, they being Creatures whose
prime or principal distinction from other, consisteth in that they
are *reasonable*, and such as have reason as a thing *essential* to
them; wherefore the excellency that you have discoursed of, is
30 none other then the excellency and goodness that is of this
World, such as in the first Principles of it is common to
Heathens, Pagans, Turks, Infidels: and that as evidently dictates
to those that have not heard the Gospel (I mean as to the Nature
the good and evil) as it doth in them that sit under the sound
35 thereof; and is the self same which our late ungodly Heriticks the
Quakers have made such a stir to promote and exalt it, only in
the description thereof you seem more ingenious then they: for
whereas they erroniously call it Christ, the light of Christ, Faith,

9 why said you not such] *errata*; such   25 is more in] *errata*; is in
36 exalt it] *errata*; exalt

Grace, Hope, the Spirit, the Word that is nigh, &c. you give it
the names due thereto, *viz. A complexion or complication and
combination of all the virtue of the Soul, the humane Nature, the
dictates of it, the Principles of reason, such as are self-evident, than
which there is nothing Mankind doth naturally assent to,* Page 6, 7, 8,   5
9, 10, 11. only here as I have said, you glorifie your errors also,
with Names and Titles that are not to be found, but in your own
deluded Brains: As that the virtues of the Souls can keep
themselves *incommixed*, that there is yet in us the *purity* of the
humane Nature or *such* a disposition, that can both by light and   10
power give a man to see, and powerfully incline him to, and bring
him under the government of all those good and practical
principles, that are made known either by Revelation, Nature, or
the use of Reason.

But I say, these principles thus stated by you, being the   15
principles, and the goodness of this World, and such as have not
faith, but the law, not the holy Ghost, but humane nature in
them; they cannot be those which you affirm, was or is the
design, the great, the only, and ultimate design of Christ, or his
Gospel to promote, and propagate in the World; neither with   20
respect to our justification before God from the curse; neither
with respect to the workings of his Spirit, and the faith of Jesus in
our hearts, the true Gospel or evangelical Holiness.

First, It is not the righteousness that justifieth us *before God*
from the curse; because it is that which is properly *our own*; and   25
acted and managed by principles of *our own*, arising originally in
the roots of it, from *our own.* There is the righteousness of Men,
and the righteousness of God: that which is the righteousness
of Men, is that which we do work from matter and principles of
our own; but that which is the righteousness of God, is that which   30
is wrought from matter and principles purely Divine, and of the
Nature of God. Again, that which is our own righteousness, is
that which is wrought in and by *our own persons as Men*; but that
which is the righteousness of God, is that which is wrought in
and by the second person in the Trinity, *as God and Man* in one   35
person; and that resideth onely in that person of the Son. I speak
now of the righteousness by which we stand just before God,
from the curse of the Law. Now this righteousness of ours, *our
own* righteousness, the Apostle always opposeth to the righteousness of God, saying, *They going about to establish their OWN*   40

*righteousness, have not submitted themselves to the righteousness of
God.* Farther, This righteousness of *our own*, Paul counts *loss* and   Rom. 10. 3.
dogs-meat, in comparison of that other, far more glorious
righteousness, which he calleth as it is in truth, *the righteousness of*
5 *God*, which as I said but now, *resideth in the person of the son.*
Therefore saith *Paul*, I cast away my own righteousness, *and do
count it loss, and but dung, that I may win Christ, and be found in
him, not having my own righteousness, which is of the law, but that
which is through the faith of Christ, the righteousness which is of God*
10 *by faith.* The righteousness therefore, that is *our own*, that ariseth
from matter and principles of *our own*, (such as that which you
have described) justifieth us not *before God* from the curse.

Secondly, The righteousness that you have described, justifieth
15 us not as before, because it is the righteousness which is of the
moral law, that is, it is wrought by us, as walking in the law. Now
it mattereth not, whether you respect the law in its first
principles, or as it is revealed in the table of the ten
Commandments, they are in nature but one, and the same, and
20 their substance and matter is written in our Hearts, as we are
Men. Now this righteousness, the Apostle casteth away, as was
shewed before; not having mine own righteousness, (saith he)
which is of the law; why? Because the righteousness that saveth us
from the wrath of God, is the righteousness of God; and so a
25 righteousness that is without the law. *But now the righteousness of
God without the law is manifest, being witnessed by the law and the*   Rom. 3. 21, 22,
prophets, even the righteousness of God, which is by faith of Jesus   23.
Christ, unto all, and upon all them that believe. Rom. 3. The
righteousness of God without the law; the righteousness of
30 Christ who is naturally God; wherefore such a righteousness, as
was accomplished by him, that was Lord, and the very God of
the law; whose nature was infinite, and not that which the law
could command or condemn; neither was the command of the
law, the great and principal argument with him, no, not in its first
35 and highest principles, to do or continue to do it; but even that
which the law commanded of us, that he did, *not by the law*, but
by *that spirit* of life, that eternal Spirit, and God-head, which was
essential to his very being: He did naturally and infinitely that
which the law required of us, from higher, and more mighty
40 principles then the law could require of him: for I should reckon

it a piece of prodigious blasphemy, to say, that the Law could
command his God, the Creature, his Lord and Creator: but this
Lord God, Jesus Christ, even he hath accomplished rightous-
ness, even righteousness that is without, that is above, higher,
and better then that of the Law: and that is the righteousness   5
that is given to, and put upon all them that believe. Wherefore
the Lord Jesus Christ, in his most blessed life, was neither
prompted to actions of holiness, nor managed in them, by the
purity of human nature, or those you call first principles of
morals, or as he was simply a reasonable Creature; but being the   10
natural Son of God, truly, and essentially, eternal as the Father;
by the eternal Spirit, his God-head, was his man-hood governed,
and acted, and spirited to do and suffer. *He through the eternal*

Heb. 9. 14.   *spirit offered himself without spot to God*; which offering respects
not onely his act of dying, but also that by which he was   15
capacitated to dye without spot in his sight; which was the infinite
Dignity, and Sinlessness of his person; and the perfect justice of
his Actions. Now this person, thus acting, is approved of, or
justified by the Law to be good: for if the righteousness of the
Law be good, which Law is but a creature, the righteousness of   20
the Lord, the God of this Law, must needs be much more good;
wherefore here is the Law, and its perfection swallowed up, even as
the light of a Candle, or Star is swallowed up by the light of the
Sun. Thus then is the believer made, not the righteousness of
the Law, *but the righteousness of God in Christ*; because Christ   25

2 Cor. 5. 21.   Jesus who is the righteousness of the Christian, did walk in this
world, in, and under the Law; not by legal and humane
principles, which are the excellencies of men, but in, and by
those that are divine, even such as were, and are of his own
nature, and the essence of his eternal God-head. This is the   30
righteousness *without* the Law, accompanied by a person, and
principles, far otherwise, then is he, or those you make
description of; and therefore yours cannot be that, by which we
stand just before the justice of God *without* the Law; Now if it be
a righteousness *without* the Law, then it is a righteousness   35
without Men, a righteousness that cannot be found in the World;
For take away the Law, the rule, and you take away, not onely the
righteousness, but that by which men, as men, work righteousness in the World: *Mine own righteousness which is of the Law*. The
righteousness then by which a man must stand just in the sight of   40

God from the curse, is not to be found in men, nor in the Law, but in him, and him onely, who is greater, and also, *without the Law*; For albeit, for our sakes he became under the Law, even to the curse and displeasure of God; yet the principles by which he
5 walked in the World to God-ward, they were neither humane, nor legal, but heavenly, and done in the Spirit of the Son: Wherefore it is not the righteousness you have described, by which we stand just before God.

Thirdly, the righteousness you have described, cannot be that
10 which justifieth us before God, because of its imperfections, and that both with respect to the principle, and the power with which it is managed: For though you have talked of a sound complexion of Soul, the purity of the humane nature, and that with this addition of power, as to be able to keep it self incommixt with
15 that which is not of it self; yet we Christians know, and that by the words of God, that there is in man, as man, now no soundness at all, but from the *crown of the head, to the sole of the foot, Botches, and Boyls, Putrifactions, and Sores. We are ALL an*   Isa. 1. 6. *unclean thing; and our righteousness, as filthy ulcerous raggs. If there*   Isa. 64. 6.
20 *had been a Law given that could have given life, verily, righteousness*   Gal. 3. 21. *should have been by the Law.* Could a man perform the Law to the liking of the justice of the eternal majesty, then would the Law give life to that man; but because of the perfection of an infinite justice, and the weakness and unprofitableness of the Law   Rom. 8.3.
25 through our flesh, therefore, though you speak yet farther of the excellency of your sound complexion, and of the purity of the humane nature, you must flie from your self, to another righteousness for life, or at the last stick in the jaws of Death and everlasting Desperation. *For by the works of the Law shall no flesh*
30 *be justified.* Gal. 2. 16.

It is therefore no better then error, thus to ascribe to poor man, *that hath drunk iniquity like water*, a soundness of soul, a purity of humane nature. Wherefore *Jude* saith of you, and of all such naturalists, *That even in the things that you know naturally, as*
35 *the bruit, in them you corrupt your selves.* Jude 10. even in the very principles, the first or original dictates of your nature, or humanity. There is none that understandeth or is good, therefore there is none that doth good, *no not one*: that is, none as continuing in a natural state; none by the power or principles of
40 nature; for he meaneth here, in your own sense, as men by

natural principles have to do with the justice of the Law.

Fourthly, The righteousness which you have described, cannot be that which justifieth us before God, because it is that which is not of faith. *The Law is not of faith, but the man that doth them shall live in them.* Gal. 3. The Apostle also in the 10*th.* 5 *Chapter* of the *Romans* tells us, that the righteousness that is compleated by doing the Law is one, and another, besides the righteousness of faith. For faith in the justification of a sinner from the curse and wrath of God, respecteth onely the mercy of God, and forgiveness of sins for the sake of Christ. *God for* 10 *Christs sake hath forgiven him, that is enabled to believe, that is, trust to, and venture the eternal concern of his soul upon the righteousness that is no where to be found, but in the person of the Son of God.* For there is justice more then answerable to all the demands of the Law, and equal to the requirements of the eternal justice of God, 15 and he is our justice; He is made unto us of God, righteousness, or justice; that is the righteousness or justice that is in him; is by God accounted the mans that shall accept thereof by faith, that he might be made the justice or righteousness of God in him. For the righteousness that saveth a sinner from damnation, must 20 be equal to that in the eternal Deity: but where can that be found but in him that is naturally God, as is indeed the son of the Father; in him therefore, and not in the Law, there is a righteousness fit for faith to apply to. Besides, the Law is not, neither can be the object of faith to men; for that which is the 25 object of faith (I speak now as to justifying righteousness) it must be a righteousness already compleated, and as I said, a righteousness to be received, and accepted, being now perfected and offered, and given to us by the kindness and mercy of God: but a man may believe long enough in the Law, before that 30 performs for him a perfect righteousness. The Law can work nothing unless it be wrath. *Rom.* 4. No thou must work *BY*, and not *believe IN* the Law. Besides, all that cometh out of the mouth

Gal. 3.10.

of the Law is, *Cursed is every one that continueth not in every thing which is written in the book of the Law to do them*; which no man is 35 capable of doing, so as to escape the curse by doing, that hath once, or first transgressed the same. Wherefore it is a vain thing, yea an horrible wickedness in you, thus to abuse the Law, and

15 and equal to the] *errata*; and the   34 *marg.* Gal. 3. 10.] Gal. 3. 13.

the weakness of man, by suggesting that the onely, the ultimate, or grand design of Christ Jesus was, or is, *the promoting of a righteousness by the Law*, that is performed by humane principles in us.

5   I could double, yea ten times double the number of these arguments against you, but I will pass from this to the second thing. *The righteousness you have described, is not the true Gospel inward holiness.*

I told you before, that the principles which you have
10 described, are not evangelical principles; and now I will adde, that as they are not such in themselves, so neither do they fetch in, or obtain by our adhering to them, those things which alone can make, or work in the Soul, those truly Gospel inward acts of holiness.

15   There are three things which are essential to the inward Gospel holiness; of which as your description is utterly destitute, so, neither can they by that be obtained, or come into the heart.

1. *The holy Ghost.*
2. *Faith in Christ.*
20 3. *A new Heart, and a new Spirit.*

Without these three, there is no such thing as Gospel holiness in Man, as before I have also hinted at. But now as there is none of these three found in your discription of inward Holiness; so neither can you, or other, by all your inclinations, either to those
25 you call first principles of natural reason, or the dictates of humane nature, obtain or fetch in the Soul, the least dram of that which is essential, to that which is indeed according to the Gospel description of inward Gospel holiness: as will further be manifest in this that followeth.

30   1. The holy Ghost is not obtained by your description, that consisting only in principles of Nature, and in putting forth it self in acts of Civility and Morality. When the Apostle would convince the bewitched *Galathians*, that your Doctrine which was also the Doctrine of the false Apostles, was that, which
35 instead of helping forward, did hinder, and pervert the Gospel of Christ; he applieth himself to them in this manner. *This onely* Gal. 3. 2, 3. *would I learn of you; Received you the Spirit by the works of the Law, or by the hearing of Faith?* By the works of the Law, that is, by putting of your principles into practice. Nay, may I not adde,
40 by putting of your principles into practice, by a more bright, and

clear rule, then in the beginning of your description is inserted
by you; for the Law as written and engraven in stones, with the
addition of all the Mosaical precepts, was a more ample, and full
Rom. 3. 1, 2, 3. discovery of the mind of God, then can be obtained by your
virtues of Soul, your purity of humane nature, or the first 5
principles of morals, as they are written in the heart of man; and
originally dictates of humane nature. Yet by these, by following
these, by labouring to live up to the light of these, their own
experience told them, that they neither could, nor did obtain the
enjoyment of the holy Ghost; but that rather their now declining 10
the word of Faith, by which indeed they receive it at first
(whatever pretences of holiness, and godliness were the arguments
to prevail with them so to do) was in truth none other but the
very witch-craft, and inchantments of the Devil.

Farther, The Apostle sets this your Spirit and Principles; and 15
that which indeed is the Spirit of God, in a line *Diametrically*
opposite one against another; yea the receiving of the one,
opposeth the receiving of the other. *Now we have received*, saith
he, *NOT the Spirit of the World* (that is, your spirit, and principles
of humanity) to walk by it, or live in it; *but the Spirit which is of* 20
God, that we may know the things that are freely given us of God. 1
Cor. 2. 12. But what is the Spirit of the World? He tells us in
the verse before, it is the Spirit of a man; *which Solomon calls, the*
Candle of the Lord; that which searcheth all the inward parts of
the Belly. *Prov.* 20. 27. by humane principles, good motions to 25
moral duties, workings of reason, dictates of nature to obey God
as Creator. These things flow from the *Spirit of a man*, which is
the Spirit of *all the World*. They that preach, or speak by this
Spirit; they preach or speak *of the World*, of the virtues of the
World; and the World, *the whole World heareth them*, or know in 30
1 Joh, 4. 5. themselves what they say.

Now when this Spirit is received, imbraced and followed, as
the Spirit *that is of God*, then it must be branded with the mark of
the Spirit of error, and of Antichrist; because the act in so doing,
is most wicked; yea, and Christ himself is made head against, by it. 35

But I say, the holy Ghost is not obtained by these principles,
nor by the pursuit of them.

2. Faith is not obtained by the pursuit of your principle; but
by hearing of another doctrine. He that presseth men to look to,
and live by the purity of humane nature, principles of natural 40

reason, or by the Law, *as written in the heart, or Bible*; he sets the
word of Faith *out of the World*; for these doctrines are as opposite,
as the Spirits I spake of before; For *Moses describeth the
righteousness that is of the Law, that the man that doth these things
5 shall live by them.* Now he that receiveth this Law, to do, and live
by; he hath set up, and is in pursuit of a doctrine of another
nature, then that which is called the righteousness of faith;
that being such, as for justification, and deliverance from the
curse, maketh no mention at all of hearing the Law, or of doing
10 good works; but of hearing of the mercy of God, as extended to
sinners; and of its coming to us through the death, and
resurrection of Christ Jesus. *The righteousness which is of Faith,
speaketh on this wise; say not in thine heart, who shall ascend into
Heaven (that is to bring Christ down from above) or who shall descend
15 into the deep, (that is to bring up Christ again from the dead) but what
saith it? The word is nigh thee, even in thy mouth, and in thy heart;
that is the word of faith which we preach; That if thou shalt confess
with thy mouth the Lord Jesus; and shall believe in thine heart that
God hath raised him from the dead, thou shalt be saved.* Rom. 10. 5,
20 9. This *then* is the doctrine of faith; or the righteousness with
which faith hath to do. Now as old covenant-works are begotten
in men *by the doctrine of works*; so faith is begotten *by the doctrine of
faith.* Therefore after he had said, *faith cometh by hearing*; he
insinuates it to be the hearing the preaching of the Gospel of
25 peace (peace by the blood of the cross) and the glad tidings of
good things, (*ver.* 14, 15, 16, 17.) of good things promised for the
sake of the Lord Jesus; not for the sake of good deeds done of us,
by humane principles, or the dictates of our nature.

Faith, Then the second essential, comes into the heart, not by
30 the preaching, or the practice of your principles; but by another,
a higher, and far more heavenly doctrine. And hence the Apostle
compleatly puts the difference betwixt the worker of good works
in the Spirit of the Law; and the believer that taketh hold of
grace by Christ, that he may be saved thereby. The one he calls
35 *Them that are of the works of the Law*: the other, *They which are of* Gal. 3.
Faith. This being done, he tells us, that as they differ in the
principles, to wit, of Faith, and Works, so they shall differ in
conclusion: *For the Law is not of faith; the promise is onely made to
faith, therefore they onely that are of faith, are blessed with faithful
40 Abraham.*

3. The third essential is, *a new Heart*, and *a new Spirit* or *mind*, and this also comes not by your principle, that being but the old covenant that gendreth to bondage, and that holds its *Ismaels* under the curse for ever: there comes no new heart by the Law, nor new Spirit. It is by the new Covenant, even the Gospel, that   5 all things are made new. *Jer.* 31. 33. *Ezek.* 36. *Heb.* 8. 2. 2 *Cor.* 5. 17, 18, 19.

The Apostle after a large discourse of the two ministrations, and their excellencies. (2 *Cor.* 3.) tell us that the heart is nothing changed, so long as it abideth in the works of the Law; but   10 remaineth blind, and ignorant; Nevertheless, saith he, *when it shall turn* (from the Law) *to the Lord, the vail shall be taken away.* But what is it to turn (from the Law) to the Lord? Why even to leave, and forsake your Spirit, and principles, and works from those principles; and flie to the grace, and merits; *the glory of the*   15 *Lord Jesus Christ.* Now when the heart is turned to Christ, then the vail of *Moses* is taken off; wherefore then the soul *with OPEN face, beholding as in a glass the glory of the Lord, is changed from glory to glory, even as by the Spirit of the Lord.* 2 Cor. 3. 14, 18.

Object. But it seems a paradox to many, That a man should live   20 to the Law, that is devote himself to the works of the ten Commandments, the most perfect rule of life; and yet not be counted one changed, or new.

Answ. Though it seemeth an untruth, yet it is most true; That by the works of the Law, no heart is made new, no man made   25 new. A man from principle of nature, and reason, (which principles are of himself, and as old) may give up himself to the goodness of the Law: Yet these principles are so far off from being new, that they are as old as *Adam* in Paradise; and come into the world with all the children of men. To which principles   30 the Law, or the first principles of morals, so equally suit, that as you have said, page 8. *they are self-evident; then which there is nothing man-kind doth more naturally assent unto,* page 11. Now Nature is no new principle, but an old; even our own and of our selves. The Law is no new principle, but old, and one with our   35 selves (as also you well have called it) *first written in mens hearts, and originally dictates of humane nature.* Let a man then be as devout, as is possible for the Law, and the holiness of the Law.

20 *object*] *objct*

Yet if the principles from which he acts; be but the habit of Soul, the purity (as he feigns) of his own nature; principles of natural reason, or the dictates of humane nature; all this is nothing else but the old Gentleman in his Holy-day-cloaths; the old Heart,
5 the old Spirit; the Spirit of the man, not the Spirit of Christ is here.

And hence the Apostle, when he would shew us a man alive, or made a new man indeed; as he talketh of the holy Ghost and faith, so he tells us such *are dead to the Law*, to the Law, as a Law
10 of works; to the Law as to principles of nature. *Wherefore my brethen you are also becom dead to the Law* (the moral Law, and the ceremonial Law) *by the body of Christ, that you should be married to another* (another then the Law) *even to him, who is raised from the dead, that we should bring forth fruit unto God.* Rom. 7. 4.

15 Ye are become dead to the Law: dead to the Law! Why? That you should be married to another: Married to another! Why? *That you should bring forth fruit unto God.* But doth not a man bring forth fruit unto God, that walketh orderly according to the ten Commandments? NO, if he do it before faith make this in
20 the Spirit of a man, by the dictates of humane nature, respecting the Law, as that, by the obeying of which, he must obtain acceptance with God. This is bringing forth fruit unto himself; for all that he doth, he doth it as a man, as a Creature, from principles natural, and of himself, his own and for none other
25 then himself; and therefore he serveth in an old Spirit, the oldness of the letter, and for himself. But now, (that is, *ye being dead to the Law, and married to Christ*) that (the Law) being dead; by which (while in our selves) we were held; *Now we are delivered from that law*, both as to its use and impositions; as it stands a
30 Law of works in the heart of the world; we serve in newness of the Spirit, and not in the oldness of the letter. *v.* 6. A man must first then, be dead to your principles, both of nature, and the Law; if he will serve in a new Spirit, if he would bring forth fruit unto God. Wherefore your description of the principle of
35 holiness in man, and also the principles by which this holiness is put forth by him into righteous acts, they are such as are altogether void of the true essentials of inward Gospel-holiness, and righteousness.

19 faith make this in] *errata*; faith in

But there is one thing more in this description, or rather effect thereof, which I shall also inquire into: And that is your saying, *As it was the errand of Christ to effect our deliverance out of that sinful state we had brought our selves into: so to put us again into possession of that holiness which we HAD LOST.* page 12. The proof of this position is now your next business: that is, if I understand your learning, the remaining part of your book, which consisteth of well nigh 300 pages, is spent for proof thereof; which I doubt not but effectually to confute with less than 300 lines. Onely first by the way, I would have my reader to take notice that in this last Clause. [*to put us again into possession of that holiness which we had lost*] is the sum of all this large description of his holiness in the foregoing pages: that is, the holiness and righteousness that Mr. *Fowler* had been describing; and adds, that Christs whole business when he came into the world was, as to effect our deliverance from sin; *so to put us again in possession of that holiness which we had lost.* The holiness therefore that here he contendeth for, is that, and onely that which was in *Adam* before the fall, which he lost by transgression; and we by transgressing in him. A little therefore to inquire into this, if perhaps his reader and mine, may come to a right understanding of things.

First then, *Adam* before the fall, even in his best and most sinless state, was but a pure natural man, consisting of body and soul; these (to use your own terms) were his pure essentials: In this mans heart, God also did write the Law; that is, (as you term them) *the first principles of morals.* This then was the state of *Adam*, he was a pure natural man; made by God sinless; all the faculties of his soul, and members of his body were clean. *God made man upright.* But he made him not then a *Spiritual man; The first* Adam *was made a living Soul, howbeit that was not first which was Spiritual: but that which was natural, and afterwards that which is Spiritual. The first man is of the earth, earthy.* 1 Cor. 15. A living Soul he was; yet but a *natural man,* even in his first and best estate: but earthly, when compared to Christ; or with them that believe in Christ. So then, the holiness of *Adam in his best estate,* even that which he LOST, and we in him, it was none other, then that which was natural, even the sinless state of a natural man. This holiness then was not of the nature of that, which hath for its root the holy Ghost; for of that we read not at all in him, he

page 11.

page 8.

Eccle. 7.

1 Cor. 15.

onely was indued with a *living Soul*; his holiness then could not
be Gospel, nor that which is a branch of the second covenant: his
acts of righteousness, were not by the operations of the Spirit of
Grace, but the dictates of the Law in his own natural heart. But
5 the Apostle when he treateth of the Christian inherent holiness;
first excluding that in *Adam*, as earthly; he tells us, it is such as is
in Christ: *As is the earthly, such are they, that are earthly; and as is
the heavenly such are they that are heavenly.* Let then those that are
the Sons of *Adam*, in the state of nature as he, though not so
10 pure, and spotless as he, be reckoned to bear his image and
similitude: but let them that are the children of Christ, though
not so pure as he, bear the image and similitude of Christ; *for*   Rom. 8. 29
they are conformable to the image of the Son of God. The holiness
therefore that was in *Adam*, being but that which was natural,
15 earthly, and not of the holy Ghost, cannot be that which Christ
came into the world to give us possession of.

Secondly, *Adam* in his best, and most sinless state, was but a
type or figure: *The figure of him that was to come.* A type in what? A
type or figure doubtless, in his sinless and holy estate; a type and   Rom. 5. 14.
20 figure of the holiness of Christ: But if Christ should come from
heaven, to put us in possession of this sinless holiness that was in
Adam, or that we lost in him: To what more would his work
amount, then to put us into the possession of a natural,
figurative, shadowish, righteousness or holiness. But this he
25 never intended; therefore it is not the possessing of his people
with that holiness, that was the great errand Christ came into the
world upon.

Thirdly, The holiness and righteousness that was in (and that
we lost by) *Adam* before the fall; was such as stood in, and was to
30 be managed by his natural perfect compliance with a covenant
of works. For, *Do not this sin and die*, were the terms that was
from God to *Adam*. But Christ at his coming brings in another, a
better a blessed Covenant of Grace; and likewise possesseth his
Children, with the Holiness, and Priviledges of that Covenant;
35 Not with *Adams* heart nor *Adams* mind; but a *new* Heart, a *new*
Spirit, a *new* Principle to act by; and walk in a new Covenant.
Therefore the Holiness that was in *Adam* before, or that we lost
in him by the Fall, could not be the Holiness that Christ at his
coming made it his great or onely business to put us in
40 possession of.

Fourthly, The Holiness that was in *Adam* before, and that we lost in him by the Fall, was such as might stand with *perfect ignorance of the Mediation of Jesus Christ*: For Christ was not made known to *Adam* as a Saviour, before that *Adam* was a Sinner; neither needed he at all to know him to be his Mediator, before he knew he had offended. But Christ did not come into the World to establish us in, or give us possession of such Holiness as might stand with perfect Ignorance of his Mediatorship. No; The Holiness that we Believers have, and the righteous acts that we fulfil, they come to us, and are done by us, through the knowledge of the Lord Jesus, and of his being the Messias promised.

Fifthly, The Holiness that was in *Adam*, was neither given him *through* the *Promise*, neither encouraged *by* the *Promise*. *Adam* had *no* promise to possess him with a Principle of holiness; it came to him by Creation; neither had he *any promise* to strengthen or encourage him in Holiness. All he had was *Instructions* concerning his Duty, and *Death threatned if he did it not*. But Christ came not to give us possession of an holyness or Righteousness, that came to us by our Creation, without a Promise; and that hath no promise to encourage us to continue therein; but of an Holiness that comes to us by the best of Promises, and that we are encouraged to by the best of Promises. Therefore it was not his great Errand when he came from Heaven to Earth, to put us in possession of that Promiseless holiness that *Adam* had before, and that was lost in him by the Fall.

Lastly, In a word; The Holiness that *Adam* had before, and that we lost in him by the Fall; it was a natural shadowish old Covenant, promiseless holiness; such as stood and might be walked in, while he stood perfectly ignorant of the Mediator Christ. Wherefore it is rather the Design of your *Apollo* the Devil, whom in *Page* 101. you bring forth to applaud your Righteousness; I say, it is rather his Design then Christs, to put men upon an indeavour after a possession of that: For that which is truely Evangelical, is the Spiritual, Substantial, New Covenant, promised holiness; that which cometh to us by, and standeth in the Spirit, Faith and Knowledge of the Son of God, not that which we lost in *Adam*. Wherefore the Song which there you learnt of the Devil, is true, in the sense he made it, and in the

Gen. 3.

Ephes. 4. 21, 22.

2 Pet. 1. 3.

Gen. 2. 15, 16, 17.

5

10

15

20

25

30

35

40

sense for which you bring it; which is, to beget in men, the highest esteem of their own humane nature; and to set up this natural, shadowish, promiseless; ignorant holiness, in opposition to that which is truely Christs.

5   *To dwell in Heaven doth not more please him, then*
     Within the Souls of Pious mortal Men.

This is the Song; but you find it not in *Matthew, Mark, Luke,* or *John,* but among the Heathens who were his Disciples; and who were wont to enquire at his mouth, and learn of him.

10   Thus have I *Rased* the foundation of your Book, even by overthrowing the Holiness, and Righteousness, which by you is set up, as that which is the onely true Gospel, and Evangelical. Wherefore it remaineth, that the rest of your Book, *viz.* whatever therein is brought, and urged for the proof of this your

15   Description of Holiness, *&c.* it is but the abuse of Christ, of Scripture, and Reason; it is but a wresting and corrupting of the Word of God, both to your own destruction, and them that believe you.

But to pass this, and to come to some other passages in your

20   Book; And first to that in Page 5*th.* where you say, *The Holiness, which is the Design of the Religion of Christ Jesus, is not such as is subjected in any thing without us; or is made ours by a meer external, or outward application,* &c.

1. These words secretly smite at the Justification that comes by   *Answ.*

25   the imputation of that most glorious Righteousness that alone resideth in the Person of the Lord Jesus; and that is made ours by an act of eternal Grace, we resting upon it by the Faith of Jesus.

2. But if the Holiness of which you speak, be not subjected in

30   any thing without us; then it is not of all that fulness which it pleased the Father should dwell in Christ: For the Holiness and Righteousness, even the inward Holiness that is in Saints; it is none other then that which dwelleth in the Person of the Son of God in Heaven: Neither doth any man partake of, or enjoy the

35   least measure thereof, but as he is united by Faith to this Son of God. *The thing is as true in him, as in us; in him as the Head, and*   1 Joh. 2. 8. *without measure*; and is originally seated in him, not in us. *Of his*

29 in] *errata*; to   36 *him, as in us*] *errata*; *him in us*

fulness have we all (Saints) *received, and grace for grace.* Wherefore the holiness that hath its original from us; from the purity of the humane nature (which is the thing you aim at) and that originally, as you term it, is the dictates thereof, is the Religion of the *Socinians*, *Quakers*, *&c.* and not the Religion of Jesus Christ.

And now I will come to your indifferent things, *viz.* those which you call, *positive Precepts; things* say you, *of an indifferent nature; and absolutely considered, are neither good nor evil; but are capable of becoming so; onely by reason of certain Circumstances: Of these positive indifferent Precepts,* you say, *you know but three in the Gospel; but three that are purely so* viz. *That of coming to God by Christ, the Institutions of Baptisme, and the Lords Supper.* This we have in *Page* 7. and 9.

Answ.

1. These words, as I hinted before, are highly derogatory to the Lord the King of Glory, and trample as much upon the Blood of the Son of God, as words can likely do.

For first, If coming to God by Christ, be in it self but an Indifferent thing, then, as I also hinted before, it is not of the substance of Christianity; but a man may be truely a Christian without it; may be saved, and go to heaven without it; This is in truth the Consequence of your words: for things purely of an indifferent nature, do not in themselves either make or marre the Righteousness that justifieth us from the Curse before God. Wherefore by your Argument, if a man remain ignorant of that positive Precept, of *coming to God by Christ*; he remaineth ignorant but of an Indifferent thing, a thing that in its self is neither good nor evil, and therefore not essentially material to his Faith or justifying Righteousness.

2. An indifferent thing *in it self* is next to nothing, neither good nor evil, then but a thing betwixt them both.

Then is the Blood of the Lord Jesus, *in it self,* of no value at all; nor Faith in him, of it self, any more then a thing of nought; their virtue and goodness onely dependeth upon *certain Circumstances* that make them so. For the indifferency of the thing lyeth not simply in coming to God, but in coming to him *by Christ*: Coming otherwise to God, even in this mans eyes, being the All in All; but in *this* coming, in coming to him *by Christ*, there lyeth the indifferency. *I marvel what injury the Lord Jesus hath done this man, that he should have such indifferent thoughts of coming to God by him?*

But hath he no better thoughts of his own good deeds, which are by the Law? Yes doubtless, *for those* (saith he) *are of an*
5 *indispensible, and eternal obligation, which were first written in mens hearts, and originally dictates of human nature. page* 8. Mark, Not a dictate of humane nature, or necessary conclusion or deduction from it, is of an indifferent, but of an indispensible; not of a transient, but of an eternal obligation. It is onely *going to God by*
10 *Christ,* and two other things, that he findeth in the Gospel, that of themselves, are of an indifferent nature.

But how indifferent? Even as indifferent in it self, as the blood of a silly Sheep, or the ashes of an Heifer; for these are his very words. *SUCH* (that is such ordinances as in themselves are of an
15 indifferent nature) *were all the Injunctions and Prohibitions of the Ceremonial Law; and some few SUCH we have under the Gospel.* page 7. Then in *page* 9, he tells you what these positive Precepts under the Gospel or things indifferent are, *THAT of going to God by Christ, is one; and the other two, are Institutions of Baptisme, and*
20 *the Lords Supper. SUCH* therefore as were the Ceremonies of the Law, *such* (even) *SUCH* (saith he) *is that of going to God by Christ,* &c.

Wherefore he that shall lay no more stress upon the Lord Jesus to come to God by, then this man doth, would lay as much (were
25 the old Ceremonies in force) upon a silly Sheep, as upon the Christ of God. For these are all alike, *positive Precepts, such* as were the Ceremonies of the Law, *things in themselves* neither good nor evil, but absolutely considered, of an indifferent nature.

So that to come to God by Christ, is reckoned, of it self, by
30 him, a thing of a very *indifferent* nature, and therefore this man cannot *do it*, but with a very *indifferent* heart, his *great*, and most *substantial* coming to God must needs be by some *other* way: But why should this *THIEF* love thus to *Clamber*, and seek to go to   Joh. 10. 1. God by *other* Means; *such* which he reckoneth of a more
35 indispensible nature; and eternal; seeing Christ onely (as indifferent as he is) is the *onely* way to the Father. *I am the Way* (saith he) *the Truth, and the Life; No man cometh to the Father but by me.* If he be the *onely* Way, then there is *none* other; if he be *thus*

35 indispensible] *errata*; dispensible

the *Truth*, then is all other the *Lye*; and if he be here the *Life*,
then is all other the *Death*; let him call them indispensible and
eternal never so often.

So then, how far off this mans Doctrine is, of sinning against
the Holy Ghost, let him that is wise consider it. For if coming to   5
God by Christ, be in it *self*, but a thing *indifferent*, and onely made
a *Duty* upon the account of certain *Circumstances*: then to come to
God by Christ is a *duty* incumbent upon us *onely* by reason of
certain Circumstances, not that the thing in it self is good; or that
the nature of sin, and the Justice of God layeth a necessity on us   10
so to do. But what be these certain Circumstances? For it is
because of these, (if you will believe him) that God the Father,
yea, the whole Trinity, did consult in Eternity, and consent, that
Christ should be the Way to Life: Now I say, it is partly because
by Him was the greatest safety, he being naturally, the Justice,   15
Wisdome, and Power of God; and partly, because it would (we
having sinned) be utterly impossible we should come to God by
other means and live. He that will call *these* Circumstances, that
is, things over and above besides the Substantials of the Gospel,
will but discover his unbelief and ignorance, *&c.*   20

As for your saying, That *Calvin*, *Peter Martyr*, *Musculus*,
Zanchy, and *others*, did not question, but that God could have
Pardoned sin, without *any other* Satisfaction, then the Repentance
of the Sinner. *page* 84, It matters nothing to me, I have neither
made my Creed out of them, nor other, then the Holy Scriptures   25
of God.

But if Christ was from before all Worlds *ordained* to be the
Saviour, then was he from all Eternity so *appointed* and prepared
to be: And if God be, as *you say*, *infinitely*, page 136, and I will
add, *Eternally*, *just*; how can he Pardon without he be presented   30
with that Satisfaction for Sin, that to all points of the highest
perfection doth answer the Demands of this Infinite, and Eternal
Justice? unless you will say, that the *Repentence* of a Sinner is
sufficient to answer whatever could be justly demanded as a
Satisfaction thereto; which if you should, you would in   35
consequence say, that Man *is*, or *may* be in himself, *just*, that is,
equal with God; or that the sin of Man was not a transgression of
the Law that was given, and a procurer of the Punishment that is

11 to do.] *errata*; to.

threatened, by that Eternal God that gave it. (But let me give you
a Caution, Take heed that you belye not these men) Christ cryes,
If it be possible let this Cup pass from me. If *what* be possible? why,   Mat. 26. 39.
that Sinners should be *saved without* His Blood. *Ought not Christ*   Heb. 9. 22.
Luke 24. 26.
5   *to have suffered? Christ must needs have suffered*, not because of   Acts 17.3.
some certain Circumstances; but because the Eternal Justice of
God, could not consent to the salvation of the Sinner, without a
Satisfaction for the Sin committed. Of which more in the next; if
you shall think good to reply.

10   Now that my Reader may see, that I have not abused you, in
this Reply to your sayings, I will repeat your words at large, and
leave them upon you to answer it.

You say, *Actions may become dutyes, or sins, two wayes: first as they
are compliances with, or transgressions of Divine positive Precepts:*
15   *These are the declarations of the arbitrary Will of God, whereby he*
restraineth our liberty, for great and wise reasons in things that are of
an indifferent nature, and absolutely considered are neither good nor
evil; and so makes things not good in themselves (and are capable of
becoming so, onely by reason of certain Circumstances) Duties; and
20   *things not evil in themselves, sins. SUCH were all the Injunctions and*
Prohibitions of the Ceremonial Law; and some few SUCH we have
under the Gospel. page. 7. Then *page* 9. you tell *us, That the reason*
of the Positive Laws (that is, concerning things in themselves
indifferent) *in the Gospel are declared; of which*, say you, *I know but*
25   *three that are purely so*, viz. *That of Coming to God by Christ, the*
Institution of Baptisme, and the Lords Supper.

Here now let the Reader *note*, That the *positive* Precepts,
declarations of the arbitrary Will of God, in things of an
indifferent nature, being such, as absolutely considered, are
30   neither good nor evil; some few *SUCH* (say you) we have under
the Gospel, namely, that of coming to God by Christ, *&c.* I am
the more punctual in this thing, because you have confounded
your weak Reader with a crooked Parenthesis in the midst of the
Paragraph, and also by deferring to spit your intended venome at
35   Christ, till again you had puzzled him, with your Mathematicks,
and Metaphysicks, *&c.* putting in another Page, betwixt the
beginning, and the end of your blasphemy.

Indeed in the seventh Chapter of your Book, you make a great

22 *us*] *ts*

noise of the Effects and Consequences of the Death of Christ, as
that it was *a Sacrifice for sin*, an *expiatory*, and *propitiatory*
Sacrifice. (*page* 83.) Yet, he that well shall weigh you, and
compare you with your self, shall find that *words* and *sense*, with
you are *two* things; and also, that you have learned of your   5
Brethren of old, to *dissemble* with Words, that thereby your own
heart-errors, and the *Snake* that lyeth in your *bosome*, may *yet*
there abide the more *undiscovered*. For in the conclusion of that
very Chapter, even *in* and *by* a *word* or *two*, you take away *that*
glory, that of *right* belongeth to the *Death* and *Blood* of Christ,   10
and lay it upon other things. For you say,

   *The Scriptures that frequently affirm; that the end of Christs Death
was the forgiveness of our sins, and the reconciling of us to the Father,
we are not SO to understand, as if the blessings were absolutely thereby
procured for us.* (page 91) *any otherwise, then upon the account of our* 15
effectual believing. I answer.

   By the Death of Christ was the Forgiveness of Sins effectually
obtained for all that shall be saved, and they even while yet
Enemies, by that were reconciled unto God. So that, as to
forgiveness from God, it is purely upon the account of grace in   20
Christ; *We are justified by his Blood, we are reconciled to God by the*
Death of his Son. Rom. 5. Yea peace is made by the Blood of his
Cross; And God for Christs sake hath forgiven us. So then, our
effectual believing, is not a procuring cause in the sight of God;
or a condition of ours foreseen by God, and the motive that   25
prevaileth with him to forgive us our manifold transgressions:
Believing being rather that which makes Application, of that
Forgiveness, and that possesseth the Soul with that Peace, that
already is made for us with God, by the Blood of his Son Christ
Jesus; *Being justified by Faith, we have Peace with God through our* 30
Lord Jesus Christ. The peace and comfort of it cometh not to the
Soul, but by believing. Yet the Work is finished, Pardon
procured, Justice being satisfied already, or before, by the
precious Blood of Christ.

   Observe; I am commanded to believe, but what should I   35
believe? or what should be the object of my Faith in the matter of
my justification with God? Why, I am to believe in Christ. I am to
have Faith in his Blood. But what is it to believe in Christ? and

Col. 1. 20.
Ecclus. 4. 31.

Rom 5.1.

28 Soul] *errata*; Son

what to have faith in his Blood? Verily, To believe that while we were yet sinners Christ dyed for us; That even then when we were Enemies, we were Reconciled to God by the *Death* of his Son: To believe that there is a Righteousness *already* for us
5 compleated.

I had as good give you the Apostles Argument and Conclusion in his own language. *But God commended his love towards us, in*   Rom. 5. 6, 7, 8. *that while we were YET sinners, Christ dyed for us; much more then being NOW justified by his Blood, we shall be saved from wrath*
10 *through him.* And note that this word [*now*] respects the same time with [*yet*] that went before. *For if when we were enemies we were reconciled to God, by the Death of his Son; much more being Reconciled, we shall be saved by his life*: or Intercession.

Believing then (as to the business of my deliverance from the   1 Tim. 1. 15.
15 Curse before God) is an *accepting* of, a *trusting* to, or a *receiving*   Ephes. 1. 12, 13. the benefit that Christ hath already obtained for me; by which act   Joh. 1. 12. of Faith, I see my interest in that *Peace* that is made *before* with God by the Blood of his Cross: For if Peace be made *already* by his Blood, then is the Curse taken away from his sight; if the
20 Curse be taken away from his sight, then there is no sin with the Curse of it to be charged from God by the Law, for so long as sin is charged by the Law, with the Curse thereto belonging, the Curse, and so the Wrath of God remaineth.

But (say you) *Christ dyed to put us into a capacity of pardon.* page
25 91.

Answ. True; But that is not all, *He dyed to put us into the Personal Possession of Pardon*: Yea, to put us into a personal Possession of it; and that before we know it.

But (say you) *the Actual removing of our Guilt is not the necessary*
30 *and immediate Result of his Death*, Pag. 91.

Answ. Yea, but it is, *from before the Face of God*; and from the Judgement and Curse of the Law; For before God the Guilt is taken away, by the Death and Blood of his Son, immediately, for all them that shall be saved; else how can it be said we are
35 Justified by his Blood; He hath made Peace by his Blood; *He loved us, and washed us from our Sins in his own Blood*,. and that we   Rev. 1. 5. are Reconciled to God by the Death of his Son; which can by no means be: If notwithstanding, his Death and Blood, Sin in the

14 deliverance] deliveranc

Guilt, and Consequently the Curse that is due thereto, should
yet remain in the sight of God. But what saith the Apostle? *God*
2 Cor. 5.   *was in Christ Reconciling the World to himself; not Imputing their*
Trespasses unto them. Those that are but *Reconciling*, are not yet
Reconciled: I mean, as *Paul*, not yet come aright over in their   5
own Souls by Faith: Yet to these he imputeth not their
Trespasses: Wherefore? because they have none: or because he
forgiveth them as they Believe and Work: Neither of both; but
because he hath, First, made his Son to be Sin for them; and
lay'd all the Guilt and Curse of their Sin upon him; that they   10
might be made the Righteousness of God in him. Therefore
even because by him their Sin and Curse is taken off, from
before the Law of God; therefore, God for the sake of Christ,
seeketh for, and beseecheth the Sinner to be Reconciled: That
is, to believe in, and imbrace his Majesty.   15

No (say you) *The Actual Removing of Guilt, is not the necessary*
and immediate Result of his Death; but Suspended until such time as
the formentioned Conditions, by the help of his Grace are performed by
us.

Answ. 1. Then may a Man have the Grace of God within him;   20
Yea, the Grace and Mercy of the New-Covenant; *viz. Faith*, and
the like, that *yet* remaineth under the *Curse* of the Law; and so
hath *yet* his Sins untaken away from before the Face of God: For
where the Curse is *onely* suspended, it may stand there:
Notwithstanding, in Force against the Soul. Now, let the Soul   25
stand accursed, and his Duties must stand accursed: For, First,
Gen. 4.   the Person, and then the Offering must be accepted of God.
God accepted not the Works of *Cain*, because he had not
accepted his Person: But having first accepted *Abel's* Person, he
Hebr. 11   therefore did accept his Offering. And hence it is said, that *Abel*   30
Offered by Faith: He believed that his Person was accepted of
God, for the sake of the promised *Messias*; and therefore
believed also that his offering should be accepted.

2. Faith, As it respecteth Justification in the sight of God,
must know nothing to rest upon, but the *Mercy* of God, through   35
Christ's Blood: But if the *Curse* be not taken away, *Mercy* also
hangeth in Suspence; yea, lyeth as drowned, and hid in the
bottom of the Sea. This Doctrine then of yours, overthroweth

30 hence] *errata*; here   31 believed] belived

Faith, and rusheth the Soul into the Works of the Law, the Moral Law; and so quite Involveth it in the fear of the Wrath of God, maketh the Soul forget Christ, taketh from it the Object of Faith; and if a Miracle of Mercy prevent not, the soul must dye
5 in everlasting Desperation.

But (say you) *it is Suspended till such time as the forementioned Conditions, by the help of his Grace, be performed by us, Pag.* 92.

Answ. Had you said the *Manifestation* of it is kept from us; it might, *with some Allowance*, have been Admitted: But yet the
10 *Revelation* of it *in the Word*, which in *some Sence* may be called a Manifestation thereof, is first Discovered to us by the Word: Yea, is seen by us; and also believed as a truth *Recorded*; before 1 John 5. 11. the Injoyment thereof be with comfort in our own Souls.

But, you Proceed and say, *Therefore, was the Death of Christ*
15 *Designed, to Procure our Justification, from all Sins past, that we might by this means be Provoked to become New Creatures.*

Answ. That the Death of Christ is a mighty Argument to perswade with the Believer, to Devote himself to God, in Christ, in all things, as becometh one that hath received Grace, and
20 Redemption, by his Blood, is *True*: But that it is in *Our* Power, as is here Insinuated, to become *New Creatures*, is as *Untrue*. The *New* Creature, is of God; yea, *Immediately* of God; Man being as 2 Cor. 5. 17, 18. Uncapable to make himself *A-new*, as a Child to Beget himself; Neither is our Conformity to the Revealed Will of God, any
25 thing else, (if it be Right) then the Fruit and Effect of that: All things are already, or before become New in the Christian Man. But to return:

After all the Flourish you have made about the Death of Christ, even as he is an *Expiatory*, and *Propitiatory* Sacrifice;
30 In Conclusion, you Terminate the Business far short of that for which it was intended of God: For you almost make the Effects thereof but a bare Suspension of present Justice, and Death for Sin: or that which hath delivered us at present from a *Necessity* of dying; that we might live unto God: That is,
35 according as you have Stated it; 'That we might from Principles of Humanity, and Reason, act towards the First Principles of Morals, &c. till we put our selves into a Capacity of Personal and Actual Pardon.'

30 of that for which] *errata*; of which

Answ. The Sum of Your Doctrine therefore is, That Christ by his Death onely holds the Point of the Sword of Justice, *Not that he Received it into his own Soul.* That he Suspends the Curse from us; *Not that himself was made a Curse for us*; that the Guilt might be Remitted by our Vertues: *Not that he was made to be our Sin*: But *Paul* and the New Testament, giveth us Account far otherwise: *viz. That Christ was made our Sin, our Curse, and Death; that we by him* (not by the Principle of pure Humanity, or our Obedience to your first Principles of Morals; &c.) *should be set free from the Law of Sin and Death.*

If any Object that Christ hath designed the Purifying our Hearts and Natures; I Answer,

But he hath not designed to Promote, or to Perfect that righteousness that is Founded on, and Floweth from, the Purity of our Humane Nature: for then he must design the setting up Mans righteousness; that which is of the Law: and then he must design also the setting up of that which is directly in opposition, both to the Righteousness, that of God is designed to Justifie us: and *that* by which we are inwardly made Holy. As I have shewed before.

You have therefore, Sir, in all that you have yet Asserted, shewed no other Wisdom then a Heathen, or of one that is short, even of a Novice in the Gospel.

In the next place, I might Trace you Chapter, by Chapter; and at large Refute, not only the whole design of your Book, by a particular Replication to them; but also sundry, and damnable Errors, that like venome drop from your Pen.

But, as before I told you in general, so here I tell you again, That neither the Scriptures of God, the Promise, or Threatnings, the Life, or Death, Resurrection, Assention, or coming again of Christ to Judgement; hath the least Sillable, or Tendency in them, to set up *Your* Heatherish, and Pagan Holiness, or Righteousness: Wherefore your whole Discourse is but a meer abuse of, and Corrupting the Holy Scriptures, for the fastening, if it might have been, your Errors upon the Godly. I Conclude then upon the whole, that the Gospel hath cast out Mans Righteousness to the Dogs: and Conclude that there is no such thing as a Purity of Humane Nature, as a Principle in us, thereby

2. Cor. 5. 21.

Gal. 3. 13.

5 *he*] errata; *Sin* must   18 to the] *errata*; also to the   35 might] *errata*;

to Work Righteousness withal. Farther, It never thought of
returning us again, to the Holiness we lost in *Adam*: or to make
our perfection to Consist in the Possession of so Natural, and
Ignorant a Principle as that is, in all the things of the Holy
5 Gospel: But hath declared another, and far better way, which
you can by no means understand by all the Dictates of your
Humanity.

I will therefore content my self at present, with gathering up
some few Errors, out of those abundance which are in your
10 Book; and so leave you to God, who can either Pardon these
grievous Errors, or Damn you for your Pride and Blasphemies.

You pretend in the beginning of your Second Chapter, to
prove your Assertion; *Viz. That the great Errand that Christ came
upon, was to put us again into possession of that Holiness which we had
15 lost.* For Proof whereof you bring *John* the Baptist's Doctrine,
and the Angels saying to *Zacharias*, and the Prophet *Malachi*
(*Mat.* 3.12. *Luke* 1. 16, 17. *Mal.* 3. 1, 2, 3.) In which Texts there
is as much for your purpose, and no more, then there is in a
perfect *Blanck*: For which of them speak a *Word* of the
20 Righteousness or Holiness which we have lost? Or, where is it
said, either by these mentioned, or by the whole Scripture, that
we are to be restored *TO*, and put again into Possession of
that Holiness? These are but the Dictates of your Humane
Nature.

25 *John's* Ministry was, *To make ready a People prepared for the Lord
Jesus*: not to Possess them with *themselves*, and their own (but
now lost) Holiness. And so the Angel told his Father, saying,
Many of the Children of Israel *shall he turn to the Lord their God*:
Not to *Adam's* Innocency, or to the Holiness that we lost by him.
30 Neither did the Prophet *Malachi* Prophesie that Christ at his
coming should put men again in Possession of the Holiness we
had lost. And I say again, As you here fall short of your Purpose,
so I Challenge you to produce but one piece of a Text, that in the
least looketh to such a thing. The whole Tenor of the Scripture,
35 that speaks of the Errand of Christ Jesus, tells us another
Lesson, to wit, That he *himself* came to *save* us, and *that* by his
own Righteousness; not *that* in *Adam*, or which we have *lost* in
him, unless you can say, and prove, that we had *once*, even *before*

30 Prophesie] Prohhesie

we were Converted, the Holiness of Christ within us, or the Righteousness of Christ upon us.

But you yet go on, and tell us, *That this was also the Prophesie of the Angel to* Joseph, (Pag. 14.) *in these Words, HE* (Jesus) *shall save his People from their sins. Not* (say you) *from the Punishment of them: although that be a true Sence too: but not the Primary, but Secondary, and implyed onely, and the Consequence of the former Salvation, Pag.* 15.

Answ. Thus *PEN* the Quaker and you run in this, in one and the self same Spirit: He Affirming that Sanctification is antecedent to Justification, but not the Consequence thereof.

2. But what Salvation? *Why Salvation?* say you: *First from the Filth*: For *that is the Primary and First Sence: Justification from the Guilt, being the never-failing Consequence of this.* But how then must Jesus Christ, first save us from the Filth? You add in Pag. 16. *That he shall bring in, instead of the Ceremonial Observations, a far more Noble,* viz. *An Inward Substantial Righteousness: and by Abrogating that* (namely of the Cerimonies) *he shall Establish onely this inward Righteousness.* This is, that Holiness, or Righteousness you tell us of, in the end of the Chapter going before, that *You* acknowledge we had *lost*; so that the Sum of all that you have said, is, *That the way that Christ will take to save his People from their Sins, is, First to Restore unto them, and give them Possession of the Righteousness that they had lost in* Adam: *And having established this in them, he would accquit them also of Guilt.* But that this is a shameless Error, and Blasphemy, is apparent from which hath already been asserted of the Nature of the Holiness, or Righteousness, that we have lost: viz. *That it was only Natural of the Old Covenant, Tipical:And such as might stand with perfect Ignorance of the Mediation of Jesus Christ*: And now I add, That for Christ to come to Establish this Righteousness, is alone; as if he should be sent from Heaven, to overthrow, and Abrogate the eternal Purpose of Grace, which the Father had purposed should be manifested to the World by Christ: but Christ came not to Restore, or to give us Possession of that which was once our own Holiness, but to make us Partakers of that which is in him, *That we might be made Partakers of HIS Holiness.* Neither (were it granted that you speak the truth;) is it possible for a man

33 but] *errata*; For

to be filled with inward Gospel-Holiness, and Righteousness, Heb. 12.
that yet abideth, as before the Face of God, under the Curse of
the Law, or the Guilt of his own Transgressions. The Guilt must
therefore, first be taken off, and we set free by Faith in that
5 Blood, that did it, before we can Act upon Pure Christian
Principles: Pray tell me the meaning of this one Text; which
speaking of Christ, saith, *Who when he had by himself Purged our*
Sins, sat down on the Right Hand of the Majesty on High, Heb. 1.3.
Tell me, I say, by this Text, whether is here intended the Sins of
10 all that shall be saved? If so, what a kind of Purging is here
meant, seeing thousands, & thousands of thousands, of the
Persons intended by this Act of Purging were not then in being,
nor their Personal Sins in Act? And note, he saith, he *Purged*
them, before he sat down at the Right hand of God: Purging
15 then, in this place, cannot First, and Primarily, Respect the
Purging of the Conscience: But the taking; the compleat taking
of the Guilt; and so the Curse from before the face of God,
according to other Scriptures: *He hath made him to be Sin, and*
accursed of God for us. Now he being made the Sin which we
20 committed, and the Curse which we deserved; there is no more
Sin nor Curse: I mean to be charged by the Law, to Damn them
that shall believe; not that their believing takes away the Curse;
but puts the Soul upon trusting to him, that before Purged this
Guilt, and Curse: I say, before he sat down on the Right Hand of
25 God: Not to Suspend, (as you would have it) but to *take away* the   Isaiah 53.
Sin of the World. *The Lord hath LAID upon him the Iniquities of us*   1 Pet. 2.
all: And he BARE them in his own Body on the Tree: Nor yet that he   24
should OFTEN Offer himself; for then must he OFTEN have suffered
since the Foundation of the World: But NOW, (and that at *Once*) *in*
30 *the end of the World, hath he Appeared, to put away Sin, by the*   Heb. 9. 24, 25,
Sacrifice of himself. Mark, he did put it away by the Sacrifice of his   26.
Body and Soul, *when* he dyed on the Cross: but he could not then
put away the inward Filth of *those,* that then remained
Unconverted; or *those* that as yet wanted being in the World. The
35 putting away of Sin therefore, that the Holy Ghost here
intendeth, is, *such* a putting of it away, as respecteth the Guilt,
Curse, and Condemnation thereof, as it stood by the Accusations
of the Law, against all Flesh before the Face of God; which

8 Heb. 1. 3.] *errata;* Heb. 1. 13.   17 so the] so the the   29 at] at)

Guilt, Curse, and Condemnation, Christ himself was made in
that day, when he dyed the Death for us. And this is the First and
Principle Intendment of the Angel, in that blessed saying to
Godly *Joseph*, concerning Christ; *He shall save his People from
their Sins*; from the Guilt and Curse due to them, first: and
afterwards from the Filth thereof. This is yet manifest, farther;
because *the Heart is Purified by Faith*, and Hope, *Acts* 9. 15. 1 *John*
3. 3, 4. Now it is not the Nature of Faith; I mean, of Justifying
Faith; to have any thing for an Object; from which it fetcheth
Peace with God, & Holiness before, or besides the Christ of
God himself, for he is the way to the Father: and no Man can
come to the Father, but by him. Come; that is, so as to find
Acceptance, and Peace with him: The Reason is, because
without his Blood, Guilt remains, *Heb.* 9. 22. He hath made
Peace by the Blood of his Cross: so then, Faith in the first place
seeketh Peace: But why Peace First? because till Peace is fetched
into the Soul, by Faiths laying hold on the blood of Christ, Sin
remains in the Guilt and Curse, though not in the sight of God,
yet upon the Conscience, through the Power of Unbelief: *He that
believeth not stands yet Condemned.* Now, so long as Guilt, and the
Curse in Power remains, there is not Purity, but Unbelief: not
Joy, but Doubting; not Peace, but Peevishness: not Content, but
Murmuring, and Anger, against the Lord himself. *The Law
Worketh Wrath*, Rom. 4. Wherefore, as yet there can be no Purity
of Heart; because that Faith yet wants his Object: But having
once found Peace with God by believing what the Blood of
Christ hath done, Joy followeth, so doth Peace, Quietness,
Content, and Love; *Which is also the fulfilling of the Law*: Yet not
from such Dungish Principles as yours: For so the Apostle calls
them, *Phil.* 3. But from the Holy Ghost it self; which God, by
Faith, hath granted to be received by them that believe in the
Blood of his Jesus.

But you add, *That Christ giveth, First Repentance, and then
forgiveness of Sins.* Page 17.

Answ. 1. This makes nothing for the Holiness which we lost
in *Adam*: for the Proof of which you bring that Text, *Acts* 5. 31.

2. But for Christ to take away Guilt, and the Curse, from
before the Face of Gods is one thing; and to make that discovery
is another.

John 3. 18, 19.

9 which it] *errata*; which   38 Gods] Cods

3. Again, Christ doth not give forgiveness for the sake of that Repentance, which hath it's rise, Originally from the Dictates of our own nature, which is the thing you are to prove; for that Repentance is called the Sorrow of this World; and must be again Repented of: But the Repentence mentioned in the Text, is that which comes from Christ: But,

4. It cannot be for the sake of Gospel Repentance, that the forgiveness of Sins is Manifested, because both are his Peculiar Gift.

5. Therefore, both Faith, and Repentance, and Forgiveness of Sins, are given by Christ; and come to us, for the sake of that Blessed Offering of his Body, once for all: For after he Arose from the Dead, having led Captivity Captive, and taken the Curse from before the Face of God: therefore his Father gave him Gifts for Men, even all the things that are Necessary, and Effectual, for our Conversion, and Preservation in this World, &c. *Ephes.* 4. 6, 7, 8.

This Text therefore, with all the rest you bring, falleth short of the least shew of Proof, *That the great Errand for which Christ came into the World was—to put us in Possession of the Holiness that we had lost.*

Your Third Chapter is as Empty of the Proof of your Design, as that through which we have passed: there being not one Scripture therein cited, that giveth the least intimation, that ever it entred into the Heart of Christ to put us again into Possession of that Holiness which we had before we were Converted: for such was that we lost in *Adam.*

You tell us the Sum of all is, *That we are Commanded to add to to, our Faith, Vertue,* &c. Page 35. I suppose you intend a Gospel Faith, which if you can prove *Adam* had before the fall, and that we lost this Faith in him; and also that this Gospel Faith is none other, but that which Origianally ariseth from, or is the Dictates of Humane Nature, I will confess you have Scripture, and Knowledge beyond me. In the mean time you must suffer me to tell you you are as far in this from the mind of the Holy Ghost, as if you had yet never in all your days heard whether there be a Holy Ghost, or no.

Add to your Faith. The Apostle here lays a Gospel Principle,

24 cited *errata*] Tited

viz. Faith in the Son of God: which Faith layeth hold of the forgiveness of Sins, alone for the sake of Christ: Therefore he is a great way off, of laying the Purity of the Humane Nature, the Law, as written in the heart of natural man, as the Principle of Holiness; from whence is produced good Works in the Soul of the Godly.

In your Fourth Chapter also (Pag. 28.) even in the beginning thereof; even with one Text you have overthrown your whole Book.

This Chapter is to prove, that the onely Design of the Promises, and Threatnings of the Gospel, is to Promote, and put us again in Possession of the Holiness we had lost: (For that the Reader must still remember, is the onely Design of your Book, *Pag.* 12) Whereas the First Text you speak of, maketh mention of the Divine Nature, or of the Spirit of the Living God, which is also received by the Precious Faith of Christ, and the Revelation of the Knowledge of him; this Blessed Spirit, and therefore not the Dictates of Humane Nature, is the Principle that is laid in the Godly: But *Adam*'s Holiness had neither the Knowledge, or Faith, or Spirit of the Lord Jesus, as it's Foundation, or Principle: Yea, Nature was his Foundation, even his own Nature was the Original, from whence his Righteousness and good Works arose.

The next Scriptures also (*viz.* 2 *Cor.* 7. 1. *Rom.* 12. 1.) overthrow you; for they urge the Promises as Motives to stir us up to Holiness. But *Adam* had neither the Spirit of Jesus, or Faith in him, as a Principle; nor any Promises to him as Motives: Wherefore this was not that to which, or which we Christians are Exhorted to seek the Possession of; but that which is Operated by that Spirit which we receive by the Faith of Jesus, and that which is encouraged by those Promises, that God hath *since* given to them that have closed by Faith with Jesus.

The rest also, (in *Pag.* 29.) not one of them doth promise us the Possession of the Holiness we have lost, or any mercy to them that have it.

You add: *And whereas the Promises of Pardon, and of Eternal Life, are Frequently made to believing; there is nothing more Evidently declared, then that this Faith is such as Purifieth the Heart, and is Productive of good Works*, Pag. 30.

4 Principle] Prenciple

2 Pet. 1.

Answ. If the Promise be made *at all* to believing, it is *not* made to us upon the account of the Holiness we had lost; for I tell you yet again, that Holiness *is not of Faith*, neither was *Faith the Effect thereof.* But,

5   2. The Promises of Pardon, though they be made to such a Faith as is Fruitful in good Works: Yet not to it, as it is Fruitful in doing, but in receiving Good. Sir, the quality of Justifying Faith, is this, *Not to Work but to Believe*, as to the Business of pardon of Sin: and that not onely, because of the Sufficiency that this

10 Faith sees in Christ to Justifie, but also for that it knows those whom God thus Pardoneth, *he Justifieth as ungodly. Now to him that Worketh not, but believeth*; (Mark, here Faith and Works are Opposed) *Now to him that Worketh not, but Believeth in him that Justifieth the Ungodly, his Faith is counted for Righteousness,*

15 Rom. 4.

You add farther, *That the Promises may be Reduced to these three Heads; that of the Holy Spirit, of Remission of Sins, and Eternal Happiness, in the Injoyment of God.*

Answ. If you can prove that any of these Promises were made

20 to the Holiness that we had lost, or that by these Promises we are to be Possessed with that Holiness again; I will even now lay down the Bucklers. For albeit, The time will come when the Saints shall be absolutely, and perfectly Sin-less; yet then shall they be also Spiritual, Immortal, and Incorruptible; which you

25 cannot prove *Adam* was, in the best of his Holiness, even that which we lost in him.

The Threatnings you speak of (*Pag.* 35.) are every one made against Sin, but not one of them to drive us into a Possession of that Holiness that we had lost: Nay, contrariwise, he that looks

30 to, or seeks after *that*, is as sure to be Damned, and go to Hell, as he that Transgresseth the Law; because that is not the Righteousness of God, the Righteousness of Christ, the Righteousness of Faith, nor that to which the Promise is made.

35 And this was manifested to the World betimes, even in that day when God drove the Man and his Wife out of *Eden*, and placed Cherubines, and a Flaming Sword in the way by which they came out, to the end, that by going back by *that* way, they might rather be *Killed* and *Dye*, then lay hold of the *Tree of Life*,

40 *Gen.* 3.

Which the Apostle also Respects, when he calleth the way of
the Gospel, the *New* and *Living* Way, even that which is made by
the Blood of Christ; Concluding by this Discription of the Way
that is by Blood, that the other is *Old*, and the *Way* of *Death*; even
that which is by the *Morral* Law, or the Dictates of our Nature,   5
or by that fond Conceit of the Goodly Holiness of *Adam*,
Heb. 10.

Your Fifth Chapter tells us that the Promoting of Holiness
was the design of our Saviours whole Life and Conversation
among Men, *Pag.* 36.   10

Answ. 1. Were this granted, it reacheth nothing at all the
Design, for which you in your way Present us with it: For,

2. That which you have Asserted is, *That the Errand about
which Christ came, was,* as the Effecting our Deliverance out of
that Sinful State we had brought our selves into; *so to put us*   15
again in Possession of that Holiness which we had LOST: For that
you say, is the Business of your Book (*Pag.* 12.) Wherefore you
should have told us in the Head of this Chapter, not so much
that our Saviour Designed the Promoting of Holiness, in
General, by his life; *but that the whole Design of our Saviours Life*   20
and Conversation, was to put us again into Possession of THAT
Holiness which we had lost, into a Possession of *that* Natural, Old
Covenant, Figurative, Ignorant Holiness. But it seems you count
that there is no other, then that now lost, but never again to be
obtained, Holiness, that was in *Adam*.   25

3. Farther: You also Faulter here, as to the Stating of the
Proposition; for in the Beginning of your Book you state it thus;
That the Enduing Men with inward Real Righteousness, or True
Holiness, was the Ultimate end of our Saviours coming into the World;
still meaning the Holiness we lost in *Adam*. You should therefore   30
in this place also, have minded your Reader, of this your
Proposition, and made it manifest if you could, *that the Ultimate*
End of our Saviours whole Life and Conversation, was the Induing
Men with this Adamitish Holiness. But HOLINESS, and THAT
Holiness is alone with you; and to make it his End, and whole   35
End; his Business, and the whole Business of his Life, is but the
same with you.

But you must know that the whole Life and Conversation of
our Saviour, was intended for another Purpose, then to drive us

back to, or to Indue us with such an Holiness, and Righteousness, as I have Proved this to be.

You have therefore in this your Discourse, put an unsufferable
Affront upon the Son of God, in making all his Life and
5 Conversation to Center and Terminate in the Holiness we had
lost: As if the Lord Jesus was sent down from Heaven, and the
Word of God made Flesh; that by a Perfect Life and
Conversation he might shew us how Holy *Adam* was before he
fell; or what an Holiness that our Holiness was, which we had
10 before we were Converted.

Your Discourse therefore of the Life and Conversation of the
Lord Jesus, is none other then Heathenish: For you neither
Treat of the Principle (his Godhead) by which he did his Works;
neither do you in the least, in one Sillable, Aver the First, the
15 main and Prime Reason of this his Conversation; only you Treat
of it so far, as a mean Man might have considered it. And indeed
it stood not with your Design to Treat aright with these things:
For had you Mentioned the First, though but once, your Babel
had tumbled about your Ears: For if in the Holy Jesus *did dwell*
20 *the Word, One* of the *Three* in Heaven; or if the Lord and Saviour
Jesus Christ, was Truly, Essentially, and Naturally God; then
must the *Principle* from whence his *Works* did *Proceed*, be *better*
then the Principle from whence Proceeded the Goodness in
Adam; otherwise *Adam* must be God and Man. Also you do, or
25 may know that the self same act may be done from several
Principles: And again, that it is the Principle from whence the act
is done, and not the bare doing of the act, that makes it better or
worse Accepted, in the Eyes either of God or Men.

Now then to *shew you* the Main, or Chief Design of the Life
30 and Conversation of the Lord Jesus.

First, It was, not to shew us what an Excellent Holiness we
once had in *Adam*; But that thereby God, the Eternal Majesty,
according to his Promise, might be seen by, and dwell with
Mortal Men: For the Godhead being altogether in it's own
35 Nature Invisible, and yet desirous to be seen by, and dwell with
the Children of Men; therefore was the Son, who is the self same
Substance with the Father, closed with, or Tabernacled in our

28 Accepted, in] *errata*; Accepted, or not in

Flesh; that in that Flesh the Nature, and Glory of the Godhead, might be seen by, and dwell with us: *The Word was made Flesh,*

Iohn 1. 14.

and dwelt among us, (and we beheld his Glory: What Glory? The Glory, as of the onely Begotten of the Father) full of Grace and Truth.

1 Iohn 1. 2, 3
Col 1. 15.

Again, *The Life* (that is, the Life of God, in the Works and Conversations of Christ) *was Manifest; and we have seen it, and bear Witness, and shew unto you that Eternal Life which was with the Father, and was Manifested unto us.* And hence he is called *the Image of the Invisible God;* or he by whom the Invisible God is most perfectly presented to the Sons of Men. Did I say before that the God of Glory is desirous to be seen of us? Even so also,

Iohn 14.

have the Pure in Heart, a desire that it should be so: *Lord,* say they, *shew us the Father, and it suffiseth us*: And therefore the promise is

Mat. 5.

for their comfort, that *they shall see God*: But how then must they see him? Why, in the Person, and by the Life, and Works of Jesus. When *Philip* under a mistake, thought of seeing God some other way, then in and by this Lord Jesus Christ; What is the Answer? *Have I been so long time with you,* saith Christ, *and hast thou not known me* Philip? *He that hath seen me hath seen the Father, and how sayest thou then, shew us the Father; Believest thou not that I am in the Father, and the Father in me? The Words that I speak unto you, I speak not of my self, but the Father that dwelleth in me, he doth the Works. Believe me, that I am in the Father, and the Father in me;*

Iohn 14.

or else Believe me for the very Works sake. See here, that both the Words and Works of the Lord Jesus, were not to shew you, and so to call you back to the Holiness that we had lost, but to give us Visions of the Perfections that are in the Father. *He hath given us*

2 Cor. 4. 6

the Knowledge of the Glory of God, in the Face of Jesus Christ. And hence it is that the Apostle, in that brief Collection of the wonderful Mystery of Godliness, placeth this in the Front

1 Tim. 3. 16.

thereof, *God was Manifested in the Flesh*: Was Manifested, *viz.* In and by the Person of Christ: when in the Flesh he lived among us: Manifest, I say, for this, as one Reason, that the Pure in heart, who long after nothing more, might see him. I beseech thee, said *Moses, shew me thy Glory. And will God indeed dwell with Men on the Earth*, saith *Solomon*?

Now to fullfil the desires of them that fear him, hath he shewed himself in Flesh unto them; which Discovery Principally is made by the Words and Works of Christ. But,

Secondly, Christ by his Words and Works of Righteousness, in

the days of his Flesh, neither shewed us which was, nor called us back to the Possession of the Holiness that we had lost; but did Perfect, in, and by himself, the Law for us, that we had Broken. Man being Involved in Sin and Misery, by reason of Transgression
5 Committed against the Law, or Ministration of Death, and being utterly unable to Recover himself there-from, the Son of God himself, Assumeth the Flesh of Man, and for Sin Condemned Sin in that Flesh. And that, First, by walking through the Power of his Eternal Spirit, in the highest Perfection to every point of
10 the whole Law, in it's most Exact and full Requirements; which was to be done, not onely without Commixing Sin in his doing, but by one that was perfectly without the least being of it in his Nature: yea, by one that now was God-Man, because it was God whose Law was broken, and whose Justice was offended. For,
15 were it now possible to give a Man Possession of that Holiness that he hath lost in *Adam*, that Holiness could neither in the Principle, nor Act, deliver from the Sin by him before Committed. This is Evident by many Reasons: First, because it is not a Righteousness able to answer the Demands of the Law
20 for Sin; that requiring not onely a perfect abiding in the thing Commanded, but a satisfaction by death, for the Transgression Committed against the Law. *The Wages of Sin is Death.* Wherefore he that would undertake the Salvation of the World, Rom. 6. must be one who can do both these things: One that can
25 perfectly do the Demands of the Law, in Thought, Word, and Deed, without the least Commixture of the least Sinful thought, in the whole Course of his Life: He must be also able to give by Death, even by the Death that hath the Curse of God in it, a compleat satisfaction to the Law for the breach thereof. Now this
30 could none but Christ accomplish; none else having Power to do it. *I have Power*, said he, *to lay down my Life, and I have Power to take it again: And this Commandment have I Received of my Father.* This Work then must be done, not by another Earthly *Adam*, but by the Lord from Heaven; by one that can Abollish Sin, Destroy
35 the Devil, Kill Death, and Rule as Lord in Heaven and Earth. Now the Words and Works of the Lord Jesus, declared him to be such a one. He was first, *without* Sin; then he *did no Sin*; neither could either the Devil, the whole World, or the Law, find any Deceit in his mouth. But by being under the Law, and walking in
40 the Law, by that Spirit which was the Lord God of the Law, he

not onely did always the things that pleased the Father, but by that means in mans Flesh, he did perfectly accomplish, and fullfil, that Law which all Flesh stood Condemned by. It is a Foolish, and an Heathenish thing, nay worse, to think that the Son of God should onely, or specially, fullfil, or perfect the Law, and the Prophets, by giving more and higher Instances of Morral Duties, then were before expressly given (*Pag.* 17.) This would have been but the Lading of men with heavy Burthens. But know then, whoever thou art that Readest, that Christ's Exposition of the Law, was more to shew thee the Perfection of his own Obedience, then to drive thee back to the Holiness thou hadst lost. For God sent him to fullfil it, by doing it, and dying, to the most sore Sentence it could Pronounce: not as he stood a single Person, but common, as Mediator between God and Man; making up in himself the breach that was made by Sin, betwixt God and the World. For,

Thirdly, He was to dye as a *Lamb,* as a *Lamb* without *Blemish,* and without *Spot,* according to the Type: *Your Lamb shall be* Exod. 12. *without Blemish:* But because there was none such to be found *by,* 1, 2, 3, 4, 5, 6. and *among* all the Children of Men; therefore God sent *his* from Iohn 1. 29. Heaven. Hence *John* calls him *the Lamb of God;* and *Peter,* him 1 Pet 1. 18, 19. that was *without Spot,* who Washed us by his Blood. Now wherein doth it appear that he was *without Spot,* and *Blemish,* but as he walked in the Law. These words therefore *WITHOUT SPOT,* are the Sentence of the Law, who searching him could find nothing in him, why he should be slain, yet he dyed because there was Sin; Sin! where? Not in him, but in his People; *For the* Isa. 53. *Transgression of my People was he stricken* (Isa. 53.) He dyed then for our Sins, and qualified himself so to do, by coming Sin-less into the World, and by going Sin-less through it; for had he not done both these, he must have dyed for himself. But being God, even in Despite of all that stumble at him, he Conquered Death, the Devil, Sin, and the Curse, by himself, and then sat down at the Right Hand of God.

Fourthly, And because he hath a Second Part of his Priestly Heb. 7. Office to do in Heaven, therefore it was thus Requisite that he should *thus* manifest himself to be Holy, and Harmless, Undefiled, and Seperate from Sinners on the Earth: As *Aron First* put on the Holy Garments, and *then* went into the Holiest of all. The Life therefore, and Conversation of our Lord Jesus, was

to shew us with what a Curious Robe and Girdle he went into the Holy Place. And not to shew us with what an Adamitish Holiness he would Possess his own. *Such an High Priest became us, who is Holy, Harmless, and Undefiled, Seperate from Sinners,*
5 *and made Higher then the Heavens,* that he might always be Accepted, both in Person and Offering, when he Presenteth his Blood to God, the Attonement for Sin: Indeed in some things he was an Example to us to follow him; but mark; It was not as he was *Mediator,* not as he was *under the Law to God,* not as he *dyed for*
10 *Sin,* nor as he *maketh Reconciliation for Iniquity.* But in these things Consist the Life of our Soul, and the beginning of our Happiness. He was then Exemplary to us as he carried it Meekly, and Patiently, and Self-denyingly towards the World: But yet not so neither, to any, but such to whom he first offered justification
15 by the means of his own Righteousness. For before he saith *Learn of me,* he saith, *I will give you Rest*; Rest from the Guilt of Sin, and fear of Everlasting Burnings, *Mat.* 11. And so *Peter,* first tells us, *he dyed for our Sins*: And next, that he left us an Example. But should it be granted that the whole of Christ's Life, and
20 Conversation among men, was for our Example, and for no other end at all, but that we should learn to live by his Example, yet it would not follow, but be as far from truth, as the ends of the Earth are assunder, that by this means he sought to Possess us with the Holiness we had lost; for *that* he had not in himself; 'tis
25 true, he was born without Sin, yet *born God and Man*; he lived in the World without Sin, but he lived *as God-Man*; he walked in, and up to the Law, but it was *as God-Man.* Neither did his Manhood, even in those acts of Goodness, which as to action, most properly respected *it*; do ought without, but by, and in
30 Conjunction with his Godhead. Wherefore all, and every whit of the Righteousness, and good that he did, was that of *God-Man*; the Righteousness of *God.* But this was not *Adam*'s Principle, nor any Holiness that we had lost.

Your Fifth Chapter, therefore Consisteth of Words spoken to
35 the Ayr.

Your Sixt Chapter tells us, 'That to make Men truly Vertuous and Holy, was the Design of Christ's Unimitable Actions, or mighty Works and Miracles; and these did onely tend to Promote it,' *Pag.* 68.
40 He neither did, nor needed, so much as one small piece of a

Miracle to perswade men to seek for the Holiness which they
had lost; or to give them again Possession of *that*: For *that* as I
have shewed, though you would fain have it otherwise, is not at
all the Christian, or Gospel Righteousness. Wherefore, in one
word, you are as short by this Chapter to prove your Natural, old   5
Covenant, Promise-less, Figurative Holiness, to be here Designed,
as if you had said so much as amounts to nothing. Farther, Christ
needed not to Work a Miracle to perswade men to fall in Love
with *themselves*, & their own Natural Dictates; to perswade them
that they have a *Purity* of the Humane Nature in them; or that   10
the Holiness which they have lost, is the *onely True*, Real, and
Substantial Holiness: These things, both Corrupted Nature, and
the Devil, have of a long time fastned, and fixed in their minds.

His Miracles therefore tend rather to take Men off of the
Pursuit after the Righteousness or Holiness that we had lost; and   15
to Confirm unto us the truth of a far more Excellent, and Blessed
thing; to wit, the Righteousness of God, of Christ, of Faith, of
the Spirit, which, *that* you speak of never knew: neither is it
possible that he should know it, who is hunting for your sound
Complexion, your Purity of Humane Nature, or it's Dictates, as   20
the onely True, Real, and Substantial Righteousness. *They are
Ignorant of God's Righteousness, that go about to Establish their own
Righteousness*; and neither have, nor can, without a Miracle,
submit themselves unto the Righteousness of God. They cannot
submit THEMSELVES thereto; talk thereof they may, notion it   25
they may, profess it too they may; but for a man to submit *himself*
thereto, is by the mighty power of God.

1 Cor. 14. 22.   Miracles and Signs are for them that *believe not*: Why for them?
That they *might* believe, therefore their State is reckoned fearful,
that have not *yet* believed for all his wondrous Works. *And though*   30
Iohn 12.   *he did so many Miracles among them, yet they believed him not*: But
37, 38, 39, 40.   what should they believe? That Jesus is the true *Messias*, the
Christ that should come into the World. *Do you say that I
Blaspheme* (saith Christ) *because I said I am the Son of God; if I do
not the Works of my Father believe me not; but if I do, though you*   35
*believe not me, believe the Works, that ye may know, and believe, that
the Father is in me, and I in him*, John 10.37, 38. But what is it to
believe that he is *Messias*, or Christ? Even to believe that this
Man, Jesus, was ordained, and appointed of God, (and that
before all Worlds) to be the Saviour of Men, by accomplishing in   40

himself an Everlasting Righteousness for them, and by bearing their Sins in his Body on the Tree; that it was he that was to Reconcile us to God, by the Body of his Flesh, when he hanged on the Cross. This is the Doctrine that at the beginning Christ
5 Preached to that Learned Ignorant *Nicodemus*. *As* Moses (said he) *lifted up the Serpent in the Wilderness, so must the Son of Man be* Iohn 3.14, 15. *lifted up, that whosoever believeth in him should not Perish, but have Everlasting Life.* The Serpent was lifted up upon a Pole; *Christ was hanged on a Tree*: the Serpent was lifted up for Murmurers: Numb. 21.
10 *Christ was hanged up for Sinners*: the Serpent was lifted up for 1, 2, 3, 4, 5, 6, 7, them that were bitten with Fiery Serpents, the fruits of their 8, 9, 10. wicked Murmuring: *Christ was hanged up for them that are bitten with Guilt, the rage of the Devil, and the fear of Death, and wrath*: the Serpent was hanged up to be looked on: *Christ was hanged up*
15 *that we might believe in him, that we might have Faith in his Blood*: They that looked upon the Serpent of Brass lived: *They that believe in Christ shall be saved*, and shall never perish. Was the Serpent then lifted up for them that were good and Godly? No, but for the Sinners: *So God commended his Love to us, in that, while*
20 *we were yet Sinners Christ dyed for us.* But what if they that were Stung, could not, because of the swelling of their face, look up to the Brazen Serpent? then without remedy they dye: *So he that believeth not in Christ shall be Damned.* But might they not be healed by humbling themselves? one would think that better then
25 to live by looking up onely: No, onely looking up did it; when death swallowed up them that looked not. This then is the Doctrine, *Christ came into the World to save Sinners*: according to the Proclamation of *Paul, Be it known unto you therefore, Men and Brethren, that through this Man is Preached unto you the forgiveness of*
30 *Sins; and by him, all that believe are Justified from all things, from which they could not be Justified by the Law of Moses.* The forgiveness of Sins: But what is meant by forgiveness? Forgiveness doth *strictly* respect the Debt, or Punishment that by Sin we have brought upon our selves. But how are we by this Man
35 forgiven this? Because by his Blood he hath answered the Justice of the Law, & so made amends to an offended Majesty. Besides, this Man's Righteousness is made over to him, that looks up to him for Life: Yea, that man is made the Righteousness of God in him. This is the Doctrine, that the Miracles were wrought to
40 confirm, and that both by Christ, and his Apostles; and not that

Holiness, and Righteousness, that is the fruit of a feigned Purity
of our Nature.

Take two or three Instances for all.

The Jews *came round about him, and said unto him, How long dost
thou make us to doubt? If thou be the Christ, tell us plainly.* Jesus
*answered them I told you, and you believed not; the Works that I do in
my Fathers name, they bear witness of me; but ye believe not, because ye
are not of my Sheep,* John 10. 24, 25, 26.

By this Scripture the Lord Jesus testifies what was the end of
his Words, and wondrous Works; *viz. That men might know that
he was the Christ*; that he was sent of God to be the Saviour of the
World: and that these Miracles required of them, first of all, that
they accept of him by *believing*: (a thing little set by, by our
Author) for in *Pag.* 299. he preferreth his doing Righteousness
far before it, and above ALL things else; his words are Verbatim
thus, *Let us exercise our selves unto Real and Substantial Godliness*,
(such as he hath Described in the first part of his Book: *viz.* That
which is the Dictates of his Humane Nature, &c.) *and in keeping
our Consciences void of Offence, both towards God, and towards Men;
and in studying the Gospel to enable us, not to Discourse, or onely to
BELIEVE, but also and above ALL things to DO WELL.* But
Believing, though not with this man, yet by Christ and his
wondrous Miracles, is expected first, and *above ALL* things, from
men; and to *do well*, in the *best Sence* (though his Sence is the
worst,) is that which by the Gospel *is to come after.*

Secondly, *Go into all the World, and Preach the Gospel unto every
Creature; He that Believeth and is Baptized shall be saved; and he that
Believeth not shall be Damned. And these signs shall follow them that
Believe: In my Name shall they cast out Devils, they shall speak with
New Tongues, they shall take up Serpents, and if they drink any deadly
thing it shall not hurt them, &c.* Mark. 16. 16, 17, 18.

Mark you *here*, it is *Believing, Believing*; It is, I say, *Believing* that
is here required by Christ. Believing what? The Gospel; even
good Tydings to Sinners by Jesus Christ; good Tydings of Good,
glad Tydings of good things. Mark how the Apostle hath it:
the glad Tydings is, *that through Jesus is Preached the forgiveness of
Sins; and by him all that BELIEVE are Justified from ALL things,
from which they could not be Justified by the Law of* Moses. Acts 13.
33–39.

These Signs shall follow them that Believe: Mark, Signs *before*,

and Signs *after*, and all to Exite *to*, and Confirm the weight *of
Believing. And they went forth and Preached every where; the Lord
working with them, and Confirming the Word with Signs following,*
Amen. Mark 16. 20.

5   Thirdly, *Therefore we ought to give the more earnest heed to the
things that we have heard, least at any time we should let them slip.
For if the Word spoken by Angels was stedfast, and every Transgression,
and Disobedience received a just Recompence of Reward, how shall we
escape if we neglect so great Salvation? which at the first began to be*
10   *spoken by the Lord, and was Confirmed to us by them that heard him;
God also bearing them Witness with Signs and Wonders, and with
divers Miracles, and Gifts of the Holy Ghost, according to his own
will,* Heb. 2. 1, 2, 3, 4.

Here we are Excited to the *Faith* of the Lord Jesus, under
15   these Words (*so great Salvation.*) As if he had said, *Give earnest
heed*, the *most* earnest heed, to the Doctrine of the Lord Jesus,
because it is *SO great Salvation.* What this Salvation *is*, he tells
us, it is that which was Preached by the Lord himself; *That God
so loved the World, that he gave his onely Begotten Son, that whosoever*
20   *Believed in him should not Perish, but have Everlasting Life,* John
3.God *SO* Loved, that he gave his Son to be *SO* great Salvation.
Now as is expressed in the Text, to be the better for this
Salvation, is, to give heed to *hear* it; *Faith cometh by hearing.*   Rom. 10.

He saith not, give heed to *doing*, but to the *Word you have*
25   *HEARD*, Faith (I say) cometh by *Hearing*, and *Hearing* by *the
Word of God*, Rom. 10. But that this *hearing* is the *hearing of Faith*,
is farther Evident:

1. Because he speaketh of a *great Salvation*, accomplished by
the Love of God in Christ, accomplished by his *Blood. By his own*
30   *Blood he entred into Heaven it self, having Obtained Eternal
Redemption for us*, Heb. 9.

2. This Salvation is set in Opposition to that which was
Propounded before, by the Ministration of Angels, which
Consisted in a Law of Works; that which *Moses* received to give
35   to the Children of *Israel*. For the Law (a command to Works and
Duties) was given by *Moses; but Grace and Truth came by Jesus
Christ.* To live by doing Works is the Doctrine of the Law, and   Iohn 1.
Moses: but to live by *Faith*, and *Grace*, is the Doctrine of Christ,
and the Gospel.

40   Besides, the threatning being pressed with an *HOW shall we*

escape? Respects still a Better, a *Freer*, a more *Gracious Way of Life*, then either the *Morral*, or *Ceremonial* Law; for both these were long before; but here comes *in another Way*, not that Propounded by *Moses*, or the Angels, but since by the *Lord himself. How shall we escape if we neglect so great Salvation?* which *at First began to be spoken by the Lord, and was Confirmed to us by them that heard him.*

Now Mark, It is *this* Salvation, *this SO* great, and Eternal Salvation, that was obtained by the Blood of the Lord himself: It was this, even to Confirm *Faith in this*, that the God of Heaven himself came down, to Confirm by Signs and Wonders; *God bearing them Witness, both with Signs and Wonders, and with divers Miracles, and Gifts of the Holy Ghost, according to his own Will.*

Thus we see, that to establish a Holiness that came from the First Principles of Morrals in us, or that ariseth from the Dictates of our Humane Nature, or to drive us back to that Figurative Holiness that we had *once*, but *lost* in *Adam*, is little thought on by Jesus Christ, and as little intended by any of the Gospel Miracles.

A Word or two more. The Tribute Money you mention, *Pag.* 72. was not as you would clawingly Insinuate for *no* other Purpose, then to shew Christs Loyalty to the Magistrate: But First, and above all, to shew his Godhead, to Confirm his Gospel, and then to shew his Loyalty, the which Sir, the Persons you secretly smite at, have respect for, as much as you.

Again, Also the Curse of the Barren Fig-Tree, mentioned, *Pag.* 73. was not (if the Lord himself may be believed) to give us an Emblem of a Person void of good Works; but to shew his Disciples the Power of *Faith*, and what a wonder-working thing that blessed Grace is. Wherefore when the Disciples wondred at that sudden Blast, that was upon the Tree, Jesus answered not, Behold an Emblem of one void of Morral Vertues; but, *Verily, I say unto you, if you have Faith, and doubt not, ye shall not onely do this which is done to the Fig-Tree, but also if you shall say unto this Mountain, be thou removed, and be thou cast into the Sea, it shall be done; and all things whatsoever ye shall ask in Prayer, Believing, ye shall Receive.* Again *Mark* saith, *When* Peter *saw the Fig-tree, that the Lord had Cursed, dryed up from the Roots, he said to his Master, Behold the Fig-tree which thou Cursed'st is withered away.* Christ now doth not say as you, this Tree was an Emblem of a Professor

void of good Works; but, *Have Faith in, or the Faith of God; For,*
verily I say unto you, whosoever shall say unto this Mountain, Be thou
removed, and be thou cast into the Sea, and shall not doubt in his
Heart, but shall believe that those things which he saith shall come to
5 *pass, he shall have whatsoever he saith; Therefore I say unto you, what*
things soever you desire when you pray, believe that you receive them,
and you shall have them. (Mat. 21. Mark 11.) Christ Jesus
therefore had a higher, and a better end, then that which you
propound, in his cursing the Barren Fig-tree, even to shew, as
10 himself Expounds it, the mighty power of *Faith*; and how it lays
hold of things in Heaven, and tumbleth before it things on Earth.
Wherefore your Scriptureless Exposition, doth but lay you even
Solomon's Proverb, *The Legs of the Lame are not equal,* &c.

I might Inlarge; but enough of this; Onely here I add, that the
15 Wonders and Miracles, that attend the Gospel, were wrought,
and are Recorded, to perswade to Faith in Christ. By Faith in
Christ, men are Justified from the Curse, and Judgement of the
Law. This Faith worketh by Love, by the Love of God it brings
up the Heart to God, and Goodness; but not by *your Covenant,* Ezek. 16. 61.
20 not by Principles of Humane Nature, but of the Spirit of God;
not in a Poor, Legal, Old Covenant, Promiseless, Ignorant,
Shadowish, Natural Holiness, but by the Holy Ghost.

I come now to your Seventh Chapter; but to that I have spoken
briefly already, and therefore here shall be the shorter.
25 In this Chapter you say, *that to make Men Holy was the Design of*
Christ's Death.

Answ. But not with your Described Principles of Humanity,
and Dictates of Humane Nature: He Designed not, as I have
fully proved, neither by his Death, nor Life, to put us into a
30 Possession of the Holiness which we had lost, though the Proof
of that be the business of your Book.

2. To make men holy, was Doubtless, Designed by the Death
and Blood of Christ: But the way and manner of the Proceeding
of the Holy Ghost therein, you write not of; although the First
35 Text you mention (*Pag.* 78. 79.) doth fairly present you with it:
For the way to make men inwardly Holy, by the Death and Blood
of Christ, is, First, to Possess them with the Knowledge of this,
that their Sins were Crucified with him; or that he did bear them
in his Body on the Tree: *Knowing this, that our Old Man is*
40 *Crucified with him, that the body of Sin might be Destroyed, that*

henceforth we should not serve Sin, Rom. 6.6. So he dyed for all, that they that live, should not henceforth live unto themselves (as you would have them) nor to the Law or Dictates of their own Nature, as your Doctrine would perswade them; but to him that 2 Cor. 5. 14 dyed for them, and rose again.

There are two things, in the right stating of the Doctrine of the Effects of the Death and Blood of Christ, that do Naturally Effect in us an Holy Principle, and also a life becoming such a Mercy.

First, For that by it we are set at liberty (by Faith therein) from the Guilt, and Curse that is due to Guilt, from Death, the Devil, and the Wrath to come: NO Incouragement to Holiness, like this, like the Perswasion, and Belief of *this*; because *this* carrieth in it the greatest *expression of Love*, that we are Capable of Hearing, or Believing; and there is nothing that worketh on us so Powerfully as Love. *And herein is Love! not that we Loved God, but* 1 John 4. 10. *that he Loved us, and gave his Son to be the Propitiation for our Sins.* He then that by Faith can see that the Body of his Sin did hang upon the Cross, by the Body of Christ, and that can see by that action, Death and Sin, the Devil and Hell, destroyed for him; 'tis he that will say, *Bless the Lord, O my Soul, and all that is within me Bless his Holy Name*, &c. Psa. 103. 1, 2, 3, 4.

Secondly, Moreover, the Knowledge of this giveth a man to understand this Mistery, That Christ and himself are united in one: For Faith saith, *If our Old man was Crucified with Christ*, then were we also Reckoned in him, when he hanged on the Cross, *I* Gal. 2. 20. *am Crucified with Christ*: All the Elect did Mystically hang upon the Cross in Christ. We then are Dead to the Law, and Sin, First, by the Body of Christ, *Rom.* 7. 4. *Now he that is Dead is free from Sin; now if we be dead with Christ, we Believe that we shall live with him, knowing that Christ being raised from the Dead, Dyeth no more, Death hath no more Dominion over him; for in that he dyed, he dyed unto Sin once; but in that he liveth, he liveth unto God: Likewise reckon your selves also dead unto Sin, but alive unto God, through Jesus Christ our Lord.* This also *Peter* doth lively Discourse of, *Forasmuch then* (saith he) *as Christ hath suffered for us in the Flesh, Arm your selves likewise with the same mind; for he that hath suffered in the Flesh hath ceased from Sin*, 1 Pet. 4. 1, 2. By which Words he Insinuateth the Mystical Union, that is between Christ the Head, and the Elect his Body; Arguing, from the Suffering of a

Part, there should be a Sympathy in the whole: If Christ then
suffered for us, we were (even our Sins, Bodies and Soul)
reckoned in him, when he so suffered. Wherefore, by his
sufferings, the Wrath of God for us is appeased, the Curse is
5 taken from us: For as *Adam* by his acts of Rebellion, made all
that were in him Guilty of his Wickedness; so Christ by his acts,
and doings of Goodness, and Justice, made all that were
reckoned in him good, and Just also: But as *Adam*'s Transgression
did First, and immediately Reside with, and remain in the Person
10 of *Adam* onely, and the Imputation of that Transgression to them
that sprang from him; so the Goodness, and Justice, that was
accomplished by the Second *Adam*, First, and Immediately
Resideth in him, and is made over to his also, by the Imputation
of God. But again, As they that were in *Adam*, stood not onely
15 guilty of Sin, by Imputation, but Polluted by the Filth that
Possessed him at his fall; So the Children of the Second *Adam*,
do not onely (though first) stand Just by Vertue of the Imputation
of the Personal acts of Justice, and Goodness done by Christ, but
they also receive of that inward quality, the Grace, and Holiness
20 that was in him, at the Day of his rising from the Dead.

Thus therefore come we to be Holy, by the Death, and
Blood of the Lord: This also is the Contents of those other
Scriptures, which abusively you Cite, to Justifie your Assertion,
to wit:

25 *That the great Errand of Christ in coming into the World, was—to*
put us again into Possession of the Holiness which we had lost: And
that *onely* Designed the Establishing such a Holiness, as is seated
Originally in our Natures, and Originally Dictates of the
Humane Nature. The rest of the Chapter being spoken to
30 already, I pass it, and Proceed to the next.

Your Eighth Chapter tell us, *That it is onely the Promoting of the*
Design of making Men Holy, that is Aimed at by the Apostles, Insisting
on the Doctrines of Christ's Resurrection, Assention, and coming again
to Judgement.

35 Though this should be granted, as indeed it ought not; yet
there is not one Sillable in all their Doctrines, that tendeth in the
least to drive Men back to the Possession of the Holiness we had
lost; which is still the thing Asserted by you, and that, for the

27 seated] *errata*; Sealed

Proof of which you make this noise, and adoe. Neither did Christ
at all Design the Promoting of Holiness, by such Principles as
you have Asserted in your Book; neither doth the Holy Spirit of
God, either help us in, or excite us to our Duty, *Simply* from
such Natural Principles.   5

But the Apostles in these Doctrines you mention, had far
other Glorious Designs; such as were truly Gospel, and tended
to strengthen our Faith yet farther: As,

First, For the Resurrection of Christ; They Urge *that*, as an
Undeniable Argument, of his doing away Sin, by his Sacrificing,   10
and Death: *He was delivered for our Offences*, because he put
himself into the Room, and State of the Wicked, as undertaking
their Deliverance from Death, and the Everlasting Wrath of
God: Now putting himself into their Condition, he bears their
Sin, and dyes their Death; but how shall we know that by   15
undertaking this Work he did accomplish the thing he intended?
The answer is, *He was raised again for our Justification*, Rom. 4.
25. even to make it manifest that by the Offering of himself he
had Purged our Sins from before the Face of God. For in that he
was raised again, and that by him, for the appeasing of whose   20
Wrath he was delivered up to Death; it is evident that the Work
for us, was by him effectually done: *For God raised him up again.*
And hence it is that *Paul* calls the Resurrection of Christ, *the
sure Mercies of* David, Act. 13. *And as concerning that he raised him
up from the Dead, now no more to return to Corruption; he saith on* 25
this wise, I will give thee the sure Mercies of David. For Christ
having Conquered and overcome Death, Sin, the Devil, and the
Curse, by himself, as 'tis manifest he did, by his rising from the
Dead; what now remains for him, for whom he did this, but
Mercy and Goodness for ever?   30

Wherefore the Resurrection of Christ is that which Sealeth
the truth of our being delivered from the Wrath by his Blood.

Secondly, As to his Ascension, they urge, and make use of that,
for divers weighty Reasons also.

1. A a farther Testimony yet, of the Sufficiency of his   35
Righteousness to Justifie Sinners withal: For if he that under-
taketh the Work, is yet entertained by him, whose Wrath he was
to appease thereby: What is it? but that he hath so compleated
that Work. Wherefore he saith, that the Holy Ghost shall
Convince the world, that he hath a sufficient righteousness, and   40

that because he went to the Father (*John* 16.) And *they saw him no more*; because he, when he Ascended up to the Father, was there Entertained, Accepted, and Imbraced of God. That is an Excellent Word. *He is Chosen of God, and Precious*: Chosen of
5 God, to be the Righteousness, that his Divine Majesty is pleased with, and takes Complacency in; God hath Chosen, Exalted, and set down Christ at his own Right Hand; for the sweet Savour that he smelled in his Blood, when he dyed for the Sins of the World.

10 2. By his Ascension he sheweth how he *returned Conqueror*, and *Victor* over our Enemies. His Ascention was his going home, *from whence* he came, to deliver us from Death: Now it is said, that when he returned home, or *Ascended, he led Captivity Captive*, Eph. 4. that is, carried them Prisoners, whose Prisoners we were:
15 He rode to Heaven in Triumph, having in Chains the Foes of Believers.

3. In that he Ascended, it was, that he might perform for us, the Second Part of his Priestly Office, or Mediator-ship. He is gone into Heaven it self, there, *now to appear in the presence of God*
20 *for us*. Wherefore, he is able to save to the uttermost, all that Heb. 9. 7. come to God by *him*, (as indifferent a thing as you make it to be) *seeing he ever-liveth* (*viz.* in Heaven, whether he is Ascended) *to make Intercession for them*.

4. He Ascended, that he might be Exalted not onely above,
25 but be made head over all things to the Church. Wherefore now in Heaven, as the Lord in whose hand is all Power, he Ruleth over, both Men, and Devils, Sin, and Death, Hell, and all Calamities, for the good and profit of his body, the Church, *Eph.* 1. 19, 20, 21.
30 5. He Ascended to prepare a place for us, who shall live and dye in the Faith of Jesus, *John* 14. 1, 2, 3.

6. He Ascended, because there he was to receive the Holy Ghost, *the great Promise of the New Testament*; that he might Communicate of *that* unto his chosen ones, to give them light to
35 see his wonderful Salvation, and to be as a Principle of Holiness in their Souls: *For the Holy Ghost was not yet given, because that Jesus was not yet Glorified*. But when he Ascended on High, even as he led Captivity Captive, so he received Gifts for Men; by

7 Christ at] Christ at at

which Gifts he meaneth the Holy Ghost, and the Blessed and saving Opperations thereof, *Luke* 24. *Acts* 1. 2.

Thirdly, As to his coming again to Judgement, that Doctrine is urged, to shew the benefit, that the Godly will have at that day, when he shall gather together his Elect, and Chosen, from one end of Heaven unto the other. As also to shew you what an end he will make with those, who have not obeyed his Gospel, *Mat.* 25. 2 *Thes.* 1. 8. 2. *Pet.* 3. 7, 8, 9, 10, 11.

Now 'tis true, all these Doctrines do Forcibly Produce an Holy, and Heavenly life, but neither from your Principles, nor to the end you Propound; to wit, that we should be put into Possession of our first Old Covenant Righteousness, and act from Humane, and Natural Principles.

Your Ninth Chapter is spent, as you suppose, to shew us the Nature, and Evil of Sin; but because you do it more like a Heathen Philosopher, then a Minister of the Gospel, I shall not much trouble my self therewith.

Your Tenth Chapter Consisteth in a Commendation of Vertue, but still of that, and no other, though Counterfeited for another, then at first you have Described, (*Chap.* 1.) even such, which is as much in the Heathens you make mention of, as in any other man, being the same both in Root, and Branches, which is Naturally to be found in all men, even as is Sin and Wickedness it self. And hence you call it here, *A living up to your feigned highest Principle, like a Creature Possessed of a Mind and Reason.* Again, *While we do thus, we act most agreeable to the right frame and temper of our Souls; and Consequently most Naturally; and all the actions of Nature, are confessedly very sweet and Pleasant*; of which very thing you say, *the Heathens had a very great Sence.* Pag. 113, 114.

Answ. No marvel, for it was their Work, not to search the deep things of God, but those which be the things of a man, and to Discourse of that Righteousness, and Principle of Holiness, which was Naturally founded, and found within themselves, as Men; or, as you say, *as Creatures Possessed with a mind, and Reason*: But as I have already shewed, all this may be, where the Holy Ghost and Faith is absent, even by the Dictates, as you call them, of Humane Nature; a Principle, and actions, when trusted to that, as much please the Devil, as any Wickedness, that is committed by the Sons of Men. I should not have thus boldly Inserted it, but that your self did (*Pag.* 101.) tell me of it: but I

believe it was onely Extorted from you; your Judgement, and
your *Apollo* suit not here, though indeed the Devil is in the right;
for this Righteousness and Holiness which is *our own*, and of *our
selves*, is the greatest enemy to Jesus Christ: the Post, against his
5 Post, and the Wall, against his Wall. *I came not to call the Righteous*
(puts you *quite* of the World) *but Sinners to Repentance.*

Your Eleventh Chapter, is, to shew what a miserable Creature
that man is, that is Destitute of your Holiness.

Answ. And I add, as miserable is he, that hath, or knoweth no
10 better: For such an one is under the Curse of God, because he
abideth in the Law of Works, or in the Principles of his own
Nature, which neither can cover his Sins from the sight of God,
nor Possess him with Faith or the Holy Ghost.

There are two things in this Chapter, that Proclaim you to be
15 Ignorant of Jesus Christ.

First you say, *It is not possible a Wicked Man should have God's
Pardon.* Pag. 119. Pag. 130.

Secondly, You *Suppose it to be impossible for Christ's Righteousness to be Imputed to an unrighteous man.* Pag. 120.

20 *Answ.* To both which., a little briefly God doth not use to
Pardon *Painted* Sinners, but such as are *Really so. Christ dyed for
SINNERS, and God Justifieth the UNGODLY*, even him that
worketh not, nor hath no Works to make him Godly. Besides,
Pardon supposeth Sin; now he that is a Sinner, is a Wicked man;
25 by Nature a Child of Wrath, and as such an Object of the Curse
of God, because he hath broken the Law of God. But such God
Pardoneth; not because they have made themselves Holy, or
have given up themselves to the Law of Nature, or the Dictates
of their Humane Principles, but because he will be Gracious, and
30 because he will give to his beloved Son Jesus Christ the benefit
of his Blood.

As to the Second Head; What need is there, that the
Righteousness of Christ should be *Imputed*, where men are
Righteous first? God useth not thus to doe; his Righteousness is
35 for the *stout hearted, and for them that are far from Righteousness*,
Isa. 46. 12, 13.

The Believing of *Abraham* was, while yet he was Uncircumcised; and Circumcision was added, not to save him by, but as a

Tim 1. 15.
Rom, 5. 6, 7, 8,
9.

Rom. 4. 3, 4, 5.
Rom. 9. 18,
Isa. 33. 11.

14 be] *errata*; be an

Rom. 2.

Seal of *the Righteousness of THAT Faith, which he had, being yet Uncircumcised.* Now we know that Circumcision in the Flesh, was a Type of Circumcision *in the heart*; wherefore the Faith that *Abraham* had, before his outward Circumcision; was to shew us, that Faith if it be right, layeth hold upon the Righteousness of   5 Christ, before we be Circumcised inwardly: and this must needs be so; for if Faith doth *Purifie* the Heart; then it must be there *before* the Heart is Purified. Now this inward Circumcision is a Seal, or Sign of this; That that is the onely saving Faith, that layeth hold upon Christ before we be Circumcised: But he that   10 believeth, before he be inwardly Circumcised, must believe in another, in a Righteousness without him, and that as he standeth at present in himself Ungodly, for he is not Circumcised; which Faith, if it be right, approveth it self also, *so to be,* by an after Work of Circumcising inwardly. But, I say, the Soul that   15 *thus* layeth hold on Christ, taketh the onley way to please his God, because this is that also, which himself hath determined shall be accomplished upon us. *But unto him that worketh, is the Reward, not reckoned of Grace, but of Debt; but to him that Worketh not, but Believeth in him that Justifieth the UNGODLY, his Faith is*   20 *counted for Righteousness,* Rom. 4. He that is Ungodly hath a want of Righteousness, even of the inward Righteousness of Works: But what must become of him? Let him Believe in him that Justifieth the Ungodly, because for that purpose there is in him a Righteousness. We will now return to *Paul* himself; he had   25 *Righteousness* before he was *Justified by Christ*; yet he chose to be Justified, *rather* as an unrighteous man, then as one Indued with so brave a Qualification. *That I may be found in him, not having mine own Righteousness*; away with mine own Righteousness; I chuse rather to be Justified as Ungodly by the Righteousness of   30 Christ, than by mine own, and his together, *Phil.* 3.

You Argue therefore like him that desireth to be a Teacher of the Law, (nay worse) that neither knoweth what he saith, nor where of he Affirmeth. But you say,

Were it possible that Christ's Righteousness could be imputed to an   35 *Unrighteous man, I dare boldly affirm that it would signifie as little to his Happiness, while he continueth so, as would a Georgeous, and Splendid Garment, to one that is almost starved,* &c.

Answ. 1. That Christ's Righteousness is Imputed to men, while Sinners is sufficiently testified by the Word of God, *Ezek.*   40

16.1,–8. *Zech.* 3. 1, 5. *Rom.* 3. 24, 25. *Chap.* 4. 1,–5. *Chap.* 5. 6,–
9. 2 *Cor.* 5. 18,–21. *Phil.* 3. 6, 7, 8. 1 *Tim.* 1. 15, 16. *Rev.* 1. 5.

2. And that the Sinner, or unrighteous Man, *is happy in this Imputation*, is also as abundantly Evident. For,

1. The Wrath of God, and the Curse of the Law, are both taken off, by this Imputation.

2. The Graces, and Comforts of the Holy Ghost, are all Intailed to, and followers of this Imputation. *Blessed is he, to whom the Lord will not Impute Sin*: It saith not, that he is Blessed that hath not Sin to be imputed; *but he to whom God will not Impute them, he saith*, Therefore the non Imputation of Sin, doth not argue a non being thereof in the Soul, but a Glorious act of Grace, Imputing the sufficiency of Christ's Righteousness, to Justifie him that is yet Ungodly.

But what Blessedness doth follow, the Imputation of the Righteousness of Christ, to one that is yet Ungodly?

Answ. Even the Blessing of *Abraham*, to wit, *Grace, and Eternal Life: For Christ was made the Curse, and Death that was due to us, as Sinners; that the Blessing of* Abraham *might come upon the Gentiles, through Faith in Jesus Christ: That we might receive the Promise of the Spirit through Faith*, Gal. 3. 13, 14. Now Faith hath it's eye upon two things, with respect to it's act of Justifying. First, it acknowledgeth that the Soul is a Sinner, and then that there is a sufficiency in the Righteousness of Christ, to Justifie it in the sight of God, though a Sinner.

We have Believed in Jesus Christ, that we might be Justified by the Faith of Christ, and not by the Works of the Law. Therefore they that believe aright, receive Righteousness, even the Righteousness of another, to Justifie them, while yet in themselves they are Sinners.

Why do they believe in Christ? The answer is, That they MIGHT be Justified, not because in their own Eyes they are. They therefore at present stand Condemned in themselves, and *therefore* they believe in Jesus Christ, that they *might* be set free from present Condemnation. Now being Justified by his Blood as Ungodly, they shall be saved by his Life, that is, by his Intercession: For whom he Justifieth by his Blood, he saveth by his Intercession: For by that is given the Spirit, Faith, and all Grace that preserveth the Elect unto Eternal Life and Glory.

I Conclude therefore, that you argue not Gospelly, in that you so boldly Affirm, *that it would signifie as little to the Happiness of one, to be Justified by Christ's Righteousness, while a Sinner; as would a Gorgeous and Splendid Garment to one that is ready to perish.* For farther, Thus to be Justified is Meat and Drink to the Sinner; and so the beginning of Eternal Life in him. *My Flesh is Meat* 5 *indeed*, said Christ, *and my Blood is Drink indeed: And he that Eateth my Flesh, and Drinketh my Blood, hath Eternal, or Everlasting Life.* He Affirmeth it once again. *As the living Father hath sent me, and I live by the Father, so he that Eateth me, even he shall live by me,* John 6. Here now is a Man an Hungred; what must he feed 10 upon? Not his pure Humanity, not upon the sound Complexion of his Soul, nor yet on the Dictates of his Humane Nature, nor those neither, which you call, *truly Generous Principles*: But upon the Flesh, and Blood of the Son of God, which was once given for the Sin of the World. Let *those then*, that would be saved from 15 the Devil, and Hell, and that would find a Fountain of Grace in themselves, first receive, and feed upon Christ, as Sinners, and Ungodly. Let them believe that both his Body, and Blood, and Soul, was offered for them, as they were Sinners. The believing of this, is the Eating of Christ; this eating of Christ, is the 20 beginning of Eternal Life, to wit, of all Grace, and health *in* the Soul; and of Glory to be Injoyed most perfectly in the next World.

Your Twelfth Chapter is to shew, *That Holiness being Perfected, is Blessedness it self; and that the Glory of Heaven Consisteth chiefly in* 25 *it.*

Answ. But none of your Holiness, none of that inward Holiness which we have *Lost* before Conversion, shall ever come to Heaven: That being as I have shewed, a Holiness of another Nature, and arising from another Root, then that we shall in 30 Heaven injoy.

Pag. 123.
124

2. But farther, Your Description of the Glory that we shall Possess in Heaven, is questionable, as to your notion of it; your notion is, *That the substance of it Consists in a perfect resemblance to the Divine Nature.* 35

Answ. Therefore not in the Injoyment of the Divine Nature it self: For that which in *Substance* is but a bare *Resemblance*, though it be a most perfect one, is not the thing it self, of which it is a Resemblance. But the Blessedness that we shall enjoy in Heaven, in the very *Substance* of it, Consisteth not wholly, nor 40

Principally, in a Resemblance *of*, but in the Injoyment of God *himself; Heirs of God.* Wherefore there shall not be in us a Likeness onely to, but the very Nature of God: *Heirs of God, and joynt Heirs with Christ*, Rom. 8. Hence the Apostle tells us, that Rom. 8.
5 he *rejoyced in hope of the Glory of God*, Rom. 5. Not onely in hope of a Resemblance of it. *The Lord is my Portion, saith my Soul.* But this is like the rest of your Discourse. You are so in Love with your Adamitish Holiness, that with you it must be God in Earth, and Heaven.

10 Who they are that hold, our Happiness in Heaven, shall come by a *meer fixing our Eyes upon the Divine Perfections?* I know not; But thus I Read, *We shall be like him*: Why? or how? For we shall see him as he is. Our Likeness then to God, even in the very Heavens, will in great part come by the Visions of him. And to
15 speak the truth, our very entrance into eternal life, or the beginnings of it here, they come to us thus, *But we all* (every one of us that shall be saved, come by it onely thus) *with open Face, beholding as in a Glass, the Glory of the Lord, are changed from Glory to Glory, even as by the Spirit of the Lord*, 2, Cor 3. 18.

20 And whereas you tell us, *pag.* 124. *That the Devils themselves have a large measure of some of the Attributes of God, as Knowledge, Power*, &c. though themselves are unlike unto him.

In this you most Prodigiously Blaspheme.

Your Thirteenth Chapter is to shew, *That our Saviours*
25 *prefering the Business of making Men Holy, before any other, witnesseth, that this is to do the best Service to God.*

But still respecting the Holiness, you have in your first Chapter Described, which still the Reader must have his eye upon, it is false, and a slander of the Son of God. He never
30 intended to Promote, or Prefer, your Natural Old Covenant, Holiness, *viz.* that which we had lost in *Adam*, or that which yet from him, in the Dregs thereof, remaineth in Humane Nature; but that which is of the Holy Ghost, of Faith, of the New Covenant.

35 I shall not here again take notice of your 130 Page, nor with the Error Contained therein, about Justification by Imputed Righteousness.

But one thing I observe, that in all this Chapter you have nothing Fortified what you say, by any Word of God; no, though
40 you Insinuate (*Pag.* 129. and *Pag.* 131.) that some Dissent from

your Opinion. But instead of the Holy Words of God, being as you Feign, Conscious to your self, you cannot do it *SO* well, as by another Method, *viz.* The Words of Mr. *John Smith*; therefore you Proceed with his, as he with *Plato's*, and so wrap you up the Business.   5

You come next to an Improvement upon the whole, where you make a Comparison between the Heathens and the Gospel: shewing how far the Gospel helpeth the Light the Heathens had, in their Pursuit after your Holiness. But still the Excellency of the Gospel, as you have vainly Dreamt, is, to make Improvement,   10 First of the Heathens Principles; such good Principles, say you, *as were by the Light of Nature Dictated to them.* Pag. 133, 134, 135. As,

1. That there is but one God; that he is Infinitely perfect, &c.
2. That we owe our lives, and all the comforts of them to him.   15
3. That he is our Soveraign Lord.
4. That he is to be Loved above all things.

Answ. 1. Seeing all these are, and may be known, as you your self confess, by them that have not the Gospel; and I add, nor yet the Holy Ghost, nor any saving Knowledge of God, or Eternal   20 Life: Therefore it cannot be the Design of Jesus Christ, by the Gospel, to Promote, or help forward this Knowledge, simply from this Principle: *viz.* Natural Light, and the Dictates of it. My Reason is, because when Nature is trained to the highest Pin, it is but Nature still; and so all the improvement of it's Light, and   25 Knowledge, is but an increase of that which is but Natural. Now, saith *Paul, The Natural Man receiveth not the things of the Spirit of god, for they are foolishness unto him, neither can he know them, because they are Spiritually discerned,* 1 Cor. 2.

But the Gospel is the Ministration of the Spirit; a Revelation   30 of another thing then is found in, or can be acquired to, by Heathenish Principles of Nature.

I say a Revelation of another thing; or rather, another discovery of the same. As,

1. Concerning the Godhead; The Gospel giveth us another   35 discovery of it, then is *possible* to be obtained by the Dictates of Natural Light, even, a discovery of a Trinity of Persons, and yet Unity of Essence, in the same Deity. 1 *John* 5. 1, 5, 8.

2. The Light of Nature will not shew us, that God was in Christ, Reconciling the Wordld to himself.   40

3. The Light of Nature will not shew us, that we owe what we are, and have, to God, because we are the Price of the Blood of his Son.

4. The Light of Nature will not shew, that there is such a thing as Election in Christ.

5. Or, that there is such a thing, as the Adoption of Children to God, through him.

6. Nor that we are to be saved by Faith in his Blood.

.7. Or, that the Man Christ shall come from Heaven, to Judgement.

These things, I say, the Light of Nature teacheth not; but these things are the Great and Mighty things of the Gospel, and those, about which it chiefly bendeth it self, touching upon other things, still as those that are knowable, by a Spirit Inferior to this of the Gospel.

Besides, as these things are not known by the Light of Nature, so the Gospel, when it comes, as I also told you before, doth Implant in the Soul, another Principle, by which they may be received, and from which the Soul should act and do, both towards God, and towards Men; as Namely, the Holy Ghost, Faith, Hope, the Joy of the Spirit, &c.

The other things you mention, *Pag.* 138, 140, 142, 143. *viz.*

1. *The Immortality of the Soul.*

2. *The Doctrine of Rewards, and Punishments in the Life to come.*

3. *Of the forgiveness of Sin upon true Repentance,* &c.

Answ. all these things may be Assented to, where yet the Grace of the Gospel is not; but yet the Apprehension must be such, as is the Light, by which they are discovered; but the Light of Nature cannot discover them, according to the Light and Nature of the Gospel; because the Gospel Knowledge of them, ariseth also from another Principle: So then, *these Doctrines are not Confirmed by the Gospel, as the Light of Nature teacheth them*: Wherefore, *Paul,* speaking of the things of the Gospel, and so consequently of these, he saith, *Which things also we speak, NOT* 1 Cor. 2, 13. *in the WORDS which MAN'S Wisdom teacheth, but which the HOLY GHOST teacheth, comparing Spiritual things with Spiritual.* As if he should say, We speak of God, of the Soul, of the Life to come, of Repentance, of Forgiveness of Sins, &c. Not as

37 should] shoul

Philosophers DO, nor yet in *their* Light; but as Saints, Christians, and Sons of God; as such who have received, not the Spirit of the World, but the Spirit which is of God; that we may know the things that are freely given to us, of God.

But you add (for the Glory of the Gospel) *That we have other things, which no man could, without Divine Revelation, once have Dream'd of.* As,

1. That God hath made miserable Sinners the Objects of such Transcendent Love, as to give them his onely begotten Son.

Answ. I must confess, If this one Head had by you been handled well, you would have Written like a Worthy Gospel Minister. But you add, *Pag.* 146.

1. *That when Christ was sent, it was to shew us upon what terms God was Reconcileable to us: viz. By laying before us all the Parts of Holiness, which are necessary to Restore our Natures to his Likeness; and most Pathetically, moreover to intreat us to do what lyeth on our Parts to put them in Practice, that so to Eternity it may be well with us.*

What these things are, you mention not here; therefore I shall leave them to be spoken to, under the Third Head.

2. A Second thing you mention is, *That this Son of God Conversed upon equal terms with Men, becoming the Son of Man, born of a Woman:* (*a great Demonstration that God hath a liking to the Humane Nature.*) But little to the purpose as you have handled it.

3. *That the Son of God taught men their Duty, by his own Example, and did himself perform what he required of them; and that himself did tread before us EVERY' step of that which he hath told us leadeth to Eternal Life.*

Answ. Now we are come to the point: *viz. That the way to Eternal Life, is, First of all to take Christ for our example, treading his step*: And the Reason, if it be true, is weighty; *For he hath trod every step before us, which he hath told us leads to Eternal Life.*

1. *Every step.* Therefore he went to Heaven by Vertue of an Imputative Righteousness; *For this is one of our steps thither.*

2. *Every step.* Then he must go thither, by Faith in his own Blood, for Pardon of Sin; *For this is another of our steps thither.*

3. *Every step.* Then he must go thither, by Vertue of his own Intercession at the Right Hand of God, before he came thither; *For this is one of our steps thither.*

15 *Reconcileable*] errata; *Rconciled*

4. *Every step*. Then he must come to God, and ask mercy for some great Wickedness, which he had Committed; *For this is also one of our steps thither*.

But again, we will Consider it the other way.

1. *Every step*. Then we cannot come to Heaven, before we first be made accursed of God; *For so was he before he came thither*.

2. *Every step*. Then we must first make our Body and Soul an Offering for the Sin of others; *For this did he before he came thither*.

3. *Every step*. Then we must go to Heaven for the sake of our own Righteousness; *For that was one of his steps thither*.

O Sir! What will thy Gallant, Generous mind do here? Indeed you talk of his being an Expiatory Sacrifice for us, but you put no more trust to that, then to Baptism, or the Lords Supper; counting that, with the other two, but things indifferent in themselves, *Pag.* 6, 7, 8.

You add again, *That this Son of God being raised from the Dead, and Ascended to Heaven, is our High Priest there*: But you talk not at all, of his sprinkling the Mercy Seat with his Blood, but clap upon him, the Heathens *Demons*, Negotiating the Affairs of Men with the Supream God; and so wrap up, with a testification that it is needless to enlarge on the Point. *Pag.* 150.

But to be plain, and in one word to tell you; About all these things you are Heathenishly dark; there hath not in these 150 Pages, one Gospel truth been Christianly handled by you; but rather a darkening of truth, by Words without Knowledge. What Man that ever had Read, or Assented to the Gospel, but would have spoken (yet kept within the bounds of truth) more Honourably of Christ, then you have done? His Sacrifice must be stept over, as the Spider stradleth over the Wasp, his Intercession is needless to be Inlarged upon. But when it falleth in your way to talk of your Humane Nature, of the Dictates, of the first Principles of Morrals within you, and of your Generous mind to follow it: Oh what need is there now of Amplifying, Inlarging, and Pressing it on Mens Consciences! As if that poor Heathenish, Pagan Principle, was the very Spirit of God within us: And as if Righteousness done by *that*, was *that*, and *that* onely, that would or *could* fling Heaven Gates off the Hinges.

Yea, a little after you tell us, 'That the Doctrine of sending the Holy Ghost, was to move, and Excite us to our Duty; and to Assist, Chear, and Comfort us in the Performance of it: Still meaning our close Adhering by the Purity of our Humane Nature to the Dictates of the Law, as Written in our hearts as Men. Which is as false as God is true. For the Holy Ghost is sent into our Hearts, not to Excite us to a Compliance with our Old and Wind-shaken Excellencies, that came into the World with   5 us, but to Write new Laws in our Hearts; even the Law of Faith, the Word of Faith, and of Grace, and the Doctrine of Remission of Sins, through the Blood of the Lamb of God; that Holiness might flow from thence.

Your 15th. Chapter is to shew, *That the Gospel giveth far greater*   10 *helps to an Holy Life, then the Jewish Ceremonies did of Old.* I Answer.

But the Reader must here well weigh, that in the Gospel you find also, some possitive Precepts, that are of the same Nature with the Ceremonies under the Law; of which, *that of coming to*   15 *God by Christ*, you call *one*, and Baptism, and the Lords Supper, the other two. So then by your Doctrine, the Excellency of the Gospel doth not lye in that we have a Christ to come to God by; but in things as you feign more substantial. What are they? 'Inward Principles of Holiness, *Pag.* 159. Spiritual Precepts, *P.*   20 162.' That height of Vertue, and true Goodness, that the Gospel Designeth to raise us to: All which are General Words, falling from a staggering Conscience, leaving the World, that are Ignorant of his mind, in a Muse; but tickling his Brethren with the Delights of their Morral Principles, with the Dictates of their   25 Humane Nature, and their gallant Generous Minds. Thus making a very Stalking-horse of the Lord Jesus Christ, and of the Words of Truth and Holiness, thereby to slay the silly one; making the Lord of Life and Glory, instead of a Saviour, by his Blood, *the Instructer, and School-Master onely of Humane Nature, a*   30 *Chaser away of evil Affections, and an Extinguisher of Burning Lusts*; and that not so neither, but by giving perfect Explications of Morral Precepts, (*Pag.* 17.) and setting himself an Example before them to follow him, *Pag.* 297.

Your Sixteenth Chapter Containeth an answer to those that   35 Object against the Power of the Christian Religion to make Men Holy.

Answ. And to speak truth; what you at first render as the cause of the Unholiness of the Professors thereof (*Pag.* 171) *is to the Purpose*, had it been Christianly Managed by you, as namely,   40

Mens Gross Unbelief of the truth of it; *for it Effectually Worketh in them that Believe* (1 Thes. 2. 13.) but that you onely touch, and away, neither shewing what is the Object of Faith, nor the cause of it's being so Effectual to that Purpose; neither do you at all
5 treat of the Power of Unbelief, and how all Men by Nature are shut up therein, *Rom.* 11. 32. But presently, according to your Old and Natural Course, you fall *First*, upon a supposed Power in Men, to imbrace the Gospel, both by closing with the Promise, and shuning the threatning (*Pag.* 172) farther adding,
10 'That mankind is *Indued with a Principle of Freedom*, and that this Principle is *as Essential*, as any other, *to the Humane Nature*' (Pag. 173.) By all which it is Manifest, that however you make mention of Unbelief, *because the Gospel hath laid the same in your way*; yet *your* Old Doctrine, of the Purity of the Humane Nature, now
15 broken out into a *freedom of Will*, and that as an Essential of the Humane Nature, is your great Principle of Faith, and your following of that, as it Dictateth to you Obedience to the first Principles of Morrals, the Practice of Faith, by which you think to be saved. That this is so, must unavoidably be gathered from
20 the good opinion you have your self of coming to God by Christ: *viz.* That in the Command thereof, it is one of these Positive Precepts, and a thing in it self absolutely considered indifferent, and neither Good nor Evil. Now he that looketh upon coming to God by Christ, with such an Eye as this, cannot lay the stress of
25 his Salvation upon the Faith, or Belief thereof; *Indifferent* Faith, will serve for *Indifferent* things: Yea, a Man must look beyond that, which he Believeth is but *one* with the *Ceremonial* Laws, but not the same with Baptism, or the Lord's Supper; for with those you compare *that* of coming to God by Christ. Wherefore Faith,
30 with you, must be turned into a Chearful, and Generous Complying with the Dictates of the Humane Nature, and Unbelief, into that which Opposeth this, or that makes the Heart backward, and sluggish therein. This is also gathered from what you aver of the Divine Morral Laws, that they be of an
35 Indispensible, and Eternal Obligation (*Pag.* 8.) things that are *good in themselves* (Pag. 9.) Considered in an Abstracted Notion (*Pag.* 10) Wherefore things that are good in themselves, must needs be better then those that are in themselves but *Indifferent*:

14 *your*] *errata*; our

neither can a Positive Precept make that which of it self is neither
Good nor Evil, better then that which in it's own Nature
remaineth the Essentials of Goodness.

I Conclude then, by Comparing you with your self, by
bringing your Book to your Book, that you understand neither   5
Faith, nor unbelief, any farther then by obeying, or disobeying
the Humane Nature, and it's Dictates in Chief; and that of
coming to God by Christ, as one of the things that is indifferent
in it self.

But a little to touch upon your Principle of Freedom, which in   10
Pag. 9. you call *an undestanding and liberty of Will.*

Answ. First, That there is *no* such thing in Man by Nature, as
Liberty of Will, or a Principle of *Freedom,* in the saving things of
the Kingdom of Christ, is Apparent by several Scriptures.
Indeed there is in Men, as Men, a willingness to be saved their   15
own way, even by following (as you) their own Natural
Principles, as is seen by the Quakers, as well as your self; but that
there is a freedom of will in Men, as Men, to be saved by the way
which God hath Prescribed, is neither asserted in the Scriptures
of God, neither standeth with the Nature of the Principles of the 20
Gospel.

The Apostle saith, *The Natural Man receiveth not the things that
be of the Spirit of God.* And the Reason is, not because, not
Principally because he layeth aside a *Liberty of Will,* but because
they are foolishness to him (1 Cor. 2.) Because in his Judgement   25
they are things of no Moment, but things (as you have imagined
of them) that in themselves are but indifferent. And that this
Judgement that is passed by the Natural Man, concerning the
things of the Spirit of God (of which, that of coming to God by
Christ, is the chief) is that which he cannot but do as a Man; is   30
Evident from that which followeth; *neither CAN he know them,
because they are Spiritually Discerned*: Neither CAN he know them
as a Man, because they are Spiritually Discerned. Now if he
cannot *know* them, from what Principle should he *will* them: For
Judgement, or Knowledge must be, *before the Will can act.* I say,   35
again, a Man must know them to be things in chief, that are
Absolutely, and Indispensibly Necessary, and those in which
resteth the greatest Glory; or else his *Will* will not Comply with

19 which] wich

them, nor Center, and Terminate in them, as such, but still count themselves (as you) though somewhat Convinced that he ought to adhere unto them things that in themselves, are onely indifferent, and absolutely Considered neither Good nor Evil.

5 A farther inlargement upon this Subject, will be time enough, if you shall Contradict.

Another Reason, or cause which you call an immediate one, of the unsuccessfulness of the Gospel, is, Mens unaccountable mistaking the Design of it ([not to say worse) as to conceive no

10 better of it, then as a Science, and a matter of Speculation, &c. *Pag.* 173.

Answ. If this be true, you have shewed us the Reason, why your self have so base and unworthy thought thereof: For although coming to God by Christ, be the very chief, first, the

15 substance, and most Essential part of obedience thereto; yet you have reckoned this but like one of the Ceremonies of the Law, or as Baptism with Water, and the Lord's Supper, *Pag.* 7, 8, 9. Falling more Directly upon the Body of the Morral Law, as written in the Heart of Men, and inclining more to the teaching,

20 or Dictates of Humane Nature, (which were neither of them both ever any Essential part of the Gospel) then upon that which indeed is the Gospel of Christ.

And here I may (if God will) timely Advertise my Reader, that the Gospel, and it's Attendants, are to be accounted things

25 Distinct: The Gospel properly taken, being *Glad Tidings of good things*; or, the Doctrine of the forgiveness of Sins freely by Grace, through the Redemption that is in Christ Jesus. For to speak strictly; neither is the Grace of Faith, Hope, Repentance, or Newness of Life, the Gospel; but rather things that are

30 wrought by the Preaching thereof; things that are the Effects of it; or its unseperable Companions, to all them that shall be saved. Wherefore the Gospel is said to be Preached in all Nations, for _{Rom. 16.} the obedience of Faith: Hope also is called, the Hope of the Gospel, not the Gospel it self. So again, the Gospel is Preached

35 that Men should repent, but it is not Preached that men should Gospel.

But your Gospel, which Principally, or Chiefly Centers in the Dictates of Humane Nature, and your Faith, which is chiefly a

3 them] them)   7 which] (which

subjecting to those Dictates, are so far off from being at all, any
near attendants of the Gospel, that they never are urged in the
New Testament, but in order to shew men they have forgotten to
act as men, *Rom.* 1. 19, 20, 21. Chap. 2. 14, 15. 1 Cor. 11. 14.

Your last Reason is, because of several untoward opinions, the   5
Gospel is very unsuccessful. *Pag.* 175.

Answ. But what these opinions are, we hear not; nor how to
shun them you tell us here nothing at all. This I am sure, there
are no Men in this day have more opposed the Light, Glory, and
Lustre of the Gospel of Christ, then those (as the Quakers and   10
others) that have set up themselves, and their own Humanity, as
the Essential parts of it.

You in Answer to other things add many other Reasons to
prove they are mistaken that count the Gospel a thing of but
mean Operation to work Holiness in the heart: at which you   15
ought your self to tremble, seeing the Son himself, who is the
Lord of the Gospel, is of so little esteem with you, as to make
coming to God by him so trivial a business as you have done.

Your large Transcript of other mens sayings, to prove the
good success of the Gospel of Old, did better become that   20
People and age, then you & yours; they being a people that lived
in the power thereof, but you such Bats as cannot see it. That
Saying you mention of *Rigaltias*, doth better become you and
yours: *Those now adays do retain the Name, and the Society of
Christians, which live altogether Antichristian Lives: For take away*   25
Publicans, and a wretched Rable, &c. *And your Christian Churches,*
will be lamentable, weak, small, and insignificant things.

I shall add to yours another reason of the unsuccessfulness of
the Gospel in our days, and that is, because so many ignorant Sir
Johns, on the one hand, and so many that have done Violence to   30
their former Light, and that have Damned themselves in their
former Anathematizing of others, have now for a long time, as a
Judgement of God, been permitted to be, and made the mouth to
the People: Persons whose Lives are Debauched, and who in
the Face of the World, after seeming serious Detestings of   35
Wickedness have for the Love of filthy Lucre, and the
Pampering their idle Carcasses, made Shipwrack of their former
Faith, and that Feigned good Conscience they had. From which
number if you, Sir, have kept your self clear, the less Blood of
the Damned will fall upon your head: I know you not by Face;   40

much less your Personal Practice; yet I have heard as if Blood might pursue you, for your Unstable Weathercock Spirit, which doubtless could not but stumble the Weak, and give advantage to the Adversary to speak Vilifyingly of Religion.

5 As to your Seventeenth and Eighteenth Chapter, I shall say little, onely I wish that your Eighteenth had been more express in discovering how far a man may goe, with a notion of the truth of the Gospel, and yet perish because he hath it not in Power.

Onely in your *Inveighing* so much against the *Pardon* of Sin, 10 while you seem so much to *cry* up *Healing*; you must know that Pardon of Sin is the beginning of Health to the Soul: *He Pardoneth our Iniquities, and Healeth all our Diseases*, Psa. 103. 3. And where he saith, by the stripes of Christ we are healed, it is Evident that healing beginneth at Pardon, and not Pardon after 15 healing, as you would rather have it, 1 *Pet.* 2. 24. compare, *Isa.* 53. As for your Comparison of the Plaister, and the Physitians Potion, *Pag.* 217. I say, you do but abuse your Reader, and muddy the way of the Gospel. For the first thing of which the Soul is sick, and by which the Conscience receiveth wounding, it 20 is the guilt of Sin, and fear of the Curse of God for it. For which is provided the wounds and Precious Blood of Christ, which Flesh and Blood, if the Soul eat thereof by Faith, giveth deliverance there-from. Upon this the filth of Sin appears most odious, for that it hath not onely at present Defiled the Soul, but 25 because it keeps it from doing those Duties of Love, which by the Love of Christ it is constrained to endeavour the perfecting of. For Filth, appears Filth; that is irksome, and odious to a contrary Principle now Implanted in the Soul; which Principle had its Conveyance thither by Faith in the Sacrifice and death of 30 Christ going before. *The Love of Christ constraineth us, because we thus judge; That if one dyed for all, then are all Dead; and that he dyed for all, that they which live should not henceforth live unto themselves, but to him that dyed for them, and rose again,* 2 Cor. 5. 14. The man that hath received Christ, desireth to be Holy, because the 35 Nature of the Faith that layeth hold on Christ (although I will not say as you, it is of a Generous mind) worketh by love, and longeth, yea, greatly longeth that the Soul may be brought, not onely into an universal Conformity to his Will, but into his very

28 Implanted] *errata*; implant

likeness; and because that State standeth not with what we are
now, but with what we shall be hereafter: Therefore in this we

2 Cor. 5.
1, 2, 3, 4, 5, 6, 7,
8.

groan, being burthened (with that which is of a contrary Nature)
to be cloathed upon with our House which is from Heaven:
Which state is not that of *Adam*'s Innocency; but that which is   5
Spiritual, and Heavenly, even that which is now in the Lord in
Heaven.

But I will Descend to your Nineteenth Chapter, it may be
more may be discovered there.

Your Nineteenth Chapter is to shew; *That a right understanding*   10
of the Design of Christianity (viz. as you have laid it down) *will give*
satisfaction concerning the true Notion.

First, *Of Justifying Faith.*

Secondly, *Of the Imputation of Christ's Righteousness,* Pag. 221.

First, of Justifying Faith; *It is* (say you) *such a Belief of the truth of*   15
the Gospel, as Includes a sincere Resolution of Obedience to all it's
Precepts.

Answ. To this I shall Answer; First, that the Faith which we

2. Pet. 1. 1.
Iude 20.

call Justifying Faith, *is like Precious Faith with all the Elect,* and
that which *is most Holy:* but those Acts of it, *which Respect our*   20
Justification with God from the Curse of the Law that is due for Sin;
are such, as respect not any good Work done by *us,* but the
Righteousness that *Resideth* in the Person of Christ; and is made
ours by the imputation of Grace. This Faith I say, accounteth
him in whom it is now a Sinner, and without Works; yea, if he   25
have any that in his own eyes are such, this Faith rejects them,
and throweth them away; for it seeth a Righteousness in the
Person of Christ sufficient; even such as is verily the Righteousness of God. *Now to him that worketh not, but believeth. Works* and
Faith are put *here* in opposition, Faith being considered as   30
Justifying, in the sight of God from the Curse. The Reason is,
because the Righteousness by which the Soul must thus stand
Justified, *is a Righteousness* of God's *appointing,* not of his
Prescribing us; a Righteousness that *Intirely* is Included in the
Person of Christ. The Apostle also, when he speaks of God's   35
saving the Election, which hangeth upon the same Hinge, as this
of Justification doth, to wit, on the Grace of God; he opposeth it
to Works; and that, not to this or that sort onely, but even to
Work, in the *Nature* of *Work (Rom.* 11.) *If it be of Grace, then it is no*
more of Works; otherwise Grace is no more Grace; but if it be of Works,   40

then it is no more of Grace; otherwise Work is no more Work. By this
Text, I say, the Apostle doth so throughly Distinguish between
Grace and Works, as that which so ever standeth in the Case, the
other must be Annihilated: If it be by Grace, then must *Works* be
no more, *then it is no more of Works*: but if it be of Works, then is
Grace no more, *then it is no more of Grace.*

But this, notwithstanding, you urge farther; *That Faith*
Justifieth, as it includes, a sincere Resolution, &c.

Answ. Although, as I have said before, the *Faith* which is the
Justifying Faith, is that of the Holiest Nature, yet in the *Act,* by
which it layeth hold of *Justifying* Righteousness, it respects it,
simply, as a Righteousness offered by *Grace,* or given unto the
Person that by Faith layeth hold thereon as he stands yet ungodly
and a Sinner.

Faith Justifieth not seperate from the Righteousness of Christ
as it is a Grace in us, nor as it subjecteth the Soul to the
obedience of the Morral Law, but as it receiveth a Righteousness
offered to that Sinner, that as *such* will lay hold on, and accept
thereof. *Christ Jesus came into the World to save Sinners, by being*   1 Cor. 1. 30.
their Redemption, and Righteousness himself.

But you add, *The Faith that Intaileth the Sinner to SO High a*
Priviledge as that of Justification, must needs be such as complyeth with
all the purposes of Christ's coming into the World, &c.

Answ. By this supposition, *Faith Justifieth, not by receiving of the*
Righteousness that Christ by himself accomplished for Sinners; but by
falling in with *all* good Works, which because they cannot be
known, much less *done,* by the Soul at first, his Faith being then,
as to the perfection of knowledge of Duties, weak, he standeth
still before God unjustified, and so must stand until he doth comply
with *all* those purposes of Christ's coming into the World.

But yet again you recall your self, and distinguish *one* purpose
from the *rest,* as a *grand* one, *Pag.* 222. *And that is to receive Christ*
as Lord, as well as a Saviour.

Answ. 1. Although the Soul that in truth receiveth Christ,
receiveth him wholly, and intirely as Christ, and not as chopt,
and pul'd in Pieces: Yet I distinguish between the act of Faith,
which layeth hold of Christ for my Justification from the Curse
before God, and the consequences of that act, which are to
engage me to newness of Life. And indeed, as it is impossible for
a Man to be a new Man, before he be Justified in the sight of

God; so it is also as impossible, but that when Faith hath once layed hold on Christ for Life, it should also follow Christ by Love. But,

2. Christ may be received at first as Lord, and that in our Justification, and yet not at all be considered as a Law-giver, for so he is not the Object of Faith for our Justification with God, but a requirer of Obedience to Laws, and Statutes of them that already are Justified by the Faith that receiveth him as Righteousness. But Christ is as well a Lord *for* us, as *to*, or *over* us, and it *highly* concerneth the Soul, when it believeth in, or trusteth to the Righteousness of Christ, for Justification with God, to see that this Righteousness *Lords it* over Death, and Sin, and the Devil, and Hell for us; The Name wherewith he shall be called, is, *The Lord our Righteousness*. Our Righteousness, then is *Lord*, and Conqueror over all, and we more then Conquerours through this Lord that loved us. The Author to the *Hebrews* calls him *King of Righteousness*, because by his Righteousness he ruleth as *Lord* and *King*, and can reign and *Lord it*, at all times over all those that seek to separate us from the presence, and Glory of God.

Now, how you will brook this Doctrine I know not; I am sure he stands in need thereof, that is *Lorded over by the Curse of the Law, the guilt of Sin, the Rage of the Devil, and the fear of Death and Hell*; He, I say, would be glad to know that in Christ there is a Righteousness that *Lords it*, or that Christ, as he is Righteousness, *is Lord*.

Wherefore Reader, when thou shalt Read or Hear, that Jesus Christ is Lord, if thou art at the same time under guilt of Sin, and fear of Hell, then do thou Remember that Christ is Lord more ways then one, he is Lord *as he is Righteousness*; he is Lord as he is *Imputative Righteousness*; he is the Lord *OUR* Righteousness. Of the same import is that also, *he is a Prince, and a Saviour*, he is a Prince *as* he is a Saviour; because the Righteousness by which he saveth, *beareth Rule in Heaven, and Earth*. And hence we Read again, that even when he was in the Combat with our Sins, the Devils, the Curse, and Death, upon the Cross, he even in that place made *a shew of them openly*, *and triumphed over them*. Now in these things he is Lord *for us*, and *the Captain of our Salvation*; as also in that he hath Led Captivity Captive; all which places, with many more, being Testimonies to us, of the

Rom. 8.

Heb. 7.

Jere. 23. 6.

Colos. 2. 15, 16.
Eph. 4. 8, 9.

sufficiency of that Righteousness which saveth us from the
Justice of the Law and Wrath of God. But you respect not this
his manner of *Lording*; but will have him be a Saviour, as he
giveth Laws, especially those you call *Indispensible*, and *Eternal*,
5 the Morral Law. You would have him a *Saviour*, as he bringeth
us back *to the Holiness we had lost*. But this is none other then
Barbarous Quakerisme, the stress of their Writing, also tending
to no other purpose.

But you tell us, *That you scarcely admired at any thing more in all*
10 *your Life, then that any, worthy Men especially, should be so difficultly*
perswaded, to receive or imbrace this account of Justifying Faith, and
should perplex, and make intricate, so plain a Doctrine.

Answ. And doubtless they far more groundedly stand amazed
at such as you, who while you pretend to shew the design of the
15 Gospel, make the very Essential of it, *a thing in it self indifferent;* Page 7.
and absolutely considered neither good nor evil, that makes obedience to   8.
the Morral Laws, more Essential to salvation, then that of going to   9.
God by Christ, that maketh it the great Design of Christ, *to put us*   10.
into a Possession of that promiseless, natural old Covenant holiness   11.
20 *which we had lost long since in Adam,* that maketh as if Christ,   12.
rejecting *all other* Righteousness, or Holiness, *hath Established*   Page 16.
onely this: Yea, that maketh the very Principle of this Holiness to
consist *in a sound Complexion of Soul, the Purity of Humane Nature*
in us, a habit of Soul, truly Generous Motives and Principles, Divine
25 *Morral Laws, which were first written in Mens Hearts, and Originally*
Dictates of Humane Nature. All this Villany against the Son of
God, with much more as bad, is Comprised within less then the
first sixteen Pages of your Book.

But, say you, what pretence can there be for thinking that Faith is
30 *the Condition, or Instrument of Justification, as it complyeth with*
onely the Precept of relying upon Christ's Merits, for the obtaining of it:
especially when it is no less manifest then the Sun at Noon-day, that
obedience to the other Precepts must go before obedience to this: And
that a Man may not rely upon the merits of Christ, for the forgiveness
35 *of his Sins, and he must be presumptuous in so doing, and puts an*
affront upon his Saviour too, till he be sincerely willing to be reformed
from them, Pag. 223.

Answ. That the Merits of Christ, for Justification, are made

10 *difficultly*] *difficutly*

over to *that* Faith that receiveth them, while the Person that believeth it, stands in his own account, by the Law a Sinner, hath already been shewed. And that they are *not* by God appointed for another purpose, is manifest through all the Bible.

1. In the Type when the bloody Sacrifices were to be offered, and an Atonement made for the Soul, the People were *onely* to confess their Sins over the head of the Bullock, or Goat, or Lamb, by laying their *Hands* thereon, and *so* the Sacrifice was to be slain. They were onely to acknowledge their Sins. And observe it, in the day that these offerings were made, they were *not to Work at all; For he that did any Work therein, was to be cut off from his People*, Lev. 4. ch. 16. ch. 23.

2. In the Antitype thus it runs; *Christ dyed for our Sins; Christ gave himself for our Sins; He was made to be Sin for us; Christ was made a Curse for us.*

Yea, but, say you, *What pretence can there be, that Faith is the Condition, or Instrument of Justification, as it Complyeth with onely the Precepts of relying upon Christ's Merits*; that is, first, or before the Soul doth other things.

Answ. I say (avoiding your own Ambiguous terms) that it is the Duty, the indispensible Duty of all that would be saved, *First, Immediately, now* to close in by Faith with that work of Redemption, which Christ by his blood hath purchased for them, as they are Sinners.

1. Because God doth *hold it forth*, yea, hath *set* it forth to be received by us, as such, *Rom.* 3. 23. to 27.

2. Because God hath *Commanded us* by Faith to receive it as such, *Act.* 16.

And I add, If the Jaylor was altogether ignorant of what he must do to be saved; and *Paul* yet bids him *then*, before he knew any thing else, *Believe in the Lord Jesus Christ, and he should be saved*, that then Believing (even Believing on Christ for a Righteousness to justifie, and save him) must go *first*, and *may*, nay *ought to be pressed*, even then, when the Soul stands ignorant of what else he ought to do, *Act.* 16. 30, 31, 32.

But, you say, *It is evident as the Sun at Noon-day, that obedience to the other Precepts must go before obedience to THIS; that is, before Faith in Christ.*

11 *Work at all*] errata; *Work all*

Answ. This you say; But *Paul* said to the ignorant Jaylor, that knew nothing of the mind of God in the Doctrine of Justification, that he should *first* believe on the Lord Jesus Christ; and *so* should be saved. Again when *Paul* Preached to the *Corinthians*,
5 The *first* Doctrine that he delivered unto them was, *That Christ dyed for their Sins, according to the Scriptures*, &c. 1 Cor. 15. 1, 2, 3, 4.

But what be these other Precepts? Not Baptism, nor the Supper of the Lord; for these you say are (as poor and
10 inconsiderable) as that of coming to God by Christ, even all three, things in themselves neither good nor evil, but of an indifferent Nature; they must be therefore, some more weighty things of the Gospel, then these positive Precepts. But what things are they? It is good that you tell us, seeing you Tacitely
15 forbid all men upon pain *of Presumption*, and of doing *affront to Jesus Christ*, that they rely not on the merits of Christ for forgiveness; till they be sincerely willing to perform them first; yet I find not here one particular Precept instanced by you: But perhaps we shall hear of them hereafter, therefore now I shall let
20 them pass. You tell us farther, *that such a relyance as that, of acting* Page 223.
Faith, First, on the Merits of Christ for Justification, is ordinarily to be found amongst Unregenerate, and even the worst of Men.

Answ. This is but a falshood, and a slander, for the 1 Iohn 3.
Unregenerate know him not; how then can they believe on him:
25 Besides, the worst of men, so far as they pretend Religion, set up *your* Idol in their hearts; *viz.* their own good meanings, their own good Nature, the Notions and Dictates of their Nature, living that little which they do live upon the Snuff of their own Light, the Sparks of their own fire, and therefore woe unto them.

30 But you add, *How can it be otherwise, then that that act of Faith must needs have a Hand in Justifying, and the special Hand too, which distinguisheth it from that which is found in such Persons.*

Answ. 1. There is no Act of Faith doth more distinguish true Faith from false, and the Christian from the painted
35 Hypocrite, then that which first lays hold on Christ, while the Person that hath it stands in his own esteem, ungodly; all other like your self, being fearful and unbelieving (*Rev.* 20. 8.) despite it, and wonder, and perish (*Act.* 13. 40, 41.)

2. And this Faith, by thus acting, doth more subdue Sin
40 (though it doth not Justifie, as subduing, but as applying Christ's

Righteousness) then all the Wisdom and Purity of Humane Nature, or the Dictates of that Nature, that is found in the whole World.

But you add farther; What *good ground can Men have for this fancy, when as our Saviour hath Merited the Pardon of Sin for this end, that it might be an Effectual motive to turn from it?*

Answ. Although you speak this in great Derision to Faith when it worketh right, yet know that therefore (seeing you would hear it) I say, therefore hath our Saviour merited pardon, and bestowed it on men freely, and bid them believe or receive it, and have it; that thereby they might be incouraged to live to him, and love him, and comply with his commandements. *For scarcely for a Righteous Man will one dye, yet peradventure for a good Man some would even dare to dye: But God commended his love to us, in that while we were yet Sinners Christ dyed for us. Much more then being NOW Justified, we shall be saved from Wrath through him.* Now, as here we are said to be Justified by his Blood, that is, as his Blood appeaseth the Justice of God; so again, it is said that this Blood is set forth by God for us to have Faith in it, by the term of a Propitiation. *Whom God hath set forth to be a Propitiation* (or a Sacrifice to appease the displeasure of God) *through Faith in his Blood. To declare at this time his Righteousness, that he might be Just, and the justifier of him that believeth in Jesus,* Rom. 3.

Again, As we are thus Justified by Blood in the sight of God, by Faith in it, so also it is testified of his Blood, that it sprinkleth the Conscience of the faithful, but still onely as it is received by Faith. But from what is the Conscience sprinkled, but from those dead Works that remain in all that have not yet been Justified by Faith in this Blood. Now if Faith in this Blood doth sprinkle the Conscience, and so doth purge it from all dead Works, then must Faith go first to the Blood of Christ for Justification, and must bring this home to the Defiled Conscience, before it be delivered from those dead Works that are in it, and made Capable of serving the Living God, *Rom.* 5. 7, to 10. *ch.* 3. 24, 25. *Heb.* 9. 14. *ch.* 10. 19, 20, 21, 22.

But you say, *you will never trust your discoursive faculty so long as you live, if you are mistaken here, Pag.* 224.

Tell not me of your discoursive faculty: The Word of God is

21 (or])or

plain: And never challenge Man, for he that Condemneth your way to Heaven, to the very Pit of Hell, as *Paul* doth, can yet set forth a better.

I come now to the Second thing; *viz.* The Doctrine of the imputation of Christ's Righteousness, which you thus Expound.

It Consists in dealing with sincerely Righteous Persons, as if they were perfectly so, for the sake, and upon the account of Christ's Righteousness, Pag. 225, 226.

Answ. 1. Any thing but truth; But I would know how sincerely Righteous they were that were Justified without Works? or how sincerely Righteous they were, whom God Justified, as Ungodly? *Rom.* 4. 3, 4, 5.

2. Your Explication of the imputation of Christ's Righteousness makes it respect our *Works* rather then our *Persons; It Consists, say you, in dealing with sincerely Righteous Persons, as if they were Perfectly so*: That is, it Justifieth their imperfect Righteousness First, and so Secondarily their Persons for the sake of that.

But Observe a few things from this Explication.

1. This Concludeth that a man *may* be sincerely Righteous in God's account, WITHOUT the Righteousness of Christ: for that is to be imputed to *such*, and *none* but such.

2. This Concludeth that Men *may* be sincerely Righteous, BEFORE Christ's Righteousness is imputed: For this sincere Righteousness is Precedent to the Imputation of Christ's.

3. This Concludeth that a Man *may* have *true*, yea, *saving* Grace in great and mighty action in him, before he hath Faith in the Righteousness of Christ. For if a Man must be sincerely Righteous first; then he must not onely have that we call the *Habit*, but the powerful *Acts* of Grace.

Besides, if the Righteousness of Christ is not to be looked to *First*, but Secondarily; not *before*, but after we be made sincerely Righteous; then may not Faith be thus acted if a man should have it, until he be first a sincerely Righteous Person.

4. This Concludeth that a Man may be brought from under the Curse of the Law in God's sight, before he have Faith in the Righteousness of Christ, yea, before it be imputed to him: For he that in God's account is reckoned sincerely Righteous, is beloved of his God.

5. This Concludeth that a Man may be from under the Curse

of God, without the Imputation of the Righteousness of Christ:
For if a Man must be sincerely Righteous in God's account
without it, then he is from under the Curse of God without it.

6. This Doctrine teacheth farther, that Christ came to call,
and Justifie the Righteous, contrary to his express Word. In
short, By this account of things, first, we must be healed, and
then the Plaister comes.

Yea, so Confident is this Man in this his Assertion, that he
saith, *it is not possible any other notion of this Doctrine should have
truth in it*, Pag. 226. O this Jesus! this Rock of offence! But he
that believeth on him shall not be Confounded.

But Blessed be God for Jesus Christ, and for that he took our
Nature, and Sin, and Curse, and Death upon him: And for that
he did also by *himself*, by *one* Offering Purge our Sins. We that
have *believed* have found *rest*, even *there* where God and his
Father hath smelled *a sweet savour of rest*; because we are
presented to God, *even now* compleat in the Righteousness of
him, and stand discharged of guilt, even by the Faith of him:
Yea, as Sins past, so Sins to come, were taken up and satisfied
for, by that offering of the Body of Jesus, we who have had a due
sense of Sins, and of the Nature of the Justice of God, we know
that *no* Remission of the guilt of *any one* can be, but by
Attonement made by Blood, *Heb.* 9. 22. We also know that where
Faith in Jesus Christ is wanting, there can be neither *good*
Principle, nor *good Indeavour*; for Faith is the first of all Graces,
and without it there *is nothing but Sin.* We know also, that Faith
as a Grace in us, severed from the Righteousness of Christ, is
onely a beholder of things, but not a Justifier of Persons, and that
if it lay not hold of, and applyeth not that Righteousness which is
in Christ, it carrieth us no farther then to the Devils. We know
that this Doctrine killeth Sin, and curseth it, at the very roots; I
say, we know it, *who have mourned over him whom WE have pierced*,
and who have been confounded to see that God by his Blood
should be pacified towards us, for all the Wickedness we have
done. Yea, we have a double Motive to be Holy, and Humble
before him; one because *he dyed for us on Earth*, another because
he now appears for us in Heaven, there sprinkling for us the
Mercy-Seat with his Blood, there ever-living to make Intercession
for them that come unto God by him. *If any man Sin, we have an
Advocate with the Father, Jesus Christ the Righteous, who is the*

Rom. 14.

Zech. 12. 10.

Ezek. 16. 63.

Propitiation for our Sins; Yet this Worketh in us no looseness, nor   1 John 2. 1, 2, 3.
favour to Sin, but so much the more an abhorrence of it: *She*
loveth much, for much was forgiven her: Yea, she weeps, she   Luk. 7. 47.
washeth his Feet, and wipeth them with the hairs of her Head, to
5 the confounding of *Simon* the Pharisee, and all such ignorant
Hypocrites.

But I pass this, and come to the Twentieth Chapter, which is
to learn us by what Measure, and Standard we are to Judge of
Doctrines; and that is, *by the Design of Christianity*, as stated, you
10 must know, by Mr. *Fowler*: Wherefore it will be requisite here
again, that a Collection of Principles, and Doctrines be gathered
out of this Book, that the Man that hath a short Memory may be
helped the better to bear them in mind, and to make them, if he
shall be so bewitched by them, instead of the Bible, a Standard
15 for Truth, and a Rule for him to obtain Salvation by.

First, Then he must know that the Principle by which he
must walk, must be the Purity of the Humane Nature, a Divine
or God-like Nature, which yet is but an Habit of Soul, or more
plainly the Morral Law, as Written in the Heart, and Originally
20 the Dictates of Humane Nature, a Generous Principle, such an
one as although it respects Law, yet acts in a Sphere above it;
above it as a Written Law, that acts even in the first Principles of
it, *Pag.* 7, 8, 9, 10.

Secondly, He must know, that the Holiness Christ designed to
25 Possess his People with, is that which we had lost in *Adam*, that
which he had before he fell, that Natural Old Covenant Christless Holiness, *Pag.* 12.

Thirdly, He must put a difference between those Laws of the
Gospel that are Essential to Holiness, and those Positive
30 Precepts that in themselves are indifferent, & absolutely
considered neither good nor evil; but must know also that of
these Positive Precepts he alloweth but three in the Gospel, but
three that are purely such; to wit, *that of coming to God by Christ*,
the Institutions of Baptism, and the Lord's Supper, *Pag.* 7, *and* 9.

35 *Fourthly*, He must hold for certain, that the Faith which
Intituleth a Sinner to so high a Priviledge as that of Justification,
must needs be such as Complieth with all the purposes of
Christ's coming into the world; (whither at present it understands
them or not) & it is no less necessary it should Justifie as it doth
40 so, *P.* 222.

Fifthly, He must know that a Man may not rely upon the Merits of Christ for the forgiveness of his Sins, before he have done other good Works first, *Pag.* 223.

Sixthly, And that the right explication of the imputation of Christ's righteousness, is this, that it Consisteth in having to do with persons that are sincerely Righteous, *Pag.* 225. For it is not possible for Christ's Righteousness to be imputed to an unrighteous Man, *Pag.* 120.

These things, with many like to them, being the main points by this Man handled, and by him asserted to be the design of Christianity, by these we must, as by a Rule, and Standard, understand how to Judge of the truth of Doctrines. And (saith he) *Seeing the Design of Christianity is to make Men Holy*, (still meaning from Principles of Humanity, and by Possessing us again, with the often repeated Holiness which we had lost) *whatsoever opinions do either directly, or in their evident Consequences obstruct the promoting of it, are perfectly false.* Pag. 227, 228.

Answ. Thus with one Word, as if he were Lord, and Judge himself, he sendeth to the Pit of Hell, all things that Sanctifie, or make Holy the hearts of Men, if they oppose the Design of *his* Christianity. But what if the *Holy Ghost* will become a Principle in the hearts of the Converted, and will not now suffer them to act *simply*, and *alone*, upon the Principles of *pure Humanity*; or what now if *Faith* will become a Principle to act by, instead of these that are Originally Dictates of Humane Nature? Or, what if a Man should act now as a *Son*, rather than simply as a *Creature* indued with a Principle of Reason? I question here, whether these things thus doing do not obstruct, put by, yea, and take the way of his Pure Humanity, Dictates of Human Nature; and instead thereof, Act, and Govern the Soul by, and with their own Principles. For albeit, there be the Dictates of Humane Nature in the Sons of Men, yet neither is this Nature, nor yet the Dictates of it, laid by Jesus Christ as the truly Christian Principles in his. But you add:

Those Doctrines which in their own Nature do evidently tend to the serving of THIS design of Christianity, we may conclude are most True, and Genuine, Pag. 229.

Answ. The Holiness which you so often call the Design of Christianity, being by your self said to be that which we had lost (for this one Sentence is it on which your whole Book is built (*P.*

12.) whatsoever Doctrine, or Doctor it be that asserts it, both that Doctrine is of the Devil, and that Doctor an Angel of darkness, or rather a Minister of Satan, become as a Minister of Righteousness. For where is it said in all the whole Book of God,

5 that ever the Lord Christ Designed, yea made it his Errand from Heaven, to put us again in Possession of the Holiness which we had lost? Yet this you affirm, and tell us the business of your Book is to prove it: But blessed be God, your shifts are discovered, and your Fig-leaves rent from off you, and the

10 Righteousness or Holiness so much cryed up by you, proved to be none of the Holiness of the Gospel, but that which stood with perfect ignorance thereof. I might speak to what yet remains of falshood, in the other part of this Chapter; but having overthrown the Foundation, and broken the Head of your Leviathan; what

15 remains falleth of it self, and dyeth of it's own accord.

What you say of Modes, or Forms, and Sticklers for little Trifles, such as place their Religion in meer Externals, you may fasten them where of due they belong: Yet I tell you, the least of the Commandments of Christ is better then your Adamitish

20 Holiness.

Your Twenty first Chapter tells us (if we will believe you) how we shall Judge of the necessity of Doctrine, to be imbraced, or rejected; also , you say it giveth us a brief discourse of the Nature of Fundamentals. But because your discourse of them is general,

25 and not any one Particularized, I might leave you in your generals, till you dealt more Candidly, both with the Word of God, and your abused Reader.

Indeed you tell us of Primary Fundamentals, such as without the Knowledge, and belief of which it is impossible to acquire that inward

30 *Righteousness, and Holiness which the Christian Religion Aimeth at; but the Particulars of these*, say you, *I shall not enumerate, because (as will appear from what will be said anon) it is not needful to have a just table of them.*

Answ. Deep Divinity! *First*, They are such as without the

35 Knowledge and Belief of them, it is not possible we should acquire your true Holiness; and yet for all that it is not needful that we be told what they are, or that we should have a just Table of them.

Secondly, But if they be things necessary, things without the

40 Knowledge of which it is impossible we should be truly Holy,

then is it needful that we understand what they are: Yea, then is it needful that they be written, and presented only by one unto us, that our Knowledge of them being distinct and full, we may the better be able to obtain or acquire your Glorious (so pretended) Holiness.

But I know your Primary Fundamentals, they are your first Principles of Morals, not Faith in the Righteousness of Christ, for that is comprehended in your possitive, and in themselves indifferent things: Your Morrals are the things in themselves absolutely necessary, of an indispensible and Eternal Obligation, *Pag.* 8, 9.

But Secondly you tell us of Points of Faith that are Secondarily Fundamental; the disbelief of which cannot consist with true Holiness, in those to whom the Gospel is sufficiently made known.

Answ. The Secondary Fundamentals also, are all kept close, and hid, and not otherwise to be understood, but by implication; however the disbelief of these is not of so sad a consequence as is that of the former; because, say you, *They are not in their own Nature, Holiness,* Pag. 235. Yea, he insinuateth that the disbelief of them may stand with true Holiness in those to whom the Gospel is not sufficiently made known.

Of these Secondary Fundamentals therefore, (whatever is their number) this is one, even coming to God by Christ; for as in Page 7, and 9. he calleth it a Possitive Precept, a thing that in it self is neither good nor evil; so here he speaks of such as are not in their own Nature Holy; not such, as that Holiness is not in some degree or other attainable without the belief of them.

That one of these Secondary Fundamentals is intended by Mr. *Fowler, that of coming to God by Christ*; I farther gather, because he saith, that *in the number of these, are all such Doctrines, as are with indisputable clearness revealed to us* (that is, by the Holy Scriptures of the New Testament, *Pag.* 235) For therein is this Revealed to be a Fundamental; but he saith, not a Primary one, because, that in it self it is but indifferent, and not in it's own Nature good. *Now the belief of these,* saith he, *though it is not in it self any more, then in higher, or lower degrees profitable,* (Confusion! Darkness! Confusion!) *yet it is absolutely necessary from an External cause*: That is, with such abundant clearness, as that nothing can cause men to refuse to admit them, but that which argueth them to be stark naught.

Answ. 1. Then, hence it seems that the reason why you admit these Secondary sort of Fundamentals, is not from any Internal Power, but an External Declaration onely.

2. Nay, and you do but ADMIT them neither, and that too, for some External cause; not because of the worthiness of the Nature of the points themselves.

3. And were it not, but that you are loath to be counted stark naught in the eyes of Men, so far as I can descern, you would not at all make profession of them, with pretence as unto God: For, say you, *We must take notice here, that all such Points (*viz. *these Fundamentals) are not of equal necessity to be received by all Christians, because that in regard of the Diversity of their Capacities, Education, and other means and advantages, some of them may be most plainly perceived by some to be delivered in the Scriptures, which cannot be so by others, with the like ease.*

Answ. From these words I take notice of four things.

1. That by this Universal (*all Christians*) is Comprehended the Heathen, and Pagan People, that give heed to, and mind to follow that light, that Originally, and Naturally stirreth them to Morral Duties. These be they that want the Education, and advantages of others, and are not in such a Capacity, as they to whom these things are delivered by the Scriptures.

2. That this People, notwithstanding they want a Scripture Revelation of these Secondary Fundamentals, yet have the more necessary, the first sort of Fundamentals: For the secondary sort, say you, are not in their own Nature such, as that Holiness is not in some degree or other attainable without the belief of them.

3. That therefore these Secondary sort of Fundamentals, are onely necessary to be believed by them that have the indisputable (the Scripture) Revelation of them; and that in truth the others may be saved without them.

4. But yet, even those that are made capable by education, and other advantages, to obtain the belief of them, ought notwithstanding, not to have the same respect for them, as for those of the first sort of Fundamentals, because they are not in their own Nature such.

But will this man know that Christ is not onely a Fundamental,

---

21 advantages of others] *errata*; Vantages of other,

but the very foundation of all other Fundamental truths, revealed both in the Old Testament, and the New? and that his pure Humane Nature, with the Dictates of it, with his feigned Adamitish Holiness is no Fundamental at all; I mean no Fundamental of Faith, no Gospel Fundamental, 1 *Co.* 3. 14. *Eph.*   5
2. 19, 20. Yea, will he know that from Heaven there is none other Name given, then the Name of Jesus Christ, whereby we must be saved, none other Name given under the whole Heavens, *Act.* 4. 12.

Oh the Witchcrafts by which some Mens Spirits are In-   10
toxicated! and the strength of delusion, by which some are infatuate, and turned aside from the simplicity that is in Jesus Christ! But I proceed:

Your great Question, or rather Urim and Thummim, by which you would have all men make Judgement of their saveable, or   15
damnable state, *Pag.* 236. is according to your description of things, most Devilish and Destructive. For to obey God and Christ, in all things with you, is to do it from Principles purely Humane in the Faith of this; that Christ hath designed to possess us again with that Holiness we had lost. Again, to obey God,   20
and Christ with you, is, so to obey all their Laws, as respecting the first Principles of Morrals, and our obedience to them, far more indispensible then that of coming to God by Christ. Farther, he that obeys them in all things with your directions, must not look upon Faith in the Blood of Christ, and   25
Justification by his Righteousness, as the main and first, but the second part of our duty; other Commands or Precepts more naturally Holy, and Good, first being imbraced and lived in the practise of by, us.

This, I say, being the Doctrine you have asserted, and the   30
Foundation on which your Urim and Thummim stands; the Foundation, with your tryal are both from the Devil and Hell, as hath at large been proved, and discovered in this Book.

And I now will add (and bid you take advantage) that should a man with all his might strive to obey all the Morral Laws, either   35
as they are contained in the first Principles of Morrals, or in the express Decalogue, or Ten Commandments, without Faith, First, in the Blood, and Death, and Resurrection of Christ, &c. For his Justification with God; his thus doing would be counted Wickedness, and he in the end accounted a Rebel against the   40

Gospel, and shall be Damned for want of Faith in the Blood of
the Lord Jesus.

Your Twenty Second Chapter saith *That the Design of
Christianity teacheth us what Doctrines and Practises we ought as*
5 *Christians to be most Zealous for, or against,* Pag. 237.

Answ. But there is not by that (it being rightly stated) one
Sillable that tendeth to incourage any Man, to have lower
thoughts of *coming to God by Christ,* then of keeping the Morral
Law. For even the first Text you bring, doth utterly overthrow it.
10 *Contend, say you, for the Faith:* I Answer then, not for the Law of
Work; for the Law is *not of Faith,* but the Man that doth these
things shall live in them, by them. *Contend earnestly for the Faith,
for there are certain men crept in unawares, which were before of old
ordained unto his Condemnation;* (even the Condemnation that is
15 to come upon them to Contend against the Faith;) for these
ungodly Men turn the Grace of God into Lasciviousness, and
deny the onely Lord God, and our Lord Jesus Christ. Now these
creeping ungodly Men, may be divided into three Rancks.

1. Such as by Principle, and Practice both, say, *Let us do evil,*
20 *that good may come thereon;* and their Damnation is Just, *Rom.* 3. 8,
9.

2. Such as by Practice onely, appear to be such, denying to
profess the Principle thereof, such are they that made excuse and
delay, when invited to come to the Wedding, *Mat.* 22. 1, 2, 3.
25 *Luke* 14.

3. There is yet *another* sort; And they are *such* as seem to deny
it, both in Principle, and Practice also; onely they do it *Covertly,*
PRIVILY bringing in Damnable Heresies, even denying the Lord
that bought them. *These bring upon themselves swift destruction,* 2.
30 Pet. 2. 1.

This Third sort, make of the Doctrine of Grace, and of the
forgiveness of Sins, through the Faith of the Righteousness of
Christ, a Loose, and Licentious Doctrine, or a Doctrine that
giveth liberty to the Flesh: By reason of THESE *the way of truth*
35 *is evil spoken of,* and the Hearts of Innocent ones Alienated
therefrom: *These* will not stick to charge it upon the very chief of
the Brethrern, if they shall say, As Sin abounded, Grace hath
much more abounded; that they press men to do evil, that good
may come of it, *Rom.* 3. 8, 9. But (as I said) these Vilifie Christ,
40 not with *open* Words, but *Covertly;* PRIVILY they bring in their

Blasphemy under a *Cloak*, crying, the *Law*, *Holiness*, *Strictness*, *good Works*, &c. Besides, *these* cloath their Doctrines with *Names* and *Notions* that belong not at all unto them; as of *Christ*, *Grace*, the *Spirit*, the *Gospel*, when there is onely there, the *Devil*, and his *Angels*, and *Errours*, as Angels of Light, and Ministers of Righteousness. Of this last sort, are you, and the subject matter of your Book; for you bring into the World an Antigospel Holiness, Antigospel Principles, and Antigospel Fundamentals; and that these things might be Worshiped by your Disciples, you give them the Name of Holiness, the Design of Christ, and of Christianity; by which means you remove the Christ of God, from before, and set him behind, *forbiding Men to believe on him*, *till they have Practiced your things first*: Nay, after they have Practiced yours, they then must come to God by him; still respecting the Principles and Dictates of Humanity, as things of the *greatest weight*, things that are *good in themselves*; Still considering that '*coming to God by Christ*, is not good in it self, but so, onely upon the account of certain Circumstances; a thing in it self of an indifferent Nature, and absolutely considered neither good nor evil.'

Wherefore, Sir, laying aside all fear of men, not regarding what you may procure to be inflicted upon me, for this my plain dealing with you, I tell you again, that your self is one of them, that have *Closely*, *Privily*, and *Devishly*, by your Book, turned the Grace of our God into a Lascivious Doctrine, bespattering it with giving liberty to looseness, and the hardening of the ungodly in Wickedness, against whom shall you persist in your Wickedness; I shall not fail (may I live, and know it, and be helped of God to do it) to discover yet farther the rottenness of your Doctrine, with the accursed tendencies thereof.

What you say about *doubtful Opinion, alterable Modes, Rites, and Circumstances in Religion*, Pag. 239. I know none so wedded thereto as your selves, even the whole gang of your rabling counterfeit Clergy; who generally like the *Ape* you speak of, lye blowing up the Aplause and Glory of your Trumpery, and like the *Tail*, with your Foolish and Sophistical arguings, you cover the filthy parts thereof; as you sweetly argue in the next Chapter, *Pag.* 242 saying, *Whatsoever of such are Commended by the custome of the place we live in, or commanded by Superiors, or made by ANY*

Circumstance convenient to be done, our Christian liberty Consists in
this, that we have leave to do them. So that do but call them things
indifferent, things that are the customs of the place we live in, or
made by ANY Circumstance convenient, and a man may not
5 doubt but he hath leave to do them, let him live at *Rome*, or
Constantinople, or amidst the greatest Corruption of Worship and
Government. These are therefore doubtless, a *Third* sort of
Fundamentals, by which you can *Wrastle* with Conviction of
Conscience, and stifle it; by which you can suit yourself for every
10 Fashion, Mode, and Way of Religion. Here you may hop from
Presbiterianism, to a Prelatical Mode; and if time and chance
should serve you, backwards, and forwards again: Yea, here you
can make use of several Consciences, one for this way now,
another for that anon; now putting out the Light of this by a
15 Sophistical Delusive Argument, then putting out the other, by an
argument that best suits the time. Yea, *how oft is the Candle of the*
Wicked put out, by such glorious Learning as this. Nay, I doubt
not, but a man of your Principles, were he put upon it, would not
stick to count those you call Gospell-possitive Precepts, of no
20 Value at all in the Christian Religion; for now, even now, you do
not stick to say that, *that* even *that* of going to God by Christ, is
one of these, and that such an one, as if *absolutely Considered* in it
self, is neither good nor evil. How then, if God should cast you
into *Turky*, where *Mahomet* Reigns *as Lord*? It is but reckoning
25 that it is the Religion, and Custome of the Country, and that
which is Authorized by the Power that is there; wherefore it
is but sticking to your Dictates of Humane Nature, and
remembring that coming to God by Christ is a thing of an
indifferent Nature in it self, and then for peace sake, and to sleep
30 in a whole skin, you may comply, and do as your Superiour
commands. Why? Because in *Turky*, are your first sort of
Fundamentals found: These are Men that have Humane
Nature, and the Law of Morrals written in their hearts; they have
also the Dictates thereof written within them, which teach them,
35 those you call the Eternal Laws of Righteousness; wherefore you
both would agree in your Essential, and immutable differences of
good and evil, *Pag.* 6. and differ onely about these possitive
Laws, *Indifferent things*. Yea, and *Mahomet* also for the time,
because by a custome made convenient, might be now accounted

worshipful, and the Circumstances that attend his Worship, especially *those* of them, that *clash* not with the Dictates of *your* Humane Nature, might also be swallowed down.

Behold you here then (good Reader) a glorious Latitudinarian, that can, as to Religion, turn and twist like an Eel on the Angle; or rather like the Weather-cock that stands on the Steeple.

But (saith he) *our refusing to comply with these can hardly proceed from any thing better then a proud affection of singularity, or at best, from Supersticious Scrupulosity*, Pag. 242.

Do but believe him therefore in what he saith, and you cannot chuse but be ready with him to comply with all Modes, that may serve for advantage.

Besides, he saith, *that the Word Superstition, in the* Greek *implyeth, a frightful, and over-timerous apprehension of the Divine Nature; and consequently a base and under-valuing conception of it.*

So that to be tender of Conscience, especially in things of Divine Worship, binding up the Soul to the words of the everlasting Testament, in such things especially, as a Fool can call little, and insignificant trivial matters, rendreth a man such an one as hath a very Errorious Conscience.

But he would not be understood (*Pag.* 244.) as if he here intended to vilifie things that are plainly commanded, or to tolerate that which is plainly forbidden, onely he would have all things that may fall within the reach of these two general Heads, be examined by this general Rule, HIS discription *of the Design of Christianity.*

Answ. But I could tell him, that whatsoever is imposed as a part of God's Worship, is Judged by a better rule then his, both as to it's goodness and badness, neither can we account any thing indifferent that is a part thereof. Besides, whatsoever is reputed a part of God's Worship, layeth hold on the Conscience of the Godly: Although a ranting Latitudinarian may say, *If the Devil should Preach, I would hear him, before I would suffer Persecution*: (As a brave fellow which I could name, in his Zeal was pleased to declare.)

But *what* trust should any man put to the rule to which you direct him for help, and relief therein; *seeing* that from the *beginning* to the *end*, from the *top* to the *bottom*, it is a cursed

2 especially] *errata*; especiall

Blasphemous Book; a Book that more vilifieth Jesus Christ, then many of the Quakers themselves: for which of them said worse of him, and make coming to God by him, a more insignificant thing, then you by your pretended design of Christianity have
5 done.

We have therefore a more sure *Word of the Prophets*, to the which *we do well to take heed*; by which, both your Doctrine, and practice, is already judged to be naught, as will be farther discovered time enough, when you shall Justifie or Condemn
10 Particulars. 2 Pet. 1. 19.

Your Twenty Fourth Chapter I shall now pass by, until I can better compare you and Popery, against which you there so stoutly diggle together.

Your Twenty Fifth Chapter carrieth in it an hideous outcry
15 against many of *your* Ministers and *Guides*, complaining, and confessing, *That nothing hath so conduced to the Prejudice of your Church of* England, *and done the separating parties so much service, as the* Scandalous *lives of some that exercise your Ministerial Function*, P. 258.
20 *Answ.* I will grant it, if you respect these poor carnal People, who yet have been shamed from your Assemblies, by such Vicious Persons you mention; But the truly Godly, and Spiritually Judicious have left you from other Arguments, of which I shall not here Dilate.
25 But from Page 261. to the end of the Chapter, you take upon you to particularize other of your Ministers that are an offence to you, and to the Design of your Christianity.

1. *Such as affect to make people stare at their high flown bumbast Language, or to please their Phantacies with foolish Jugglings, and*
30 *Pœdantick or Boyish wit; or to be admired for their ability in dividing of an hair, their Metaphysical Acuteness, and Scholastick subtilety, or for their Doughty Dexterity in Controversial Squabbles.* And I add, had you joyned herewith, such as vilifie, and trample upon the Blood of the Lord Jesus, preferring the Snivel of their own
35 brains before him, you had herein but drawn your own Picture, and given your Reader an Emblem of your self.

2. The Second sort you blame, are *such as seek to approve themselves to their Auditories to be Men of* Mysteries, *and endeavour to make the plain and the easie Doctrines of the Gospel as* Intricate
40 *and obscure as ever they are* Able. I will add to these, such as take

away the Doctrine of Faith, and that set themselves and their
Works in the room thereof: Such as have sought to overturn the
Foundation, Jesus Christ, and have made coming to God by him,
in it self of a far more indifferent Nature then the Dictates of our
Humanity.   5

3. Another sort (you say) are *such as Preach upon free Grace, and
Christian Priviledges, otherwise then as Motives to cite to obedience,
and never scarce insist upon any Duties, but those of believing, laying
hold on Christ's Righteousness, applying the promises, and renouncing
our own Righteousness, which they that have none at all to renounce,* 10
have a mightly kindness for.

Answ. 1. Who they are that Preach free Grace in your
Church, to excite Men to uncleanness, you may know better then
I. But if these Words (otherwise then to Cite men to obedience)
be thus thrust in, of purpose thereby to speak evil of the   15
Preachers of free Grace, and the exalters of the imputed
Righteousness of Christ, then look to it; for such venome
Language as this, doth but involve you within the bowels of that
most dreadful Prophecy, concerning the false Prophets of the
last days, that shall privily bring in damnable Heresies, even   20
denying the Lord that bought them.

2. The Preaching of free Grace, pressing to believing, and
laying hold on Christ's Righteousness, is the most available
means under Heaven, to make Men Holy, and Righteous: 1.
Before God. 2. Then before Men.   25

3. The Preaching of these are first, and principally to *beget*
Faith, to *beget* Life, to *beget* Souls to God, yea, to *beget* in Men
such a Principle, whereby they may serve God acceptably, with
reverence and Godly fear.

4. But to Preach *free Grace*, doth much condemn your *freewill*;   30
to Preach *Christ's Righteousness* doth utterly Curse, and Condemn
yours; and to Preach the *Promise* of Grace, doth quite shut out a
Covenant of Works: Therefore no marvel if you, who are so
Wedded to these things, be such an Enemy to free Grace, the
Righteousness of Christ, and the Gospel-promises, that you   35
make even these things a Characteristical note (first abusing the
Consequences of them) of a Church-troubling-Preacher.

5. You tauntingly proceed, saying, *Such Preachers also press us*

26 Preaching] Phreaching

to renounce our own Righteousness, which they that have none at all to
renounce, have a mighty kindness for.

Answ. Indeed those that have a Righteousness of their own, as
the Pharisees, and Hypocrites of old, had never much kindness
5 for the Doctrine of Grace, and the Ministers of Christ, but the
Publicans and harlots had: and therefore these (while they that
had Righteousness stumbled and fell) entred into the Kingdom
of Heaven. *The Publicans and Harlots entred the Kingdom of
Heaven, before you.* But what Righteousness have you of your
10 own, to which you so dearly are Wedded, that it may not be let
go, for the sake of Christ? seeing also so long as you go about to　Rom. 10. 3
establish it, *you submit not your self to the Righteousness of God*: Yea,
Why do you taunt those Ministers that perswade us to Renounce
our own Righteousness, and those also that follow their
15 Doctrine? seeing this was both the Doctrine and Practice of *Paul*
and all others, save onely those that had *Moses* Vail over their
Hearts.

Another sort of Ministers that you say are Enemies to the
promoting of Holiness, are *such as are never in their Element, but
20 when they are talking of the* Irrespectiveness *of God's Decrees, the*
absoluteness *of his promises, the* utter *disability, and* perfect
impotency of Natural Men, to do *any thing towards their* own
*Conversion, and that insists with great Emphasis, and Vehemency,
upon such like* false, *and* dangerous *opinions.* Pag. 262.

25 *Answ.* The Men that Preach these things, being rightly stated,
Preach the truth of God, if the Scriptures may bear sway; they
having all been prooved the truth of the Gospel, both by the
Prophets and Apostles: And when you shall think meet by
argument to contradict them, either I, or some other may shew
30 you the folly of your undertaking. In the mean time let the
Reader take notice that here you have judged not by Scripture,
nor by Reason, but upon a bare Presumption, arising from your
Pride or Ignorance. Wherefore pray you in your next, shew us.

1. What is in Man that the decree of Election should respect
35 as a thing fore-seen of God, to prevail with him to predestinate
him to Eternal life by Jesus Christ our Lord.

2. Make it manifest that in the Word of God there neither is,
nor can be any absolute promise contained.

3. Shew us what ability there is in a Natural Man, as such, to
40 do things towards his own Conversion; I mean things immediately

tending to, and that must infallibly consummate therein, and let us see what things they are: And know that when you have well done all this, according to the Scriptures of truth, that then it will be time enough to condemn the contrary, for false, and dangerous opinions.   5

But shall I speak the truth for you? The reason of this your presumptuous exclamation, and condemnation of these things, is because they stand in the way of promoting your ignorant, tottering, promiseless, and Gospelless Holiness, they stand in the way of old *Adam*, they stand in the way of your dunghil   10 rebellious Righteousness, they stand in the way of your freedom of will, and a great rable more of such like pretended Vertues. Yea, they do, and must, and shall stand there, when you and the rest of the *Socinians*, and *Quakers*, have said their all against them.   15

There is yet another sort of Preachers whom you condemn, and so do I as well as you, though not in your Spirit, nor to advance your Pestiferous Principles: and they are *such as make it their great business, to advance the petty interest of any party whatsoever, and concern themselves more about doing this, then about*   20 *promoting, and carrying on that, wherein consists the chief good of all Mankind, and are more Zealous to make Prosilites to their particular Sects, then Converts* (I will add first to Jesus Christ, and then) *to an Holy Life, and press more exact and ridged conformity to their Modes and Forms, then to the Laws of God, and the Essential Duties of the*   25 *Christian Religion.*

Lastly, the Caution which you give to Ministers, because there wanteth for it, among *you*, a Foundation, is to be esteemed but an Error, and an abuse of the words, and practices of the Apostle. And as for your subtile and close incensing the power to   30 persecute Non-conformists, know that we are willing, God assisting, to overcome you with truth, and patience, not sticking to Sacrifice our lives, and dearest concerns in a faithful Witness-baring against your filthy errors, Compiled and Foiled into the World, by your Devilish design to promote Paganism, against   35 Christianity, *Pag.* 265, 266.

I come now to your Twenty Sixth Chapter, which is spent to prove, *that an obedient temper of mind is a necessary, and excellent qualification to prepare men for a firm belief, and a right understanding of the Gospel of Christ*, Pag. 267.   40

Answ. 1. For as much as the obedient temper you mention, is
Precedent to, or *before Faith*, and the right understanding of the
Gospel, it must needs be also, that which stands with unbelief,
and ignorant of the same. Now that this should be an excellent,
5 and necessary qualification, to a firm belief, and right under-
standing of the Gospel, is altogether without proof, and truth.
But this is affirmed for the farther promoting of your Humane
Nature, and the things; that Originally are Dictates thereof. But,

2. The obedience or inclination to obedience that is before
10 Faith, or the understanding of the Gospel, is so far off from
being an excellent preparative, or good qualification for Faith,
and the knowledge of the Gospel, that in its own Nature (which
is more then in its Consequences) it is a great obstruction
thereto.

15 For, while a Man remains faithless and ignorant of the
Gospel, to what doth his obedient temper of mind incline? Not to
Faith, nor the Gospel of Christ; for with these, as yet you
suppose he hath not to doe; therefore he inclineth to the Law of
Morrals, either as it was delivered in Tables of Stone from *Sinai*,
20 or as written in the hearts of all the Children of Men, to it under
the last consideration, (which is in truth the most Heathen and
Pagan) to it, as so you intend your obedient temper of mind
should incline, *Pag.* 7, 8, 9, 10.

Now this Doctrine being in it self of quite another Nature
25 then the Doctrine of Faith, and also, *as such*, a Covenant by it
self, it requireth the mind by vertue of it's Commands, to stand
to THAT, and to rest in THAT: For of necessity the heart and
mind of a Man, can go no farther, then it seeth, and hath learnt;
but by this Morral Doctrine, the heart and mind is bound and
30 limited to it self, by the power of the Dictate to obedience, and
the promise of obtaining the Blessing, when the preceptive part 2 Cor. 3.
of it is fulfilled. Hence *Paul* tells us that though that Ministration,
that was *Written, and Ingraven in Stones*, (which in Nature is the
same with this) *is glorious*, yet these imperfections attended the
35 Man that was in it.

1. He was but within the bounds of the *Ministration of Death*.

2. In this estate he was *blind*, and could not see how to be
delivered therefrom: *The vail is over their heart*, so that they could
not heretofore, neither can they now see to the *end* of that which
40 was commanded, neither to the perfection of the command, nor

their own insufficiency to do it, nor to the Death and Curse of
God, that attended him, that in every thing continued not in that
was Written in the Book of the Law to do them.

3. Every Lecture, or Reading of this Old Law, is as a fresh
Hood-winking of it's Disciples, and a doubling of the hindrance   5
of their coming to Christ for life. *But their minds were blinded, for
until this day the same Vail remaineth untaken away, in reading of the
Old Testament, which Vail is done away in Christ; But even unto this
day when* Moses *is read, the Vail is over their Hearts,* 2 Cor. 3. 6, to
15.   10

And let the Reader note, that all these things attend the
Doctrine of Morals; the Ceremonies being in themselves more
apt to instruct Men in the Knowledge of Christ, they being by
God's Ordaination, Figures, Shadows, Representations, and
Emblems of him; but the Morals are not so, neither as Written   15
in our Natures, nor as Written and Engraven in Stones.
Wherefore your so highly commended obedient temper of mind
(you intending thereby an hearty complyance before Faith, with
Morals for Righteousness) is so far off from being an excellent
temper, and a necessary qualification, to help a Man to a firm   20
belief, and right understanding of the Gospel; that it is the
most ready way of all ways in the World, to keep a man
perpetually blind, and ignorant thereof. Wherefore the Apostle
saith, *that the Vail*, the Ignorance cannot be taken away, but when
the Heart shall turn to the Lord, that is from the Doctrine of   25
Morals as a Law and Covenant in our Natures, or as it was
Written, and Ingraven in Stones, to Christ for mercy to pardon
our transgressions against it, and for imputative Righteousness
to Justifie us from it. *While* Moses is *Read, the Vail is over the Heart*;
that is, while Men with their minds stand bending also to do it: 30
But mark, *when it, the Heart, shall turn to the Lord*, or to the Word
of the Gospel, which is the Revelation of him, *then the Vail shall
be taken away.*

And hence it will not be amiss, if again we consider how the
Holy Ghost compareth, or setteth one against another, these two   35
Administrations.

The *Law* he calls the *Letter*, even the Law of Morals, that
Law that was Written and Engraven in Stones. The other
Ministration he calls the Ministration of the *Spirit*, even that
which Christ offered to the World, upon believing.   40

Gal. 3. 24.

Again, he denyeth himself to be a Minister of *the Law* of
Morrals. He hath made us able Ministers of the New Testament;
not of the *Letter* (or Law) but of the *Spirit* (or Gospel.) The
reason is, for the *Letter*, or Law, can do nothing but kill, Curse,
5 or Condemn, but the Spirit of the Gospel, giveth life. Farther, in
comparing, he calls the Law, the *Ministration of Death*; or that
which layeth Death at the Doors of all Flesh; but the Gospel the
Ministration of Righteousness, because by this Ministry there is
a Revelation of *that* Righteousness that is fulfilled *by the Person* of
10 Christ, and to be imputed *for Righteousness* to them that believe,
that they might be delivered from the Ministration of death. How
then? hath the Ministration of God *no* Glory? Yes, forasmuch as
it is a Revelation of the Justice of God, against Sin. But yet
again, it's *Glory* is turned into no Glory, when it is compared with
15 that which *excelleth. For if the Ministration of Death, Written and
Graven in the Stones was glorious, so that the Children of Israel could
not stedfastly behold the face of* Moses, *for the Glory of his
countenance; which Glory was to be done away: how shall not the
Ministration of the Spirit be rather Glorious: For if the Ministration of*
20 *Condemnation be Glory, much more doth the Ministration of
Righteousness exceed in Glory: For even that which was made Glorious
hath no Glory in this respect, by reason of the Glory that excelleth*, 2
Cor. 3. 9, 10.
So then, your obedient temper of mind, forasmuch as it
25 respecteth the Law of Morrals, and that too, *before* Faith, or a
right understanding of the Gospel, is nothing else but an
obedience to the Law, a living to Death, and the Ministration of
Condemnation, and is a perswading the World, that to be
obedient to that Ministration, that is not the Ministration of the
30 Gospel, but holdeth it's Disciples in blindness and ignorance, *in
which* it is impossible Christ should be revealed, is an excellent,
yea, a necessary qualification to prepare Men for a firm belief,
and a right understanding of the Gospel of Christ, which yet
even blindeth, and holdeth all blind that are the followers of that
35 Ministration. I come now to your *Proof*, which indeed is *no* Proof
of this Antigospel Assertion, but Texts abused, and wrestled out
of their place, to serve to underprop your erronious Doctrine.
The First is, *If any Man will do his will, he shall know of the
Doctrine, whether it be of God, or whether I speak of my self* John 7.
40 17. *P.* 268.

Answ. This Scripture respecteth not at all the Morral Law, or obedience to the Dictates of Humane Nature, as an acceptable qualification precedent to Faith, or that, for the sake of which God will give Men Faith in, and a right undertanding of the Gospel, *but is it self an immediate exhortation to believing, with a*   5
promise of what shall follow; as who shall say, The Father hath sent me into the World to be Salvation to it, through Faith in my Blood: My Fathers will therefore is, *that Men believe in me*; and if any will do his will, *he shall know of the Doctrine*, he shall feel the power thereof, by the peace and comfort that will presently   10
possess the Soul, and by the holy effects that follow.

That this is the true exposition of this place, will be verified if you consider, that to do the will of God, in a New Testament sence, is to be taken under a double consideration. 1. As it respecteth Christ. 2. Man.   15

1. As it respecteth Christ, so it concerns his compleating the Redemption of Man by himself, by his own personal performances, *John* 6. 38, 39. *Heb.* 10. 5, 6, 7, 8, 9, 10.

2. As it respecteth Man, it doth first, and immediately respect our believing on him for Remission of Sins, and Eternal Life.   20
And this is the Will of the Father which sent me, (saith Christ) *that every one that seeth the Son, and believeth on him, may have everlasting Life, and I will raise him up at the last day*, John 6. 40. This then is the will of God; That Men do believe in Jesus Christ.   25

Again, when the *Jews* asketh Jesus Christ what they should do, that they might work the works of God, he did not send them first to the Morral Precept, or to it's first Principles in the hearts of Men, by obeying that, to fit themselves for Faith; but immediately he tells them, *This is the Work of God, that ye believe*   30
in him whom he hath sent, John 6. 29. *This* is the Work of God; that is, *this is his Commandement, that we believe in the Name of his Son Jesus Christ*, &c. *and love one another as he gave us Commandement.* 1 John 3. 23. If any Man will do his will, he shall know of the Doctrine, that is, (as I have said) he shall feel, and   35
have the Authourity of this Faith in his heart, both to give Peace, and Joy in his heart, and assurance, and the Sealing of his Soul to Glory. For all these things come in upon believing, *First* in Christ.

20 Remission] Remssion

1. By *Faith* we have *Peace* with God, *Rom.* 5. 1.

2. We have *Joy* and *Peace*, through *Believing, Rom.* 15. 13.

3. *Assurance* comes also through *Believing,* Joh. 6. 69. *Heb.* 10. 22.

5　4. Yea, and the Sealings up to Eternal Life; *In whom also after that ye believed, ye were sealed with that Holy Spirit of Promise,* Eph. 1. 13.

5. Sanctification, and a right obedient temper, is not to be found in Men *before,* but *after* they have believed; *He purified their*
10　*hearts by Faith.* Yea, Heaven and Eternal Happiness is promised to them who are Sanctified *by Faith* which is in Christ, *Act.* 15. 9. Chap. 26. 18.

This *First* Text therefore, hath been by you abused, in that you have ungodlily strained it, (but in vain) to make it warrant your
15　Heathenish preparations to Faith.

The *Second* Scripture; *He that is of God heareth Gods Words; ye therefore hear them not, because you are not of God,* John 8. 47.

Answ. This Scripture supposeth Men must first be of God, before they can hear God's Word; before they can hear it with
20　the hearing of Faith; and therefore nothing respecteth those that before they have Faith, live in the Law of Works; and least of all, those that become obedient thereto, that thereby they may obtain everlasting life: For *these* are *not* of God, *not* of him in a *New Testament* Sence; not *Sons,* because they are born of Men, of the
25　will of Men, of the Law, and according to the Wisdom of Flesh and Blood, *John* 1. 12, 13.

Your Third Scripture is; *And as many as were ordained to Eternal Life, believed,* Act. 13, 48. Which Text you thus expound: *That as many of the* Gentiles *as were disposed, or in a ready*
30　*preparedness for Eternal Life, believed; that is those which were Proselites of the Gate, who were admitted by the* Jews, *to the hope of Eternal Life, and to have a Portion in the Age to come, without submitting to the whole Law, or any more then owning the God of* Israel, *and observing the Seven Precepts of* Noah.

35　*Answ.* 1. That obedience to the Morral Law, is not a preparative to Faith, or an excellent and necessary qualification to the right understanding of the Gospel I have proved.

2. That to be a Jewish Proselite, was to live in the Faith of

14 ungodlily] *errata;* ungodly

Messias to come, is the strain of all the Scriptures that have to deal with them.

3. But that ordaining men to Eternal Life, respects an act of the *Jews* or that the Jews did dispence with the *Gentile* Proselites, in their casting off all their Laws, but the *seven Precepts of* Noah.   5

4. Or that God counted this a fit, or forerunning qualification to Faith in Jesus Christ, neither stands with the Word of God, nor the Zeal of that People.

5. Besides, the Words presently following seem to me to insinuate more; *viz.* That the *Jews*, and Religious Proselites, that   10
adhered to *Paul*, at his first Sermon, *verse* 43. did Contradict and Blaspheme at his second, *verse* 45. And moreover, that it was they that raised Persecution upon him, and expelled him out of their Coasts, *verse* 50. When the *Gentiles*, even those that were more Barbarously ignorant at his coming, when they heard that   15
by Christ there was offered to them the forgiveness of Sins, they believed, *verse* 48 and Glorified the Word of the Lord. The Wisdom of Heaven so disposing such of their hearts, that were before by *him* not by *Jews*, ordained to Life. *And as many as were ordained to Eternal Life, believed.*   20

But you come again in *Pag.* 269. to the Scripture first urged by you; *If any man will do his will*, &c. and you tell us, That this must also needs be *implyed, he shall rightly understand and the Doctrine too.* Which word (understand) you so carry, as may best help you, in case you should meet with an Adversary. As if any   25
should thus object, that here you have granted that the Words make promise of an understanding of the Gospel; yea, require in it the very *first act of the will*; then you readily shift it, by saying, That this this is *implyed* onely, suggesting that obedience to Morrals is *expressed*, and therefore must *first* be thought on, and   30
done. But if one of your Brotherhood stop here, and make the objection; then you add, It is Knowledge, at least, in all the necessary points thereof, absolutely necessary, and Essential parts; from among which, you long since did cast out, *Coming to God by Jesus Christ*: Yea, you add; *That by* (that which you call) *the*   35
design of the Gospel, it may be presumed, that whosoever considereth it, with a design of being so, (that is, of living up to Humane Principles, and that desireth to be possessed again of the Holiness he hath lost; for that is it, for the proof of which you have Written above 300 Pages,) *he must needs believe the Gospel to*   40

have come from God, and also be inlightned in the true Knowledge of,
at least the necessary points of it; viz. All Morral Duties contained
therein, which are never a one of them as such an Essential of
the Gospel, but are such Duties as are consequential to the belief
5 thereof.

Wherefore (although you feign it) *this honest temper*, as you call
it, will not help you, 1. To judge of the Gospel without
Prejudice; nor, 2. To evidence it with satisfaction; nor, 3. Secure
those in whom it is, from Error and Delusion; No Man being
10 more Bruitish or Heathenish, nor so void of satisfaction about it,
nor more involved in Error concerning it, then your self; being
truly what you charge upon others. 1. Grosely ignorant. 2. Too
highly Opinionate. 3. Proud in affection. 4. Liquorish. 5. A Self-
Lover. 6. And for your Blasphemy under the just Judgement of
15 God. *If our Gospel be hid, it is hid to them that are lost: In whom the*
God of this World hath blinded the minds of them that believe not;
least the light of the Glorious Gospel of Christ, who is the Image of
God, should shine unto them, 2 Cor. 4. 3, 4.

I am come now to your last Chapter, *Pag.* 281. which tells us
20 wherein *the essence and life of Christianity Consisteth*: viz. *In a good*
state and habit of mind, in a holy frame and temper of Soul.

Answ. 1. It consisteth in a *Life of Faith*, when I live in the *belief*
of *this*, that Christ loved me, and gave himself for me. *The Life*
that I now live in the Flesh (saith *Paul*) *it is by the Faith of the Son*
25 *of God, who loved me, and gave himself for me.*

2. And besides, a good state and habit of mind, or an Holy
frame and temper of Soul, in your notion of them, which
respecteth purely obedience to Morrals, from Natural Impulses,
or Dictates of our Humanity, they are rather Heathenish then
30 Christian, and being alone, end in Death, rather then Life. *As*
many as are of the Works of the Law, are under the Curse; (he saith
not, they that Sin against it, but they that are OF the Works of it)
such as do Justice, Righteousness, Charity, Goodness, Mercy,
Patience, and all kind of Morral Duties, from Principles
35 Humane, Natural, or as Men, they are under the Curse, because
they have sinned first, and also are infirm and weak in their
pursuit after the perfections they desire. *These follow after*
Righteousness, but that *flyes* from them; wherefore they do not

13 Liquorish] Lignorish   22 Consisteth] Censisteth

obtain it, because they seek it not by Faith in Christ, but as it were by the Works, the Righteousness, Good, and Holy Works of the Law. But you add;

It is such a habit of mind, such a frame and temper of Soul, as esteemeth God as the chiefest good, and preferreth him and his Son Jesus Christ before all the World; and that prizeth above all things an interest in the Divine Perfections, &c.

Answ. 1. God must needs be esteemed the chiefest good, by all that have but, and are ruled by the light of Nature, because they see him by his Works, to be Almighty, Merciful, and Eternal; but this may be where the Knowledge of the Man, the Mediator is not, therefore this, in *this*, and in *your* sence, cannot be of the Essence of Christianity, for that it is common to all the World. That estimation of God, which is common to Natural Men, cannot be of the Essence of Christianity, because they want that knowledge of him, that comes by Jesus Christ, and so are not capable to esteem of him under a Christian consideration.

But, you say, *it is that good habit, and temper of mind, that preferreth God, and his Son Jesus Christ, before all the World.*

Answ. He that esteemeth God above all, must needs, at least in his Judgement, so prefer him; but whereas you add (and his Son Jesus Christ) you put in them Words, but as a Cloak; For your self have not preferred his Son Jesus Christ, no, not before a Morral Law; no, not before your obedience to it, although but by Humane Principles; Yea, you have accounted the Command of God, by which we are injoyned by him, to come to God, a thing in it self but like Levitical Ceremonies, or as Baptism, and the Lord's Supper; a thing in it self indifferent, and absolutely considered neither good nor evil, *Pag.* 7, 8, 9.

You add; *It is such a temper as prizeth above all things, an interest in the Divine Perfections; such as Justice, and Righteousness, Universal Charity, Goodness, Mercy, Patience, and all kind of Purity.*

Answ. Seeing by these expressions you onely intend Morral Vertues, and those that are inherent in you, and originally operations of Humanity, it is evident that you have but Impiously, and Idolatrously Attributed to your own goodness, so high, and blessed a Title. For whatsoever is in your Nature, and Originally the Dictates thereof, and whatsoever proficiency you make therein, by Humane Principles, and helps of Natural Indowments; these things are but of your self, your *own* Justice,

5

10

15

20

25

30

35

40

your *own* Righteousness, your *own* Charity, Goodness, Mercy, Patience, Kindness, &c. Now to call these the *Divine* Perfections, when they are onely your *own* Humane Vertues, bespeaks you, I say, *Fond, Impious,* and *Idolatrous,* and shews you, in the midst of
5 all your pretended design to Glorifie God, such an one, who have set up your own goodness with him, yea, and given it the Title of his blessed Grace and Favour.

That Scripture you mention, *Rom.* 14. 17. Although by the Word (*Righteousness*) there, is intended obedience to the Morral
10 Law, yet to it by persons already Justified by Christ's Righteousness; hence they are said to do it *in the Joy, and Peace of the Holy Ghost*; or by the Joy and Peace, which they had by Faith in Christ's Righteousness, as Revealed to them by the Spirit of God. Hence again, they are said in IT to *serve Christ,* or to
15 receive the Law *at his hand,* which he giveth to them to walk after, having first justified them from the Curse thereof by his Blood.

2. The Law was given twice on *Sinai; the last time,* with a Proclamation of Mercy going before, and he that receiveth it
20 *thus,* receiveth it after a Gospel manner. For they as Justified persons are dead to the Law, as a Covenant of Works, by the Body of Christ, that they might live to another, even to him that   Rom. 7.
is raised from the Dead. But you by this Scripture intend not this   Gal. 2. 19.
Doctrine, for you make Justification by Christ, come after, not
25 before obedience to the Law: Yea, you make obedience thereto, the Essential, *and coming to God by Christ,* but a thing of a more remote Nature, from true and substantial Gospel-Righteousness.

In Page 283. you speak again of the old Principle, and thus you comment. *A Principle of Holiness that respecteth Duty, as with respect*
30 *to the Nature of the Command, so not with respect to the Duty as occasioned by certain External Inducements, and Motives, but from a good temper, and disposition of Soul.*

Answ. This I say, still respecting your old Principle of Humanity, and the Purity of your Nature, the most amounts but
35 to this: Your Principle is confined to a liberty of Will and Affections, with respect to doing of the Law of Work, which many have professed to *have,* and *do,* before you, and yet have come short of the Glory of God. For as I told you before, I tell you now again, that the Gospel-Principles are the Holy Ghost

5 pretended] prentended

and Faith, which help that Soul in whom they dwell, to count
believing in Jesus Christ the great & Essential part of our
Christianity, and our reckoning our selves pardoned, for the sake
of him: *And thus being set free from Sin, we become the Servants of
God, and have our fruit unto Holiness, and the end everlasting Life,*   5
Rom. 6. 20.

Your description of a Child of *Abraham*, you meaning in a new
Testament sence, is quite beside the truth: For albeit, the Sons
of *Abraham* will live Holy Lives, & become obedient to the
substantial Laws; yet it is not their subjection to *Morrals*, but   10
Faith in Jesus, that giveth them the *Denomination* of Children of
Abraham. *Know ye therefore that they that are of Faith, are the*

Gal. 3.7, 9.   *Children of faithful* Abraham: *They that are of Faith, the same are
the Children of* Abraham: *Yea, they that are of Faith, are blessed with
faithful* Abraham. In Pag. 284. You say, 'That there is not one   15
Duty more affectionately recommended to us in the Gospel,
then is Alms-giving.'

Answ. Yes, That there is, and that which more immediately
respecteth our Justification with God, then Ten Thousand such
Commandements; and that is Faith in Christ. Alms-Deeds is   20
also a blessed Command; yet but *one* of the *Second* Table, such as
must flow from Faith going before; Faith I mean that layeth hold
on Christ's Righteousness, if it be accepted of God. For before
the Heart be good, the Action must be naught; now the Heart is
good by Faith, because Faith, by applying Christ's Righteous-   25
ness, makes over whole Christ to the Soul, of whose fulness it
receiveth, and Grace, for Grace, *John* 1. 16. Many things in this
last Chapter, are worthy Reprehension, but because you tell us,
in the last two Pages thereof, is the Sum of all that need to be
said, I will immediately apply my self to what is there contained.   30

You say, (*Pag.* 296) *It is not possible we should not have the design
of Christianity accomplished in us, and therefore that we should be
destitute of the power of it, if we make our Saviours most excellent life,
the Pattern of our Lives.* (By our Saviours Life (as by a
Parenthesis) you also express) you mean, as your self hath in   35
short Described it, *Chap.* 5. *viz. The greatest Freedom, Affability,
Courtesie, Candor, Ingenuity, Gentleness, Meekness, Humility, Contempt
of the World, Contentation, Charity, Tenderness, Compassion, Patience,
Submission to the Divine Will, Love of God, Devoutest temper of mind
towards him, mighty Confidence and trust in God,* &c.   40

Answ. Our Saviours Life, in not onely these, but all other Duties that respected Morrals, was not Principally, or First, to be imitated by us, but that the Law, even in the preceptive part thereof, might be fully, and perfectly fulfilled for us. *Christ is the*
5 *end of the Law for Righteousness*; the end, not onely of the Ceremonial Law, but the ten Commandments too: For if the word (Righteousness) respecteth in special *them. Jesus increased in favour with God.* This respecteth him as made under the Law, and his pleasing of God in that Capacity. So also doth that, *In*
10 *him I am well pleased.* Now I say, as Jesus stood in this Capacity, he dealt with the Law in it's greatest force, and severity, as it *immediately* came from God, *without* the advantage of a *Mediator*; and stood by his perfect complying with, and fulfilling every Title thereof. Besides, as Jesus Christ had *thus* to do with the Law, he
15 did it in order to his *finishing transgression, and putting an end to Sin*; and so consequently as Mediator, and Undertaker for the World: For his perfect complying withal, and fulfilling every Title of the Law, respected nothing his own private person, that he for himself might be Righteous thereby; for in himself he was
20 eternally Just and Holy, even as the Father, but it respected us, even us; For US he was made under the Law, that *we*, by his fulfilling the Law, might by him be Redeemed from under the Law, and also receive the Adoption of SONS. For we having sinned, and transgressed the Law, and the Justice of God, yet
25 requiring obedience thereto, and the Law being too weak through our Flesh to do it, God therefore *sent his own Son in the likeness of sinful Flesh*; who himself for *us* did first of all, Walk in the Law, and then for Sin suffered also in his Flesh, the Sentence, and Curse pronounced against *us* by the Law: For it
30 was nothing less necessary, when the Son of God became undertaker for the Sin of the World, that he should walk in obedience to the whole of the Precepts of the Law, to deliver us from the Judgement of the Law; I say it was no less necessary he should so do, then that he should bear our Curse and Death: For
35 it would have been *impossible* for him to have overcome the *last*, if he had not been *Spotless* touching the *first*: For *therefore* it was impossible he should be *holden* of Death, because he did *nothing worthy* of Death; *no*, not in the Judgement of the *Law*, to which he *immediately* stood. Now as Christ Jesus stood thus *to*, and
40 walked in the Law, it is Blasphemy for any to presume to *imitate*

Luk. 2. 52
Mat. 3. 17.

Dan. 9. 24.

Gal. 4. 4, 5.

him; because thus to do, is to turn *Mediator* and *Undertaker* for the *Sin* of the World. Besides, whoso doth attempt it, undertakes an *impossibility*, for *no* Man can stand by the Morral Law, as it *immediately* comes from the Divine Majesty; he having *Sinned* first, even *before* he goeth about to fulfil it: And in this sence is 5 that to be understood, as many as are of the Works of the Law, are *under* the Curse, held accursed, because they have sinned first; accursed in their *performances*, because of *imperfection*, and therefore *assuredly* accursed at *last*, because they come *short* of the Righteousness thereof. 10

1. Christ Jesus did never set himself forth for an example, that we by imitating his steps in *Morrals*, should obtain Justification with God, from the Curse of that Law; For this would be to overthrow, and utterly abolish the Work which himself came into the World to accomplish, which *was* not to be 15 our example, that we by treading his steps might have Remission of Sins, but that through the Faith of him, through Faith in his Blood we might be reconciled to God.

2. Besides, thus to *imitate* Christ, is to make of him of a Saviour, not by *Sacrifice*, but by *example*: Nay, to speak the whole, 20 this would be to make his *Mediatorship* wholly to center, rather in *prescribing* of *Rules*, and *exacting* obedience to *Morrals*, *then in giving himself a ransome for Men*. Yea, I will add, to *imitate* Christ, as *you* have prescribed, may be done by *him*, that yet may be ignorant of the excellency of his Person, and the chief end of his 25 being made Flesh: For in all these things which you have discoursed in that fifth Chapter of him; you have onely spoken of that, *something* of which is apprehended by the light of Nature. Yea, Nature it self will teach, that men should trust in God, which is the most excellent Particular that there you mention: 30 Wherefore our Lord Jesus himself foreseeing, that in Men there will be a proudness, to content themselves with that Confidence, he intimateth that it would be in *us* insignificant, if it stand without Faith in himself; *Ye believe naturally in God*, saith he,

John 14. 1, 2. *Believe also in me.* Faith in Jesus is as absolutely necessary as to 35 believe immediately in the Divine being: Yea, without Faith in Jesus, whosoever believeth in God is sure to perish, and burn in
John 8. 24. Hell. *If you belive not that I am he, ye shall dye in your Sins.* And to

32 content] *errata*; contentent

take Jesus in *Morrals* for *example*, is no where *called* believing *in*
him; neither is there one promise of eternal life, annexed to such
a practice. But you say, *If we tread in his blessed steps, and be such,*
according to our measure, and capacity, as we have understood he was
5   *in this World.*

    Answ. I say, for a Man to confine himself, onely to the life of
the Lord Jesus for an example, or to think it enough to make
him, in his life, a pattern for us to follow, leaveth us, through our
shortness in the end, with the Devil and his Angels, for want of
10 Faith in the Doctrine of Remission of Sins: For Christ did no
where make another Mediator between God and him, nor did he
ever trust to another Man's Righteousness, to be thereby
Justified from the Curse of the Law, neither did he at all stand in
need thereof, without which *WE must be Damned*, and Perish:
15 Now I say, these things being no where practiced by him, he
cannot therein be an example to us: And I say again, seeing that
in these things, by Faith in them, is *immediately* wrapped up *our*
Reconciliation with God, it followeth, that though a Man take
the Lord Christ in his whole life, for an *example* in the end, that
20 notwithstanding, he abideth unreconciled to God. Neither will
that clause (and be such) help such a person at all: For
Justification with God, comes not by imitating Christ as
exemplary in Morrals, but through Faith in his Precious Blood.
In the Law I read, that the Paschal Lamb was neither to be eaten
25 *Sodden*, nor *Raw*, but *Roast* with fire, must it be eaten, *Exod.* 12.
Now to make Salvation Principally to depend upon imitating
Christ's Life; it is to feed upon him *Raw*, or at most as *Sodden*, or
Sanctified and Holy: But the precept is, *Eat it Roast with fire*, is,
the Antitype, as accursed of God for Sin, and induring the   Exod. 19.
30 punishment for it. The Law is compared to fire, and it's Curse to   Deut. 33. 2.
a *burning Oven*: Now under the Curse of this fiery Law, was the   Mal. 4. 1.
Lord Jesus afflicted for the Sins of the World: Wherefore, as *so*
considered, our Faith must lay hold upon him, for Justification
with God. *This is the Law of the Burnt Offering (which was the*
35 *Offering for Sin;) It is the Burnt Offering, because of the burning upon*
the Altar all night, unto the morning, and the fire of the Altar shall be
burning in it, Levit. 6.9. But now I would inquire; Had *Israel* done
the Commandment, if they had eaten the Passover Raw, or
Boiled in Water? or if they had offered that Offering, that was to
40 be burnt as a Sin Offering, *otherwise* then it was commanded?

Even so, to feed upon Christ, as he is Holy, and of *good* life *onely*;
and also as taking him *therein* for for an example to *us*, to follow
his steps for *Justification with God*; this is to eat the Passover *Raw*,
and not as *Rost* with *Fire*; this is to *feed* upon Jesus, without
respecting him as accursed of God for our Sin, and so   5
consequently to miss of that eternal life, that by his Blood he
hath obtained for every one that believeth on him. I have been
pleased with this observation, *that none of the Signs and Wonders in*
Ægypt, *could deliver the Children of* Israel *thence, till the Lamb was*
slain, and Roast with fire, Exod. 12. 1. And I have been also   10
pleased with this, *that the Father, not* Moses, *gave the Manna from*
Heaven, which was a Type of the Flesh, and Blood of Christ, that
whoso feedeth on, shall live for ever, *John* 6. 32. Yea,
Circumcision also, which was a Type of inward, and Heart-
Holiness, *was not of* Moses, *but of the Fathers*, and Principally a   15
consequence of the *Faith of* Abraham, John 7. 22. Whence I gather,
That no Wonder, but the Blood of Christ can save: That no
Kindness, but the Mercy of God can *give* this to us: And that no
Law, but the *Law* of Faith, can make us *truly Holy in heart.* But
you add, *Those that sincerely, and industrously indeavour to imitate*   20
the Holy Jesus in his Spirit, and Actions, can never be ignorant what it
is to be truly Christians. Those that follow Jesus in his Spirit, must
first receive that Spirit from Heaven, which Spirit is received, as
I have often said, by applying first, by Faith, the Merits of Christ
to the Soul, for Life, and Justification with God. The Spirit is *not*   25
received by the *Works* of the Law, but by the *hearing of Faith*;
neither *comes* it in the *Ministry*, or Doctrine of *Morrals*, but in and
by the *Ministry of Faith; and the Law is NOT of Faith.* Wherefore
seeing you have, in Page 223. of your Book, forbidden Sinners to
come first to Jesus for Justification with God; the Spirit you talk   30
of, however you call it the Spirit Jesus, can be no other then the
Spirit of a Man; which you also your self, in Pag. 7, 8, 9 call the
Purity of Humane Nature, a Principle of Reason, the first Principles of
Morrals, or those that are Originally Dictates of Humane Nature.
Wherefore by these Words (in his Spirit) you do but Blaspheme   35
the Holy Ghost, and abuse your ignorant Reader; calling now
(Quaker-like) the Dictates of your Humanity, and your Socinian
Complyances therewith, the Spirit of Holy Jesus. I conclude
therefore, that the way of Salvation, or the design of Christianity
as prescribed by you, is none other then the Errors of your own   40

brain, the way of Death, the Sum and Heart of Papistical
Quakerism, and is quite denyed by the Lord Jesus, and by his
blessed Testament. And now go your ways, and imitate the Lord
Jesus, and take the whole History of his life for your example,
5 and walk in his steps, and be such as much as you can, yet
without Faith in his Blood, first; yea, and if you stand not Just
before God through the imputation of his Righteousness, your
imitating will be found no better then rebellion, because by that,
instead of Faith in his Blood, you hope to obtain remission of
10 Sins, thrusting him thereby from his Office, and Work, and
setting your dunghil Righteousness up, in his stead.

I come now to Your Conclusion. First, in Page 298. *You press
men to betake themselves to find* (that which you call) *the design of
Christianity, accomplished in their hearts and lives.*

15 *Answ.* Seeing that the Holiness that your erronious Book hath
exalted, is none other but *THAT which we have LOST*; Yea, and
again seeing you have set this in the Head of, and before the
Righteousness of Christ, I admonish my Reader to tremble at the
Blasphemy of your Book, and account the whole design therein
20 to be none other, but that of an enemy to the Son of God, and
Salvation of the World: For that Holiness as I have shewed, is
none other, but a Shadowish, Christless, Graceless Holiness,
and your so exalting of it, *very Blasphemy.* You proceed, saying,
Let us exercise our selves unto real, and substantial Godliness; (still
25 meaning your Adamitish Holiness) *Let us study the Gospel not to
discourse, or onely to believe, but also, and above ALL things, to do
well.*

Answ. Herein still you manifest, either ignorance of, or malice
against the Doctrine of Faith; that Doctrine, which above all
30 Doctrines, is the quintessence of the new Testament, because
therein (and not Principally, as you feign, by doing well) is the
Righteousness of God revealed, and that from *Faith* to *Faith*; not
from *Faith* to *Works*, nor yet from *Works* to *Faith.* Besides, the
Gospel is Preached in all Nations for the *obedience of FAITH*: Rom. 16.
35 Neither Works, the Law, the Dictates of Humanity, nor the first
Principles of Morrals, knowing what to do with the Righteousness
of the Gospel, which is a Righteousness imputed by God, not
wrought by us; a Righteousness *given*, not *earned*, a Righteousness

17 before the] before the the

received by believing, not that which floweth from *our* obedience
to *Laws*, a Righteousness which *comes* from *God* to *us*, not one
that *goeth* from *us* to *God.* Besides, as I also have hinted before;
the Apostle, and you are directly opposite. You cry, *above ALL
things, DO* well: that is *Work* and *do* the *Law*; but he, *Above ALL*   5
take the *SHIELD* of *Faith, wherewith* are quenched *ALL the fiery
Darts of the Wicked*, Eph. 6.

But you add, *Pag.* 300. *Let us do what lyeth in us to convince our
Atheist, that the Religion of the blessed Jesus, is no trick or device, and
our wanton and loose Christians, that it is no notional business,*   10
speculative Science.

Answ. This you cannot do by your Morral Natural Principles
of Humanity: For even some of your *BRAVE* Phylosophers,
whose Godliness you have so much *aplauded*, were even *then* in
the *midst* of their, and your *Vertues*, Atheistically ignorant of the   15
Religion of Jesus. And as to the *loose* Christian; Christ neither
hath need of, nor will he bless your *Blasphemous* opinions, nor
feigned Godliness, but Real ungodliness, to make them Converts
to his Faith and Grace; neither can it be expected it should,
seeing you have not onely dirty thoughts, but vilifying Words,   20
and sayings of his Person, Work, and Righteousness. You have
set *your* Works before *his, Pag.* 223. calling them *Substantial,
Indispensible*, and *Real*; but coming to God by *him*, a thing *in it self*
Indifferent, *P.* 7, 8, 9. You go on, and say, *Let us declare—that we
are not hearty relyers on Christ's Righteousness*, by being imitators of   25
it. *Pag.* 300. You cannot leave off to Contemn and Blaspheme
the Son of God. Do you not yet know that the Righteousness of
Christ, on which the sinner ought to rely for life, is such, as
consisted in his standing to, and doing of the Law, without a
Mediator? And would you be doing this? What know you not,   30
that an Essential of the Righteousness he accomplished for
Sinners when he was in the World? is, *That he was Conceived by
the Holy Ghost, Born without Sin, did all things in the Power of, and
Union with his own eternal God-head.* And are you able thus to
imitate him? Again, the Righteousness on which we ought to rely   35
for life, is that which hath in it the *Merit of Blood: We are Justified
by his Blood, through Faith in his Blood: Is this the Righteousness you
would imitate?* Farther, the Righteousness on which poor Sinners

Rom. 5. 4.

should rely, is that, for the sake of which, God forgiveth the Sins of him, that resteth by Faith thereupon. But would · you be imitating, of, or accompishing such a Righteousness?

Your Book Sir is begun in Ignorance, mannaged with Errour, and ended in Blasphemy.

Now the God of Glory, if it may stand with his Glory, give you a sight of your Sins, against the Son of God, that you may as Saul, lye trembling, and being astonished cry out, to be Justified, with the Righteousness of God, without *the Law, even* that *which is by Faith of Jesus Christ,* unto all, *and* upon all *them that believe.*

Many other gross Absurdities, which I have omitted in your whole Book, may (perhaps) be more throughly gathered up, when you shall have taken the oportunity to reply. In the mean time I shall content my self with this.

Behold the Lamb of God that taketh away the Sin of the World, Joh. 1. 29.

Even Jesus, who delivered us from the Wrath to come, 1 Thes. 1. 10.

Who when he had by himself purged our Sins, sat down on the Right Hand of the Majesty on High, Heb. 1. 3.

Christ dyed for our Sins, 1 Cor. 15. 1, 2, 3.

God hath made him to be Sin for us, 2 Cor. 5. 21.

Christ was made a Curse for us. Gal. 3. 13.

He bare our Sins in his own Body on the Tree, 1 Pet. 2. 24.

He loved us, and washed us from our Sins in his own Blood, Rev. 1. 5.

God for Christ's sake hath forgiven you, Eph. 4. 23.

We have Redemption through his Blood, even the forgiveness of our Sins, according to the riches of his Grace, Eph. 1. 7.

Now unto the King, Eternal, Immortal, Invisible, the onely Wise God, be Honour, and Glory, for ever, and ever. *Amen.*

The Conclusion.

That my Reader may farther perceive that Mr. *Fowler,* even by the chief of the Articles of the Church of *England,* is adjudged Erronious, and besides the very Fundamentals of the Doctrine of Jesus Christ, and that in those very Principles that are the main (I say,) and that most immediately concern Christ, Faith, and Salvation, will be evident to them that compare his Design of Christianity, with these Articles hereunder Recited.

The Articles concerning Free-will.

THe condition of Man after the fall of Adam, is such, that he cannot turn, and prepare himself, by his own Natural strength, and good Works, to Faith, and calling upon God: Wherefore we have no power to do good Works, pleasant and acceptable to God, without the Grace of God by Christ preventing us, that we may have a good will; and working with us when we have that good will.

The Article concerning justification.

WE are accounted Righteous before God, ONELY for the Merit of our Lord and Saviour Jesus Christ, by Faith, and not for our own Works, or Deservings: Wherefore that we are justified by Faith ONELY, is a most wholesome Doctrine, and full of Comfort, &c.

The Article of Works before justification.

WOrks done before the Grace of Christ, and the inspiration of his Spirit, are not pleasant to God, for as much as they spring not of Faith in Jesus Christ, or deserve Grace of Congruity: Yea, rather for that they are not done as God hath willed, and commanded them to be done, we doubt not but they have the NATURE of Sin.

These Articles, because they respect the points in controversie betwixt Mr. *Fowler*, and my self; and because they be also Fundamental truths of the Christian Religion (as I do heartily believe) let all Men know that I quarrel not with him, about things wherein I discent from the Church of *England*, but do contend for the truth continued, even in these very Articles of theirs, from which he hath so deeply revolted, that he clasheth with every one of them, as may farther be shewn when he shall take heart to reply.

But to wind up this unpleasant Scrible, I shall have done when I have farther shewed, how he joyneth with Papist, and Quaker, against these wholsome, and Fundamental Articles.

Mr. *Fowler's* Doctrine compared with *Campian* the Jesuite, upon that question whether Faith onely Justifieth: saith *Campian*

1. *Campian.*

5 We (Papists) say, that as Grace is put into us in Justification, so also our Righteousness is inlarged through Good Works, and is inherent in us; therefore *it is not true* that God doth Justifie by Faith ONELY.

Fowler Pag. 221.

10 *Justifying Faith is such a belief of the truth of the Gospel as includeth a sincere resolution of obedience unto all its Precepts; and that it justifieh AS it doth SO: In short, is it possible that Faith in Christs Blood, for the forgiveness of Sin, should be the onely act which justifieth* Pag. 22. *a Sinner?*

15 ### 2. *Campian*

So that *Faith* is urged, *but not* Faith *ONELY*; again, by Faith is meant *all Christianity*, and the whole Religion of Christians.

Fowler, Pag. 222.

For surely the Faith which intaileth the Sinner to so high a 20 *Priviledge, as that of justification, must needs be such as complyeth with all the purposes of Christ's coming into the World; especially with his grand purpose, as Lord, and that it is no less necessary that it should justifie as it doth this.*

3. *Campian.*

25 Though Works void of Christ are nothing; yet through Grace they serve to Justification.

Fowler, Pag. 225, 226.

Of the Imputation of Christ's Righteousness, this is the true Explication; It consisteth in dealing with sincerely Righteous Persons: 30 *as if they were perfectly so, for the sake and upon the account of Christ's Righteousness: The grand intent of the Gospel being to make us partakers of an inward real Righteousness; and it being a Secondary one, that we should be accepted, and rewarded, as if we were compleatly Righteous.*

4. *Campian.*

Speaking of Faith, Hope, and Charity, he confesseth, that Faith in Nature is before them, but it doth not Justifie before   5
they come.

Fowler, Pag. 223.

What pretence can there be for thinking that Faith is the condition, or Instrument of Justification, as it complyeth with onely the Precept of relying on Christ's Merits, for the obtaining of it: especially when it is   10
no less manifest than the Sun at Noon Day, that obedience to the other Precepts, or Works of Love, must go before obedience to this.

Pag. 284.

5. *Campian.*

I deny (that Faith ONELY doth Justifie) for you have not in all the Word of God, that Faith ONELY doth Justifie.   15

Fowler, Pag. 225.

And for my part, I must confess, that I would not willingly be he that should undertake to Encounter one of the Champions of that foul Cause, with the Admission of this Principle, That Faith Justifieth, onely as it apprehendeth (resteth or relyeth on, Pag. 224.) the Merits,   20
and Righteousness of Jesus Christ, I must certainly have great luck, or my Adversary but little Cunning, if I were not forced to repent me of such an engagement.

6. *Campian.*

Abraham being a Just Man, was made more Just by a living   25
Faith.

Fowler, Pag. 283.

He onely is a true Child of Abraham, *who in the Purity of the Heart obeyeth those substantial Laws, that are imposed by God, upon him.*
                                                                              30

7. *Campian.*

I say that Charity and good Work, are not excluded (in the causes of our Justification.)

Fowler, Pag. 215.

For we have shewn, not onely that Reformation from the practice, and purification of Heart from the liking of Sin, are as plainly as can be asserted in the Gospel, to be absolutely necessary to give Men a right to the Promises of it, but also that its great Salvation doth even consist in it.

Mr. *Fowler*'s Doctrine compared with *William Pen* the Quaker.

1. Pen's *Sandy Foundation*, Pag. 19.

Life and Salvation is to them that follow Christ the Light, in all his Righteousness, which every man comes onely to experience, as he walks in a holy Subjection to that measure of Light and Grace, wherewith the fulness hath inlightned him.

Fowler, Pag. 8.

That is, those which are of an indispensible, and Eternal Obligation, which were first written in mens hearts, and Originally Dictates of Humane Nature.

2. *Pen, Pag.* 32.

I really confess that Jesus Christ fullfilled the Fathers Will, and offered up a most satisfactory Sacrifice, but not to pay God, or help him to save Men.

Fowler, Pag. 85.

Christ was set forth to be a Propitiatory Sacrifice for Sin; I will not say that his Father (who is perfectly sui Puris) *might be put by this means into a Capacity of forgiving it.*

3. *Pen, Pag.* 16.

God's Remission is grounded on Man's Repentance, not that it's impossible for God to pardon without a Plenary Satisfaction.

3 our] ruo

Fowler, Pag. 84.

There are many that do not question but that God could have pardoned Sin, without any other satisfaction, then the Repentance of the Sinner, &c.

4. Pen, Pag. 27.

Justification doth not go before, but is subsequential to the Mortification of Lusts.

Fowler, Pag. 14, 15.

This Blessing of making Men Holy, was so much the design of Christ's coming, that he had his very Name from it: Observe the Words; He shall save his People from their Sins; not from punishment of them, &c. And that is the Primary sense of them which is most plainly expressed in them; That he shall save his People from the punishment of Sin, is a true sence too; but it is Secondary, and implyed onely, as this latter is the never failing, and necessary consequence of the former Salvation.

5. Pen, Pag. 25.

Since therefore there can be no admittance had, without performing that Righteous Will, and doing those Holy, and Perfect sayings; Alas! to what value will an imputative Righteousness amount? &c.

Fowler, Pag. 16.

Christ shall bring in an inward substantial, and everlasting Righteousness, and by abrogating the outward (Ceremonial) and establishing ONELY this Righteousness, he should inlarge the Jewish Church, an accession of the Gentiles, *being by that means made unto it.*

6. Pen, Pag. 24, 25.

Since God hath prescribed an inoffensive life, as that which onely can give acceptance with him; and on the contray hath determined not to justifie the Wicked, &c. Will not the abomination appear greatest of all, when God shall be found Condemning the just, on purpose to justifie the wicked; and that he is thereto compelled, or else no Salvation? which is the

tendency of their Doctrine, who imagine the Righteous, and merciful God to condemn and punish his righteous Son, that he being satisfied for our Sins, we might be justified (while unsanctified) by the imputation of his perfect Righteousness. O
5 why should this horrible thing be contended for by Christians!

Fowler, Pag. 119.

If it were possible (as it hath been proved it is not) that a Wicked Man should have God's pardon, it would not make him cease to be miserable.

10 ### Fowler, Pag. 120.

*Were it possible that Christ's Righteousness could be imputed to an unrighteous man, I dare boldly affirm it would signifie as little to his happiness, as would a Gorgeous and Splendid Garment, to one that is almost starved with Hunger, or that lyeth racked by the torturing
15 Diseases of the Stone, or Cholick.*

Fowler, Pag. 130.

To justifie a Wicked Man, while he continueth so, if it were possible for God to do it, would far more disparage his Justice, and Holiness, then advance his Grace and Kindness.

20 ### 7. Pen, Pag. 26.

Unless we be doers of the Law, which Christ came not to destroy, but as our example to fulfil, we can never be justified before God.

Fowler, Pag. 296.

25 *It is impossible we should not have the design of Christianity accomplished in us, and therefore that we should be destitute of the power of it, if we make our Saviours most excellent Life, the pattern of our lives. Those that sincerely, and industriously indeavour to imitate the Holy Jesus in his Spirit and Actions, can never be ignorant what it
30 is to be truly Christians, nor can they fail to be so.*

8. Pen, Pag. 26.

Nor let any fancy that Christ hath so fulfilled it for them, as to

3 satisfied] *errata B*; sanctified   4 unsanctified] *errata B*; unsatisfied

exclude their obedience, from being requisite to their acceptance, but onely as their pattern.

Fowler, Pag. 148.

This Son of God taught Men their Duty, by his own example, and *did himself perform among them, what he required of them. Now that* 5 *he should tread before us EVERY step of that way, which he hath told* *us leadeth to Eternal Happiness, and commend those Duties which are* *most ungrateful to our corrupt inclinations, by his own practice; our* *having so brave an example is no small incouragement, to a chearful* *performance of all that is commanded.* 10

Understand thou what thou Readest.

The End.

A CONFESSION OF MY FAITH,
AND A REASON OF MY PRACTICE

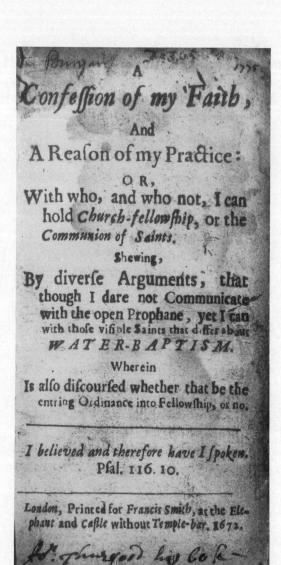

Title-page of *A Confession of my Faith, and A Reason of my Practice* (1672)

A CONFESSION OF MY FAITH, AND A REASON OF MY PRACTICE

Note on the Text

One edition of this work was published in Bunyan's lifetime. Only two copies are extant. The publisher was Francis Smith who was also responsible for *A Defence of the Doctrine of Justification, by Faith* (1672). Appended to *Defence* was a list of works printed by Smith that included *A Confession*. Smith was also the printer for two responses to Bunyan's *A Confession*: John Denne's *Truth Outweighing Error* (1673) and Thomas Paul's *Some Serious Reflections* (1673). The number of printer's errors in *A Confession* suggests that the work was produced hurriedly. Some changes were apparently made during production, for the copy at Union Theological Seminary in New York City contains a paragraph which is not in the Manchester Central Library copy. There are also a few other differences between the two copies.

Title-page: A | *Confession of my Faith*, | And | A Reason of my Practice: | OR, | With who, and who not, I can| hold *Church-fellowship*, or the | *Communion of Saints*. | Shewing, | By diverse Arguments, that | though I dare not Communicate | with the open Prophane, yet I can | with those visible Saints that differ about | *WATER-BAPTISM*. | Wherein | Is also discoursed whether that be the | entring Ordinance into Fellowship, or no. | [rule] | *I believed and therefore have I spoken,* | Psal. 116. 10. | [rule] | *London*, Printed for *Francis Smith*, at the *Ele-|phant* and *Castle* without *Temple-bar*, 1672.

Collation: 12⁰; [A1 missing], [A2], A3, A4 (misprinted A5), [A5, A6]; B–F¹², G¹⁰; pp. [i–x]+140 = 150. The following page numbers are misprinted: 15 (wrongly) for 16, 71 for 81, 74–5 for 84–5, 78–9 for 88–9, 82–3 for 92–3, 86–98 for 96–108, probably 100 for 109 (pen and ink corrections, especially in the Manchester Central Library copy, sometimes obscure the original printed numbers), 100–1 for 110–11, 78 for 112, 103–30 for 113–40. The following page numbers are placed on the inside (wrongly) of the running title: 16 (misprinted 15), 17, 18, 19, 20, 21, 40, 44; 45 and 48 Manchester Central Library only; 71, 72, 73; 130, 133, 136 (misprinted 120, 123, 126) Union Theological Seminary copy only. Signature B2 is misprinted A2, B4 is misprinted A4, and D is misprinted C. Signatures are printed on the first four leaves for B and C, and on the first five leaves for D–G.

Contents: A2ʳ title-page, A2ᵛ blank, A3ʳ–A6ʳ to the reader, A6ᵛ errata, B1ʳ–

G10^v text. A6^r is signed 'J. B.' A row of ornaments on B1^r is followed by '*A* |
Confession of my Faith; | *and a reason of my pra-|crice in worship,* &*c.*' The end of
the section on B9^v is followed by a rule. The end of the text is followed by
'*FINIS.*' In contrast to the copy at Manchester Central Library, the Union
Theological Seminary copy has a 20-line paragraph numbered '6'. on C11^r
(p. 45), accommodated by adjustments of lines (including blank lines) through
C12^v (p. 48). In addition, the catchwords are thus different, the page numbers
'45' and '48' are at the outside margin (correctly) rather than the inside margin
of the running title, and the words 'Practice' and 'Worship' are capitalized in
the title of the section beginning on C12^v (A reason of My Practice in
Worship) as are 'Faith' and 'Worship' in the first sentence of the section. It
should also be noted that page numbers 130, 133, and 136 (misprinted 120,
123, and 126) are wrongly placed at the inside margin of the running title in
the Union Theological Seminary copy but correctly placed at the outside
margin of the Manchester Central Library copy.

Running Titles: To the Reader: '*To the Reader.*' beginning on A3^v. Text: B1^v–
C12^r '*A Confession of Faith.*' None on C12^v. D1^r–F12^v '*A Reason of* | *my Practise
in worship.*' G1^r repeats the second part. G1^v–G10^r '*A Reason of* | *my Practice in
worship.*' G10^v '*A Reason of*'.

Catchwords (selected): B3^r *That*, C6^v *cause*, D9^v *Church*, E5^r *that*, F1^v
exceeding, G5^r *them*.

Copies collated: Union Theological Seminary, New York City; Manchester
Central Library. There is no copy in the British Library, although one is listed
there by Wing.

The following text is based on the Union Theological Seminary copy.

TO THE
READER

SIR,

5 I Marvail not that both your self, and others do think my long
   Imprisonment strange (or rather strangely of me for the sake of that)
   for verily I should also have done it my self, had not the Holy Ghost
   long since forbidden me. 1 Pet. 4, 12. 1 Joh. 3. 13. Nay verily that
   notwithstanding, had the adversary but fastened the supposition of guilt
   upon me; my long tryalls might by this time have put it beyond dispute:
10 for I have not hitherto been so sordid, and so stand to a Doctrine right
   or wrong; much less when so weighty an argument, as above eleven
   years imprisonment, is continually dogging of me to weigh and pause,
   and pause again, the grounds and foundation of those principles, for
   which I thus have suffered: but having not only at my tryall asserted
15 them, but also since, even all this tedious tract of time, in cool blood, a
   thousand times by the word of God examined them, and found them
   good; I cannot, I dare not now revolt or deny the same, on pain of
   eternal damnation.

   And that my principles, and practice may be open to the view and
20 judgment of all men (though they stand, and fall to none but the word
   of God alone) I have in this small treatise presented to this generation,
   A Confession of my Faith, and a Reason of my Practise in the
   Worship of God; by which although it be brief; Candid Christians,
   may I hope, without a violation to faith or love, judge, I may have the
25 root of the matter found in me.

   Neither have I in this relation abusively presented my Reader, with
   other doctrine or practices, then what I held, professed, and preached
   when apprehended, and cast in Prison. Nor did I then, or now retain a
   Doctrine besides, or which is not thereon grounded. The Subject I
30 should have Preached upon, even then when the Constable came, was,
   Dost thou believe on the Son of God? from whence I intended to
   shew, the absolute need of Faith in Jesus Christ; and that it was also a
   thing of the highest concern, for men to inquire into; and to ask their
   own hearts whether they had it or no.
35 Faith, and Holiness, are my professed principles, with an endeavour,

so far as in me lyeth, to be at peace with all men. What shall I say, let mine enemies themselves be judges, if anything in these following doctrines, or if ought that any Man hath heard me preach, doth, or hath according to the true intent of my words, savoured either of heresie or rebellion. I say again, let they themselves be judges, if ought they find 5
in my writing or preaching, doth render me worthy of almost twelve years imprisonment, or one that deserveth to be hanged, or banished for ever, according to their tremendous Sentence. Indeed my principles are such, as lead me to a denial to communicate in the things of the Kingdom of Christ, with ungodly and open prophane; neither can I in, 10
or by the superstitious inventions of this world, consent that my Soul should be governed, in any of my approaches to God, because commanded to the contrary, and commended for so refusing. Wherefore excepting this one thing, for which I ought not to be rebuked; I shall I trust in despite of slander and falsehood, discover my self at all times a 15
peaceable, and an obedient Subject. But if nothing will do, unless I make of my conscience a continual butchery, and slaughter-shop, unless putting out my own eyes I commit me to the blind to lead me, (as I doubt is desired by some) I have determined the Almighty God being my help, and shield, yet to suffer, if frail life might continue so long, 20
even till the moss shall grow on mine eye-browes rather then thus to violate my faith and principles. Will a man leave the Snow of Lebanon, *that cometh from the rock of the field? or shall the cold flowing waters, that come from another place be forsaken?* Jer. 18. 14.
Hath a Nation changed their Gods which yet are no Gods? For 25
all People will walk every one in the name of his God, and we will walk in the name of the Lord our God for ever and ever. *Micah* 4. 5.

 Touching my Practice as to Communion with visible Saints, although not Baptized with Water; I say, it is my present Judgement so 30
to do, and am willing to render a farther reason thereof; shall I see the leading hand of God thereto.

  Thine in Bonds
  for the Gospel.

             J. B. 35

  5 *or*] *of* 9 *in the*] *in the the*

A
Confession of my Faith; and a reason of my practice in worship, &c.

I believe, that there is but one, onely true God, and there is none other but he. *To us there is but one God the Father of whom are all things. And this is life eternal that they might know thee, the only true God,* &c. Mar. 12. 32, 1 Cor, 8. 8. Joh. 17. 3, Acts. 17, 24.

2. I believe, that this God is Almighty, Eternal, Invisible, Incomprehensible, &c. *I am the Almighty God, walk before me and be thou perfect. The eternall God is thy refuge. Now unto the king eternall, Immortal, invisible, the only wise God, be honour and glory for ever and ever.* Gen. 17. 1. Deut. 33. 26, 27. 1 Tim. 1. 17. Job. 11. 7. Rom. 11. 33.

3. I believe, that this God is unspeakably perfect in all his attributes of power, wisdom, justice, truth, holyness, mercy, love, *&c.* his power is said to be *eternall,* his understanding and wisdom, *infinite*; He is called the *just Lord* in opposition to all things; he is said to be truth it self and the God thereof: There is none holy as the Lord. *God is love. Canst though by searching find out God; canst thou find out the Almightly unto perfection?* Rom. 1. 20. Psa. 147. 5. Zeph. 3. 5. 2 Thes. 2. 10. Deut. 32. 4 Job. 11. 7.

4. I believe that in the Godhead, there are *three persons* or subsistances. *There are three that bare record in heaven. The Father, the Word, and the holy Ghost.* 1 Joh. 5. 7. see also, Gen. 1. 26. chap. 3. 22. chap. 11. 7. and Esa. 6 8.

5. I believe, that these three are in Nature, Essence, and Eternity, *equally one. These three are one.* 1 John. 5. 7.

6. I beleive, *there is a World to come.* Heb. 2. 5. chap. 6. 5.

7. I believe that there shall be a resurrection of the dead, both of the just, and unjust. *Many that sleep in the dust of the earth shall awake, some to everlasting life, and some to everlasting shame and contempt. Marvail not at this. For the hour is coming, in which all that are in their graves shall hear his voice, and shall come forth, they that have done good, to the resurrection of life, and they that have done evil,*

to the resurrection of Damnation. Act. 24. 15. Dan. 12. 2. Joh. 5. 28.

8. I believe, that they that shall be counted worthy of that world, and of the resurrection from the dead, neither marry nor are given in marriage, neither can they dye any more, *for they are* 5
equall to the Angels, and are the children of God, being the children of the resurrection. Luk. 10. 34. 35, 36. Joh. 10. 27, 28, 29. Rev. 7. 16. chap. 20. 6.

9. I believe, that those that dye impenitent, shall be tormented with the Divel and his Angels, and shall be cast with them into 10
the Lake that burns with fire and brimstone, *where their worm dyeth not, and the fire is not quenched.* Rev. 21. 8. Mar. 9. 43. 48. Mat. 25 41. 46. Joh. 5. 29.

10. I believe, that because God is naturally holy and just, even as he is Good and Mercifull; therefore (all having sinned) none 15
can be saved, *without the means of a redeemer. Then he is gracious unto him, and saith, deliver him from going down to the pit, I have found a ransome. We have redemption through his blood, even the forgiveness of our sins. For without shedding of blood, is no remission,* Job. 33. 24. Col. 1. 14. Hebr. 9. 22. 20

11. I believe, that Jesus Christ our Lord himself is the redeemer. *They remembred that God was their rock, and the high God their redeemer. Forasmuch as ye know, that ye were not redeemed, with corruptible things, as silver and Gold, from your vain conversation received by tradition from your Fathers; But with the* 25
precious blood of Christ, as of a Lamb without blemish, and without spot. Psa. 78. 35. 1 Pet. 1. 18, 19.

12. I believe, that the great reason why the Lord, the second person in the God-head, did cloth himself with our flesh and blood, was that he might be capable of obtaining the redemption, 30
that before the world, was intended for us. *Forasmuch then as the children were made partakers of flesh and blood, he also himself likewise took part of the same; (mark) that through death he might destroy him that had the power of death, that is the Divel, and deliver them who through fear of death, were all their life time subject to* 35
bondage. When the fulness of the time Was Come, God sent forth his Son made of a woman, made under the Law to redeem them that were under the Law. Wherefore it behooved him in all things to be made like

19 *without*] *which out*

unto his brethren; that he might be a mercifull, and faithfull high priest
in things pertaining to God; To make reconciliation for the sins of the
people. For in that himself hath suffered being tempted, he is able also
to succour them that are tempted. Christ hath redeemed us from the
5 curse of the Law, being made a curse for us. As it is written cursed is
every one that is hanged on a tree. That the blessing of Abraham might
come upon the Gentiles, through faith in Jesus Christ. Heb. 2. 14, 15.
Gal. 4, 4. Heb. 2. 17, 18. Gal. 3, 13, 14.

13. I believe, that the time when he clothed himself with our
10 flesh, was in the dayes of the reign of *Cæsar Augustus*; then, I say,
and not till then, was the word made flesh, or clothed with our
nature. *And it came to pass in those days, that there went out a decree
from* Cæsar Augustus, *that all the world should be taxed; And Joseph
went up from Galilee, out of the City of Nazareth unto Judah, unto the*
15 *city of David, which is called Bethlehem; because he was of the house
and linage of David, to be taxed with Mary his espoused wife being
great with child; And so it was, that while they were there, the dayes
were accomplished, that she should be delivered. This child was he of
whom godly Simeon was told by the holy Ghost, when he said, That he*
20 *should not see death untill he had seen the Lord Christ.* Joh 1. 14. 1
Tim. 3. 16. Luk. 2. 1, 2, 3, 6. 25, 26, 27.

14. I believe, therefore that this very child, as afore is testified
is both God and man; the Christ of the living God. *And she
brought forth her first born son, and wrapt him in swadling clothes,*
25 *and laid him in a manger; Because there was no room for them in the
inn. And there were in the same Countrey shepheards keeping watch
over their flock by night, And Lo, the Angel of the Lord came upon
them, and the Glory of the Lord shined round about them: and they
were sore afraid. And the Angel said unto them fear not; for behold I*
30 *bring you good tidings of great joy, which shall be to all people. For unto
you is born this day in the City of David, a saviour, which is Christ the
Lord.*

*And this shall be a sign unto you; you shall find the babe wrapped in
swadling clothes lying in a manger. Again. But while he thought on*
35 *these things, behold the Angel of the Lord appeared unto him; saying,
Joseph, thou son of David, fear not to take unto thee Mary thy Wife,
for that which is conceived in her is of the holy Ghost. And she shall
bring forth a son, and thou shalt call his name Jesus; for he shall save*

22 testified) testifiied

*his people from their sins. Now all this was done, that it might be
fullfilled which was spoken of the Lord by the prophet, saying; Behold a
virgin shall be with child, and shall bring forth a son, and they shall
call his name Immanuel, which being interpreted is God with us.* Luk.
2. 7–12. Mat. 1. 21, 22.

15. I believe, therefore that the righteousness, and redemption,
by which we, that believe, stand just before God, as saved from
the curse of the Law, is the righteousness, and redemption, that
consists in the personal acts, & performances of this child Jesus;
this God man the Lords Christ: it consisteth, I say, in his
personal fulfilling the law for us, to the utmost requirement of
the justice of God. *Do not think (said he) that I am come to destroy
the Law, or the Prophets; I am not come to destroy, but to fulfill.* By
which means he became the end of the Law for righteousness to
every one that believeth. *For what the Law could not do in that it
was weak through the flesh; God sending his own son in the likeness of
sinfull flesh, and for sin, condemned sin in the flesh.* So finishing
transgressions and making an end of sins, and making reconciliation for iniquity, *he brought in everlasting righteousness.* Math. 5.
17. Rom. 10. 3. chap. 8. 3. 1 Joh. 3. 8. 2 Tim. 1. 9. Hebr. 10. 5,
6, 7, 8, 9, 10, Dan. 9. 24.

16. I believe, that for the compleating of this work, he was
always sinless; did always the things that pleased God's
Justice, that every one of his acts, both of doing and suffering,
and rising again from the dead, was really and infinitely perfect,
being done by him as God-man: Wherefore his acts before he
dyed, are called, *the righteousness of God,* his blood, *the blood of
God*; and *herein perceive we the love of God in that he laid down his
life for us.* The Godhead which gave vertue to all the acts of the
humane nature, was then in perfect union with it, when he
hanged upon the cross for our sins. Heb. 4. 15. chap. 7. 26, 27,
28. Joh. 8. 29. Acts. 10. 30. Rom. 3. 21, 22. Act. 20. 28. 1 Joh. 3.
16. Joh. 20. 28. Rom. 1. 4.

17. I believe, then that the righteousness that saveth the
sinner from the wrath to come, is properly and personally
Christs, and ours but as we have union with him; God by grace
imputing it to us. *Yea doubtless, and I count all things less for the
excellency of the knowledge of·Christ Jesus my Lord, for whom I have*

17 *and for*] *and and for*

suffered the loss of all things, and do count them but dung that I may win Christ and be found in him, not haveing my own righteousness, which is of the Law, but that which is through the faith of Christ, the righteousness which is of God by faith. For of him are ye in Christ
5 *Jesus, who of God is made unto us wisdom and righteousness, and sanctification, and redemption. For he hath made him to be sin for us who knew no sin, that we might be made the righteousness of God in him.* Phil. 3, 8, 9. 1 Cor. 1. 30. 2 Cor. 5. 20, 21.

18. I believe, that God, as the reward of Christs undertakings
10 for us, hath exalted him to his own right hand, as our mediatour, and given him a name above every name; and hath made him Lord of all, and judge of quick and dead: and all this that we who believe might take courage to believe, and hope in God. *And being found in fashion as a man, he humbled himself unto death, even*
15 *the death of the cross,* (where he dyed for our sins) *wherefore God hath highly exalted him; and given him a name above every name; That at the name of Jesus every knee should bow, both of things in heaven, and things in earth, & things that are under the earth. And that every tongue should confess that Jesus Christ is Lord to the glory of*
20 *God the Father. And he commanded us to preach unto the people, and to testify, that it was he that was ordained of God to be the judge of quick and dead. Who verily was foreordained, before the foundation of the world, but was manifest in these last times for you, who by him do believe in God, who raised him from the dead, and gave him glory that*
25 *your faith and hope might be in God,* Ph. 2. 5.–10. Eph. 1. 18,–22. Act. 10 42. ch. 17, 31. 1 Pet. 1. 19, 20, 21.

19. I believe, that being on the right hand of God in heaven, he doth there effectually exercise the office of his excellent priesthood, and mediatorship, presenting himself continually
30 before God, in the righteousness which is accomplished for us, when he was in the world. For by the efficacy of his blood, he not onely went into the holy place, but being there, and having by it obtained eternal redemption for us; now, as receiving the worth and merit thereof from the Father; doth bestow upon us grace,
35 repentance, faith, and the remission of sins: Yea he also received for us, the holy Ghost to be sent unto us, to ascertain us of our adoption and Glory: *For if he were on earth he should not be a Priest; seeing then we have a great high priest, that is entred into the heavens,*

16 *exalted*] alted

Jesus the son of God. Let us hold fast our profession. For there is one God, and one mediatour between God and men, the man Christ Jesus. For by his own blood he entred into the holy place, having obtained eternal redemption for us. For Christ is not entred into the holy places made with hands, which are the figure of the true; but into heaven it self, now to appear in the presence of God for us. Therefore being by the right hand of God exalted; and having received of the Father, the promise of the holy Ghost; he hath shed forth this which ye now see and hear. Hebr. 8. 4. 1 Tim. 2. 5. Hebr. 9. 12. 24. Act. 5. 31. chap. 2. 33.

20. I believe, that being there, he shall so continue till the restitution of all things, and then he shall come again in Glory, and shall sit in judgment upon all flesh. And I believe; that according to his sentence, so shall their judgment be. *Repent ye therefore and be converted, that your sins may be blotted out when the times of refreshing shall come, from the presence of the Lord; and he shall send Jesus Christ, which before was preached unto you whom the heaven must receive, untill the restitution of all things, spoken of by the mouth of all the holy prophets, since the world began. For this same Jesus which ye have seen go up into heaven, shall so come, in like manner, as ye have seen him go into heaven. For the Lord himself shall descend from heaven with a shout, with the voice of the Arch-angel, and the trumphet of God, &c. When the son of man shall come in his glory, and all the holy Angels with him, then he shall sit upon the throne of his Glory. And before him shall be gathered all nations; and he shall separate them one from another, as a shepheard divideth his sheep from the Goats. And he shall set his sheep on his right hand, but the Goats on the left. Then shall the King say to them on his right hand, Come ye blessed of my Father, inherit the kingdom prepared for you from the foundation of the world. Then shall he say to them on the left hand, Depart from me ye Cursed into everlasting fire prepared for the Divel and his Angels; And these shall go away into everlasting punishment, but the righteous into life eternal. For the day of the Lord will come as a thief in the night, in the which the heavens shall pass away with a great noise, and the elements shall melt with fervent heat; the earth also and the works that are therein shall be burnt up. Seeing then that all these things must be dissolved. What manner of persons ought we to be in all holy conversation, and godliness; looking for and*

38 *godliness*] godlinels

hastening unto the coming of the day of God. Wherein the heavens being on fire shall be dissolved, and the elements shall melt with fervent heat. Act. 3. 19, 20, 21. 1 Thes. 4. 16. Act. 1. 11. Mat. 25. 31, 32, 33, 41, 46. 2 Pet. 3. 10, 11, 12.

5   21. I believe that when he comes, his saints shall have a reward of grace, for all their work and labour of Love which they shewed to his name in the world. *And every man shall receive his own reward, according to his own labour. And then shall every man have praise of God. And behold I come quickly, and my reward is with* 10 *me, to give to every man according as his work shall be. Wherefore my beloeved brethren, be stedfast, unmoveable always abounding in the work of the Lord; forasmuch as ye know your labour is not in vain in the Lord, Knowing that of the Lord ye shall receive the reward of inheritance, for you serve the Lord Christ,* 1 Cor. 3. 8. chap. 4. 5. 15 Rev. 22. 12. 1 Cor. 15. 58. Col 3. 24.

How Christ is made ours; or by what means this or that man, hath that benefit by him, us to stand just before God now, and in the day of judgement.

1. I believe, we being sinfull Creatures in our selves, that no   *Of justification.* 20   good thing done by us, can procure of God the imputation of the righteousness of Jesus Christ. But that the imputation thereof, *is an act of grace,* a free gift without our deserving. *Being justified freely by his grace through the redemption that is in Jesus Christ. He called us, and saved us, with an holy calling; Not according* 25 *to our works but according to his own purpose and grace, which was given us in Christ Jesus.* Rom. 3. 24. chap. 5. 17. 2 Tim. 1. 9.

2. I believe also, that the power of imputing righteousness resideth onely in God by Christ: 1. Sin being the transgression of the Law; 2. The soul that hath sinned, being his creature, and 30 the righteousness also his, and his onely. *Even as David also describeth the blessedness of the man, to whom God imputeth righteousness without works; saying, Blessed are they whose iniquities are forgiven, and whose sin is covered; Blessed is the man to whom the Lord will not impute sin.* Hence therefore it is said again, *that men* 35 *shall abundantly utter the memory of his great goodness, and sing of his righteousness. For he saith in Moses, I will have mercy, on whom I will*

24 *Christ*] Chrlst

have mercy, and I *will have compassion, on whom I will have compassion, So then, it is not in him that willeth, nor in him that runneth, but in God that sheweth mercy.* Rom. 4. 6, 7. Psal. 145. 7, Rom. 9. 15, 16.

3. I believe, that the offer of this righteousness, as tendered in the Gospell, is to be received by faith: we still in the very act of receiving it, judging our selves sinners in our selves. *Oh wretched man that I am! who shall deliver me from the body of this death. I thank God through Jesus Christ. Believe in the Lord Jesus Christ, and thou shalt be saved. The Gospel is preached in all nations for the obedience of faith. Being justified freely by his grace, through the redemption that is in Jesus Christ; whom God hath set forth to be a propitiation* (*a sacrifice to appease* the displeasure of God) *through faith in his blood. To declare his righteousness for the remission of sins that are past through the forbearance of God; to declare I say, at this time his righteousness; that he might be just, and the justifyer of him that believeth on Jesus. Be it known unto you therefore, men and brethren, that through this man is preached unto you the forgiveness of sins; And by him all that believe are justifyed from all things, from which they could not be justifyed by the law of Moses.* Rom. 7. 24. Act. 16. 31. Rom 3. 24, 25 Act. 13. 38, 39.

4. I believe, that this faith, as it respecteth the imputation of this righteousness, for justification before God; doth put forth it *self in such acts, as purely respect the offer of a gift* it receiveth, accepteth of, imbraceth, or trusteth to it. *As many as received him to them he gave power to become the sons of God, even to them that believe on his name. This is a faithfull saying, and worthy of all acceptation, that Jesus Christ came into the world to save sinners; of whom I am chief, In whom ye also trusted, after that ye heard the word of truth, the Gospell of your salvation: In whom also after that ye believed ye were sealed with the holy spirit of promise.* I believe therefore, that as to my justification from the curse of the Law, I am, as I stand in my self, ungodly, to receive, accept of, imbrace, and trust to the righteousness, that is already provided by, and wrapt up in the personal doings and sufferings of Christ: it being faith in that, and that onely, that can justify a sinner in the sight of God. Joh. 1. 12. 1 Tim. 1. 15. Heb. 11. 13. Eph. 1. 13.

5. I believe, that the faith that so doth is not to be found with any but those, in whom the Spirit of God by mighty power doth work it; all others being fearfull and incredulous, dare not

venture their souls and eternity upon it. And hence it is called
the faith that is wrought by the *exceeding great and mighty power of
God*: The faith *of the operation of God*. And hence it is that others
are said to be *fearfull*, and so unbelieving. These with other
5 ungodly sinners *must have their part in the lake of fire*. Eph. 1. 18,
19. Col. 2. 12. Eph. 2. 8. Phil. 1. 19. Rev. 21. 8.

    6. I believe, that this faith is effectually wrought in none, but
those which before the world, were appointed unto Glory. *And as
many as were ordained unto eternal life believed, That he might make
10 known the riches of his Glory, upon the vessels of mercy, which he had
before prepared unto Glory. We give thanks unto God alwayes for you
all, making mention alwayes of you in our prayers; remembring
without ceasing your work of faith, and labour of love, and patience of
hope in our Lord Jesus Christ in the sight of God; knowing brethren,
15 beloved, your election of God*, But of the rest he saith, ye believed
not because ye are not of my sheep, as I said which latter words,
relate to the 16 *v*. which respecteth the election of God. Joh.
10. 26.

    *Therefore they could not believe, because Esaias said again: he hath
20 blinded their eyes, and hardened their hearts that they should not see
with their eyes; nor understand with their heart, and I should heal
them* . Act. 13. 48. Rom 9. 23. 1 Thes. 1. 2, 3, 4. Joh. 10. 26.
chap. 12, 38, 39, 40.

Of Election.

25 1. I believe that Election is free and permanent, being founded
in *Grace*, and the unchangeable will of God. *Even so then at
this present time also there is a remnant according to the election of
Grace: And if by Grace, then it is no more of works; otherwise grace is
no more grace. But if it be of works, then it is no more of grace,
30 otherwise work is no more work. Nevertheless the foundation of God
standeth sure, having this Seal, the Lord knoweth who are his. In
whom also we have obtained an inheritance, being predestinated,
according to the purpose of him who worketh all things after the council
of his own will.* Rom. 11. 5, 6. 2 Tim. 2. 19. Eph. 1. 11.

35   2. I believe that this decree, choyce or election, was before the
foundation of the world; and so before the elect themselves, had
being in themselves; For God who quickeneth the dead, and
calleth those *things* which be not as though they were, stayes not
for the being of things, to determine his eternal purpose by; but

having all things present to, and in his wisdome, he made his choice before the world was. Rom. 4. 17. *Eph.* 1. 4. 2 *Tim* 1. 9.

3. I believe, that the decree of election is so far off, from making works in us foreseen, the ground or cause of the choyce, that it containeth in the bowels of it, not onely the persons, but the graces that accompany their salvation. And hence it is, that it is said; *We are predestinated to be conformed to the image of his son;* not because we *are,* but; that we *should be holy and without blame before him in love. For we are his workmanship, created in Christ Jesus, unto Good workes, which God hath before ordained that we should walk in them. He blessed us according as he chose us in Christ.* And hence it is again that the salvation and calling of which we are now made partakers, is no other then what was *given us in Christ Jesus before the world began;* according to his eternal purpose which he purposed in Christ Jesus our Lord. *Eph.* 1. 3, 4. *chap.* 2. 10. *chap.* 3. 8, 9, 10, 11. 2 *Tim.* 1. 9. *Rom.* 8. 26.

4. I believe that Christ Jesus is he in whom the elect are alwayes considered, and that without him there is neither election, Grace, nor salvation. *Having predestinated us to the adoption of children, by Jesus Christ to himself; according the good pleasure of his will; to the praise of the glory of his grace: Wherein he hath made us accepted in the beloved, In whom we have redemption through his blood, the forgiveness of sins according to the riches of his grace. That in the dispensation of the fullness of times, he might gather together in one, all things in Christ, both which are in heaven, and which are in earth even in him. Neither is their salvation in any other: for there is none other name under heaven given among men, whereby we must be saved.* Eph. 1. 5, 6, 7. 10. Act. 4. 12.

5. I believe, that there is not any impediment attending the election of God, that can hinder their conversion, and eternal salvation. *Moreover whom he did predestinate, them he also called; and whom he called, them he also justifyed; and whom he justifyed them he also glorifyed: What shall we say to these things; if God be for us, who can be against us? Who shall lay any thing to the charge of Gods elect? It is God that justifieth: Who is he that condemneth?* &c. *What then? Israel hath not obtained that which he seeketh for; but the election hath obtained it, and the rest were blinded. For Israel hath not been forsaken, nor Judah of his God, of the Lord of hosts; though their*

24 *dispensation*] dispensasation

land was filled with sin, against the holy one of Israel. When *Ananias* made intercession against *Saul*, saying, Lord I have heard by many of this man, how much evil he hath done to thy saints at Jerusalem, and here he hath authority from the high-priest to
5 bind all that call upon thy name. What said God unto him? *Go they way, for he is a chosen vessel unto me, to bear my name before the Gentiles, and Kings, and the children of Israel*, Rom. 8. 30, 31, 32, 33, 34. chap. 11. 7. Jer. 51. 5. Act. 9. 12, 13, 14, 15.

6. I believe that no man can know his election, *but by his*
10 *calling.* The vessels of mercy, which God afore prepared unto Glory, do thus claim a share herein: *Even us, say they, whom he hath called, not onely of the Jews, but also of the Gentiles; As he also saith in Osee; I will call them my people, which were not my people, and her beloved, which was not beloved*, Rom. 9. 23, 24, 25.

15 7. I believe therefore, that election doth not forestall or prevent the means which are of God appointed to bring us to Christ, to grace and glory; but rather putteth a necessity upon the use and effect thereof; because they are chosen to be brought to heaven that way: that is by the faith of Jesus Christ, which is
20 the end of effectual calling. *Wherefore the rather brethren give diligence to make your calling and election sure.* 2 Thes. 2. 13, 1 Pet. 1. 12. 2 Pet. 1. 10.

Of Calling.

1. I believe, that to effectual Calling the holy Ghost must
25   accompany the word of the Gospel, and that with mighty power: I mean that calling, which of God is made to be the fruit of electing love *I know* saith *Paul*, to the Thessalonians, *brethren, beloved your election of God: for our Gospell came not unto you in word onely; but also in power, and in the holy Ghost, and in much*
30 *assurance*, &c. 1 Thes. 1. 4. 8. Otherwise men will not, cannot, hear and turn. *Samuell* was called *four* times, before he knew the voice of him that spake from heaven. It is said of them in *Hosea*, That as the Prophets called them so they went from them; And instead of turning to them, *sacrificed to Balaam, and burnt incense to*
35 *Graven Images.* 1 Sam 4. 6. 10. Hos. 11. 2. The reason is, because men by nature, are not only dead in sins, *but enemys in*

11 herein] sherein

their minds by reason of wicked works: The call then is; *Awake thou that sleepest, and arise from the dead, and Christ shall give thee light* Eph. 5. 14. Understand; therefore that effectual calling is like that word of Christ that raised *Lazarus* from the dead: A word attended with an arm, that was omnipotent. *Lazarus come forth*: was a word to the dead; but not onely so: It was a word for the dead; a word that raised him from the dead; a word that outwent all opposition; and that brought him forth of the grave, though bound hand and foot therein. *Joh.* 11. 43. *Eph.* 2. 1, 2. *Heb.* 10. 32. *Gal.* 1. 15. *Act.* 9. And hence it is that calling, is sometimes expressed by quickening, awakening, illuminating, or bringing them forth of darkness to light that amazeth, and astonisheth them. For as it is a strange thing for a man that lay long dead, or never saw the light with his eyes, to be raised out of the grave, or to be made to see that which he could not so much as once think of before, so it is with effectual calling 1 Pet. 2. 9. Hence it is that *Paul*, when called, stood *trembling and was astonished*: and that *Peter* saith, *he hath called us out of darkness into his marvellous light* Eph. 4. 21. Act. 7. 2. In effectual calling the voyce of God is heard, and the gates of heaven are opened: when God called *Abraham*, he appeared to him in glory. Oh that of *Ananias* to *Saul* is experienced but by few. *The God of our Fathers hath chosen thee*, saith he, *that thou shouldest know his will, and see that just one, and shouldest hear the voyce of his mouth*. Act. 22. 14. True; *Sauls* call was out of the ordinary way, but yet as to the matter, and truth of the work, twas no other then all the chosen have, *viz.*

1. An effectual awakening about the evil of sin, and especially of unbelief. *Joh.* 16. 9. And therefore when the Lord God called *Adam*, he also made unto him, asn effectual discovery of sin; insomuch that he stript him of all his righteousness. *Gen.* 3. Thus he also served the Gaoler. Yea it is such an awakening, as by it, he sees he was without Christ, without hope, and a stranger to the common-wealth of *Israel*, and without God in the word. *Act.* 16. 29, 30. *Eph.* 2. 12. Oh the dread and amazement that the guilt of sin brings with it, when tis revealed by the God of heaven: and like to it is the sight of mercy, when it pleaseth God, *who calleth us by his grace, to reveal his son in us.*

32 Gaoler] Gealer

2. In effectual calling, there is great awakenings about the world to come, and the glory of unseen things; The resurrection of the dead; and eternal judgement; The salvation that God hath prepared for them that love him; with the blessedness that
5 will attend us, and be upon us, at the coming of our Lord Jesus Christ, are great things in the soul that is under the awakening calls of God. And hence we are said to be *called to Glory, to the obtaining of the Glory of our Lord Jesus Christ.* 1 Thes. 2. 12. 2 Thes. 2. 13, 14.

10 3. In effectual calling, there is also a sanctifying vertue; And hence we are said to be called with an holy calling, with an heavenly calling: Called to glory and vertue. *But ye are a chosen Generation, a royall priesthood, an holy nation, a peculiar people, that you should shew forth the praises of him who hath called you out of*
15 *darkness into his marvellous light.* Heb. 3. 1. 1 Thes. 4. 7. 1 Pet. 1. 8, 9. Yea effectual calling hath annexed to it, as its unseparable companion, the promise of through sanctification. *Faithfull is he that hath called you, who also will do it.* 1 Thes. 5. 22, 23, 24.

1. I believe, that effectual calling doth therefore produce.
20 1. *Faith*; and therefore it is said, that faith cometh by hearing; by hearing the word that calleth us unto the grace of Christ. For by the word that calleth us is Jesus Christ held forth to us; and offered to be our righteousness; and therefore the Apostle saith again, *that God hath called us unto the fellowship of his son*
25 *Jesus Christ*; that is to be made partakers of the riches of grace, and the righteousness that is in him. *Rom.* 10. 17. *Gasl.* 1. 6. 1 *Cor.* 1. 9.

2. It produceth hope; It giveth a ground to hope; and therefore hope is said to be the *hope of our calling.* And again,
30 *Even as you are called in one hope of your calling.* Eph. 1. 18, 19. chap. 4. 4. Now the Godly wise know, whoso misseth of effectual calling, misseth of eternal life; because God justifyeth none but them whom he calleth; and glorifyes none but those whom he justifyes: And therefore it is that *Peter* said before, *Make your*
35 *calling, and* (so) *your election sure*: make it sure, that is prove your calling right, by the word of God. For whoso staggereth at the certainty of his calling, cannot comfortably hope for a share in eternal life. *Remember the word unto thy servant, whereon thou hast*

30 *as*] *us*

caused me to hope. My soul fainted for they salvation, but I hope in thy word. Psa. 119. 49, 81.

3. It produceth repentence; For when a man hath heaven, and hell before his eyes, (as he will have if he be under the power of effectual calling) or when a man hath a revelation of the mercy and justice of God, with an heart-drawing invitation, to lay hold on the tender forgiveness of sins; and being made also to behold the goodly beauty of holiness; it must needs be, that repentance appears, and puts forth it self, unto self-revenging acts, for all its wickedness which in the dayes of ignorance, it delighted in. And hence is that saying, *I came not to call the righteous but sinners to Repentance.* For the effecting of which, the preaching of the word of the Kingdom, is most proper: *Repent for the Kingdom of God is at hand.* Mar. 2. 17. chap. 1. 10.

Of Repentance.   1. Repentance is a turning the heart to God in Christ: a turning of it from sin, and the Divel, and darkness; to the goodness and grace, and holyness that is in him. Wherefore they that of old are said to repent are said to loath, and abhor themselves, for all their abominations. *I abhor myself; said* Iob, *and repent in dust, and ashes.* Ezek. 6. 9. chap, 2. 43. chap. 36. 31. Job. 42. 5, 6. Ezek. 16. *v.* last.

2. Godly repentance: doth not onely affect the soul with the loathsome nature of sin that is past; but filleth the heart with godly hatred of sins that yet may come; When *Moses* feared that through his being overburthened, with the care of the children of *Israel,* some unruly, or sinfull passions might shew themselves in him; what saith he? *I beseech thee kill me out of hand, if I have found grace in thy sight, and let me not see my wretchedness.* Num. 14. 13, 14, 15.

See also, how that, that *Paul* calleth godly repentance, wrought in the upright *Corinthians. Behold* saith he, *this self same thing that ye sorrowed after a Godly sort; what carefulness it wrought in you? what clearing of your selves? yea what fear? yea what vehement desire, yea what zeal, yea what revenge? In all things you have approved your selves to be clear in this matter.* 2 Cor. 7. 9, 10, 11.

4. It produceth also Love: Wherefore *Paul* when he had put the church in remembrance that they were called of God; addes, That concerning brotherly Love, they had no need that he

15 Repentance] *errata*; Repentane

should write unto them. 1 Thes. 4. 17. 19. As who should say, If *OfLove.*
God be so kind to us, to forgive us our sins, to save our souls,
and to give us the kingdom of heaven; let these be motives
beyond all other, to provoke us to love again. Farther; If we that
5 are thus beloved of God, are made members of one mans body,
all partakers of his grace; clothed all with his glorious righteousness; and are together appointed to be the children of the next
world; why should we not love one another? *Beloved, if God so
loved us we ought also to love one another.* 1 Joh 4. 11. And truly so
10 we shall, if the true grace of God be upon us; because we also see
them to be the called of Jesus. Travellers, that are of the same
countrey, love, and take pleasure one in another, when they meet
in a strange Land, why? we sojourn here in a strange countrey;
with them that are heirs together with us of the promised
15 kingdom and glory. Heb. 11. 9. Now as I said, this holy love,
worketh by love; Mark, Love in God, and Christ, when
discovered, constraineth us to love. 2 Cor. 5. 14.

The name, therefore, and word, and truth of God in Christ,
20 together with the sincerity of Grace, of faith, and holyness in us,
are the delightfull objects of this love. *Psa.* 119. 47, 127, 159.
Psa. 5. 11, *and* 69. 36. *and* 119. 132. *and* 101. 6. For it imbraceth
with delight, and complacency, but as it discerneth the image of
God, and of Christ in the Soul, his presence in the ministery;
25 and a suitableness in our worship to the word, and mind of
Christ. *Psa.* 26. 8. *and* 27. 4. *and* 84. 4. 1 *Thes.* 5. 13. *Phil.* 1. 3 7.
Eph. 4. 32.

Love also hath a blessed faculty, and heavenly; in bearing and
suffering afflictions, putting up wrongs, overlooking the infirmities
30 of the brethren, and in serving in all Christian offices the
necessities of the Saints *Charity suffereth long, and is kind, charity
envyeth not, charity vaunteth not it self, is not puffed up, doth not
behave it self unseemly; seeketh not her own; is not easily provoked;
thinketh no evil, rejoyceth not in iniquity, but rejoyceth in the truth;*
35 *beareth all things, believeth all things; hopeth all things, endureth all
things; charity never faileth.* 1 Cor. 13. 1 Pet. 4. 8. Gal. 5. 13. In a
word it designeth a holy conversation in this world; that God,
and Christ, and the word of Christ *may be glorified thereby.* 2 Cor.
11. 10, 11, 12 1 Pet. 1. 12 chap. 3. 16.

38 of Christ *may*] *errata*; of *may*

Of the Scriptures.

TOuching which word of God. I thus believe and confess.
1. That all the holy scriptures are the words of God. *All scriptures is given by inspiration of God. For the prophecy of the scripture came not in old time by the will of man; but holy men of God, speak as they were moved by the holy Ghost.* 2 Tim. 3. 16. 2 Pet. 1. 21.

2. I believe that the holy scriptures, of themselves, without the addition of humane inventions, are able to make the man of God perfect in all things; and *thoroughly to furnish him unto all good works.* They are able *to make thee wise unto salvation through faith in Jesus Christ*; and to instruct thee in all other things, that either respect the worship of God, or thy walking before all men. 2 Tim. 3. 14, 17. 2 Pet 1. 19, 20, 21.

3. I believe, the great end why God committed the Scriptures to writing was; that we might be instructed to Christ, taught how to believe, encouraged to patience, and hope, for the grace that is to be brought unto us, at the revelation of Jesus Christ; also, that we might understand what is sin, and how to avoid the commission thereof. *Joh.* 20. 31. 1 *Joh.* 5. 13. *Rom.* 15. 4 *Concerning the Works of men* (said David) *by the word of thy lips, I have kept me from the pathes of the destroyer.* Through thy precepts I get understanding, *therefore I hate every false way.* I have hid thy word in my heart, that I might not sin against thee. *Psa.* 17. 4. *and* 119, 104. *v.* 11.

4. I believe that they *cannot be broken*, but will certainly be fulfilled in all the prophecies, threatnings, and promises, either to the salvation, or damnation of men. They are like that flying roll, that will go over all the earth to cut off and curse; In them is contained also the blessing; they preach to us also the way of salvation; *Take heed therefore lest that come upon you which is written in the prophets, Behold ye despisers, and wonder and perish, For I work a work in your dayes, a work which you shall in no wise believe, though a man declare it unto you.* Gal 3. 8. Acts 13. 40, 41. John. 10. 35. chap. 12. 37. 41. chap. 3. 17, 18, 19. Zach. 5. 2. 3, 4.

5. I believe Jesus Christ, by the word of the scriptures, will judge all men at the day of doom; For that is the book of the Law

12 to instruct] *errata*; to

of the Lord, according to *Pauls* Gospel, *Joh.* 12. 41, 49. *Rom.* 2. 16.

6. I believe, *that this God made the world, and all things that are therein, for in Six dayes the Lord made Heaven and Earth, the Sea,*
5 *and all that in them is; also that after the time of the making thereof, be disposed of it to the children of men, with a preserve thereof for the children of God, that should in all ages be born thereunto. When the most high divided to the nations their inheritance, when he separated the Sons of* Adam; *he set the bounds of the people according to the*
10 *number of the children of* Israel, *for as he made of one blood all nations of men for to dwell upon the face of the earth, so he hath determined the times before appointed, and the bounds of their habitation.* Acts 17. 24, Exo. 24. 19, Deu. 32. 8, Acts 17. 26.

Of Magistracy.

15 I believe, that Magistracy is Gods ordinance, which he hath appointed for the government of the whole world; And that it is a judgment of God, to be without those ministers of God, which he hath ordained *to put wickedness to shame.* Judg. 18. 7.

Whosoever therefore resisteth the power, resisteth the ordinance of
20 *God; and they that resist, shall receive to themselves damnation; For rulers are not a terror to good works but to the evil; Wilt thou not then be afraid of the power, do that which is Good and thou shalt have praise of the same: For he is the minister of God to thee for good. But if thou do that which is evill, be afraid, for he beareth not the sword in*
25 *vain, For he is the minister of God, a revenger to execute wrath upon him that doth evil: Wherefore, ye must needs be subject; not onely for wrath, but also for conscience sake: For his cause pay ye tribute also; for they are Gods ministers attending continually unto this very thing.* Rom. 13. Many are the mercyes we receive, by a well qualified
30 Magistrate, and if any shall at any time be otherwise inclined, *let us shew our christianity in a patient suffering for well doing, what it shall please God to inflict by them.*

A reason of my Practise in Worship,

Having thus made confession of my Faith, I now come to
35 shew you my practise in Worship, with the reasons thereof.

3 6. *I believe* .. Acts 17, 26.] *om. Manchester Central Library copy* 31 *our*] *ovr*
33 *Practice in Worship*] *practise in worship Manchester copy* 34 Faith] faith
Manchester copy 35 Worship] worship *Manchester copy*

The which I shall have occasion to touch, under two distinct heads.

1. *With whom I dare not hold communion.*
2. *With whom I dare.*

Only, first, Note, that by the word Communion I mean 5
fellowship *in the things of the Kingdom of Christ,* or that which is commonly called Church communion, the Communication of Saints. For in civil affairs and in things of this World that are honest, I am not altogether tyed up from the fornicators thereof, (*Cor.* 5. 9, 10.) Wherefore in my following discourse understand 10
me in the first sense.

Now, Then, *I dare not have communion with them that profess not faith and holiness*; or that are not visible Saints by calling: but note that by this assertion, I meddle not with the elect; but as he is a visible Saint by calling; neither do I exclude the secret 15
Hypocrite, *if he be hid from me by visible Saint ship.* Wherefore I dare not have communion with men from a single supposition, that they may be elect, neither dare I exclude the other from a single supposing that he may be a secret Hypocrite. I meddle not here with these things; I onely exclude him that is not a visible 20
Saint: Now he that is visibly or openly prophane, cannot be then a visible Saint, for he that is a visible Saint must profess faith, and repentance, and consequently holyness of life: And with none else dare I communicate.

First, Because God himself hath so strictly put the difference; 25
both by word and deed; For from the beginning, he did not only put a difference between the Seed of the woman and the children of the wicked, onely the instinct of grace and change of the mind as his own, but did cast out from his presence the father of all the ungodly, even cursed *Cain* when he shewed 30
himself open prophane, and banished him to go into the Land of the Runnagate or Vagabond, where from Gods face, and so the priviledges of the communion of Saints he was ever after hid. *Gen.* 3. 15. *chap.* 4. 9, 10, 14, 15, 16.

Besides, when after this, through the policy of Satan, the 35
children of *Cain*, and the seed of *Seth*, did commix themselves in worship, and by that means had corrupted the way of God: what followed, but first, God judged it wickedness, raised up *Noah* to preach against it, and after that, because they would not be reclaimed, he brought the floud, upon the whole world of these 40

ungodly; and saved onely *Noah* and his alive because he had
kept himself righteous. *Gen.* 6. 1, 2 *v.* 3. 11, 12, 13.

Here I could inlarge abundantly, and add many more
instances of alike nature but I am here onely for a touch upon
5 things.

Secondly, Because it is so often commanded in the Scriptures,
That all the congregation should be holy. *I am the Lord your God,
ye shall therefore sanctifie your selves; and ye shall be holy for I am
holy. Ye shall be holy, for I the Lord your God am holy. Sanctifie your
10 selves therefore and be ye holy, for I am the Lord your God.* Besides,
1. The Gates of the temple were to be shut against all other.
*Open ye the gates, that the righteous nation, that keepeth the truth may
enter in: This Gate of the Lord into which the righteous shall enter.
Thus saith the Lord, no stranger uncircumcised in heart, or
15 uncircumcised in flesh shall enter into my sanctuary of any stranger
which is amongst the children of Israel.* 2. Because, the things of
worship are holy; *Be ye holy that bear the vessels of the Lord.* 3.
Because all the limits, and bounds of communion are holy. *This
is the law of the house, upon the top of the mountain, the whole limit
20 thereof shall be most holy: Behold this is the Law of the house. Lev.* 11.
44. chap. 19. 2. chap. 20. 7. 1 Pet. 1. 15, 16. Esa. 26. 2. Psa. 128.
20. Eze, 43. 12. chap. 44. 9. Esa. 52. 11.

Thirdly, I dare not have communion with them; Because the
example of new testament churches before us, have been a
25 community of visible Saints. Paul to the Romanes, writes thus:
To all that are at Rome, beloved of God, called to be Saints, And to
the rest of the Churches thus: *Unto the Church of God which is at
Corinth; to them that are sanctified in Christ Jesus, called to be Saints.*
To the Saints that are at *Ephesus,* and to the faithfull in Christ
30 Jesus; To all the Saints that are at *Philippi* with the Bishops and
Deacons. To the Saints and faithfull brethren which are at
Colosse. To the Church of the *Thessalonians,* which is in God the
Father; and in our Lord Jesus Christ; *&c.* Thus you see under
what denomination, those persons went of old, who were
35 counted worthy to be members of a visible Church of Christ.
Rom. 1. 7. 1 *Cor.* 1. 2. *Eph.* 1. 1. *Col.* 1. 2. *Phil* 1. 1. 1 *Thes.* 1. 1.
Besides, the members of such Churches, go under such
characters as these.

1 and his alive] *errata*; alive   4 touch] *errata*; truth

1. *The called of Christ Jesus.* Rom. 1. 6.

2. Men that have drank into the spirit of Jesus Christ. 1 *Cor.* 12. 13.

3. Persons in whom was God the Father. *Eph.* 4. 6.

4. They were all made partakers of the joy of the Gospell *Phil.* 1. 7.

5. Persons that were circumcised inwardly. *Col.* 2. 11.

6. Persons that turned to God from Idols, to serve the living and true God. 1 *Thes.* 1. 4.

7. Those that were the body of Christ, and members in particulars that is those that were visibly such; because they made profession of faith, of holyness, of repentance, of love to Christ, and of self denyal, at their receiving into fellowship.

Fourthly, I dare not hold communion with the open prophane:

1. Because it is promised to the Church, that she shall dwell by her self; that is, as she is a Church, and spiritual; *Lo the people shall dwell alone, and shall not be reckoned among the nations.* Num. 23. 9.

2. Because this is their priviledge. *But ye are a chosen generation, a royall priesthood, an holy nation, a peculiar people; that ye should shew forth the praises of him, who hath called you out of darkness into his marvellous light.* 1 Pet. 1. 9, 10.

3. Because this is the fruit of the death of Christ, who gave himself for us, that he might redeem us from all iniquity; and purify unto himself a peculiar people zealous of good works. *Tit.* 3. 14.

4. Because this is the Commandment: *Save your selves from the untoward generation.* Act. 2. 40.

5. Because with such it is not possible we should have true and spiritual communion. *Be not unequally yoked together with unbelievers: For what fellowship hath righteousness, with unrighteousness? And what communion hath light with darkness? And what concord hath Christ with Belial? Or what part hath he that believeth with an infidell? Or what agreement hath the temple of God with Idols? For ye are the temple of the living God, as God hath said, I will dwell in them and walk in them, and I will be their God, and they shall be my people. Wherefore, Come out from among them, and be ye separate saith the Lord, and touch not the unclean thing, and I will receive you,*

17 *alone*] a-alone

and I will be a Father unto you saith the Lord Almightly. 2 Cor. 6,
14–18.

Fifthly, I dare not hold communion with the open prophane.

1. Because this would be plowing with an Ox, and an
5 Ass together: heavenly things suit best for communion in
heavenly matters. *Deut,* 22. 10.

2. It subjecteth not to the nature of our discipline, which is
not forced, but free, in a professed subjection to the will and
commandment of Christ: others being excluded by God's own
10 prohibition, *Levit.* 1. 3. *Rom.* 6. 17, 2 *Cor.* 8. 12. *chap.* 9. 7, 13.
chap. 8. 5.

Paul also when he exhorteth *Timothy* to follow after righteousness; Faith, Charity, Peace, *&c.* (which are the bowels of Church
communion) he saith, *do it with those that call on the name of*
15 *the Lord, out of a pure heart.* 2 Tim. 2. 22.

Sixthly, In a word, to hold communion with the open
prophane, is most pernicious and destructive.

1, 'Twas the wicked multitude, that fell a lusting, and that
tempted Christ in the desert, *Num.* 11. 4.

20 2, It was the prophane, heathen, of whom Israel learned, to
worship Idols. *They were mingled among the heathen, and learned
their works, and served their Idols, which were a snare to them.* Psa.
106. 25, 26, 27.

3, It is the mingled people that God hath threatned to plague
25 with those deadly punishments of his, with which he hath
threatned to punish *Babylon* it self: saying; When a sword is upon
her lyars, her mighty, her chariots and treasures; a sword also
shall be upon the mingled people that are in the middest of her.

And no marvail: for,

30 1, Mixed communion polluteth the ordinances of God. Say to
the rebells saith the Lord God. *Let it suffice you, of all your
abominations, that you have brought into my sanctuary strangers,
uncircumcised in heart, and uncircumcised in flesh; to be in my
sanctuary to pollute it; even my house, when ye offered my bread and*
35 *the fat, and the blood: And they have broken my Covenant, because of
all their abominations.* Eze. 44. 6, 7, 8.

2. *It violateth the law; her priests have violated my Law, and
prophaned my holy things;* (how) *they have put no difference, between*

*the holy and prophane; neither have they shewed difference between the
unclean, and the clean.* Eze. 22. 6.

3, It prophaneth the holyness of God: *Judah hath dealt
treacherously, and an abomination is committed in Israel, and
Jerusalem: For Judah hath prophaned the holyness of the Lord which he   5
loved, and hath married the daughter of a strange God.* Mal. 2. 11.

4. It defileth the truly Gracious; *Know ye not that a little
Leaven, leaveneth the whole lump: Look diligently therefore lest any
root of bitterness springing up trouble you, and thereby many be defiled.*
1 Cor. 5, 6, Heb. 12, 15, 16.   10

Lastly, To conclude, as I said before, it provoketh God to
punish with severe judgments: And therefore heed well.

1. As I said before, The Drowning of the whole world was
occasioned, by the sons of God commixing themselves with the
daughters of men; and the corruption of worship that followed   15
thereupon, *Gen.* 6, *and* 7 *chapters.*

2, He sent a plague upon the children of Israel, for joyning
themselves unto the people of Moab; and for following their
abominations in worship: And let no man think, that now I have
altered the state of the question: for it is all one with the Church   20
to Communicate with the prophane; and to sacrifice, and offer
their gifts to the Divel: the reason is, because such have by their
sin forsaken the protection of heaven, and are given up to their
own heartlusts; and left to be overcome of the wicked to whom
they have joyned their selves. *Num.* 25. 1, 2, 3, 4, 5. *Jos.* 22. 17.   25
Deut. 32. 16, 19. *Psa.* 106. 36, 40. *Deut.* 12. *Deut.* 7. 1, 26. *Neh.*
13. 26.

Joyn not your selves, saith God, to the wicked, neither in
religion nor marriages; *for they will turn away thy son from
following me, that they may serve other Gods; so will the anger of the*   30
Lord be kindled against you, and destroy thee suddainly. Did not
Solomon *King of* Israel *sin by these things? yet among many nations
was there no King like him who was beloved of his God.*

Hear how Paul handleth the point; *This I say,* saith he, *That the
things which the Gentiles or openly prophane sacrifice; they sacrifice*   35
*to Devils, and not to God: And I would not that you should have
fellowship with Divels. Ye cannot drink of the Cup of the Lord, and the
cup of Divels: Ye cannot be partakers of the table of the Lord & of the*

5 the] th

table of Divels, Do we provoke the Lord to Jealousie? Are we stronger then he? 1 Cor. 10. 21, 22, 23. I conclude that therefore it is an evil, & a dangerous thing to hold Church-communion with the open prophane, and ungodly. It polluteth his ordinances: It violateth his Law: It prophaneth his holiness: It defileth his people; and provoketh the Lord to severe, and terrible judgments.

Object. But we can prove in all ages, there have been the open prophane in the Church of God.

Answ. In many ages indeed it hath been so; but marke, they appeared not such, when first they were received unto Communion neither was they with Gods liking, as such to be retained among them, but in order to their admonition repentance and amendment of life: of which if they failed; God presently threatened the Church; and either cut them off from the Church, as he did the Idolaters, Fornicators, murmurers, Tempters, Sabbath-breakers; with *Korah, Dathan, Achan* and others: or else cut of them with the Church and all, as he served the ten tribes at one time, and the two tribes at another. *My God shall cast them away, because they did not hearken to him, and they shall be wanderers among the nations.* Exod, 12. 48. 2 Cor. 6. 1 Cor. 5. 4, 5; 10. 12, 13. Exo. 32. 25. Numb. 25. 1, 9. chap. 21, 5, 6 chap. 14. 37. chap. 16. chap. 15. 32, 36. Josh. 7. 2. Kin. 17. Ezek. 22. chap. 23. Hos. 9. 17. Neh. 13. 1, 2, 3, I might here greatly enlarge but I only intend brevity; yet let me tell you, that when *Nehemiah* understood by the book of the Law of the Lord, that the *Ammonite*, and the *Moabite* should not come into the congregation of God; they *separated from* Israel *all the mixed multitude.* Many have pleaded for the prophane; that they should abide in the Church of God; but such have not considered, that Gods wrath at all times hath with great indignation been shewed against such offenders and their conceits. Indeed they like not for to plead for them under that notion, but rather as *Korah*, and his company. *All the congregation is holy every one of them* Num. 16. 3. But it maketh no matter by what name they are called; if by their deeds they shew themselves openly wicked; for names, and notions, sanctify not the heart, and nature: they make not vertues of vice, neither can it save such advocates, *from the heavy curse both of God and Men. The righteous men they shall judge*

17 off] of

them after the manner of adulteresses; and after the manner of women that shed blood, because they are adulteresses, and blood is in their hands. Pro. 17. 15. chap. 24. 24. Eze. 23. 45.

Thus have I shewed you with whom I dare not have communion: And now to shew you with whom I dare. But in order thereto, I desire you first to take notice; That touching shaddowish, or figurative ordinances; I believe that Christ hath ordained but two in his Church, *viz.* Water baptism and the Supper of the Lord: both which are of excellent use to the Church, in this world; they being to us representations of the death, and resurrection of Christ, and are as, God shall make them, helps to our faith therein; But I count them not the fundamentals of our Christianity; nor grounds or rule to communion with Saints: servants they are, and our mystical Ministers, to teach and instruct us, in the most weighty matters of the Kingdom of God: I therefore here declare my reverent esteem of them; yet dare not remove them, as some do, from the place, and end, where by God they are set and appointed; nor ascribe unto them more, then they were ordered to have in their first, and primitive institution: Tis possible to commit Idolatry, even with Gods own appointments: But I pass this, and come to the thing propounded.

Secondly, then, *I dare have communion; Church communion with those that are visible Saints by calling*; with those that by the word of the Gospell, have been brought over to faith and holyness. And it maketh no matter to me, what their life was heretofore, *if they now be washed, if they be sanctified. if they be justified in the name of our Lord Jesus Christ, and by the Spirit of our God.* 1 Cor. 6. 9, 10, 11. Now in order to the discovery of this faith and holyness, and so to fellowship in Church communion: I hold it requisite that a faithful relation be made thereof by the party thus to be received; yea if need be by witnesses also, *for the satisfaction of the church, that she may receive in faith and judgment,* such as best shall suit her holy profession. Acts 9. 26, 27, 28. 1 Cor. 16. 10. 2 Cor. 8. 23. Observe it; these Texts do respect extraordinary officers; and yet see, that in order to their reception by the Church, there was made to them a faithfull relation, of the faith and holyness of these very persons; For no man may intrude himself upon, or thrust himself upon, or thrust himself into a Church of Christ:

11 Christ] Chtist

without the Church have first the knowledge, and liking of the person to be received; If otherwise there is a door opened for all the hereticks in the world; yea for Divels also if they appear in
5 humane shapes. But *Paul* shews you the manner of receiving, by pleading (after some disgrace thrown upon him by the false Apostles) for his own admission of his companions: *Receive us,* saith he, *we have wronged no man; we have defrauded no man; we have corrupted no man*: and so concerning Timothy; *If* Timothy
10 *come,* saith he, *see that he may be with you without fear; for he worketh the work of the Lord, as I also do.* 2 Cor. 7. 2. 1 Cor 16. 10. Also when Paul supposed that *Titus* might be suspected by some; see how he pleades for him: *If any do enquire of* Titus; *he is my partner, and fellow helper, concerning you; or our brethren be enquired*
15 *of, they are the messengers of the Churches, and the glory of Christ.* 2 Cor. 8. 23. *Phæbe* also when she was to be received by the Church at *Rome*; see how he speaketh in her behalf: *I commend unto you* Phæbe *our sister, which is a servant of the Church, which is at* Cenchrea; *that ye receive her in the Lord, as becometh Saints; and*
20 *that you assist her in whatsoever business she hath need of you; for she hath been a succourer of many, and of myself also.* Rom. 16. 1, 2. Yea when the Apostles, and brethren sent their Epistles, from Jerusalem to *Antioch*: under what characters do those go, that were the messengers to them? *It seemed good, unto the holy Ghost,*
25 *and to us to send chosen men unto you, with our beloved* Barnabas, and Saul, *men that have hazarded their lives for the name of our Lord Jesus Christ,* &c. Acts 15. 25, 26. 27. Now though the occasion upon which these commendations were written, were not simply, or onely, in order to Church relation, but also for other causes;
30 yet because the persons concerned were of the Churches to be received as faithfull, and such who would partake of Church priviledges with them, they have therefore, their faith, and faithfulness related to the Churches, as those that were particularly imbodyed there. Besides *Timothy* and *Titus* being extraordinary
35 officers, stood as members and officers in every Church where they were received: Likewise *Barnabus,* and *Saul, Judas,* and *Silas,* abode as members, and officers there where they were sent. 'Twas requisite therefore that the Letters of recommendation, should be in substance the same with that relation, that ought to

Saul was in Antioch before, but being brought into suspicion by false Apostles, he had need of a new commendation.

18 Cenchrea] Ceuchrea

be made to the Church, by or for the person, that is to be imbodyed there. But to return; *I dare have communion, Church-communion with those that are visible Saints by calling.*

Quest. *But by what rule would you receive him into fellowship with your selves.*

Answ. Even by a discovery of their faith and holyness; *and their declaration of willingness to subject themselves to the laws and government of Christ in his Church.*

Quest. But do you not count that by *water-baptism*, and not otherwise that being the initiating, and entering ordinance, they ought to be received into fellowship.

Answ. No; But tarry, and take my sense with my word. For herein lyes the mistake, To think that because in time past, Baptism was administred upon conversion, *that therefore it is the initiating, and entring ordinance* into Church-communion: when by the word no such thing is testifyed of it. Besides, that it is not so, will be manifest, if we consider the nature, and power of such an ordinance.

That ordinance then, that is the initiating or entering ordinance as before, Doth give to them that partake thereof, a right to, and a being of membership, with that particular Church, by which it is administered. I say, a right to, and a being of membership, without the addition of another Church-Act. This is evident by the Law of circumcision, which was the initiating Law of old, For by the administration of that very ordinance, the partaker thereof was forthwith a member of that congregation, *without the addition of another Church-act.* Gen. 17. This is declared in its first institution, and therefore it is called the token of the Covenant: The token or sign of righteousness of *Abrahams* Faith, and of the visible membership of those that joyned themselves to the Church with him; the very inlet into Church-communion; that gave a being of membership among them. And thus *Moses* himself expounds it; *Every Man-servant* saith he, *that is bought with money when thou hast circumcised him, he shall eat of the passover:* without the addition of another Church-act, to impower him thereunto; his circumcision hath already given him a being there, and so a right to, and priviledge in the blessing of Church-relation: *A Forreigner and an hired servant shall not eat thereof.* (because not circumcised) *but when a stranger that sojourneth with thee, will keep the Passover to the Lord, let all his males be circumcised, and then let*

him come near and keep it. (for then he is one of the Church) *and he shall be as one born in the Land; for no uncircumcised person shall eat thereof.* Exo. 12. 43, 45, 46, 47, 48, 49. Neither could any other thing, according to the Law of Circumcision, give the
5 devoutest person that breathed, a being of membership with them. *He that is born in thine house, & he that is bought with thy money, must needs be circumcised, & the uncircumcised man-child, whose flesh of his foreskin is not circumcised, that Soul shall be cut off from his people.* Gen. 17, 13, 14. Note then, that that which is the
10 initiating ordinance, admitteth none into Church-communion, but those that first partake thereof; The Angel sought to kill *Moses* himself, for attempting to make his child a member without it. Note again, that as it admitteth of none to membership without it, so as I said, *the very act of circumcising*
15 *them, without the addition of another Church act*, gave them a being of membership with that very Church, by whom they were circumcised. *Exo.* 4. 24, 25, 26. But none of this can be said of Baptism: First there is none debarred or threatened to be cut off from the Church, if they be not first baptized: Secondly, neither
20 doth it give to the person baptized, a being of membership, with this or that Church, by whose members he hath been baptized. *John* gathered no particular Church, yet was he the first, and great baptizer with water; he preached Christ to come, and baptized with the baptism of repentance, and left his Disciples to
25 be gathered by him. Acts 19. 3, 4, 5. *And to him shall the gathering of the people be* Gen, 49. 10, Besides after Christs ascension, *Phillip* baptized the *Eunuch*; but made him, by that, no member of any particular Church: We onely read, that *Phillip* was caught away from him, and that the *Eunuch* saw him no more, but went
30 on his way rejoycing to his Masters and countrey of *Ethiopia. Acts* 8. 35, 40. Neither was *Cornelius* made a member of the Church at *Jerusalem*, by his being baptized at *Peters* commandment at *Cæsarea. Acts* 10. *chap.* 11. Neither were they that were converted at *Antioch*, by them that were scattered from the Church at
35 *Jerusalem*, by their baptism (if they were baptized at all) joyned to the Church at *Jerusalem*. Acts 11. 19. No, they were after gathered, and imbodyed among themselves, by other Church acts. *Acts* 16. What shall I say? Into what particular Church was *Lydia* baptized by *Paul*, or those first converts at *Philippi*? Yea
40 even in the second of the Acts, Baptizing and adding to the

Church, appear to be acts distinct: but if Baptism were the initiating ordinance, then was he that we Baptized made a member; made a member of a particular Church, by the very Act of water baptism: Neither ought any by Gods ordinance to have Baptized any, but with respect to the admitting them by that Act, to a being of membership in this particular Church. For if it be the initiating ordinance, it entereth them into the Church: What Church? Into a visible Church; Now there is no Church visible but that which is particular; The Universal being utterly invisible, and known to none but God. The person then that is baptized stands by that, a member of no Church at all, neither of the visible, nor yet of the invisible. A visible Saint he is, but not made so by Baptism; for he must be a visible Saint before, else he ought not to be baptized *Acts* 8. 37. *Acts* 9. 17. *Acts* 16. 33.

Take it again; *Baptism makes thee no member of the Church, neither particular nor universall: neither doth it make thee a visible Saint: It therefore gives thee neither right to, nor being of membership at all.*

Quest. But why then were they Baptized.

Answ. That their own Faith by that figure might be strengthened in the death and resurrection of Christ. And that themselves might see, that they have professed themselves, dead, and buryed, and risen with him to newness of life. It did not seal to the Church that they were so (their satisfaction as to that arose from better arguments) but taught the party himself, that he ought so to be. Farther, It confirmed to his own conscience and forgiveness of sins, if by unfeigned faith he laid hold upon Jesus Christ. *Col.* 2. 12. *Rom.* 6. 3, 4. *Gal.* 3. 26. 1 *Cor.* 15. 29. *Acts* 2. 38. *Acts* 22, 16. 1 *Pet.* 3, 21.

Now then, if Baptism be not the initiating ordinance, we must seek for entring some other way, by some other appointment of Christ; unless we will say, that without rule, without order and without an appointment of Christ, we may enter into his visible Kingdom. The Church under the Law had their initiating and entering ordinance, it must therefore be; unless we should think that Moses was more punctual and exact then Christ, but that also our Lord hath his entering appointment. Now that which by Christ is made the door of enterance into the Church, by that we may doubtless enter; and seeing Baptism is not that ordinance, we ought not to seek to enter thereby, but may with good conscience enter without it.

Quest. But by what rule, then would you gather persons into Church-communion?

5 Answ. *Even by that rule, by which they are discovered to the Church to be visible Saints; and willing to be gathered into their body and fellowship.* By that word of God therefore, by which their Faith, experience, and conversation (being examined) is found Good; by that the Church should receive them into fellowship with

10 them. Marke; Not as they practise things that are circumstantial; but as their faith is commended by a word of faith, and their conversation by a moral precept. Wherefore that is observable, that after *Paul* had declared himself sound of faith; he falls down to the body of the Law: *Receive us, saith he, we have wronged no*

15 *man, we have corrupted no man, we have defrauded no man,* he saith not, I am baptized; but I have wronged no man, *&c.* 2 *Cor.* 5. 18, 19, 20, 21. *chap.* 7. 2. And if Churches after the confession of faith, made more use of the ten commandments, to judge of the fitness of persons by; they might not exceed by this seeming

20 strictness christian tenderness towards them, they receive to communion.

I will say therefore, that by the word of faith and of good works; moral duties Gospellized; we ought to judge of the fitness of members by, by which we ought also to receive them to

25 fellowship: *For he that in these things proveth sound,* he hath the antitype of circumcision, which was before the entering ordinance. *For he is not a Jew, which is one outwardly; neither is that circumcision which is outward in the flesh. But he is a Jew which is one inwardly; and circumcision is that of the heart in the spirit,*

30 *whose praise is not of men but of God.* Rom. 2. 28, 29. Phil. 3. 1, 2, 3, 4.

Now a confession of this by word and life, makes this inward circumcision visible; When you know him therefore to be thus circumcised, you ought to admit him to the Lords passover: he, if

35 any hath a share, not onely in Church communion, but a visible right to the Kingdom of Heaven.

Again, *For the Kingdom of God,* or our Service to Christ, *consisteth not in meats or drinks, but in righteousness, peace, and joy in*

26 circumcision] circumsion   28 *circumcision] circumsion*
32 circumcision] circumsion

the holy Ghost; And he that in these things serveth Christ is accepted of God, and approved of men. Rom. 14. 18. Deut. 28. 47. By which word righteousness he meaneth as *Iames* doth; the royal Law, the perfect Law which is the moral precept Evangelized or delivered to us by the hand of Christ. *James* 2. 8, 9. The Law was given   5
twice on *Sinai*; The last time it was given with a proclamation of grace and mercy of God, and of the pardon of sins going before. *Exo* 19, *and chap.* 34. 1, 10. The second giving is here intended; for so it cometh after faith, which first receiveth the proclamation of forgiveness; hence we are said to do this righteousness in the   10
joy and peace of the holy Ghost. Now he that in these things serveth Christ, is accepted of God, and approved of men. For who is he that can justly find fault with him that fullfilleth the royal Law from a principle of Faith and Love. *If ye fullfill the royal Law according to the Scriptures, Thou shalt love they neighbour as thy*   15
self; ye do well; ye are approved of men. Again, he that hath loved another hath fullfilled the Law, for love is the fulfilling of the Law. He then that serveth Christ, according to the royal Law, from faith and love going before, he is a fit person for Church-communion; God accepteth him, Men approve him.   20
Now that the royal Law is the moral precept; read the place. *James* 2. 8, 9, 10, 11, 12. It is also called the law of liberty, because the bondage is taken away by forgiveness going before; and this is it by which we are judged, as is said, meet or unmeet for Church-communion, *&c.*   25

Therefore I say, the rule by which we receive Church-members; it is the word of the Faith of Christ, and of the moral precept Evangelized, as I said before, *I am under the Law to Christ,* saith Paul. So when he forbideth us, communion with men, they be such as are destitute of the Faith of Christ, and live   30
in the transgression of a moral precept: I have *written unto you, saith he, not to keep company, if any man that is called a brother, be a fornicator, or covetous, or an Idolater, or a railer, or a drunkard, or an extortioner, with such an one no not to eat.* He saith not, if any man be not Baptized, have not hands laid on him, or joyne with the   35
unbaptized: these are fictions, scriptureless notions. For this, *Thou shalt not commit Adultery; Thou shalt not Kill; Thou shalt not Steal; Thou shalt not bear false witness; Thou shalt not Covet. And if there be any other Commandment, it is briefly comprehended in this saying. Thou shalt Love thy Neighbour as thy self. Love thinketh no*   40

ill to his Neighbour; therefore Love is the fullfilling of the Law. Rom.
13. 9, 10.

The word of Faith, and the moral precept, is that which *Paul*
injoyns the Galathians and Philippians; still avoiding outward
5 circumstances: hence therefore when he had to the Galathians
treated of Faith, he falls point blank upon moral duties. *For in
Christ Jesus neither circumcision availeth any thing, nor uncircumcision,
but a new creature: And as many as walk according to this rule, peace
be on them, and mercy, and upon the Israel of God.* Gal. 6. 15, 16. As
10 many as walk, according to this rule; What rule? The rule by
which men are proved new creatures: The word of Faith and the
moral precept. Wherefore *Paul* exhorteth the Ephesians, not to
walk as other Gentiles, in the vanity of their mind; seeing they
had received Christ, and had heard him, and had been taught by
15 him, as the truth is in Jesus; that they would put off the old man;
what is that? Why, the former conversation, which is corrupt
according to the deceitfull lusts; Lying, Anger, Sin, giving place
to the Divel, corrupt communication, all bitterness, wrath,
clamor, evil speaking, with all malice; and that they would put on
20 the new man; What is that? That which is created in
righteousness and true holyness; A being renewed in the spirit of
their mind, and a putting away all these things. *Eph.* 4. *For in
Christ Jesus*, these words are put in of purpose, to shew us the
nature of new Testament administrations; And how they differ
25 from the old: In *Moses* an outward conformity, to an outward
and carnal ordinance was sufficient to give (they subjecting
themselves thereto) a being of membership with the Jews: But in
Christ Jesus it is not so: of *Abrahams* flesh was the national
Jewish congregation; but it is *Abrahams* Faith that makes new
30 testament Churches; *They that are of Faith, are the children of
faithfull Abraham. They that are of Faith, the same are the children of
Abraham.* So then the seed being now spiritual, the rule must
needs be spiritual also *viz.* the word of Faith and holyness; This
is the Gospel concision knife; sharper then any two edged sword,
35 and that by which new testament Saints are circumcised in heart,
ears, and lips. *For in Christ Jesus*, no outward and circumstantial
thing; but the new creature; none subjects of the visible
Kingdom of Christ but visible Saints by calling; Now that which

24 administrations] administratinons

manifesteth a person to be a visible Saint, must be conformity to
the word of Faith and Holyness. *And they that are Christs, have
crucified the flesh with the affections and lusts.* Hearken how
delightfully *Paul* handleth the point? The new creatures, are the
Israel of God. The new creature hath a rule by himself to walk   5
by; And as many as walk according to this rule, peace be on
them, and mercy, and upon the Israel of God. *Paul* to the
Philippians commandeth as much; where treating of his own
practice in the doctrine of Faith and Holyness, requireth them to
walk by the same rule, to mind the same thing. I desire to be   10
found in Christ; saith he, I reach forward toward the things that
are before; my conversation is in heaven, and flatly opposite to
them, whose God is their belly, who glory in their shame; and
who mind earthly things. *Brethren*, saith he, *be ye followers together
with me; and mark them that walk so*; Mark them; For what? For   15
persons that are to be received into fellowship and the choycest
communion of Saints. And indeed this is the safest way to judge
of the meetness of persons by. For take away the confession of
Faith and holyness; and what can distinguish a Christian from a
Turk? He that indeed receiveth faith, and that squareth his life   20
by the royal, perfect, moral precept; and that walketh there, in
the joy and peace of the holy Ghost; no man can reject him; he
cannot be a man if he object against him; not a man in Christ;
not a man in understanding. *The Law is not made for a righteous
man*; neither to debar him the communion of Saints if he desire   25
it, nor to cast him out if he were in. *But for the Lawless and
disobedient, for the ungodly and for sinners, for unholy and prophane:
For murtherers of fathers and for murtherers of mothers; for
manslayers, for whoremongers: for them that defile themselves with
mankind; for manstealers, for perjured persons; and if there be any 30
other thing contrary to sound doctrine, according to the glorious Gospell
which is committed to my trust.* 1 Tim, 1. 9, 10, 11. *Paul also*, when
he would leave an everlasting conviction upon the Ephesians
concerning his Faith and Holyness; treating first of the
sufficiency of Christs blood, and the grace of God to save us; he   35
adds, *I have coveted no mans Silver, or Gold, or Apparell*, he bringth
them to the moral precept, to prove the sincerity of his good
conversation by. *Acts* 20. 28. 32, 33. And when men have juggled

23 against] a-against   32 when] wen

what they can, and made never such a prattle about religion; yet if their greatest excellency, as to the visibility of their Saintship, lyeth in an outward conformity, to an outward circumstance in religion; their profession is not worth two mites. *Let us walk*
5 *honestly, as in the day, not in rioting, and drunkeness; not in chambering and wantonness; not in strife and envy; but put ye on the Lord Jesus Christ, and make no provision for the flesh, to fulfill the lusts thereof.* Rom. 13. 13, 14. And it is observable, That after the Apostle had in the 9th and 10th verses of this chapter told us,
10 that the moral precept is the rule of a good conversation; and exhorted us to make no provision for the flesh; he adds (these things provided) we may receive any that believe in Christ Jesus, unto communion with us; how weak soever and dark in circumstantialls; and chiefly designs the proof thereof, in the
15 remaining part of his Epistle. For he that is of sound Faith, and of conversation honest in the world; no man, however he may fail in circumstances, may lightly reproach or vilify him. And indeed such persons are the honour of Christian congregations. Indeed he is prejudiced, for want of light in those things about which he
20 is dark; as of Baptism or the like; but seeing that is not the initiating ordinance, or the visible character of a Saint; yea seeing it maketh no breach in a good and holy life; nor intrencheth upon any mans right but his own; and seeing his Faith may be effectual without it, and his life approved by the worst of his enemies; why
25 should his friends, while he keeps the Law, dishonour God by breaking of the same? *Speak not evil one of another brethren: he that speaketh evil of his brother, and judgeth his brother; speak evil of the Law and judgeth the Law: But if thou judge the Law thou are not a doer of the Law, but a judge.* Jam. 4. 11. He that is judged, must
30 needs fail somewhere in the apprehension of him that judgeth him, else why is he judged, But he must not fail in substance, for then he is worthy to be judged. 1 *Cor.* 5. 12. his failure is then in a circumstance, *for which he ought not to be judged.*

Object. But notwithstanding all that you have said: Water
35 baptism ought to go before Church-membership; shew me one in all the New Testament, that was received into fellowship without it.

Answ. 1. That Water-baptism hath formerly gone first is granted: But that it ought of necessity so to do, I never saw proof.

---

5 *drunkeness*] *drunkenss*　　　18 are the] *errata*; are

2. None ever received it without light going before, unless
they did play the Hypocrite: And besides no marvail though in
the primitive times it was so generally practised first, for the
unconverted themselves know, it belonged to the Disciples of
Jesus Christ. *Joh* 1. 24, 25, 26, 27. Yet that all that were received   5
into fellowship, were even then baptized first, would strain a
weak mans wit to prove it, if arguments were closely made upon
these three texts of holy scriptures (1 *Cor.* 1. 14, 15, 16 *Gal.* 37.
27. *Rom* 6. 3.) But I pass them, and say, If you can shew me the
Christian, that in the primitive times remained dark about it, I   10
will shew you the Christian that was received wthout it.

But should I grant more then can be proved; *viz.* That
Baptism were the initiating ordinance; and that it once did, as
circumcision of old, give a being of membership to the partakers;
yea set the case that men were forbidden then to enter into   15
fellowship without it: yet the case may so bee, that these
things notwithstanding, men might be received into fellowship
without it. All these things intailed to circumcision; That was the
initiating ordinance; that gave being of membership; that was it
without which it was positively commanded, none should be   20
received into fellowship. *Jos.* 5. Yet for all this more then six
hundred thousand were received into the Church without it; yea
received, and also retained there and that by *Moses* and *Joshua*,
even those to whom the Land was promised, when the
uncircumcised were cut off. But why then were they not   25
circumcised? Doubtless there was a reason; either they wanted
time, or opportunity, or instruments, or something. But they
could not render a bigger reason then this. *I have no light therein*:
which is the cause at this day that many a faithful man denyeth to
take up the ordinance of Baptism, But I say what ever the   30
hinderance was, it mattereth not; our brethren have a manifest
one, an invicible one, one that all the men on earth nor Angels in
heaven cannot remove; *For it is God that createth light*; and for
them to do it without light would but prove them unfaithfull to
themselves, and make them sinners against God; *For whatsoever*   35
is not of Faith is sin. Rom. 14. If therefore *Moses* and *Joshuah*
thought fit to communicate with six hundred thousand uncircumcised persons; when by the Law not one such ought to

2 no] on   28 render] *errata*; rnder

have been received among them; why may not I have communion,
the closest communion with visible Saints as afore described,
although they want light in, and so cannot submit to that, which
of God was never made the wall of division betwixt us. I shall
5 therefore hold communion with such.

First. Because the true visible Saint hath already subjected to
that which is better; even to the righteousness of God, which is
by Faith of Jesus Christ; by which he stands just before God; he
also hath made the most exact and strict rule under heaven, that
10 whereby he squares his life before men. He hath like precious
Faith with the best of Saints, and a conversation according to
light received, becoming the Gospell of Christ: He is therefore
to be received, received I say, not by thy light, not for that in
circumstances he jumpeth with thy opinion; but according to his
15 own Faith which he ought to keep to himself before God.
*Conscience I say, not thine own, but of the other; For why is my liberty
judged by another mans conscience?* 1 Cor. 10. 29. Some indeed do
object that what the Apostles wrote, they wrote to gathered
Churches and so to such as were baptized. And therefore the
20 arguments that are in the Epistles about things circumstantial,
respect not the case in hand. But I will tell such, that as to the
first part of their objection, they are utterly under a mistake. The
first to the *Corinthians*, The Epistle of *James*, both them of *Peter*,
and the first Epistle of *John*, were expressly written to all the
25 Godly, as well as particular Churches. Again; if Water-baptism,
as the circumstances with which the Churches were pestered of
old, trouble their peace, wound the consciences of the Godly;
dismember and break their fellowships, it is although an
ordinance for the present to be prudently shunned; for the
30 edification of the Church as I shall shew anon, is to be preferred
before it.

Secondly, and observe it; *One Spirit, one Hope, one Lord, one
Faith, one Baptism* (not of Water, for by one spirit are we all
Baptized into one body) one God and Father of all, who is above
35 all and through all, and in you all; is a sufficient rule for us to
hold communion by, & also to endeavour the maintaining that
communion, and to keep it in unity, within the bond of peace
against all attempts whatsoever. *Eph*. 4. 1. 6. 1 *Cor*. 12. 16.

15 keep to] *errata*; keep

Thirdly, I am bold therefore to have communion with such
Heb. 6. 2. Because they also have the doctrin of Baptisms: I say
the doctrins of them; For here you must note, I distinguish
between the doctrin and practise of Water-baptism; The Doctrin
being that which by the outward sign is presented to us, or which
by the outward circumstance of the act is preached to the
believer: *viz. The death of Christ; My death with Christ; also his
resurrection from the Dead, and mine with him to newness of life.* This
is the doctrin which Baptism preacheth, or that which by the
outward action is signifyed to the believing receiver. Now I say,
he that believeth in Jesus Christ; that richer and better then that,
viz. is dead to sin, and that lives to God by him, he hath the
heart, power and doctrine of Baptism: all then that he wanteth, is
but the sign, the shadow, or the outward circumstance thereof;
Nor yet is that despised, but forborn for want of light. The best
of Baptisms he hath; he is Baptized by that one spirit; he hath the
heart of Water-baptism, he wanteth only the outward shew,
which if he had would not prove him a truly visible Saint; it
would not tell me he had grace in his heart. It is no
Characteristical note to another, of my Sonship with God.
Indeed 'tis a sign to the person Baptized, and an help to his own
Faith; he should know by that circumstance, that he hath
received remission of sins; if his Faith be as true, as his being
Baptized is felt by him. But if for want of light, he partake not of
that sign, his Faith can see it in other things, exceeding great and
precious promises. Yea as I also have hinted already, if he appear
not a Brother before, he appeareth not a Brother by that, And
those that shall content themselves to make that the note of
visible Church-membership; I doubt make things not much
better, the note of their sonship with God.

Fourthly, I am bold to hold communion with visible Saints as
afore; because God hath communion with them; whose example
in the case, we are streightly commanded to follow. *Receive you one
another as Christ Jesus hath received you,* saith Paul *to the glory of*
*The Strongest
may sometimes be
out of the way.* *God.* Rom. 15. 7. Yea though they be Saints of opinions contrary
to you; though it goeth against the mind of them that are strong.
*We that are strong ought to bear the infirmities of the weak; and not to
please our selves.* What infirmityes? Those that are natural are
incident to all, they are infirmityes then that are sinfull, that

35 Rom. 15. 7] Rom. 15. 16.

cause a man for want of light, to erre in circumstantials; And the reason upon which he ground this admonition is, *that Christ pleased not himself; but as it is written, the reproaches of them that reproached thee, have fallen upon me.* You say, to have communion
5 with such weak brethren, reproacheth your opinions, and practise; Grant it, your dulness and deadness, and imperfections also reproach the holyness of God. If you say no, for Christ hath born our sins; The answer is still the same, Their sins also are fallen upon Christ; He then that hath taken away thy sins from
10 before the throne of God; hath taken away their shortness in conformity to an outward circumstance in religion. *Both your infirmityes are fallen upon Christ*; yea if notwithstanding thy great sins; thou standest by Christ compleat before the Throne of God; why may not thy Brother, notwithstanding his little ones,
15 stand compleat before thee in the Church.

Vain man! Think not by the streightness of thine order, in outward and bodily conformity, to outward and shadowish circumstances, that thy peace is maintained with God; for peace with God is by Faith in the blood of his cross; who hath born the
20 reproaches of you both. Wherefore he that hath communion with God for Christs sake, is as good and as worthy of the communion of Saints as thy self. He erreth in a circumstance, thou errest in a substance; who must bear these errors? Upon whom must these reproaches fall? *Phil.* 1. 10. Some of the things of God that
25 are excellent have not been approved by some of the Saints: What then? Must these for this be cast out of the Church? No, these reproaches by which the wisedom of heaven is reproached have fallen upon me, saith Christ. But to return; *God hath received him, Christ hath received him*, therefore do you receive
30 him. There is more solidity in this argument, *then if all the Churches of God had received him.* This receiving then, because it is set an example to the Church is such as must needs be visible to them; and is best described by that word which discovereth the visible Saint: Whoso therefore you can by the word, judge a
35 visible Saint, one that walketh with God; you may judge by the self same word that God hath received him. Now him that God receiveth and holdeth communion with, him you should receive and hold communion with. Will any say we cannot believe that God hath received any such as are Baptized? I will not suppose a
40 Brother so stupifyed; and therefore, to that I will not answer.

Receive him to the Glory of God; [To the Glory of God] is put in on purpose, to shew what dishonour they bring to God who despise to have communion with them; who yet they know have communion with God. For how doth this man or that Church glorify God, or count the wisdom and holyness of heaven beyond   5
them, when they refuse communion with them; *concerning whom, they are by the word convinced, that they have communion with God.*

Now the God of patience and consolation, grant you to be like minded one towards another, according to Christ Jesus. Rom. 15. 5.   10
By this word Patience, Paul insinuateth how many imperfections, the choycest Christians, do mingle their best performances with. And by this of consolation, how readily God overlooks, passeth by them and comforteth you notwithstanding. Now that this mind should be in Christians one to another; is manifest;   15
because Paul praies that it might be so. But this is an heavenly gift, and therefore must be fetched from thence. But let the patience of God, and the willingness of Christ to bear the reproaches of the weak, and the consolations that they have in God, notwithstanding, moderate your passions and put you upon   20
prayer, to be minded like Jesus Christ.

Fifthly, Because a failure in such a circumstance as Water doth not unchristian us; This must needs be granted, not onely from what was said before; but for that thousands of thousands that could not consent thereto, as we, have more gloriously, then   25
we are like to do, acquitted themselves and their Christianity before men, and are now with the innumerable company of Angels, and with spirits of just men made perfect: What is said of Eating or the contrary may as to this be said of Water baptism. Neither if I be Baptized, am I the better, neither if I be not, am I   30
the worse: Not the better before God; not the worse before men; still meaning as Paul doth, provided I walk according to my light with God: otherwise 'tis false; For if a man that seeth it to be his duty, shall despisingly neglect it; or if he that hath no Faith therein shall foolishly take it up; both these are for this the worse,   35
being convicted in themselves for transgressors. He therefore that doth it according to his light, doth well; and he that doth it not, or dare not do it for want of light doth not ill; for he

11 word] wotd   16 because] bcause   22 circumstance] circumstatce

approveth his heart to be sincere with God: he dare not do
anything but by light in the word. If therefore he be not by Grace
a partaker of light, in that circumstance which thou professest;
yet he is a partaker of that liberty and mercy by which thou
5 standest. He hath liberty to call God Father, as thou. And to
believe he shall be saved by Jesus: His Faith, as thine, hath
purifyed his heart: He is tender of the Glory of God as thou art:
and can claim by Grace an Interest in Heaven; which thou must
not do because of Water: Ye are both then Christians before
10 God and men without it: He that can let him preach to himself
by that: He that cannot let him preach to himself by the
promises; But yet let us rejoyce in God together; let us exalt his
name together, Indeed the Baptized can thank God for that, for
which another cannot; But may not he that is unbaptized thank
15 god for that which the baptized cannot? Wouldst thou be content
that I should judge thee, because thou canst not for my light
give thanks with me? Why then should he judge me for that I
cannot give thanks with him for his? *Let us not therefore judge one*
another any more: but judge this rather, that no man put a stumbling
20 *block, or occasion of offence in his Brothers way.* Rom. 14. 1. And
seeing the things wherein we exceed each other, are such as
neither make nor marre Christianity; let us love one another and
walk together by that glorious rule above specifyed, leaving each
other in all such circumstances to our own Master, to our own
25 Faith. *Who art thou that judgest another mans servant? To his own*
Master he standeth or falleth; yea he shall be holden up, for God is able
to make him stand. Rom. 14. 4.

Sixthly, I am therefore for holding communion thus, because
the edification of Souls in the Faith and holyness of the Gospell,
30 is of greater concernment, then an agreement in outward things;
I say, 'tis of greater concernment with us, and of far more profit
to our Brother; then our agreeing in, or contesting for the
business of Water-baptism. *Joh.* 16. 13. 1 *Cor.* 14, 26. 2 *Cor.* 10.
8. *chap.* 12. 19. *Eph.* 4. 12. 2 *Tim.* 3. 10, 17. 1 *Cor.* 8. 1. *chap.* 13.
35 1, 2. That the edification of the Soul, is of the greatest concern,
is out of measure evident: because heaven and eternal happiness
are so immediately concerned therein. Besides, this is that for
which Christ dyed, for which, the holy Ghost was given, yea for

35 of the Soul] *errata*; of Soul

which the Scriptures and the gifts of all the Godly are given to
the Church; yea and if gifts are not bent to this very work, the
persons are said to be proud or uncharitable that have them; and
stand but for cyphers or worse among the Churches of God.
Farther, Edification is that that cherisheth all grace, and maketh   5
the Christians quick and lively, and maketh sin lean and
dwindling, and filleth the mouth with thanksgiving to God. But
to contest with gracious men, with men that walk with God; to
shut such out of the Churches; because they will not sin against
their Souls, rendereth thee uncharitable, *Rom.* 14. 15. 20. *Thou*   10
seekest to destroy the work of God; thou beggetest contentions,
janglings, murmurings, and evil surmisings; thou ministrest
occasion for whisperings, back-bitings, slanders and the like,
rather then godly edifying; contrary to the whole current of the
scriptures and peace of all communityes. Let us therefore leave   15
off these contentions, and follow after things that make for
peace, *and things wherewith one may edify another.* Rom. 14. 19.
And know that the edification of the Church of God dependenth
not upon, neither is tyed to this or that circumstance. Especially
when there are in the hearts of the Godly; different perswasions   20
about it: then it becometh them in the wisedom of God, to take
more care for their peace and unity; then to widen or make large
their uncomfortable differences.

Although *Aaron* transgressed the Law, because he eat not the
sin offering of the people; yet seeing he could not do it with   25
satisfaction to his own conscience; *Moses* was content that he left
it undone. *Lev.* 10. 16–20.

Joshuah was so zealous against *Eldad* and *Medad*, for prophesying
in the camp; without first going to the Lord to the door of the
tabernacle, as they were commanded, that he desired *Moses* to   30
forbid them; *Num.* 11. 16: 26. but *Moses* calls his *zeal*, envy, and
praies to God for more such Prophets; knowing that although
they failed in a circumstance, they were right in that which was
better. The edification of the people in the camp was that which
pleased *Moses*.   35

In *Hezekiahs* time; Though the people came to the passover in
an undue manner; *and did eat it otherwise then it was written*; yet
the wise King would not forbid them; but rather admitted it,
knowing that their edification was of greater concern, then to
hold them to a circumstance or two. 2 *Chro*: 30. 13–27. Yea   40

God himself, did like the wisdom of the King, and healed, that
is, forgave the people at the prayer of *Hezekias*. And observe it,
notwithstanding this disorder, as to circumstances; the feast was
kept with great gladness; and the Levites and the priests praised
5 the Lord, day by day, singing with loud instruments unto the
Lord: yea there was not the like joy in *Jerusalem*, from the time of
Solomon unto that same time. What shall we say, all things must
give place to the profit of the people of God. Yea sometimes
Laws themselves, or their outward preservation; much more for
10 Godly edifying; When Christs disciples plucked the ears. of corn
on the Sabbath (no doubt for very hunger) and were rebuked by
the Pharisees for it, as for that which was unlawfull; How did
their Lord succour them? By excusing them, and rebuking their
adversaries. *Have ye not read, said he, what David did when he was*
15 *an hungred; and they that were with him, how he entred into the house*
of God, and did eat the shew-bread, which was not lawfull for him to
eat, neither for them that were with him, but for the Priests onely; or
have ye not read in the Law, how that on the Sabbath-day, the Priests
in the Temple prophaned the Sabbath and were blameless? Why
20 blameless? Because they did it in order to the edification of the
people. *Mat.* 12, 1. 6. If Laws and ordinances of old, have been
broken and the breach of them born with (when yet the
observance of outward things was more strictly commanded then
now) when the profit and edification of the people, came in
25 competition, how much more may not we have communion,
Church-communion, now Law where is transgressed thereby.

Seventhly, Therefore I am for holding communion thus,
because Love, which above all things we are commanded to put
on; is of much more worth then to break about Baptism; *Love is*
30 *also more discovered when it receiveth for the sake of Christ, and grace;*
then when it refuseth for want of Water. And observe it, as I have
also said before, this exhortation to Love is grounded upon the
putting on of the new creature; which new creature hath
swallowed up all distinctions, that have before been common
35 among the Churches. As I am a Jew, you are a Greek; I am
circumcised, you are not: I am free, you are bound. Because
Christ was all in all these, *Put on therefore,* saith he, (*as the elect of*
God, holy and beloved) *bowels of mercyes kindness, humbleness of*

36 circumcised] circumcicised

mind, long suffering, that is, with reference to the infirmities of the weak, *forbearing one another, and forgiving one another, If any man have a quarrel against any; even as Christ forgave you, so also do ye: And above all things put on charity, which is the bond of perfectness.* Col, 3. 8, 9, 10, 11, 12, 13, 14. Which forbearing and forgiving respecteth not onely private and personal injuries, but also errours in judgment about inclinations and destinctions tending to divisions; and separating upon the grounds laid down in v. 11th, which how little soever they now seem to us who are beyond them, were strong, and of weight to them who in that day were intangled with them. Some Saints then, were not free to preach to any but the Jews; denying the word of Life to the Gentiles, and contending with them who preferred it to them: which was a greater error then this of Baptism. *Act.* 11. 1, 2, 3: 19. But what should we do with such kind of Saints? Why love them still, forgive them, bear with them, and maintain Church communion with them. Why? Because they are new creatures, because they are Christ's; For these swallow up all distinctions. Farther, because they are elect and beloved of God. Divisions and distinctions are of shorter date then election; let not them therefore that are but momentary and hatcht in darkness, break that bond that is from everlasting. It is Love, not Baptism that discovereth us to the world to be Christs Disciples. It is Love that is the undoubted character of our interest in, and sonship with God: I mean when we Love as Saints, and desire communion with others, because they have fellowship with God the Father, and his Son Jesus Christ. 1 *Joh.* 1. 2. And now though the truth and sincerity of our Love to God, be then discovered when we keep his commandments, in Love to his name; yet we should remember again, that the two head and chief Commandments, are Faith in Jesus, and Love to the brethren: 1 *Joh.* 3. 23. So then he that pretendeth to Love, and yet seeks not the profit of his Brother in chief; he Loveth, but they are his own opinions and froward notions. *Jam.* 4. 11. *Rom.* 14. 21. *Love is the fulfilling of the Law*; but he fulfills it not who judgeth, and setteth at nought his Brother; that stumbleth, offendeth and maketh weak his Brother, and all for the sake of a circumstance, that to which he cannot consent, except he sin against his own soul, or Papist like, live by an implicite Faith. Love therefore is sometimes more seen and shewed, in

forbearing to urge and press what we know, then in publishing
and imposing. I could not saith *Paul,* (Love would not let me)
speak unto you as unto spiritual, but as unto carnal, even as unto Babes
in Christ: I have fed you with Milk and not with strong meat, for
5 *hitherto you have not been able to bear it; neither yet now are you able.*
1 Cor. 3. 1, 2. The Apostle considered not onely the knowledge
that he had in the mysteries of Christ; but the temper, the
growth, and strength of the Churches, and accordingly kept
back, or communicated to them, what might be for their profit.
10 *Act* 20. 18, 19, 20. So Christ, *I have many things to say unto you,*
but ye cannot bear them now. It may be some will count these old
and threadbare texts; but such must know, that the word of the
Lord must stand for ever. *Isa.* 40. 8. And I should dare to say to
such: if the best of thy new shifts, be to slight, and abuse old
15 Scriptures; It shewes thou art more fond of thy unwarrantable
opinion, then swift to hear, and ready to yield to the authority
that is unfallible. But to conclude this, when we attempt to force
our Brother beyond his light, or to break his heart with grief, to
thrust him beyond his Faith, or to bar him from his priviledge:
20 how can we say, I Love? What shall I say? To have fellowship one
with another for the sake of an outward circumstance, or to
make that the door to fellowship which God hath not; yea to
make that the including, excluding charter: The bounds, bar,
and rule of Communion, when by the word of the everlasting
25 testament there is no warrant for it (to speak charitably). If it be
not for want of Love, it is for want of knowledge in the mysteries
of the Kingdom of Christ. Strange! Take two Christians equal in
all points but this, nay let one go beyond the other far, for grace
and holyness; yet this circumstance of Water shall drown and
30 sweep away all his excellencies, not counting him worthy of that
reception, that with hand and heart shall be given a novice in
religion; because he consents to Water.

Eighthly, But for Gods people to divide into parties, or to shut
each other from Church-communion; though from greater
35 points, and upon higher pretences, then this of Water-baptism;
hath heretofore been counted carnal, and the actors herein babish
Christians: Paul and *Apollo, Cephas,* and *Christ* were doubtless
higher things then those about which we contend: yet when they
made divisions for them; *how sharply are they rebuked?* Are ye not
40 *Carnall, Carnall, Carnall?* For whereas there are among you,

envyings, strife, divisions, or factions: *are you not carnall*: 1 Cor.
1. 11, 12, chap. 3. 1, 2, 3, 4. While one saith I am of *Paul*, and
another I am of *Apollos; are you not carnall?* See therefore from
whence arise, all thy indeavours, zeal and labour to accomplish
divisions, among the Godly; Let *Paul* or *Cephas*, or Christ   5
himself be the burthen of thy song, yet the heart from whence
they flow *is carnall*, and thy actions, *discoveries of childishness.* But
doubtless when these contentions were among the Corinthians,
and one man vilifyed that another might be promoted; *a lift with*
a carnall Brother, was thought great wisedom to widen the breach. But   10
why should he be rebuked, that said he was for Christ? because
he was for him in opposition to his holy Apostles. Hence he
saith, *Is Christ divided*; or separate from his servants. Note
therefore that these divisions are deserted by the persons the
divisions were made about; Neither *Paul* nor *Apollos*, nor *Cephas*,   15
nor *Christ* is here. Let the cry be never so loud, Christ, order, the
rule, the command, or the like; Carnality is but the bottom, and
they are but babes that do it; their zeal is but a puffe, 1 *Cor*, 4. 6.
And observe it, the great division at Corinth, was helped forward
by Water-baptism: This the *Apostle* intimates by; *Were ye Baptized*   20
in the name of Paul? *Ah Brethren! Carnall Christians with outward*
circumstances, will if they be let alone, make sad work in the Churches
of Christ, against the spiritual growth of the same. But I thank God,
saith Paul, *that I Baptized none of you*, &c. Not, but that it was
then an ordinance of God, but they abused it, in making parties   25
thereby. I Baptized none of you, but *Crispus* and *Gaius, and the*
household of Stephanus; men of note among the Brethren, men of
good judgement, and reverenced by the rest; they can tell you I
intended not to make a party to my self thereby. *Besides I know not*
whether I Baptized any other. By this negligent relating, who were   30
Baptized by him; he sheweth that he made no such matter of
Baptism, as some in these dayes do; nay, that he made no matter
at all thereof, with respect to Church-communion; for if he
did not heed who himself had Baptized; he much less heeded,
who were Baptized by others; but if Baptism had been the   35
initiating or entering ordinance, and so appointed of God; no
doubt he had made more conscience thereof, then so lightly to
pass it over. *For Christ sent me not to Baptize, but to Preach the*
Gospel. The Gospel then may be effectually preached, and yet
Baptism neither administred nor mentioned. The Gospel being   40

good tidings to sinners, upon the account of free grace through Christ; but Baptism with things of like nature, are dutyes injoyned such a people who received the Gospel before: I speak not this, because I would teach men to break the least of the
5 Commandments of God; but to perswade my brethren of the Baptized way, not to hold too much thereupon; not to make it an essential of the Gospel of Christ, nor yet of communion of Saints. *He sent me not to Baptize*: These words are spoken with holy indignation against them that abuse this ordinance of
10 Christ. So when he speaketh of the Ministers themselves, which also they had abused; in his speaking, he as it were, trampleth upon them; as if they were nothing at all. *Who then is Paul? and who is Apollos?* He that planteth is not any thing; neither is he that watereth: *but God that giveth the increase*: 1 Cor. 3. 5: 7. Yet for all
15 this, the Ministers and their ministry are a glorious appointment of God in the World. Baptisme also is a holy ordinance, but when Sathan abuseth it, and wrencheth it out of its place; making that which was ordained of God, for the edification of believers; the only weapon to break in pieces, the love, the unity,
20 the concord of Saints; then *what is Baptism*; then *neither is Baptism any thing* And this is no new doctrine; For God by the mouth of his Prophets of old; cryed out against his own institutions, when abused by his people: *To what purpose is the multitude of your sacrifices to me? saith the Lord, I am full of burnt*
25 *offerings, of rams; and the fat of fed Beasts: I delight not in the blood of Bullocks, or of Lambs, or of he Goats: When you come to appear before me, Who hath required these things at your hands, to tread my Courts? Bring no more vain oblations, incense is an abominatien to me: The new Moons and the Sabbaths, and the calling of assemblyes, I cannot*
30 *away with; it is iniquity, even the solemn meeting. Your new Moons, and your appointed Feasts my Soul hateth, they are a trouble to me, my Soul hateth, I am even weary to bear them.* Isa. 1. 11, 12, 13, 14. And yet all these were his own appointments. But why then did he thus abhor them? Because they retained the evil of their
35 doings, and used them as they did other of his appointments. *viz. For strife and debate, and to strike with the fist of wickedness.* chap. 58. 4. Wherefore when that of God, that is great, is overweighed by that which is small; it is the wisedom of them that see it, to put load to the other end of the scale; untill the things thus abused,
40 poise in their own place. But to pass this, and proceed.

Ninthly, If we shall reject visible Saints by calling, Saints that have communion with God; that have received the Law, at the hand of Christ, that are of holy conversation among men; they desiring to have communion with us, as much as in us lyeth, we take from them their very priviledge, and the blessings to which they are born of God: For *Paul* saith, not only to the gathered Church at Corinth, but to all scattered Saints that in every place call upon the name of Lord: *That Jesus Christ is theirs, That Paul and Apollos, and the World, and Life, and Death, and all things are theirs*, because they are Christs, and Christ is Gods. But saith he, let no man glory in men, such as *Paul* and *Cephas*, though these were excellent: because this priviledge comes to you upon another bottom, even by Faith of Jesus Christ. *Drink you all of this*, is intailed to Faith, not Baptism: Nay Baptized persons may yet be excluded this; when he that discerneth the Lords body hath right, and priviledge to it. 1 *Cor.* 11. 28, 29. But to exclude Christians from Church communion, and to debar them their Heaven-born priviledges, for the want of that which yet God never made a wall of division between us.

1. This looks too like a *spirit of persecution*. Job. 19. 25, 26, 27, 28.

2. It respecteth more a *form, then the spirit*, and power of Godliness. 2 *Tim.* 3. 5.

3. This is to make Laws, where God hath made none, and to be wise above what is written; contrary to Gods word, and our own principles.

4. It is a directing of the Spirit of God.

5. It bindeth all mens Faith and light to mine opinion.

6. It taketh away the Childrens Bread.

7. It withholdeth from them the increase of Faith.

8. It tendeth to harden the hearts of the wicked.

9. It tendeth to make wicked the Hearts of weak Christians.

10. It setteth open a door to all temptations.

11. It tempteth the Divel to fall upon those that are alone, and have none to help them.

12. It is the Nursery of all vain janglings, backbitings, and strangenes among the Christians.

13. It occasioneth the World to reproach us.

14. It holdeth staggering consciences, in doubt of the right way of the Lord.

15. It giveth Occasion to many to turn aside to most dangerous heresies.

16. It abuseth the holy Scriptures; It wresteth Gods ordinances out of their place.

17. It is a Prop to Antichrist.

18. Shall I add, Is it not that which greatly prevailed to bring down these judgments, which at present we feel and groan under; I will dare to say, it was the cause thereof.

Tenthly, and Lastly: Bear with one word farther: What greater contempt can be thrown upon the Saints; then for their Brethren to cast them off, or to debar them Church-communion? Think you not that the World may groundly say, some great iniquity lyes hid in the skirts of your Brethren, when in truth the transgression is yet your own? But I say what can the Church do more to the sinner or open prophane? Civil commerce you will have with the worst, and what more have you with these? Perhaps you will say we can pray and Preach with these, and hold them Christians, Saints, and Godly. Well but let me ask you one word farther: Do you believe, that of very conscience, they cannot consent, as you, to that of Water-baptism? And that if they had light therein, they would as willingly do it as you? When then as I have shewed you our refusal to hold communion with them is without a ground from the word of God.

But can you commit your Soul to their Ministry, and joyne with them in Prayer; and yet not count them meet for other Gospel priviledges? I would know by what Scripture you do it? Perhaps you will say I commit not my Soul to their Ministry, only hear them occasionally for tryall. If this be all the respect thou hast for them and their Ministry, thou mayest have as much for the worst that pisseth against the Wall. But if thou canst hear them as Gods Ministers, and sit under their Ministry as Gods ordinance; then shew me where God hath such a Gospel Ministry, as that the persons Ministring, may not though desiring it, be admitted with you to the closest communion of Saints. But if thou sitest under their Ministry for fleshly politick ends, thou hearest the word like an Atheist, and art thy self, while thou judgest thy Brother, in the practise of the worst of men. But I say, where do you find this peicemeal communion with men that profess Faith and Holyness as you, and separation from the World.

If you object that my Principles lead me to have communion with all; I answer with all as afore described; if they will have communion with me.

Object. Then you may have communion with the members of Antichrist.

Answ. If there be a visible Saint yet remaining in that Church; let him come to us, and we will have communion with him.

Quest, What! Though he yet stand a member of that sinfull number, and profess himself one of them?

Answ. You suppose an impossibility; For it cannot be that at the same time, a man should visibly stand a member of two bodys, diametrically opposite one to another Wherefore it must be supposed, that he who professeth himself a member of a Church of Christ; must forthwith, nay before, forsake the Antichristian one. The which if he refuseth to do, it is evident he doth not sincerely desire to have fellowship with the Saints.

But he saith he cannot see that that company to which you stand opposite, and conclude Antichristian, is indeed the Antichristian Church.

· If so: he cannot desire to joyn with another, if he know them to be professedly, and directly opposite.

I hold therefore to what I said at first; That if there be any Saints in the Antichristian Church, my heart, and the door of our Congregation is open to receive them, into closest fellowship with us.

Object. But how if they yet retain some Antichristian principles?

Answ. If they be such as eat out the bowels of a Church, so soon as they are detected, he must either be kept out, while out, or cast out, if in: For it must be the prudence of every community, to preserve its own unity with peace and truth: The which the Churches of Christ may do; and yet as I have shewed already, receive such persons as differ upon the point of Water-baptism: For the doing or not doing of that, neither maketh nor marreth, the bowels or foundation of Church communion.

Object. But this is receiving for opinion sake; as before you said of us.

Answ. No, We receive him for the sake of Christ, and grace, and for our mutual edification in the Faith; and that we respect

28 either be] *errata*; be either be

not opinions, I mean in lesser matters, 'tis evident; for things
wherein we differ are no breach of communion among us; We let
every man have his own Faith in such things to himself before
God.

5   *I now come to a short Application.*

1, Keep a strict separation, I pray you, from communion with
the open prophane; and let no man use his liberty in Church
relation, as an occasion to the flesh; but in Love serve one
another; Looking diligently least any root of bitterness (any
10 poisonfull herb. *Deut.* 29. 18.) springing up trouble you, and
thereby many be defiled. And let those that before were reasons
for my separation; be motives to you to maintain the like: and
remember that when men have said what they can for a sinfull
mixture in the worship of God, the arm of the Lord is made bare
15 against it.

2. In the midst of your zeal for the Lord, remember that the
visible Saint is his; and is priviledged in all those spiritual things,
that you have in the word, and live in the practice of, and that he
is to partake thereof, according to his light therein. Quarrel not
20 with him about things that are circumstantial; but receive him in
the Lord as becometh Saints; if he will not have communion with
you, the neglect is his, not yours. But saith the open prophane;
Why cannot we be reckoned Saints also? We have been
Christened, we go to Church, we take the Communion. Poor
25 People! This will not do; for so long as in Life and Conversation
you appear to be open prophane; we cannot unless we sin,
receive you into our fellowship: For by your ungodly lives you
shew that you know not Christ; and while you are such by the
word, you are reputed but Beasts: Now then judge your selves, if
30 it be not a strange community that consisteth of men and Beasts:
Let Beasts be with the Beasts, you know your selves do so; you
receive not your Horse nor your Hog to your Table; you put
them in a room by themselves. Besides I have shewed you before,
that for many reasons we cannot have communion with you.
35   1. The Church of God must be Holy. *Lev.* 11. 44. *chap.* 19. 2.
chap. 20. 7. 1 *Pet.* 1. 15, 16. *Isa.* 26. 2. *Psa.* 128. 20. *Ezek.* 43. 12.
chap. 44. 9. *Isa.* 52. 11.

12 to you to maintain] *errata*; to you maintain

2. The example of the Churches of Christ before, hath been a community of visible Saints. *Rom.* 1. 7. 1 *Cor.* 1. 2. *Eph.* 1. 1, 2. *Col.* 1. 1. 1 *Thes. 1. 1,* 2. 2 *Thes.* 1. 1. Poor carnal man, there are many other reasons urged in this little book, that shew why we cannot have communion with thee: Not that we refuse of pride   5 or stoutness, or because we scorn you as men: No, we pity you, and pray to God for you; and could if you were converted, with joy receive you to fellowship with us: Did you never read in *Daniel, That Iron is not mixed with miry Clay?* Dan. 2. 43. No more can the Saints with you, in the worship of God, and fellowship of   10 the Gospel. When those you read of in the fourth of *Ezra,* attempted to joyn in Temple work with the children of the captivity; what said the children of *Judah?* you have nothing to do with us, to build an house to the Lord our God; but we our selves together will build unto the Lord God of *Israel. &c.*   15 *Ezra.* 4. 1, 2, 3.

I return now to those that are visible Saints by Calling, that stand at a distance one from another, upon the accounts before specifyed: Brethren: Close; Close; Be one as the Father and Christ is one.   20

1. This is the way to convince the World that you are Christs, and the Subjects of one Lord; whereas the contrary makes them doubt it. *Joh.* 13. 34, 35. *Joh.* 17. 23.

2. This is the way to increase Love; that Grace so much desired by some, and so little enjoyed by others. 2 *Cor.* 7. 14, 15.   25

3. This is the way to savour and taste the Spirit of God in each others experience; for which if you find it in truth you cannot but bless (if you be Saints) the name our Lord Jesus Christ. 1 *Thes.* 1. 2, 3, 4.

4. This is the way to increase knowledge, or to see more in   30 the word of God: for that may be known by two; that is not seen by one. *Isa.* 52. 8.

5. This is the way to remove secret jealousies, and murmurings one against the other; yea this is the way to prevent much sin, and greatly to frustrate that design of hell, *Prov.* 6. 16, 17, 18, 19.   35

6. This is the way to bring them out of the World into fellowship, that now stand off from our Gospel priviledges, for the sake of our vain janglings,

21 This is the] *errata*; This the

7. This is the way to make Antichrist shake, totter and tumble. *Isa* 11. 13, 14.

8. This is the way to leave *Babylon*, as an habitation for Divels only; and to make it an hold for foul Spirits, and a cage only for every unclean and hatefull bird.

9. This is the way to hasten the work of Christs Kingdom in the World; and to forward his coming to the eternal judgment.

10. And this is the way to obtain much of that Well done, Good and Faithfull Servant, when you stand before his face.

I beseech you Brethren suffer the word of exhortation; for I have written a Letter unto you in few words. *Heb.* 13. 22.

Finis.

DIFFERENCES IN JUDGMENT ABOUT WATER-BAPTISM, NO BAR TO COMMUNION

Differences in Judgment
ABOUT
VVater-Baptilm,
No Bar to *Communion*:
OR,
To Communicate with *Saints*, as *Saints*, proved lawful.

In ANSWER to a Book written by the *Baptists*, and published by Mr. *T. P.* and Mr. *W. K.* entituled, *Some serious Reflections on that part of Mr. Bunyan's Confession of Faith, touching Church-Communion with Unbaptized Believers.*

Wherein,
Their Objections and Arguments are Answered, and the Doctrine of Communion still Afferted and Vindicated.

Here is also Mr. *Henry Jeffe's* Judgment in the Case, fully declaring the Doctrine I have Afferted.

By *John Bunyan.*

Should not the multitude of words be answered? and should a man full of talk be justified? Should thy lyes make men hold their peace? and when thou mockest, shall no man make thee an answer? Job 11. 2, 3.
I am for Peace, but when I speak they are for War. Pfal. 120. 7.

London, Printed for John Wilkins, and are to be fold at his Shop in Exchange-Alley, next door to the Exchange-Coffee-House, over against the Royal-Exchange, 1673.

1, 6, 174.

Title-page of *Differences in Judgment About Water-Baptism, No Bar to Communion* (1673)

DIFFERENCES IN JUDGMENT ABOUT WATER-BAPTISM, NO BAR TO COMMUNION

Note on the Text

One edition of this work was published in Bunyan's lifetime. At least fifteen copies survive. The publisher was John Wilkins, whose shop was located in Exchange Alley 'by the Exchange-Coffee-House, over against the Royal-Exchange'. Wilkins was also the publisher of *History of the Administration of Cardinal Ximenes* (1670), and *Index Biblicus Multi-jugus* (second edition, 1672).[1]

Title-page: [within single rules] Differences in Judgment | ABOUT | Water-Baptism, | No Bar to *Communion*: | OR, | To Communicate with *Saints*, as *Saints*, | proved lawful. | In ANSWER to a Book written by the *Baptists*, | and published by Mr. *T. P.* and Mr. *W. K.* | entituled, *Some serious Reflections on that* | *part of Mr.* Bunyan's *Confession of Faith*, | *touching Church-Communion with* Unbaptized | *Believers.* | Wherein, | Their Objections and Arguments are Answered, and | the Doctrine of Communion still Asserted | and Vindicated. | Here is also Mr. *Henry Jesse's* Judgment in the Case, | fully declaring the Doctrine I have Asserted. | [rule] | By *John Bunyan.* | [rule] | *Should not the* *multitude of words be answered? and should a man* | *full of talk be justified? Should* *thy lyes make men hold their* | *peace? and when thou mockest, shall no man make thee* *an an-*|*swer?* Job. 11. 2, 3. | *I am for Peace, but when I speak they are for War.* Psal. 120. 7. | [rule] | *London*, Printed for *John Wilkins*, and are to be sold at his Shop | in Exchange-Alley, next door to the Exchange-Coffee-House, | over against the Royal-Exchange, 1673.

Collation: 8⁰, A⁸–H⁷; pp. 122+[4] = 126. Signature A1 is not printed, otherwise signatures are printed on the first four leaves. Page number 69 is misprinted 45 in the copies at William Andrews Clark Memorial Library, Los Angeles; J. Pierpont Morgan Library; Regents Park College, Oxford; Dr Williams's Library. The copy at Regents Park College, Oxford lacks H7.

Contents: A1ʳ title-page, A1ᵛ blank, A2 to the reader, A3ʳ–H5ᵛ text (G2ᵛ errata, G3ʳ–H5ᵛ Henry Jessey's judgment), H6ʳ–H7ʳ books printed and sold by John Wilkins. A double row of ornaments on A2ʳ is followed by 'Courteous | READER,'. A2ᵛ is signed '*John Bunyan.*' followed by a single rule. A double

---

[1] Plomer, 315.

row of ornaments on A3ʳ is followed by '*Differences in Judgment about* Wa-|ter-Baptism *No Bar to* Com-|munion.' A single row of ornaments on E5ʳ is followed by 'I come now to your *Fourteen | Arguments*, and shall im-|partially consider them.' A single row of ornaments on F7ʳ is followed by the catchwords 'I come' and a second single row of ornaments. A single row of ornaments on F7ᵛ is followed by '*I come now to your* Questions; | *which although they be mixed | with Gall, I will with patience see | if I can turn them into Food.*' A single rule on G2ᵛ is followed by 'ERRATA.' A single row of ornaments on G3ʳ is followed by a single rule and 'Here followeth Mr. | *Henry Jessey's* Judg-|ment upon the same | *Argument.*' A single rule on H5ᵛ is followed by '*FINIS.*' A single row of ornaments on H6ʳ is followed by '*Books Printed and are to be sold by* John | Wilkins, *at his Shop next door to the | Exchange* Coffee-house *in Exchange-|Alley, over against the* Royal-Ex-|change, *London.*' The conclusion of the list of books on H7ʳ is followed by a single row of ornaments, a single rule, eight blank lines, and a second single row of ornaments.

Running Titles: To the reader: 'To the Reader.' on A2ᵛ only. Text: '*Differences about Water-Baptism,* | *no Bar to Communion.*' None on A3ʳ. The '*n*' is omitted from *Communion* on B7ʳ, D7ʳ, and G7ʳ. List of books: '*Books sold by* John Wilkins.' on H6ᵛ and H7ʳ.

Catchwords (selected): A8ʳ her, D4ᵛ Exhor-, F3ʳ the, G1ʳ Quest. 5., H3ᵛ and.

Copies collated: Bodleian, Oxford; British Library; William Andrews Clark Memorial Library, Los Angeles; Elstow Moot Hall, Bedfordshire; Glasgow University; Huntington Library; J. Pierpont Morgan Library; Regents Park College, Oxford; John Rylands Library, University of Manchester; Folger Shakespeare Library; University of Texas, Austin; Union Theological Seminary Library, New York City; Williams College Library, Williamstown, Massachusetts; Dr Williams's Library. The copy at the Rosenbach Museum and Library, Philadelphia was missing and presumedly mis-shelved at the time of this collation.

The following text is based on the Bodleian copy.

Courteous

READER,

BE intreated to believe me, I had not set Pen to Paper about this Controversie, had we been let alone at quiet in our Christian Communion. But being assaulted for more than sixteen years; wherein the Brethren of the Baptized-way (as they had their opportunity) have sought to break us in pieces, meerly because we are not in their way all baptized first: I could not, I durst not, forbear to do a little, if it might be, to settle the Brethren, and to arm them against the attempts, which also of late they begin to revive upon us. That I deny the Ordinance of Baptism, or that I have placed one piece of an Argument against it, (though they feign it) is quite without colour of truth. All I say, is, That the Church of Christ hath not: Warrant to keep out of their Communion the Christian that is discovered to be a visible Saint by the Word, the Christian that walketh according to his Light with God. I will not make Reflections upon those unhandsom brands that my Brethren have laid upon me for this, as that I am a Machivilian, a man devilish, proud, insolent, presumptuous, and the like; neither will I say as they, The Lord rebuke thee; words fitter to be spoke to the Devil, then a Brother. But Reader, read and compare, lay aside Prejudice and Judge. What Mr. Kiffin hath done in the matter I forgive, and love him never the worse, but must stand by my Principles because they are peaceable, godly, profitable, and such as tend to the Edification of my Brother, and as I believe will be justified in the day of Judgment.

I have also here presented thee with the Opinion of Mr. Henry Jesse, in the Case, which providentially I met with, as I was coming to London to put my Papers to the Press, and that it was his Judgment is Asserted to me, known many years since to some of the Baptists, to whom it was sent, but never yet Answered; and will yet be Attested if need shall require. Farewel.

Thine in all Christian Service,
according to my Light and Power,
John Bunyan.

Differences in Judgment about Water-Baptism *no Bar to* Communion.

SIR.

YOur seemingly serious reflections upon that part of my plain-hearted Confession of Faith, which rendreth a Reason of my freedom to Communicate with those of the Saints and Faithful, who differ from me about *Water-Baptism*, I have *read*, and *considered*, and have *weighed* them so well as my *rank* and abilities will admit me to do. But finding yours (if I mistake not) *far short* of a candid Replication; I thought convenient, not only to tell you of those *impertinencies* everywhere scattered up and down in your Book; but also, that in *my* simple opinion, your *rigid* and Church-disquieting-Principles are not fit for any Age and state of the Church.

But before I enter the body of your Book, give me leave a little to discourse you about your Preamble to the same, wherein are *two* miscarriages unworthy *your* pretended seriousness, because void of love, and humility.

The first is, In that you closely disdain my Person, because of my *low* descent among men, stigmatizing me for a Person of THAT Rank, that *need* not to be heeded, or attended unto, *Page* 1.

Answ. What it is that gives a man reverence with you, I know not; but for certain, *He that despiseth the Poor, reproacheth his Maker:* yet a *poor man is better than a lyar.* To have gay-cloathing, or gold-rings, or the Persons that wear them in admiration; or to be partial in your judgment, or respects, for the sake, or upon the account of flesh and blood, doubtless convicteth you to be of the Law a transgressor, and not without partiality, &c. in the midst of your seeming sanctity.

Again you say: *I had not medled with the Controversie at all, had I found any of parts that would divert themselves to take notice of YOU.* *pag.* 2.

A. What need you, before you have shewed one syllable of a reasonable Argument in opposition to what I Assert, thus

trample my Person, my Gifts, and Grace (have I any) so
disdainfully under your feet? What a kind of a YOU am I? And

Read
Psal. 1. 1, 2.

why is MY Rank so mean, that the *most* gracious and godly
among you, may not duly and soberly consider of what I have
said? Was it not the art of the false Apostles of old to say thus? to   5
bespatter a man, that his Doctrine might be disregarded. Is not

2 Cor. 10. 10.

this the Carpenter? and, *His bodily presence is weak and
contemptible,* did not use to be in the mouths of the Saints; for

Joh. 3. 8.

they knew the *Wind blew where it listed.* Neither is it high birth,
worldly breeding, or wealth; but electing love, grace, and wisdom   10

Jam. 3. 17.

that comes from Heaven, that those who strive for strictness of
order in the things, and Kingdom of Christ, should have in
regard, and esteem. Need I reade you a Lecture? *Hath not God*

1 Cor. 1. 27, 28.

*chosen the foolish, the weak, the base, yea and even things that are not,
to bring to nought things that are?* Why then do you despise my   15
rank, my *state,* and *quality* in the World?

As for my Confession of Faith, which you also secretly
despise, *pag.* 1. If it be good, and godly, *why may it not be accepted*?
If I have spoken evil, *bear witness of the evil*; but if well, why
smitest thou me? If you, and the Brethren of your way, did think   20
it convenient to shew to the World what you held; if perhaps by
that means you might escape the Prison: why might not I, after
above 11 years indurance there, give the World a view of my
Faith and Practice; if peradventure, wrong Thoughts, and false
Judgments of me, might by that means be abated, and removed.   25

But you suggest; I did it, *because I was so willing to be known in
the World by my SINGULAR Faith, and Practice.*

How singular my Faith and Practice is, may be better known
to you hereafter: but that I did it for a popular applause and
fame, as your words seem to bear (for they proceed from a   30
taunting Spirit) that will be known to you better in the day of

Luke 12. 1, 2, 3,
4.

God, when your evil surmizes of your Brother, and my designs in
writing my Book, will be published upon the house-tops.

And even *now*, before I go any further, I will give you a touch
of the Reason of my publishing that part thereof which you so   35
hotly oppose.

It was because of those continual Assaults that the rigid
Brethren of your way, made, not only upon this Congregation, to
rent it; but also upon many others about us: if peradventure they
might break us in pieces, and draw from us Disciples after them.   40

Assaults (I say) upon this Congregation by times, for no less than these sixteen or eighteen years: Yea, my self they have sent for, and endeavoured to perswade me to break Communion with my Brethren; also with many others they have often tampered, if haply their seeds of Division might take. Neither did they altogether fail of their purpose, for some they did rent and dismember from us; but none but those, of whom now they begin to be ashamed. The Judgment of God so following their design, that the Persons which then they prevailed upon, are now a stink, and reproach to Religion. Neither were these Spirits content with that discord they did sow among us, but they proceeded to seize upon others. But to pass these: The wild, and unsound Positions they have urged to maintain their Practice, would be too large here to insert.

Now, Sir, to settle the Brethren (the Brethren of our Community) and to prevent such disorders among others, was the cause of my publishing my Papers: and considering my Concern in the House of God, I could do no less than to give them warning, *That every man might deliver his Soul.*

You proceed, saying, *It is my liberty, as well as others into whose hands it falls, to weigh what you have said in Truths ballance, and if it be found too light, to reject it whether you will or no.*

Answ. Do but grant me, without *mocking* of me, the liberty you desire to take, and God helping me, I desire no more to shift for my self among you.

As to your saying, that I *proudly* and *imperiously* insult, because I say they are *Babes and Carnal, that attempt to break the Peace and Communion of Churches, though upon better pretences than Water.* You must know I am still of that mind, and shall be so long as I see the Effects that follow, *viz. The breach of Love, taking off Christians from the more weighty things of God; and to make them quarrel and have heart-burnings one against another.*

Where you are pleased to charge me with *Raging*, for laying those Eighteen particular Crimes to the charge of SUCH who *exclude Christians from Church-Communion, and debar them their Heaven-born Priviledges, for the want of that, which yet God never made, the Wall of Division between us.* (pag. 116).

I say, when you can prove, That God hath made Water-Baptism that Wall, and that the stress of the after Eighteen Charges lye wholly and only in that; then you may time enough

call my language such as wanteth Charity: but I question though
that was granted, whether your saying, I *RAGE*, will be justified
in the day of Judgment.

My *great noise* (as you call it) *about an initiating Ordinance*,
you say, *you shall take no notice of.* pag. 3.   5

Answ. 1. Although you do not, I must: For If Baptism be not
that, but another; and if visible Saints may enter into Fellowship
by that other, and are no where forbidden so to do, because they
have not light into Water-Baptism: it is of weight to be
considered by me; yea, and of others too who are unprejudiced.   10

2. How ignorant you are of such as hold it the initiating
Ordinance I know not: nor how long you have been of that
perswasion I know not. This I know, that men of your own Party,
as serious, godly, and it may be more learned than your self, have
within less than this twelve-month urged it. Mr. *D.* in my   15
hearing, did from *Rom.* 6. 1, 2. in the Meeting in *Lothbury* affirm
it: Also my much esteemed Friend Mr. *D. A.* did twice in a
Conference with me Assert it.

3. But whatever you say, whether for, or against, 'tis no
matter; for while you deny it to be the entering Ordinance, you   20
account it the Wall, Bar, Bolt, and Door; even that which
must separate between the righteous and the righteous; nay, you
make want of Light therein, a ground to exclude the most Godly
your Communion, when every Novice in Religion shall be
received into your bosom, and be of esteem with you because he   25
hath (and from what ground God knows) submitted to Water-
Baptism.

I am glad that in *page* 4. you conclude with me what is the
initating Ordinance: but withal, give me leave to correct, as I
think, one extravagant expression of yours.   30

You say, *'Tis CONSENT on all hands and NOTHING else, that
makes them Members of particular Churches, and not Faith and
Baptism.* pag. 4.

You might have stopped at [and nothing else] you need not in
particular have *rejected* Faith: your first Error was bad enough,   35
what? *NOTHING* else but *Consent?* What? not so much as a
respect to the *matter* or *end?* Why then are not all the
Communities of all the High-way-men in the Land, truly
Constituted Churches of Christ; unless you can prove that they
hold together, *but not by consent.*   40

What? Consent and nothing else? But why do YOU throw out
FAITH? why, *I* throw out Baptism; which because you cannot as
to the case in hand *fetch in again*, therefore OUT must Faith go
too. Your action is much like that Harlots, that stood to be   1 King. 3.
5   judged by *Solomon*, who because her own Child was dead, would
have her Neighbours killed also. Faith (Sir) both in the
Profession and Confession of it, is of immediate and also
absolute concern, even in the very act of the Churches
reception, of this or another Member. Throw out Faith, and
10 there is no such thing as a Christian, neither visible nor invisible:
You ought to receive no man, but upon a comfortable satisfaction
to the Church, that you are now receiving a Believer. Faith,
whether it be savingly there or no, is the great Argument with the
Church in receiving any: we receive not men as men, but the
15 man immediately under that supposition; *He hath Faith, he is a*
Christian. Sir, Consent, simply without Faith, makes no man a
Member of the Church of God; because then would a Church
not cease to be a Church, whoever they received among them.
Yea, by his Assertion you have justified the Church of *Rome* it
20 self, to be to this day both good, and godly, unless you can prove
that they did at first, and do now receive their unbelieving
Members, without their own Consent.

The Church hath no such Liberty to receive men without
respect to Faith; yea Faith and Holiness, must be the Essentials,
25 or Basis, upon, and for the sake of which you receive them:
Holiness (I say) yet not such as is circumstantial, but that which
is such in the very heart of it: Pray you in your next therefore
word it better, lest while you slight and trample upon me, you
stand before all blame-worthy your self.
30 The Scriptures you speak of, I did not in my first (*pag.* 68.)
produce to shew persons unbaptized might hold Communion
with the Church (though I am fully convinced they may) but to
shew, that knowledge of those Persons, of their Faith and
Holiness in general, ought first to be shewed to the Church,
35 before she can lawfully receive them, *Acts* 9. 25, 26, 27. 1 *Cor.*
16. 10. 2 *Cor.* 8. 23.

As to my Answer to a Question (*pag.* 70.) which you have at
pag. 5. of yours corrupted, and then abused: I tell you again,
That a discovery of the Faith and Holiness, and a Declaration of

26 Holiness] Hoiness

the willingness of a Person to subject himself to the Laws and the
Government of Christ in his Church, is a ground sufficient to
receive such a Member.

But you descant; *Is Baptism none of the Laws of Christ?*

Answ. It is none of those Laws, neither any part of them, that   5
the Church, as a Church, should shew her Obedience by. For
albeit that Baptism be given by Christ our Lord to the Church,
yet not for them to worship him by as a Church. Shew me what
Church-Ordinance it is; and when, or where the Church, as a
Church is to practise it, as one of those Laws and Appointments   10
that he hath commanded his Church to shew to him her
Obedience by.

Again, That submitting to Water-Baptism, is a sign or note,
that was ever required by any of the Primitive Churches, of him
that would hold Fellowship with them; or that it infuseth such   15
Grace and Holiness into those that submit thereto, as to
capacitate them for such a Priviledge; or that they did
acknowledge it a sign thereof, I find not in all the Bible.

I find not (as I told you in my first) that Baptism is a sign to
any, but the Person that is baptized. The Church hath her   20
satisfaction of the Person, from better proof, *Col.* 2. 12. *Rom.* 6.
1, 2, 3, 4. 1 *Cor.* 15. 29. *Acts* 2. 38. & 22. 16. 1 Pet. 3. 21.

I told you also, That Baptism makes thee no Member of the
Church, neither doth it make thee a visible Saint; *It giveth thee,*
therefore, neither right to, nor being of Membership at all. Why, Sir, 25
did you not Answer these things? but slip them with others, as if
you were unconcerned; troubling your Reader with such kind of
insinuations, as must needs be unsavoury to godly ears.

You make the Moral Law none of Christs, but *Moses*'s; not the
Sons, but the Servants: and tell me, because I plead for Faith,   30
and Holiness, *according to Moral Duties Gospellized* (they are my
words, *pag.* 79.) whereby we ought to judge of the fitness of
Members; that therefore *Moses* is more beholding to me than
Christ. *pag.* 6.

Sir, Know you not yet, that a difference is to be put betwixt   35
those Rules that discover the Essentials of Holiness, and those
that in themselves are not such; and that that of Faith and the
Moral Law is the one, and Baptism, &c. the other?

Is not Love to God, abhorrence of Idols, to forbear
Blaspheming, to honour our Parents, to do no Murther, to   40

forbear Theft, not to bear False witness, nor Covet, &c. are not (I say) these the Precepts of the Lord Jesus, because delivered by *Moses*? Or, are these such as may better be broken, than for want of light to forbear Baptism with Water? Or, doth a man while he
5 liveth in the neglect of these, and in the mean time bustle about those you call Gospell-Commands, most honour Christ, or best fit himself for Fellowship with the Saints? Need I tell you, That the Faith of Christ, with the Ten Commandments, are as much now Gospel-Commands as Baptism; and ought to be in as much,
10 and far more respect with the holy ones than that, or other the like.

Yea, shall I tell you; That Baptism will neither admit a man into Fellowship, nor keep him there, if he be a transgressor, of a Moral Precept; and that a man who believeth in Jesus, and
15 fulfilleth the Royal Law, doth more glorifie God, and honour Religion in the World, than he that keepeth (if there were so many) ten thousand figurative Laws.

As to those Commands that respect God's Instituted Worship in a Church, as a Church, I have told you that Baptism is none of
20 them, and you have been driven to confess it: The Church then must first look to Faith, then to good Living according to the Ten Commandments; after that she must respect those Appointments of our Lord Jesus, that respects her outward order and discipline, and then she walks as becomes her, sinning if she
25 neglecteth either; sinning if she over-valueth either.

But why did you not Answer those Texts I produced for the strengthening of my Argument, *viz. Rom.* 14. 18. *Deut.* 23. 47. *Jam.* 2. 8.–12. 1 *Cor.* 9. 21. *&* 5. 9, 10, 11. *Gal.* 6. 15, 16. *Phil.* 3. 1 *Tim.* 1. 9, 10, 11. *Acts* 20. 28, 32. *Rom.* 13. 13. *Jam.* 4. 11.
30 1 *Cor.* 5. 12.

Deal fairly; Answer those Texts, with the Argument made upon them; and when you have after a godly manner done that, you may the more boldly condemn.

You tell me, That in *page* 93 of mine, I say, *None ever received*
35 *Baptism without light therein.*

What if I did? (as I did not) but you grant it; And now I will ask you, and pray deal fairly in your Answer, May a man be a visible Saint without light therein; May he have a good Conscience without light therein? And seeing that Baptism is none of the
40 worship that Christ Instituted in his Church for them to practise

Pag. 40. *of your Book*

as a Church, must he be kept dark about all other things concerning the Worship of God in his Church, until he receive light therein?

You have answered already, *pag.* 7. *That ought to be ashamed, and to repent of that abomination* (their sprinkling) *BEFORE they come to have a sight of the pattern of the House of God, the goings in and the comings in thereof,* Ezek. 43. 10, 11.

But, Sir, where do you find that want of Light in Water-Baptism, or because a man hath been Sprinkled, that he is to be kept dark in all other Temple-Institutions, till he be ashamed and repent of that? Pray produce the Texts, for *Ezekiel* helps you nothing: He speaks *only* of the Pattern of the *HOUSE*, the goings *out*, and comings *in* thereof. As for the coming *IN*, you have already confessed, That Baptism is not the entering Ordinance. And as for the Worship that Christ hath Instituted in his Church, as a Church, I say (and you also have said it *page* 40) Baptism is none of the Forms thereof, none of the Ordinances thereof, none of the Laws thereof: for Baptism is, as to the Practice of it, that which is without the Church, without the House of God: Then by your own Text, if a man do repent him of his Christening in his Childhood, he may be received into Fellowship without submitting to Baptism: but I will not strain you too far.

You add, *Is it a Persons Light that giveth being to a Precept?*

Answ. Who said it? Yet it's his Light and Faith about it, that can make him to do it acceptably.

You ask again, *Suppose men plead want of Light in other Commands?*

Answ. If they be not such, the forbearance of which, discapacitates him of Membership, he may yet be received to Fellowship.

But what if a man want Light in the Supper? pag. 7.

Answ. There is more to be said in that case than in the other; for that is a part of that Worship which Christ hath Instituted for his Church, to be Conversant in as a Church; presenting them as such, with their Communion with their Head, and with one another as Members of him. *The Cup of blessing which we bless, is it not the Communion of the Blood of Christ? The Bread which we break, is it not the Communion of the Body of Christ? For we being many are*

29 discapacitates] discapaciates

one Bread, and one Body; for we are all partakers of that one Bread, 1
Cor. 10. 16, 17. Wherefore this being a Duty incumbent on the
Church, as a Church; and on every Member of that Body as
such, they are obliged in that case more closely to deal with the
5 Members, than in that wherein they are not SO concerned; and
with which as such, they have NOTHING to do. No man
baptizeth by virtue of his Office in the Church; no man is
baptized by virtue of his Membership there.

But what if a man want Light in his Duty to the Poor? pag. 8.
10 *Answ.* If he doth, God must give it him; I mean to know his
Duty as a Church-Member. Now I will add, But what if he that
can give a shilling, giveth nothing? I suppose all that the Church
can do in that case, is but to warn, to exhort, and charge him, and
to shew him his Duty; and if he neglect, to shew him, *That he that*
15 *soweth sparingly, shall not reap plentifully,* 1 Cor. 9. 6. But to cut a
man off for this, as you forwardly urge, *pag.* 8. would argue that
Church (at least I think so) a little too bold with so high and
weighty a censure. I plead not here for the *Churle,* but seek to
allay your heat: And should it be granted that such deserve as
20 you would have it, this makes no matter to the case in hand.

Now whereas you suggest, *That Moral Evils are but sins against
men,* pag. 8. You are too much unadvised; The Moral Evil (as
you call it) whether you respect the breach of the first or second
Table, is first and immediately a sin against God; and more
25 *insufferable,* yea and *damnable,* than for a man for want of Light to
forbear either Baptism or the Lord's Supper.

But say you, *We have now found an Advocate for Sin against
GOD, in the breach of one of HIS holy Commands?*

Answ. As if none of the Moral Precepts were HIS, But, Sir,
30 who have I pleaded for, in the denyal of any one Ordinance of
God? Yea, or for their neglect of it either? What I say, is but that
men *must* have *Light,* that they may not do in *darkness,* or *Papist-
like, live by an implicite Faith.*

But I see you put no difference, between an open breach of
35 the Law, and a forbearing that which to him is doubtful. But I
will suppose a case; There is a man wants Light in Baptism, yet
by his Neighbour is pressed to it: he saith he seeth it not to be his
Duty; the other saith, he sins if he doth it not: Now seeing
whatsoever is not of Faith, is Sin; what should this man do? If you · Rom. 14.
40 say, Let him use the means: I say so too. But what, if when he

hath used it, he still continueth dark about it; what will you
advise him now? If you bid him wait, do you not encourage him
to live in sin, as much as I do? Nay, and seeing you will not let
him for want of Light in that, obey God in other his Institutions,
what is it, but to say, Seeing you live for want of Light in the   5
neglect of Baptism, we will make you, while you continue so, live
(though quite against your Light) in the breach of all the rest;
And where you are Commanded *thus*, you may shew the place
when you find it.

Now where you urge, that you are one of them that say, *The*   10
Epistles were writ to particular Churches, and so serve nothing at all
for our kind of Communion: Urging further, *That it will be difficult*
for me to prove, that they were also directed to particular Saints.

Answ. I wish there were nothing harder that were good for me
to do.   15

But what should be the reason that our Author, with others of
his Opinion, should *stickle* so hard to prove all the Epistles were
wrote to particular Churches? Why, because those Members
were, as they think, every one baptized; and so the Epistles from
which we fetch our Arguments for the Love and Concord of   20
Saints, to be only proper to themselves. But if this be true, there
is virtue indeed, and more than ever I dreamed of, in partaking of
Water-Baptism: For if that shall take away the Epistles, and
consequently the whole Bible, from all that are not baptized;
then are the other Churches, and also particular Saints, in a very   25
deplorable condition. For he asketh me very devoutly, *Whether*
any unbaptized Persons were concerned in these Epistles? pag. 9. But
why would they take from us the Holy Scriptures? Verily, that we
might have nought to justifie our practice withal: For if the
Scriptures belong only to baptized Believers, they then belong   30
not to the rest; and in truth, if they could perswade us to yield
them this grant, we should but sorrily justifie our practice. But I
would ask these men, *If the Word of God came out from them? or if it*
came to them only? Or, whether Christ hath not given his *whole*
Word to every one that believeth, whether they be baptized, or in,   35
or out of Church Fellowship? *Joh*. 17. Or, whether every Saint in
some sort, hath not the keyes of the Kingdom of Heaven, which
are the Scriptures and their Power?

Would to God they had learnt more modesty, than thus to
take from all others, and appropriate to themselves, and that for   40

Pag. 9.

Joh. 17. 14
1 Cor. 14. 36.

the sake of their observing a Circumstance in Religion, *so high*, and glorious a Priviledge.

But we will come a little to proof: What Church will this Author find in *Rome*, that time the Epistle was sent to the Brethren there, besides that Church that was in *Aquila*'s house, although many more Saints were then in the City? Yea, the Apostle in his salutation at the beginning, imbraceth them *only* as Brethren, without the least intimation of their being gathered into Fellowship; *To all that be at Rome, beloved of God, called to be Saints, Grace to you, &c.* Chap. 1. 7. To *all* there, to *all* in that City, beloved of God, and that are Converted to the Lord Jesus Christ. A Church there was in *Aquila*'s house, and that there were many more Saints besides is (and that by the Text) as manifest. Besides, considering the Rules that are given them in the 14 and 15 Chapters about their receiving one another, doth yet strongly suggest to me, that they were not yet in fellowship, but as it were now about it, when *Paul* wrote his Epistle to them.

The first Epistle written to *Corinth*, was also wrote to *all them that in every place called upon the Name of the Lord Jesus Christ*, *Chap.* 1. 2. But it will be hard work for our Author to make it manifest, that *none* in those dayes *did call on the Name of our Lord*, but those that were *first* baptized.

The second Epistle also, was, not only written to the Church at *Corinth*, but also *to all the Saints which were in all Achaia.* To the *Galatians* and *Thessalonians* indeed, his salutation was only to the Churches there: but the three Epistles before were as well to *all other*, as also that to the *Ephesians*, *Philippians*, and *Colossians*, in which the *Faithful*, and *Saints* in Christ Jesus were also every one comprehended. Besides, To what particular Church was the Epistle to the *Hebrews* wrote? or the Epistle of *James*? both those of *Peter*, and the first of *John*? Nay, that of *John* was wrote to some at that time out of Fellowship, *that they might have fellowship with the Church*, Chap. 1. 1, 2, 3, 4. So that these Brethren must not have all the Scriptures: we have then a like priviledge with all Saints, to use the Scriptures for our godly edifying, and to defend our selves thereby, from the assaults of those that would make spoyl of us. But to pass this, and come to the next.

You object for that I said, *If Water-Baptism (as the Circumstances with which the Church was pestred of old) trouble the Peace, and wound the Consciences of the Godly, dismember and break their*

Rom. 16. 5, *&c.*

2 Cor. 1. 1.

Fellowships; it is, although an Ordinance, for the present prudently to
be shunned. (pag. 86).

At this (as I said) you object (*pag.* 10, 11.) and say, *Did I ever*
find Baptism a Pest or Plague to Churches? And did ever God send an
Ordinance to be a Pest and Plague to his People?

I answer; I said not that God did send it for any such end at all:
God's Ordinances are none of this, in themselves; nor if used as,
and for the end for which God sent them. But yet both Baptism,
and the Supper of the Lord, have (by being wrested out of their
place) been a great affliction to the Godly both in this and other
Ages. What say you to breaking of Bread, which the Devil, by
abusing, made an Engine in the hand of *Papists* to burn, starve,
hang-and-draw thousands? What say you to *John* of *Leyden*?
What work did he make by the abuse of the Ordinance of Water-
Baptism? And I wish this Age had not given cause, through the
Church-renting-Spirits that some are possessed with, to make
complaint of this matter; who have also had for their Engine the
Baptism with Water: Yea, your self Sir, so far as I can perceive,
could you get but the opportunity; your self (I say) under
pretence of this innocent Ordinance, as you term it, would not
stick to make in-roads, and out-roads too, in all the Churches,
that suit not your fancy, in the Land. For you have already been
bold to affirm, *That all those that have baptized Infants, ought to be*
ashamed and repent, before they be shewed the Pattern of the House:
And what is this but to threaten, that could you have your will of
them, you would quickly take from them their present Church-
priviledges, and let them see nothing thereof, till those qualifications, especially subjection to Water-Baptism, was found to
attend each of them.

As to the Persons you speak of, *Who have rent Churches in*
pieces, by making Preaching by Method, Doctrine, Reason and Use,
to be Antichristian; Or, because they could not have other
Ministrations performed after their fancies (*pag.* 11, 12.) *the*
imprudence of such with your selves, hath been heart-breaking to
many a gracious Soul; an high occasion, of stumbling to the
weak, and a reproach to the wayes of the Lord. That it may be
prudently shunned, I referred you then for proof, to what should
be offered after: but at this you cry out, and so pass it.

And now *Reader,* although this Author hath thus objected
against *some* passages in this my first Argument for Communion

with Persons unbaptized; yet the *body* of my Argument he
misseth, and passeth over, as thing not worth the Answering;
whether because he forgot, or because he was conscious to
himself, that he knew not what to do therewith, I will not now
5 determine.

1. I effectually prove, *That Baptism is not the initiating
Ordinance.* pag. 71.–75.

2. I prove, *That though it was, yet the case may so fall out, that
Members might be received without it.* pag. 82, 83.

10 3. I prove, *That Baptism makes no man a visible Saint, nor giveth
any a right to Church-Fellowship.* pag. 76.

4. I prove, *That Faith, and a Life becoming the Law of the Ten
Commandments, should be the chief and most solid Argument with
true Churches to receive Saints to Fellowship.*

15 5. I prove, *That Circumcision in the Flesh, which was the entring
Ordinance of old, was a Type of Circumcision in the heart, &c.* p. 79,
80.

These things, with others, our Author letteth pass; although in
the proof of them abideth the strength of this first Argument; to
20 which I must intreat him in his next, to cast his eye, and give fair
Answer; as also to the Scriptures on which each are built, or he
must suffer me to say, I am abused. Further, I make a question
upon three Scriptures, Whether all the Saints, even in the
Primitive times, were baptized with Water? to which also he
25 answereth nothing; whereas he ought to have done it, if he will
take in hand to Confute. (The Scriptures are, 1 *Cor.* 1. 14, 15,
16. *Rom.* 6. 3. *Gal.* 3. 27.) Yet were they effectually answered, my
Argument is Nothing weakened.

You come to my second Argument, drawn from *Eph.* 4. 4, 5, 6.
30 Upon which a little more now to inlarge, and then to take notice
of your *Objection.*

The Apostle then in that Fourth of the *Ephesians,* exhorteth
the Church there, with *all lowliness, and meekness, with long-
suffering, and forbearing one another, to ENDEAVOUR to keep the
35 Unity of the SPIRIT in the bond of PEACE,* vers. 2, 3. This done,
he presents them with such Arguments, as might fasten his
Exhortation to purpose upon them.

The first is, Because the *Body* is *ONE; There is one Body*;
therefore they should not divide: For if the Church of Christ be
40 a *Body,* there ought not to be a rent or Schism among them.

1. Cor. 12.
22, 23, 24. 25,
26.

2. His second Argument is, There is *one Spirit*, or one
quickning Principle by which the Body is made to live: for having
Asserted before that Christ hath indeed a Body, it was meet that
he shewed also, that this Body hath life, and motion. Now that
life, being none other, than that nourishment, or Spirit of life,   5
from which the *whole Body fitly joyned together, and compact, by that
which every joynt supplyeth, according to the effectual working of the
measure in every part, maketh increase of the body, to the edifying of it
self in love*, Eph. 4. 16. Now this Spirit, being first, and chiefly, in
the Head, therefore none other but those that hold the Head can   10
have this nourishment ministred to them: Besides, This is the Spirit
that knits the Body together, & makes it increase with the
increase of God, *Col.* 2. 16. *This* is the *Unity* of the *Spirit* which
he before exhorts them to keep.

3. The third Argument is, Because their *Hope* is also but *one*.   15
Even as you are called (saith he) *in one Hope of your calling*: As who
should say, My Brethren, if you are called with one calling, if
your Hope, both as to the Grace of Hope, and also the Object,
be *but one*: if you hope for *one* Heaven, and for *one* Eternal Life;
then maintain *that Unity* of the Spirit, and Hope, while here, in   20
love, and the *bond of peace.*

4. The fourth Argument is, *There is one Lord*, or Husband, or
Prince, to whom this Church belongs: Therefore if we have
Husbands but *one*, Lord, and Prince but one, let us not rent into
many Parties, as if we had many Husbands, Lords, and Princes,   25
to govern us, as his Wife, his House, and Kingdom. *Is Christ
divided?*

1 Cor. 1.

5. The fifth Argument is, *There is one Faith*, by which we all
stand justified by *one* Lord Jesus Christ; *one Faith* by which we
escape the Wrath of God; *one Faith* by which only they that have   30
it are blessed; yea, seeing there is but *one Faith*, by which we are
all put into *one way* of Salvation, let us hold together as such.

6. The sixth Argument, *There is one Baptism.*
Now we are come to the pinch, *viz.* Whether it be that of
Water, or no? which I must positively deny.   35

1. Because Water-Baptism hath nothing to do in a Church, as
a Church; it neither bringeth us into the Church, nor is any part
of our Worship when we come there; how then can the Peace
and Unity of the Church depend upon Water-Baptism? Besides,
he saith expresly, It is the *Unity of the Spirit*, (not Water), that is   40

here intended: and the Arguments brought to inforce it, are such as wholly and immediately relate to the Duty of the Church, as a Church.

2. Further, That other Text, that treateth of our being *baptized into a body*, saith expresly it is done by the Spirit; *For by one Spirit we are all baptized into one body*, 1 Cor. 12. 16. Here is the Church presented as under the notion of a *Body*; here is a Baptism mentioned, by which they are brought, or initiated into this Body: Now that this is the Baptism of Water, is utterly against the words of the Text; *For by one spirit are we all baptized into one body*: besides, if the Baptism here be of Water, then is it the initiating Ordinance; but the contrary I have proved, and this Author stands by my Doctrine. So then, the Baptism here, respecting the Church as a Body, and Water having nothing to do to enter men into the Church, nor to command them to practise it as a Church, in order to their Peace, or Communion, or respecting the Worship of God as such: And (I say again) the Baptism in the sixth Argument, being urged precisely for no other purpose, but with respect to the Churches peace as a Body; it must needs be THAT Baptism, by virtue of which, they were initiated, and joyned together in one: and that Baptism being only that which the Spirit executeth; this therefore is that one Baptism.

7. The other Argument is also effectual; There is *one God and Father of all, who is above all, and through all, and in you all.* If we are *one Body*; if to it there be but *one Spirit*; if we have but *one Hope, one Faith*, and be all baptized by *one Spirit* into that *one* Body; and if we have but *one Lord, one God*, and he in every *one* of us; let us be also *one*: and let them that are thus qualified, both *joyn* together, and *hold* in *one*.

But our Author against this, objecteth, That, *now I imploy my Pen against every man; and give the lye to all Expositors, for they hold this one Baptism, to be none other than that of Water.* pag. 13.

Answ. What if I should also send you to Answer those *Expositors* that expound *certain* Scriptures for *Infant-Baptism*, and that by *them* brand us for *Anabaptists*; must this drive you from your belief of the Truth? *Expositors* I reverence, but must *live by mine own Faith*: God hath no where bound himself to *them* more than to *others*, with respect to the revelation of his Mind in his Word.

(margin notes) 1 Cor. 12. 13. Vers. 6. Hab. 2. 4.

But it becomes not you to run thus to Expositors, who are, as to your notions in many things, but of yesterday: *To the Law, and to the Testimony*: For out of the mouth of Babes the Lord hath ordained strength.

But you bid me tell you, *What I mean by Spirit-Baptism*?   5

Answ. Sir, you mistake me, I treat not here of our being baptized with the Spirit, with respect to its coming from Heaven into us; but of that act of the Spirit, when come, *which baptizeth us into a Body, or Church*: It is one thing to be baptized *with* the Spirit in the first sense; and another to be baptized *by* it in the   10
sense I treat of: for the Spirit to come upon me, is one thing; and for that when come, to implant, imbody, or baptize me into the body of Christ, is another.

Your Question therefore is grounded on a mistake, both of my Judgment, and the words of the Apostle. Wherefore thus I soon   15
put an end to your Objections (*pag.* 14.) For the Spirit to come down upon me *is one thing*; and for the Spirit to baptize, or implant me into the *Church, is another*: for to be possessed with the Spirit, is *one thing*; and to be led by that Spirit, is *another*. I conclude then; Seeing the Argument taken from that one   20
Baptism, respecteth Church-Fellowship properly; and seeing Water-Baptism medleth not with it as such; it is the other, even, that in 1 *Cor.* 12. 16. that is here intended, and no other.

But you add, *If nothing but extraordinary Gifts are called the baptism of the Spirit in a strict sense; then that baptism,* 1 Cor. 12.   25
must be Water-baptism, as well as that in the Ephesians.

Hold: You make your Conclusions before you have cause; First prove that in the *Ephesians* to be meant of Water-baptism, and that the Baptism in 1 *Cor.* 12, 16. is the Baptism you would have it; and then conclude my Argument void.   30

That it is the Baptism of the Holy Ghost according to the common notion, *I say not*; for you to *assert* it is the Baptism of Water, *gives the lye to the Text*: But that it is an act of the Holy ghost, baptizing the Saints *into a Body*, or Church, you will hardly be able to make the contrary appear to be truth.   35

But behold, while here you would have this to be Baptism with Water, how you contradict and condemn your own Notion: You say Water-baptism is not the *entering* Ordinance; yet the Baptism here is such as baptizeth us *into* a Body: Wherefore before you say next time that this in 1 *Cor.* 12. 16. is meant of Water-   40 baptism; affirm, that Water-baptism is the *initiating* or *entering* Ordinance, that your Opinion and Doctrine may hang better together.

We come to my third Argument; *Which is to prove, It is lawful to*
5 *hold Church-Communion with the godly sincere Believer, though he hath not been baptized with Water, because he hath the DOCTRINE of Baptisms,* Heb. 6. Which *Doctrine* I distinguish from the *Practice* of it; the *Doctrine* being that which by the outward-sign is presented to us; or which by the outward-circumstance of the act
10 is preached to the Believer, *viz.* the Death of Christ, my death with Christ; also his Resurrection from the dead, and mine with him to newness of life. *This our Author calleth one of the strangest Paradoxes that he hath LIGHTLY observed.*

Answ. How *light* he is in his Observation of things, I know not:
15 This I am sure, the Apostle makes mention of the *Doctrine* of Baptism; Now that the *Doctrine* of a man, or Ordinance, is the signification of what is Preached, is apparent to very sense. What is Christ's Doctrine, *Paul*'s Doctrine, Scripture-Doctrine, but the Truth couched under words that are spoken? So the
20 Doctrine of Baptism, yea and the Doctrine of the Lord's Supper, are those Truths or Mysteries that such Ordinances preach unto us. And that the *Doctrine* of Baptism in this sense, is the great end for which that, and the Lord's Supper was instituted, is apparent from all the Scriptures: it is that which the Apostle
25 seeketh for in that eminent sixth of the *Romans, Know you not that so many of us as were baptized into Jesus Christ, were baptized into his Death? Therefore we are buried with him by Baptism, that like as Christ was raised from the Dead by the Glory of the Father; so we should walk in newness of Life. For if we have been planted together in*
30 *the likeness of his Death, we shall be also in the likeness of his Resurrection,* Rom. 6. 3, 4, 5. What is here discoursed, but the Doctrine of, or that which Baptism teacheth; with an intimation, that that was the chief, for the sake of which that Shadow was Instituted; as also that they that have the *Doctrine,* or that which is
35 signified *thereby,* they only must reign with Christ.

Again, This is that which he seeketh for among the *Corinthians; If the dead rise not at all,* saith he; *why then were you baptized for the dead?* 1 Cor. 15. 22. Why then were you baptized? what did Baptism teach you? What *Doctrine* did it preach to you?
40 Further, *Buried with him in Baptism, wherein also you are risen*

*again with him, through the Faith of the operation of God, who
raised him from the dead.* What is here in chief asserted, but the
Doctrine only which Water-baptism preacheth? with an intimation,
that they, and they only, are the saved of the Lord, that have heard,
received, and that live in this Doctrine, *Col.* 2. 12, 13.   5

The same may be said of the Lord's Supper, it also hath its
Doctrine. But against this our Author objecteth, saying, *That this
is called the Doctrine of Baptism, I am yet to learn.*

Answ. Your ignorance of the Truth makes it not an Error: But
I pray you, what is the *Doctrine* of Baptism, if not that which   10
Baptism teacheth, even that which is signified thereby? As that is
the Doctrine of Christ, and the Scriptures; which he and they
teach as the mind of God.

But you say, *I took the Doctrine of Baptism to be the Command
that a Believer should be baptised, for such ends as the Gospel*   15
expresseth.

Answ. To assert that a figurative Ordinance is of God, is one
thing; but the *Doctrinal* signification of that Ordinance is
another: A man may preach the Command, yet none of the
Doctrine which Baptism preacheth. The *Doctrine* lyeth not in the   20
Command, but the mystery discovered to Faith, by the act.

You object, *If the Resurrection be the Doctrine of Baptism, why
doth the Apostle make that, and the Doctrine of Baptism, things
distinct, in* Heb. 6.

Answ. The Resurrection simply considered, is not the   25
Doctrine of Baptism, but Christ's, and mine by him. Besides,
there is more in it than the Mystery of this Resurrection; there is
my death first, and then my rising with him.

But you add, *Under the Law, all the Sacrifices of that
Dispensation, with their Sabbaths, were Types of that Christ, who was*   30
*the substance of all those Ceremonies. If any of them then that professed
Faith in the Messias to come, should upon scruples, or want of
pretended Light, neglect the whole, or part of that Typical Worship;
why may not a man say of them, as this Advocate of the Practice under
Debate, they had the richer and better Sacrifice.*   35

Answ. First, That the Brethren which refuse to be baptized, as
you and I would have them, refuse it for want of *pretended* Light,
becomes you not to imagine, unless your boldness will lead you
to judge, that *all* men want *sincerity*, that come not up to *our*
judgment. Their Conscience may be better than either *yours* or   40

mine; yet God, for purposes best known to himself, may forbear
to give them conviction of their Duty in this particular. But what?
Because they are not baptized; have they not Jesus Christ? Or,
must we now be afraid to say Christ is *better* than *Water-/baptism*?
5 Yea, God himself for the *sake* of this *better thing*, hath suffered in
his Church a *suspension* of some of his Ordinances, yet owned
them for his truly Constituted Congregation. What say you to the
Church in the Wilderness? *I touched you with it in my first*, but
perceive you listed not to meddle therewith. That Church
10 received Members, the way which was not prescribed by, but
directly against the revealed Mind of God; yet stood a true
Church, their Members true Members; also that Church in that
state, was such before whom, among whom, and to whom, God
continually made known himself to be their God, and owned
15 them for his peculiar treasure.

And now I am faln upon it, let me a little inlarge: This
Church, according to the then Instituted Worship of God, had
Circumcision for their entering-Ordinance, *Gen.* 17. 13, 14.
without which it was unlawful to receive any into Fellowship with
20 them: yea, he that without it was received, was to be cut off, and
cast out again. Further; As to the Passeover, the Uncircumcized
was utterly forbidden to eate it, *Exod.* 12. Now if our Brethren
had as express prohibition to justifie their groundless Opinion, as
here is to exclude the Uncircumcised from the Communion of
25 the Church and the Passeover; (I say) if they could find it
written, *No Unbaptized Person shall enter, no Unbaptized Person
shall eat of the Supper*; what a *noise* would they make about it? But
yet the *Reader* observe, that although Circumcision was the
entering-Ordinance, and our Author saith Baptism is not; yea,
30 though this Church was expresly forbidden to receive the
Uncircumcised (and we have not a syllable now to forbid the
Unbaptized) yet this Church received Members without, and
otherwise than by this entering-Ordinance. They also admitted
them to the Passeover; yea, entertained, retained, and held
35 Communion with them so long as forty years without it. I say,
again, That the number of this sort of Communicants was not so
few as six hundred thousand. Moreover, to these Uncircumcised
was the Land of *Canaan* given, yea, a possession of part thereof
before they were Circumcised; but the old Circumcised ones
40 might not enter therein. I am the larger in this, because our

Author hath over-look'd my first mention thereof. And now I
ask, What was the reason that God *continued* his Presence with
this Church notwithstanding *this* transgression? Was it not
because they had that *richer* and *better* thing, *the Lord Jesus Christ?*
For they did all eat of that spiritual Bread, and drank of that spiritual   5
Rock which followed them, and that Rock was Christ, 1 Cor. 10. I
confess I find them under rebukes and judgments in the
Wilderness, and that they were *many* times threatned to be
destroyed; but yet I find not so much as *one* check for their
receiving of Members Uncircumcised. Further, In the New   10
Testament where we have a *Catalogue* of their *sins*; and also of
their punishment for them; we find not a word about Circumcision,
nor the *smallest* intimation of the *least* rebuke for neglecting the
entering-Ordinance, 1 *Cor.* 10. 5, 10. I will therefore say of
them, as I have also said of my Brethren, *They had the richer and*   15
better thing.

But you object, *That this putteth the whole of God's Instituted*
Worship both under the Law and Gospel, to the highest uncertainties,
p. 17.

Answ. This putteth our Opposers out of their road, and   20
quencheth the flame of their unwarrantable zeal. For if the
entering-Ordinance, if the Ordinance without which no man
might be added to the Church, was laid aside for forty years; yea,
if more than six hundred thousand did Communicate with them
without it: I say again, If they did it, and held Communion with   25
God, that notwithstanding; yea, and had not (that we read of) all
that time, one small check for so doing; why may not we now
enter Communion, hold Communion, maintain Communion,
Church-Communion, without being judged, and condemned by
you? because we cannot for want of Light be all baptized before;   30
especially considering Baptism makes no man a Saint, is not the
entering-Ordinance, is no part of the Worship of God injoyned
the Church as a Church. To conclude, Although we receive
Members unbaptized, we leave not God's Instituted Worship at
uncertainties, especially what he hath commanded us as his   35
Church; we only profess our want of Light in some things; but
see no Word to warrant the forbearance of our Duty in all, for
want of perswasion in one.

You object, *I call Baptism a Circumstance, a shew, an outward-*
shew, I NICK-NAME it.   40

Answ. Deep reproof! But why did you not shew me my evil in thus calling it, when opposed to the Substance, and the thing signified? Is it the Substance, *is it the thing signified*? And why may not I give it the Name of *a Shew*; when you call it a symbole, and compare it to a Gentleman's Livery? *pag.* 52.

But you say, I call it *an OUTWARD shew.*

Answ. Is it an *Inward* one? What is it?

It is a Command?

Answ. But doth that install it in that place and dignity, that was never intended for it?

You object further, *They cannot have the Doctrine of Baptism that understand not our way of administring it.* pag. 18.

This is your mistake, both of the *Doctrin* and *Thing* it self. But if you will not SCORN to take NOTICE of me, I advise you again to consider, That a man may find Baptism to be Commanded, may be informed who ought to administer it: may also know the proper Subject: and that the manner of baptizing is Dipping; and may desire to practise it because it is Commanded, and yet know *nothing* of what Water-baptism preacheth; or of the Mystery baptism sheweth to Faith. But that the *Doctrine* of Baptism is not the Practice of it, not the outward act, but the thing signified; and that every Believer hath that, must argue you more than too bold to deny it.

But say you, *Who taught you to divide betwixt Christ and his Precepts, that you word it at such a rate?* That he that hath the one, &c.

Answ. To say nothing of Faith, and the Word: verily Reason it self teacheth it. For if Christ be my *Righteousness*, and not Water; if Christ be my *Advocate*, and not Water; if there be that good and blessedness in Christ, that is not in Water; then is Jesus Christ better than Water; and also in these to be eternally divided from Water; unless we will make them Co-Saviours, Co-Advocates, and such as are equally good, and profitable to men.

But say you, *I thought that he that hath Christ, had an orderly right to all Christ's Promises and Precepts; and that the Precepts of Christ, are part of the riches that a Believer hath in and by Christ.*

Answ. A Believer hath more in Christ, then either Promise or Precept; but all Believers know not all things, that of God are given to them by Christ. But must not they use, and enjoy what they know, because they know not all? Or must they neglect the weightier matters, because they want Mint, and Annise, and Commin? Your pretended orderly right is your fancy; there is not a syllable in the whole Bible, that bids a Christian to forbear his Duty in other things, because he wanteth (as you term it) the symbole, or Water-baptism.

But say you, *He that despiseth his Birth-right of Ordinances, our Church-priviledges, will be found to be a prophane Person, as Esau, in God's account.*

Baptism is not the Priviledge of a Church, as such. But what? are they all *ES All'S* indeed? Must we go to Hell, and be damned for want of Faith in Water-baptism? And take notice, I do not plead for a *despising* of Baptism, but a bearing with our Brother, that *cannot* do it for *want* of *Light*. The *best* of Baptism he hath, *viz.* the signification thereof; he wanteth only the outward *shew*, which if he *had*, would *not* prove him a truly *visible* Saint; it would not tell *me* he had the Grace of God in *his* heart; it is no Characteristical note to another of *my* Sonship with God.

But why did you *not* Answer these parts of my Argument? Why did you only cavil at words? which if they had been left out, the Argument yet stands good. *He that is not baptized, if yet a true Believer, hath the Doctrine of Baptism; yea, he ought to have it before he be Convicted, it is his duty to be baptized, or else he playeth the Hypocrite. There is therefore no difference between that Believer that is, and he that is not yet baptized with Water; but only his going down into the Water, there to perform an outward Ceremony of the Substance which he hath already; which yet he is not Commanded to do with respect to Membership with the Church; but to obtain by that further understanding of his Priviledge by Christ, which before he made Profession of, and that as a visible Believer.*

But to come to my fourth Argument, which you so *tenderly* touch as if it *burnt* your fingers: *I am bold* (say I) *to have Communion with visible Saints as before, because God hath Communion with them, whose example in the case we are strictly* commanded to follow. *Receive ye one another, as Christ Jesus hath received you, to the glory of God.* Yea, though they be Saints in Opinion contrary to you, or I. *We that are strong, ought to bear the infirmities of the weak, and not to please our selves.* Infirmities that are *Sinful*: for they that are *Natural*, are incident to all. Infirmities therefore they are, that for want of Light, cause a Man to err in

Rom. 15. 7.

Rom. 15. 1.

Circumstantials: And the reason upon which *Paul* groundeth this admonition is; *For Christ pleased not himself, but as it is written, the* Vers. 3. *reproaches of them that reproached thee are fallen upon me.*

5   You say to this, pag. 20. *That it is Paul's direction to the Church at* Rome *how to receive their Brethren Church-Members,* pag. 20.

I answer.

1. What? are not the poor Saints now in this City? are not they concerned in these instructions? or is not the Church by these 10 words at all directed how to carry it to those that were not yet in fellowship? A bold Assertion! but grounded upon nothing, but that *you would have it so.*

2. But how will you prove that there was a Church, a rightly constituted Church at *Rome*, besides that in *Aquila's* house? 15 *Chap.* 16. Neither doth this Epistle, nor any other in the whole Book of God affirm it. Besides, since *Paul* in this last Chapter saluteth the Church, as in this Mans house, but the other only as particular Saints, it giveth farther ground of Conviction to you, that those others were not as yet imbodyed in such a fellowship.

20   3. But suppose there was another Church besides; it doth not therefore follow, that the Apostle exhorteth them only to receive persons already in fellowship; *but him*, even every *him, that there* Rom. 14. 1. *was weak in the Faith, but not to doubtful disputations.*

4. Suppose again, The *receiving* here exhorted to, be such as 25 you would have it; yet the *Rule* by which they are directed to do it, is that by which we perceive *that Christ hath received them*: But Christ did not receive them by Baptism, but as given to him by the Father: Him therefore concerning whom we are convinced, that he by the Father is given to Christ, *Him should we receive.*

30   5. But what need I grant you that which cannot be proved? yet if you could prove it, it availeth nothing at all; because you may not, cannot, ought not to dare to limit the Exhortation to receiving of one another into each others affections only; and not also receiving Saints into Communion.

35   But you object: *To make God's receiving the Rule of our receiving, in all cases will not hold.* pag. 21.

Answ. Keep to the thing Man: If it hold in the case in hand, it is enough, the which you have not denied. And that it holds thus, is plain, because commanded. But let the Reader know, that your 40 putting in that way of his receiving which is invisible to us, is but

an unhandsome stradling over my Argument, which treateth only
of a visible receiving; such as is manifest to the Church: This you
knew, but sought by evading, to turn the Reader from
considering the strength of this my Argument. *The receiving then*
(said I, p. 29.) *because it is set an example to the Church, is such as*   5
must needs be visible unto them; and is best discovered by that word
that describeth the visible Saint: Whoso then you can judg a visible
Saint, one that walketh with God, you may, nay ought to judg by the
same Word, God hath received him. Now him that God receiveth, him
should you receive. But will any object; they cannot believe that   10
God receiveth the unbaptized Saints? I will not suppose you so
much stupified, and therefore shall make no answer. But you
seem to be much offended, because I said, *Vain Man! Think not*
by the straightness of thine Order in outward, and bodily conformity to
outward and shadowish Circumstances, that thy peace is maintained   15
with God?

But why so much offended at this?

Because, you intend by this the Brethren of the Baptized way.

A. If they be *vain Men,* and set up their *OWN* Order; how
straight soever they make it, they are worthy to be reproved: *If*   20

Jer. 8. 9.   *they have rejected the Word of the Lord, what wisdom is in them.* And
as you suggest the first, I affirm the second. But if you would be
justified in excluding those, with whom yet you see God hath
Communion, because they yet see not a shadow with you;
ɔroduce the Scripture for such Order, that we may believe it is   25
the Order of God: But deal fairly, lest we shew your nakedness,
and others see your shame.

You tell me of the *Order of the Colossians, Chap.* 2. 5. but if you
can prove that that Church refused to hold Communion with
that Saint whom they knew to be received by Christ, and held   30
Communion with him, or that none but those that are baptized
are received by, and hold Communion with him, then you justifie
your Order. In the mean while the whole of mine Argument
stands firm against you; *You must have Communion with visible*
Saints, because God hath Communion with them, whose Example in   35
the Case we are strictly Commanded to follow.

But you ask me, *If outward and bodily Conformity be become a*
crime? pag. 23.

Answ. I no where said it: But know that to glorifie God with
our bodies, respecteth chiefly far higher and more weighty things   40

than that of Water-baptism, *Whatsoever is not of Faith is sin*; and   Rom. 14.
to set up an Ordinance, though an Ordinance of God, that by it
the Churches may be pull'd in pieces, or the truly visible Saints
excluded Communion with their Brethren; I say again, To make
5 Water-baptism a bar and division betwixt Saint and Saint, every-
whit otherwise gracious and holy alike: This is *like fasting for
strife, and debate, and to smite with the fist of wickedness*; and is not
to be found within the whole Bible, but is wholly an order of your
own devising. As to the Peace you make an Objection about (*pag.*
10 23.) you have granted me what I intended; and now I add
further, That for Church-peace to be founded in Baptism, or   Eph. 4. 31, 32.
any other external Rite, not having to do with the Church as a   Phil. 2. 1, 2, 3.
Church, is poor Peace indeed: Church-peace is founded in
blood; and love to each other for Jesus sake; bearing with, and
15 forbearing one another, in all things Circumstantial, that
concern not Church-worship as such: And in my other I have
proved that Baptism is not such, and therefore ought not to be
urged to make rents and divisions among Brethren.

But you ask, *Is my peace maintained in a way of disobedience? and
20 conclude if it be, you fear it is false.* pag. 24.

A. If the *first* were true, you need not to *doubt* of the *second*; but
it may be thought he hath little to say in the Controversie, who is
forced to stuff out his Papers, *with such needless prattles as these.*

My fifth Argument is, *That a failure in such a Circumstance as
25 Water-baptism, doth not un-Christian us; This* you are compelled
to grant, *pag.* 25. And I conclude with your words, Persons ought
to be Christians before, visible Christians; such as any Congregation in the Land may receive to Communion with
themselves, because God hath shewed us that he hath received
30 them. *Receive him to the Glory of God*: [To the Glory of God] is
put on purpose, to shew what dishonour they bring to him, who
despise to have Communion with such, whom they know do
maintain Communion with God. I say again, How doth this
Man, or that Church glorifie God, or count the Wisdom and
35 Holiness of Heaven beyond them, when they refuse Communion
with them, concerning whom yet they are convinced, that they
have Communion with God.

But my Argument you have not denied; nor medled with the
Conclusion at all; which is, *That therefore, even because a failure
40 here, doth not un-Christian us, doth not make us insincere*; and I add,

Doth not lay us open to any revealed judgment or displeasure of God;
(if it doth, shew where) *therefore it should not, it ought not to make
us obnoxious to the displeasure of the Church of God.*

But you say, *I rank Gospel-Precepts, with Old-Testament
abrogated Ceremonies.* pag. 25.

Answ. You should have given your *Reader* my words, that he
might have judged from my own mouth: I said then (speaking
before of Christianity *it self*, pag. 94.) *that thousands of thousands
that could not Consent to Water, as we, are now with the innumerable
company of Angels, and the Spirits of just men made perfect.* What was
said of Eating, or the contrary, may *as to this* be said of Water-
baptism; Neither if I be baptized, am I the better? neither if I be
not, am I the worse? not the better before God, not the worse
before Men; still meaning as *Paul*, Provided I walk according to
my Light with God; otherwise 'tis false. For if a man that seeth it
to be his Duty, shall despisingly neglect it; or if he that hath not
Faith about it, shall foolishly take it up: both these, are for this
the worse; I mean, as to their own sense, being convicted in
themselves, as transgressors. He therefore that doth it according
to his Light, doth well; and he that doth it not, for want of Light,
doth not ill; for he approveth his heart to be sincere with God,
even by that his forbearance. And I tell you again, It is no where
recorded, that this man is under any revealed threatning of God,
for his not being baptized with Water, he not having Light
therein, but is admitted through his Grace to as many Promises
as you. If therefore he be not a partaker of that Circumstance, yet
he is of that Liberty, and Mercy, by which you stand with God.

But that I practise Instituted Worship, upon the same account
as *Paul* did Circumcision, and shaving, is too bold for you to
presume to imagine. What? Because I will not suffer Water to
carry away the Epistles from the Christians; and because I will
not let Water-baptism be the Rule, the Door, the Bolt, the Bar,
the Wall of Division between the Righteous, & the Righteous;
must I therefore be judged to be a Man without Conscience to
the Worship of Jesus Christ? The Lord deliver me from
Supersititous, and Idolatrous thoughts about any the Ordinances
of Christ, and of God. But my fifth Argument standeth against
you untouched; you have not denyed, much less confuted the
least syllable thereof.

4 But] Bnt

You tell me my sixth Argument is, *Edification.*

A. If it be, why is it not imbraced? But my own words are these;

I am for holding Communion thus; because the Edification of Souls
5 *in the Faith, and holiness of the Gospel is of greater concern than an*
agreement in outward things; I say, 'tis of greater concern with us, and
of far more profit to our Brother, than our agreeing in, or contesting for
Water-baptism, Joh. 16. 13. 1 Cor. 14. 12. 2. Cor. 10. 8. Chap.
12. 19. Ephes. 4. 12. 1 Cor. 13. 1, 2. Chap. 8. 1. Now why did
10 you not take this Argument in pieces, and answer those
Scriptures, on which the strength thereof depends; But if to
contest, and fall out about Water-baptism, be better than to
edifie the House of God, produce the Texts, that we may be
informed. You say; *Edification is the end of all Communion, but all*
15 *things must be done in Order, orderly,* pag. 26.

Answ. When you have proved that there is no such thing as an
orderly edifying of the Church without Water-baptism, precede,
then it will be time enough to think you have said something.

You add; *Edification as to Church-fellowship being a building up,*
20 *doth suppose the being of a Church; but pray you shew us a Church*
without Baptism. p. 26.

A. See here the spirit of these Men, who for the want of
Water-baptism, have at once un-Churched all *such* Congregations
of God in the World; but against this I have, and do urge, That
25 Water-baptism giveth neither being, nor well-being to a Church,
neither is any part of that Instituted Worship of God, that the
Church, as such, should be found in the Practice of. Therefore
her Edification as a Church may, yea and ought to be attained
unto without it.

30 But you say, *Shew us a New-Testament-Church without Baptism.*
pag. 26.

A. What say you to the Church all a-long the *Revelation* quite
through the Reign of Antichrist? Was that a New-Testament-
Church, or no?

35 Again, If Baptism be without the Church, as a Church, if it
hath nothing to do in the Constituting of a Church; if it be not
the door of entrance into the Church, if it be no part of Church-
worship as such; then, although all the Members of that Church
were baptized, yet the Church is a Church without Water-

20 *Church*] *Chuch*

baptism. But all the Churches in the New-Testament were such:
Therefore, &c.

Again, If Baptism respect Believers, as particular Persons
only; if it respects their own Conscience only; if it make a man no
visible Believer to me, then it hath nothing to do with Church-   5
membership: Because, that which respects my own Person only,
my own Conscience only: that which is no Character of my
visible Saintship to the Church, cannot be an Argument unto
them to receive me into fellowship with themselves. But this is
true, Therefore, &c.   10

You proceed, *If by Edification, be meant the private increase of*
Grace, in one another, in the use of private means, as private
Christians in meeting together; how doth the Principle you oppose
hinder that? Endeavour to make men as holy as you can, that they may
be fitted for Church-fellowship, when God shall shew them the orderly   15
way to it. pag. 26.

Answ. What a many private things have we now brought out to
publick view? Private Christians, private Means, and a private
increase of Grace. But, Sir, Are none but those of your way the
publick Christians? Or, ought none but them that are baptized to   20
have the publick means of Grace? Or, must their Graces be
increased by none but private means? Was you awake now? Or,
are you become so high in your own phantasies, that none have,
or are to have but private means of Grace? And, are there no
publick Christians, or publick Christian-Meetings, but them of   25
your way? I did not think that all but Baptists, should only abide
in holes.

But you find fault because I said, Edification is greater than
contesting about Water-baptism. pag. 27.

A. If it be not, confute me; if it be, forbear to cavil. Water-   30
baptism, and all God's Ordinances, are to be used to Edification;
not to beget heats and contentions among the Godly, wherefore
Edification is best.

Object. *I had thought that the Preaching, and opening Baptism,*
might have been reckoned a part of our Edification.   35

Answ. The act of Water-baptism hath not place in Church-
worship, neither in whole nor in part; wherefore pressing it upon
the Church is to no purpose at all.

Object. *Why may you not as well say that Edification is greater*
than breaking of Bread. pag. 27.   40

Answ. So it is, else that should never have been Instituted to edifie withal; that which serveth, is not greater than he that is served thereby. Baptism and the Lord's-Supper both, were made for us, not we for them; wherefore both were made for our
5 Edification, but no one for our destruction.

But again, The Lord's-Supper, not Baptism, is for the Church, as a Church; therefore as we will maintain the Church's edifying, that must be maintained in it; yea, used oft, to shew the Lord's Death till he come, 1 *Cor.* 11. 22, 26.

10 Besides, because it is a great part of Church-worship, as such, therefore it is pronounced blessed, the Lord did openly bless it before he gave it; yea and we ought to bless it also; (The Cup of blessing which we bless) not to say more, Therefore your reasoning from the one to the other will not hold.

15 Object. *How comes contesting for Water-baptism to be so much against you?*

Answ. First, because weak Brethren cannot bear it; whom yet we are commanded to receive but not to doubtful disputation; doubtful to them, therefore for their sakes, I must forbear it.
20 *Rom.* 14. 1.

Secondly, Because I have not seen any good effect, but the contrary, where-ever such hot Spirits have gone before me: For where Envie and Strife is, there is Confusion (or Tumults) and every Evil-works. *Jam.* 3. 16, 17.

25 Thirdly, Because by the Example of the Lord, and *Paul*, we must consider the present state of the Church, and not trouble them with what they cannot bear. *Joh.* 16. 13. 1 *Cor.* 3. 1, 2, 3.

I conclude then, Edification in the Church is to be preferrerd above what the Church, as a Church, hath nothing to do withal.
30 All things (dearly beloved) are for our Edifying. 1 *Cor.* 14. 5. & 12. 26. 2 *Cor.* 12. 19. *Eph.* 4. 26. *Rom.* 15. 2. 1 *Cor.* 14. 3. 2 *Cor.* 10. 8. & 13. 10. *Rom.* 14. 19. Before I wind up this Argument, I present you with several Instances, shewing that some of the breach of God's Precepts have been born with, when they come
35 in competition with Edification. As First, That of *Aaron*, who let the Offering for Sin be burnt, that should have indeed been eaten, *Levit.* 10. Yet because he could not do it to his Edification, *Moses* was content. But the Law was thereby transgressed, *Chap.* 6. 26. The Priest that offereth it for Sin, shall eat it.

31 *Eph.*] *Epg.*   34 breach] brecah

To this you Reply, *That was not a constant, continued, forbearing of God's Worship, but a suspending of it for a season.*

Answ. We also suspend it but for a season; when Persons can be baptized to their Edification, they have the liberty.

But secondly, This was not a bare suspension, but a flat transgression of the Law: Ye should indeed have eaten it: Yet *Moses* was content. *Levit.* 10. 16–20.

But say you, *Perhaps it was suspended upon just and legal grounds, though not expressed.*

Answ. The express Rule was against it; *Ye should indeed* (said *Moses*) *have eaten it in the Holy place, as I commanded*, vers. 18. But good Sir, are you now for unwritten verities? for legal grounds, though not expressed? I will not drive you further, here is Rome enough.

As for *Eldad* and *Medad*, it cannot be denyed, but that their edifying of the People, was preferred before their conforming to every Circumstance. *Numb.* 11. 16.–26.

You add, *That Paul for a seeming low thing did withstand Peter.*

Sir, If you make but a seeming low thing of Dissembling, and teaching others so to do (especially where the Doctrine of Justification is endangered) I cannot expect much good Conscience from you.

Gal. 2. 11, 12, 13.

As for your Answer to the case of *Hezekiah*, it is faulty in two respects:

1. For that you make the Passeover a Type of the Lord's Supper, when it was only a Type of the Body and Blood of the Lord: For even Christ our Passeover is Sacrifice for us. 1 *Cor.* 5. 7.

2. In that you make it an Example to you to admit Persons unprepared to the Lord's-Supper. *pag.* 29.

Answ. May you indeed receive Persons into the Church unprepared for the Lord's Supper; yea, unprepared for that, with other solemn Appointments? For so you word it, *page* 29. O what an Engine have you made of Water-baptism.

Thus, gentle *Reader*, while this Author teareth us in pieces for not making Baptism the orderly Rule for receiving the Godly, and Conscientious into Communion; he can receive Persons if baptized, though unprepared for the Supper, and other solemn Appointments? I would have thee consult the place, and see if it countenanceth such an act, That a man who pleadeth for Water-

baptism above the Peace and Edification of the Church, ought to be received (although unprepared) into the Church to the Lord's-Supper, and other solemn Appointments; especially considering the Nature of right Church Constitution, and the

5 severity of God towards those that came unprepared to his Table of old. 1 *Cor.* 11. 28, 29, 30. A Riddle indeed. That the Lord should, without a word, so severely command, that all which want Light in Baptism, be excluded Church-priviledges; and yet against his Word, admit of Persons unprepared, to the Lord's

10 Table, and other solemn Appointments.

But good Sir, why so short-winded? why could not you make the same work with the other Scriptures, as you did with these? I must leave them upon you unanswered; and standing by my Argument conclude, That if Laws and Ordinances of old have

15 been broken, and the breach of them born with (when yet the Observation of outward things was more strictly Commanded than now) if the Profit and Edification of the Church come in competition; how much more, may not we have Communion, Church-Communion, when no Law of God is transgressed

20 thereby. And note, That all this while I plead not (as you) for Persons unprepared, but godly, and such as walk with God.

We come now to my seventh Argument, for Communion with the Godly, though unbaptized Persons; which you say is *Love*. *pag.* 20.

25 My Argument is this; *Therefore I am for Communion thus; because Love, which above all things we are Commanded to put on, is of much more worth than to break about Baptism.* And let the *Reader* note, That of this Argument you deny not so much as one syllable, but run to another story; but I will follow you.

30 I add further, That Love is more discovered when we receive for the sake of Christ, than when we refuse his Children for want of Water: And tell you again, That this Exhortation to Love is grounded not upon Baptism, but the putting on of the new Creature, which hath swallowed up all distinctions. *Col.* 3. 9.–

35 14. Yea, there are ten Arguments in this one, which you have not so much as touched; but thus object, *That man that makes Affection the Rule of his walking, rather than judgment, it is no wonder if he go out of the way.*

Answ. Love to them we are perswaded that God hath received,

40 is Love that is guided by Judgment; and to receive them that are

such, because God hath bidden us (*Rom.* 14.) is Judgment guided by Rule. My Argument therefore hath forestalled all your noise, and standeth still on its legs against you.

As to the Duties of Piety, and Charity you boast of, *pag.* 30. sound not a Trumpet, tell not your left hand of it; we are talking now of Communion of Saints, Church-Communion, and I plead that to Love, and hold together as such, is better than to break in pieces for want of Water-baptism. My Reason is, because we are exhorted above all things to put on Love; the Love of Church-Communion: contrariwise you oppose, Above all things put on Water. For the best Saint under Heaven that hath not that, with him you refuse Communion. Thus you make Baptism, though no Church-Ordinance, a bar to shut out the Godly, and a Trap-door to let the unprepared into Churches, to the Lord's Supper, and other solemn Appointments. *pag.* 29.

But you object, *Must our Love to the unbaptized indulge them in an act of disobedience? Cannot we love their Persons, Parts, Graces, but we must love their Sins*: pag. 30.

Answ. We plead not for indulging. But are there not with you, even with you sins against the Lord your God? 2. *Chron.* 28. 10. But why can you indulge the Baptists in many acts of disobedience? For to come unprepared into the Church, is an act of disobedience: To come unprepared to the Supper is an act of disobedience; and to come so also to other solemn Appointments, are acts of disobedience.

But for these things, you say, *you do not cast, nor keep any out of the Church.*

But what acts of disobedience do we indulge them in?

In the Sin of Infant-baptism.

Answ. We indulge them not; but being Commanded to bear with the Infirmities of each other, suffer it; it being indeed in our eyes such; but in theirs they say a duty, till God shall otherwise perswade them. If you be without infirmity, do you first throw a stone at them: They keep their Faith in that to themselves, and trouble not their Brethren therewith: we believe that God hath received them, they do not want to us a proof of their Sonship with God; neither hath he made Water a Wall of Division between us, and therefore we do receive them.

Obj. *I take it to be the highest act of friendship to be faithful to these Professors, and to tell them they want this one thing in Gospel-order, which ought not to be left undone.* pag. 30.

Answ. If it be the highest piece of Friendship, to preach
5 Water-baptism to unbaptized Believers, the lowest act thereof must needs be very low. But contrariwise, I count it so far off from being any act of Friendship, to press Baptism in our Notion on those that cannot bear it; that it is a great abuse of the Peace of my Brother, the Law of Love, the Law of Christ, or the
10 Society of the Faithful. Love suffereth long, and is kind, is not easily provoked: Let us therefore follow after the things that make for Peace, and things wherewith one may edifie another: Let every one of us please his Neighbour, for his good to Edification: Bear you one anothers burdens, and so fulfil the
15 Law of Christ. 1 *Cor.* 13. *Rom.* 14. 19. *Chap.* 15. 2. *Gal.* 6. 2.

But say you, *I doubt when this comes to be weighed in God's ballance, it will be found no less than flattery, for which you will be reproved.* pag. 31.

Answ. It seems you do but doubt it, wherefore the Principle
20 from which you doubt it, of that methinks you should not be certain; but this is of little weight to me; for he that will presume to appropriate the Epistles to himself and fellows for the sake of Baptism, and that will condemn all the Churches of Christ in the Land for want of Baptism, and that will account his Brother as
25 prophane *Esau* (*pag.* 20.) and rejected, as Idolatrous *Ephraim* (page. 32.) because he wanteth his way of Water-baptism; he acts out of his wonted way of rigidness, when he doth but doubt, and not affirm his Brother to be a flatterer. I leave therefore this your Doubt to be resolved at the Day of Judgment, and in the
30 mean time trample upon your harsh, and unchristian surmises.

As to our Love to Christians in other cases, I hope we shall also endeavour to follow the Law of the Lord; but because it respects not the matter in hand, it concerns us not now to treat thereof.

35 My Argument treateth of Church-Communion; in the prosecution of which I prove,

1. That Love is grounded upon the new Creature, *Col.* 3. 9, *&c.*

2. Upon our fellowship with the Father and Son, 1 *Joh.* 1. 2, 3.

3 *undone*] *undon*

3. That with respect to this, it is the fulfilling of the Royal Law, *Jam.* 4. 11. *Rom.* 14. 21.

4. That it shews it self in acts of forbearing, rather than in publishing some Truths: Communicating only what is profitable, forbearing to publishing what cannot be born, 1 *Cor.* 3. 1, 2. *Acts* 5 20. 18, 19, 20. *Joh.* 16. 17.

5. I shew further, That to have fellowship for, to make that the ground of, or to receive one another chiefly upon the account of an outward Circumstance; to make Baptism the including, and excluding Charter; the Bounds, Bar, & Rule of Communion, 10 when by the Word of the everlasting Testament, there is no Word for it; (to speak charitably) if it be not for want of Love, it is for want of light in the Mysteries of the Kingdom of Christ. Strange! Take two Christians equal in all Points but this; nay, let one go beyond the other in Grace and Goodness, as far as a Man 15 is beyond a Babe, yet Water shall turn the Scale, shall open the Door of Communion to the less; and command the other to stand back: Yet is no proof to the Church of this Babes Faith and Hope, hath nothing to do with his entering into fellowship, is no part of the Worship of the Church. These things should have 20 been answered, seeing you will take upon you so roundly to condemn our practice.

You come now to my eighth Argument; which you do not only render falsly, but by so doing abuse your *Reader,* I said not that the Church of *Corinth* did shut each other out of Communion; 25 but, For God's People to divide into Parties, or to shut each other from Church-Communion, though for greater Points, and upon higher Pretences, than that of Water-baptism, hath heretofore been counted carnal, and the actors therein Babish-Christians; and then bring in the Factions, that was in the 30 Church at *Corinth.* But what! May not the evil of denying Church-Communion now, if proved naught by a less crime in the Church at *Corinth,* be counted Carnal and Babish; but the breach of Communion must be charged upon them at *Corinth* also? 35

That my Argument is good you grant, *pag.* 32. saying, *The Divisions at the Church at Corinth were about the highest Fundamental Principles, for which they are often called carnal*; yet you cavil at it. But if they were to be blamed for dividing, though for the highest Points: Are not you much more for condemning your 40

Brethren to perpetual banishment from Church-Communion, though sound in all the great Points of the Gospel, and right in all Church-Ordinances also, because for want of Light they fail only in the Point of Baptism?

5 As to your quibble about *Paul* and *Apollos*, whether they, or others, were the Persons (though I am satisfied you are out) yet it weakeneth not my Argument; For if they were blame-worthy for dividing, though about the highest Fundamental Principles (as you say) how ought you to blush for carrying it as you do to

10 Persons, perhaps, more godly than ourselves, because they jump not with you in a Circumstance?

That the divisions at *Corinth* were helped on by the abuse of Baptism, to me is evident, from *Paul*'s so oft suggesting it; *Were you baptized in the Name of* Paul? *I thank God I baptized none of you,*

15 *lest any should say, I had baptized in my own Name.*

I do not say, that they who baptized them *designed* this, or that Baptism in it self *effected* it; nor yet (though our Author feigns it) *that they were most of them baptized by their Factious Leaders*, pag. 55. But that they had their Factious Leaders, is evident; and that

20 these Leaders made use of the Names of *Paul*, *Apollos*, and *Christ*, is as evident; for by these Names they were beguiled by the help of *abused* Baptism.

But say you, *Wherein lies the force of this man's Argument against Baptism as to its place, worth, and continuance?*

25 I answer; I have no Argument against its place, worth, or continuance, although thus you seek to scandalize me. But this kind of sincerity of yours, will never make me one of your Disciples.

Have not I told you even in this Argument, *That I speak not as I*

30 *do, to perswade or teach men to break the least of God's Commandments; but that my Brethren of the Baptized-way may not hold too much THEREUPON, may not make it an Essential of the Gospel, nor yet of the Communion of Saints.* Yet he feigns that I urge two Arguments against it, *p.* 36. & 38. But *Reader*, thou

35 mayst know I have no such reason in my Book. Besides, I should be a Fool indeed, were I against it, should I make use of such weak Arguments. My words then are these;

I thank God (said *Paul*) *that I baptized none of you but* Crispus, *&c. Not but that then it was an Ordinance, but they abused it in*

40 *making Parties thereby, as they abused also* Paul, *and* Cephas. *Besides*

(said he) *I know not whether I baptized any other. By this negligent relating who were baptized by him; he sheweth that he made no such matter thereof, as some in these dayes do. Nay, that he made no matter at all thereof with respect to a Church-Communion. For if he did not heed who himself had baptized, much less did he heed* 5 *who were baptized by others? But if Baptism had been the initiating-Ordinance, (and I now add) Essential to Church-Communion; then no doubt he had made more Conscience of it, than thus lightly to pass it by.*

I add further, where he saith, He was not sent to baptize; that 10 he spake with an holy Indignation against those that had abused that Ordinance. *Baptism is an Holy Ordinance, but when Satan abuseth it, and wrencheth it out of its place, making that which is Ordained of God, for the Edification of Believers, the only Weapon to break in pieces the Love, Unity, and Concord of the Saints; than as* 15

1 Cor. 3. 5, 6, 7. *Paul said of himself, and fellows, What is Baptism? Neither is Baptism any thing? This is no new Doctrine, for God by the mouth of the* Isa. 1. 11, 12, 13, 14, 15. *Prophet of old, cryed out against his own Appointments, when abused by his own People, because they used them for strife, and debate, and to* Isa. 58. 4. *smite with the fist of wickedness.* But to forbear, to take notice thus 20 of these things, my Argument stands firm against you: *For if they at* Corinth *were blame-worthy for dividing, though their divisions were (if you say true) about the highest Fundamentals, you ought to be ashamed, thus to banish your Brethren from the Priviledges of Church-Communion for ever, for the want of so low a thing as Water-baptism.* 25 I call it not low, with respect to Gods appointment, though so, it is far from the highest place, but in comparison of those Fundamentals, about which, you say, *the Corinthians made their divisions.*

You come next to my ninth Argument, and serve it as *Hanun* 30 served *David*'s Servants, 2 *Sam.* 10. 4. you have cut off one half of its Beard, and its Garments to its Buttocks, thinking to send it home with shame. You state it thus;

That by denying communion with unbaptized Believers, you take from them their Priviledges to which they are born, pag. 40. 35

Answ. Have I such an Argument in all my little Book? Are not my words *verbatim* these? *If we shall reject visible Saints by calling, Saints that have communion with God; that have received the Law at the hand of Christ; that are of an holy conversation among men, they desiring to have communion with us; as much as in us lyeth, we take* 40

*from them their very priviledges, and the blessings to which they were
born of God.*

This is mine Argument: now confute it.

Paul saith, (1 *Cor.* 1. 1, 2. *&* 3. 22.) not only to the Gathered
5 Church at *Corinth*, but to all scattered Saints, that in every place
call upon the Name of the Lord, *that Jesus Christ is theirs; that*
Paul, *and* Apollos, *and* Cephas, *and the World, and all things else
was theirs.*

But you answer, *We take from them nothing, but we keep them
10 from a disorderly practice of Gospel-Ordinances, we offer them their
priviledges, in the way of Gospel-Order.*

Answ. Where have you one word of God, that forbiddeth a
person, so qualified, as is signified in mine Argument, the best
Communion of Saints for want of Water? There is not a syllable
15 for this in all the Book of God. So then, you in this your
plausible defence, do make your Scriptureless Light, which in
very deed is darkness, (*Isa.* 8. 20, 21.) the Rule of your Brothers
Faith; and how well you will come off for this in the Day of God,
you might, were you not wedded to your wordless Opinion,
20 soon begin to conceive.

I know your Reply, *New-Testament Saints were all baptized first.*

Answ. Suppose it granted; Were they baptized, that thereby
they might be qualified for their right to communion of Saints, so
that without their submitting to Water, they were to be denyed
25 the other? Further, Suppose I should grant this groundless
Notion, Were not the Jews in Old Testament times to enter the
Church by Circumcision? For that, though water is not, was the   *Gen.* 17.
very entering-Ordinance. Besides, as I said before, there was a   *Exod.* 12.
full forbidding all that were not circumcised from entering into
30 fellowship, with a threatning to cut them off from the Church if
they entered in without it: Yet more than six hundred thousand
entred that Church without it. But how now, if such an one as
you had then stood up and objected, *Sir Moses,* What is the
reason that you transgress the Order of God, to receive
35 Members without Circumcision? Is not that the very entring-
Ordinance? Are not you commanded to keep out of the Church
all that are not circumcised? Yea, and for all those that you thus
received, are you not commanded to cast them out again, *to cut
them off from among this people?* (*Gen.* 17. 13, 14. *Exod.* 12. 24, 25,
40 26.)

I say, Would not this man have had a far better argument to have *resisted* Moses, than you in your wordless Notion have to shut out men from the Church, more holy than many of our selves? But do you think that *Moses* and *Joshua*, and all the Elders of *Israel*, would have thanked this Fellow, or have concluded that he spake on God's behalf? Or, that they should then, for the sake of a better than what you call Order, have set to the work that you would be doing, even to break the Church in pieces for this?

But say you, *If any will find or force another way into the Sheep-fold, than by the footsteps of the Flock, we have no such custom, nor the Churches of God*, pag. 41.

Answ. What was done of old, I have shewed you, that *Christ*, not Baptism, *is the way to the Sheep-fold*, is apparent: and that the person, in mine Argument, is intituled to all these, to wit, Christ, Grace, and all the things of the Kingdom of Christ in the Church, is, upon the Scriptures urged, as evident.

But you add, *That according to mine old confidence, I affirm, That drink ye all of this, is intailed to Faith, not Baptism: A thing, say you, soon said, but yet never proved.*

Answ. 1. That it is intailed to *Faith*, must be confessed of all hands. 2. That it is the priviledge of him that discerneth the Lord's Body, and that no man is to deny him it, is also by the Text as evident, (and so let him eat) because he is worthy. Wherefore he, and he only that *discerneth* the Lord's Body, he is the worthy Receiver, the worthy Receiver *in God's estimation*; but that none discern the Lord's Body but the Baptized, is both fond and ridiculous once to surmise.

Wherefore to exclude Christians, and to debar them their Heaven-born Priviledges, for want of that which yet God never made the Wall of Division betwixt us: This looks too like a Spirit of Persecution, (*Joh.* 19. 25, 26, 27, 28, *&c.*) and carrieth in it those eighteen absurdities which you have so hotly cryed out against. And I do still add, *Is it not that which greatly prevailed with God to bring down those Judgments, which at present we* (*the People of God*) *groan under, I will dare to say, it was** *A cause thereof*: Yea, I will yet proceed; I fear, I strongly fear, that the Rod of God is not yet to be taken from us; for what more provoking sin among Christians, than to deny one another their Rights and Priviledges to which they are born of God? and then to Father these their

1. Cor. 11. 29.

* *And so it was in my first Copy, but for* A, *the Printer put in* the.

doings upon God, when yet he hath not commanded it, neither
in the New Testament nor the Old?

But, I may not *lightly* pass this by, for because I have gathered
eighteen absurdities from this *abuse* of God's Ordinances, or
5 from the *sin* of binding, the Brethren to observe Order, *not*
founded on the *Command* of God; (and I am sure you have none
to shut out men as good, as holy, and as sound in Faith as our
selves, from Communion). Therefore you call my Conclusion
devilish, (pag. 43.) *Top-ful of ignorance*, and *prejudice*, (p. 41.) and
10 *me*, one of *Machiavels* Scholars, (p. 42.) also proud, presumptious,
impeaching the Judgment of God.

Answ. But what is there in my Proposition, that men,
considerate, can be offended at? These are my words; *But to
exclude Christians from Church-Communion, and to debar them their*
15 *Heaven-born Priviledges, for the want of that which yet God never
made a wall of division between us: This looks too like a Spirit of
Persecution: This respecteth more the form, than the spirit and power of
Godliness, &c. Shall I add, Is it not that which greatly prevailed to
bring down those Judgments which at present we feel and groan under?*
20 *I will dare to say, it was a cause thereof.* (p. 116, 117.) *A*, was in my
Copy, instead whereof the Printer put in *the*; for this, although I
speak only the truth, I will not beg of you belief; besides, the
Bookseller desired me, because of the Printers haste, to leave the
last sheet to be over-looked by him, which was the cause it was
25 not among the Errata's.

But, I say, wherein is the Proposition offensive? Is it not a
wicked thing to make *bars* to Communion, where *God* hath made
none? Is it not a wickedness, to make that a Wall of Division
betwixt us, which God never commanded to be so. If it be not,
30 justifie your practice; if it be, take shame. Besides, the
Proposition is universal, why then should you be the chief
intended? But you have in this, done like to the Lawyers of old,
who when Christ reproved the Pharisees of wickedness before
them, said, *Master, thus saying thou reproachest us also*, Luk. 11.
35 45.

But you feign, and would also that the World should believe,
that the Eighteen Absurdities which naturally flow from the
Proposition, I make to be the Effects of Baptism, saying to me,
None but your self could find an innocent Truth big with so many
40 *monstrous Absurdities*. pag. 42.

I Answer; This is but speaking wickedly for God, or rather to justifie your wordless Practice. I say not that Baptism hath any Absurdity in it, though your abusing it, hath them all, and many more, while you make it, without warrant from the Word, as the flaming Sword, to keep the Brotherhood out of Communion, because they after *your* manner cannot consent thereto.

And let no man be offended, for that I suggest that Baptism may be abused to the breeding such monstrous Absurdities, for greater Truths than that have been as much abused. What say you to, *This is my Body*? To instance no more, although I could instance many, are not they the words of our Lord? are not they part of the Scriptures of Truth? and yet behold, even with those words, *the Devil by abusing them*, made an *Engine* to let out the heart-blood of thousands. Baptism also may be abused, and is, when more is laid upon it by us, than is Commanded by God. And that you do so, is manifest by what I have said already, and shall yet say to your *Fourteen Arguments*.

My last Argument, you say is this;

The World may wonder at your carriage to those Unbaptized Persons, in keeping them out of Communion?

Ans. You will yet set up your own words, and then fight against them: but my words are these, *What greater contempt can be thrown upon the Saints, than for their Brethren to cut them off from, or to debar them Church-Communion!*

And now I add, Is not this to deliver them to the Devil, 1 *Cor.* 5. or to put them to shame before all that see your acts? There is but one thing can hinder this, and that is, by-standers see, that these your Brethren, that you thus abuse, are as holy men as our selves. Do you more to the open Prophane, yea, to all Wizards and Witches in the Land? For all you can do to them (I speak now as to Church-acts) is no other than debar them the Communion of Saints.

And now I say again, *The World may well wonder*, when they see you deny holy-men of God that liberty of the Communion of Saints which you Monopolize to your selves. And though they do not understand the grounds of Profession, or Communion; yet they can both see, and say, these Holy-men of God, in all visible acts of Holiness, are not one inch behind you. Yea, I will put it to your selves, If those many, yea very many, who thus severely (but with how little ground, is seen by men of God) you deny

Communion with, are not of as good, as holy, as unblameable in life, and as sound, if not sounder in the Faith than many among our selves: Here only they make the stop, they cannot, without Light, be driven into Water-baptism, I mean after our Notion of
5 it: but what if they were, 'twould be little sign to me that they were sincere with God.

To conclude this; when you have proved that Water-baptism (which you yourself have said is not a Church-Ordinance, p. 40.) is Essential to Church-Communion, and that the Church
10 may, *by the Word of God*, bolt, bar, and for ever shut out those, far better than *our* selves, that have not, according to our Notion, been baptized with Water; then 'twill be time enough, to talk of ground for so doing. In the mean time I must take leave to tell you, *There is not in all the Bible one syllable for such a Practice,*
15 *wherefore your great cry about your Order is wordless, and therefore faithless, and is a meer Humane Invention.*

I come now to your *Fourteen Arguments*, and shall impartially consider them.

Y Our first Argument to prove it lawful to reject the
20 Unbaptized Saint, is, *Because the great Commission of Christ,* Matth. 28. *from which all Persons have their Authority for their Ministry, (if any Authority at all) doth clearly direct the contrary. By that Commission, Ministers are first to Disciple, and then to Baptize them so made Disciples, and afterward to teach them to observe all that*
25 *Christ Commanded them, as to other Ordinances of Worship. If Ministers have no other Authority to teach them other parts of Gospel-Worship, before they believe and are baptized; it may be strongly supposed, they are not to admit them to other Ordinances before they have passed this first injoyned in the Commission.*
30 *Answ.* 1. That the Ministers are to Disciple and Baptize, is granted. But that they are prohibited (by the Commission; *Matth.* 28.) to Teach the Disciples other parts of Gospel-Worship, that have not Light in Baptism, remains for you to prove. Shall I add, This Position is so absurd and void of truth, that none that have
35 ever read the Love of Christ, the Nature of Faith, the End of the Gospel, or of the Reason of Instituted Worship (which is Edification) with understanding, should so much as once imagine.

But where are they here *forbidden* to teach them other Truths, *before* they be baptized? *This Text as fairly denieth to the unbaptized Believer, Heaven, and Glory.* Nay our Author in the midst of all his flutter about this 28th of *Matthew*, dare venture to gather no more therefrom, but that it *may be strongly supposed.* Behold therefore, gentle *Reader*, the ground on which these Brethren lay the stress of their separation from their Fellows, is *nothing else but a supposition*, without warrant, skrewed out of this blessed Word of God. *Strongly Supposed*! but may it not be as strongly supposed, that the Presence and Blessing of the Lord Jesus, with his Ministers, is laid upon the same ground also? for thus he concludes the Text, *And lo, I am with you always, even to the end of the World.* But would I say, any man from these words, conclude, That Christ Jesus hath here promised his Presence only to them that after discipling, baptize those that are so made; and that they that do not baptize, *shall neither have his Presence, nor his Blessing?* I say again, Should any so conclude hence, would not all Experience prove him void of Truth? The words therefore must be left, by you, as you found them, they favour not at all your groundless supposition.

To conclude, these words have not laid Baptism in the way to debar the Saint from Fellowship of his Brethren, no more than to hinder his inheritance in Life and Glory. *Mark* reads it thus; *He that believeth and is baptized, shall be saved; but he that believeth not, shall be damned*, Mark 16. 16. letting Baptism, which he mentioned in the promise, fall, when he came at the threatning.

God also doth thus with respect to his Worship in the Church, he commands all and every whit of his will to be done, but beareth with our coming short in this, and that, and another Duty. But let's go on.

Your second Argument, is:

That the Order of Christ's Commission, as well as the matter therein contained to be observed, may easily be concluded, from God's severity towards them that sought him not according to due order, 1 Chron. 15. 13. Was God so exact with his People then, that all things to a Pin must be according to the Pattern in the Mount, Heb. 7. 16. & 9. 11. whose Worship then comparatively, to the Gospel, was but after the Law of a Carnal Commandment; and can it be supposed he should be so indifferent now to leave men to their own liberty, to time and place

*his Appointments, contrary to what he hath given in express Rule, for
in his Word as before?* Ezek. 44. 7, 9, 10. *It was the Priest's Sin
formerly to bring the uncircumcised in heart and flesh into his house.*

Answ. That there is no such Order in that Commission as you
5 feign, I have proved. As for your far-fetch'd Instance (1 *Chron.*
15.) 'tis quite besides your purpose. The express Word was, *That
the Priest, not a Cart, should bear the Ark of God*: Also they were not
to touch it, and yet *Uzza* did, *Exod.* 25. 14. 1 *Chron.* 15. 12, 13,
14, 15. *Numb.* 4. 15. 1 *Chron.* 13. Now, if you can make that 28th
10 of *Matthew* say, *Receive none that are not baptized first; or that Christ
would have them of his, that are not yet baptized, kept ignorant of all
other Truths that respect Church-Communion*; then you say
something, else you do but raise a mist before the simple *Reader*:
but who so listeth, may hang on your sleeve.

15 As for the Pins and Tacks of the Tabernacle, they were
expresly commanded; and when you have proved by the Word of
God, That you ought to shut Saints out of your Communion for
want of Baptism, then you may begin more justly to make your
Parallel. How fitly you have urged *Ezek.* 44. to insinuate that
20 unbaptized Believers are like the uncircumcised in heart and
flesh, I leave it to all Gospel-Novices to consider.

Your third Argument, is,

*The practice of the first Gospel-Ministers, with them that first
trusted in Christ, discovers the truth of what I assert. Certainly, they
25 that lived at the spring-head, or fountain of Truth, and had the Law
from Christ's own mouth, knew the meaning of his Commission better
than we: but their constant practice in conformity to that Commission,
all along the Acts of the Apostles, discovers that they never arrived to
such a latitude as men plead for now a-dayes. They that gladly received
30 the Word were baptized, and they (yea they only) were received into the
Church.*

Answ. How well you have proved what you have asserted, is
manifest by my Answer to the two former Arguments. I adde,
That the Ministers, and Servants of Jesus Christ in the first
35 Churches (for that you are to prove) were Commanded to
forbear to Preach other Truths to the Unbaptized Believers; or
that they were to keep them out of the Church: or that the
Apostles, and first Fathers, have given you to understand by their
Example, that you ought to keep as good out of Churches as your

selves, hath not yet been shewed by the Authority of the Word. The second of the *Acts* proveth not, That the three thousand were necessitated to be baptized in order to their Fellowship with the Church, neither doth it say THEY, yea they *only*, were received into the Church. But suppose all this, as much was done   5 at the first Institution of Circumcision, &c. yet afterwards thousands were received without it.

Your fourth Argument is,

None of the Scripture-Saints ever attempted this Church-priviledge without Baptism, (if they did, let it be shewn). The Eunnuch first   10 *desired Baptism before any thing else*; Paul *was first baptized before he did essay to joyn with the Church. Our Lord Christ, the great Example of the New Testament, entred not upon his publick Ministry, much less any other Gospel-Ordinance of Worship, till he was Baptized.*

Answ. That none of the Scripture-Saints (if there be any   15 unscripture ones) so much as *attempted* this Church priviledge first, remains for you to prove. But suppose they were all Baptized, because they had light therein, what then? Doth this prove that Baptism is essential to Church-Communion? Or, that Christ commanded in the 28th of *Matthew*, or gave his Ministers   20 by that *authority*, not to make known to Believers other parts of Gospel-Worship, if they shall want light in Baptism? The Eunuch, *Paul*, and our blessed Lord Jesus, did none of them, by their Baptism, set themselves to us Examples how to enter into Church-Communion, what Church was the Eunuch Baptized   25 into, or made a Member of; but where is it said, that the unbaptized Believer, *how excellent soever in Faith and Holiness*, must, for want of Water-baptism, be shut out from the communion of Saints, or be debarred the Priviledge of his Fathers House? This you are to prove.   30

Your fifth Argument is,

If Christ himself was made manifest to be the SENT of God by Baptism, as appears Mark 1. 9, 10. Then why may not Baptism, as the first Fruits of Faith, and the first step of Gospel-Obedience, as to Instituted Worship, be a manifesting, discovering Ordinance upon   35 *others who thus follow Christ's steps.*

Answ. That Jesus Christ was *manifested* as the SENT of God by Baptism, or that Baptism is the first Fruit of Faith, and the

first step of Gospel-Obedience, as to instituted Worship, is both
without proof and truth; the Text saith not, he was manifest to be
the *sent* of God by Baptism; nay it saith not, that by that he was
manifest to others to be any thing: you have therefore but
5 wronged the Text, to prove your wordless Practice by. Yea, *John*
himself, though he knew him before he was baptized, to be a
Man of God, (for, saith he, *I have need to be Baptized of thee, and
comest thou to me*) *and knew him after to be the SENT of God*; yet not
in, or by, but after he was Baptized, to wit, by the descending of
10 the Holy Ghost, after he was come out of the Water, *as he was in
Prayer*, for the Heavens were opened to *John*, and he saw, and
bare Record, because he saw the Spirit descend from Heaven,
and abide upon Jesus, after his Baptism, *as he was in Prayer*, Mat.
3. 13, 14, 15, 16. Luk. 3. 21, 22. Thus we find him made known
15 before, and after, but not at all by Baptism, to be the SENT of
God.

    And that Baptism is the first fruits of Faith, or that Faith ought
to be tyed to take its first step in Water-baptism, in the instituted
Worship of God, (this you must prove) is not found expressed
20 within the whole Bible. *Faith acts according to its strength, and as it
sees*, it is not tyed or bound to any outward Circumstance; one
believeth he may, and another believeth he may not, either do
this or that.

25 Your sixth Argument is,

    *If Baptism be in any sence any part of the foundation of a Church, as
to order*, Heb. 6. 1, 2. *it must have place here or no where: why are
those things called first Principles, if not first to be believed, and
practised? Why are they rendred by the learned the A. B. C. of a*
30 *Christian, and the beginning of Christianity, Milk for Babes, if it be no
matter whether Baptism be practised or no? If it be said Water-baptism
is not there intended, let them shew me how many Baptisms there are
besides Water-baptism? Can you build and leave out a stone in the
Foundation? I intend not Baptism a Foundation any other way, but in*
35 *respect of order, and it is either intended for that or nothing.*

    Answ. Baptism is in no sense the Foundation of a Church. I
find no foundation of a Church, *but Jesus Christ himself*, Mat. 16.
18. 1 Cor. 3. 11. Yea, the Foundation mentioned, *Heb.* 6. 1, 2. is
nothing else but this very Christ. For he is the Foundation, not only

    4 thing:] *errata*; thing thereby:

Mat. 3. 14.
Joh. 1. 30, 31,
32, 33, 34.

of the Church, but of all that good that at any time is found in
her. He is the Foundation OF our *Repentance*, and OF our *Faith*
towards God, *vers.* 1, 2. Further, Baptisms are not here
mentioned, with respect to the Act in Water, but of the Doctrine, 5
that is, the signification thereof. *The Doctrine of Baptisms.* And
observe, neither *Faith*, nor *Repentance*, nor *Baptisms*, are called
here Foundations: Another thing, for a Foundation, is here by
the Holy Ghost intended, even a Foundation for them all; a
Foundation OF Faith, OF Repentance, OF the Doctrine of 10
Baptisms, OF the Resurrection of the Dead, and OF eternal
Judgment. And this Foundation is Jesus Christ himself, and
these are the first Principles, the Milk, the A. B. C. and the
beginning of Christian Religion in the World.

I dare not say, No matter whether Water-Baptism be practised 15
or no. But it is not a stone in the Foundation of a Church, no not
respecting order; it is not, to *another*, a sign of *my* Sonship with
God; it is not the *door* into Fellowship with the Saints, it is *no*
Church Ordinance, as you, your self have testified, *pag.* 40. So
then as to Church-work, it hath no place at all therein. 20

Your seventh Argument is,

If Paul *knew the* Galatians *ONLY upon the account of Charity,
NO other wayes to be the Sons of God by Faith; but by this part of their
Obedience, as he seems to import, then the same way we judge of the
truth of mens profession of Faith, when it shews it self by this self-same* 25
Obedience, Gal. 3. 26, 27. *Baptism being an Obligation to all
following Duties.*

Answ. This your Argument, being builded upon no more than
a SEEMING *Import*, and having been above ten times overthrown
already; I might leave still with you, till your seeming Import is 30
come to a real one, and both to a greater perswasion upon your
own Conscience. But verily Sir, you grosly abuse your Reader;
Must *Imports*, yea, must *seeming Imports* now stand for Arguments,
thereby to maintain your confident separation from your
Brethren? Yea, must such things as these, be the Basis on which 35
you build those heavy Censures and Condemnations you raise
against your Brethren, that cannot comply with you, because you
want the word? *A seeming Import.* But *are these words of Faith*, or
do the Scriptures only help you to *seeming Imports*, and *me-hap-
soes* for your practice? No, nor yet to them neither, for I dare

boldly affirm it, and demand, if you can, to prove, that there is so much as a *seeming IMPORT* in all the Word of God, that countenanceth your shutting men, better than our selves, from the Things and Priviledges of our Fathers House.

5   That to the *Galatians*, saith not, that *Paul knew them to be the Sons of God by Faith, NO other way, but by THIS part of their Obedience*; but puts them upon concluding themselves the Sons of God, if they were baptized into the Lord Jesus, which could not (ordinarily) be known but unto themselves alone; because,
10 being thus baptized, respecteth a Special Act of Faith, which onely God, and him that hath, and acteth it, can be privy to. It is one thing for him that administreth, to Baptize in the Name of Jesus, and another thing for him that is the Subject, by that to be baptized INTO Jesus Christ: Baptizing INTO Christ, is rather
15 the Act of the Faith of him that is baptized, than his going into Water and coming out again: But that *Paul* knew this to be the state of the *Galatians* NO other way, but by their external Act of being baptized with Water, is both wild and unsound, and a miserable IMPORT indeed.

20   Your eighth Argument is.

    If being baptized into Christ, be a putting on of Christ, as Paul *expresses, then they have not put on Christ, in that sense he means, that are not baptized; if this putting on of Christ, doth not respect the visibility of Christianity; assign something else as its signification; great*
25 *mens Servants are known by their Masters Liveries, so are Gospel-Believers by this Livery of Water-baptism, that all that first trusted in Christ submitted unto; which in it self is as much an Obligation to all Gospel-Obedience, as Circumcision was to keep the whole Law.*

    Answ. For a reply to the first part of this Argument, go back to
30 the Answer to the seventh.

    Now that none have put on Christ in *Paul*'s sense; yea, in a saving, in the best sense but them that have, as you would have them, gone into Water, will be hard for you to prove, yea, is ungodly for you to assert.

35   Your comparing Water-baptism to a Gentlemans Livery, by which his Name is known to be his, is fantastical.

    Go you but *ten doors* from where men have knowledge of you, and see how many of the World, or Christians, will know you by

27 *which*] *which is*

this goodly Livery, to be one that hath put on Christ. What! known by Water-baptism to be one that hath put on Christ, as a Gentlemans man is known to be his Masters Servant, by the gay Garment his Master gave him. Away fond man, you do quite forget the Text. *By THIS shall all men know that you are my* 5 *Disciples, if you have love one to another*, John 13. 35.

That Baptism is in it SELF obliging, to speak properly, it is false, for set it by it self, and it stands without the stamp of Heaven upon it, and without its signification also: and how, as such, it should be obliging, I see not.   10

Where you insinuate, it comes in the room of, and obligeth as
Acts 15. 1, 2. Circumcision: You say, you know not what. Circumcision was the
Gal. 5. 1, 2, 3, 4. initiating Ordinance, but this you have denyed to Baptism. Further, Circumcision THEN bound men to the whole Obedience of the Law, when urged by the false Apostles, and received by an 15 erroneous Conscience. Would you thus urge Water-baptism!
Rom. 2. 28, 29. would you have men to receive it with such Consciences?
Phil. 3. 3. Circumcision in the flesh, was a Type of Circumcision in the heart, and not of Water-baptism.

Your ninth Argument is,   20

If it were commendable in the Thessalonians, *that they followed the foot-steps of the Church of* Judea, 1 *Thes.* 2. 24. *who it appears followed this order of adding Baptized-Believers unto the Church; Then they that have found out another way of making Church-Members, are not by that Rule praise-worthy, but rather to be blamed;* 25 *it was not what was since in corrupted times, but that which was from the beginning: the first Churches were the purest Patern.*

Answ. That the Text saith there was *a Church OF Judea*, I find not, (1 *Thess.* 2. 14.) And that the *Thessalonians* are commended for refusing to have communion with the unbaptized Believers, 30 (for that is our question) prove it by the word, and then you do something. Again, that the commendations (1 *Thess.* 2. 14.) do chiefly, or at all, respect their being Baptized: *Or, because they followed the Churches of God, which in* Judea *were in Christ Jesus*, in the Example of Water-Baptism is quite beside the word. The 35 Verse runs thus, *for the Brethren, became followers of the Churches of God, which in* Judea *are in Christ Jesus, for ye also have suffered like things of your own Countrey-men, even as they have of the Jews*, &c. This Text then commends them, not for that they were baptized

with Water, but, for that they stood their ground, although baptized with suffering, like them in *Judea*, for the Name of the Lord Jesus. *For suffering like things of their own Countreymen, as they did of the Jews.* Will you not yet leave off to abuse the Word
5 of God, and forbear turning it out of its place, to maintain your unchristian practice of rejecting the People of God, and excluding them their blessed Priviledges.

The unbaptized Believer, instead of taking shame for entering into fellowship without it, will be ready, I doubt, to put you to
10 shame for bringing Scriptures so much besides the purpose, and for stretching them so miserably to uphold you in your fancies.

Your tenth Argument is,

If so be, that any of the Members at Corinth, Galatia, Coloss, Rome, *or them that* Peter *wrote to, were not baptized, then* Paul's
15 *Arguments for the Resurrection to them, or to press them to holiness from that ground* (Rom. 6. Col. 2. 1 Cor. 15.) *was out of doors, and altogether needless, yea, it bespeaks his ignorance, and throweth contempt upon the Spirits Wisdom,* (Heb. 6. 1 Pet. 3. 12.) *by which he wrote; if that must be asserted as a ground to provoke them to such*
20 *an end, which had no beeing; and if all the Members of all those Churches were baptized, why should any plead for an exemption from Baptism, for any Church-Member now?*

Answ. Suppose all, if all these Churches were baptized, what then? that answereth not our Question. We ask where you find it
25 written, that those that are baptized, should keep men as holy, and as much beloved of the Lord Jesus as themselves, out of Church-Communion, for want of light in Water-Baptism.

Why we plead for their admission, though they see not yet, that that is their Duty, is because we are not *forbidden*, but
30 *commanded* to receive them, because God and Christ hath done it, *Rom.* 14, & 15.

Your eleventh Argument is,

If unbaptized Persons must be received into Churches onely, because they are Believers, though they deny Baptism; Then why may not
35 *others plead for the like privilege, that are negligent in any other Gospel-Ordinance of Worship, from the same ground of want of light, let it be what it will. So then as the consequence of this Principle, Churches may be made up of visible sinners, instead of visible Saints.*

244 Differences About Water-Baptism

Answ. 1. I plead not for Believers simply because they are Believers, but for such Believers of whom we are perswaded by the Word, that God hath received them.

2. There are some of the Ordinances that, be they neglected, the being of a Church, as to her visible Gospel-Constitution, is taken quite away; but Baptism is none of them, it being no Church-Ordinance as such, not any part of Faith, nor of that Holiness of heart, or life, that sheweth me to the Church to be indeed a visible Saint. The Saint is a Saint before, and may walk with God, and be faithful with the Saints, and to his own Light also, though he never be baptized. Therefore to plead for his admission, makes no way at all for the admission of the open prophane, or to receive, as YOU profess YOU do, *Persons unprepared to the Lord's Table, and other solemn Appointments.* pag. 29.

Your twelfth Argument is,

Why should Professors have more Light in breaking of Bread, than Baptism? That this must be so urged for their excuse: Hath God been more sparing in making out his mind in the one, rather than the other? Is there more Precepts of Precedents for the Supper, than Baptism? Hath God been so bountiful in making out himself about the Supper, that few or none, that own Ordinances, scruple it: And must Baptism be such a rock of offence, to Professors? That very few will inquire after it, or submit to it? Hath not man's wisdom interposed to darken this part of God's Counsel? By which Professors seem willingly led, though against so many plain Commands and Examples, written as with a Sun-beam, that he that runs may read? And must an Advocate be entertained to plead for so gross a piece of ignorance, that the meanest babes of the first Gospel-times were never guilty of?

Answ. Many words to little purpose:

1. Must God be called to an account by you, why he giveth more Light about the Supper, than Baptism? May he not shew to, or conceal from this, or another of his Servants, which of his Truths he pleaseth? Some of the Members of the Church of *Jerusalem* had a greater Truth than this kept from them, for ought I know, as long as they lived, (*Acts* 11. 19.) yet God was not called in question about it.

---

1 *Answ.* 1.] *Answ.*

2. Breaking of Bread, not Baptism, being a Church-Ordinance, and *that* such also, as must be *often* reiterated; yea, it being an Ordinance SO full of blessedness, as lively to present Union and Communion with Christ to all the Members that worthily eat
5 thereof; I say, The Lord's-Supper being *such*, that while the Members sit at that feast, they *shew* to each other the Death and Blood of the Lord; as they ought to do, *till he comes*, (1 *Cor.* 10. 15, 16, 17. & 11. 22, 23. 24, 25, 26.) the Church, as a Church, is much more concerned in THAT, than in *Water-baptism*, both as
10 to her Faith, and *Comfort*; both as to her Union, and *Communion*.

3. Your supposition, That very few Professors will seriously enquire after Water-baptism, *is too rude.* What! must all the Children of God, that are not baptized for want of Light, be still stigmatized, with want of serious inquiry after God's mind in it.
15 4. That I am an Advocate, entertained, to plead for so gross a piece of ignorance, as want of Light in Baptism, is but like the rest of your jumbling. I plead for Communion with men, *godly* and *faithful*, I plead that they may be received, that *God hath shewed us* he hath received, and commanded we should receive
20 them.

Your thirteenth Argument is,

If Obedience must discover the truth of a man's Faith to others, why must Baptism be shut out? as if it was no part of Gospel-Obedience. Is there no Precept for this Practice, that it must be thus despised? as a
25 *matter of little use, or shall one of Christ's precious Commands be blotted out of a Christians Obedience, to make way for a Church-fellowship of man's devising?*

Answ. 1. This is but round, round, the same thing, over and over: That my obedience to Water, is *not* a discovery of my Faith
30 to others, is evident, from the body of the Bible, we find nothing that affirms it.

And I will now add, That if a man cannot shew himself a Christian without Water-baptism, *He shall never shew either Saint, or Sinner, that he is a Christian by it.*
35 2. Who they are that despite it, I know not but that Church-membership may be without it, (seeing, even you your self have concluded, it is no Church-Ordinance, *p.* 40, not the entering-Ordinance, *p.* 3, 4.) standeth both with Scripture and Reason, as mine Arguments make manifest. So that all your Arguments

prove no more but this, *That you are so wedded to your wordless Notions, that Charity can have no place with you.* Have you all this while so much as given me one small piece of a *Text* to prove it unlawful for the Church to receive those whom she, by the Word, perceiveth the *Lord God* and her Christ *hath* 5 received? No: and therefore you have said so much as amounts to nothing.

Your last Argument is,

If the Baptism of John *was so far honoured, and dignified, that they that did submit to it, are said to justifie God; and those that did it not,* 10 *are said to reject his counsel against themselves: so that their receiving, or rejecting the whole Doctrine of God, hath its denomination from this single Practice. And is there not as much to be said of the Baptism of Christ, unless you will say, it is inferior to* John's, *in worth and use.*

Answ. 1. That our denomination of Believers, and of our 15 receiving the Doctrine of the Lord Jesus, is not to be reckoned from our Baptism, is evident; Because according to our Notion of it, they only that have before received the Doctrine of the Gospel, and so shew it us by their Confession of Faith, they only ought to be baptized. This might serve for an Answer for all: 20 But,

2. The Baptism of *John* was *the Baptism of Repentance, for the*
Matt. 3. 4, 5, 6.
Luk. 3. 3. *Remission of Sins,* of which Water was but an outward signification, *Mark* 1. 4. Now, what is the Baptism of Repentance, but an unfeigned acknowledgement that they were Sinners, and so 25
Chap. 7. 29, 30.
Cha. 18 9.
Chap. 10. 29.
Chap. 15. 7. stood in need of a Saviour, Jesus Christ: This Baptism, or Baptism under this Notion, the *Pharisees* would not receive, *For they trusted to themselves that they were righteous, that they were not as other men, that they had need of NO repentance*: Not, but that they would have been baptized with Water, might that have been 30
Mat. 3. 7. without an acknowledgement that they were Sinners: wherefore seeing the Counsel of God respected, rather the Remission of
Eph. 1. 7, 8, 11. sins by Jesus Christ, than the outward act of Water-baptism, ye ought not, as you do, by this your Reasoning, to make it rather, at least in the revelation of it, to terminate in the outward act of 35 being baptized, but in unfeigned and sound Repentance, and the receiving of Jesus Christ by Faith.

Further, A *desire* to submit to *John's* Water-baptism, or of being *baptized* by him in Water, did not demonstrate by that

SINGLE act, the receiving of the whole Doctrine of God, as you
suggest.

Why did John *reject the Pharisees that would have been baptized?*
and Paul *examine them that were?* Matth. 3. 7. Acts 19. 2, 3.

5   If your Doctrine be true, why did they not rather say, Oh!
seeing you *desire* to be baptized, seeing you *have* been baptized,
you need not to be questioned any further your submitting to
John's Water; to us is a sufficient testimony, *even that single act,*
that you have received the whole Doctrine of God.

10   But I say, why did *John* call them *Vipers?* and *Paul* ask'd them,
Whether they had *yet received the Holy Ghost*: Yea, it is evident,
that a man may be desirous of Water that a man may be baptized,
and neither own the Doctrine of Repentance, nor know on
whom he should believe: evident, I say, and that by the same

15 Texts (*Matth.* 3. 7. *Acts* 19. 2, 3, 4.)

You have grounded therefore this your last Argument, as also
all the rest, upon an utter mistake of things.

I come now to your Questions; *which although they be*
mixed with Gall, I will with patience see if I can turn them
20   *into Food.*

Your first Question is,

I Ask *your own heart, whether popularity and applause of variety of*
Professors, be not in the bottom of what you have said; that hath
been your snare to pervert the right wayes of the Lord, and to lead
25 *others into a path wherein we can find none of the foot-steps of the*
Flock in the first Ages?

Answ. Setting aside a retaliation, like your Question, I say, and
God knows I speak the truth, I have been tempted to do what I
have done, by a provocation of sixteen years long; tempted, I say,
30 by the Brethren of your way: Who, when-ever they saw their
opportunity, have made it their business to seek, to rend us in
pieces; mine own self they have endeavoured to perswade to
forsake the Church; some they have rent quite off from us,
others they have attempted, and attempted to divide and break
35 off from us, but by the mercy of God, have been hitherto
prevented.

A more large account you may have in my next, if you think

good to demand it; but I thank God that I have written what I have written.

Quest. 2. *Have you dealt Brotherly, or like a Christian, to throw so much dirt upon your Brethren, in print, in the face of the World, when you had opportunity to converse with them of reputation amongst* 5 *us, before printing, being allowed the liberty by them, at the same time for you to speak among them?*

Answ. I have thrown no dirt upon them, nor laid any thing to their charge, if their Practice be warrantable by the Word; but *you* have not been offended at the *dirt*, your selves have thrown at 10 all the Godly in the Land that are not of our Perswasion, in counting them unfit to be communicated with, or to be accompanyed with in the House of God. *This dirt you never complained of,* nor would, I doubt, to this day, might you be still let alone to throw it. As to my Book, it was Printed before I spake 15 with any of you, or knew whether I might be accepted of you. As to them of reputation among you, I know others not one tittle inferior to them, and have my liberty to consult with who I like best.

Quest. 3. *Doth your carriage answer the Law of Love or Civility,* 20 *when the Brethren used means to send for you for a conference, and their Letter was received by you, that you should go out again from the City after knowledge of their desires, and not vouchsafe a meeting with them, when the glory of God, and the vindication of so many Churches is concerned?* 25

Answ. The reason why I came not amongst you, was partly because I consulted mine own weakness, and counted not my self, being a dull-headed man, able to engage so many of the chief of you, as I was then informed intended to meet me; I also feared, in personal Disputes, heats and bitter contentions might 30 arise, a thing my Spirit hath not pleasure in: I feared also, that both my self and words would be misrepresented; and that not without cause, for if they that Answer a Book will alter, and scrue Arguments out of their place, and make my Sentences stand in their own words, not mine, when (I say) my words are in a Book 35 to be seen. What would you have done, had I in the least, either in matter or manner, though but seemingly miscarried among you?

15 Printed] Prineed

As for the many Churches which you say are concerned, as also the Glory of God, I doubt not to say they are only your wordless Opinions that are concerned; the Glory of God is vindicated: *We receive him that God hath received, and that to the*
5 *glory of God*, Rom. 15. 16.

Quest. 4. *Is it not the Spirit of* Diotrephes *of old, in you, who loved to have the preheminence, that you are so bold to keep out all the Brethren, that are not of your mind in this matter, from having any entertainment in the Churches or Meetings to which you belong, though*
10 *you your self have not been denied the like liberty, among them that are contrary-minded to you? Is this the way of your retaliation? Or are you afraid lest the Truth should invade your quarters?*

Answ. I can say, I would not have the Spirit you talk of, what I have of it, God take it from me. But what was the Spirit of
15 *Diotrephes*? Why, *not to receive the Brethren into the Church, and to forbid them that would*, (3 John 9, 10.) This do not I; I am for Communion with Saints, because they are Saints: I shut none of the Brethren out of the Churches, nor forbid them that would receive them. I say again, shew me the man that is a visible
20 Believer, and that walketh with God; and though he differ with me about Baptism, the Doors of the Church stand open for him, and all our Heaven-born Priviledges he shall be admitted to them. But how came *Diotrephes* so lately into our parts? Where was he in those dayes that our Brethren of the Baptized-way,
25 would neither receive into the Church, nor pray with men as good as themselves, because they were not baptized; but would either, like *Quakers*, stand with their Hats on their heads, or else withdraw till we had done.

As to our not suffering those you plead for to preach in our
30 Assemblies, the Reason is, because we cannot yet prevail with them, to repent of their Church-renting Principles. As to the Retaliation, *mind the hand of God*, and remember *Adonibezek*, Judg. 1. 7.

Let the Truth come into our quarters and welcome, but *sowers* Prov. 6. 19.
35 *of Discord*, because the Lord hates it, we also ourselves will *avoid* Rom. 16. 17, 18. them.

Quest. 5. *Is there no contempt cast upon the Brethren, who desired your satisfaction, that at the same time, when you had opportunity to speak to them; instead of that, you committed the Letters to others, by*
40 *way of reflection upon them?*

Answ. It is not contempt at all to consult men more wise and judicious than him that wrote, or my self either. But why not consult with others, *is Wisdom to die with you?* Or do you count all that your selves have no hand in, *done to your disparagement?*

Quest. 6. *Did not your presumption prompt you to provoke THEM to printing, in your Letter to them, when they desired to be found in no such practice, lest the Enemies of Truth should take advantage by it?*

Answ. What provoked you to Print, will be best known at the Day of Judgment, whether your fear of losing your wordless Opinion, or my plain Answer to your Letter: the words in my Letter are, *As for my Book, never defer its Answer till you speak with me, for I strive not for mastery but Truth.* Though you did not desire to write, yet with us there was continual labour to rend us to pieces, and to prevent that, was my first Book written. And let who will take advantage, so the Truth of God, and the edification of my Brother be promoted.

Quest. 7. *Whether your Principle and Practice is not equally against others as well as us, viz; Episcopal, Presbyterians, and Independents, who are also of our side, for our practice, (though they differ with us about the subject of Baptism) Do you delight to have your hand against every man?*

Answ. I own Water-baptism to be God's Ordinance, but I make no Idol of it. Where you call now the *Episcopal* to side with you, and also the *Presbyterian,* &c. you will not find them easily perswaded to conclude with you against me. They are against your manner of Dipping, as well as the Subject of Water-baptism; neither do you, for all you flatter them, agree together in all but the Subject. Do you allow their Sprinkling? Do you allow their signing with the Cross? Why then have you so stoutly, an hundred times over, condemned these things as Antichristian. I am not against every man, though by your abusive language you would set every one against me, but am for Union, Concord, and Communion with Saints, as Saints, and for that cause I wrote my Book.

To conclude.

1. In ALL I have said, I put a difference between my Brethren of the Baptized-way; I know some are *more moderate than some.*

2. When I plead for the *unbaptized*, I chiefly intend *those* that are not SO baptized as *my* Brethren judge right, *according to the first pattern.*

3. If any shall count my Papers worth the scribling against, let him deal with mine Arguments, and things immediately depending upon them, *and not conclude he hath confuted a Book, when he hath only quarrelled at words.*

4. I have done, when I have told you, that I strive not for Mastery, nor to shew myself singular; *but, if it might be, for Union and Communion among the godly.* And count me not as an enemy, *because I tell you the Truth.*

5. *And now, dissenting Brethren, I commend you to God, who can pardon your sin, and give you more grace, and an inheritance among them that are sanctified by Faith in Jesus Christ.* Amen.

Here followeth Mr. *Henry Jessey*'s Judgment upon the same *Argument*.

Rom. 14. 1.

Such as are weak in the Faith, receive you, &c.

Whereas some suppose the receiving there mentioned, was but receiving into brotherly Affection, such as were in Church-Fellowship; but not a receiving of such as were weak into the Church.

For answer unto which consider,

That in the Test are *two things* to be enquired into.

First, What weakness of Faith this is, that must not hinder receiving.

Secondly, By whom, and to what, he that is weak in the Faith, is to be received?

To the *First*, What weakness of Faith this is that must not hinder receiving, whether was it weakness in the Graces of Faith, or in the Doctrine of Faith? It's conceived the *First* is included, but the *Second* principally intended.

Mar. 9. 24.
Luke. 24. 25.

First, That some of the Lord's People are weak in the Graces of Faith, will be confessed by all, and that the Lord would have his *Lambs* fed as well as his *Sheep*, and his *Children* as well as *grown* Men, and that he hath given the right to Gospel-priviledges, not to *degrees of Grace*, but to the *Truth; Him that is weak in the Faith, receive you*: or UNTO you, as some GOOD Translations read it. *Rom.* 14. 1.

Secondly, It's supposed, this Command of receiving *him* that is weak in the Faith, doth principally intend, that is weak in the *Doctrine* of Faith, and that not so much in the Doctrine of Justification, as in Gospel-Institutions, as doth appear by the second and sixth verses, which shews, that it was in matters of Practice, wherein some were weak, and at which others were offended; notwithstanding the Glorious Lord who bears all his *Israel* upon his heart receives, vers. 3. and commandeth, *him that is weak in the Faith receive you*, or unto you.

Therefore, here we are to enquire of the receiving in the Text, *By whom, and to what*, he that is weak in the Faith, should be received.

In which enquiry there are *Two parts.*

    First, By whom?

    Secondly, To what?

    To the *First.* The Text makes answer, *Him that is weak in the*
5 *Faith, receive you,* or unto you; which must be the Church at
Rome, to whom the Epistle was writ, as also, to all beloved of
God, called to be Saints, *Rom.* 1. 7. And as to them, so unto all
Churches, and Saints, *Beloved* and *called* throughout the World.

    Note, *That Epistles are as well to direct how Churches are to carry*
10 *things toward Saints without, as to Saints within; and also toward all*
men so as to give no offence to Jew or Gentile, nor to the Church of
God. 1. Cor. 10. 32.

    The second part of the Enquiry is, to what he that is weak in
the Faith is to be received? whether only unto mutual affection,
15 as some affirm, as if he were in Church-Fellowship before, that
were weak in the Faith? or whether the Text doth as well, if not
rather intend, the receiving such as were, and are weak in the
Faith. Not only unto mutual affection if in the Church, but unto
Church-fellowship also, if they were out. For clearing of which,
20 consider, To whom the Epistle was written, *Rom.* 1. 7. Not only
to the Church there, but unto all that were beloved of God, and
called to be Saints in all Ages. And as at *Rome* it is like there then
were, and in other places now are Saints weak in the Faith, both
in and out of Church-Fellowship; And it is probable there then
25 were, and elsewhere now are those that will cast such out of their
mutual affection. And if they will cast such out of their mutual
affection that are within, no doubt, they will keep out of their
Church-Fellowship those that are without.

    Arg. 1. Whereas the Lord's care extends to all his, and if it
30 were a good Argument in the third verse, for them to receive
those within, because God hath received them, it would be as
good Argument to receive in those without, *for God hath received*
them also: unless it could be proved, that all that were and are
weak in the Faith, were and are in Church-Fellowship, which is
35 not likely; For if they would cast such out of their Affection that
are within, they would upon the same account keep them out of
Church-fellowship that were without: Therefore as it is a Duty
to receive those within unto mutual Affection, SO it is no less a

27 no] do

duty, *by the Text*, to receive such weak ones as are without, into Church-Fellowship.

Arg. 2. Is urged from the words themselves which are, *Receive him that is weak in the Faith*, wherein the Lord puts NO limitation, in this Text or in any other, and *who* is *he* then that *can* restrain it, *unless he will limit the Holy One of Israel?* and how would such an interpretation, foolishly charge the Lord, as if he took *care ONLY* of those within, but not LIKE care of those without? whereas he commandeth them to receive *them*, and useth this Motive, he had received them, and he receiveth those that are weak in the Faith, if without, as well as those within.

From the Example, (to wit) *That God had received them*; whereas, had he been of the Church, they would have been perswaded of that before the Motive was urged: For no true Church of Christ's would take in, or keep in any, whom they judged the Lord had not received, but those weak ones were such as they questioned whether the Lord had received them, else the Text had not been an answer sufficient for their receiving them: There might have been objected, They hold up *Jewish* observations of Meats, and Dayes, which by the Death of Christ were abolished, and so did deny some of the Effects of his Death; yet the Lord who was principally *wronged* could pass *this* by, and *commandeth* others to receive them also. And if it be a good Argument to receive such as are weak in any thing, whom the Lord hath received, *Then there can be no good Argument to reject for any thing for which the Lord will not reject them*; For else the Command in the first verse, and his Example in the third verse were insufficient, without some other Arguments unto the Church, *beside his Command and Example.*

Some Object, *Chap.* 15. 7. *Receive you one another, as Christ hath received us unto the Glory of God,* and from thence supposing they were all in Church-fellowship before, whereas the Text saith not so: For if you consider the 8th and 9th verses, you may see he speaks unto *Jews* and *Gentiles* in *general*, that if the *Jews* had the receiving, *they* should receive *Gentiles*; and if the *Gentiles* had the *receiving, they* should receive *Jewes*; For had they not been on both sides commanded, The *Jewes* might have said to the *Gentiles*, you are commanded to receive us, but we are not commanded to receive you; and if the weak had the receiving, they should receive the strong; and if the strong had the

receiving, they should not keep out the weak; and the Text is
reinforced with the Example of the *Sons receiving us unto the Glory
of God*, that as he receiveth *Jewes*, and poor *Gentiles*, weak, and
strong; in Church-fellowship, or out of Church-fellowship: So
should they, to the Glory of God. And as the Lord Jesus received
some, though they held some things *more* than were Commanded,
and some things *less* than were Commanded, and as those that
were weak and in Church-fellowship, so those that were weak
and out of Church-fellowship; and that not only into mutual
Affection, but unto Fellowship with himself; and *so* should they,
not only receive such as were weak within into mutual Affection,
but such as were without, both to mutual Affection and to
Church-fellowship: Or else such weak ones as were without, had
been excluded by the Text. Oh! how is the heart of God the
Father and the Son set upon this, to have his Children in his
House, and in one anothers hearts as they are in his, and are
born upon the shoulders and breasts of his Son their High-
Priest? and as if all this will not do it, but the Devil will divide
them still whose work it properly is; *But the God of Peace will come
in shortly, and bruise Satan under their feet*, as in *Rom.* 16. 20. And
they will agree to be in one House, when they are more of one
Heart; in the mean time pray as in *Chap.* 15. 5. *Now the God of
Patience and Consolation grant that we be like-minded one towards
another according to Christ Jesus.*

    I shall endeavour the answering of some *Objections*, and leave it
unto Consideration.

    Obj. Some say this *bearing, or receiving, were but in things
indifferent.*

    Answ. That eating, or forbearing upon a civil account, are
things indifferent, is true: But not when done upon the account
of Worship, as keeping of Dayes, and establishing *Jewish*
observations about Meats, which by the Death of Christ are
taken away, and it is not fairly to be imagined the same Church at
Rome look'd so upon them as indifferent; nor that the Lord doth;
That it were all alike to him to hold up *Jewish* Observations, or to
keep Days or no Days, right Days or wrong days, as indifferent
things, which is a great mistake, and no less than to make God's
Grace little in receiving such: For if it were but in things wherein
they had not sinned, it were no great matter for the Lord to
receive, and it would have been as good an Argument or Motive

to the Church, to say the things were indifferent, as to say the
Lord had received them.

Whereas the Text is to set out the Riches of Grace to the
Vessels of Mercy, as *Rom.* 9. 15. That as at first he did freely
chuse and accept them; so when they fail and miscarry in many   5
things, yea about his Worship also, although he be most injured
thereby, yet he is first in passing it by, and perswading others to
do the like; That as the good *Samaritan* did in the Old
Testament, so our good *Samaritan* doth in the New, when Priest
and Levite pass'd by, Pastor and People pass by; yet he will not,   10
but pours in Oyl, and carries them to his Inn, and calls for
receiving, and setting it upon his account.

Object. *That this bearing with, and receiving such as are weak in
the Faith, must be limited to Meats, and Dayes, and such like things
that had been old Jewish Observations, but not unto the being ignorant*   15
in, or doubting of any New-Testament-Institution.

Answ. Where the Lord puts no limitation, men should be wary
how they do it, for they must have a Command for Example,
before they can limit this Command; for although the Lord took
this occasion from their difference about Meats and Dayes to   20
give this Command, yet the Command is not limited there, no
more than *Mat.* 12. 1, 2, 3, 4, 5, 6, 7. That when they made use
of his good Law rigorously in the Letter, he presently published
an Act of Grace, in the 7th verse, and tells them, *Had they known
what this meaneath, I will have Mercy and not Sacrifice, they would*   25
not have condemned the guiltless; as also *Mat.* 9. 13. *Go learn what
this meaneth, I will have Mercy and not Sacrifice*, which is not to be
limited unto what was the present occasion of publishing the
Command, but observed as a general Rule upon all occasions,
wherein Mercy and Sacrifice comes in competition, to shew the   30
Lord will rather have a Duty omitted that is due to him, then
Mercy to his Creatures omitted by them. So in the Text, When
some would not receive such as were weak in the Faith, as to
matters of Practice, the Lord was pleased to publish *this ACT of
Grace; Him that is weak in the Faith, receive you, but not to doubtful*   35
disputation. Now unless it be proved, that no Saint can be weak in
the Faith in any thing but Meats and Days, or in some Old-
Testament-Observation, and that he ought not to be judged a
Saint, that is weak in the Faith, as it relates to Gospel-
Institutions, in matters of practice, you cannot limit the Text,   40

and you must also prove his weakness SUCH, *as that the Lord will not receive him*; else the Command in the first verse, and the Reason or Motive in the third verse, will both be in force upon you, to wit, *Him that is weak in the Faith, receive you, or unto you,*
5 *for God hath received him.*

Object. *But some may object from* 1 Cor. 12. 13. For by one Spirit are we all baptized into one body, whether we be Jews or Gentiles. *Some there are that affirm this to be meant of Water-baptism, and that particular Churches are formed thereby, and all*
10 *persons are to be admitted and joyned unto such Churches by Water-baptism.*

Answ. That the Baptism intended in the Text, is the Spirits-baptism, and not Water-baptism; and that the Body the Text intends, is not principally the Church of *Corinth*, but all
15 Believers, both Jews and Gentiles, being baptized into one Mystical Body, as *Ephes.* 4. 4. *There is one Body, and one Spirit*, wherein there is set out the *Uniter* and the *United*; therefore in the third verse they are exhorted to keep the *unity* of the *Spirit* in the Bond of Peace. The United are all the Faithful, in one body;
20 into whom? in the fifth verse, in one Lord Jesus Christ; by what? one Faith, one Baptism, which CANNOT be meant of Water-baptism; for Water-baptism doth not unite all this Body, for some of them never had Water-baptism, and are yet of this Body, and by the Spirit gathered into one Lord Jesus Christ, *Ephes.* 1.
25 10. both which are in Heaven and in Earth, Jew and Gentile, *Ephes.* 2. 16. that he might reconcile both unto God in one Body by his Cross; the Instrument you have in *vers.* 18. *by one Spirit*, Ephes. 3. 6. That the Gentiles should be Fellow-Heirs of the same Body, *vers.* 15. *of whom the whole family in Heaven and Earth*
30 *is named.* And the Reasons of their keeping the Unity of the Spirit, in *Eph.* 4. 3. is laid down in *v.* 4, 5. being one Body, one Spirit, having one Hope, one Lord, one Faith, one Baptism, whether they were Jews or Gentiles, such as were in Heaven or in Earth, which CANNOT be meant of Water-baptism, for in
35 that sense, they had not all one Baptism, nor admitted and united thereby: So in 1 *Cor.* 12. 13. *For by one Spirit we are all baptized into one Body, whether Jews or Gentiles, whether we be bond or free, we having been all made to drink into one spirit*; which CANNOT be meant of Water-baptism, in regard all the Body of Christ,
40 Jews and Gentiles, bond and free, partook not thereof.

Object. *But* Ephes. 4. 5. *saith, there is but* one Baptism; *and by what hath been said, if granted, Water-baptism will be excluded, or else there is more Baptisms than one.*

Answ. It followeth not that because the Spirit will have no corrival, that therefore other things may not be in their places: That because the Spirit of God taketh the preheminence, therefore other things may not be subservient: 1 *John* 2. 27. The Apostle tells them, That *the anointing which they have received of him, abideth in them; and you need not,* saith he, *that any man teach you, but as the same anointing teacheth you all things.* By this some may think, *John* excludes the Ministry; no such matter, though the Holy Ghost had confirmed and instructed them so in the Truth of the Gospel, as that they were furnished against Seducers in *v.* 26. yet you see *John* goes on still teaching them in many things: As also in *Ephes.* 4. 11, 12, 13. he gave some Apostles, some Prophets, some Evangelists, some Pastors, and Teachers, *vers.* 12. for the perfecting of the Saints, for the work of the Ministry, for the edifying of the Body of Christ; *vers.* 13. *Till we all come in the unity of the Faith, and of the knowledge of the Son of God, unto a perfect man, unto the measure of the stature of the fulness of Christ.* So in the Spirits-baptism, though it have the preheminence, and appropriateth some things, as peculiar to it self, it doth not thereby destroy the Use and End of Water-baptism, or any other Ordinance in its place: for Water-baptism is a means to increase Grace, and in it, and by it Sanctification is forwarded, and Remission of sins more cleared and witnessed; yet the giving Grace, and regenerating and renewing, is the Holy Spirit's peculiar. Consider *Tit.* 3. 5. *By the washing of Regeneration, and renewing of the Holy Ghost,* Baptism being the outward sign of the inward Graces wrought by the Spirit, a representation or figure, as in 1 *Pet.* 3. 21. *The like Figure, whereunto Baptism doth now also save us, not the putting away of the filth of the flesh, but the answer of a good Conscience towards God, by the Resurrection of Jesus Christ,* not excluding Water-baptism; but shewing, That the Spiritual part is chiefly to be looked at: Though such as slight Water-baptism as the *Pharisees* and *Lawyers* did *Luke* 7. 30, reject the Counsel of God against themselves not being Baptized; And such as would set Water-baptism in the Spirit's place, exalt a duty against the Deity and dignity of the Spirit, and do give the Glory due unto him, as God blessed for ever, unto a duty.

By which mistake of setting up Water-baptism in the Spirit's place, and assigning it a work, which was never appointed unto it
5 of forming the Body of Christ, either in general, as in 1 *Cor.* 12. 13. *Eph.* 4, 5. or as to particular Churches of Christ, we may see the fruit, that instead of being the means of uniting as the Spirit doth, that it hath not only rent his seamless Coat, but divided his Body which he hath purchased with his own blood, and opposed
10 that great design of Father, Son, and Spirit, in uniting poor Saints, thereby pulling in pieces what the Spirit hath put together. *Him that is weak in the Faith receive you, for God hath received him*; being such as the Spirit had baptized and admitted of the Body of Christ, he would have his Churches receive them
15 also: whose Baptism is the ONLY Baptism, and so is called the ONE Baptism: Therefore consider, whether such a Practice, hath a Command or an Example, that Persons must be joyned into Church-fellowship by Water-baptism; For *John* baptized many, yet he did not baptize some into one Church, and some
20 into another, nor all into one Church (as the Church of *Rome* doth); And into what Church did *Philip* baptize the *Eunuch*, or the Apostle the Jaylor and his house? And all the rest they baptized, were they not left free to joyn themselves for their convenience, and Edification? All which I leave to
25 Consideration. I might have named some inconveniences, if not absurdities that would follow the Assertion; As to father the mistakes of the Baptizers on the Spirit's act, who is not mistaken in any He baptizeth; no false Brethren creep in unawares into the Mystical Body by him; and also, how this manner of forming
30 Churches would suit a Country, where many are converted, and willing to be baptized; but there being no Church to be baptized into, how shall such a Church-state begin? The first must be baptized into no Church, and the rest into him as the Church, or the Work stand still for want of a Church.

35 *Obj.* But God is a God of Order, and hath ordained Order in all the Churches of Christ; and for to receive one that holds the Baptism he had in his Infancy, there is no Command nor Example for, and by the same Rule Children will be brought in to be Church-members.

Answ. That God is a God of Order, and hath ordained Orders

in all the Churches of Christ, is true; and that this is one of the
Orders to receive him that is weak in the Faith, is as true. And
though there be no Example or Command, in so many words,
receive such an one that holds the Baptism he had in his infancy,
nor to reject such a one; but there is a Command to receive him   5
that is weak in the Faith, without limitation, and it is like this
might not be a doubt in those dayes, and so not spoken of in
particular.

But the Lord provides a remedy for all times, in the Text, *Him
that is weak in the Faith, receive you*, for else receiving, *would not be*   10
upon the account of Saintship; but upon knowing, and doing all
things according to Rule and Order, and that must be perfectly,
else for to deny any thing, or to affirm too much is disorderly,
and would hinder receiveing: But the Lord deals not so with his
People, but accounts *LOVE the fulfilling of the Law*, though they   15
be ignorant in many things, both as to knowing, and doing; and
receives them into Communion and Fellowship with himself,
and would have others do the same also: And if he would have so
much bearing in the Apostle's dayes, when they had infallible
helps to expound Truths unto them, much more now, the   20
Church hath been so long in the Wilderness and in Captivity,
and not that his People should be *driven away in the dark day*,
though they are sick and weak, *Ezek.* 34. 16, 21. And that it
should be supposed such tenderness would bring in Children in
Age to be Church-members, yea, and welcome, if anybody could   25
prove them in the Faith, though never so weak; for the Text is,
Him that is weak in the Faith, receive you: It is not He, and his
Wife, and Children, unless it can be proved, they are in the
Faith.

Object. *By this, some Ordinances may be lost or omitted, and is it to*   30
be supposed the Lord would suffer any of his Ordinances to be lost or
omitted in the Old or New-Testament, or the right use of them, and yet
own such for true Churches, and what reason can there be for it?

Answ. The Lord hath suffered some Ordinances to be omitted
and lost in the Old Testament, and yet owned the Church.   35
Though Circumcision were omitted in the Wilderness, yet he
owned them to be his Church, *Acts* 7. 38. and many of the
Ordinances were lost in the Captivity; See *Ainsworth* upon *Exod.*
28. 30, *&c.* which shewed what the High-Priest was to put on,
and were not to be omitted upon pain of death, as the *Urim* and   40

Thummim, yet being lost, and several other Ordinances, the Ark, with the Mercy-Seat and Cherubims, the Fire from Heaven, the Majesty and Divine Presence, *&c.* yet, he owns the Second Temple, though short of the First, and filled it with his Glory,
5 and honoured it with his Son, being a Member and a Minister therein. *Mal.* 3. 1. *The Lord whom you seek will suddenly come to his Temple*: So in the New-Testament, since their Wilderness condition and great and long Captivity, there is some darkness and doubts, and want of Light in the best of the Lord's People,
10 in many of his Ordinances, and that for several Ages, and yet how hath the Lord owned them for his Churches, wherein he is to have *Glory and Praise throughout all Ages*, Eph. 3. 21. And so should we own them, *unless we will condemn the Generation of the Just*: It must be confessed, That if exact Practice be required,
15 and clearness in Gospel-Institutions before Communion; who dare to be so bold as to say his hands are clean, and that he hath done all the Lord Commands, as to Institutions in his Worship? and must not confess the Change of Times doth necessitate some Variation, if not Alteration either in the matter or manner
20 of things according to Primitive Practice, yet owned for true Churches, and received as visible Saints, though ignorant either wholly or in great measure, in laying on of hands, singing, washing of feet, and anointing with oyl, in the Gifts of the Spirit, which is the *Urim* and *Thummim* of Gospel? and it cannot be
25 proved that the Churches were so ignorant in the Primitive times, nor yet that such were received into Fellowship; yet now herein it is thought meet there should be bearing, and why not in Baptism, especially in *such as own it for an Ordinance*, though in some things miss it, and do yet shew their love unto it, and unto
30 the Lord, and unto his Law therein, that they could be willing to die for it rather than to deny it, and to be baptized in their blood; which sheweth, they hold it in Conscience their duty, while they have further Light from above, and are willing to hear and obey as far as they know, though weak in the Faith, as to clearness in
35 Gospel-Institutions; surely the Text is on their side, or else it will exclude all the former, *Him that is weak in the Faith receive you, but not to doubtful disputations*, Rom. 14. 5. Let every man be fully perswaded in his own mind, and such the Lord hath received.

    As to the Query, *What reason is there, why the Lord should suffer*
40 *any of his Ordinances to be lost?*

Answ. If there were no Reason to be shown, it should teach us
silence, for he doth nothing without the highest Reason; and
there doth appear some Reasons, in the Old Testament, why
those Ordinances of *Urim* and *Thummim*, &c. were suffered to
be lost in the Captivity, that they might long, and look for the   5
Lord Jesus, the Priest, that was to stand up with *Urim* and
Thummim, Ezra. 2. 63. Neh. 7. 65. which the Lord by this puts
them upon the hoping for, and to be in the expectation of so
great a mercy, which was the promise of the Old Testament, and
all the Churches losses in the New Testament: By all the dark   10
night of ignorance she hath been in, and a long captivity she hath
been under, and in her wandering wilderness-state, wherein she
hath rather been fed with Manna from Heaven, than by men
upon Earth; and after all her crosses and losses, the Lord lets
Light break in by degrees, and deliverance by little and little; *and*   15
she is coming out of the Wilderness leaning upon her Beloved; and the
Lord hath given the Valley of *Achor* for a Door of Hope, that e're
long she may receive the Promise of the Gospel richly, by the
Spirit to be poured upon us from on High, *Isa.* 32. 15. and the
Wilderness be a fruitful Field, and the fruitful Field become a   20
Forrest, and then the Lord will take away the covering cast over
all people, *Isa.* 25. 7. and the Vail that is spread over all Nations;
Isa. 11. 9. *For the Earth shall be filled with the Knowledge of the*
Lord, as the Waters cover the Sea. vers. 13. *Then* Ephraim *shall not*
envy Judah, *and* Judah *shall not vex* Ephraim. Thus will the God   25
of Peace bruise Satan under-foot shortly; and one Reason why
the Lord may suffer all this Darkness and Differences that have
been, and yet are, is, that we might long and look for this blessed
Promise of the Gospel, the pourings out of the Spirit.

Object. But many Authors do judge, that the weak and strong were   30
all in Church-fellowship before, and that the receiving Rom. 14. 1.
was but into mutual affection.

Answ. It ought to be seriously weighed how any differ from so
many worthy Authors, is confessed, to whom the World is so
much beholding for their help in many things; but it would be of   35
dangerous consequence to take all for granted they say and
unlike the noble *Bereans*, Acts 17. 11. Though they had some
infallible Teachers, yet they took not their Words or Doctrine
upon trust; and there may be more ground to question
Expositors on this Text, in regard their Principles necessitate   40

them to judge that the sense; for if it be in their Judgments a
Duty to compel all to come in, and to receive all, and their
Children, they must needs judge by that Text, they were all of
the Church, and in Fellowship, before their scrupling Meats and
5 Dayes, because that is an Act of grown persons at ycars of
discretion; and therefore the receiving is judged by them to be
onely into mutual affection, for it is impossible for them to hold
their Opinion, and judge otherwise of the Text; for in Baptism,
they judge Infants should be received into Church-fellowship;
10 and then scrupling Meats and Dayes must needs be after
joyning. Their Judgements might as well be taken, that it is a
Duty to baptize Infants, as that they can judge of this Text
rightly, and hold their practice.

Object. *But no uncircumcised Person was to eat the Passeover,*
15 Exod. 12. *And doth not the Lord as well require, the sign of Baptism
now, as of Circumcision then? and is there not like reason for it?*

Answ. The Lord, in the Old Testament, expressly commanded
no uncircumcised Person should eat the Passeover, *Exod.* 12. 28.
and in *Ezek.* 34. 9. that no stranger, uncircumcised in heart, or
20 uncircumcised in flesh, should enter into his Sanctuary: And had
the Lord commanded, that no unbaptized Person should enter
into his Churches, it had been clear: And no doubt, Christ was
as faithful as a Son in all his House, as *Moses* was as a Servant;
and although there had been like reason, if the Lord had
25 commanded it so to be, yet in God's Worship we must not make
the likeness of any thing in our reason, but the Will of God, the
Ground of Duty; for upon such a Foundation some would build
the baptising of Infants, because it would be like unto
Circumcision, and so break the Second Commandment, in
30 making the likeness of things of their own contrivance, of force
with Institutions in the Worship of God.

The most that I think can be said is, That we have no Gospel-
Example for receiving without Baptism, or rejecting any for want
of it: Therefore it is desired, what hath been said, may be
35 considered, lest while we look for an Example, we do not
overlook a Command upon a mistake, supposing that they were
all in Church-fellowship before; where as the Text saith not
so, but, *Him that is weak in the Faith receive you,* or unto you.

We may see also how the Lord proceeds under the Law,
40 though he accounts those things that were done contrary to his

Law, sinful, though done ignorantly; yet never required the Offender to offer Sacrifice till he knew thereof, *Levit.* 5. 5. *comp.* with 15, & 16 verses. And that may be a mans own sin through his ignorance; that though it may be anothers Duty to endeavour to inform him in, yet not thereupon to keep him out of his 5 Father's House; for surely the Lord would not have any of his Children kept out, without we have a word for it. And though they scruple some Meats in their Fathers House, yet it may be dangerous for the stronger Children to deny them all the rest of the dainties therein, till the weak and sick can eat strong Meat; 10 whereas *Peter* had Meat for one, and Milk for another; and *Peter* must feed the poor Lambs as well as the Sheep; and if others will not do it, the Great Shepheard will come ere long and look up what hath been driven away, *Ezek.* 34. 4, 11. *Isa.* 40, 11. He will feed his Flock like a Shepheard; he shall gather the Lambs into 15 his Bosom, and gently lead those that are with Young.

Finis.

PEACEABLE PRINCIPLES
AND TRUE

PEACEABLE PRINCIPLES
AND TRUE

Note on the Text

Apparently only one edition (1674) of this work was published in Bunyan's lifetime. Charles Doe listed 'Peaceable Principles &c. 1674' in the 'catalogue-table' of the *1692 Folio*, and in a later catalogue noted that it was published 'in about 2 Sheets in 12⁰.'[1] W. T. Whitley locates copies of a 1688 reprint at the British Library and the John Rylands Library, but neither library actually has any copy of this work.[2] In fact, the only extant copy is in the collection of the American Baptist Historical Society in Rochester, New York. It is in 8⁰, and lacks the title-page, pp. 15–16, and apparently a last page that contained Bunyan's poem 'Of the Love of Christ.' In the 1860's the copy was owned by a Robert Cole of Bayswater. The earliest extant publication of the 'complete' work is in *The Works of that Eminent Servant of Christ, Mr John Bunyan*, ii (1737), ed. Samuel Wilson. Wilson includes much of the title-page, but not information on publisher, place, or date. He also includes the love poem at the end.[3]

Title-page (from Wilson): Peaceable Principles and True: | OR, | A brief Answer to Mr. Danver's and Mr. Paul's | Books against my Confession of Faith, and Differen-|ces in Judgment about Baptism no Bar to Com-|munion|WHEREIN | Their Scriptureless Notions are overthrown, and my Peaceable principles | still maintained. | [rule] | *Do ye indeed speak Righteousness, O Congregation? do ye judge uprightly, O ye Sons of* | *Men?* Psal. 58. 1. | [rule]

Collation: 8⁰; [A1 missing], A2, A3, A4, [A5, A6, A7], [A8 missing]; B–C⁸; [pp. 1–2, 15–16 missing] = pp. 48. The copy and text begin with the printed page number 3 and end with the printed page number 48. Signature B3 is misprinted B5. Signatures are printed on the first four leaves.

Contents: A2^r–C8^v text. A row of ornaments on A2^r is fillowed by '*Peaceable Principles*, &c.' The end of the section on C3^v is followed by a rule. A row of ornaments on C4^r is followed by '*The Conclusion.*' C8^v is signed 'J. BUNYAN.' The content held in common is the same in the American Baptist Historical

---

[1] *1692 Folio*, p. [871]; 'An Exact Catalogue of All Mr. John Bunyan's Writings,' in Bunyan's *The Heavenly Foot-Man* (4th edn., 1708), B3^v.

[2] W. T. Whitley, *A Baptist Bibliography* (1916–22), i. 103.

[3] For 'Of the Love of Christ', see Oxford Bunyan, vi. 131–2.

Society Copy and the Wilson version except for some differences of capitalization.

Running Titles: None.

Catchwords (selected): A2^v Question, B2^r *wonder*, B7^v *Such*, C2^r Bap-, C8^r God.

Copy collated: American Baptist Historical Society.

The following text is based on the American Baptist Historical Society copy with missing portions supplied from the Wilson version in the Dr Williams's Library.

Peaceable Principles, &c.

SIR

I Have received and considered your *short Reply* to my *Differences in judgment about* Water-Baptism *no Bar to Communion*; and observe, that you *touch* not the Argument at all; but rather labour what you can, and beyond what you ought, to throw *odiums* upon your Brother for reproving you for your Error; to wit, *That those Believers that have been baptized after confession of Faith made by themselves, ought, and are in duty bound to exclude from their Church-Fellowship, and Communion at the Table of the Lord, those of their holy Brethren that have not been so baptized.* This is your *Error*: Error I call it, because it is not founded upon the Word, but a meer humane Device; for although I do not deny, but acknowledge, that Baptism is God's Ordinance, yet I have denied, that Baptism was ever ordained of God *to be a wall of Division between the Holy* and *the Holy*: the Holy that are, and the Holy that are not *So* baptized with Water as we. You on the contrary, both by Doctrine and Practice, *assert that it is*; and therefore do separate your selves from all your Brethren that in that matter differ from you; accounting them, notwithstanding their saving faith and holy lives, *not fitly qualified for Church-communion*, and all because they have not been, as you, baptized: Further, you count their communion among *themselves, unlawful*, and therefore *unwarrantable*; and have concluded, *they are joyned to Idols, and that they ought not to be shewed the pattern of the House of God, until they be ashamed of their sprinkling in their Infancy, and accept of and receive Baptism as you*. Yea, you count them as they stand, not the Churches of God; saying, *We have no such Custom, nor the Churches of God.*

At this, I have called for your proofs; the which you have attempted to produce; but in conclusion, have shewed none other, but, *That the Primitive Churches had those they received, baptized before so received.*

I have told you, that this, though it were granted, cometh not up to the Question; *for we ask not, whether they were so baptized? but, whether you find a word in the Bible that justifieth your*

Your Reflections, p. 7.

p. 32.

p. 26.

p. 41.

concluding that it is your Duty to exclude those of your holy Brethren that have not been SO baptized? From this you cry out, that I take up the Arguments of them that plead for Infant-Baptism: I answer, I take up no other Argument but your own, *viz. That there being no Precept, President nor Example in all the Scripture for our excluding our holy Brethren that differ in this point from us; therefore we ought not dare to do it,* but contrariwise to receive them; because God hath given us sufficient proof that himself hath received them, whose example in this case he hath commanded us to follow, *Rom.* 14. 15.

This might serve for an Answer to your Reply. But because, perhaps, should I thus conclude, some might make *an ill use* of my brevity; I shall therefore briefly step after you, and examine your *short Reply*; at least, where shew of Argument is.

Your first five Pages are spent to prove me either *proud* or a *liar,* for inserting in the Title-page of my *Differences,* &c. *that your Book was written by the Baptists,* or Brethren of your way.

In answer to which; whoso* readeth your *second,* your *fifth* and *sixth* Questions to me, may not perhaps be easily perswaded to the contrary; but the two last in your Reply, are omitted by you; whether for brevities sake, or because you were conscious to your self, that the sight of them would overthrow your insinuations, I leave to the sober to judge. But put case I had failed herein, *doth this warrant your unlawful practice?*

You ask me next, *How long 'tis since I was a Baptist?* and then add, *'Tis an ill Bird that bewrays his own Nest.*

Answ. I must tell you (avoiding your *slovenly* Language) I know none to whom that Title is so proper as *to the Disciples of* John. And since you would know by what Name I would be distinguished from others; I tell you, I would be, and hope I am, *a Christian*; and chuse, if God shall count me worthy, *to be called a Christian, a Believer* or other such Name which is approved by the Holy Ghost. And as for those Factious Titles of *Anabaptists, Independents, Presbyterians,* or the like, I conclude, that they came neither from *Jerusalem,* nor *Antioch,* but rather from *Hell* and *Babylon*; for they naturally tend to divisions, *you may know them by their Fruits.*

Next, you tell us of your *goodly harmony in* London; or of the *amicable Christian correspondency betwixt those of divers perswasions there, until my turbulent and mutineering Spirit got up.*

* *If unbyassed.*

p. 5.

p. 6.

Act. 11. 26.

p. 7.

Answ. The cause of my writing, I told you, which you have neither disapproved in whole, nor in part. And now I ask *what kind* of Christian correspondency you have with them? *Is it such as relateth to Church-communion;* or *such* only as you are
5 commanded to have with every Brother that walketh disorderly, that they may be ashamed of their Church-communion, which you condemn? if so, *your great flourish will add no praise to them*; and why they should glory in a correspondency with them as Christians, who yet count them, under such deadly sin, which
10 will not by any means, as they now stand, *suffer you to admit them* to their Father's Table, to me is not easie to believe.

Farther, Your Christian correspondency (as you call it) will not keep you *now* and *then*, from *fingering* some of their members from them; nor from teaching them that you *so* take away, to judg
15 and condemn them that are left behind: *Now who boasteth in this besides your self, I know not.*

Touching Mr. *Jesse's* Judgment in the case in hand, *you know it condemneth your Practice*; and since in your first, you have called for an Author's testimony, I have presented you with one, whose
20 Arguments you have not condemned.

For your insinuating my abusive and unworthy behaviour, as the cause of the Brethrens attempting to break our Christian communion; it is not only false, but ridiculous: *False*; for they have attempted to make *me* also one of their Disciples, and sent *to** me, and *for* me
25 for that purpose. Besides, it is *ridiculous*; surely their *pretended* order, and as they call it, our *disorder*, was the cause; or they must render themselves very malicious, to seek the overthrow of a whole Congregation, for (if it had been so) the unworthy behaviour of one.

    * This attempt began above sixteen years ago.

30 Now since you tell me, *pag.* 9. *That Mr.* Kiffin *had no need of my foregiveness for the wrong he hath done me in his Epistle.*

I ask, did he tell you so? But let it lie as it doth; I will at this time turn his Argument upon him, and desire his direct Answer: *There being no Precept, President or Example for Mr.* Kiffin *to exclude*
35 *his holy brethren from Christian Communion that differ with him about Baptism, he ought not to do it; but there is neither Precept, President, nor Example; therefore,* &c.

You blame me for writing his Name at length; but I know he is not ashamed of his Name: and for you, though at the remotest
40 rate, to insinuate it, *must needs be damage to him.*

Your artificial squibbing suggestions to the world about my
self, imprisonment, and the like, I freely *bind* unto me as an
Ornament among the rest of *my Reproaches*, till the Lord shall
wipe them off at his coming. *But they are no Argument that you
have a word that binds you to exclude the holy Brethren Communion.*   5

Now what if (as you suggest) the sober Dr. *Owen*, though he
told me and others at first, he would write an Epistle to my Book,
yet waved it afterwards; *this is also to my advantage*; because it was
through the earnest solicitations of several of you that at that
time stopped his hand: *And perhaps, 'twas more for the Glory of*   10
*God, that Truth should go naked into the world, than as seconded by so
mighty an Armour-bearer as he.*

p. 6.   You tell me also, that some of the sober Independents have
shewed dislike to my writing on this Subject: What then? If I
should also say, as I can without lying, *that several of the Baptists*   15
have wished yours burnt before it had come to light; is your Book ever
the worse for that?

In *p.* 13. *You tell us, you meddle not with Presbyterians,
Independents, mixt Communionists* (a new name) *but are for liberty
for all according to their light.*   20

Answ. I ask them, suppose an holy man of God, that differeth
from you, as those above-named do, in the manner of Water-
Baptism; I say, suppose such an one should desire communion
with you, yet abiding by his own light, as to the thing in question,
would you receive him to fellowship? If no, *do you not dissemble*?   25

But you add, *If unbaptized Believers do not walk with us, they may
walk with them with whom they are better agreed.*

Answ. Then it seems you do but flatter them: You are not, for
all you pretend to give them their liberty, *agreed they should have it
with you*: Thus do the Papists give the Protestants their liberty,   30
because they can neither will nor chuse.

Again, But do you not follow them with clamours and out-
cries, that their communion even amongst themselves, is
unwarrantable? Now how then do you give them their liberty?
Nay, do not even these things declare that you would take it away   35
if you could?

For the time that I have been a Baptist (say you) *I do not remember
that ever I knew, that one unbaptized person did so much as offer
themselves to us for Church-fellowship.*

Answ. This is no proof of your love to your Brethren; but   40 rather an Argument that your *rigidness* was from that day to this so apparent, that those good souls despaired to make such attempts; we know they have done it elsewhere, where they hoped to meet with encouragement.

In *p.* 14. You seem to retract your denial of Baptism to be the initiating Ordinance. And indeed Mr. *Danvers* told me, that you must retract that Opinion, and that he had or would speak to you to do it; yet by some it is still so acknowledged to be; and in particular, by your great helper. Mr. *Denne*, who strives to maintain it by several Arguments; but your denial may be a sufficient confutation to him; so I leave you together to agree about it, and conclude you have overthrown him.

Denne's *Truth outweighing*, &c. *p.* 46.

But it seems though you do not now own it to be the inlet into a particular Church; yet (as you tell us in *p.* 14. of your last) *you never denied that Baptism doth not make a Believer a member of the universal, orderly, Church-visible.* And in this Mr. *Danvers* and you agree. *Persons enter into the Visible Church thereby,* saith he.

Treatise of Bapt.

Answ. Universal, that is, the *whole* Church; This word now comprehendeth all the parts of it, even from *Adam* to the very world's end, whether in Heaven or Earth, &c. Now that Baptism makes a man a member of this Church, I do not yet believe, nor can you shew me why I should.

2. The *Universal, Orderly Church*: What Church this should be (if by orderly, you mean Harmony or Agreement in the outward parts of Worship) I do not understand neither.

And yet thus you should mean, because you add the word *VISIBLE* to all at the last; *The Universal, Orderly, Visible Church.* Now I would yet learn of this Brother where this church is; for if it be *Visible*, he can *tell* and also *shew* it. But to be short, there is no such Church: The universal Church cannot be visible; a great part of that vast Body being already in Heaven, and a great part as yet (perhaps) unborn.

But if he should mean by *Universal*, the whole of that part of this Church that is on Earth, then neither is it *Visible* nor *Orderly*. 1. Not *Visible*; for the greatest part remains alwayes to the best mans eye utterly invisible.

2. This Church is not *Orderly*; that is, hath not Harmony in its outward and visible parts of worship; some parts opposing and contradicting the other most *severely*. Yea, would it be uncharitable to believe, that some of the members of this Body could

willingly die in opposing that which others of the Members hold to be a Truth of Christ? As for instance at home; could not some of those called *Baptists*, die in opposing Infant-Baptism? And again, some of them that are for Infant-Baptism, *die for that as a Truth?* Here therefore is no Order, but an evident contradiction; and that *too* in *such* parts of worship, as both count visible parts of worship indeed.

So then by *Universal, Orderly, Visible Church*, this Brother must mean those of the Saints only, that have been, or are baptized as we; this is clear, because Baptism (saith he) maketh a Believer a member of *this Church*; his meaning then is, that there is an *Universal, Orderly, Visible Church*, and they *alone* are the *Baptists*; and that every one that is baptized, is by that made a member of the *Universal, Orderly, Visible Church of Baptists*, and that the whole number of the rest of Saints are utterly excluded.

But now if other men should do as this man, how many Universal Churches should we have? An *Universal, Orderly, Visible Church* of *Independents*; an *Universal, Orderly, Visible Church* of *Presbyterians*, and the like. And who of them, if as much confused in their Notions as this Brother, might not (they judging by their own light) contend for *their Universal Church*, as *he* for *his?* But they have more wit.

But suppose that this *unheard-of* fictitious Church were the only true Universal Church; yet *whoever they baptize*, must be a Visible Saint first; and *if* a Visible Saint, *then* a Visible Member of Christ; and if *so*, then a *Visible Member* of his Body, which is the Church, before they be baptized; now he which is a Visible Member of the Church already, *that which hath so made him, hath prevented all those claims that by any may be made or imputed to this or that Ordinance to make him so.* His visibility is already; he is already a Visible Member of the Body of Christ, and after that baptized. His Baptism then neither makes him a Member, nor Visible Member, of the Body of Jesus Christ.

You go on, *That I said it was consent that makes Persons Members of particular Churches is true.*

Answ. But that it is Consent and *NOTHING* else, Consent *WITHOUT* Faith, *&c.* is false. Your after-endeavour to heal your unsound saying, will do you no good; *Faith gives being to, as well as Probation for Membership.*

Act. 8. 37, & 19. 17. & 16. 33.

Pag. 4. of your first

23–21 (facing page) But suppose . . . *How can we*] Wilson 1737

What you say *NOW* of the Epistles that they were written to particular Saints, and those *too* out of Churches as well as in, I always believed: But in your first you were pleased to say, *you were one of them that objected against our proofs out of the Epistles,* Your Reflections, p. 9.
5 *because they were written to particular Churches* (intending these baptized) *and that they were written to other Saints, would be hard for me to prove:* but you do well to give way to the Truth.

What I said about Baptism's being a *PEST*, take my Words as they lie, and I stand still thereto; *Knowing that Satan can make any*
10 *of God's Ordinances a PEST and Plague to his People, even Baptism, the Lord's Table, and the holy Scriptures; yea, the Ministers also of Jesus Christ may be suffered to abuse them, and wrench them out of their place.* Wherefore I pray, if you write again, either consent to, or deny this Position, before you proceed in your
15 Outcry.

But I must still continue to tell you, tho' you love not to hear thereof; That supposing your Opinion hath hold of your Conscience, *if you might have your will, you would make inroads and outroads too, in all the Churches that are not as you in the Land.*
20 You reckon that Church-privileges belong not to them who are not baptized as we; saying, *How can we take these priviledges from them before they have them, we keep them from a disorderly practice of* p. 37. of your Reply *Ordinances, ESPECIALLY among our selves;* intimating you do what you can also among others: And he that shall judge those he
25 walketh not with, or, say as you, that they like *Ephraim, are joined to an Idol, & ought to repent & be ashamed of that Idol before they* Your Reflect. p. 32. p. 26, p. 30. p. 7. *be SHEWED the pattern of the House;* and then shall back all with the citation of a Text; doth it either in *jest* or in *earnest*; if in *jest*, it is *abominable*; if in *earnest*, his Conscience is *engaged*; and
30 being *engaged*, it putteth him upon doing what he can to extirpate the thing he counteth Idolatrous and abominable, out of the Churches abroad, as well as that he stands in relation unto. This being thus, 'tis reasonable to conclude, you want not an heart, but opportunity for your Inrodes and Outrodes among
35 them.

Touching those five things I mentioned in my second; *you should not have counted* they were found *no where*, because not found under that Head which I mention: And now lest you should miss them again, I will present you with them here.

40 1. *Baptism is not the initiating Ordinance.*

2. *That though it was, the case may so fall out, that Members might be received without it.*

3. *That Baptism makes no man a visible Saint.*

4. *That Faith, and a life becoming the ten Commandments, should be the chief and most solid Argument with Churches to receive to Fellowship.*

5. *That Circumcision in the flesh was a type of Circumcision in the heart, and not of Water-Baptism.*

To these you should have given fair answers, then you had done like a workman.

Now we are come to *p.* 22, and 23 of yours; where you labour to insinuate, *that a transgression against a positive precept, respecting instituted worship, hath been punished with the utmost severity that God hath executed against men, on record, on this side Hell.*

Treat. of Baptism. *Answ.* Mr. *Danvers* says, *That to transgress a positive Precept respecting Worship, is a breach of the first and second Commandment.* If so, then 'tis for the breach of *them*, that these severe rebukes befal the Sons of men.

2. But you instance the case of *Adam his eating the forbidden fruit*; yet to no great purpose. *Adam*'s first transgression was, that he violated the Law that was written in his heart; in that he hearkned to the tempting voice of his Wife; and after, because he did eat of the Tree: He was bad then before he did eat of the *Gen.* 3. Tree; which badness was infused over his whole Nature; and *Mat.* 7. then he bare this evil fruit of eating things that God had 17. forbidden. *Either make the Tree good, and his Fruit good; or the Tree Luke* 6. 43, 44. *bad, and his Fruit bad*: Men must be bad, ere they do evil; and good, ere they do good.

Again, Which was the greatest judgment, to be *defiled* and *depraved*, or to be put out of Paradise, do you in your next determine.

But as to the matter in hand, *What positive Precept do they transgress that will not reject him that God bids us receive*, if he want light in Baptism?

As for my calling for Scripture to prove it lawful thus to exclude them; blame me for it no more: verily I still must do it; and had you but *one* to give, I had *had it* long before this. *But you p.* 23. *wonder I should ask for a Scripture to prove a Negative.*

Answ. Are you at that door, my Brother? If a Drunkard, a Swearer, or Whoremonger should desire communion with you,

and upon yor refusal, demand your grounds; would you think his
Demands such you ought not to answer? would you not readily
give him by *SCORES*? So doubtless would you deal with us, *but
that in this you are without the Lids of the Bible.*

5   2. But again, you have acted as those that must produce a
positive Rule. *You count it your Duty, a part of your Obedience to
God, to keep those out of Church-fellowship that are not baptized as
you.* I then demand what Precept bids you do this? where are you
commanded to do it?

10   You object, That in *Eph.* 4. and 1 *Cor.* 12. is not meant of   p. 24.
Spirit-Baptism. But Mr. *Jesse* says it is not, cannot be the
Baptism with water; and you have not at all refuted him.

And now for the Church in the wilderness; *You thought, as*   p. 26, 27.
you say, I could have answered my self in the thing but as yet I have
15 not, neither have you. But let us see what you urge for an
Answer.

1. (Say you) *Though God dispensed with their obedience to*   Gen. 17.
Circumcision in that time, it follows not that you or I should dispense   Ex. 12.
with the Ordinance of Water-Baptism now.

20 *Answ.* God commanded it, and made it the initiating
Ordinance to Church-communion. But *Moses*, and *Aaron*, and
Joshuah, and the Elders of *Israel* dispensed with it for forty years;
therefore the dispensing with it *was ministerial*, and that with
God's allowance, *as you affirm.* Now if they might dispense with
25 Circumcision, though the initiating Ordinance; why may not we
receive God's Holy ones into Fellowship, since we are not
forbidden it, but commanded; yea, why should we make Water-
Baptism, which God never ordained to that end, a Bar to shut
out and let in to Church-communion?

30   2. You ask, *Was Circumcision dispensed with for want of Light, it
being plainly commanded?*

Answ. Whatever was the cause, want of Light is as great a
cause: And that it must necessarily follow, they must needs see it,
because commanded, savours too much of a Tang of Free will,
35 or of the sufficiency of our understanding; and intrencheth too
hard on the glory of the Holy Ghost; whose work it is *to bring all
things to our remembrance, whatsoever Christ hath said to us*, John
14. 26.

3. You ask, *Cannot you give your self a reason, that their moving,*
40 *travelling state, made them uncapable, and that God was merciful?*

Can the same reason, or any thing like it, for refusing Baptism, be given now?

Answ. I cannot give my self this reason, nor can you by it give me any satisfacation.

First, Because their travelling state could not hinder; if you consider, that they might, and doubtless did lie still in one place years together.

1. They were forty years going from *Egypt* to *Canaan*; and they had but forty two journies thither.

2. They at times went several of these journies in one and the same year. They went (as I take it) eleven of them by the end of the third Moneth after they came out of the Land of *Egypt.* compare *Exod.* 19. 1. with *Numb.* 33. 15.

3. Again, in the fortieth year we find them in Mount *Hor,* where *Aaron* died, and was buried. Now that was the year they went into *Canaan*; and in that year they had nine Journies more, or ten, by that they got over *Jordan, Numb.* 33. 38, &c. Here then were twenty journies in less than an year and an half. Divide then the rest of the time to the rest of the Journies, and they had above thirty eight years to go their two and twenty Journies in. And how this should be such a travelling moving state, as that it should hinder their keeping this Ordinance in its season, to wit, *to circumcise their Children the eighth day*; especially considering, to circimcise them in their Childhood, as they were born; might be with more security, than to let them live while they were men, I see not.

If you should think that their Wars in the Wilderness might hinder them; I answer, They had, for ought I can discern, ten times as much fighting in the Land of *Canaan,* where they were circumcised, as in the Wilderness where they were not. And if carnal or outward safety had been the Argument, doubtless they would not have circumcised themselves in the sight (as it were) of one and thirty Kings; I say, they would not have circumcised their *six hundred thousand Warriors* and have laid them open to the attempts and dangers of their enemies. No such thing therefore as you are pleased to suggest, was the cause of their not being as yet circumcised.

Fourthly, An extraordinary Instance to be brought into a standing Rule, are no parallels: That's the sum of your Fourth.

Answ. The Rule was ordinary; which was Circumcision; the

Josh. 5.
Ch. 12.

laying aside of this Rule became as ordinary, so long a time as forty years, and that *in the WHOLE Church also*. But this is a poor shift, to have nothing to say, but that the case was extraordinary, when it was not.

5 But you ask, *Might they do so when they came into* Canaan?

Answ. No, no. No more shall we do as we do now, *when that which is perfect is come*.

You add, *Because the Church in the Wilderness*, Rev. 12. *could not come by Ordinances*, &c. *therefore when they may be come at, we need*
10 *not practise them*.

Answ. No body told you so. But are you out of that wilderness mentioned *Rev.* 12? Is Antichrist down and dead to ought but your Faith? Or are we only out of that *Egyptian* darkness, that in Baptism have got the start of our Brethren? For shame be silent:
15 your selves are yet under so great a Cloud, as to imagine to your selves a *Rule of practice* not found in the Bible; that is, *to count it a sin to receive your Holy Brethren, though not forbidden, but* Ro. 14. *commanded to do it*. chap. 15.

Your great Flourish against my fourth Argument, I leave to
20 them that can judge of the weight of your words; as also what you say of the fifth or sixth.

For the instance I give you of *Aaron*, *David*, and *Hezekiah*, who did things not commanded, and that about Holy matters, and yet were held excusable; you, nor yet your Abettors for you, can by Levit. 6. 26.
25 any means overthrow. *Aaron transgressed the Commandment*; ch. 10 18. David *did what was not lawful* and they in *Hezekiah's* time *ate the* Mat. 12. 3, 4. *Passeover otherwise than it was written*, 2 Chron. 30. 18. But here I perceive the Shoe pincheth; which makes you glad of Mr. *Denne's* evasion for help. At this also Mr. *Danvers* (but yet to no p. 29.
30 purpose) cries out, charging me with asserting, *that Ignorance absolves from Sin of Omission and Commission*. But first, fairly take from me the Texts, with others that I can urge; and then begin to accuse.

You have healed your suggestion of unwritten verities poorly.
35 But any shift to shift off the force of truth. After the same manner also, you have helped your asserting, *that you neither keep out, nor cast out from the Church, if Baptized, such as come unprepared to the Supper, and other solemn appointments*. Let us leave yours and mine to the pondering of wiser men.

40 My seventh Argument (as I said) you have not so much as Pag. 31.

touched; nor the ten in that one, but only derided at the ten. But we will shew them to the Reader.

1. *Love, which above all things we are commanded to put on, is much more worth, than to break about Baptism*, Col. 3. 14.

2. *Love, is more discovered, when we receive for the sake of Christ and Grace, than when we refuse for want of Water.*

3. *The Church at* Colosse, *was charged to receive, and forbear the saints, because they were new Creatures.*

4. *Some Saints were in the Church at* Jerusalem, *that opposed the Preaching of Salvation to the Gentiles; and yet retained their Membership.*

5. *Divisions, and distinctions among Saints, are of later date, than Election, and the Signs of that; and therefore should give place.*

6. *It is Love, not Baptism, that discovereth us to the World to be Christ's Disciples*, Joh. 13. 35.

7. *It is Love that is the undoubted Character of our Interest in, and Fellowship with Christ.*

Gal. 6. 16.
Phil. 3. 16.
1 Joh. 1. 2.
Ro. 12. 10.
ch. 14. 18.
v. 10.
Jam. 4. 11.

8. *Fellowship with Christ is sufficient to invite to, and the new Creature the great Rule of our fellowship with, Christ.*

9. *Love is the fulfilling of the Law, wherefore he that hath it is accepted with God, and ought to be approved of Men; but he fulfils it not, who judgeth and setteth at nought his Brother.*

10. *Love is sometimes more seen, and shewed in forbearing to urge and press what we know, than in publishing and imposing*, John. 16. 12. 1 Cor. 3. 1, 2.

11. *When we attempt to force our Brother beyond his Light, or to break his heart with grief, to thrust him beyond his Faith, or bar him from his priviledges, how can we say I love?*

12. *To make that the Door to Communion which God hath not; to make that the including, excluding Charter, the Bar, Bounds and Rule of Communion, is for want of Love.* Here are two into the bargain.

If any of these, Sir, please you not in this dress give me a Word; and I shall as well as my Wit will serve, give you them in a Syllogistical mode.

Now that you say (practically) *for some speak with their feet,* (their walking *Prov.* 6. 13.) *that Water is above Love*; and all other things is evident; because have they all but Water, you refuse them for want of that; yea, and will be so hardy, though without God's Word, to refuse Communion with them.

Pag. 32.

In our discourse about the Carnality that was the cause of the

Divisions that were at Corinth, you ask *who must the charge of Carnality fall upon, them that defend, or them that oppose the Truth?* Pag. 33:

Answ. Perhaps upon both; but be-sure upon them that oppose; wherefore look you to your selves, *who without any command of God to warrant you, exclude your Brother from Communion; your Brother whom god hath commanded you to receive.*

My ninth Argument, you make your self merry with in the beginning; but why do you by and by so cut, and hack, and cast it as it were in the Fire. Those seventeen absurdities you can by no means avoid. *For if you have not*, as indeed you have not (though you mock me for speaking a word in Latin) not one word of God, that commands you to shut out your Brethren for want of Water-Baptism, from your Communion; I say, if you have not one word of God to make this a duty to you, then unavoidably,

1. *You do it by a Spirit of Persecution.*

2. *With more respect to a Form, than the Spirit and Power of Godliness.*

3. *This also, makes Laws, where God makes none; and is to be wise above what is written.*

4. *It is a directing the Spirit of the Lord.*

5. *And bindeth all mens Consciences to our Light and Opinion.*

6. *It taketh away the Childrens Bread.*

7. *And with-holdeth from them the increase of Faith.*

8. *It tendeth to make wicked the hearts of weak Christians.*

9. *It tendeth to harden the hearts of the wicked.*

10. *It setteth open a Door to all Temptations.*

11. *It tempteth the Devil to fall upon them that are alone.*

12. *It is the Nursery of all vain janglings.*

13. *It occasioneth the World to reproach us.*

14. *It holdeth staggering Consciences in doubt of the right ways of the Lord.*

15. *It abuseth the Holy Scriptures.*

16. *It is a prop to Antichrist.*

17. *And giveth occasion to many to turn aside to most dangerous Errors.*

And though the last is so abhorred by you, that you cannot contain yourselves when you read it; yet do I affirm, as I did in my first (p. 116.) *That to exclude Christians from Church-Communion, and to debar them their Heaven-Born Priviledges, for the want of that which God never yet made a wall of Division between us;*

did, and doth, and will prevail with God to send those Judgments we
have, or may hereafter feel. Like me yet as you will.

Pag. 41.
I come next to what you have said in justification of your
fourteen Arguments. *Such as they were* (say you) *I am willing to*
stand by them: What I have offered, I have offered modestly; according 5
to the utmost Light I had into those Scriptures upon which they are
bottomed; having not arrived unto such a peremptory way of
Dictatorship, as what I render must be taken for Laws binding to others
in Faith and Practice; and therefore express my self by Suppositions,
Reflections. *strong Presumptions, and fair seeming Conclusions from the Premises.* 10

Answ. Your Arguments, as you truly say, are builded upon, or
drawn from Suppositions and Presumptions; and all because you
Pag. 51. want for your help the words of the Holy Scripture. *And this let*
the Reader note. For as I have often called for the Word, but as yet
could never get it, because you have it not, *neither in Precept,* 15
President nor Example, therefore come you forth with your
seeming Imports and Presumptions.

The judicious Reader will see in this last, that not only here,
but in other Places, what poor shifts you are driven to, to keep
your Pen going. 20

But, sir, since you are not peremptory in your Proof; *how come*
you to be so absolute in your Practice? For notwithstanding all your
seeming modesty, you will neither grant these Communion with
you; nor allow their Communion among themselves, that turn
aside from your *seeming Imports*; & that go not with you in your 25
strong Presumptions. You must not; you dare not, lest you
Pag. 30, 31, 32. countenance their Idolatry; *and nourish them up in sin*; they live in
Of your
Reflections. the breach of Gospel-order; and *Ephraim-like are joyned to an*
Idol. And as for your Love, it amounts to this, you deal with
them, and withdraw from them, and all because of some strong 30
Presumptions and Suppositions.

But you tell me *I use the Arguments of the Pædo-Baptists, to wit,*
But where are Infants forbidden to be Baptized?

But I ingenuously tell you, I know not what *Paedo* means; and
how then should I know his Arguments. 35

2. I take no mans Argument but Mr. *K's.* (I must not name
him farther) I say I take no mans Argument but his, *now*, viz.
That there being no Precept, President, or Example, for you to shut
your Holy Brethren out of Church-Communion; therefore you should
not do it. That you have no command to do it, is clear, and you 40

must of necessity grant it. Now where there is no Precept for a foundation; 'tis not what you by all your reasonings can suggest; can deliver you from the guilt of adding to his Word.

Are you commanded to reject them? If yea, where is it? If nay,
5 for shame be silent.

Let us say what we will (say you) for our own Practice; unless we bring positive Scriptures that yours is forbidden, though no where written, you will be as a man in a rage without it; and would have it thought you go away with the Garland.

10 *Answ.* 1. I am not in a rage, but contend with you earnestly for the Truth. And say what you will or can, though with much more squibbing, frumps and taunts, than hitherto you have mixed your writing with, Scripture, Scripture we cry still. And 'tis a bad sign that your cause is naught, when you snap and snarl because I call
15 for Scripture.

2. Had you a Scripture for this practice that you ought to shut your Brethren out of Communion for want of water-Baptism, I had done; but you are left of the Word of God, and confess it!

3. And as you have not a Text that justifies your own; so
20 neither that condemns our Holy and Christian Communion: we are commanded also *to receive him that is weak in the Faith, for God hath received him.* I read not of Garlands, but those in the *Acts*; take you them. And I say moreover, that honest and holy Mr. *Jesse* hath justified our practice, and you have not condemned his
25 Arguments. They therefore stand all upon their feet against you.

I leave your 2, 3, 4, 5 and 6 Argument under my Answers where they are suppressed. In your seventh you again complain, for that I touch your *seeming imports; saying, I do not use to say as* John Bunyan, *this I say, and I dare to say. I please my self by*
30 *commending my apprehensions soberly, and submissively to others much above me.*

Answ. 1. Seeming imports are a base and unworthy foundation for a practice in Religion; and therefore I speak against them.

2. Where you say, you submit your apprehensions soberly to
35 those much above you; 'Tis false; unless you conclude none are above you, but those of your own opinion. Have you soberly, and submissively commended you apprehensions to those Congregations, in *London* that are not of your perswasion in the case in hand? and have you consented to stand by their Opinion?
40 Have you commended your apprehensions *soberly and submissively*

to those you call Independents, and Presbyters? And are you
willing to stand by their Judgment in the Case? Do you not
reserve to your self the liberty of judging what they say? and of
choosing what you judg is right, whether they conclude with you
or no? If so; why do you so much dissemble with all the World in   5
Print; to pretend you submit to others judgment, and yet abide to
condemn their judgments? you have but one help: perhaps you
think they are not above you; and by that *Proviso*, secure your
self; but it will not do.

Reflection
p. 52.
p. 46.

For the offence you take at my Comment upon your calling   10
Baptism, *a livery*: and *for your calling it the Spirits metaphorical
description of Baptism*: both Phrases are boldness without the
Word. Neither do I find it called a lifting Ordinance, nor the
solemnization of the Marriage betwixt Christ and a Believer. But
perhaps you had this from Mr. *D'anvers*, who pleaseth himself   15
with this kind of wording it: and says moreover in justification of
you, *That persons entred into the visible Church thereby* (by Baptism,
which is untrue, though Mr. *Baxter* also saith it) *are by consent
admitted into particular Congregations, where they may claim their
priviledges due to Baptized Believers, being orderly put into the Body,*   20
*and put on Christ by their baptismal Vow and Covenant: for by that
publick declaration of consent, is the Marriage and solemn Contract*

*This is in the 3
last pages of his
Treatise of
Baptism.*

made betwixt Christ and a Believer in Baptism. And (saith he) *if it be
preposterous and wicked for a Man and Woman to cohabit together,
and to enjoy the priviledges of a Married Estate, without the passing of*   25
*that publick solemnity: So it is NO less disorderly upon a spiritual
account, for any to claim the priviledges of a Church, or be admitted to
the same, till the passing of this solemnity by them.*

Answ. But these words are very black.

First, here he hath not only implicitly forbidden Jesus Christ   30
to hold Communion with the Saints that are not yet his by
Baptism; but is bold to charge him with being as preposterous
and wicked if he do, as a man that liveth with a woman in the
priviledges of a married state, without passing that publick
solemnity.   35

Secondly, He here also chargeth him as guilty of the same
wickedness, that shall but dare to claim Church-Communion
without it; yea, and the whole Church too, if they shall admit
such Members to their Fellowship.

And now since cleaving to Christ by Vow and Covenant, will   40

not do without Baptism, after personal confession of Faith; what a state are all those poor Saints of Jesus in, that have avowed themselves to be his a thousand times without *this* Baptism: yea, and what a case is Jesus Christ in too, by your Argument, to hold
5   that Communion with them, that belongeth only unto them that are Married to him by this Solemnity!

Brother, God give him Repentance. I wot that through ignorance, and a preposterous Zeal he said it: unsay it again with tears, and by a publick renunciation of so wicked and horrible
10   words; but I thus sparingly pass you by.

I shall not trouble the World any farther with an answer to the rest of your Books: The Books are publick to the World: let men read and judge. And had it not been for your endeavouring to stigmatize me with reproach and scandal, (a thing that doth not
15   become you) I needed not to have given you two lines in answer.

And now, my angry Brother, if you shall write again, pray keep to the Question, namely, *what Precept, President, or Example have you in God's Word to exclude your holy Brethren from Church-Communion for want of Water-Baptism?*
20   Mr. *Denn's* great Measure, please your self with it, and when you shall make his Arguments your own, and tell me so, you perhaps may have an Answer, but considering him, and comparing his Notions with his Conversation, I count it will be better for him to be better in Morals, before he be worthy of an
25   Answer.

The Conclusion.

Eader, when *Moses* sought to set the *Brethren* that strove against each other, at one, *He* that did the wrong *thrust him away*, as unwilling to be hindred in his ungodly attempts; but
30   *Moses* continuing to make peace betwixt them, the same person attempted to charge him with a murderous and bloody design, *saying, Wilt thou kill me as thou didst the Egyptian yesterday?* a thing too commonly thrown upon those that seek peace and insue it. *My soul*, saith David, *hath long dwelt with him that hateth Peace. I*
35   *am for Peace*, said he, *but when I speak, they are for War.* One would think that even Nature it self should count *Peace and Concord* a thing of greatest worth among Saints, especially since they above all men, know themselves: for he that best knoweth himself, *is*

Exod. 2.
Acts. 7.

Psa. 120. 6, 7.

Heb. 5. 2.
best able to pity and bear with another; yet even amongst these, such will arise, as will make divisions among their Brethren, *and seek to draw away Disciples after them*; Crying still that they, even they are in the *right*, & all that hold not with them in the *wrong*, and to be withdrawn from.

Acts 20. 30.
Ro. 16. 17.
Prov. 6. 16, 17,
18, 19.

But when every *HE* hath said all that he can, it is one of the things which the Lord hateth, *to sow discord among Brethren.*

Yet many years experience we have had of these mischievous attempts, as also have others in other places, as may be instanced if occasion requireth it, and that specially by those of the rigid way of our Brethren, the Baptists *so called*, whose principles will neither allow them to admit *TO* Communion, *That Saint that differeth from them* about Baptism, nor consent they should Communicate in a Church-state among themselves; but take occasion still ever as they can, both to reproach their Church-state, and to finger from amongst them who they can to themselves. These things being grievous to those concerned (as we are) though perhaps those at quiet are too little concerned in the matter *therefore when I could no longer forbear*, I thought good to present to publick view the *warrantableness* of our Holy-Communion, and the *unreasonableness* of their seeking to break us to pieces. At this Mr. *Will. K.*, Mr. *Thomas Paul*, and Mr. *Henry D'anvers*, and Mr. *Den*, fell with might and main upon me; some comparing me to the Devil, others to a Bedlam, others to a sot and the like, for my seeking Peace and Truth among the Godly. Nay, further, they began to cry out *MURDER*, as if I intended nothing less than to accuse them to the Magistrate, and to render them uncapable of a share in the Common-wealth, when I only struck at their heart-breaking, Church-renting-Principles, and Practice, in their excluding their Holy Brethrens Communion from them, and their Condemning of it amongst themselves. They also follow me with Slanders and reproaches, counting (it seems) such things Arguments to defend themselves.

My second Book
p. 34. 78.
His Reply p. 42.

But I in the mean time call for Proof, Scripture-Proof to convince me, 'tis a Duty to refuse Communion with those of the Saints that differ from them about Baptism; at this Mr. *P.* takes offence, calling my demanding of Proof for their rejecting the unbaptized Believer, *how excellent soever in Faith and Holiness*, a clamorous calling for Proof, with high and swelling words, which he counteth not worthy of answer; but I know the reason,

he by this demand is shut out of the Bible, as himself also
suggesteth: wherefore, when coming to assault me with Arguments, he can do it but by seeming imports, suppositions, and
strong presumptions, and tells you farther in his Reply, *that this is*
5 *the utmost of his light in the Scriptures urged for his Practice*, of which
light thou mayst easily judge, Good Reader', that hast but the P. 41.
Common Understanding of the mind of God concerning
Brotherly Love. Strange! that the Scripture that every where
commandeth and presseth to Love, to forbearance and bearing
10 the burden of our Brother; should yet imply, or implicitly import
that we should shut them out of our Fathers House; or that those
Scriptures that command us to receive the weak, should yet
command us to shut out the strong! Thinkest thou, Reader, that
the Scripture hath two Faces, and speaketh with two Mouths? yet
15 it must do so, by these mens Doctrine. It saith expresly, *Receive*
one another, as Christ also received us to the Glory of God. But these Ro. 15.
Men say 'tis not Duty, 'tis preposterous, and Idolatrous; P. 41. of Mr. *P.*
concluding that to receive this Brother, is not a Custom of them; *Reflections.*
nor yet of the Churches of God: consequently telling thee, that those
20 that receive such a Brother are not (*let them talk while they will*)
any of the Churches of God: see their Charity, their Candor and
Love, in the midst of their great pretensions of Love.

But be thou assured, Christian Reader, that *for these* their
uncharitable words and actions, they have not footing in the
25 Word of God, neither can they heal themselves with suggesting
their amicable correspondence to the World; Church-Communion
I plead for, Church-Communion they deny them, yet Church-
Communion is Scripture-Communion, and we read of none
other among the Saints. True, we are commanded to withdraw 2 *Thes.* 3.
30 from every Brother that walks disorderly, that they may be
ashamed, yet not to count him as an Enemy, but to admonish
him as a Brother. If this be that they intend, for I know not of
another Communion that we ought to have with those, to whom
we deny Church-Communion; then what ground of rejoycing
35 those have that are thus respected by their Brethren, I leave it to
themselves to consider of.

In the mean-while, I affirm, that Baptism with Water, *is neither*
a Bar nor Bolt to Communion of Saints, nor a Door nor Inlet to
Communion of Saints. The same which is the Argument of my
40 Books; and as some of the moderate among themselves have

affirmed, that neither Mr. *K.* Mr. *P.* nor Mr. *D'anvers*, have
made invalid, though sufficiently they have made their assault.
For Mr. *Den*, I suppose they count him none of themselves,
though both *He*, and Mr. *Lamb* (like to like) are brought for
Authors and abetters of their practice, and to resell my peaceable   5
Principle. For Mr. *Den*, if either of the three will make his
Arguments their own, *they may see what their Servant can do*: but I
shall not bestow Paper and Ink upon *Him*, nor yet upon Mr.
Lamb; the one already, *having given his profession the lye*, and for
the other perhaps they that know his Life, will see little of   10
Conscience in the whole of his Religion, and conclude him not
worth the taking notice of. Besides Mr. *P.* hath also concluded
against Mr. *Den*, *that Baptism is not the initiating Ordinance*, and
that his utmost strength for the justification of his own practice
is, *suppositions, imports and strong presumptions*, things that they   15
laugh at, despise and deride, when brought by their Brethren to
prove Infant-Baptism.

Railing for Railing, I will not render, though one of these
Opposers (Mr. *Dan.* by name) did tell me, that Mr. *Pauls* reply
when it came out, would sufficiently provoke me to so beastly a   20
work: but what is the reason of his so writing, if not the
peevishness of his own Spirit, or the want of better matter.

This I *thank* God for, that some of the Brethren of this way,
are of late more moderate than formerly, and that those that
retain their former sowreness still, are left by their Brethren, *to*   25
the vinegar of their own spirits, their Brethren ingenuously
confessing, that could these of their company bear it, *they have*
liberty in their own souls to Communicate with Saints as Saints,
though they differ about Water-Baptism.

Well, God banish bitterness out of the Churches, and pardon   30
them that are the maintainers of Schisms and Divisions among
the Godly. *Behold how good and how pleasant it is for Brethren to*
dwell together in Unity. It is like the precious Oyntment upon the head,
that ran down upon the Beard, even Aaron's *Beard, and that went*
down to the skirts of his Garment: (farther) it is as the Dew of   35
Hermon, *that descended upon the Mountains of* Sion. Mark, *for there*
the Lord commanded the blessing, even Life for ever more, Psal. 133.

I was advised by some, who considered the Wise Mans
Proverb, not to let Mr. *Paul* pass with all his bitter invectives, but

5 resell] resel

I consider that the wrath of Man worketh not the Righteousness
of God; therefore I shall leave him to the censure and rebuke of
the sober, where I doubt not but his unsavoury ways with me will
be seasonably brought to his remembrance.

FAREWEL

> *I am thine to serve thee,*
> *Christian, so long as I*
> *can look out at those*
> *Eyes, that have had so*
> *much dirt thrown at*
> *them by many.*

J. BUNYAN

Of the Love of CHRIST

THE love of Christ, poor I! may touch
upon;
But 'tis unsearchable. Oh! There is none
It's large Dimensions can comprehend,
Sould they dilate thereon, world without end.
 When we had sinned, in his Zeal he sware,
That he upon his back our Sins would bear.
And since unto Sin is entailed Death,
He vowed, for our Sins he'd lose his Breath.
 He did not only say, vow, or resolve,
But to Astonishment did so involve
Himself in man's distress and misery,
As for, and with him both to live and die.
To his eternal Fame and sacred Story,
We find that he did lay aside his Glory,
Stept from the Throne of highest Dignity;
Became, poor man, did in a manger lie;
Yea was beholden upon his for bread,
Had of his own, not where to lay his head:
Tho' rich, he did, for us, become thus poor,
That he might make us rich for evermore.
 Nor was this but the least of what he did;
But the outside of what he suffered.

God made his blessed Son under the Law;
Under the Curse, which, like the Lyon's
    Paw,
Did rent and tear his Soul, for mankind's Sin,
More than if we for it in Hell had been.   5
His Cries, his Tears, and bloody Agony,
The Nature of his Death doth testify.
   Nor did he of constraint himself thus give,
For Sin, to Death, that Man might with
    him live.   10
He did do what he did most willingly,
He sung, and gave God thanks, that he
    must die.
   But do Kings use to die for Captive
    Slaves?   15
Yet we were such, when Jesus dy'd to save's.
   Yea, when he made himself a Sacrifice,
It was that he might save his Enemies.
And, tho' he was provoked to retract,
His blest Resolves, for such, so good an   20
    Act.
By the abusive Carriages of those,
That did both him, his Love, and Grace
    oppose.
Yet he, as unconcerned with such things,   25
Goes on, determines to make Captives
    Kings;
Yea, many of his Murderers he takes
Into his Favour, and them Princes makes.

13–29 (over) Of the Love . . . Princes makes.] Wilson 1737.

A CASE OF CONSCIENCE
RESOLVED

A Case of Conscience

RESOLVED.

VIZ.

Fuller, Brussels Sale, June, 18-6

Whether, where a Church of Christ is Situate, it
is the Duty of the Women of that Congregation, Ordinarily, and by Appointment, to Separate themselves from their Brethren, and so to
Assemble together, to perform some parts of Divine Worship, as Prayer, &c. without their
Men?

AND

The Arguments made use of for

that Practice, Examined.

By JOHN BUNYAN.

London, Printed for Benj: Alsop, at the Angel and Bible
in the Poultrey. 1683.

A3 e 290 (12)   1214. e 3.

Title-page of *A Case of Conscience Resolved* (1683)

A CASE OF CONSCIENCE
RESOLVED

Note on the Text

One edition of this work was published in Bunyan's lifetime, and only one copy survives. The publisher was Benjamin Alsop whose shop was located at the sign of the Angel and Bible over against the stock market in the Poultry. He also published Bunyan's *Holy War* (1682) with Dorman Newman. In the following year he issued *A Holy Life* and *Seasonable Counsel*. Alsop gave up his shop to receive a commission in Monmouth's army, and after its defeat apparently lived in exile in Holland.[1]

Title-page: **A Case of Conscience** | RESOLVED. | *VIZ.* | *Whether, where a Church of Christ is Situate, it* | *is the Duty of the Women of that Congregati-|on, Ordinarily, and by Appointment, to Sepa-|rate themselvate from their Brethren, and so to* | *Assemble together, to perform some parts of Di-|vine Worship, as Prayer, &c. without their* | *Men?* | AND | The Arguments made use of for | that Practice, Examined. | [rule] | *By* JOHN BUNYAN. | [rule] | *London*, Printed for *Benj: Alsop*, at the Angel and Bible | in the *Poultrey.* 1683.

Collation: 4⁰; A–E⁴; pp. 44. The first printed page number is 5. Signatures are printed on the first two leaves.

Contents: A1ʳ title-page; A1ᵛ blank; A2ʳ–A2ᵛ epistle dedicatory; A3ʳ–E4ʳ text; E4ᵛ blank. A2ʳ begins 'The Epistle Dedicatory to those God-|lyWomen concerned in the | following Treatise.' A2ᵛ is signed 'John Bunyan.' A row of ornaments on A3ʳ is followed by 'A | *Case of Conscience Resolved, &c.*' The end of the text on E4ʳ is followed by a rule, 'FINIS.', and another rule.

Running titles: None.

Catchwords (selected): A3ʳ Now, B2ᵛ Se-, C1ʳ in, C4ʳ Christ, D2ᵛ 4.

Copy collated: Bodleian, Oxford. There is no copy at the British Library, although one is listed there by Wing.

The following text is based on the Bodleian copy.

---

[1] Plomer, 5.

The Epistle Dedicatory to those Godly
Women concerned in the following Treatise.

Honoured Sisters,

T*is far from me to despise you, or to do any thing to your*
5   *reproach. I know* you *are beloved of God for the sake of*
   Christ, and that you *stand fixed for ever by Faith upon the*
same foundation with us. *I also know that the Lord doth put* no
difference betwixt Male *and* Female, *as to the communications of*
his Saving Graces, *but hath often made many of your Sex eminent for*
10 *piety; yea, there hath been of* YOU, *I speak now of ordinary*
Christians, that for Holiness of life have out gone many of the
Brethren: Nor can their vertuous lives but be renown *and Glory to*
YOU, *and conviction to those of* US *that have come behinde you in*
Faith and Holyness. The love of Women in Spirituals (as well as
15 *Naturals) oft times out-goes that of Men.*

   When Christ was upon Earth, we read not that any Man did to,
and for *him, as did the* Woman *that was a sinner,* Joanna,
Susanna, *and many others,* Luk. 7. 36, 37, 38. Chap. 8. 1, 2, 3.

   And as they have shewed themselves eminent for piety, so for
20 *Christian valour and fortitude of minde, when called of God to bear*
witness to, and for his Name in the World: as all Histories of that
Nature doth sufficiently testifie. They were Women, *as I take it, as*
well as Men, that were tortured, and that would not accept of
deliverance that they might obtaine a better resurrection, Heb. 11. 35.
25 *Wherefore I honour and praise your eminencie in vertue; and desire to*
be provoked by the exceeding piety of any of you, in all Holy
conversation and Godlyness.

   And although, as you will find, I have not with out a cause, made a
Question of the Lawfulness of your assembling together, by your
30 selves, to perform, without your Men, solemn Worship to God:
Yet I dare not make your selves the Authors of your own miscarriage in
this. I do therefore rather impute it to your Leaders; who whether of a
fond respect to some seeming abilities they think is in you for this, or
from a perswasion that you have been better then themselves in other
35 *things, or whether from a preposterous zeal, they have put you upon a*

work so much *too heavy for you: I shall not at this time concern my self to inquire into. But this is certaine, at least 'tis so in my apprehension, that in this matter you are tempted by them to take too much upon you.*

I am not insensible but that for my thus writing, though I thereby have designed your Honour and good Order, I am like enough to run the Gantlet *among you, and to partake most smartly of the scourge of the Tongues of some, and to be soundly Brow-beaten for it by others: Specially by our Author, who will finde himself immediately concerned, for that I have blamed him for what he hath irregularly done both* with *the Word,* to *you, and me. I look also to be sufficiently Scandalized, and counted a man not for Prayer, and Meetings for Prayer, and the like, but I will labour to bare them with Patience, and seek their good that shall be tempted to abuse me.*

I had not, indeed I had not spoke a Word to this question in this manner, had not Mr. K. sent his Paper broad, and amongst us, for the encouraging this practise with us, in Opposition to our peace. I do not say he designed *our breach, but his Arguments* tended *thereto; and had not our People been of a wise and quiet temper, his Paper might have set us into a Flame. But thanks be to God we are at quiet, and walk in love, notwithstanding the* Lists *that have been to make us do otherwise.*

There are also the mouths of some opened against me for this, who lie at wait for Occasions, and shew that they are glad to take them before they are given by mee: to whom I now shew by this ensuing discourse, that I had a reason to do what I did.

I commend you to God, and to the Word of his Grace, which is able to build you up, and to give you an inheritance among them that are Sanctified by Faith in Jesus Christ: to whom be Honour and Glory for ever.

And remaine your Faithfull Friend and Brother to Pray for you, to love you in the Gospel, and to do you what Christian Service I can.

John Bunyan.

A

Case of Conscience Resolved, &c.

THE occasion of my meddling in this manner with this
Controversie, is this: After I had (for reasons best
known to my self) by searching, found, that those
called the *Womens meetings*, wanted for their support,
a bottom in the Word: I called them in our Fellowship into
question. Now having so done, my reasons for so doing (as was
but reason) were demanded; and I gave them, to the Causing of
that practise with us to cease. So subject to the *Word* were our
Women, and so willing to let go what by *that* could not be proved
a duty for them to be found in the Practise of. But when I had
so done, by what means I know not, Mr. *K*, hearing of my
proceeding in this matter (though I think he knew little of
question or Answer) sets Pen to Paper, and draws up four
Arguments for the Justification of those *Meetings*. The which,
when done, were sent down into our parts; not to me, but to
some of his own perswasion, who *kept* them, or *sent* them, or *lent*
them whether they thought good: And so about two years after,
with this note immediately following, they were conveyed to my
hand.

 Bro: Bunyan, *This enclosed, was sent to me from godly Women,
whose Custom for a long time hath bin to meet together to pray: who
hearing of your contrary Opinion, sent this. It came from Mr.* K, *who
would desire to know what objections you have against it: and he is
ready to give his further advice. Pray be pleased to give your Answer
in writing, for Mr.* K. *Expects it.*

Pray be pleased   your Friends in the
to leave your   Lord, *S. B.*
Answer with   *S. F.*
 S. F.
in Bedford.

Now having received the Papers, and considering the contents thereof: I was at First at a question with my self, whether the thing was feigned, or true; and *to that purpose*, writt to these *Women* again: But calling to minde, that I had heard something of this before, I concluded there was ground to believe as I doe: 5
And so resolved to Answer his Demand and Expectation.

But to say nothing more as to this, I will next present you with the Arguments he sent, and then with my manner of handling of them.

First he begins with this question, *Whether Women fearing God*   10
may Meet to pray together, and whether it be Lawfull for them so to do? which done, he fals to a Wonderment, saying, It seems very strange to me, that any who profess the Fear of God, can make any question touching the Lawfulness thereof: The rule for praying being so General to all, and there being so many Instances for the Practice   15
thereof, upon several occasions in the Word of God, for their incouragement therein.

In the next place he presents us with his Arguments, which are in *Number* four, but in *Verity not one*, to prove that thing for the which he urgeth them: as I hope to make appear by that I have   20
done.

First, *saith he, If Women may prayse God together for Mercies received for the Church of God, or for themselves: Then they may pray together: the Proof whereof is plain,* Exod. 15. 20, 21. *If it be objected the Case was Extraordinary, and that* Miriam *was a Prophetess; To*   25
which I Answer, That the danger of Ruin and Destruction, and our deliverance from it (if the Lord grant it) cannot be looked at but as Extraordinary: The designs of ruin to the Church, and Servants of God, being as great as at that time when God delivered his People from the hand of Pharoah. *And will call for praises, if the Lord please to*   30
send it, as then. And Whereas it is further objected, that Miriam *was an Extraordinary Person; To which I Answer, That the Duty it self of praising God for the Mercie, was incumbent upon all, in as much as they were all partakers of the Mercie. And the same Spirit of Christ that was in her, is also in all his Servants: Given for the same End,*   35
both to Pray for Mercies, we stand in need of, and to praise God for.

Secondly, *If Women have in eminent danger to themselves and the Church of God, Prayed joyntly together for deliverance, and God hath Answered and approved of the same: then may Women joyntly pray together. The instance we have is famous,* Esther. 4. 16. *We there see*   40

shee and her Maidens did pray and fast together, and the Lord gave a
gracious Answer and deliverance.

Thirdly, *If God hath in Gospel times promised the powring out of*
his Spirit to Women, to that very end that they may pray together apart
5 *from Men; Then it is not only their Liberty, but Duty to Meet and*
Pray together. But God hath promised his Spirit to that end. Zech.
12. 10, 11, 12, 13. *Which Scripture, 'tis plain, is a promise of Gospel*
times. And it is to be noted that the Text doth not in the singular
number, say, HE shall Pray apart, and HIS Wife apart. But THEY
10 *shall Pray apart, and THEIR Wives apart. And* Malachi 3. 16. *God*
takes notice of all them that speak often together, and CALL upon his
name.

Fourthly, *If God hath so approved of Womens Meeting together to*
Pray in Gospel times, as then, and at that time to take an advantage to
15 *make known to them his mind and will concerning Jesus Christ: then it*
is Lawfull for Women to Pray together. But, God hath so approved of
their Meeting to Pray together, Acts. 16. 13. *By which Text it*
appeareth it was a frequent practise for Women to Meet and Pray
together.

20 These are Mr. *K*'s Arguments, the Conclusion of his Paper
Follows.

And besides ALL these particular instances (says he) *what means*
those General rules to build up one another in our most Holy Faith,
and Pray in the Holy Ghost, Jude 20. *But it extends to all that believe,*
25 both Men and Women; *unless any will say Women are not to be*
built up in their most Holy Faith. Therefore let not any hinder you
from a Duty so incumbent upon you in a special manner, in such a day
as this is. Cannot many Women that have used this practise, by
experience, say, they have met with the Lord in it, and have found
30 *many blessed returns of prayer from God, both to themselves and the*
Church, wherein God hath owned them? Therefore what God hath
Born Witness to, and approved of, let no Man deter you from. Pray
turn to the Scriptures quoted, which I hope will give you full
Satisfaction.

35 These are his Arguments, and this his Conclusion, in which
I cannot but say, there is, not only Boldness, but Flattery.
Boldness, in *Fathering* of his mis-understanding upon the
Authority of the Word of God: and *Flattery,* in Soothing up
Persons in a way of their own, by making of them the Judges in
40 their own cause: the which I hope to make further appear anon.

For since his Women in their Letter told me that Mr. K. expects my Answer, I count my self *called* to shew the unsoundness of his Opinion. Indeed he would, as they insinuate, confine me to Answer *by Writing*: But his Papers have been I know not where, and how to put check to his Extravagancies, that also, I know not, but by Scattering mine abroad. And as I will not be confined to an *Answer* in Writing: So neither to his methods of Argumentation. What Scholar he is, I know not; for my part, I am not ashamed to Confess, that I neither know the *Mode* nor *Figure* of a Sylogism, nor scarce which is *Major* or *Minor*. Methinks I perceive but little *sence*, and far less *truth* in his Arguments: also I hold that he has stretched and strained the Holy Word out of place, to make it, if it might have bin, to shore up his fond conceits. I shall therefore First take these Texts from the Errors to which he hath joyned them, and then fall to picking the bones of his Sylogismes.

But as I shall not confine my self to his mode and way of Arguing: So neither shall I take notice of his question upon which he stateth the matter in Controversie. But shall propound the same question here, which for the substance of it, was *handled* among us, when the thing it self was in *doubt* among us, Namly,

Whether, where a Church of Christ is Situate, it is the Duty of the Women of that Congregation, Ordinarily, and by Appointment, to Separate themselves from their Brethren, and so to Assemble together, to perform some parts of Divine Worship, as Prayer &c. without their Men?

This was our question, this we debated, and this Mr. K. might have sent for, and spoken to, since he will needs be a confuter.

And courteous Reader, since I have here presented thee with the Question, I will also present thee with the method which I took when I handled it among my Brethren.

1. I opened the Termes of the Question.
2. Then shewed what Assemblies they were that used to perform divine Worship to God.
3. And so shewed whose Prayers in such Worship was *used*, or by *Paul* and others *desired*.

For the First.

1. By *Church* of Christ, I mean, one gathered or Constituted by, and walking after the Rule of the Word of God.

2. By *Situate*, I mean, where such Church shall happen to be, in whole, or in the parts thereof.

3. By *Separating*, I mean, their Meetings together by appointment of their own, and as so met, to attempt to performe
5   divine Worship, *Prayer*, without their Men.

Having thus explained the Question; I, as a preparatory to a solution thereof, come next to shew what manner of Assemblies they were that used to perform divine Worship to God of Old.

Now I finde that there have been three Sorts of Assemblies, in
10   which divine Worship has been performed:

1st. It has been performed in mixed Assemblies; in Assemblies made up of Saints and Sinners. I say divine Worship has been performed IN such Assemblies, for that there the Saints have been Edified, Sinners convinced and converted, and made to
15   confess their Sins, to the Glory of God. Of these Assemblies we read, *Matt.* 5. 1. *Chap.* 13. 1. *Chap.* 23. *Marc.* 4. 1. *Chap.* 2. 1. *Chap.* 6. 2. *Chap.* 10. *Luk.* 5. *Chap.* 8. *Chap.* 12. *Chap.* 13. *Chap.* 15. *Chap.* 20. 1. *Cor.* 14. 24. And in many other Scriptures.

2ly. I also find that the Church, by herself; or as distinct from
20   the World, have met together to perform it by themselves. *Mar.* 4. 34. *Acts.* 12, 4. *Chap.* 13. 1, 2. *Chap.* 15. 4. *Chap.* 20. 7, 8. *Joh.* 20. 19, 26.

3ly. I find also that Assemblies for divine Worship have been made up of the Elders, and Principal Brethren of the Church,
25   none of the rest of the Congregation being present, *Matt.* 10. 1. *Luk.* 9. 1. *Acts* 1. 3. *Chap.* 2. 17, 18. *Gal.* 2. 1. 2. with several other Scriptures beside.

But in all the Scripture, I find not that the Women of the Churches of Christ, did use to separate themselves from their
30   Brethren, and as so separate, performe Worship together among themselves or in that *their* Congregation: or that they made, by allowance of the Word, appointment so to do. Thus far therefore this must stand for a humane invention, and Mr. *K.* for the promoter thereof.

35   3ly. This done, in the third place, I come to shew you *whose* Prayers, or by *whose* mouth Prayer in such Assemblies, as are above proved Lawful, *used* to be made, or by *Paul* or others were *desired*.

1. Whose Prayers were used, or who was the mouth; and I
40   find them called the Prayers of the Church in General, or of the

Principal Men thereof in particular, *Judg* 2. 4, 5. *Chap.* 20. 8, 26.
Joel 1. 14. *Chap.* 2. 15, 16. *Acts* 12. 5. *Acts* 13. 1, 3.

2. Also when *Paul,* or others *desired* that Prayers should be
made of others for them: They either desired the Prayers of the
Church in General, or of the Brethren in particular (but never   5
desireth, or biddeth a Womans Meeting, that Prayers might
there be made for them.)

1. He desireth the Prayers of the Church in General, *Col.* 4.
2. *Philipi.* 1. 9. *Chap.* 4. 6. 1 *Thes.* 5. 17. *Heb.* 13. 18.

2. Or if he desireth Prayers of certain Persons, he only calls   10
upon the Men and Brethren in particular, but never upon a
Woman by name nor Sex, to do it, 1 *Thes.* 5. 25. 2 *Thes.* 3. 1.
Rom. 15. 30. 1 *Tim.* 2. 8. Nor was, as I said, the Apostle alone in
this thing. Christ speaks a Parable to this end, that MEN ought
always to Pray. *James* saith the effectual fervent Prayer of a   15
righteous MAN. *Moses* sent the young Men to Sacrifice: And the
People in the time of *Zacharias,* sent their MEN to Pray before
the Lord, *Luk.* 18. 1. *Jam.* 5. 16. *Exod.* 24. 5. *Zach.* 7. 2. I do not
believe that by any of these, the Prayers of Women are despised,
but by these we are taught, who, as the mouth in Assemblies to   20
Pray, is commended unto us.

One Word more, The Women in the time of *Jeremy* the
Prophet, when they had made their Cakes to the Queen of
Heaven, (tho the thing which they did was as right in their own
eyes, as if they had done true Worship indeed) and was   25
Questioned by the Prophet for what they had done, could not
Justifie what they had done, as to the Act, but by pleading, *They
did it not without their Men.* Jer. 44.17, 18, 19.

*Thus having premised these few things, I shall now come more
directly to discourse of the Question it self, TO WIT, Whether, where a*   30
*Church of Christ is Situate, it is the Duty of the Women of that
Congregation, Ordinarily, and by appointment, to separate themselves
from their Brethren, and as so separate, to assemble together to perform
divine Worship, Prayer, without their Men?*

This was our Question, and this I will now give a *Negative*   35
Answer unto. For I find not in Christs Testaments any command
so to do; no nor yet Example: and where there is none of these, it
cannot be a Duty upon them; no, nor yet Liberty, but
presumption to attempt it.

The Command, says Mr. *K.* is General to All. But I Answer,   40 yet limited, and confined to Order, and manner of Performance: Women may, yea ought to Pray; what then? Is it their Duty to help to carry on Prayer in Publick Assemblies with Men, *as they*? Are they to be the audible mouth there, before all, *to God*? No verily, and yet the command is General to all to Pray. Women of the respective Churches of Christ, have no command to separate themselves from the Men of their Congregations, to perform Prayer in their own Company without them, and yet the command is General to all to Pray.

We must therefore *distinguish* of Persons and performances, though we may not *exclude* either. The manner also, and Order in which such and such Duties must be done, Mr. *K.* know knows is as Essential, in some cases, as the very matter of VVorship.

But we will come to my reasons for my dissenting from Mr. *K.* in this. After which I will consider his Arguments, and the Scriptures that he would under-prop them with. As for my reasons for my dissenting from him, they are these.

First, To appoint Meetings for divine VVorship, either in the whole Church or in the parts of it, *Is an Act of Power*: which Power, resideth in the Elders in particular, or in the Church in General. But never in the VVomen as considered by themselves. Mr. *K.* indeed doth insinuate that this Power also resideth in them; for he saith, God hath in Gospel times promised the Spirit to Women *to that very end that* they may Pray together, apart from Men. Now if the Spirit is given them to THIS very end, that they may do it apart from Men, then they have a Power residing in themselves to call their own Sex together to do it. And what brave doings will such a conclusion make, even the blind himself will perceive. But further of this anon; mean while we will our *own* assertion attend.

Namely, That to call the Church or parts thereof together to perform divine Worship to God, is an ACT of POWER, which power resideth in the Church in General, or in the Elders in particular. We will treat of the last first.

First, *For the Eldership*, *Moses* and *Aaron* of Old were they, with the Priests, that were to call the Church together to perform divine Worship to God, and that both as to the whole, or as to the parts of it, *Numb.* 10. 7. 8. *Deut.* 4. 14. *Chap.* 31. 11, 12. *Exo.* 4. 29. *Chap.* 12. 21. *Chap.* 17. 5.

Also in after times, they were the Elders and chief of the

Church, that did it, *Josh.* 24. 1. *Ezra* 10. 5, 6, 7, 8, 9. *Acts* 14. 26, 27. *Chap.* 15. 3.

Or if their calling together to performe divine Worship, was not by the Elders alone: Yet it was by the Power that resided in the Church for that thing, who joyntly ordered the same, *Judg.* 20. 8, 18. *Ezra* 3. 1. *Zeph.* 2. 1, 2, 3. *Acts* 12. 12. 1 *Cor.* 5. 4. *Chap.* 11. 20.

All these are plain cases. But never, as I ever did read of in the Bible, did Women, Ordinary beliving ones, assume this Power of the Elders, or of the Church, to themselves.

If it be asked who did appoint that Meeting made mention of *Acts* 12. 12?

I Answer, 'Twas appointed by the Power of the Church, who for her own conveniencie (if she cannot come all into one place at once, to perform the Duty, as 'tis not likely four or five thousand should, in times of persecution, which was their case) may meet, some here; some, there; for their Edification, and comfort; compare Vers. 5. with Vers. 12, and Vers. 17.

Nor, do I Question the Lawfulness of this or that part of the Churches Assembling together for Prayer: Tho the Elders, and greatest part of the Brethren be absent: If first such MEN that call such Assemblies are countenanced by the Elders, or Church, to do it, 1 *Tim.* 2. 8. 2 *Tim.* 2. 22. But that the Sisters of this or that Church, may call their own Sex together to perform such Worship by themselves to God (for this is the thing in debate) I finde no warrant for.

Secondly; *Because, This kind of Worship, when done in and by a Company, is MINISTERIAL to that Company, as well as petitionary to God.* That is, they that as the mouth in Assemblies Pray to God, teach that Assembly, as well as beg mercies of him. And I finde not that Women may Assemble to do thus. That such Prayer is a kind of Ministring in the Word to Standers by, consider well 1 *Cor.* 14. 15, 16, 17, 18, 19. Wherefore let them keep silence in the Church, and in the parts thereof, when Assembled to Worship God.

In all Publick Worship by Prayer, Teaching is set on foot, two wayes.

1. By propounding to that Assembly the things that must by agreement be Prayed for:

2. And by proving them to suit with the will of God, that Prayer may be made in Faith (1 *Joh.* 5. 14.)

For all such Prayer must be made for the things agreed upon first: and consequently for things that by the Word are proved good, and sutable for the Seasons, Persons, or thing, for, or about which such Prayers are made. For they that have Meetings
5 for Prayer, without this, Pray at random, and not by Rule.

If two of you shall agree on earth, as touching any thing that they shall ask (according to Gods will) it shall be done for them, saith Christ, *of my Father which is in Heaven*, Matt. 18. 19.

Now, I say, if things Prayed for in Assemblies, must first be
10 joyntly agreed upon; then must such things by some one, or more of that Assembly, be first *Propounded, Expounded*, and *Proved* to be good by the Word. Good for such Persons, Seasons, or things, for which such Prayer is made. And besides the Gifts required to do this, if this is not Teaching, I am out. And yet this
15 must first be done to instruct all present, to help their Faith, and to quicken their Spirits *to*, and *in* that Worship. That they may as one Man have their Eyes unto the Lord, *Zech.* 9. 1.

But that this Power is given to Women, to Ordinary believing ones that are in the highest account in Churches, I do not
20 believe. I do not believe they should Minister to God in Prayer before the whole Church, for then I should be a Ranter or a Quaker; Nor *do* I believe they should do it in their own Womanish Assembly, for the reason urged before.

And I will add, if Brethren not heretofore called by the
25 Church to open Scriptures, or to speak in the Church to God in Prayer, are not at first to be admitted to do this, but before the Elders or Principal Brethren, that they may hear and Judge (1 *Cor.* 14. 26, 27, 28, 29.) how can it be thought to be meet or lawful for Women, of whom it must be supposed, that they have
30 received no such Gifts, that they should use this Power? I say, how can it be imagined that the Women should be bound of God to do this in such Sort as doth utterly exclude the Elders and all the Men in the Congregation from a possibility of understanding and of Judging of what they do? And yet this is the Doctrine of
35 Mr. *K.* For he saith, *that the Spirit of God is promised to Women to this very end, that they may Pray together, apart from Men.* But God is not the Author of this Confusion in the Churches.

2ly. But Secondly, As teaching by Prayer in Assemblies, is thus set on foot; so every one also that shall in such Meetings be
40 the mouth of the whole, to God, Ministreth, SO, Doctrine to

that Assembly, as well as presenteth petitions to God. Else how can that Assembly say AMEN at their Prayer or giving of thanks? For to say, AMEN, is an effect of Conviction, or of Edification received of the stander by, from him that now is so Ministring in that Assembly before God, 1 *Cor.* 14. 15, 16, 17. 5

Yea, I believe that they that Pray in Assemblies, or that shall give thanks for Mercies received there, Ought to labor to speak, not only with fervency of *Words*, but with such soundness of *Doctrine*, while they mention, urge, or plead the promise with God, that that whole Assembly may be enlightned, taught, taken, 10 and carried away in their Spirits, on the wing of that Prayer, and of Faith, to God, whose face they are come to seek, and whose Grace they are gathered together to beg. Now this is called Praying and Praising, to the *Teaching* and *Edifying* of others, as by the Scripture afore named is made appear, 1 *Cor.* 14. 14, 15, 16, 15 17, 18, 19. But by what Word of God the Sisters of the respective Churches may set up this way of Teaching of one another in their Assemblies, I am ignorant of. For.

Thirdly, The Holy Ghost doth particularly insist upon the inability of Women, as to their well managing of the Worship *now* 20 under Consideration, and therefore it ought not to be presumed upon by them. They are forbidden to teach, yea to speak in the Church of God. And why forbidden, but because of their inability. They cannot orderly manage that Worship to God that in Assemblies is to be performed before him (I speak now of our 25 Ordinary believing ones, and I know none Extraordinary among the Churches.) They are not builded to manage such Worship, *they are not the Image and Glory of God*, as the Men are, 1 *Cor.* 11. 7. They are placed beneath, and are *called the Glory of the Man.* Wherefore they are weak, and not permited to perform Publick 30 Worship to God. When our first Mother, who was not attended with those weaknesses, either Sinful, or Natural, as our Women now are, stept out of her place but to speak a good Word for Worship, you see how she was baffled, and befooled therein; she utterly failed in the performance, tho she briskly attempted the 35 thing. Yea she so failed there-about, that at one clap she over-threw, not only (as to that) the reputation of Women for ever, but her Soul, her Husband, and the whole World besides, *Gen.* 3. 1, 2, 3, 4, 5, 6, 7.

The fallen Angel knew what he did when he made his Assault 40

upon the Woman. His subtilty told him that the Woman was the
weaker Vessel. He knew also that the Man was made the Head in
Worship, and the keeper of the Garden of God. The Lord God
took the Man, *said* unto the Man, *commanded* the Man, and made
5 him keeper of the Garden, *Gen.* 2. 15, 16, 17. Wherefore the
management of Worship belonged to him. This, the Serpent, as
I said, was a ware of: And therefore he comes to the Woman,
sayes to the Woman, and deals with the Woman about it, and so
overcomes the World. Wherefore it is from this consideration
10 that *Paul* tells *Timothy* that he permited not a Woman to teach,
nor to usurp Authority over the Man, but to be in silence. (But to
call the Church or parts thereof together, to perform solemn
Worship, and in such a call to exclude or shut out the Men, is an
usurping of that Authority over them to an high degree.)
15 And he renders the reason of this his prohibition thus, *For
Adam was first formed, then Eve*, (and therefore had the Headship
in Worship) *And Adam was not deceived, but the Woman being
deceived, was in the Transgression.* 1 Tim. 2. 15, 16.
But again, it should seem, methinks, if Women must needs be
20 managers of Worship in Assemblies, they should do it, as *Eve*,
before *Adam*, in presence of the Men: But that I think none will
allow, though that would be the way best to correct miscarriages;
how then should it be thought convenient for them to do it alone.
If Children are not thought fitt to help to guide the ship with the
25 *Marriners*; shall they be trusted so much as with a Boat at Sea,
alone. The thing in hand is a Parallel case: For,
Fourthly. If the weightiness of *this* Worship be, as indeed it is,
so great, that the Strongest, and best able to perform it, do
usually come off with Blushing, and with repentance for their
30 shortness, as to the well performance thereof; though they
ingage therein by good and Lawful Authority: What will they do
who are much weaker here, and when, as *Eve*, they set to it in a
way of usurping of Authority, and of their own *Head*, and *will*.
To Offer strange fire with incense (which was a type of Prayer)
35 you know what it cost *Nadab* and *Abihu*, though *Men*, and the
Sons of *Aaron*. Mr *K.* cryes the Sisters, the Women, the Womens
Meetings, and the like, and how they have prevailed with
Heaven. Poor Man, I am sorry for his weakness, and that he
should shew that himself is so *Nunnish* in such a day as this.
40 But to return, as all Worship in Assemblies ought to be

performed with the most exact order and solemnity; So this of
Prayer with that, if possible, that is more then all the rest; and
therefore this makes it more heavie still. When Men Preach, they
have to do with Men, but when they Pray in Assemblies, they
have to do both with Men, and with God at once. And I say, if it   5
be so great a matter to speak to Men *before* God: *How* great a
matter is it to speak to Men and God at once: To God by way of
petitition, and to Men by way of Instruction. But I am perswaded
if those most fond of the Womens Meetings for Prayer, were to
petition the King for their lives, they would not set Women to be   10
their Advocates to him: Specially if the King should declare
before hand by Law, that he permitted not a Woman in an open
Auditory to speak before him.

There are also many temptations that attend the Duty of
Praying in Assemblies: especially those that are immediately   15
imployed therein. These temptations, they awake, are aware of,
are forced to wrestle with, and greatly to groan under. Wherefore
we put not the weak upon this Service; not the weak, though they
be Men: Not they in the presence of the strong. How then
should the weakest of all, be put upon it, and that when together   20
by themselves. Men though strong and though Acting by Lawfull
Authority in this, are not able but with unutterable grones to do
it: How then shall all those that attempt it without that Authority,
perform it, as acceptable Worship to God? This work therefore,
is as much too heavy for our Women, now, as that about which   25
Eve ingaged in at first, was too heavy for her. But

Fifthly, If this Worship may be managed by the Sister-hood of
the Churches, being congregated together in absence of their
Men: Of what Signification is it that Man is made the Head of
the Woman, as well in *Worship*, as in nature? (1 *Cor.* 11. 3, 7.)   30

Yea more, why are the Elders of the Churches called
Watchmen, Overseers, Guides, Teachers, Rulers, and the like?
If this kind of Worship may be performed, without their Conduct
and Government? *Ezek.* 3. 7. *Chap.* 33. 7. *Acts* 20. 28. *Ephes.* 4.
11. *Psal.* 78. 72. *Heb.* 13. 17.   35

First, Why is man made the Head of the Woman in Worship,
in the Worship now under debate, in that Worship that is to be
performed in Assemblies? and why are the Women commanded
silence there, if they may Congregate by themselves, and set up
and manage Worship there? Worship was ordained before the   40

Woman was made, wherefore the Word of God at the first did
not immediately come to her, (*Gen.* 2. 16, 17, 18. 1 *Cor.* 14. 35,
36.) but to him that was first formed, and made the Head in
Worship. And hence it is that women are so strictly tied up to
this Headship, that if they will learn, they must ask their
5 Husbands at home (not appoint Meetings of their own Sex to
Teach one another) *vers.* 35. *But what must they do that have
unbelieving ones? and what must they do that have none?* Answer.
Let them attend upon those Ordinances that God has appointed
for the building up and perfecting of the Body of Christ, and
10 learn as the Angels do, *Ephes.* 4. 11, 12, 13. *Chap.* 3. 10.
1 *Pet.* 1. 12.

2ly. But I say, if they *must* do as Mr. *K.* says they are *in duty
bound*, to witt, meet by themselves apart from their Men, and as
so met, perform this most solemn Worship to God: How shall
15 the Elders and Overseers, the Watchmen, Rulers, and Guides in
Worship, perform their Duty to God, and to the Church of God,
in this, since from this kind of Worship they are quite excluded,
and utterly shut out of Dores: Unless it be said, that to *Watch*, to
Oversee, and to *Guide*, in the matter and manner of performance
20 of this Worship in Assemblies, is no part of the Watchman or
Overseers work: or in their Lawful absence, the work of the
principal Men of the Church. Nor will the Faithful and Dutiful
Overseer, leave Worship, no, not in the best part of the
Congregation Assembled to Worship, to be performed by every
25 weak Brother, though I believe it might with more Warrant be
left to them, then to the strongest among our Ordinary ones of
the other Sex.

Also our Elders and Watchmen covet, (if we have unbelievers
to behold) that our Worship be performed *by the most able*: How
30 then shall it be thought that they should be so silly, to turn a
Company of weak Women loose to be abused by the fallen
Angels? Can it be thought that their Congregation, since they
have it without a command, shall fare better among those
envious Spirits, then those that are Lawfully called, shall fare
35 before the World? *Watchman, Watchman*, see to thy Duty, look
well to the manner of Worship that is to be performed according
to thy commission. Trust not *Eve* as *Adam* did, with Worship,
and with its defence. Look that all things be done in Worship as

2 but] ut.

becomes thee, a Head, both in Nature, and by Office: And leave not so solemn a part of Worship, as Prayer in Company, is, and ought to be accounted, to be done, thou canst by no means tell how. Watch *in* and *over* all *such* Worship thy self. *Be diligent to know the state of thy flocks*, whether they be flocks of Men, or Women, and look well to *thy herds*, and thou shalt have Milk enough, not only for Men and Babes, but also *for the maintenance and life of thy Maidens.* So that they need not go with their pitchers to seek water, there where their God has not sent them (*Pro.* 27. 23, 24, 25, 26, 27.) Besides the Shepherds Tents is provision sufficient for them, *Cant.* 1.

But for a Conclusion of this, I will ask this Man, If he doth not, by pleading for these Womens Meetings, declare, that the Women without their Men, are better able by themselves to maintain divine Worship, then the Men are, without their Elders? for as much as he himself will not alow that the Men should always perform Worship, without his oversight and inspection: and yet will plead for the Women, to have such Worship in their Congregation, among themselves, Excluding forever the Men therefrom. For saith he, The Spirit is promised to be given to them to that very end, *that they may Meet together*, *to Pray apart without their Men.*

And now for Mr. *K's.* Arguments, which as I said, are in number four.

1. VVe will take the Scriptures from them, and
2. Then pick the bones of their carkases.

Yet in my taking of the Scriptures from his Arguments, I will doe it in a way that is most to his advantage, making of each of them as formidable an Objection as I can against my self.

1. *Object.* Miriam *took a timbrill in her hand, and went out, and all the Women went out after her, praising God with Timbrils and dances for their deliverances. Therefore the Women of the Churches of Christ may appoint Meetings of their own, as separate from their Brethren, and then and there perform divine Worship, Prayer, in that their Congregation without their Men.* Exo. 15. *Vers.* 20, 21.

1. *Answer.* Miriam was a *Prophetess*, and I suppose that none of our Women will pretend to be such.

And though Mr. K. labours to gett over this, by saying that the work of Praising *was incumbent upon all*: yet by his leave, Judgment and discretion, and a Spirit of Conduct Sutable to the

Duty (as we read of) was found (among the Women) *in none but shee.* Why is it else said, *Miriam* led them forth, *Miriam* the *Prophetess* did it. Another by Mr. K's. Argument, might a done it as well. Thus degrades he the *Prophetess*, that he may gett favour
5 with the Ordinary Women, and prompt them on to a Work that he has a superstitious affection for.

2. But his assertion is of no weight. The Women were not left in that *Extraordinary* service, to the Spirit of Ordinary Believers. Nor can I count it but crooked dealing, to bring in
10 *Extraordinary* Persons, in their *Extraordinary* Acts, to prove it Lawful for Ordinary Persons, to do that which is not commanded them.

3. But though *Miriam* did *go forth*, or come out *with* the Women; yet not *from* the Men, into some remote place in the
15 Wilderness, to Worship by themselves. Shee rather went or came out, and the Women followed her, *from the place by the Sea, where now they were*, after *Moses*, to sing as her Sex became her; for she, though an Extraordinary Woman, might not make her self an Equall with *Moses* and *Aaron*, therefore shee came behind
20 in Worship, yet with the Body of the People, as it is said. *So* Moses *brought Israel from the red Sea*, Vers. 22. Women, though Prophetesses, must wear some badge or other of inferiority, to those that are Prophets indeed, (1 *Cor.* 11. 3, 4, 5, 6, 7, 8.) And I chuse to understand that *Miriam* did this,

25 1. Because the Text last mentioned, says so.

2. Because *Miriam* and all the Women did Sing with the *Words of the Men*, Vers. 1. compared with 21.

3. For that they did Sing them *after the Men*, as taking them from their mouth. For saith the Text, Miriam *answered them*, and
30 so handed it down *to them of her Sex; saying, Sing ye to the Lord for he hath Triumphed Gloriously.* Vers. 1. and Vers. 21.

4. For that she commanded the Women that they should Sing the *same* Song: hence it is called the *Song of Moses*, not of *Miriam*, Revel. 15. 3.

35 5. From all which I conclude that *Miriam* did not draw the Women away into some such place where neither *Moses* nor *Aaron*, nor the Elders of Israel could see, behold, and observe their manner of VVorship. But that she, as her modestie became her, did lead them out from that place where they were, to Sing
40 and to Dance, and to praise God, after the Men.

6. This Scripture therefore, favoreth not this Mans Oppinion, To wit. *That it is the Duty of the Women of the Churches of Christ to separate themselves from the Brethren, and as so separate, to perform divine Worship by themselves.*

2. *Object.* Esther *the Queen performed with her Maidens this Duty of Prayer without their Men: Therefore the Women of Gospel Churches may separate themselves from their Brethren, and perform it among themselves.* Est. 4. 16.

1. Answer. *Esther* was in the house of the Kings Chamberlain, and could not at this time come to her Brethren: No, not to her Uncle *Mordecai*, to consult how to prevent an aproaching Judgment: Yea, *Mordecai* and shee were fain to speak one to another by *Hatach* whom the King had appointed to attend upon the Queen, *Vers.* 5. 6, 7, 8, 9. So she could by no means at that time have communion with the Church: No marvel therefore if she fasted with her Maidens alone: For so she must now do, or not do at all. But I will here ask this our Argumentator, whether *Esther* did count it a burden or a Priviledge, thus now to be separated from her Brethren, and so forced to perform this Work as she did? If a Priviledge, let him prove it. If a burden, he has little cause to make use of it, to urge that her Practise then, for a ground to Women that are at liberty to separate from their Brethren to performe such Worship by themselves in *their* Company, without their Men.

2. We do not read that she desired that any of the Women that were at Liberty should come from the Men to be with her; whence we may gather that she preferred their Liberty to Worship with Men, far beyond a Womans Meeting. She counted that too many, by her self and her Maidens, were in such bondage already.

3. Neither did she attempt to take that *unavoidable* Work upon herself, but as begging of the Men, that Shee might by their Faith and Prayers, be Born up therein, clearly concluding that Shee did count such work too hard for Women to perform by themselves, without the help of their Men, *Vers.* 15. 16.

4. Besides this Womans Meeting (as Mr. *K.* would have it) was made up of none but the Queen and her Houshold Maides, and with but few of them; nor will we complaine of our honest Women, when the case is so that they cannot go out to the Church to do this, if they Pray with their Maids at home.

5. But what if *Esther* did Pray with her Maids in her Closet, because Shee could not come out to her Brethren: Is it fair to make the necessity of a Woman in Bondage, a Law to Women at Liberty? This Argument therefore is erronious, and must not have this Text to shore it up, we therefore take it away from his Words, and proceed to a sight of his next.

3. Object. *But it is said by the Prophet* Zecharias, *that the Spirit is promised to be given in new Testament times, to Women, that they may Pray together apart from Men,* Zech. 12. 11, 12, 13.

Answ. The Text says nothing so, but is greatly abused by this Man. Indeed it says their Wives shall mourn apart, but it saith not, they shall do so *together.* Yea, that they shall separate themselves by the dictate of God, from their Brethren, to do so, Is that which this Text knows nothing of. Sometimes, many may be together apart from others; but why Mr. K. to serve his purpose, should wrack and strain this Text to Justifie his Womans Meeting, I see no reason at all.

My reason against him is, for that the *look here* upon him whom we have peirced, which is to be the cause of this mourning, is to be by an immediate revelation of the Holy Ghost, who doth not use to tell before hand when he will so come down upon us. But such a Meeting as Mr. K. intends must be the product of Consultation and time. *I will pour,* saith God, *upon the House of David, the Spirit of Grace and supplication, and then they shall look*; that is, when that Spirit so worketh, with them, as to enable them so to do. Now I say, I would know, since this mourning is to be the effect of this look, and so before one is aware (Song. 6. 12.) whether Mr. K. can prove that these Women were to have an Item before hand when they should have this Look: But as it would be Ridiculous thus to conclude, so as Ridiculous is it to think to prove his Womens Meetings from hence.

Nor doth the Conclusion that he hath made hereupon, prove more but that he is ignorant of the Work of the Spirit in this matter, or that his fondness for the Womens Meetings hath made him forgett his own experience. For how can one that never had but one such Look upon *Jesus Christ,* draw such a Conclusion from hence.

And that all those Women should have this Look at the same time, even all the Women of the House of *David,* and of the

inhabitants of *Jerusalem*, that they might all of them by the
Direction of the Holy Ghost, separate themselves from their
Men to hold a Womans Meeting or Meetings, by themselves, for
this; is more fictitious, then one would imagin, a Man should
Dream. If he says that the Women have a promise to have this   5
Look when they please, or that they are sure to have it, cause 'tis
intailed to THEIR Meeting, (for this seems to come nearest his
conclusion: yet) what unavoidable inconveniences will flow
therefrom, I leave to any to Judge.

But I take this mourning to be according as another of the   10
Prophets say, *They shall be upon the Mountains like doves of the
valleys, all of them mourning, every one for his Iniquity*, Ezek. 7. 16.

All those Souls therefore, that shall be counted worthy to have
this look, shall mourn apart, or by themselves, when they have it.
For though a Man cannot appoint to himself when he will repent   15
of his Sins, or when the *Holy Ghost* will work: yet he shall repent
indeed; he shall do it, I say when HE doth so work, not staying
till another can do so too. And since our own Iniquity will then
make us best consider our own case, mourning apart, or every
one for their own Iniquity, is most naturally proper thereto. And   20
this is the mourning that shall be in the House of *David*,
Jerusalem, the Church, both with Men and Women, at all times
when the Holy Ghost shall help us to look upon him whom we
have pierced. Pray God give Mr. K. and my self more of these
lookes upon a Crucified Christ, for then we shall understand this   25
and other such like Scriptures, otherwise then to draw such
incoherent inferences from them as he doth.

4. Object. *Women were wont in Gospel times to meet together to
Pray. Therefore the Women in Gospel Churches may separate
themselves from their Brethren to perform divine Worship by*   30
themselves without their Men. Acts 16. 13.

This is another of his Scriptures, brought to uphold this fancy:
But,

Answ. 1. It is not said that the Women of Churches met
together alone to Pray. But that *Paul* went down to a River-side   35
where Prayer was wont to be made, and spake unto the Women
that resorted thither. It looks therefore most agreeable to the
Word, to think that there the Law was read by the *Jewish* Priests

6 sure] suer

to the proselited Women of that City, and that Prayer, as was
their custom in all such service, was intermixed therewith. But
this is but Conjecturall. And yet for all that, it is better grounded,
and hath more reason on its side, then hath any of this mans
5 Arguments for the Opinion of his Womens Meetings. But,

2. There was there at that time no Gospel Church of Christ,
nor before that any Gospel Ministry, consequently no Church
Obedience. Should it then be granted, that there were none but
women at that Meeting, and that their Custom was to meet at
10 that River-side to Pray, it doth not therefore follow, that their
Practice was to be a Pattern, a Rule, a Law to women in
Churches, to separate from their Brethren, to perform Divine
Worship, in their own Womans Congregation without their
Men.

15 3. There was there no Gospel-Believer. *Lydia* her self before
Paul came thither, had her heart shut up against the Faith
of Jesus Christ; and how a company of Strangers to Gospel
Faith, should in that their doing, be a Pattern to the women
in Churches, a Pattern of Christian VVorship, I do not
20 understand.

4. If *Pauls* Call to *Philippi* had been by the vision of a
VVoman, or VVomans Meeting; what an argument would this
man have drawn from thence to have justified his womens
Meetings? but since 'twas by a *man*, he hath lost an argument
25 thereby. Though he notwithstanding, doth adventure to say, that
God so approved of that Meeting, as then, and at that time, to
take advantage to make known his Mind and VVill to them
concerning Jesus Christ.

5. And now I am in, Since Mr. *K.* will needs have this
30 Scripture to justifie such a practice, I wonder, that he so lightly
over looked *Pauls* going to that Meeting, for thither he went to be
sure (ver. 13. 16). Yea how fairly, to his thinking, might he have
pleaded, that *Paul* by this act of his, was a great lover,
countenancer and commender of those he calls the VVomens
35 Meetings. Paul *went to the Womens Meeting at* Phillipi, *therefore it
is lawful for the women of Gospel Churches to separate from their
Brethren, and to Congregate by themselves for the performance of some
parts of Divine Worship.* I say how easily might he have said this,
and then have popt in those two verses above quoted, and so
40 have killed the old one? For the word lies liable to be abused by

the ignorance of men, and it had been better then it is, if this had been the first time that this man had served it so, for the justification of his Rigid Principles; but when men out of a fond conceit of their own abilities, or of prejudice to them that contradict their Errors, are tempted to shew their folly, they will   5
not want an opportunity from false Glosses put upon the Text, to do it.

6. But *Paul* went to that company to Preach Christs Gospel to them, not for that they merited his coming, but of the Grace of God, as also did *Peter* and *John*, when at the hour of Prayer they   10
went up into the Temple, and *Paul* into the Synagogue at *Antioch*, *Acts* 3. 1, 2, 3. *chap.* 13, 14, 15, 16. But as fairly might this man have urged, that the healing of the Lame man that lay at that time at the Gate of the Temple, and the Conversion of them by *Paul* at *Antioch*, was by the procurement of the Prayers of the   15
Sisters and by their reading of the Law in that Synagogue at *Antioch*, as to argue as he has done, that God was so well pleased, or so well approved of that VVomans Meeting as he feigns it at *Phillippi*, as to send, *&c.* to them his Minister.

7. But again, that this Womans Meeting should be so   20
deserving, and that while they were without the Faith of Christ, as to procure a Gospel Minister to be sent unto them, that Christ might to them be made known, and yet that so few of them should be converted to the Faith, seems a greater Paradox to me. For we read not that one of the women then, or of them of the   25
Town, that did use to go that Meeting, (for *Lydia* was of *Thyatira*) was ever converted to Christ; Brethren we read of several, but we hear not of any one more of those Women, Vers. 10.

But *Lydia* worshipped God, therefore her practice might   30
prevail. Although 'tis said she worshipped God, yet she was but a Proselyte, as those *Acts* 13. was, and knew no more of Christ then the *Eunuch* did, *Acts* 8. But hold, she had Faith, will that make all practice acceptable, yea, Law and Commandment to others, and the work of those that have none, Meritorious? But we must   35
touch upon these things anon.

5. Object. *But* (saith Mr. *K.*) Malachi 3. 16. *doth countenance these Meetings.*

Answ. Not at all; though Mr. *K.* has pleased to change a Term in the Text, to make it speak his mind; for he has put out   40

[thought] and put in [call] but all will not do his work, for when he has done what he can, 'twill be difficult, to make that Scripture say, It is the duty of women in Gospel-Churches to separate from their Brethren, to perform Divine VVorship
5 among themselves.

6. Obj. *But* Jude 20. *doth justifie these Meetings, except* saith he, *any will say, Women are not to be built up in their most Holy Faith.*

Answ. How fain would the man lay hold on something, onely he wants Divine Help, that is,the VVord of God, to bottom his
10 things upon.

But doth the Apostle here at all treat of the VVomen and their Meetings, or are they only the *Beloved*, and to be built up, *&c.* Speaks he not there to the Church, which consisteth of men and women? and are not men the more noble part in all the Churches
15 of Christ. But can women no other way be built up in their most holy faith, but by Meetings of their own without their men?

But, *Building up your SELVES*, I suppose is the thing he holds by. But cannot the Church, and every woman in it, build up themselves without their Womans Meetings? wherefore have
20 they the Word, their Closet, and the grace of Meditation, but to build up themselves withall? He saith not, *Build up one another,* but if he had, it might well have been done without a Womans Meeting. But any thing to save a drowning man.

This Text then is written to the Church of Christ, by which it
25 is exhorted to Faith and Prayer, but it speaks not a word of a Womans Meeting, and therefore it is fooling with the VVord to suggest it. I cannot therefore, while I see this impertinent dealing, but think our Argumentator dotes, or takes upon him to be a Head of those he thinks to rule over. The womans Letter to
30 me also seems to import the same, when they say, *Mr.* K. *would desire to know what Objections you have against it* (his Arguments) *and he is ready to give his further advice.*

Thus having taken from his Arguments those Holy Words of God which he has abused, to make them stand; I come next to
35 the Arguments themselves, and intend to pick their Bones for the Crows.

1. He saith, *That the same Spirit that was in* Miriam, *is also in all Gods Servants for the same end, both to pray for Mercies we stand in need of, and to praise God for Mercies received.*

40 1. *Answer,* But the question is, whether *Miriam* did, as she led

out the women to dance, act only as an ordinary Saint. And if you
evade this, you chuse the tongue of the Crafty, and use the words
of deceit; For she managed that work as she was *Miriam the
Prophetess*; and in your next, Pray tell your women so.

2. *But as Miriam the Prophetess*, she did not lead the women
from their men, to worship in some place remote by themselves,
as we have shewed before.

2dly, *He saith, that God hath promised to pour out his Spirit in
Gospel times to that very end, that women might Pray together apart
from men.*

Answer. Not mentioning again what was said before: I add; if
by *men*, he means the *Brethren*, the Prophet will not be his
Voucher, for he neither saith nor intimates such a thing.

2. And how far short this saying is, of making of God and his
holy Prophet, the Author of Schism in Worship, and an
encouragement unto Schism therein, 'tis best in time that he
looks to it. For if they may withdraw, *to do thus* at one time, they
may withdraw, *to do thus* at another: And if the Spirit is given to
them to *this very end*, that they may go by themselves from the
Church, to perform this Divine Worship at one time, they may,
for what bounds this man has set them, go by themselves to do
thus always. But, as I said, the *whole* of this Proposition being
false, the Error is still the greater.

3dly, *God*, saith he, *hath so well approved of women meeting
together to Pray in Gospel times, as then, and at that time, to take
occasion to make known his Mind and Will to them concerning Jesus
Christ* Acts 16. 13.

Answ. Let the Reader consider what was said afore, and now it
follows; If this Assertion be true, then Popish Doctrine of Merit
is good, yea the worst sort of it, which is, works done afore Faith.
For that we read of none of these women save *Lydia* feared or
worshipped God; and yet saith he, God so approved of that
Meeting as then, & at that time to send them his Gospel, which
is one of the Richest Blessings;nor will it help to lay *Cornelius*
now in my way, for the deservings here were, for ought we read,
of *women* that feared not God. Here *Lydia* only bare that
Character, 'tis said SHE worshipped God, but she was not *all*
the women. But Mr. *K.* saith *thus of them all.* I know also there
was Faith in some in *Messias* to come, though when he came,
they knew not his person; but this is not the case neither; *These*

women, who held up as he feigned, this Meeting, were not as we
read of, of this people.

4. *He said, That* Esther *and her Maids Fasted and Prayed, and
the Lord gave a gracious return, or answer and deliverance.* That, is to
5 the Church, that then was under the Rage of *Haman.*

Answ. Let the Reader remember what was said before, and
now I ask this man,

1. Whether *Mordecai* and the good men then did not Pray and
Fast as well as she? And if so, whether they might not obtain at
10 least, some little of the Mercy, as well as those women, If so.

2. Whether Mr. *K.* in applying the deliverance of this people
to the prayer of the Queen and her Maids, for he lays it only
there, be not deceitful arguing, and doth not tend to puff up that
Sex, to their hurt and dammage? yea whether it doth not tend to
15 make them unruly and head strong? But if they be more gently
inclined to obedience, no thanks to Mr. *K.*

3. And if I should ask Mr. *K.* who gave him authority to
attribute *thus* the deliverance of this people, to who and what
Prayers he please, I suppose it would not be easie for him to
20 answer. The Text saith not, that the Prayers of these women
procured the Blessing. But Mr. *K.* hath here a Womans Meeting
to vindicate, and therefore it is that he is thus out in his mind.

Prayers were heard and the Church was delivered. And I
doubt not but that these good women had hand and heart in the
25 work. But should all be admitted that Mr. *K.* hath said as to this
also, yet this Scripture, as hath already been proved, will not
justifie his womans Meeting.

5. *He makes his appeal to the women, if they have not obtained by
their Prayers in these their Meetings, many blessed returns of Prayer
30 from God, both to themselves and the Church of God.*

Answ. I count this no whit *better* then the very *worst* of his
Paper, for besides the silliness of his appeal, by which he makes
these good women to be Judg in their own cause, his words have
a direct tendance in them to puff them up to their destruction.

35 I have wondred sometimes, to see when something extraordinary hath happened to the Church of God for good, that a
few women meeting together to Pray, should be possessed with a
conceit, that they fetched the benefit down from heaven, when
perhaps ten thousand men in the Land prayed for the Mercy as
40 hard as they.

Yea I have observed that though the things bestowed, were not so much as thought of by them, yet they have been apt to conclude that their meeting together has done it. But poor women you are to be pittied, your *Tempter* is to bear the blame, to wit, this man and his Fellows.   5

I come now to some Objections that may yet be thought on: and will speak a word to them.

1. Object. It is said, *Where two or three are gathered together in my name, I am there in the midst of them*, Matt. 18. 20.

Answer. To gather together in Christs *Name*, is to gather   10
together by his *Authority*; That is, by his Law and Commandment, *Acts* 4. 17, 18, 30. *Chap.* 5. 28. 40. *Colos.* 3. 17. But we have no Law of Christ, nor Commandment, that the Women of *this*, or *that* Church, should separate themselves from their Brethren, to maintain Meetings among themselves, for the performing of   15
Divine Worship: and therefore such Meetings cannot be in his name; that is, by his Authority, Law, and Commandment; and so ought not to be at all.

2. Object. *But Women may, if sent for by them of their own Sex, come to see them, when they are sick, and when so come together, Pray*   20
in that Assembly before they part.

Answ. The Law of Christ is, *Is any sick among you, let him* (and the Woman is included in the Man) *call for the Elders of the Church, and let them Pray over him*, &c. and to this Injunction there is a threefold promise made.   25

1. And the Prayer of Faith shall save the Sick;
2. And the Lord shall raise him up.
3. And if he have committed Sin, they shall be forgiven him.
    Jam. 5. 14, 15.

And considering, this advice is seconded with so much Grace: 30
I think it best in all such cases (as in all other) to make the Word of God our Rule.

3. Object. *But Women have sometimes cases, which modesty will not admit should be made known to Men, what must they do then?*

Answ. Their Husband and they are one Flesh, and are no   35
more to be accounted two. Let them tell their grief to them. Thus *Rachel* asked Children of her Husband, and went not to a nest of Women to make her complaint to them, (*Gen.* 30. 1.) or let them betake themselves to their Closets, with *Rebecca* (*Gen.* 25. 20, 21, 22, 23.) or if they be in the Assembly of the Saints, let   40

them Pray in their Hearts, with *Hannah*: And if their petition be Lawfull, I doubt not but they may be Heard, 1 *Sam.* 1. 13.

Our *Author*, perhaps, will say, I have not spoken to his Question, which was, *Whether Women fearing God, may Meet to* 5 *Pray together? And whether it be Lawfull for them so to do?*

But I Answer, I have: with respect to all such Godly Women as are in the churches of the Saints, 1 *Cor.* 14. 33, 34, 35. compared with *Vers.* 15, 16, 17.

And when he has told us, that his Question respected only 10 those out of Churches, then will I confess that I did mistake him. Yes he will gett nothing thereby, for as much as his Question to be sure intends *those* in special: Also his Arguments are for the Justifying of that their Practise.

Now the reason why I waved the form of his Question, was, 15 because it was both scanty and lean of Words, as to the matter of Controversie in hand: Also I thought it best to make it more ample, and distinct, for the Edification of our Reader. And if after all, Mr. K. is not pleased at what I have done, let him take up the Question, and Answer it better. The Man perhaps may fly 20 to the case of utter necessity, and so bring forth another Question, to wit, *whether, if the Men of a Church should all die, be murdered, or cast into prison: The Woman of that Church may not Meet together to Pray? And whether it be not Lawfull for them so to do?* But when he produceth a necessity for the puting of such a 25 Question, and then shall put it to me; I will, as God shall help me, give him an Answer thereto.

But, may some say, Our Women in this, do not what they do, of their own Heads, they are allowed to do what they do by the Church.

30 I *Answer*, No Church-allowance is a Foundation sufficient to Justifie that which is neither Commanded nor Allowed by the Word. Besides, who knows not, that have their Eyes in their Heads, what already has, and what further may come into the Churches, at such a gapp as this.

35 And now to give the Reader a Cautionary Conclusion.

1. Take heed of letting the name, or good shew of a thing, begett in thy Heart a Religious reverance of that thing; but look to the Word for thy bottom, for it is the Word that Authorizeth, what ever may be done with Warrant in Worship, to God; 40 without the Word, things are of humain invention, of what

Splendor or Beauty soever they may appear to be. Without doubt
the *Fryers* and *Nunns*, and their Religious Order, were of a good
intent at first, as also compulsive vowes of chastitie, single life,
and the like: But they were all without the Word, and therefore,
as their bottom wanted divine Authority, so the Practise wanted 5
Sanctity by the Holy Ghost. The Word *Prayer*, is, of it self, in
appearance so Holy, that he forthwith seems to be a *Devil* that
forbids it: And yet we finde that Prayers have been out of joynt,
and disorderly used; and therefore may be one, without
incurring the danger of damnation, be called into Question; and 10
if, found without Order by him, he may labour to set them in
joynt again, *Matt.* 6. 5, 6, 7, 8. *Chap.* 23. 14. *Jam.* 4. 3.

I am not of the number of them, that say, *Of what profit is it, if
we should Pray unto God?* Job 21. 15: But finding no good footing
in the Word for that kind of service we have treated about above, 15
and knowing that error and humain inventions in Religion will
not offer themselves, but with wiped lipps, and a countenance as
demure as may be, and also being perswaded that this Opinion of
Mr. *K.* is vagrant, yea a meer alien as to the Scriptures, I being
an Officer, have apprehended it, and put it in the stocks, and there 20
will keep it, till I see by what Authority it has leave to pass and
repass as it lists among the Godly in this Land.

2ly. Yet by all that I have said, I never meant to intimate in the
least, but that believing Women are Saints as well as Men: And
members of the body of Christ. And I will add, that as *they*, and 25
we, are united to Christ, and made members of his mystical body,
the fulness of him that fills all in all: So there is no superiority, as
I know of, but we are all one in Christ. For, *the Man is not without
the Woman, nor the Woman without the Man in the Lord*, nor are we
counted as *Male* or *Female* in him, 1 *Cor.* 11. 11. *Galat.* 3. 28. 30
Ephes. 1. 23. Only we must observe that this is spoken of *that*
Church which is his True Mystical Body, and not of every
particular Congregation of professing Christians.

The Churches of Christ *here*, and there, are also called his
Body: But no Church *here*, though never so famous, must be 35
taken for that of which mention was made afore.

As Christ then, has a Body *Mystical*, which is called his
Members, his *Flesh*, and his *Bones*, *Ephes.* 5. 30. So he has a Body
Politick, Congregations modelled by the skill that his Ministers
have in his Word, for the bearing up of his Name, and the 40

preserving of his Glory in the World against *Antichrist*. In *this* Church, *Order*, and *Discipline*, for the nourishing up of *the* True Mystical Body of Christ, has been placed from the Foundation of the World. Wherefore in *this*, Laws, and Statutes; and Govern-
5 ment, is to be looked after, and given heed unto, for the Edification of *that*, which is to arive at last to a perfect Man: To the measure of the Stature of the Fulness of Christ, 1 *Cor.* 12. 27, 28, 29, *Ephes.* 4. 11, 12, 13.

Now where there is *Order*, and *Government* by Laws and
10 Statutes: There must, of necessity, be also a distinction of *Sex*, *Degrees*, and *Age*: Yea, *Offices*, and *Officers* must also be *there*, for our furtherance, and Joy of Faith. *From which Government and Rule, our Ordinary Women are excluded by Paul*; nor should it, since it is done by the Wisdom of God, be any offence unto them.

15 In *this* Church there are oft times many Hypocrites, and formal Professors, and Heresies: *That they which are approved may be made manifest*, 1 Cor. 11. 19. These therefore being there, and being suffered to act as they many times do, provoke the Truly Godly, to contend with them by the Word: For that these
20 Hypocrites, and formal Professors, Naturaly incline to a denial of the power of Godliness, and to set up forms of their own, in the stead thereof, *Mark.* 7. 6, 7, 8, 9. 2 *Tim.* 3. 5.

And this is done for the sake, and for the good of those that are the true Members of the body of Christ, and that are to arive
25 at his Haven of Rest: From whom those others at last shall be purged, and with them, all *their* things that offend: *Matt.* 13. 40. *Then shall the righteous shine like the Sun, in the Kingdom of their Father: He that hath Ears to hear, let him hear.*

This Church, that thus consisteth of all Righteous, that are so
30 in Gods account: they are to have an House in Heaven, and to be for Gods habitation there. Who *then*, shall be governed by their Head without those Officers and Laws, that are necessary here: And *both* at last shall be subject to him, that sometime did put all things under Christ, that God may be all in all, *Joh.* 14. 1, 2, 3.
35 *Ephes.* 2. 21. 1 *Cor.* 15. 23, 24, 25, 26, 27. Wherefore my beloved Sisters, this inferiority of yours will last but a little while: When the day of Gods Salvation is come, to wit, when our Lord shall descend from Heaven, with a shout, with the voice of the Archangel, and the Trump of God, these distinctions of Sexes
40 shall be laid a side, and every pot shall be filled to the Brim. For

with a *notwithstanding* you shall be saved, and be gathered up to
that state of Felicity; if you continue in Faith, and Charity, and
Holiness, with sobriety, 1 *Tim.* 2. 15.

Thirdly. I doubt not at all of the Lawfulness of Womens
Praying, and that both in private and Publick: Only when they   5
Pray Publickly, they should not separate from, but joyn with the
Church in that Work. They should also not be the mouth of the
Assembly, but in heart, desires, grones, and Tears, they should
go along with the Men. In their Closets they are at Liberty to
speak unto their God, who can bear with, and pitty them with us;   10
and pardon all our weakness for the sake of Jesus Christ.

And here, I will take an occasion to say, there may be a twofold
miscarriage in Prayer, one in *Doctrine*, the other in the frame of
the Heart: All are too much subject to the *last*, *Women* to the *first*.
And for this cause it is, at least, so I think, that VVomen are not   15
permitted to Teach, nor speak in Assemblies for Divine
Worship, but to *be* and to *learn* in silence, 1 *Cor.* 14. 33, 34, 35.
Chap. 15. 33.

For he that faileth as to the frame of his spirit, hurteth only
himself: But he that faileth in *Doctrine*, corrupteth them that   20
stand by.

Let the Women be alone with *Rebecca*, in the Closet; or if in
Company, Let her, with *Hanna* speak to her self and to God; and
not doubt, but if She be humble, and keep within Compass,
Shee shall be sharers with her Brethren in the Mercy.   25

Fourthly. Nor are Women, by what I have said, debarred from
any Work, or imploy, unto which they are enjoyed by the Word.
they have often been called forth to be Gods witnesses, and have
Born famous Testimony for him, against the Sons of the
Sorceress, and the Whore; I remember many of them with   30
comfort: Even of these Eminent Daughters of *Sarah*, whose
Daughters *you also are*, so long as you do well, and are not affraid
with any amazement, 1 *Pet.* 3. 1, 2, 3, 4, 5, 6.

What by the Word of God, you are called unto, what by the
Word is enjoyned, you, do; and the Lord be with you.   35

But this of the Womens Meetings: Since indeed there is
nothing for its Countenance in the Word, and since the calling
together of Assemblies for Worship, is an Act of Power, and
belongeth to the Church, Elders, or Chief Men of the same: Let
me intreat you to be content, to be under Subjection, and   40

Obedience, as also saith the Law. We hold that it is Gods Word, that we are to look to, as to all things pertaining to Worship, because it is the Word that Authorizeth, and Sanctifieth what wee do.

5 *Fifthly. Women*! They are an Ornament in the Church of God on Earth, as the *Angels* are in the Church in Heaven. Betwixt whom also there is some Comparison, for they cover their faces in Acts of Worship, *Isa.* 6. 2. 1 *Cor.* 11. 10. But as the *Angels* in Heaven, *are not Christ*, and so not admitted to the Mercie-seat to
10 speak to God, so neither are Women on Earth, *the Man*; who is to Worship with open face before him, and to be the mouth in Prayer for the rest. As the Angels then cry, *Holy, Holy, Holy*, with faces covered in Heaven: So let the Women cry, *Holy, Holy, Holy*, with their faces covered on Earth: Yea thus they should do,
15 because of the Angels. *For this cause ought the Woman to have Power*, that is a covering, *on her Head, because of the Angels*, 1 Cor. 11.10. Not only because the Angels are present, but because *Women*, and *Angels*, as to their Worship, in their respective places, have a semblance. For the Angels are inferior
20 to the great Man *Christ*, who is in Heaven; and the Woman is inferior to the Man, that Truly Worships God in the Church on Earth.

Methinks, Holy and Beloved Sisters, you should be content to wear this *Power*, or badge of your inferiority, since the cause
25 thereof, arose at first from your selves. 'Twas the *Woman* that at first the *Serpent* made use of, and by whom he then overthrew the World: Wherefore the *Woman*, to the Worlds end, must wear tokens of her *Underlingship* in all Matters of VVorship. To say nothing of *that* which she cannot shake off, to wit, her pains and
30 sorrows in Child-bearing (which God has *riveted* to her Nature) there is her *Silence*, and *shame*, and a *covering for her face*, in token of it, which she ought to be exercised with, when ever the Church comes together to VVorship, *Gen.* 3. 16. 1 *Tim.* 2. 15. 1 *Cor.* 11. 13. 1 *Tim.* 2. 9.
35 Do you think that God gave the VVoman her hair, that she might deck her self, and set off her fleshly beauty therewith? It was given her to cover her face with, in token of shame and silence, for that by the VVoman sin came into the VVorld, 1 *Tim.* 2. 9.
40 And perhaps the reason why the Angels cover their faces when

they cry, *Holy*, *Holy*, *Holy*, in Heaven, is to shew that they still bear in minde with a kind of abhorrence, the remembrance of their Fellows falling from thence. Modesty, and shame-facedness, becomes VVomen at all times, especially in times of Publick VVorship, and the more of this is mixed with their grace, and personage, the more Beautiful they are both to God and Men. *But why must the Women have shame-facedness, since they live honestly as the Men?* I Answer, In remembrance of the Fall of *Eve*, and to that the Apostle applies it. For a VVoman (necessity has no Law) to shave her head, and so look with open face in VVorship, as if she could be a leader there; is so far from doing that which becomes her, that it declares her to have forgot what God would have her for ever with shame remember.

Sixthly: In what I have said about the VVomens Meetings; I have not at all concerned my self about those VVomen, that have been *Extraordinary* ones, such as *Miriam*, *Deborah*, *Huldah*, *Anna*, or the rest, as the Daughters of *Philip* the Evangelist, *Priscilla*, the VVomen that *Paul* said laboured with him in the Gospel, or such like; for they might Teach, Prophecy, and had power to call the People together so to do.

Though this I must say concerning them, they ought to (and did, notwithstanding so high a calling, still) bear about with them the badge of their inferiority to them that were Prophets indeed. And hence 'tis said, under pain of being guilty of disorder, that if they Prayed in the Church, or Prophesied there, with their head uncovered, they then dishonoured their Head, 1 *Cor.* 11. 5.

The Prophetesses were below the Prophets, and their covering for their head was to be worn in token thereof; and perhaps 'twas for want of regard to this Order, that when *Miriam* began to perk it before *Moses*, that God covered her face with a *Leperous-Scabb*, *Numb.* 12.

Hence these VVomen, when Prophets were present, did use to lie still as to Acts of Power, and leave that to be put forth by them that was higher then they: And even *Miriam* her self, though she was one indeed, yet she came allwayes behind, not only in name, but VVorship, unless when she was in her own disorders, *Num.* 12. 1.

And it is worth your further noting, that when God tells *Israel* that they should take heed in the Plague of *Leprosie* that they diligently observed to do what the Priest and Levites taught them, that he conjoyns with that Exhortation, *that they should remember what God did to* Miriam *by the way*, Deut. 24. 8, 9. Intimating surely, that they should not give heed to VVomen, that would be perking up in matters of VVorshiping God.

5   Much less should we invest them with Powcr to call Congregations of their own, there to perform Worship without their Men.

    Yet, will I say, notwithstanding all this, that if any of these high Women, had (but we never read that they did) separate themselves
10 and others of their own Sex with them, apart to Worship by themselves: or if they had given out Commandment so to do, and had joyned Gods name to that Commandment, I should have freely consented that our Women should do so too, when lead out, and conducted in Worship, by so Extraordinary a one.

15   Yea more, If any of these high Women, had given it out for Law, that the Women of the Churches in New Testament-times, ought to separate themselves from their Men, and as so Separate, perform divine Worship among themselves: I should have Subscribed thereto. But finding nothing like this in the
20 Word of God, for the Sanctifying of such a Practise: And seeing so many Scriptures wrested out of their place to Justifie so fond a conceit: And all this done by a Man of Conceit, and of one that, as his Sisters say, expects my Answer: I found my self engaged to say something for the suppressing of this his Opinion.

25   But to return to the good Women in the Churches, and to make up my discourse with them.

    First, These Meetings of yours (honourable Women) wherein you attempt to perform divine Worship by your selves, without your Men, not having the Authority of the Word to Sanctifie
30 them, will be found *Will-Worship*, in the day when you, as to that, shall be measured with that Golden Reed, the Law of God. And *who hath required this at your hand?* may put you to your shifts for an Answer, notwithstanding all Mr. *K.* has said to uphold you, *Isa.* 1. 12. *Revel.* 11. 1, 2, 3.

35   *Secondly*, These Meetings of yours *need* not be; There are Elders of Brethren in all Churches, to call to, and manage this Worship of God, in the World: if you abide in your subjection and Worship as you are commanded.

    Thirdly, These Meetings of yours, (instead of being an

Ornament to the Church in which you are) is a shame and
blemish to those Churches. For they manifest the unruliness of
such Women, or that the Church wants skill to Govern them.
Have you not in your flock a Male? 1 Cor. 24, 25. Malach. 1. 14.

Fourthly, Suppose your Meetings in some cases were Lawful,   5
yet since by the Brethren they may be managed better, you and
your Meetings ought to give place.

That the Church together, and the Brethren, as the mouth to
God, are capable of managing this Solemn Worship best:
Consider.   10

1. The Gifts for all such service, are most to be found in the
Elders and leading Men in the Church: And not in the Women
thereof.

2. The Spirit for Conduct and Government in that Worship,
is not in the Women, but in the Men.   15

3. The Men are admitted in such Worship, to stand with
open Face before God (a token of much admitance to liberty and
boldness with God) a thing denyed to the Women, 1 *Cor.* 11. 4,
5.

4. For that when Meetings for Prayers are Commanded, the   20
Men, to be the mouth to God, are mentioned, but not an
Ordinary Woman, in all the Scriptures. Where the Women and
Children, and them that suck the brests are called, with the
Bride and Bridegroom, and the whole Land, to mourn: Yet the
Ministers, and Elders, and Chiefest of the Brethren, are they, and   25
they only that are bid to SAY, *spare thy People O Lord! and give not
thine Heritage to reproach.* Joel. 1. 13, 14. *Chap.* 2. 15, 16, 17.

5. The Word for encouragement to Pray believingly in
Assemblies is given to men. And it is the Word that makes, and
that Sanctifies an Ordinance of God: Men therfore in all   30
Assemblies for Worship, should be they that should manage it,
and let others joyn in their place.

Object. *But the Woman is included in the Man, for the same Word
signifies both.*

1. *Answer.* If the Woman is included here, let her not exclude   35
the Man. But the Man is Excluded: The Man is Excluded by this
Womans Meeting from Worship; from Worship, though he be
the Head in Worship over the Woman, and by Gods Ordinance
appointed to manage it, and this is an Excluding of the worst
Complexion, 1 *Cor.* 11. 3.   40

2. Though the Woman is included, when the Man sometimes is named, yet the Man is not Excluded, when himself as Chief is named. But to cut him off from being the Chief in all Assemblies for Worship, is to Exclude him, and that when he for that in
5 Chief is named.

3. The Woman is included when the Man is named, yet but in her place, and if she Worships in Assemblies, her part is to hold her Tongue, to learn in silence; and if she speaks, she must do it, I mean as to Worship, in her Heart to God.

10 4. Nor, do I think that any Woman that is Holy and Humble, will take offence at what I have said; for I have not in any thing sought to degrade them, or to take from them what either Nature or Grace, or an Appointment of God hath invested them with: But have laboured to keep them in their place.

15 And doubtless to abide where God has put us, is that, which not only highly concerns us, but that, which becomes us best. Sisters, I have said what I have said to set you right, and to prevent your attempting to do things in such Sort unto which you are not appointed. Remember what God did to *Miriam*, and be
20 afraid.

Be as often in your Closets as you will; the oftener there, the better. This is your Duty, this is your Priviledge: This place is Sanctified to you for service by the Holy VVord of God. Here you may be, and not make Ordinances enterfere, and not
25 presume upon the Power of your Superiors, and not thrust out your Brethren, nor put them behinde your backs in VVorship.

Be also as often as possible you can in VVorship, when the Church, or parts thereof, are Assembled for that end, according to God. And when you are there, joyn with Heart and Soul with
30 your Brethren in all Holy Petitions to God. Let the Men in Prayer be the mouth to God, and the VVomen lift after with groans and desires. Let the Men stand with open Face in this VVorship, for that they are the image and Glory of God, and let the Women be clothed in modest Apparel, with shame-
35 facedness, in token of the rembrance of what has been touched afore.

When Women keep their places, and Men manage their Worshipping God as they should, we shall have better days for the Church of God, in the VVorld, *Jer.* 29. 10, 11, 12, 13.

40 VVomen are not to be blamed for that they are forward to Pray

to God, only let them know their bounds; and I wish that *Idleness* in Men, be not the cause of their putting their good VVomen upon his VVork. Surely they that can scarce tye their Shoes, and their Garters, before they arive at the Tavern, or get to the Coffe-house dore in a morning, can scarce spare time to be a 5 while in their Closets with God. Morning-Closet-Prayers, are now by most *London*-Professors, thrown a way; and what kind of ones they make at night, God doth now (and their Conscience when awake will) know; however I have cause, as to this, to Look at home: And God mend me and all his Servants about it, and 10 wherein we else are out.

I have done, after I have said, that there are some other things, concerning VVomen, touching which, when I have an Opportunity, I may also give my Judgment. But at present, I intreat that these lines be taken in good part, for I seek Edification, not 15 Contention.

FINIS.

QUESTIONS ABOUT THE NATURE AND PERPETUITY OF THE SEVENTH-DAY-SABBATH

QUESTIONS

About the

NATURE

AND

PERPETUITY

OF THE

Seventh-day-Sabbath.

And Proof,
That the First Day of the Week
Is the true
Christian-Sabbath.

By *JOHN BUNYAN.*

The Son of man is Lord also of the Sabbath day.

LONDON:
Printed for *Nath. Ponder*, at the Peacock in the *Poultry*. 1685.

Title-page of *Questions About the Nature and Perpetuity of the Seventh-Day-Sabbath* (1685)

QUESTIONS ABOUT THE NATURE AND PERPETUITY OF THE SEVENTH-DAY-SABBATH

Note on the Text

One edition of this work was published in Bunyan's lifetime. At least eight copies survive. The work is listed in the Term Catalogues for Michaelmas Term, 1684.[1] The publisher was Nathaniel Ponder, best known for his publication of *The Pilgrim's Progress*. He also published most of the works of John Owen. Ponder's shop was first at the sign of the Peacock in Chancery Lane and later in the Poultry. In the year that Bunyan died, Ponder was in prison for debt, but he continued to issue some publications in later years.[2]

Title-page: [within double rules] QUESTIONS | About the | NATURE | AND | PERPETUITY | OF THE | **Seventh-Day-Sabbath.** | And Proof, | That the **First day** of the Week | Is the true| Christian-Sabbath | [rule] | By *JOHN BUNYAN.* | [rule] | *The Son of man is Lord also of the | Sabbath day.* | [rule] | *LONDON:* | Printed for *Nath. Ponder*, at the Pea-|cock in the *Poultry.* 1685.

Collation:12⁰; A1–A6; B–G¹²; pp. [i–xii + 144 = 156. The first printed page number is 1. The 8 type for page number 58 is damaged. Signatures A2 and A3 are printed, otherwise signatures are printed on the first five leaves. The 3 is inverted in page number 135 on G8ʳ in the copies at the British Library, Trinity College, Cambridge, and Williams College, Williamstown, Massachusetts.

Contents: A1ʳ title-page; A1ᵛ blank; A2ʳ–A6ᵛ to the reader; B1ʳ–G12ᵛ text. A double rule on A2ʳ is followed by 'TO THE | READER.' A6ᵛ is signed '*Joh. Bunyan.*' A double rule on B1ʳ is followed by 'QUESTIONS | About the | NATURE and PERPETUITY | Of the | Seventh-Day-Sabbath.', followed by a single rule and 'QUEST. I.' A single rule on B5ᵛ is followed by 'QUEST. II.' A single rule on B12ᵛ is followed by 'QUEST. III.' A single rule on C4ᵛ is followed by 'QUEST. IV.' A single rule on D4ᵛ is followed by 'QUEST. V.' The conclusion of the text on G12ᵛ is followed by a single rule, '*FINIS.*', and another single rule.

Running Titles: To the reader: 'To the Reader.' Text: B1ᵛ–B5ʳ '*The first*

---

[1] *Term Catalogues*, ed. E. Arber, p. 95.　　　　[2] Plomer, 240–1.

Question | of the Sabbath.'; B5^v–C1^r '*The second Question | of the Sabbath.*'; C1^v–C4^r '*The third Question | of the Sabbath.*'; C4^v–D3^r '*The fourth Question | of the Sabbath.*'; D3^v–G12^r '*The fifth Question | of the Sabbath.*' ['fifth' is misprinted 'th' on G8^v]; G12^v '*The fifth Question*'.

Catchwords: (selected: A5^r *God*, C2^v their, D9^r Fourthly, F2^v of, G5^r need.

Copies collated: Bodleian, Oxford; British Library; Huntington Library; Folger Shakespeare Library; J. Pierpont Morgan Library; Trinity College, Cambridge: Williams College, Williamstown, Massachusetts; Yale University.

The following text is based on the Bodleian copy.

TO THE
READER.

SOME may think it strange, since Gods Church has already been so well furnished with sound Grounds and Reasons by so many wise and godly men, for proof that the first day of the week is our true Christian Sabbath, that I should now offer this small Treatise upon the same account. But when the Scales are even by what already is put in, a little more, you know, makes the weight the better.

Or grant we had down weight before, yet something over and above, may make his work the harder, that shall be hanging Fictions on the other end, endeavour to make things seem too light.

Besides, This book being little, may best sute such as have but shallow Purses, short Memories, and but little Time to spare, which usually is the lot of the mean and poorest sort of men.

I have also written upon this Subject, for that I would, as in other Gospel-truths, be a fellow witness with good men that the day in which our Lord rose from the dead should be much set by of Christians.

I have observed that some, otherwise sound in faith, are apt to be entangled with a Jewish Sabbath, &c. and that some also that are far off from the observation of that, have but little to say for their own practice though good; and might I help them I should be glad.

A Jewish Seventh-day-Sabbath has no promise of Grace belonging to it, if that be true (as to be sure it is) where Paul says, The command to honour Parents, is the first Commandment with promise, Ephes. 6. 1, 2, 3.

Also it follows from hence, that the Sabbath that has a promise annexed to the keeping of it is rather that which the Lord Jesus shall give to the Churches of the Gentiles, Isai. 56.

Perhaps my Method here may not in all things keep the common path of Argumentation with them that have gone before me: But I trust the godly-wise will find a taste of Scripture-truth in what I present them with as to the sanction of our Christian-sabbath.

I have here, by handling four Questions, proved, that the Seventh-day-Sabbath was not moral. For that must of necessity be done, before it can be

*made appear that the First day of the week is that which is the Sabbath day
for Christians. But withal it follows, that if the* Seventh-day-sabbath *was
not moral, the first day is not so. What is it then? Why a Sabbath for holy
worship is moral; but* this *or* that *day appointed for such service, is sanctified
by Precept or by approved Example. The timeing then of a Sabbath for us lies
in God, not man; in Grace, not Nature; nor in the ministration of death,
written and engraven in stones: God always reserving to himself a power to
alter and* change *both* time *and* modes *of worship according to his own will.*

*A Sabbath then, or day of rest from wordly affairs to solemnize worship to
God in, all good men do by nature conclude is meet, yea, necessary: yet that,
not* Nature, *but* God *reveals.*

*Nor is that day or time, by God so fixed on, in its own nature, better than
any other: the holiness then of a Sabbath lies, not in the Nature or Place of a
day, but in the Ordinance of God.*

*Nor doth our sanctifying of it, to the ends for which it is ordained, lie in a
bare confession that it is such; but in a holy performance of the Duty of the day
to God by Christ, according to his Word.*

*But I will not enlarge to detain the Reader longer from the following
Sheets; but shall commit both him and them to the wise dispose of God, and
rest,*

Thine to serve thee,

Joh. Bunyan.

QUESTIONS

About the
NATURE and PERPETUITY
Of the
Seventh-Day-Sabbath.

QUEST. I.

Whether the Seventh-day-Sabbath is of, or made known to man by the Law and Light of Nature?

S Omething must be here premised, before I shew the
5 grounds of this Question.

First then, By the Law or Light of Nature, I mean, *that Law* which was *concreat* with man; that which is natural to him, being Original with, and Essential to himself; consequently that which is invariable and unalterable, as is *that* Nature.

10 Secondly, I grant that by this Law of Nature, man understands that there is one eternal God; that this God is to be worshiped according to his own will; consequently that *time* must be allowed to do it in: But whether the *Law* or *Light* of Nature teacheth, and, *that of it self*, without the help of Revelation, that the *Seventh day* of
15 the week is *that* time sanctified of God, and set apart for his Worship, that's the Question; and the grounds of it are these.

First, Because *the Law of Nature* is antecedent to this day, yea compleated as a Law before 'twas known or revealed to man that God either did or would sanctifie the *Seventh day* of the week at
20 all.

Now this Law, as was said, being natural to a man, (*for man is a Law unto himself*, (Rom. 2.) could onely teach the things of a man, and there the Apostle stints it, 1 *Cor.* 2. 11.). But to be able to determine, and that about things that were yet without being
25 either in Nature, or by Revelation, is that which belongs not to a man as a man; and the *Seventh-day-Sabbath* as yet, was such: For *Adam* was compleatly made the day before; and God did not

sanctifie the Seventh day before it was, none otherwise than by his secret Decree. Therefore by the Law of Nature *Adam* understood it not, it was not made known to him thereby.

Secondly, To affirm the contrary, is to make the *Law* of Nature *Supernatural*, which is an impossibility. Yea, they that do so, make it a Predictor, a Prophet; a Prophet about divine things to come; yea, a Prophet able to foretel *what shall be*, and that *without* a Revolution; which is a strain that never yet Prophet pretended to.

Besides; to grant this, is to run into a grievous errour; for this doth not onely make the Law of Nature the *first* of Prophets; contrary to *Gen.* 3. 10. compared with *Joh.* 1. 1. but it seems to make the will of God, made known by Revelation, a needless thing. For if the Law of Nature, as such, can predict, or foretel Gods Secrets, and that before he reveals them, and this Law of Nature is universal in every individual man in the world, what need is there of particular Prophets, or of their holy writings? (and indeed here the Quakers and others split themselves:) For if the Law of Nature can of it self reveal unto me *one thing* pertaining to instituted Worship, for that we are treating of now, and the exact time which God has not yet sanctified and set apart for the performance thereof, why may it not reveal until me more, and so still more; and at last *all* that is requisite for me to know, both as to my Salvation, and how God is to be worshipped in the Church on Earth.

Thirdly, If it be of the Law of Nature, then all men by nature are convinced of the necessity of keeping it, and that though they never read or heard of the revealed Will of God about it; but this we find not in the world.

For though it is true that the Law of Nature is common to all, and that all men are to this day under the power and command thereof; yet we find not that they are by nature under a conviction of the necessity of keeping of a *Seventh-day-Sabbath*. Yea, the Gentiles, though we read not that they ever despised the Law of Nature, yet never had, as such, a reverence of a *Seventh-day-Sabbath*, but rather the contrary.

Fourthly, If therefore the *Seventh-day-Sabbath* is not of the Law of Nature, then it should seem not to be obligatory to all.

16 individual] individal

For instituted Worship, and the necessary circumstances thereunto belonging, is obligatory but to some. The Tree that *Adam* was forbid to eat of, we read not but that his Children might have eat the fruit thereof: and Circumcision, the Passover, and other
5 parts of instituted Worship was enjoyned but to some.

Fifthly, I doubt the *Seventh-day-Sabbath* is not of the Law of Nature, and so not moral; because though we read that the Law of Nature, and that before *Moses*, was charged upon the world, yet I find not *till then*, that the prophanation of a *Seventh-day-*
10 *Sabbath* was charged upon the world: and indeed to me this very thing makes a great scruple in the case.

A Law, as I said, we read of, and that from *Adam* to *Moses* (Rom. 5. 13, 14.) The transgressions also of *that* Law we read of them, and that particularly, as in *Gen.* 4. 8. ch. 6. 5. ch. 9. 21, 22.
15 ch. 12. 13. ch. 13. 13. ch. 18. 12, 13, 14, 15. ch. 19. 5. (*Ezek.* 49 50.) ch. 31. 30. ch. 35. 2. ch. 40. 15. ch. 44. 8, 9, 10. *Deut.* 8. 19, 28. ch. 12. 2. *Psal.* 106, 35, 36, 37. and *Romans* the first and second Chapters.

But in all the Scriptures we do not read, that the breach of a
20 *Seventh-day-Sabbath* was charged upon men as men *all that time.* Whence I gather, that either a *Seventh-day-Sabbath* was not discerned by the Light of Nature, and so not by that Law imposed; or else, that men by the help and assistance of that (for we speak of men as men) in old time kept it better, than in after
25 Ages did the Church of God with better assistance by far: For they are there yet found fault with as breakers of that Sabbath (*Ezekel* 20. 13.)

It follows therefore, that if the Law of Nature doth not of it self reveal to us, as men, that the *Seventh day* is the *holy Sabbath of*
30 *God.* That that day, as to the sanction of it, *is not Moral*, but rather Arbitrary, to wit, imposed by the will of God upon his people, until the time he thought fit to change it for another day.

And if so, it is hence to be concluded, that though by the Light of Nature men might see that *time* must be allowed and set apart
35 for the performance of that Worship that God would set up in his House, yet, as such, it could not see *what* time the Lord would to that end chuse. Nature therefore saw *that* by a positive Precept, or a Word revealing it, and by no other means.

Nor doth this at all take away a whit of that Sanction which
40 God once put upon the *Seventh-day-Sabbath*; unless any will say,

and by sufficient Argument prove, that an Ordinance for divine Worship receiveth greater Sanction from the Law of Nature than from divine Precept: or standeth stronger when 'tis established by a Law humane, for such is the Law of Nature, than when imposed by Revelation of God.

But the Text will put this controversie to an end. The Sanction of the *Seventh-day-Sabbath*, even as it was the *Rest of God*, was not till after the Law of Nature was compleated; *God rested the seventh day, and sanctified it*, (Gen. 2. 3.) Sanctified it; that is, set it apart to the end there mentioned, to wit, to rest thereon.

Other grounds of this Question I might produce, but at present I will stop here, and conclude, That if a *Seventh-day-Sabbath* was an essential necessary to the instituted Worship of God, then it self also as to its sanction for that Work, was not founded by a positive Precept; consequently not known of man at first, but by revelation of God.

QUEST. II.

Whether the Seventh-day-Sabbath, as to Mans *keeping of it holy, was ever made known to or imposed by a positive Precept upon him until the time of Moses? which from* Adam *was about two thousand years.*

SOmething must also be here premised in order to my propounding of my grounds for this Question; and that is, That the *Seventh day* was sanctified *so soon* as it had being in the world, unto the rest of God (as it is *Gen.* 2. 2, 3.) and he did rest from all his works which he had made therein. But the Question is, *Whether when God did thus sanctifie* this *day to his* own rest, *he did also by the space of time above-mentioned, impose it as an holy Sabbath of rest upon men*; to the end they might solemnize Worship to him in special manner thereon? And I question this,

First, *Because we read not that it was.* And reading, I mean, of the divine Testimony, is ordained of God, for us to find out the mind of God, both as to Faith and our performance of acceptable service to him.

In reading also, we are to have regard to two things.

1. To see if we can find a Precept: or,

2. A countenanced Practice for what we do: For both these ways we are to search, that we may find out what is that good,
5 that acceptible will of God.

For the first of these we have *Gen.* 2. 16, 17. and for the second, *Gen.* 8. 20, 21.

Now as to the imposing of a *Seventh-day-Sabbath* upon men from *Adam* to *Moses*, of that we find nothing in holy Writ either
10 from Precept or Example. True, we find that Solemn worship was performed by the Saints that then lived: for both *Abel, Noah, Abraham, Isaac, Jacob* sacrificed unto God (*Gen.* 4. 4. ch. 8. 20, 21. ch. 12. 7. ch. 13. 4. ch. 35. 1.) but we read not that the *Seventh day* was the time prefixed of God for their so
15 worshipping, or that they took any notice of it. Some say, that *Adam* in eating the forbidden Fruit, brake also the *Seventh-Day-Sabbath*, because he fell on that day; but we read not that the breach of a Sabbath was charged upon him. That which we read is this; *Hast thou eaten of the tree whereof I commanded thee, that*
20 *thou shouldest not eat?* (*Gen.* 3. 11.) Some say also that *Cain* killed *Abel* on a *Sabbath day*; but we read not that in his Charge God laid any such thing at his door. This was it of which he stood guilty before God; namely, *That his brothers bloud cried unto God against him from the ground,* (*Gen.* 4. 10.)

25 I therefore take little notice of what a man saith, though he flourisheth his matter with many brave words, if he bring not with him, *Thus saith the Lord.* For that, and that onely, ought to be my ground of Faith as to how my God would be worshipped by me. For in the matters material to the Worship of God, 'tis
30 safest that thus I be guided in my Judgement: for here onely I perceive *the footsteps of the Flock* (*Ezek.* 3. 11. *Song* 1. 8.) They say further, that for God to sanctifie a thing, is to set it apart. This being true; then it follows, that the *Seventh-day-Sabbath* was sanctified, that is, set apart for *Adam* in Paradise; and so, that it
35 was ordained a Sabbath of rest to the Saints from the beginning.

But I answer, as I hinted before, that God did sanctifie it to his own rest. *The Lord also hath set apart him that is godly for himself.* But again, 'tis one thing for God to sanctifie this or that thing to an use, and another thing to command that that thing be
40 forthwith in being to us. As for instance: the Land of *Canaan*

was set apart many years for the Children of *Israel* before they possessed that Land. Christ Jesus was long sanctified; that is, set apart to be our Redeemer before he sent him into the world (*Deut.* 32. 8. *Joh.* 10. 36).

If then, by Gods sanctifying of the *Seventh day* for a *Sabbath*,   5 you understand it for a Sabbath for man, (but the Text saith not so) yet it might be so set apart for man, long before it should be, as such, made known unto him. And that the *Seventh-day-Sabbath* was not as yet made known to men, consider.

Secondly, *Moses* himself seems to have the knowledge of it at   10 first, not by *Tradition*, but by *Revelation*; as it is (*Exod.* 16. 23.) *This is that*, saith he, *that the Lord hath said*, (namely to me; for we read not, as yet, that he said it to any body else) *Tomorrow is the Sabbath of the holy rest unto the Lord.*

Also holy *Nehemiah* suggesteth this, when he saith of *Israel* to   15 God, *Thou madest known to them thy holy sabbaths* (*Neh.* 9. 14) The first of these Texts shew us, that tidings of a *Seventh-day-Sabbath* for men, came *first* to Moses from Heaven: and the second, that it was to *Israel* before unknown.

But how could be either the one or the other, if the *Seventh-*   20 *day-Sabbath* was taught men by the Light of Nature, which is the moral Law? or if from the beginning it twas given to men by a positive Precept for to be kept.

This therefore strengthning my doubt about the affirmative of the first Question, and also prepareth an Argument for what I   25 plead as to this, we have now under consideration.

Thirdly, This yet seems to me more scrupulous, because that the punishment due to the breach of the *Seventh-day-Sabbath* was *hid* from men to the *time* of *Moses*; as is clear; for that 'tis said of the breaker of the Sabbath, *They put him in ward, because it was*   30 *not as yet declared what should be done unto him,* Numb. 15. 32, 33, 34, 35, 36.

But methinks, had this *Seventh-day-Sabbath* been imposed upon men from the beginning, the penalty or punishment due to the breach thereof had certainly been known before now.   35

When *Adam* was forbidden to eat of the Tree of the Knowledge of Good and Evil, the Penalty was then, if he disobeyed, annexed to the *Prohibition*. So also it was as to *Circumcision*, the *Passover*, and other Ordinances for Worship. How then can it be thought, that the *Seventh-day-Sabbath* should   40 be imposed upon men from the beginning; and that the Punishment for the breach thereof, should be hid with God for the space of Two thousand years! *Gen.* 2. 16, 17. ch. 17. 13, 14. *Exod.* 12. 43, 44, 45, 46, 47, 48. and the same Chapter, *vers.* 19.

Fourthly, Gods giving of the *Seventh-day-Sabbath* was with respect to *stated* and *stinted* Worship in his Church; the which, until the time of *Moses*, was not set up among his people. Things till then were *adding* or *growing: Now* a Sacrifice, *then* Circumcision, then again *long after that* the Passover, *&c.* But when *Israel* was come into the Wilderness, there to receive as Gods Congregation, a *stated, stinted, limited* way of Worship, then he appoints them a *time*, and *times*, to perform this Worship in; but as I said afore, before that it was not so, as the whole five Books of *Moses* plainly shew: wherefore the *Seventh-day-Sabbath* as such a limited day, cannot be Moral, or of the Law of Nature, nor imposed till then.

And methinks Christ Jesus and his Apostles do plainly enough declare this very thing: For that when they repeat unto the people, or expound before them the moral Law, they quite exclude the *Seventh-day-Sabbath*: Yea, *Paul* makes that Law to us compleat without it.

We will first touch upon what Christ doth in his case.

As in his Sermon upon the Mount, *Matthew* chap. 5. chap. 6. chap. 7. in all that large and hevenly Discourse upon this Law, you have not one syllable about the *Seventh-day-Sabbath*.

So when the Young man came running, and kneeling, and asking what good thing he should do to inherit eternal Life, Christ bids him keep the Commandments; but when the Young man asked *which*, Christ quite leaves out the *seventh day*, and puts him upon the other.

As in *Matth.* 19. 17, 18, 19.

As in *Mark* 10. 18, 19, 20.

As in *Luke* 18. 18, 19, 20.

You will say, he left out the first, and second, and third likewise. To which I say, that was because the Young man by his Question did presuppose that he had been a doer of them: For he profess'd in his Supplication, that he was a lover of that which is naturally good, which is God, in that his Petition was so universal for every thing which he had commanded.

Paul also when he makes mention of the moral Law, quite leaves out of that the very name of the *Seventh-day-Sabbath*, and professeth, that to us Christians the Law of Nature is compleat without it.

As in *Rom.* 3. 7,–19.   5

As in *Rom.* 13. 7, 8, 9, 10.

As in 1 *Tim.* 1. 8, 9, 10, 11.

He that loveth another, saith he, *hath fulfilled the law. For this, Thou shalt not commit adultery, Thou shalt not kill, thou shalt not steal, Thou shalt not covet: and if there be any other commandment, it* 10 *is briefly comprehended under this saying, Thou shalt love they neighbour as thy self. Love worketh no ill to his neighbour, therefore love is the fulfilling of the Law.*

I make not an Argument of this, but take an occasion to mention it as I go: But certainly, had the *Seventh-day-Sabbath* 15 been *moral,* or of the Law of *Nature,* (as some would fain perswade themselves) it would not so slenderly have been passed over in all these repetitions of this Law, but would by Christ or his, Apostles have been pressed upon the people, when so fair an opportunity as at these times offered it self unto them. But they 20 knew what they did, and wherefore they were so silent as to the mention of a *Seventh-day-sabbath* when they so well talked of the Law as *moral.*

Fifthly, *Moses* and the Prophet *Ezekel* both, do fully confirm what has been insinuated by us; to wit, that the Seventh day *as a* 25 *Sabbath* was not imposed upon men until *Israel* was brought into the Wilderness.

1. *Moses* saith to *Israel, Remember that thou wast a servant in the land of* Egypt, *and that the Lord they God brought thee out thence through a mighty hand, and by a stretched-out arm; therefore the Lord* 30 *thy God commandeth thee to keep the sabbath day.*

Yea, he tells us, that the Covenant which God made with them in *Horeb,* that written in stones, *was not made with their forefathers* (to wit, *Abraham,*, *Isaac,* and *Jacob*) *but with them,* Deut. 5. 1. 2, 3, 4, 5, 6, 7, 8, 9, 10, 11, 12, 13, 14, 15.   35

2. *Ezekiel* also is punctual as to this: *I caused them,* saith God by ·that Prophet, *to go forth out of the land of* Egypt, *and brought them into the wilderness. And I gave them my statutes, and shewed them my judgements, which if a man do he shall even live in them. Moreover, I gave them my sabbaths to be a sign between me and them, that they* 40

might know that I am the Lord that sanctifieth them, Ezek. 20. 10,
11, 12, 13. Exopd. 20. 8. ch. 31. 13. ch. 35. 2.

What can be more plain? And these to be sure, are two notable
witnesses of God, who, as you see, do joyntly concur in this; to
5 wit, that it was not from Paradise, nor from the Fathers, but from
the Wilderness, and from *Sinai*, that men received the Seventh-
day-sabbath to keep it holy.

True, it was Gods Sabbath before: for on the first Seventh day
we read, that god rested thereon, and sanctified it. Hence he
10 calls it in the first place *MY Sabbath. I gave them MY Sabbath*: But
it seems 'twas not given to the Church till he had brought them
into the Wilderness.

But, I say, if it had been *moral*, it had been natural to man; and
by the Light of Nature men would have understood it, even both
15 before it was, and otherwise. But of this you see we read nothing,
either by *positive Law*, or *countenanced* Example, or *any* other way,
but rather the flat contrary; to wit, That *Moses* had the knowledge
of it *first* from Heaven, *not* by *Tradition*. That *Israel* had it, *not of*,
or from their *Fathers*, but in the Wilderness, from *him*, to wit
20 *Moses*, after he had brought them out of the Land of *Egypt*. And
that that whole Law in which this *Seventh-day-sabbath* is placed,
was given for the bounding and better ordering of them in their
Church-state for their time, till the Messias should come and put
by a better Ministration of this out of his Church, as we shall
25 further shew anon.

The Seventh-day-sabbath therefore was not from Paradise,
nor from Nature, nor from the Fathers, but from the Wilderness,
and from *Sinai*.

QUEST. III.

30 *Whether when the Seventh-day-Sabbath was given to Israel in the*
Wilderness, the Gentiles, as such, was concerned therein.

BEfore I shew my ground for this Question, I must also first
premise, *That* the Gentiles, as such, were then without the
Church of God, and pale thereof; consequently had nothing to
35 do with the essentials or necessary circumstances of that

24 of] *om.*

Worship which God had set up for himself now among the children of *Israel*.

Now then for the ground of the Question.

First, we read not that God gave it to any but to the Seed of *Jacob*. Hence it is said to *Israel*, and to *Israel* onely, *The Lord hath given* [you] *his Sabbaths*: And again, *I also gave* [them] *my Sabbaths*, Exod. 16. 29. Ezek. 2. 5, 12.

Now, if the gift of the *Seventh-day-sabbath* was onely to *Israel*, as these Texts do more than seem to say; then to the Gentiles, as such; it was not given. Unless any shall conclude, that God by thus doing preferred the Jew to a state of Gentilism; or that he bestowed on them by *thus* doing, some high Gentile Priviledge. But this would be very fictious: For, to lay aside reason, the Text always, as to preference, did set the Jew in the *first* of places, (*Rom.* 2. 10.) nor was his giving the *Seventh-day-sabbath* to them but a signe and token thereof.

But the great Objection is, Because the *Seventh-day-sabbath* is found amongst the rest of those Precepts which is so commonly called the Moral Law; for thence it is concluded *to be a perpetual duration*.

But I Answer, That neither that as given on *Sinai* is moral; I mean, as to the *manner* and *ends* of its Ministration; of which, God permitting, we shall say more in our Answer to the fourth Question, whither I direct you for satisfaction. But,

Secondly, The Gentiles could not be concerned, as such, with Gods giving of a *Seventh-day-sabbath* to *Israel*, because, as I have shewed before, it was given to *Israel considered as a Church of God*, (Acts 7. 31.)

Nor was it given to them, as such, but with Rites and Ceremonies thereto belonging, so *Levit.* 24. 5, 6, 7, 8, 9. *Numb.* 28. 9, 10. *Neh.* 13. 22. *Ezek.* 46. 4.

Now, I say, if this Sabbath hath Ceremonies thereto belonging, and if these Ceremonies were essential to the right keeping of the *Sabbath*: And again, if these Ceremonies were given to *Israel* onely, excluding all but such as were their Proselytes, then *this* Sabbath was given to them as excluding the Gentiles as such. But if it had been Moral, the Gentiles could as soon have been deprived of their Nature as of a *Seventh-day-sabbath*, though the Jews should have appropriated it unto themselves onely.

Again, to say that God gave this *Seventh-day-sabbath* to the

Gentiles, as such, (and yet so he must, if it be of the moral Law)
is as much as to say, that God hath ordained that *that* Sabbath
should be kept by the Gentiles *without*; but by the Jews, *not*
without her Ceremonies. And what Conclusion will follow from
5 hence, but that God did at *one* and the *same* time set up two sorts
of acceptable Worships in the world: one among the *Jews*,
another among the *Gentiles*? But how ridiculous such a thought
would be, and how repugnant to the wisdom of God, you may
easily perceive.

10 Yea, what a diminution would this be to Gods Church *that
then was*, for one to say, the Gentiles were to serve God with
more liberty than the Jew! For the Law was *a Yoak*, and yet the
Gentile is called the *Dog*, and said to be without God in the world,
Deut. 7. 7. *Psal.* 147. 19, 20. *Matth.* 15. 26. *Eph.* 2. 11, 12.

15 Thirdly, When the *Gentiles* at the Jews return from *Babylon*,
came and offered their Wares to sell to the Children of *Israel* at
Jerusalem on *this* Sabbath; yea, and sold them to them too: yet *not
they*, but the Jews, were rebuked as the onely breakers of *that*
Sabbath. Nay, there dwelt then at *Jerusalem* men of *Tyre*, that on
20 *this* Sabbath sold their Commodities to the Jews, and men of
Judah: yet *not they*, but the men of *Judah*, were contended with,
as the breakers of *this* Sabbath.

True, good *Nehemiah* did threaten the Gentiles that were
Merchants, for lying then about the Walls of the City, for that by
25 that means they were a temptation to the Jews to break *their*
Sabbath; but still he charged the breach thereof *onely* upon his
own people, *Neh.* 13. 15, 16, 17, 18, 19, 20.

But can it be imagined, had the Gentiles now been concerned
with *this Sabbath* by Law divine, that so holy a man as *Nehemiah*
30 would have let them escape without a rebuke for so notorious a
transgression thereof; especially considering, that now also they
were upon Gods ground, to wit, *within* and *without* the Walls of
Jerusalem?

Fourthly, Wherefore he saith to *Israel* again, *Verily my Sabbaths*
35 [ye] *shall keep*. And again, [ye] *shall keep my Sabbaths*. And
again, *The children of* Israel *shall keep my Sabbaths to observe my
Sabbaths throughout* [their] *generations*, Exod. 16. 29. ch. 31.
14, 15, 16.

What can be more plain, these things thus standing in the
40 Testament of God, than that the *Seventh-day-sabbath*, as such,

was given to *Israel*, to *Israel* onely; and that the Gentiles, as such, were not concerned therein!

Fifthly, The very reason also of Gods giving of the *Seventh-day-sabbath* to the Jews, doth exclude the Gentiles, as such, from having any concern therein. For it was given to the Jews, as was 5 said before, as they were considered Gods Church, and for a sign and token by which they should know that he had chosen and sanctified them to himself for a peculiar people, *Exod.* 31. 13, 14, 15, 16, 17. *Ezek.* 20. 12, 13. And a great token and sign it was that he had so chosen them: For in that he had given to them 10 this *Sabbath*, he had given to them (his own Rest) a Figure and Pledge of his sending his Son into the world to redeem them from the Bondage and Slavery of the Devil: of whom indeed this Sabbath was a shadow or type, *Coloss.* 2. 16, 17.

Thus have I concluded my ground for this third Question: I 15 shall therefore now propound another.

QUEST. IV.

Whether the Seventh-day-Sabbath did not fall, as such, with the rest of the Jewish Rites *and Ceremonies? Or whether that day, as a Sabbath, was afterwards by the Apostles imposed upon the Churches* 20 *of the Gentiles?*

I Would now also, before I shew the grounds of my proposing this Question, premise what is necessary thereunto; to wit, That *Time* and *Day* were both fixed upon by Law, for the solemn performance of Divine Worship among the Jews; And that *Time* 25 and *Day* is also by Law fixed, for the solemnizing of Divine Worship to God in the Churches of the Gentiles: But that the *Seventh-day-sabbath*, as such, is *that* Time, *that* Day, that still I question.

Now before I shew the grounds of my questioning of it, I shall 30 enquire in to the *nature* of *that* ministration in the bowels of which this *Seventh-day-sabbath* is placed. And

First, I say, as to that, the *nature* of that Law is *moral*, but the ministration, and Circumstances thereunto belonging, are *shadowish* and *figurative*. 35

By the *nature* of it, I mean the matter thereof: By the

Ministration and Circumstances thereto belonging, I do mean the giving of it by such hands, at such a Place and time, in such a Mode, as when 'twas given to *Israel* in the Wilderness.

5 The matter therefore, to wit, *Thou shalt love the Lord thy God with all thy heart, and with all thy soul, and with all thy mind, and with all thy strength, and thy neighbour as thy self,* is everlasting, (*Mark* 12. 29, 30, 31.) and is not from *Sinai,* nor from the *two Tables of stone,* but in Nature; for this Law commenced and took being and place that day in which man was created: Yea, it was

10 concreate with him, and without it he cannot be a rational creature, as he was in the day in which God created him. But for the ministration of it from *Sinai,* with the Circumstances belonging to that ministration, they are not Moral, not Everlasting, but Shadowish and Figurative onely.

15 That Ministration cannot be Moral for three Reasons.

1. It commenced not when Morality commenced, but two thousand years after.

2. It was not universal as the Law, as moral is, 'twas given onely to the Church of the Jews in those Tables.

20 3. Its end is past as such a *ministration,* though the same Law as to the morality thereof abides. Where are the Tables of Stone and this Law as therein contained? We onely, as to that, have the notice of such a *ministration,* and a rehearsal of the Law, with that mode of giving of it, in the testament of God.

25 But to come to Particulars.

1. The very Preface to *that* Ministration carrieth in it a type of our deliverance from the Bondage of Sin, the Devil, and Hell. *Pharoah,* and *Egypt,* and *Israels* bondage there, being a type of these.

2. The very Stones in which this Law was engraven, was a

30 figure of the Tables of the Heart. The first two were a figure of the Heart carnal, by which the Law was broken: The last two, of the Heart spiritual, in which the new Law, the Law of Grace is written and preserv'd, *Exod.* 34. 1. 2 *Cor.* 3. 3.

3. The very Mount on which *this* Ministration was given, was

35 typical of Mount *Zion:* See *Heb.* 12. where they are compared, *vers.* 18, 19, 20, 21, 22.

4. Yea, the very Church to whom *that* Ministration was given, was a figure of the Church of the Gospel that is on Mount *Zion:* See the same Scripture, and compare it with *Acts* 7. 38. *Revel.* 14.

40 1, 2, 3, 4, 5.

5. That Ministration was given in the hand and by the disposition of Angels, to prefigure how the new Law or Ministration of the Spirit was to be given afterwards to the Churches under the New Testament by the hands of the Angel of Gods everlasting Covenant of Grace, who is his onely begotten Son, *Isai.* 63. 9. *Matth.* 3. 1. *Acts* 3. 22, 23.

6. It was given to *Israel* also in the hand of *Moses*, as Mediator, to shew or typifie out, that the Law of Grace was in after-times to come to the Church of Christ by the hand and mediation of Jesus our Lord, *Gal.* 3. 19. *Deut.* 5. 5. *Heb.* 8. 6. 1 *Tim.* 2. 5. *Heb.* 9. 15. ch. 12. 24.

7. As to *this* Ministration, it was to continue *but till the Seed should come*; and then must, as such, give place to a better Ministration, *Gal.* 3. 19. *A better Covenant, established upon better promises*, Heb. 8. 6.

From all this therefore I conclude, that there is a difference to be put between the morality of the Law, and the ministration of it upon *Sinai*. The Law, as to its morality, was before; but as to *this* ministration, 'twas not till the Church was with *Moses*, and *he* with the *Angels* on Mount *Sinai* in the Wilderness.

Now in the Law as moral, we conclude a time propounded, but no *Seventh-day-sabbath* enjoyed: But in that Law, as thus ministred, which Ministration is already out of doors, we find a *seventh day*; that *seventh day* on which God rested, on which God rested from all his works, enjoyed. What is it then? why the whole Ministration as written and engraven in stones being removed, the *Seventh-day-sabbath* must also be removed; for that *the time*, nor *yet the day*, was as to your holy Sabbath, or rest, moral; but imposed with that whole Ministration, as such, upon the Church, until the time of Reformation: Which time being come, this Ministration, as I said, as such, ceaseth; and the whole Law, as to the morality of it, is delivered into the hand of Christ, who imposes it now also; but not as a Law of Works, nor as that Ministration written and engraven in Stones, but as a Rule of life to those that have believed in him, 1 *Cor.* 9. 21.

So then, that Law is still moral, and still supposes, since it teaches that there is a God, that *time* must be set apart for his Church to worship him in, according to that will of his that he hath revealed in his Word. But though by that Law *time* is required; yet by that, as moral, the time never was prefixed. The

time then of old was appointed by such a ministration of that
Law as we have been now discoursing of; and when that
Ministration ceased, that time did also vanish with it. And now
by our new Law-giver, the Son of God, he being *Lord also of the*
5 *Sabbath-day*, we have a time prefixed, as the Law of Nature
requireth, a *new* day, by him who is the Lord of it; I say,
appointed, wherein we may worship, not in the oldness of that
Letter written and engraven in Stones, but according to, and
most agreeing with, his new and holy Testament. And this I
10 confirm further by those reasons that now shall follow.

First, because we find not from the resurrection of Christ to
the end of the Bible, any thing written by which is imposed that
Seventh-day-sabbath upon the Churches. *Time*, as I said, the
Law as moral requires; but *that* time we find no longer imposed:
15 And in all duties pertaining to God and his true Worship in his
Churches, we must be guided by his Laws and Testaments: By
his old Laws, when his old Worship was in force; and by his new
Laws, when his new Worship is in force. And he hath verily now
said, *Behold, I make all things new.*

20 Secondly, I find, as I have shewed, that this *Seventh-day-
sabbath* is confined, not to the Law of Nature as such, but that
ministration of it which was given on *Sinai*: which Ministration
as it is come to an end as such, so it is rejected by *Paul* as a
Ministration no ways capable of abiding in the Church now,
25 since the ministration of the Spirit also hath taken its place, (2
Cor. 3.) Wherefore instead of propounding it to the Churches
with Arguments tending to its reception, he seeks by degrading it
of its old lustre and glory, to wean the Churches from any
likement thereof;

30 1. By calling of it the ministration of *Death*, of the *Letter*, and
of *Condemnation*, a term most frightful, but no ways alluring to
the godly.

2. By calling it a Ministration that *now* has *NO* glory, by
reason of the exceeding glory of that Ministration under which
35 by the holy Spirit the New Testament-Churches are: And these
are weaning Considerations, 2 *Cor.* 3.

3. By telling of them it is a Ministration that tendeth to *blind*
the Mind, and to *veil* the Heart as to the knowledge of their Christ:
So that they cannot, while under that, behold his beauteous face,
40 but as their heart shall turn from it to him, 2 *Cor.* 3.

4. And that they might not be left in the dark, but perfectly know what Ministration it is that he means, he saith expresly, it is *that written and engraven in stones.* See again 2 *Cor.* 3. And in that Ministration it is that this *Seventh-day-sabbath* is found.   5

But shall we think that the Apostle speaks any thing of all here said, to wean Saints off from the Law of Nature as such! No verily, that he retains in the Church, as bening managed *there* by Christ: But *THIS Ministration* is dangerous *now*, because it cannot be maintained in the Church, but in a way of contempt to   10 the Ministration of the Spirit, and is derogatory to the glory of that.

Now these, as I said, are weaning Considerations. No man, I do think, that knows himself, or the glory of a Gospel-ministration, can, if he understands what *Paul* says here, desire   15 that *such* a Ministration should be retained in the Churches.

Fourthly, This *Seventh-day-sabbath* has lost its ceremonies (those unto which before you are cited by the Texts) which was with it imposed upon the old Church for her due performance of Worship to God thereon: How then can *this* Sabbath *now* be   20 kept? Kept, I say, according to Law. For if the Church on which it was at first imposed, was not to keep it, yea, could not keep it leagally without the practising of those Ceremonies: And if those Ceremonies are long ago dead and gone, how will those that pretend to a belief of a continuation of the Sanction thereof,   25 keep it, I say, according as it is written?

If they say, they retain the day, but change their manner of observation thereof; I ask, *Who has commanded them so to do?* This is one of the Laws of *this* Sabbath: *Thou shalt take fine flour, and bake twelve cakes thereof: two tenth deals shall be in one cake. And*   30 *thou shalt set them in two rows, six on a row, upon the pure Table before the Lord. And thou shalt put pure frankincense upon each row, that it may be on the bread for a memorial, even an offering made by fire unto the Lord. Every sabbath he shall set it in order before the Lord continually, being taken from the children of* Israel *by an everlasting*   35 *covenant,* Levit. 24. 5, 6, 7, 8, 9. You may see also other places, as *Numb.* 28. 9, 10. *Neh.* 13. 22. and *Ezek.* 46. 4.

Now if these be the Laws of the *Sabbath*, this *Seventh-day-*

6 Apostle] Apostles

sabbath; And if God did never command that *this* Sabbath should by his Church be sanctified without them: And, as we said before, if these Ceremonies have been long since dead and buried, how must *this* Sabbath be kept?

5   Let men take heed, lest while they plead for Law, and pretend themselves to be the onely doers of Gods will, they be not found the biggest transgressors thereof. And why can they not as well keep the other Sabbaths, as the Sabbaths of Months, of Years, and the Jubilee? For *this*, as I have shewed, is no moral Precept,

10 'tis onely a branch of the ministration of Death and Condemnation.

Fifthly, The *Seventh-day-sabbath*, as such, was a sign and shadow of things to come; and a sign cannot be the thing signified and substance too: Wherefore when the thing signified, or substance, is come, the signe or thing shadowing ceaseth.

15 And, I say, the *Seventh-day-sabbath* being so, as a *Seventh-day-sabbath* it ceaseth also. See again, *Exod.* 31. 13, 14. *Ezek.* 20. 12, 21. *Coloss.* 2. 14.

Nor do I find that our Protestant Writers, notwithstanding their reverence of the Sabbath, do conclude otherwise; but that

20 though *time*, as to worshipping God, must needs be contained in the bowels of the moral Law, as moral; yet they for good reasons forbear to affix the *seventh day* as *that* time there too. They do it, I say, for good reasons, reasons drawn from the Scripture; or rather, for that the Scripture draws them so to conclude: yet they

25 cast not away the morality of a Sabbath of rest to the Church. It is to be granted then, that time for Gods Worship abideth for ever, but the *seventh day* vanishes as a shadow and sign; because such indeed it was, as the Scripture above cited declares as to the Sanction thereof as a *Sabbath*.

30 The *Law* of Nature then calls for Time; but the *God* of Nature assigns it, and has given power to his Son to continue SUCH time as himself shall by his eternal Wisdom judge most meet for the Churches of the Gentiles to solemnize Worship to God by him in. Hence he is said to be *Lord even of the sabbath day*,

35 *Matth.* 12. 9.

Sixthly, I find by reading Gods Word, that *Paul* by Authority Apostolical, takes away the Sanctions of all the Jews Festivals and *Sabbaths*.

This is manifest, for that he leaves the observation or non-

40 observation of them, as things *indifferent* to the *Mind* and

Discretion of the Believers. *One man esteemeth one day above another: another esteemeth every day alike. Let every man be fully perswaded in his own mind.* Rom. 14. 5.

By this last clause of the Verse, [*Let every man be fully perswaded in his own mind*] he doth plainly declare, that *such* days are now 5 stript of their Sanction: For none of Gods Laws, while they retain their Sanction, are left to the *will* and *mind* of the believers, as to whether they will observe them or no. Men, I say, are not left to their liberty in such a case; for when a stamp of Divine Authority is upon a Law, and abides, so long we are 10 bound, *not* to our *mind*, *but* to that *Law*: But when a thing, once sacred, has lost its sanction, then it falls, as to Faith and Conscience, among other *common* or indifferent things. And so the *Seventh-day-sabbath* did. Again,

Seventhly, Thus *Paul* writes to the Church of *Coloss. Let no* 15 *man judge you in meat, or in drink, or in respect of any holy day, or of the new Moon, or of the Sabbath: which are a shadow of things to come, but the body is Christ,* Coloss. 2. 16, 17. Here also, as he serveth other Holy-days, he serveth the *Sabbath*: He gives a liberty to believers to refuse the observation of it, and commands 20 that no man should judge against them for their so doing. And as you read, the reason of his so doing is, because the *body*, the substance is come: Christ, saith he, is the Body, or that which these things were a shadow or figure of. *The Body is Christ.*

Nor hath the Apostle, since he saith [or of the Sabbath] one 25 would think, left any hole, out at which mens inventions could get: but man has sought out many; and, so, many he will use.

But again, That the Apostle by this word *Sabbath* intends the *Seventh-day-sabbath*, is clear; for that it is by *Moses* himself counted for a *sign*, as we have shewed: and for that none of the 30 other Sabbaths were a more clear shadow of the Lord Jesus Christ than this. For that, and that alone, is called *the Rest of God*: in it God rested from all his works. Hence he calls it by way of eminency *MY Sabbath*, and *MY Holy-day*, Isai. 58. 13.

Yet could that Rest be nothing else but typical; for God, never 35 since the world began, really rested, but in his Son; *This is he,* saith God, *in whom I am well pleased.* This Sabbath then, was Gods Rest typically, and was given to *Israel* as a sign of his Grace towards them in Christ: Wherefore when Christ was risen, it ceased, and was no longer of obligation to bind the Conscience 40

to the observation thereof. [Or of the Sabbath] He distinctly
singleth out *THIS Seventh day*, as that which was a most noble
shadow, a most exact shadow. And then puts that with the other
together; saying, they are a shadow of things to come; and that
5   Christ has answered them all. *The body is Christ.*

Eighthly, No man will, I think, deny, but that *Heb.* 4. 4. intends
the *Seventh-day-sabbath*, on which *God rested from all his works*;
for the Text doth plainly say so: Yet may the observing Reader
easily perceive, that both it, and the Rest of *Canaan* also, made
10   mention of *vers.* 5. were typical, as to a day made mention of *Vers.*
7, and 8. which day he calls *another.* He would not *afterwards*
have made mention of *another* day. If *Joshuah* had given them
rest, he would not. Now if they had not that Rest in *Joshua*'s
days, be sure they had it not by *Moses*; for he was still before.

15   All the Rests therefore that *Moses* gave them, and that *Joshua*
gave them too, were but typical of *another* day, in which God
would give them rest, *vers.* 9, 10. And whether the day *to come*,
was Christ, or Heaven, it makes no matter: 'Tis enough that they
before did fail, as always Shadows do, and that therefore
20   mention by *David* is, and that *afterward*, made of another day.
There remains therefore a rest to the people of God. A Rest to come,
of which the *Seventh day* in which God rested, and the Land of
Canaan, was a type; which Rest begins in Christ *now*, and shall
be consummated *in glory*.

25   And in that he saith, *There remains a Rest*, referring to that of
David, What is it, if it signifies not, that the other Rests remain
not? There *remains* therefore a Rest; a Rest prefigured by the *Seventh
day*, and by the *Rest* of *Canaan*, though they are fled and gone.

There remains a Rest; a Rest which stands not now in signs or
30 ·   shadows, in the *Seventh day*, or *Canaan*; but in the Son of God,
and his Kingdom, to whom, and to which the weary are invited to
come for rest. *Isai.* 28. 12. *Matth.* 11. 28. *Heb.* 4. 11.

Yet this casts not out the Christians Holy-day or Sabbath: For
that was not ordained to be a Type or Shadow of things to come,
35   but to sanctifie the Name of their God in, and to perform that
worship to him which was also in a shadow signified by the
ceremonies of the Law, as the Epistle to the *Hebrews* doth
plentifully declare.

And I say again, the *Seventh-day-sabbath* cannot be it, for the
40   reasons shewed afore.

Ninthly, Especially if you adde to all this, that nothing of the ministration of Death written and engraven in stones, is brought by Jesus, or by his Apostles into the Kingdom of Christ, as a part of his instituted Worship. Hence it is said of *that* Ministration in the bowels of which *this Seventh-day-sabbath* is found, that it has now *NO* glory; that its glory is done away, in or by Christ, and so is laid aside, the ministration of the Spirit that excels in glory, being come in the room thereof.

I will read the Text to you.

But if the ministration of death, written and engraven in stones, was glorious, so that the children of Israel *could not stedfastly behold the face of* Moses, *for the glory of his countenance, which glory was to be done away.* (It was given at first with this Proviso, that it should not always retain its glory, that Sanction, as a Ministration). *How shall not the ministration of the Spirit be rather glorious? For if the ministration of condemnation be glory, much more doth the ministration of righteousness exceed in glory. For even that which was made glorious, had no glory in this respect, by reason of the glory that excelleth. For if that which is done away was glorious, much more that which remaineth is glorious.* 2 Cor. 3.

What can be more plain? The Text says expresly, that this ministration doth *NOT* remain; yea, and insinuates, that in its first institution it was ordained with this Proviso, *It was to be done away.* Now if in its first institution upon *Sinai* it was thus ordained; and if by the coming in of the ministration of the Spirit, this Ordination is now executed; that is, if by it, and the Apostle saith it, it is done away by a ministration that remains: then where is that *Seventh-day-sabbath*?

Thus before I have discoursed upon this fourth Question: And having shewed by this Discourse, that the old *Seventh-day-sabbath* is abolished and done away, and that it has nothing to do with the Churches of the Gentiles; I am next to shew what day it is that must abide, that must abide as holy to the Christians, and for them to perform their New Testament-church-service in. Take the Question thus.

QUEST. V.

Since it is denied that the Seventh-day-Sabbath is moral, and is found it is not to abide as a Sabbath for ever in the Church, What time is to be fixed on for New Testament Saints to perform together, Divine Worship to God by Christ in?

UPon this Question hangs the stress of all, as to the Subject now under consideration: But before I can speak distinctly to it, I must premise, as I have in order to my speaking to the Questions before, something for the better clearing of our way.

1. Then, we are not now speaking of *all* manner of worshipping God, nor of *all* times in which *all* manner of worship is to be performed; but of that Worship, which is *Church-worship*, or Worship that is to be performed by the Assembly of Saints, when by the will of God they in all parts of his Dominion assemble together to worship him; which Worship hath a prefixed time alotted to, or for its performance, and without which it cannot, according to the mind of God, be done. This is the time, I say, that we are to discourse of, and not of *ALL* time appointed for all manner of Worship.

I do not question but that Worship by the godly is performed to God every day of the week; yea, and every night too, and that time is appointed or allowed of God for the performance of such Worship. But *this* time is not fixed to the same *moment* or *hour* universally, but is left to the discretion of the Believers, as their frame of Spirit, or Occasions, or Exigencies, or Temptations, or Duty shall require.

We meddle then *onely* with that *time* that the Worship aforesaid is to be performed in; which *time* the Law of Nature as such *supposes*, but the God of Nature *chuses*. And *this* time as to the Churches of the Gentiles, we have proved is not *that* time which was assigned to the Jews, to wit, *THAT Seventh day* which was imposed upon them by the ministration of death; for, as we have shewed already, that Ministration indeed is done away by a better and more glorious Ministration, the Ministration of the Spirit; which Ministration surely would be much more inferiour than that which has now no glory, was it defective as to this. That is, if it imposed a Gospel-service, but appointed not time to perform that Worship in: or if not withstanding all its commendation, it should be forced to borrow of a Ministration inferiour to it self; *that*, to wit, the time without which by no means its most solemn worship can be performed.

This then is the Conclusion, that *TIME* to worship God in is   5
required by the Law of Nature; but that the Law of Nature doth, as such, fix it on the *Seventh day* from the Creation of the World, that I utterly deny, by what I have said already, and have yet to say on that behalf: Yea, I hope to make it manifest, as I have, that *this* Seventh day is removed; that God, by the ministration of the   10
Spirit, has changed the time to another day, to wit, *The first day of the week*. Therefore we conclude the time is fixed for the worship of the New Testament-Christians, or Churches of the Gentiles, unto *that* day.

Now in my discourse upon this Subject I shall,   15
1. Touch upon those Texts that are *more close*, yet have a divine intimation of this thing in them.
2. And then I shall come to Texts *more express*.

First, for those Texts that are *more close*, yet have a divine intimation of this thing in them.   20

First, The comparison that the Holy Ghost makes between the Rest of God from *his* Works, and the Rest of Christ from *his*, doth intimate such a thing: *He that hath entred into his rest, he also hath ceased from his own works as God did from his,* Heb. 4. 10.   25

Now God rested from his Works, and sanctified a day of rest to himself, as a signal of that Rest; which day he also gave to his Church as a day of holy rest likewise. And if Christ *thus* rested from his own Works, (and the Holy Ghost says he did *thus* rest) he also hath sanctified a day to himself, as that in which he hath   30
finished his Work, and given it also to his Church to be an everlasting Memento of his so doing, and that they should keep it holy for his sake.

And see! as the Fathers work was first, so his day went before; and as the Sons work came after, so his day accordingly   35
succeeded. The Fathers day was on the *Seventh day* from the Creation, the Sons the *First day* following.

Nor may this be slighted, because the Text says, as God finished his Work, so Christ finished his; *He also hath ceased from his own works as God did from his.* He rested, I say, as God did;   40

but God rested on his *resting* day, and therefore so did Christ.
Not that he rested on the *Fathers* resting day; for 'tis evident, that
then he had great part of his work to do; for he had not as then
got his conquest over Death, but the next day he also entred into
his Rest, having by his rising again, finished his Work, *viz.* made
a Conquest over the Powers of darkness, and brought Life and
Immortality to light through his so doing.

So then, that being the day of the Rest of the Son of God, it
must needs be the day of the Rest of his Churches also. For God
gave his resting day to his Church to be a Sabbath; *and Christ
rested from his own works as God did from his*, therefore he also
gave the day in which he rested from his Works, a Sabbath to the
Churches, as did the Father. Not that there are *TWO* Sabbaths
at once: The Fathers was imposed for a time, even until the
Son's should come; yea, as I have shewed you, even in the very
time of its imposing it was also ordained *to be done away*. Hence
he saith, that Ministration was to be done away, 2 *Cor.* 3.
Therefore we plead not for two Sabbaths to be at one time, but
that a succession of time was ordained to the New Testament-
Saints, or Churches of the Gentiles, to worship God in; which
time is that in which the Son rested from his own Works as God
did from his.

Secondly, Hence he calls himself, *The Lord even of the
Sabbath-day*, as *Luke* 5. *Matth.* 12. shews. Now to be a *LORD*, is
to have Dominion, Dominion *over* a thing, and so power to alter
or change it according to that power; and where is he that dares
say Christ has not this *absolutely*?

We will therefore conclude, that it is granted on all hands he
hath. The Question then is, Whether he hath *exercised* that
power to the demolishing or removing of the Jews *Seventh day*,
and establishing another in its room? The which I think is easily
answered, in that he did not rest from his own Works *therein*; but
chose, for his own Rest, to himself *another* day.

Surely, had the Lord Jesus intended to have established the
Seventh day to the Churches of the Gentiles, he would himself in
the first place have rested from his own Works therein; but since
he passed by *that* day, and took *no* notice of it, as to the finishing
of his own Works, as God took notice of it when he had finished
his; it remains that he fixed upon another day, even the First of
the Week; on which, by his rising again, and shewing himself to

his Disciples before his Passion, he made it manifest that he had chosen, *as Lord of the Sabbath*, that day for his own Rest. Consequently, and for the Rest of his Churches, and for his Worship to be solemnized in.

Thirdly, And on *THIS* day some of the Saints that *slept arose*, and began their eternal *Sabbath*, *Matth.* 27. 52, 53. See how the Lord Jesus had glorified *this* day! Never was such a stamp of divine Honour put upon any other day, no not since the world began. *And the graves were opened, and many bodies of Saints which slept arose and came out of their graves after his resurrection*, &c. That is, they rose as soon as he was risen: But why was not all this done on the *Seventh day*? No, that day was set apart that Saints might adore God for the works of Creation, and that Saints thorough that might look for Redemption by Christ: But now a work more glorious than that is to be done, and therefore another day is assigned for the doing of it in. A work, I say, of Redemption compleated, a day therefore by it self must be assigned for this; and some of the Saints to begin their eternal Sabbath with God in Heaven, therefore a day by it self must be appointed for this. Yea, and that this day might not want *that* glory that might attract the most dim-sighted Christian to a desire after the sanction of it, the Resurrection of Christ, and also of those Saints met together on it: *Yea, they both did begin their eternal rest thereon.*

Fourthly, The Psalmist speaks of a day that the Lord *Jehovah*, the Son of God, has made; and saith, *We will rejoyce and be glad in it.* But what day is this? Why the day in which Christ was *made the head of the corner*, which must be applied to the day in which he was raised from the dead, which is the first of the Week.

Hence Peter saith to the Jews, when he treateth of Christ before them, and particularly of his Resurrection, *This is the stone which* [was] *set at nought of you builders*, which [is] *become the head of the corner.* He *was* set at nought by them, the whole course of his Ministry unto his death, and *was* made the head of the Corner by God *that* day he rose from the dead. This day therefore is the day that the Lord *Jehovah* has made a day of rejoycing to the Church of Christ, and we will rejoyce and be glad in it.

For can it be imagined, that the Spirit by the Prophet should *thus* signalize *this* day *for nothing*, saying, *This is the day which the*

Lord hath made, to no purpose? Yes, you may say, for the resurrection of his Son.

But I adde, that that is not all, 'tis a day that the Lord has both made for *that*, and that *we might rejoyce and be glad in it*. Rejoyce,
5 that is, before the Lord while solemn divine Worship is performed on it, by all the people that shall partake of the Redemption accomplished then.

Fifthly, *God the Father* again leaves such another stamp of divine note and honour upon this day as he never before did
10 leave upon any; where he saith to our Lord, *Thou art my Son, this day have I begotten thee*, Acts 13. 33. still, I say, having *respect to the first day of the week*; for that, and no other, is the day here intended by the Apostle. *This* day, saith God, is the day: *And as concerning that he raised him up from the dead, now no more to return*
15 *to corruption, he saith on this wise, I will give thee the sure mercies of* David: wherefore he saith in another Psalm, *Thou shalt not suffer thine holy one to see corruption*. Wherefore the day in which God did this work, is greater than that in which he finished the work of Creation; for his making of the Creation saved it not from
20 corruption, but now he hath done a work which corruption cannot touch, wherefore the day on which he did this, has this note from his own mouth. *This day*, as a day that doth transcend.

And, as I said, *this* day is the *First of the Week*; for 'twas in that day that God begat his beloved Son from the dead. This first day
25 of the week therefore on it God found that pleasure which he found not in the *Seventh day* from the World Creation, for that in it his Son did live again to him.

Now shall not Christians, when they do read that God saith, *This day*, and that too with reference to a work done on it by him,
30 so full of delight to him, and so full of life and Heaven to them, set also a remark upon it, saying, *This was the day of Gods pleasure*, for that his Son did rise thereon; *and shall it not be the day of my delight in him*! This is the day in which his Son was both begotten, and born, and became the first-Fruits to God of them
35 that sleep; yea, and in which also he was made by him the chief, and *head of the corner*; and shall not we rejoyce in it? *Acts* 13. 33. *Heb.* 1. 5. *Coloss.* 1. 18. *Revel.* 1. 5.

Shall Kings, and Princes, and Great men set a remark upon the day of their Birth and Coronation, and expect that both
40 Subjects and Servants should do them high honour on that day!

and shall the day in which Christ was both begotten and born, be a day contemned by Christians! and his Name not be, but of a common regard on *that* day?

I say again, Shall God, as with his finger, point, and that in the face of the world, at *this* day, saying, *thou art my Son, this day,* &c. and shall not Christians fear, and awake from their employments, to worship the Lord on this day!

If God remembers it, well may I! If God says, and that with all gladness of heart, *Thou art my Son, this day have I begotten thee!* may not! ought not I also to set *this* day apart to sing the songs of my Redemption in?

This day my Redemption was finished.

This day my dear Jesus revived.

This day he was declared to be the Son of God with power.

Yea, this is the day in which the Lord Jesus finished a greater work than ever yet was done in the world: yea, a work in which the Father himself was more delighted than he was in making of Heaven & Earth: And shall Darkness and the shadow of Death stain *this day*! Or shall a Cloud dwell on *this day*! Shall God regard *this day* from above! and shall not his Light shine upon *this day*! What shall be done to them that curse this day, and would not that the Stars should give their light thereon? *This day*! after this day was come, God never, that we read of, made mention with delight, of the old *Seventh-day-sabbath* more.

Sixthly, Nor is that altogether to be slighted, when he saith, *When he bringeth his first-begotten into the world, Let all the Angels of God worship him,* to wit, at that very time and day, Heb. 1. 6.

I know not what our Expositors say of this Text, but to me it seems to be meant of his Resurrection from the dead, both because the Apostle is speaking of that, *vers.* 5. and closes that Argument with this Text, *Thou art my Son, this day have I begotten thee.* And again, *I will be his Father, and he shall be my Son. And again, when he bringeth his first-begotten into the world, he saith, And let all the Angels of God worship him.*

So then, for Gods bringing of his first-begotten *now* into the world, was by his raising him again from the dead after they by *crucifying* of him had turned him out of the same.

Thus then God brought him into the world, never by them to be hurried out of it again: For *Christ being now raised from the dead, dies no more; death hath no more dominion over him.*

Now, saith the Text, *when* he bringeth him thus into the world, he requireth that worship be done unto *HIM*: When? that very day, and that by all the Angels of God. And if by *ALL*, then Ministers are not excluded; and if not Ministers, then not

5 Churches; for what is said to the Angel, is said to the Church it self, *Rev.* 2. 1, 7. ch. 2. 8, 11. ch. 2. 12, 17. ch. 2. 18, 29. ch. 3. 1, 6. ch. 3. 7, 13. ch. 3. 14, and 22.

So then, if the Question be asked, when they must worship him: the Answer is, *When* he brought him into the world, *which*

10 *was on the first day of the week*; for *then* he *bringeth him again from the dead*, and gave the whole World and the Government thereof into his holy hand. This Text therefore is of weight as to what we have now under consideration, to wit, that the *First day* of the Week, the day in which God brought his First-begotten

15 into the world, should be the day of worshipping him by all the Angels of God.

Seventhly, Hence this day is called the *Lords day*, as *John* saith, *I was in the spirit on the Lords day*: the day in which he rose from the dead, *Rev.* 1. 10.

20 The *Lords day*: Every day, say some, is the *Lords day*. Indeed this for discourse-sake may be granted; but strictly, no day can so properly be called *the Lords day*, as this *First day of the week*; for that no day of the Week or of the Year has *those* badges of the Lords glory upon it, nor *such* divine Grace put upon it as has the

25 *First day* of the Week. This we have already made appear in part, and shall make appear much more before we have done therewith.

There is nothing, as I know of, that bears this title but the *Lords Supper*, and *this day*, 1 Cor. 11, 20. Rev. 1. 10. And since

30 Christians count it an abuse to allegorize the first, let them also be ashamed to fantasticalize the last; The *Lords day* is doubtless the day in which he rose from the dead. To be sure it is not the old *Seventh day*; for from the day that he *arose*, to the end of the *Bible*, we find not that he did hang so much as one twist of glory

35 upon that; but *this* day is beautiful with glory upon glory, and that both by the Father and the Son; by the Prophets and those that were raised from the dead thereon; therefore *THIS* day must be more than the rest.

22 be] by

But we are as yet but upon divine Intimations, drawn from such Texts which, if candidly considered, do very much smile upon this great truth; namely, that the *First day of the week* is to be accounted the Christian Sabbath, or Holy day for Divine Worship in the Churches of the Saints. And now I come to the Texts that are more express.

Secondly then,

First, *This was the day* in the which he did *use* to shew himself to his people, and to congregate with them after he rose from the dead. On the first first day, even on the day on which he rose from the dead, he visited his people, both when together and apart, over, and over, and over, as both *Luke* and *John* do testifie, (*Luk*. 24. *Joh*. 2.) *And preached such sermons of his resurrection, and gave unto them*; yea, and gave them such demonstration of the truth of all, as was never given them from the foundation of the world. Shewing, he shewed them his risen body; opening, he opened their Understandings; and *dissipating*, he so scattered their Unbelief on *THIS* day, as he never had done before: And this continued *one* way or *another* even from before day until the evening.

Secondly, On the next first day following the Church was within again; that is, congregated to wait upon their Lord. And *John* so relates the matter, as to give us to understand that they were not so assembled together again *till* then: *After eight days*, saith he, *again the Disciples were within*; clearly concluding, that they were not so on the days that were between, no not on the old *Seventh day*.

Now why should the Holy Ghost thus precisely speak of their assembling together upon the *first day*, if not to confirm us in this, that the Lord had chosen *that* day for the *new* Sabbath of his Church? Surely the Apostles knew what they did in their meeting together upon that day; yea, and the Lord Jesus also; for that he used *SO* to visit them when *SO* assembled, made his *practice a Law unto them*: For Practice is enough for us New Testament Saints, specially when the Lord Jesus himself is in the head of that practice, and that after he rose from the dead.

Perhaps some may stumble at the word [*after*] *after eight days*; but the meaning is, at the conclusion of the eighth day, or when they had spent in a manner the whole of *their* Sabbath in waiting

39 Sabbath] Sabbath

upon their Lord, then in comes their Lord, and finisheth that *their* days service to him with confirming of *Thomas*'s faith, and by letting drop other most heavenly treasure among them. Christ said, he must lie three days and three nights in the heart
5 of the Earth, yet 'tis evident, that he rose the third day, 1 *Cor.* 15. 4.

We must take then a part for the whole, and conclude, that from the time that the Lord Jesus rose from the dead, to the time that he shewed his Hands and his Side to *Thomas*, eight days
10 were almost expired; that is, he had sanctified unto them *two* first days, and had accepted that service they had performed to him therein, as he testified by giving of them so blessed a farewel at the conclusion of both those days.

Hence now we conclude, that this was the custom of the
15 Church at this day; to wit, upon the *first day of the week* to meet together, and to wait upon their Lord therein. For the Holy Ghost counts it needless to make a continued repetition of things) 'tis enough therefore if we have *now* and *then* mention made thereof.
20 *Obj. But Christ shewed himself alive to them at other times also, as in* Joh. 21. *&c.*

Ans. The names of all those days in which he so did are obliterate and blotted out, that they might not be idolized; for Christ did not set them apart for worship, *but this* day, *the first day*
25 *of the Week, by its name* is kept alive in the Church, the Holy Ghost surely signifying thus much, that how hidden soever other days were, Christ would have *his* day, the *first day* had in everlasting remembrance among Saints.

Churches also meet together now on the Week-days, and have
30 the presence of Christ with them too in their employments; but that takes not off from them the sanction of the *first day* of the Week, no more than it would take away the sanction of the old *Seventh day*, had it still continued holy to them: wherefore this is no let or objection to hinder our sanctifying of the first day of the
35 Week to our God. But

Thirdly, Adde to this, that upon *Pentecost*, which was the *first day of the Week*, mention is made of their being together again: For *Pentecost* was always the morrow after the *Sabbath*, the old *Seventh-day-sabbath*. Upon *this* day, I say, the Holy Ghost saith,
40 *they were again with one accord together in one place.*

But oh! the glory that then attended them, by the presence of the Holy Ghost among them: Never was such a thing done as was done on *that* first day till then. We will read the Text; *And when the day of Pentecost was fully come, they were all with one accord in one place. And suddenly there came a sound from Heaven as of a rushing mighty wind, and it filled all the house where they were sitting. And there appeared unto them cloven tongues, as of fire: And it sat upon each of them, and they were all filled with the Holy Ghost,* Acts 2. 1, 2, 3, 4.

Here's a first day glorified! Here's a countenance given to the day of their Christian assembling. But we will note a few things upon it.

First, The Church was now, as on other first days, all with one accord in one place. We read not that they came together by vertue of any precedent Revelation, nor by Accident, but contrarywise by Agreement; they was to gather *with one accord,* or by appointment, in pursuance of their duty, setting apart *that* day, as they had done the *first* days afore, to the holy service of their blessed Lord and Saviour Jesus Christ.

Secondly, we read that this meeting of theirs was not begun on the *old Sabbath,* but when *Pentecost* was *fully* come: the Holy Ghost intimating, that they had left now, and begun to leave, the *Seventh-day-sabbath* to the unbelieving Jews.

Thirdly, Nor did the Holy Ghost come down upon them till every moment of the old Sabbath was past, *Pentecost,* as was said, was *FULLY* come first: *And when the day of Pentecost was fully come, they were all with one accord in one place, and then,* &c.

And why was not this done on the *Seventh-day-sabbath?* but, possibly, to shew, that the Ministration of Death and Condemnation was not that by or thorough which Christ the Lord would communicate so good a gift unto his Churches, *Gal.* 3. 1, 2, 3, 4.

This Gift must be referred to the *Lords day,* the *first day* of the week, to fulfil the Scripture, and to sanctifie yet further this holy day unto the use of all New Testament-Churches of the Saints. For since on the *first day* of the week our Lord did rise from the dead, and by his special presence, I mean his personal, did accompany his Church therein, and *SO* preach as he did, his holy truths unto them, it was most meet that they on the same day also should receive the first-fruits of their eternal Life most gloriously.

And, I say again, since from the resurrection of Christ to *this day*, the Church then did receive upon the first day, (but as we read, upon no other) such glorious things as we have mentioned, it is enough to beget in the hearts of them that love
5 the Son of God, a high esteem of the first day of the week. But how much more, when there shall be joyned to these, proof that it was the custom of the first Gospel-Church, the Church of Christ at *Jerusalem*, after our Lord was risen, to assemble together to wait upon God on the first day of the Week *with their*
10 *Lord as leader*.

To say little more to this head, but onely to repeat what is written of *this* day of old, to wit, that it should be proclaimed the self same day, to wit, *the morrow after the Sabbath*, which is the first day of the Week, *that it may be an holy convocation unto you:*
15 *you shall do no servile work therein: it shall be a statute for ever in all your dwellings*, Levit. 23. 16, 17, 18, 19, 20, 21.

This Ceremony was about the Sheaf that was to be waved, and Bread of First-fruits, which was a type of Christ; for he is unto God *the first-fruits of them that sleep*, 1 Cor. 15. 20.
20 This Sheaf, of Bread, must not be waved on the old *Seventh day*, but on the morrow after, which is the first-day of the Week, the day in which Christ rose from the dead and waved himself as the First-fruits of the Elect unto God. Now from this day they were to count seven Sabbaths compleat, and on the morrow after
25 the seventh Sabbath, which was the first day of the week again; and this *Pentecost* upon which we now are, then they was to have a new Meat-offering, with Meat-offerings and Drink-offerings, &c.

And on the self same day they, were to proclaim that that *first*
30 *day*, should be a holy Convocation unto them. The which the Apostles did, and grounded that their Proclamation so on the Resurrection of Jesus Christ, not on Ceremonies, that at the same day they brought three thousand Souls to God, *Acts* 2. 41.

Now what another signal was here put upon the *first day of the*
35 *week*! the day in which our Lord rose from the dead, assembled with his Disciples, poured out so abundantly of the Spirit, and gathered even by the first draught that his Fishermen made by the Gospel, such a number of Souls to God.

Thus then they proclaimed, and thus they gathered sinners on
40 the first First day that they preached; for though they had

assembled together over and over with their Lord before therein, yet they began not joyntly to preach until *this* first day *Pentecost.*

Now, after this the Apostles to the Churches did never make mention of a *Seventh-day-sabbath.* For as the *Wave-sheaf* and the Bread of First-fruits were a figure of the Lord Jesus, and the *waving*, of his life from the dead: So that morrow after the Sabbath on which the Jews waved their Sheaf, was a figure of *that* in which our Lord did rise; consequently, when *their* morrow after the Sabbath ceased, *our* morrow after *that* began, and so has continued a *blessed* morrow after *their* Sabbath, as a holy Sabbath to Christians from that time ever since.

Fourthly, We come yet more close to the custom of Churches; I mean, *to the custom of the Churches of the Gentiles*; for as yet we have spoken but of the practice of the Church of God which was at *Jerusalem*; only we will add, that the Customs that were laudable & binding with the Church at *Jerusalem*, were with *reverence* to be imitated by the Churches of the Gentiles; for there was but one Law of Christ for them both to worship by.

Now then, to come to the point, to wit, that it was the custom of the Churches of the Gentiles, on the *first day of the week*, but upon no other that we read of, to come together to perform divine Worship to their Lord.

Hence it is said, *And upon the first day of the week, when the Disciples were come together to break bread*, &c. *Acts* 20. 7. This is a Text, that as to matter of fact, cannot be contradicted by any, for the Text saith plainly *they did so*, the Disciples *then* came together to break bread, the Disciples among the Gentiles *did so*.

Thus you see that the solemnizing of a first day to holy uses was not limited to, though first preached by the Church that was at *Jerusalem.* The Church at *Jerusalem* was the *Mother-church*,. and not that at *Rome*, as some falsely imagine; for from *this* Church went out the Law and the holy Word of God to the Gentiles. Wherefore it must be supposed that this meeting of the Gentiles on the first day of the Week to break bread, came to them by holy *tradition* from the Church at *Jerusalem*, since they were the first that kept the first day as holy unto the Lord their God.

And indeed, they had the best advantage to do it; for they had their Lord in the head of them to back them to it by his presence and preaching thereon.

But we will a little comment upon the Text. *Upon the* [*first day*] *of the Week.* Thus you see the day is *nominated,* and so is kept alive among the Churches: For in that the day is nominated on which this religious Exercise was performed, it is to be supposed
5 that the Holy Ghost would have it live, and be taken notice of by the Churches that succeed.

It also may *be nominated* to shew, that both the Church at *Jerusalem,* and those of the Gentiles did harmonize in their Sabbath, joyntly concluding to solemnize Worship on a day. And
10 then again to shew, that they all had left the *old* Sabbath to the unbelievers, and joyntly chose to sanctifie the day of the rising of their Lord, to this work.

They came together [*to break bread*] to partake of the Supper of the Lord. And what day so fit as the *Lords day* for this? This was
15 to be the work of that day, to wit, to solemnize that Ordinance among themselves, adjoying other solemn Worship thereto, to fill up the day, as the following part of the verse shews. This day therefore was designed for this work, the *whole* day, for the Text declares it: The first day of the week was set, by them, apart for
20 this work.

Upon [*the*] *first day*; not upon *A* first day, or upon *ONE* first day, or upon *SUCH* a first day; for had he said so, we had had from thence not so strong an argument for our purpose: But when he saith, *upon the first day of the week* they did it, he
25 insinuates, *It was their custom:* (also upon one of these, *Paul* being among them, preached unto them, ready to depart on the morrow.) Upon the first day: *what,* or *which first day* of this, or that, of the third or fourth week of the month? No, but upon the *first* day, *every* first day; for so the Text admits us to judge.

30 *Upon the first day of the Week,* [*when*] *the Disciples were come together,* supposes a Custom [*when*] or as they were *wont* to come together to perform such service among themselves to God: *then Paul* preached to them, *&c.*

It is a Text also that supposes *an agreement* among themselves
35 as to *this* thing. They came together then *TO* break bread; they had appointed to do it then, for that then was the day of their Lords Resurrection, and that in which he himself congregated after he *revived,* with the first Gospel-Church, the Church at *Jerusalem.*

40 Thus you see, *breaking of bread,* was the work, the work that by

general consent was agreed to be by the Churches of the Gentiles, performed upon the first day of the week. I say, by the *Churches*; for I doubt not but that the practice *here*, was also the practice of the rest of the Gentile-Churches, even as it had been before the practice of the Church at *Jerusalem*: For this practice *now* did become universal, and so this Text implies; for he speaks here *universally* of the practice of all Disciples as *such*, though he limits *Paul* preaching to that Church with whom he at present personally was. Upon the first day of the week, *when the Disciples were come together to break bread*, Paul being at that time at *Troas*, preached to them on that day.

Thus then you see how the Gentile-Churches did use to break bread, not on the *old Sabbath*, but on the *first day* of the week. And, I say, they had it from the Church of *Jerusalem*, where the Apostles were first seated, and beheld the way of their Lord with their eyes.

Now, I say, since we have so ample an example, not onely of the Church at *Jerusalem*, but also of the Churches of the Gentiles, for the keeping of the *first day* to the Lord, and that as countenanced by Christ and his Apostles, we should not be afraid to tread in their steps, for their practice is the *same* with Law and Commandment. But

Fifthly, We will adde to this another Text: *Now*, saith *Paul*, *concerning the collection for the Saints, as I have given order to the Churches of* Galatia, *even so do ye. Upon the first day of the week let every one of you lay by him as God has prospered him, that there be no gatherings when I come*, 1 Cor. 16. 1, 2.

This Text some have greatly sought to evade, counting the duty here, on this day to be done, a duty too inferiour for the sanction of an old *Seventh-day-sabbath*; when yet to shew mercy to an *Ass* on the old Sabbath, was a work which our Lord no ways condemns, *Luke* 13. 15. ch. 14. 15.

But to pursue our design, we have a Duty enjoyned, and that of no inferiour sort: *If charity be indeed, as it is, the very bond of perfectness*: and if without it *ALL* our doings, yea and sufferings too, are not worth so much as a rush, 1 *Cor.* 13. Coloss. 3. 14.

We have here a Duty, I say, that a *Seventh-day-sabbath*, when enforced was not too big for it to be performed in.

The work now to be done, was, as you see, to bestow their charity upon the Poor; yea, to provide for time to come: And I

say, it must be collected upon the *first day of the week.* Upon *THE* first day; not *A* first day, as signifying *one* or *two,* but upon *THE* first day, even *every* first day; for so your *ancient Bibles* have it; also our *later* must be so understood, or else *Paul* had left them to
5 whom he did write, utterly at a loss. For if he intended not *every* first day, and yet did not specifie a particular one, it could hardly even a been understood *which* first day he meant: But we need not stand upon this: This work was a work for *A* first day, for *EVERY* first day of the week.

10 Note again that we have this duty here commanded and enforced by an Apostolical Order: *I have given order,* saith *Paul,* for this; and his Orders, as he saith in another place, *are the commandments of the Lord*: you have it in the same Epistle, chap. 14. *vers.* 37.

15 Whence it follows, that there was given even by the Apostles themselves, a holy respect to the first day of the week above all the days of the week; yea, or of the Year besides.

Further, I find also by *this* Text, that this Order is *universal. I have,* saith he, *given this order not onely to you, but to the Churches in*
20 Galatia: Consequently to all other that were concerned in this Collection, 2 *Cor.* 8. and 9 chap. *&c.*

Now this, whatever others may think, puts yet more glory upon the *first day* of the week: For in that all the Churches are commanded, as to make their Collections, so to make them on
25 *THIS* day: what is it, but that *this* day, by reason of the Sanction that Christ put upon it, was of vertue to sanctifie the Offering thorough and by Christ Jesus, as the *Altar* and *Temple* afore, did sanctifie the Gift and Gold that was, and was offered on them. The Proverb is, *The better Day, the better Deed.* And I believe, that
30 things done on the Lords day, are better done, than on other days of the week, in his Worship.

Obj. But yet, say some, here are no Orders to keep this first day holy to the Lord.

Answ. 1. *That is supplied*; for that by this very Text this day
35 is appointed, above all the days of the week, to do this holy duty in.

2. You must understand that *this* Order is but additional, and now enjoyned to fill up that which was begun as to holy Exercise of religious Worship by the Churches long before.

40 3. The *universality* of the duty being enjoyned to this day,

supposes that this day was universally kept by the Churches as holy already.

4. And let him that scrupleth this, shew me, if he can, that God by the mouth of his Apostles did ever command that all the Churches should be confined to this or that *duty* on *such* a day, and yet put no Sanction upon that day; or that he has commanded that this work should be done on the first day of the week, and yet has reserved other Church-Ordinances as a publick solemnization of Worship to him, to be done of *another* day, as of a day *more* fit, *more* holy.

5. If Charity, if a general Collection for the Saints in the Churches is commanded on this day, and on no *other* day but this day; for Church-collection is commanded on no other, there must be a reason for it: And if that reason had not respect to the sanction of the day, I know not why the duty should be so strictly confined to it.

6. But for the Apostle *now* to give with this a particular command to the Churches to sanctifie that day as holy unto the Lord, had been utterly superfluous; for that they already, and that by the countenance of their Lord and his Church at *Jerusalem*, had done.

Before now, I say, it was become a custom, as by what hath been said already is manifest: wherefore what need that their so solemn a practice be imposed again upon the Brethren? An intimation now of a continued respect thereto, by the very *naming* of the day, is enough to keep the Sanctity thereof on foot in the Churches: How much more then, when the Lord is still adding *holy duty* to *holy duty*, to be performed upon *that* day. So then, in that the Apostle writes to the Churches to do this holy duty on the *first day* of the week, he puts them in mind of the Sanction of the day, and insinuates, that he would still have them have a due respect thereto.

Quest. *But is there yet another reason why this holy duty should, in special as it is, be commanded to be performed on the first day of the week?*

Answ. Yes: For that now the Churches were come together in their respective places, the better to agree about Collections, and to gather them. You know Church-worship is a duty so long as we are in the world, and so long also is this of making Collections for the Saints. And for as much as the Apostle speaks here, as I

have hinted afore, of a Church-collection, When is it more fit to
be done, than when the Church is come together upon the *first
day* of the Week to worship God?

5 2. This part of Worship is most comely to be done upon the
first day of the week, and that at the close of that days work: For
thereby the Church shews, not onely her thankfulness to God for
a Sabbath-days mercy, but also returneth him, by giving to the
Poor, that Sacrifice for their benefit that is most behoveful to
make manifest their professed subjection to Christ, *Prov.* 19. 17.
10 2 *Cor.* 9. 12, 13, 14, 15.

It is therefore necessary, that this work be done on the *first day*
of the week, for a *comely* close of the worship that we perform to
the Lord our God on that day.

3. On the first day of the week, when the Church is
15 performing of holy worship unto God, then that of Collection for
the Saints is most meet to be performed; because then, in all
likelihood, our hearts will be most *warm* with the divine
Presence; consequently most open and free to contribute to the
necessity of the Saints. You know, that a man when his heart is
20 open, is taken with some excellent thing; then, if at all, it is most
free to do something for the promoting thereof.

Why, waiting upon God in the way of his appointments, *opens*,
and makes *free*, the heart to the Poor: And because the *first day*
of the week was it in which now such solemn Service to him
25 was done, therefore also the Apostle commanded, that upon the
same day also, as on a day *most fit*, this duty of collecting for the
Poor should be done: *For the Lord loves a cheerful giver*, 2 Cor.
9. 6, 7.

Wherefore the Apostle by this, takes the Churches as it were
30 at the advantage, and as we say, while the Iron is hot, to the
intent he might, what in him lay, make their Collections, not
sparing nor of a grudging mind, but to flow from cheerfulness.
And the first day of the week, though its institution was set aside,
doth most naturally tend to this; because it is *the* day, the *onely*
35 day, in which we received such blessings from God, *Acts* 3. 26.

This is the day on which, *at first*, it rained Manna all day long
from Heaven upon the New Testament-Church, and so
continues to do this day. Oh! the resurrection of Christ, which
was on *this* day, and the riches that we receive thereby: Though it
40 should be, and is, I hope, thought on every day; yet when the

First of the week is *fully* come! Then *To* day! *This* day! This is the day to be warmed: this day he was begotten from the dead.

The thought of this, will do much with an *honest mind*: This is the day, I say, that the first Saints *DID* find, and that after-Saints *DO* find the blessings of God come down upon them; and 5
therefore this is the day here commanded to be set apart for holy Duties.

And although what I have said may be but little set by of some; yet, for a closing word as to this, I do think, could but half so much be produced from the day Christ rose from the dead quite 10
down, for the sanction of a *Seventh-day-sabbath*, in the Churches of the Gentiles, it would much sway with me. But the truth is, neither doth the Apostle *Paul*, nor any of his fellows, so much as once speak one word to the Churches that shews the least regard, as to conscience to God, of a *Seventh-day-sabbath* more. 15
No, the *first day*, the *first day*, the *first day*, is now all the cry in the Churches by the Apostles, for the performing Church-worship in to God. Christ began it on *THAT* day: Then the Holy Ghost seconded it on *THAT* day: Then the Churches practised it on *THAT* day. And to conclude, the Apostle by the command now 20
under consideration, continues the sanction of *THAT* day to the Churches to the end of the world.

But as to the old *Seventh-day-sabbath*, as hath been said afore in this Treatise, *Paul*, who is the Apostle of the Gentiles, has so taken away that whole Ministration in the bowels of which it is; 25
yea, and has so stript it of its Old Testament-grandeur, both by Terms and Arguments, that it is strange to me it should by any be still kept up in the Churches; specially, since the same Apostle, and that at the same time, has put a better Ministration in its place, 2 *Cor.* 3. 30

But when the Consciences of good men are captivated with an errour, none can stop them from a prosecution thereof, as if it were it self of the best of truths.

Obj. *But* Paul *preached frequently on the old Sabbath, and that after the Resurrection of Christ.* 35

Answ. To the unbelieving Jews and their Proselytes, I grant he did. But we read not that he did it to any New Testament-Church on that day: nor did he celebrate the Instituted worship of Christ in the Churches on that day. For *Paul*, who had before cast out the Ministration of death; as that which had *no* glory, 40 would not now take thereof any part for New Testament instituted worship; for he knew that that would veil the Heart, and blind the Mind from *that*, which yet instituted Worship was ordained to discover.

5   He preached then on the *Seventh-day-sabbath*, of a divine and crafty love to the salvation of the unbelieving Jews.

I say, he preached now on that day to them and their Proselytes, because that day was *theirs* by their estimation: He did it, I say, of great love to their Souls, that if possible, he might
10 save some of them.

Wherefore, if you observe, you shall still find, that where 'tis said that he preached on *that* day, it was to *that* people, not to the Churches of Christ. See *Acts* 9. 20. ch. 13. 14, 15, 16. ch. 16. 13. ch. 17. 1, 2, 3. ch. 18. 4.

15 Thus, though he had put away the sanction of *that* day as to himself, and had left the Christians that were weak to their liberty as to conscience to it, yet he takes occasion upon it to preach to the Jews that still were wedded to it, the Faith, that they might be saved by Grace.

20 *Paul* did also many other things that were *Jewish* and *Ceremonial*, for which he had, as then, no conscience at all, as to any Sanction that he believed was in them.

As his *Circumcising* of *Timothy*.

His *Shaving* of his Head.

25 His *submitting* to Jewish Purifications.

His *acknowledging* of himself a Pharisee.

His *implicite* owning of *Ananias* for High Priest after Christ was risen from the dead, *Acts* 16. 1, 2, 3. chap. 18. 18. chap. 21. 24, 25, 26. chap. 23. 6. chap. 23. 1, 2, 3, 4, 5.

30 He tells us also, *that to the Jew he became as a Jew, that he might save the Jew. And without Law, to them that were without Law, that also he might gain them*: Yea, he became, as he saith, *all things to all men, that he might gain the more*, as it is, 1 *Cor.* 9. 19, 20, 21, 22, 23.

35 But these things, as I said, he did not of Conscience to the things; for he *knew* that their sanction was gone: Nor would he suffer them to be imposed upon the Churches directly or indirectly; no, not by *Peter* himself, *Gal.* 2.

15 the] te

Were I in *Turkie* with a Church of Jesus Christ, I would keep the *first day* of the week *to God*, and for the edification of his people: And would also preach the Word to the Infidels on *their* Sabbath day, which is our *Friday*; and be glad too, if I might have such opportunity to try to perswade them to a love of their own salvation.

Obj. But if the Seventh-day-sabbath is, as you say, to be laid aside by the Churches of the Gentiles, Why doth Christ say to his, Pray that your flight be not in the Winter, nor on the Sabbath day? *For, say some, by this saying it appears, that the old Seventh-day-sabbath, as you have called it, will as to the Sanction of it, abide in force after Christ is ascended into heaven.*

Answ. I say first, These words was spoken to the Jewish Christians, not to the Gentile-churches: And the reason of this first hint, you will see clearer afterwards.

The Jews had several Sabbaths; as their *Seventh-day-sabbath*, their *Monthly* Sabbaths, their Sabbath of *Years*, and their *Jubile*, (Levit. 25.) Now if he means their *ordinary* Sabbaths, or that called the *Seventh-day-sabbath*, why doth he joyn the Winter thereto? for in that he joyneth the *Winter* with *that* Sabbath that he exhorteth them to pray their flight might not be in, it should seem that he meaneth rather their Sabbath of *Years*, or their *Jubile*, which did better answer one to another than *one* day and a *winter* could.

And I say again, that Christ should suppose that their flight should, or might last some considerable part of a Winter, and yet that then they should have their rest on those *Seventh-day-sabbaths*, is a little besides my reason, if it be considered again, that the Gentiles before whom they were then to fly, were Enemies to *their* Sabbath, and consequently would take opportunity at their Sabbaths to afflict them so much the more. Wherefore, I would that they who plead for a continuation of the *Seventh-day-sabbath* from this Text, would both better consider *IT*, and the incoherence that seems to be betwixt *such* a Sabbath and a Winter.

But again, were it granted that it is the *Seventh-day-Sabbath* that Christ here intendeth; yet, since, as we have proved, the Sanction *before* this was taken away; I mean, *before* this flight should be, he did not press them to pray thus because by any Law of Heaven they should then be commanded to keep it holy;

but because some would, *thorough their weakness*, have conscience
of it till then. And such would, if their flight should happen
thereon, be as much grieved and perplexed, as if it yet stood
obligatory to them by a Law.

5   This seems to have some truth in it, because among the Jews
that believed, there continued a long time many that were
wedded yet to the Law, to the ceremonial part thereof, and was
not so clearly Evangelized as the Churches of the Gentiles was.
Thou seest Brother, said *James* to *Paul*, *how many thousands of the*
10 *Jews there are that believe, and they are all zealous of the Law*, Acts
15. 5. ch. 21. 20.

Of these, and such weak unbelieving Jews, perhaps Christ
speaks, when he gives this exhortation to them to pray thus;
whose Consciences he knew would be weak, and being so, would
15 bind when they were entangled with an errour, as fast as if it
bound by a Law indeed.

Again, though the *Seventh-day-sabbath* and Ceremonies lost
their Sanction at the resurrection of Christ, yet they retained
some kind of being in the Church of the Jews, until *the desolation*
20 *spoken of by* Daniel *should be.*

Hence it is said, that *then* the Oblation and Sacrifices shall
cease, *Dan.* 9. 27. And hence it is, that *Jerusalem* and the *Temple*
are still called the holy place, even until this flight should be,
Matth. 24. 15.

25 Now if *Jerusalem* and the *Temple* are *still* called holy, even after
the Body and Substance, of which they were shadows, was come;
then no marvel though some to that day that believed were
entangled therewith, *&c.* For it may very well be supposed that
all Conscience of them would not be quite taken away, until all
30 reason for that Conscience should be taken away also. But when
Jerusalem, and the *Temple*, and the Jews Worship, by the Gentiles
was quite extinct by ruines, then in reason that Conscience did
cease. And it seems by some Texts, that all Conscience to them
was not taken away till then.

35 Quest. *But what kind of being had the Seventh-day-sabbath, and
other Jewish Rites and Ceremonies, that by Christs Resurrection was
taken away?*

Answ. These things had a *vertual* and a *nominal* being: As to
their *vertual* being, that died that day Christ did rise from the
40 dead, they being crucified with him on the Cross, *Coloss.* 2.

But now, when the *vertual* being was gone, they still with the weak retained their *name*, (among many of the Jews that believed) until the *abomination* that maketh desolate *stood in the holy place*: for in *Paul's* time they were, as to that, *but ready to vanish away.*   5

Now, I say, they still retaining their *nominal* grandeur, though not by vertue of a Law, they could not, till *Time* and *Dispensation* came, be swept out of the way. We will make what hath been said, as to this, out by a familiar similitude.

There is a Lord or great man dies; now being dead, he has lost his 10 *vertual life. He has now no relation to a Wife, to Children, vertually; yet his Name still abides, and that in that Family, to which otherwise he is dead. Wherefore they embalm him, and also keep him above ground for many days. Yea, he is still reverenced by those of the family, and that in several respects. Nor doth any thing but time and* 15 *dispensation wear this name away.*

Thus then the Old Testament-signs and shadows went off the stage in the Church of Christ among the Jews. They lost their *vertue* and signification when Christ nailed them to his Cross, *Coloss.* 2. But as to their *Name*, and the *Grandeur* that attended 20 that, it continued with many that were weak, and vanished not, *but when the abomination that made them desolate came.*

The sum then and conclusion of the matter is this; the *Seventh-day-sabbath* lost its glory when that *Ministration* in which it was, lost its: But yet the *name* thereof might abide a long 25 time with the Jewish legal Christians, and so might become obligatory still, though not by the Law, to their Conscience, even as *Circumcision* and other Ceremonies did: and to them it would be as grievous to fly on that day, as if by Law it was still in force.   30

For, I say, to a weak Conscience, that Law which has lost its life, may yet thorough their ignorance, be as binding as if it stood still upon the authority of God.

Things then become obligatory these two ways.

1. By an *Institution* of God.   35
2. By the *over-ruling* power of a mans misinformed Conscience. And although by vertue of an institution Divine Worship is acceptable to God by Christ, yet Conscience will make that a man shall have but little ease if *such* rules and dictates as it imposes be not observed by him.   40

This is my answer, upon a supposition that the *Seventh-day-sabbath* is in this Text intended: and the answer, I think, stands firm and good.

Also, there remains, notwithstanding this Objection, no divine
5 Sanction in, or upon the old *Seventh-day-sabbath.*

Some indeed will urge, that Christ here meant the *first day* of the week, which here he puts under the term of Sabbath. But this is foreign to me, so I wave it till I receive more satisfaction in the thing.

10 Quest. *But if* indeed *the first day of the week be the new Christian Sabbath, why is there no more spoken of its institution in the Testament of Christ?*

Answ. No more! What need is there of more than enough! yea, there is a great deal found in the Testament of the Lord Jesus to
15 prove its Authority Divine.

1. For we have shewed from sundry Scriptures, that from the very day our Lord did rise from the dead, the Church at *Jerusalem,* in which the Twelve Apostles were, did meet together on that day, and had the Lord himself for their Preacher, while
20 they were auditors; and thus the day began.

2. We have shewed that the Holy Ghost, the Third person in the Trinity, did second this of Christ, in coming down from Heaven upon *this day* to manage the Apostles in their preaching; and in that very day so managed them in that work, that by his
25 help then did bring Three thousand Souls to God.

3. We have shewed also, that after this the Gentile-Churches did solemnize *this* day for holy Worship, and that they had from *Paul* both Countenance and Order so to do.

And now I will adde, that more need not be spoken: *For the*
30 *practice of the first Church, with their Lord in the head of them to manage them in that practice, is as good as many Commands.* What then shall we say, when we see a first Practice turned into holy Custom?

I say moreover, that though a *Seventh-day-sabbath* is not
35 natural to man as man, yet our *Christian* Holy day is natural to us as Saints, if our Consciences are not clogged before with some old Fables, or Jewish Customs.

But if an old Religion shall get *footing* and *rooting* in us, though the grounds thereof be vanished away, yet the man concerned
40 will be hard put to it, shoud he be saved, to get clear of his

clouds, and devote himself to that service of God which is of his own prescribing.

Luther himself, though he *saw* many things were without ground which he had received for truth, had yet work hard enough, as himself intimates, to get his Conscience clear from all those *roots* and *strings* of inbred errour.

But, I say, to an *untainted* and *well-bred* Christian, we have good measure, *shaken* together, and *running* over, for our Christian *Lords day*. And I say again, that the *first day of the week*, and the spirit of *such* a Christian, *sute* one another, as *nature* suteth *nature*; for there is as it were a natural *instinct* in Christians, as such, when they understand what in a *first day* was brought forth, to fall in therewith to keep it holy to their Lord.

1. The *first day of the week*! why it was the day of our life. *After two days he will revive us*, and in the third day we shall live in his sight. *After two days*, there is the Jews *preparation*, and *Seventh-day-sabbath*, quite passed over; and *in the third day*, that's the *first day* of the week, which is the day our Lord did rise from the dead, we began to live by him in the sight of God, *Hos.* 6. 2. *Joh.* 20. 1. 1 *Cor.* 15. 4.

2. The *first day* of the week! That's the day in which, as I hinted before, our Lord was wont to preach to his Disciples after he rose from the dead; in which also he did use to shew them his Hands and his Feet, (*Luk.* 24. 38, 39. *Joh.* 20. 25.) to the end they might be confirmed in the truth of his victory over *Death* and the *Grave* for them. The day in which he made himself *known* to them in *breaking bread*: The day in which he so plentifully poured out the Holy Ghost upon them: The day in which the Church both at *Jerusalem*, and *those* of the *Gentiles*, did use to perform to God Divine Worship: all which has before been sufficiently proved. And shall we not imitate our Lord, nor the Church that was immediately acted by him in this, and the Churches their fellows? Shall, I say, the Lord Jesus do all this in his Church, and they together with him! Shall the Churches of the Gentiles also fall in with their Lord and with their *Mother* at *Jerusalem* herein! And again, shall all this be so punctually committed to sacred Story, with the day in which these things were done, under denomination, over and over, saying, These things were done on the *first* day, on the *first* day, on the *first* day of the week, while all other days are, as to name, buried in

everlasting oblivion! and shall we not take that notice thereof as
to follow the Lord Jesus and the Churches herein? Oh stupidity!

3. This day of the week! They that make but observation of
what the Lord did of old, to a many sinners, & with his Churches
5 on this day, must needs conclude, that in this day the Treasures
of Heaven were broken up, and the richest things therein
communicated to his Church. Shall the children of this world be,
as to this also, wiser in their generations than the children of
Light, and former Saints, upon whose shoulders we pretend to
10 stand, go beyond us here also.

Jacob could by observation gather that the place where he lay
down to sleep was no other but the House of God, and the very
Gate of Heaven, (*Gen.* 28. 17.)

Laban could gather by observation, that the Lord blessed him
15 for *Jacob*'s sake, (*Gen.* 30. 27.)

David could gather by what he met with upon Mount *Moriah*,
that that was the place where God would have the Temple
builded, therefore he sacrificed there (1 *Chro.* 21. 26, 27, 28. ch.
22. 1, 2. 2 Chr. 3. 1.

20 *Ruth* was to mark the place where *Boaz* lay down to sleep, and
shall not Christians also mark the day in which our Lord *rose
from the dead, Ruth* 3. 4.

I say, shall we not *mark* it, when so many memorable things
was done on it, *for*, and *TO*, and *IN* the Churches of God! Let
25 Saints be ashamed to think that such a day should be looked
over, or counted common (when tempted to it by Satan) when
kept to religious Service of old, and when beautified with so
many divine Characters of sanctity as we have proved by Christ,
his Church, the Holy Ghost, and the command of Apostolical
30 Authority it was.

But why, I say, is *this* day, on which our Lord rose from the
dead, *Nominated* as it is? Why was it not sufficient to say *he rose
again*; or, he rose again the *third day*? without a specification of
the very *name* of the day: For, as we said afore, Christ appeared
35 to his Disciples, after his resurrection, on other days also; yea,
and thereon did Miracles too: Why then did not these days live?
why was their name, for all that, blotted out, and this day, onely
kept alive in the Churches?

20 *Boaz*] *Baaz*

The day on which Christ was born of a Virgin; the day of his Circumcision, the day of his Baptism, and Transfiguration, are not by their names committed by the Holy Ghost to holy Writ to be kept alive in the world; nor yet such days in which he did many great and wonderful things: But *THIS* day, *this* day is still nominated; the first day of the week is the day. I say, why are things thus left with us? but because we, as Saints of old, should gather and separate, what is of divine Authority from the rest. For in that *this* day is so often *nominated* while all other days lie dead in their Graves, 'tis as much as if God should say, *Remember* the First day of the week to keep it holy to the Lord your God.

And set this aside, and I know not what reason can be rendered, or what Prophecy should be fulfilled by the bare *naming of the day.*

When God, of old, did sanctifie for the use of his Church a day as he did many, he always called them either by the name of the day of the Month, or of the Week, or by some other signal by which they might be certainly known. Why should it not then be concluded, that for this very reason the first day of the week is thus often nominated by the Holy Ghost in the Testament of Christ?

Moreover, he that takes away the first day, as to *this* Service, leaves us now *NO* day, as sanctified of God, for his solemn Worship to be by his Churches performed in. As for the *Seventh-day-sabbath*, that, as we see, is gone to its grave with the Signs and Shadows of the Old Testament.

Yea, and has such a dash left upon it by Apostolical Authority, that 'tis enough to make a Christian fly from it for ever, (2 *Cor.* 3.)

Now, I say; since that is removed *by God*: If we should suffer the first day also to be taken away *by man*, What day that has a divine stamp upon it, *would be left for us to worship God in?*

Alas! the first day of the week is the Christians *Market-day*, that which they so solemnly trade in for sole provision for all the week following. This is the day that they gather *Manna* in. To be sure the *Seventh-day-sabbath* is not that: For of old the people of God could never find *Manna* on *that* day. *On the seventh day*, said *Moses, which is the Sabbath, in it there shall be none*, Exod. 16. 26.

Any day of the week *Manna* could be found, but on that day it was not to be found upon the face of the ground. But now our *first day* is the *Manna-day*; the onely day that the Churches of the New Testament, even of old, did gather *Manna* in. But more of this anon.

5   Nor will it out of my mind but that it is a very high piece of ingratitude, and of uncomly behaviour, to deny the Son of God *his* day, the *Lords day*, the day that he *has made*: And as we have shewed already, this *first day of the week* is it; yea, and a great piece of *unmannerliness* is it too, for any, notwithinstanding the old *Seventh day* is so degraded as it is, to attempt to impose it on
10 the Son of God. To impose a day upon him which yet *Paul* denies to be branch of the Ministration of the Spirit, and of righteousness. Yea, to impose a great part of that Ministration which *HE* says plainly, *Was to be done away*; for that a better Ministration stript it of its glory, is a high attempt indeed, 2 *Cor.*
15 3.

Yet again, the Apostle *smites* the teachers of the Law upon the mouth, saying, *They understood neither what they say, nor whereof they affirm,* (1 Tim. 1. 7.)

The Seventh-day-sabbath was indeed Gods Rest from the
20 works of Creation; but yet the *Rest* that he found in what the *first day* of the week did produce, for Christ was born from the dead in it, more pleased him than did all the *Seventh days* that ever the world brought forth; wherefore, as I said before, it cannot be but that the *well-bred* Christian must set apart this day for solemn
25 Worship to God, and to sanctifie his name therein.

Must the Church of old be bound to remember that night in which they did come out of *Egypt*! must *Jeptha*'s daughter have *four* days for the Virgins of *Israel* yearly to lament her hard case in! Yea, must *two* days be kept by the Church of old, yearly, for
30 their being delivered from *Haman*'s fury! And must not one to the *worlds end* be kept by the Saints for the Son of God their Redeemer, for all he has delivered them from a worse than *Pharoah* or *Haman*, even from the *Devil*, and *Death*, and *Sin*, and *Hell*! oh stupidity! Exod. 12. 24. Judg. 11. 39, 40. Esth. 9. 26.–
35 32.

A day! say some, God forbid but he should have a day. But what day? oh! the old day comprized within the bounds and bowels of the Ministration of death.

And is this the love that thou hast to thy Redeemer, to keep
40 that day to him for all the service that hath done for thee, which

has a natural tendancy in it to draw thee off from the consideration of the works of thy *redemption*, to the *creation* of the world! oh stupidity!

But why must he be imposed upon? has he chosen that day? did he finish *HIS* work thereon? Is there in all the New Testament of our Lord from the day he rose from the dead, to the end of his holy Book, one syllable that signifies in the least the *tenth part* of such a thing? Where is the Scripture that saith that this Lord of the *Sabbath* commanded his Church, from that time, to do any part of Church-service thereon? Where do we find the Churches to gather together thereon?

But why the *Seventh day*? What is it? Take but the shadow thereof away: Or what shadow *now* is left in it since its institution as to Divine Service is taken long since from it?

Is there any thing in the works that was done in that day, more than shadow, or that in the least tends *otherwise* to put us in mind of Christ; and he being come, what need have we of that shadow? And I say again, since that day was to be observed by a ceremonial method, and no way else, as we find; and since Ceremonies are ceased, what way by divine appointment is there left to keep that old *Sabbath* by Christians in?

If they say, Ceremonies are ceased. By the same Argument, so is the sanction of the day in which they were to be performed. I would gladly see the place, if it is to be found, where 'tis said, *That day retains its sanction, which yet has lost that method of service which was of God appointed for the performance of worship to him thereon.*

When *Canaan*-worship fell, the *Sanction* of *Canaan* fell. When *Temple*-worship, *and Altar*-worship, and the Sacrifices of the Levitical Priesthood fell, down also came the things themselves. Likewise so, when the *service* or *shadow* and *ceremonies* of the *Seventh-day-sabbath* fell, the *Seventh-day-Sabbath* fell likewise.

On the *Seventh-day-sabbath*, as I told you, *Manna* was not to be found. But why? for that *that* day was of *Moses* and of the Ministration of death. But *Manna* was was not of him: *Moses*, saith Christ, *gave you not that bread from Heaven*, Joh. 6. 31, 32. *Moses*, as we said, gave that *Sabbath* in Tables of stone, and God gave that *Manna* from Heaven. Christ, nor his Father, gives grace by the Law, no not by that Law in which is contained the old *Seventh-day-sabbath* it self.

The Law is not of Faith, why then should Grace be by Christians expected by observation of the Law? The Law, even the Law written and engraven in stones enjoyns perfect obedience thereto on pain of the curse of God. Nor can that part
5 of it now under consideration, according as is required, be fulfilled by any man, was the Ceremony thereto belonging, allowed to be laid aside, *Isai.* 58. 13. Never man yet did keep it perfectly, except he whose name is Jesus Christ: in him therefore we have kept it, and by him are set free from that Law,
10 and brought under the ministration of the Spirit.

But why shoud we be bound to seek *Manna* on *that* day, on which God saies, *None shall be found.*

Perhaps, it will be said, *that the sanction of THAT day* would not admit that *Manna* should be gathered *on it.*

15 But that was not all, for on *that* day there *was* none to be found. And might I chuse, I had rather sanctifie that day to God on which I might gather this bread of God all day long, than set my mind at all upon that in which *no* such bread was to be had.

The *Lords day*, as was said, is to the Christians the principal
20 Manna-day.

On *this* day, even on it Manna in the morning very early gathered was by the Disciples of our Lord, as newly springing out of the ground. The true bread of God: The sheaf of First-fruits, which is *Christ from the dead*, was ordained to be waved
25 before the Lord on the morrow after the Sabbath, the day on which *our Lord ceased from his own OWN Work as God did from HIS*, Levit. 23.

Now therefore the Disciples found their green Ears of Corn indeed! Now they read life, both *IN* and *OUT* of the Sepulchre
30 in which the Lord was laid. Now they could not come together nor speak one to another, but either their Lord was with them, or they had heart-enflaming tidings from him. *Now* cries one and says, The Lord is risen: And *then* another and says, He hath appeared to such and such.

35 Now comes tidings to the Eleven that their women was early at the Sepulchre, where they had a Vision of Angels that told them their Lord was risen: Then comes another and says, The Lord is risen indeed. Two also comes from *Emmaus*, and cries, We have

13 be] *om.*

seen the Lord: and by and by, while they yet were speaking, their Lord shews himself in the midst of them.

Now he calls to their mind some of the eminent passages of his life, and eats and drinks in their presence, and opens the Scriptures to them: Yea, and opens their Understanding too, that their hearing might not be unprofitable to them; all which continued from early in the morning till late at night. Oh! what a *Manna-day* was this to the Church. And more than all this you will find, if you read but the four Evangelists upon this Subject.

Thus began the day *after* the Sabbath, and *thus* it has continued thorough all Ages to this very day. Never did the *Seventh-day-sabbath* yield *Manna* to Christians. A *new* world was now begun with the poor Church of God; for so said the Lord of the Sabbath, *Behold, I make all things new.* A *new* Covenant, and why not then a *new* resting-day to the Church? or why must the *old* Sabbath be joyned to this *new* Ministration? let him that can shew a reason for it.

Christians, if I have not been so large upon things as some might expect; know, that my brevity on this Subject is, from consideration that much needs not be spoken thereto, and because I may have occasion to write a second Part.

Christians, beware of being entangled with Old Testament-Ministrations; lest by *one* you be brought into *many* Inconveniencies.

I have observed, that though the Jewish Rites have lost their Sanction, yet some that are weak in Judgement, do bring themselves into bondage by them. Yea, so high have some been carried as to a pretended Conscience to these, that they have at last proceeded to *Circumcision*, to many Wives; and the observation of many bad things besides.

Yea, I have talked with some pretending to Christianity, who have said, *and affirmed*, as well as they could, that the Jewish Sacrifices must up again.

But do you give no heed to these Jewish Fables *That turn from the truth* (*Tit.* 1. 14.) Do you, I say, that love the Lord Jesus, keep close to his Testament, his Word, his Gospel, and observe *HIS Holy-day*.

And this Caution in conclusion I would give, to put stop to this Jewish Ceremony, to wit, That a Seventh-day-Sabbath pursued according to its imposition by Law, (and I know not that it is

imposed by the Apostles) leads to bloud and stoning to death those that do but gather Sticks thereon (*Numb.* 15. 32, 33, 34, 35, 36.) A thing which no way becomes the Gospel, that Ministration of the Spirit and of Righteousness (2 *Cor.* 3.) nor
5 yet the professors thereof (*Luke* 9. 54, 55, 56.)

Nor can it with fairness be said, that *that* Sabbath day remains, though the Law thereof is repealed. For confident I am, that there is no more ground to make such a conclusion, than there is to say, that Circumcision is still of force, though the Law for
10 cutting of the uncircumcised is by the Gospel made null and void.

I told you also in the Epistle, That if the *Fifth* Commandment was the *first* that was with promise; then it follows, that the *Fourth*, or *that* Seventh-day-Sabbath, had no promise intailed to
15 it. Whence it follows, that where you read in the Prophet of a Promise annexed to a Sabbath, it is best to understand it of our *Gospel*-Sabbath, *Isai.* 56.

Now if it be asked, *What Promise is intailed to our First-day-sabbath?* I answer, The bigest of Promises. For
20 First, The Resurrection of Christ was tyed by Promise to this day, and to none other. He rose the *Third* day after his death, and that was the *First* day of the week, *according* to what was fore-promised in the *Scriptures*, Hos. 6. 1, 2. 1 *Cor.* 15. 3, 4, 5, 6.

Second, That we should live before God by him, is a Promise
25 to be fulfilled on *this* day; *After two days he will revive us, and in the third day we shall live in his sight*, Hos. 6. 2. See also *Isai.* 26. 19. and compare them again with 1 *Cor.* 15. 4.

Third, The great promise of the New Testament, to wit, the pouring out of the Spirit, fixeth upon these days; and so he began
30 in the most wonderful effusion of it upon *Pentecost*, which was the *first day* of the week, that the Scriptures might be fulfilled, *Acts* 2. 16, 17, 18, 19.

Nor could these three Promises be fulfilled upon any other days, for that the Scripture had fixed them to the First day of the
35 Week.

I am of opinion that these things, though but briefly touched upon, cannot be fairly objected against, however they may be disrelished by some.

Nor can I believe, that any part of our Religion, as we are
40 Christians, stands in *not kindling* of *fires*, and not *seething* of

Victuals, or in binding of men not to stir out of those places on the Seventh day, in which at the dawning thereof they were found: And yet these are Ordinances belonging to *that Seventh-day-sabbath*, Exod. 16. 23, 29.

Certainly it must needs be an errour to impose these things by Divine Authority upon New Testament-Believers, our Worship standing *now* in things more weighty, spiritual, and heavenly.

Nor can it be proved, as I have hinted before, that this day was, or is to be imposed without those Ordinances, with others in other places mentioned and adjoyned, for the sanction of that day, they being made necessary parts of that worship that was to be performed thereon.

I have charity for those that abuse themselves and their Lord, by their preposterous zeal and affection for the continuing of this day in the Churches. For I conclude, that if they did either believe, or think of the incoherence that this day with its Rites and Ceremonies has with the Ministration of the Spirit, our New Testament-Ministration, they would not so stand in their own light as they do, nor to stifly plead for a place for it in the Churches of the Gentiles. But as *Paul* insinuates in other cases, there is an aptness in men to be under the Law because they do not hear it, *Gal.* 4.

Nor will it out of my mind, but if the Seventh-day-sabbath was by Divine Authority, and to be kept holy by the Churches of the Gentiles, it should not have so remained among the Jews, Christs deadliest Enemies, and a been kept so much hid from the Believers, his best Friends. For who has retained the pretended sanction of that day from Christs time quite down, in the world, but the Jews, and a few Jewish Gentiles (I will except some.) But, I say, since a Sabbath is that without which the great Worship of God under the Gospel cannot be well performed: How can it be thought, that it should, as to the knowledge of it, be confined to so blasphemous a generation of the Jews, with whom that worship is not?

I will rather conclude, that those Gentile-professors that adhere thereto, are Jewifi'd, Legaliz'd, and so far gone back from the authority of God, who from such bondages has set his Churches free.

I do at this time but hint upon things, reserving a fuller Argument upon them for a time and place more fit; where, and when, I may perhaps also shew some other wild notions of those that so stifly cleave to this.

Mean time, I entreat those who are captivated with this opinion, not to take it ill at my hand that I thus freely speak my mind. I entreat them also to peruse my Book without prejudice to my person. The truth is, one thing that has moved me to this work, is the shame that has covered the face of my Soul, when I have thought of the Fictions and Fancies that are growing among Professors: And while I see each Fiction turn it self to a Faction, to the loss of that good spirit of Love, and that oneness that formerly was with good men.

I doubt not but some unto whom this Book may come, have had seal from God, that the *first day of the week* is to be sanctified by the Church *to Jesus Christ*: Not onely from *his* testimony, which is, and should be, the ground of our Practice; but also, for that the first conviction that the Holy Ghost made upon their Consciences, to make them know that they were sinners, began with them *for breaking this Sabbath day*; which day, by that same Spirit, was told them, *was that now called the first day*, and *not* the day before, (and the Holy Ghost doth not use to begin this work with a lye) which first conviction the Spirit has followed so close, with other things tending to compleat the same work, that the Soul from so good a beginning could not *rest* until it *found* rest in Christ. Let this then to such be a second token that the *Lords day* is by them to be kept in commemoration of their Lord and his Resurrection, and of what he did on this day for their Salvation. *Amen.*

FINIS.

NOTES TO *A DEFENCE OF THE DOCTRINE OF JUSTIFICATION, BY FAITH*

p. 8, l. 24. *Smart*: suffering, penalty for offence. See *O.E.D.*

p. 12, marg. *Rom. 7. 24.* 'O wretched man that I am! who shall deliver me from the body of this death?' This biblical quotation and subsequent ones are from the Authorized Version.

p. 13, marg. *Isa. 1. 6.* 'From the sole of the foot even unto the head there is no soundness in it: but wounds, and bruises, and putrifying sores: they have not been closed, neither bound up, neither mollified with ointment.'

p. 13, marg. *Tit. 1. 15.* 'Unto the pure all things are pure: but unto them that are defiled and unbelieving is nothing pure; but even their mind and conscience is defiled.'

p. 13, marg. *Ephes. 4. 18.* 'Having the understanding darkened, being alienated from the life of God through the ignorance that is in them, because of the blindness of their heart.'

p. 13, marg. *Isa. 59. 6, 7, 8, 9, 10.* 'Their webs shall not become garments, neither shall they cover themselves with their works: their works are works of iniquity, and the act of violence is in their hands. Their feet run to evil, and they make haste to shed innocent blood: their thoughts are thoughts of iniquity; wasting and destruction are in their paths. The way of peace they know not: and there is no judgment in their goings: they have made them crooked paths: whosoever goeth therein shall not know peace. Therefore is judgment far from us, neither doth justice overtake us: we wait for light, but behold obscurity; for brightness, but we walk in darkness. We grope for the wall like the blind, and we grope as if we had no eyes: we stumble at noon day as in the night: we are in desolate places as dead men.'

p. 13, marg. *Rom. 3.* Bunyan's quotation begins with v. 10.

p. 14, marg. *Psal. 39. 5.* 'Behold, thou hast made my days as an handbreadth; and mine age is as nothing before thee: verily every man at his best state is altogether vanity. Selah.'

p. 17, marg. *1 Cor. 6. 19.* 'What? know ye not that your body is the temple of the Holy Ghost which is in you, which ye have of God, and ye are not your own?'

p. 17, marg. *1 Cor. 15.* Bunyan quotes v. 48.

p. 17, marg. *Gal. 5. 25.* 'If we live in the spirit, let us also walk in the Spirit.'

p. 17, marg. *Rom. 8. 14.* 'For as many as are led by the Spirit of God, they are the sons of God.'

p. 18, marg. *Gal. 4.* Bunyan quotes v. 6.

p. 18, marg. *Rom. 8.* Bunyan quotes v. 14.

p. 18, marg. *Eph. 1. 4; 4. 6.* 'According as he hath chosen us in him before the foundation of the world, that we should be holy and without blame before him in love.' 'One God and father of all, who is above all, and through all, and in you all.'

p. 18, marg. *Heb. 10.* Among other things, the chapter contrasts Old Testament sacrifices with the sacrifice of Christ.

p. 18, marg. *2 Cor. 5. 14, 15, 16.* 'For the love of Christ constraineth us: because we thus judge, that if one died for all, then were all dead: And that he died for all, that they which live should not henceforth live unto themselves, but unto him which died for them, and rose again. Wherefore henceforth know we no man after the flesh: yet now henceforth know we him no more.'

p. 25, marg. *Rom. 8. 3.* 'For what the law could not do, in that it was weak through the flesh, God sending his own Son in the likeness of sinful flesh, and for sin, condemned sin in the flesh.'

p. 28, marg. *Rom. 3. 1, 2, 3.* 'What advantage then hath the Jew? or what profit is there of circumcision? Much every way: chiefly, because that unto them were committed the oracles of God. For what if some did not believe? shall their unbelief make the faith of God without effect?'

p. 30, l. 6. *Jer. 31. 33.* 'The Lord hath appeared of old unto me, saying, Yea, I have loved thee with an everlasting love: therefore with loving kindness have I drawn thee.'

p. 30, l. 6. *Ezek. 36.* Verse 26 refers to a new heart and a new spirit.

p. 30, l. 6. *Heb. 8. 2.* 'A minister of the sanctuary and of the true tabernacle, which the Lord pitched, and not man.'

p. 30, ll. 6–7. *2 Cor. 5. 17, 18, 19.* 'Therefore if any man be in Christ, he is a new creature: old things are passed away; behold, all things are become new. And all things are of God, who hath reconciled us to himself by Jesus Christ, and hath given to us the ministry of reconciliation; To wit, that God was in Christ, reconciling the world unto himself, not imputing their trespasses unto them; and hath committed unto us the word of reconciliation.'

p. 32, marg. *Eccle. 7.* 'Verse 29, 'Lo, this only have I found, that God hath made man upright: but they have sought out many inventions.'

p. 32, marg. *1 Cor. 15.* Bunyan quotes vv. 45–7.

p. 33, l. 18. *A type*: Typology (the treatment of an episode or character in the

Old Testament as anticipating one in the New) was widely used in the
seventeenth century as a mode of Biblical interpretation. As Bunyan explained
in *The Pilgrim's Progress* (p. 4),

> *But must I needs want solidness, because*
> *By Metaphors I speak; was not Gods Laws,*
> *His Gospel-laws in olden time held forth*
> *By Types, Shadows and Metaphors?*

Cf. the Baptist Benjamin Keach's *Tropologia: A Key to Open Scripture Metaphors*
(1682) and Oxford Bunyan vii, Introduction.

p. 33, l. 24. *figurative, shadowish*: The Quakers also criticized such qualities in
contemporary Christianity, as well as any supposed righteousness (e.g.,
'imputed') other than real, experienced righteousness. See Oxford Bunyan,
i. xvi–xxi.

p. 33, l. 33. *Covenant of Grace*: Interest in covenant theology increased among
English Calvinist theologians in the seventeenth century. For Bunyan and
covenant theology see Oxford Bunyan, ii. xxi–xxxii.

p. 34, marg. *Ephes. 4. 21, 22.* 'If so be that ye have heard him, and have been
taught by him, as the truth is in Jesus: That ye put off concerning the former
conversation the old man, which is corrupt according to the deceitful lusts.'

p. 34, marg. Gen. 2. 15, 16, 17. 'And the Lord God took the man and put him
into the garden of Eden to dress it and to keep it. And the Lord God
commanded the man, saying, Of every tree of the garden thou mayest freely
eat: But of the tree of the knowledge of good and evil, thou shalt not eat of it:
for in the day that thou eatest thereof thou shalt surely die.'

p. 35, ll. 5–6. *To dwell . . . mortal Men.* 'The lines are from Hierocles'
commentary on the golden verses of Pythagoras, v. 1. See John Norris (trans.),
Hierocles Upon the Golden Verses of the Pythagorians (1682), p. 9. Bunyan's
reference is actually to Fowler's p. 110, misprinted 101.

p. 36, l. 5. *Socinians*: Socinians were those associated with the beliefs of the
sixteenth-century Italians Laelius and Faustus Socinus, who rejected the
doctrine of the Trinity and emphasized the humanity of Jesus. Their views
conflicted sharply with Bunyan's understanding of atonement and justification,
so that in *The Strait Gate* (1676), for example, he warned against the doctrine
of the Socinian 'who denieth to Christ that he hath made to God satisfaction
for sin' (Oxford Bunyan, v. 127). Also, on several occasions Bunyan noted the
doctrinal similarity of Socinians and Quakers (see Oxford Bunyan, i. xvi–xxx).

p. 37, l. 33. *Clamber*: climb with difficulty and effort.

p. 38, l. 21. *Calvin*: John Calvin.

p. 38, l. 21. *Peter Martyr*: Peter Martyr (1500–62) was born in Italy and
pursued Protestant scholarship in Zurich, Basle, Strasbourg, and Oxford.

394   *Notes to* A Defence of Justification

p. 38, l. 21. *Musculus*: Wolfgang Musculus (1497–1563) was a reformer and scholar who served the Protestant cause in Strasbourg, Augsburg, and Berne.

p. 38, l. 22. *Zanchy*: Jerome Zanchy (Hieronymus Zanchius, 1516–90), a Calvinist theologian, was born near Milan and taught at Strasbourg and Heidelberg.

p. 39, marg. *Heb. 9. 22.* 'And almost all things are by the law purged with blood: and without shedding of blood is no remission.'

p. 40, l. 22. *Rom. 5.* Bunyan combines portions of vv. 9 and 10.

p. 40, marg. *Col. 1. 20.* 'And, having made peace through the blood of his cross, by him to reconcile all things unto himself; by him, I say, whether they be things in earth, or things in heaven.'

p. 40, marg. *Ecclus. 4. 31.* Ecclesiasticus 4: 31. 'Let not thine hand be stretched out to receive, and shut when thou shouldest repay.' Bunyan's use of an apocryphal book is unusual, and the meaning is unclear. However, if Ecclesiastes was intended, there are only 16 verses in ch. 4, and there is no v. 31 in any of the chapters.

p. 41, marg. *Rom. 5. 6, 7, 8.* Bunyan actually quotes vv. 8–10.

p. 41, marg. *1 Tim. 1. 15.* 'This is a faithful saying, and worthy of all acceptation, that Christ Jesus came into the world to save sinners: of whom I am chief.'

p. 41, marg. *Ephes. 1. 12, 13.* 'That we should be to the praise of his glory, who first trusted in Christ. In whom ye also trusted, after that ye heard the word of truth, the gospel of your salvation: in whom also after that ye believed, ye were sealed with that holy Spirit of promise.'

p. 41, marg. *Joh. 1. 12.* 'But as many as received him, to them gave he power to become the sons of God, even to them that believe on his name.'

p. 42, marg. *2 Cor. 5.* Bunyan quotes from v. 19.

p. 43, marg. *1 John 5. 11.* 'And his is the record, that God hath given to us eternal life, and this life is in his Son.'

p. 44, marg. *2 Cor. 5. 21.* 'For he hath made him to be sin for us, who knew no sin: that we might be made the righteousness of God in him.'

p. 44, marg. *Gal. 3. 13.* 'Christ hath redeemed us from the curse of the law, being made a curse for us: for it is written, Cursed is every one that hangeth on a tree.'

p. 46, l. 8. *Pen*: The Quaker William Penn. See p. 397 note to p. 127 l. 11 below.

p. 47, marg. *Heb. 12.* Bunyan quotes from v. 10.

p. 47, marg. *Isaiah 53.* Bunyan combines part of v. 6 with portions of the additional references cited from 1 Peter and Hebrews.

p. 50, marg. *2 Pet. 1.* See v. 4.

p. 51, l. 15. *Rom. 4*. Bunyan quotes v. 5.

p. 51, l. 22. *Bucklers*: round shields. Cf. 2 Chron. 23: 9.

p. 51, l. 37. *Cherubines*: cf. Gen. 3: 24, Ezek. 1: 10.

p. 52, l. 28. *the Enduing Men with inward Real Righteousness*: the endowing or bestowing of real righteousness upon men. See *O.E.D.*

p. 54, marg. *Iohn 14*. See vv. 8–10.

p. 54, marg. *Mat. 5*. See v. 8.

p. 55, marg. *Rom. 6*. See v. 23.

p. 56, marg. *Isa. 53*. See v. 8.

p. 56, marg. *Heb. 7*. Bunyan quotes from v. 26.

p. 61, marg. *Rom. 10*. See v. 17.

p. 61, marg. *Iohn 1*. Bunyan quotes from v. 17.

p. 62, l. 22. *Loyalty to the Magistrate*: see above pp. xviii–xix, 153.

p. 63, l. 7. *Mat. 21. Mark 11*. See vv. 18–22 in Matt. and 12–14 in Mark.

p. 68, l. 16. *Heathen Philosopher*: cf. Oxford Bunyan, i. 345, and p. 406, note to p. 300 ll. 9–10 below.

p. 68, l. 22. *Root, and Branches*. Cf. Mal. 4: 1.

p. 69, ll. 4–5. *the Post . . . his Wall*: cf. Ezek. 43: 8.

p. 69, l. 5. *I came*: cf. Matt. 9: 13.

p. 70, marg. *Rom. 2*. See vv. 25–9.

p. 70, l. 6. *Circumcised inwardly*: cf. Bunyan's arguments concerning spiritual baptism in the open membership controversy, above.

p. 70, l. 31. *Phil. 3*. Bunyan quotes from v. 9.

p. 72, l. 10. *John 6*. See vv. 51–8.

p. 73, marg. *Rom. 8*. Bunyan quotes from v. 17.

p. 73, l. 5. *Rom. 5*. Bunyan quotes from v. 2.

p. 74, l. 3. *John Smith*: John Smith (1618–52) was a fellow of Queen's College, Cambridge and one of the Cambridge Platonists. Fowler's reference is on p. 131.

p. 77, l. 29. *Spider stradleth over the Wasp*: The phrase seems to be proverbial but is not to be found in Tilley or *O.D.E.P.* However, for a discussion of Bunyan's use of the emblem of the spider see Lynn Veach Sadler, *John Bunyan* (Boston, 1979], pp. 124–9.

p. 77, l. 37. *fling Heaven Gates off the Hinges*: The phrase has a proverbial ring to it but is not recorded in Tilley or *O.D.E.P.* Cf. Gen. 28: 17, 'And he [Jacob] was afraid, and said, How dreadful is this place! this is none other but the house of God, and this is the gate of heaven.'

p. 81, l. 17. *Baptism with Water, and the Lord's Supper*: cf. Bunyan's arguments in the open membership controversy, above.

p. 82, l. 19. *Your large Transcript of other mens sayings*: Bunyan claimed he did not make use of 'other men's lines', but in fact he did, of course. See *G.A.*, para. 285, p. 87 (quoted), and Oxford Bunyan, i. xvi.

p. 82, l. 23. *Rigaltias*: Nicolas Rigault (1577–1654) edited Tertullian and assisted in the editing and publication of the French statesman and historian Jacques-Auguste de Thou's (1553–1617) *History of His Time*. Fowler's reference is on p. 181.

p. 82, ll. 29–30. *Sir Johns*: priests; see *O.E.D.*, 'John'.

p. 82, ll. 39–40. *Blood of the Damned will fall upon your head*: This is possibly proverbial but does not appear in Tilly or *O.D.E.P.*

p. 83, l. 2. *Unstable Weathercock Spirit*: see Introduction, pp. xxi, xxiii.

p. 83, l. 16. *Plaister*: (plaster) medicine spread on a cloth or the like for external application to the body.

p. 84, l. 39. *Rom. 11.* Bunyan quotes v. 6.

p. 86, marg. *Rom. 8.* See vv. 38–9.

p. 86, marg. *Heb. 7.* See v. 2.

p. 89, marg. *1 Iohn 3.* See v. 6.

p. 90, l. 23. *Rom. 3.* See v. 25.

p. 92, marg. *Rom. 14.* See v. 23.

p. 95, l. 14. *the Head of your Leviathan*: cf. Ps. 74: 14.

p. 101, ll. 10–11. *hop from Presbiterianism, to a Prelatical Mode*: see above, p. xxi.

p. 103, ll. 12–13. *so stoutly diggle together*: 'Diggle' does not appear in *O.E.D.*, Tilley, or *O.D.E.P.* Bunyan may have intended 'dingle' or 'dinnle', meaning to make a noise that thrills and causes vibration, or to vibrate from such a noise. See *O.E.D.*

p. 103, l. 36. *Emblem*: For Bunyan's use of emblems, see Roger Sharrock, 'Bunyan and the English Emblem Writers', *Review of English Studies*, 21 (1945), 105–16. See also Oxford Bunyan, iii. 138, vi. 183–269, viii. 156.

p. 104, l. 19. *false Prophets*: cf. 2 Pet. 2: 1.

p. 106, l. 18. *Pestiferous*. deadly, causing plague.

p. 108, l. 15. *Emblems*: See p. 396, note for p. 103, l. 36, above.

p. 113, l. 13. *Liquorish*: in text 'Lignorish'. Lignorish does not appear in *O.E.D.*, Bunyan may have written 'liquorish', a form of 'lickerish' meaning fond of delicious fare, greedy, lecherous, lustful. See *O.E.D.* Cf. 'A lickerish tongue a lickerish tail' (Tilley, T395).

p. 114, ll. 27–28. *Baptism, and the Lord's Supper*: cf. Bunyan's arguments concerning the nature of the ordinances in the open membership controversy.

p. 115, marg. *Rom. 7*. See v. 4.

p. 116, l. 21. *Second Table*: the last six of the Ten Commandments. See J. Sears McGee, *The Godly Man in Puritan England* (New Haven, 1976), pp. ix–x, ch. 3.

p. 121, ll. 1–2. *Papistical Quakerism*: Because of their emphasis upon the Light within effecting good works and actual rather than imputed righteousness, the Quakers were sometimes accused of being crypto-Catholics. See William Penn's *Reason Against Railing* (1673), p. 7, and Oxford Bunyan, i. xix.

p. 121, marg. *Rom. 16*. See v. 26.

p. 123, l. 34. *Articles of the Church of England*: The three articles are 10, 11, and 13, the latter two of which Bunyan renders in a slightly abbreviated form. Article 11 ends 'and very full of comfort, as more largely is expressed in the Homily of Justification'. Article 13 reads 'Works done before the grace of Christ, and the inspiration of his Spirit, are not pleasant to God, forasmuch as they spring not of faith in Jesus Christ, neither do they make men meet to receive grace, or (as the School-authors say) deserve grace of congruity: yea, rather for that they are not done as God hath willed and commanded them to be done, we doubt not but they have the nature of sin.' *Articles Agreed Upon* (1669), B4.

p. 125, ll. 1–2. *Campion the Jesuite*: Edmund Campion (1540–81), born in London and educated at St John's, Oxford, was one of the first to take part in the Jesuits' English mission and to suffer martyrdom for his belief. Imprisoned in the Tower, he engaged in disputations or conferences with several divines, including one encounter on 27 Sept. 1581 with William Charke (fl. 1580), former fellow of Peterhouse, Cambridge and John Walker (d. 1588), prebendary of St Paul's cathedral. A report of the dispute by John Field was published along with others in Alexander Nowell and William Day, *A true report of the Disputation or rather private Conference had in the Tower of London, with Ed. Campion Jesuite* (1583). Those of Campion's statements to which Bunyan refers are in the report of the Charke–Walker dispute, sigs. Dd. i.[r], Dd. iiii.[r], Cc. i.[r], Dd. i.[v], Dd. iii.[v], Cc. ii.[r], Ff. iii.[r]. Of course Bunyan may have taken them from some secondary source. For Campion, Charke, Walker, Nowell, and Day, see *D.N.B.* s.vv.

p. 127, l. 11. *William Pen the Quaker*: William Penn's *The Sandy Foundation Shaken* (1668) challenged the Calvinistic view of justification and the Anselmian theory of the atonement which Bunyan accepted. Like other Quakers, Penn stressed the importance of actual experienced righteousness. Bunyan took some liberties in 'quoting' Penn's statements as he did with those of the Thirty-Nine Articles and Edmund Campion, but in general his representation of all three was not distorted. See Oxford Bunyan, i. xvi–xxx.

NOTES TO *A CONFESSION OF MY FAITH, AND A REASON OF MY PRACTICE*

p. 135, l. 7. *1 Pet. 4. 12*. 'Beloved, think it not strange concerning the fiery trial which is to try you, as though some strange thing happened unto you.'

p. 135, l. 7. *1 Joh. 3. 13*. 'Marvel not, my brethren, if the world hate you.'

p. 137, l. 1. *I believe, that there is but one, onely true God*. See Richard L. Greaves, *John Bunyan* (Studies in Reformation Theology 2, Abingdon, 1969), ch. 1.

p. 143, l. 16. *How Christ is made ours*: See Greaves, *John Bunyan*, ch. 1.

p. 145, l. 24. *Of Election*: See Greaves, *John Bunyan*, ch. 2.

p. 146, l. 4. *works in us foreseen*: Bunyan was an infralapsarian. See Greaves, *John Bunyan*, p. 52.

p. 146, l. 37. *and the rest were blinded*: Bunyan usually describes reprobation in terms of 'non-election'. Cf. Oxford Bunyan, ii. 201, ll. 34–5, viii. 352, l. 5., and Greaves, *John Bunyan*, pp. 56–8.

p. 147, l. 23. *Of Calling*: See Greaves, *John Bunyan*, ch. 2.

p. 152, l. 1. *Of the Scriptures*: See Roger Sharrock, *John Bunyan* (1968), pp. 17–18, 64–65; Oxford Bunyan i. xvi–xxx.

p. 153, l. 14. *Of Magistracy*: See Tindall, pp. 135–43; Lynn Veach Sadler, *John Bunyan*, pp. 84–5; above, pp. xviii–xix.

p. 154, l. 32. *Runnagate*: (runagate) fugitive, runaway.

p. 162, l. 4. *Quest*. Bunyan also uses such a catechetical device on other occasions. See e.g. Oxford Bunyan, i. 101–11, 309–10.

p. 167, l. 34. *concision*: cutting.

p. 168, l. 30. *perjured*: having sworn, taken an oath.

p. 169, l. 5. *chambering*: lewdness, sexual indulgence.

p. 172, l. 33. *streightly*: straightly, directly.

p. 174, ll. 27–28. *company of Angels*: See Heb. 12: 22.

p. 180, l. 17. *Carnality is but the bottom*: carnality is the basis.

p. 180, l. 18. *their zeal is but a puffe*: Bunyan's reference, 1 Cor. 4: 6., reads 'And these things, brethren, I have in a figure transferred to myself and to Apollos for your sakes; that ye might learn in us not to think of men above that which is written, that no one of you be puffed up for one against another.'

p. 182, l. 36. *janglings*: quarrels.

p. 183, l. 12. *groundly*: thoroughly, profoundly.

p. 183, ll. 12–13. *iniquity lyes hid in the skirts*: cf. Jer. 13: 22, 'And if thou say in thine heart, Wherefore come these things upon me? For the greatness of thine iniquity are thy skirts discovered, and thy heels made bare.' The saying does not appear in Tilley or *O.D.E.P.*

p. 183, l. 23. *without a ground*: without a basis.

p. 183, l. 30. *pisseth against the Wall*: cf. 'He has pissed All he has against the wall.' (Tilley, A181.)

p. 185, ll. 31–32. *you receive not your Horse nor your Hog to your Table*: This has a proverbial ring but does not appear in Tilley or *O.D.E.P.*

NOTES TO *DIFFERENCES IN JUDGMENT ABOUT WATER-BAPTISM, NO BAR TO COMMUNION*

p. 193, l. 22. *Mr. Kiffin*: William Kiffin. See above, pp. xxx–xxxi.

p. 193, ll. 26–27. *Mr. Henry Jesse*: See above, p. xxvii.

p. 195, l. 9. *rank and abilities*: Here and elsewhere Bunyan calls attention to his low rank in society. Cf. Oxford Bunyan, i. xxxviii–xli.

p. 195, ll. 24–25. *He that despiseth . . . than a lyar.* Bunyan combines portions of Prov. 14: 31 or 17: 5 and Prov. 19: 22.

p. 196, marg. *Psal. 1. 1, 2.* 'Blessed is the man that walketh not in the counsel of the ungodly, nor standeth in the way of sinners, nor sitteth in the seat of the scornful. But his delight is in the law of the Lord; and in his law doth he meditate day and night.'

p. 196, marg. *Jam. 3. 17.* 'But the wisdom that is from above is first pure, then peaceable, gentle, and easy to be intreated, full of mercy and good fruits, without partiality, and without hypocrisy.'

p. 196, marg. *Luke 12. 1, 2, 3, 4.* 'In the mean time, when there were gathered together an innumerable multitude of people, insomuch that they trode one upon another, he began to say unto his disciples first of all, Beware ye of the leaven of the Pharisees, which is hypocrisy. For there is nothing covered that shall not be revealed, neither hid, that shall not be known. Therefore whatsoever ye have spoken in darkness shall be heard in the light; and that which ye have spoken in the ear in closets shall be proclaimed upon the housetops. And I say unto you my friends, Be not afraid of them that kill the body, and after that have no more that they can do.'

p. 197, ll. 7–8. *those, of whom now they begin to be ashamed*: Possibly a reference to John Child. See above, p. xxxii.

p. 198, ll. 15–16. *Mr. D. in . . . the Meeting in Lothbury*: By this time Thomas Lamb's congregation at Lothbury had long since been dissolved and he had conformed to the Church of England (see *B.D.B.R.*, s.v., p. 405 note to p. 288 l. 4 below). However, a Nonconformist meeting was reported at Lothbury in November 1671 (*Calendar of State Papers, Domestic*, Jan.–Nov. 1671, p. 569). Mr. D. may have been Henry Danvers, John Denne, or Daniel Dyke (*B.D.B.R.*, s.vv.). Henry Denne had died in 1661.

p. 198, l. 16. *Rom. 6. 1, 2.* 'What shall we say then? Shall we continue in sin, that grace may abound? God forbid. How shall we that are dead to sin, Live any longer therein?'

p. 198, l. 17. *my much esteemed Friend Mr. D. A.* There is no one with these initials in the *Minutes*, or among Bunyan's known ministerial associates (see the first section of the Introduction, above), or in Charles E. Surman's 'Directory of Congregational Biography' card file at Dr Williams's Library. Nor is there an appropriate person to be found in *B.D.B.R.*, Wing, Plomer, or George Lyon Turner's *Original Records of Early Nonconformity* (1911–14). However, in 1659, Bunyan was reportedly using as a religious meeting place the barn of Daniel Angier of Toft, Cambridgeshire and was being entertained in his home (Thomas Smith, *The Quaker Disarm'd* [1659], B4ʳ). See also Brown, pp. 114–15, and further on Angier (Aungier) and Toft see Margaret Spufford, *Contrasting Communities: Engish Villages in the Sixteenth and Seventeenth Centuries* (1975).

p. 199, marg. *1 King. 3*. Bunyan's reference is to vv. 16–28.

p. 200, l. 4. *descant*: comment at great length.

p. 201, l. 8. *Ten Commandments*: cf. Bunyan's arguments concerning the seventh day Sabbath, above.

p. 202, l. 29. *discapacitates*: orig. 'discapaciates'. Bunyan probably intends discapacitates (incapacitates). See 'capacitates', p. 200, l. 17., and *O.E.D.*

p. 203, l. 18. *Churle*: rude or surly person.

p. 204, l. 17. *stickle*: argue insistently, haggle.

p. 204, marg. *Joh. 17. 14*. 'I have given them thy word; and the world hath hated them, because they are not of the world, even as I am not of the world.'

p. 206, l. 13. *John of Leyden*: John Beukels of Leyden (d. 1536) was 'King of Munster' during part of the radical religious revolution in that city 1533–5.

p. 206, l. 31. *Preaching*: For Bunyan's style of preaching see Tindall, ch. 8.

p. 207, ll. 26–27. *1 Cor. 1. 14, 15, 16*. 'I thank God that I baptized none of you, but Crispus and Gaius; lest any should say that I had baptized in mine own name. And I baptized also the household of Stephanas: besides, I know not whether I baptized any other.'

p. 207, l. 27. *Rom. 6. 3*. 'Know ye not, that so many of us as were baptized into Jesus Christ were baptized into his death?'

p. 207, l. 27. *Gal. 3. 27*. 'For as many of you as have been baptized into Christ have put on Christ.'

p. 208, marg. *1 Cor. 1*. See v. 13.

p. 211, l. 7. *Heb. 6*. See vv. 1–3.

p. 213, l. 9. *listed*: chose.

p. 213, l. 22. *Exod. 12*. See v. 48.

p. 215, l. 5. *Gentleman's Livery*: gentleman's distinctive attire for his servants.

p. 216, ll. 3–4. *Mint, and Annise, and Commin*: cf. Matt. 23: 23.

p. 219, marg. *Eph. 4. 31, 32*. 'Let all bitterness, and wrath, and anger, and clamour, and evil speaking be put away from you with all malice: And be ye kind one to another, tenderhearted, forgiving one another, even as God for Christ's sake hath forgiven you.'

p. 219, marg. *Phil. 2. 1, 2, 3*. 'If there be therefore any consolation in Christ, if any comfort of love, if any fellowship of the Spirit, if any bowels and mercies, Fulfil ye my joy, that ye be likeminded, having the same love, being of one accord, of one mind. Let nothing be done through strife or vainglory: but in lowliness of mind let each esteem other better than themselves.'

p. 224, marg. *Gal. 2. 11, 12, 13*. 'But when Peter was come to Antioch, I withstood him to the face, because he was to be blamed. For before that certain came from James, he did eat with the Gentiles: but when they were come, he withdrew and separated himself, fearing them which were of the circumcision. And the other Jews dissembled likewise with him: insomuch that Barnabas also was carried away with their dissimulation.

p. 225, l. 6. *1 Cor. 11. 28, 29, 30*. 'But let a man examine himself, and so let him eat of that bread, and drink of that cup. For he that eateth and drinketh unworthily, eateth and drinketh damnation to himself, not discerning the Lord's body. For this cause many are weak and sickly among you, and many sleep.'

p. 231, l. 17. *Isa. 8. 20, 21*. 'To the law and to the testimony: if they speak not according to this word, it is because there is no light in them. And they shall pass through it, hardly bestead and hungry: and it shall come to pass, that when they shall be hungry, they shall fret themselves, and curse their king and their God, and look upward.'

p. 232, l. 27. *fond*: foolish.

p. 234, ll. 25–26. *1 Cor. 5*. See v. 5.

p. 234, ll. 29–30. *Wizards and Witches*: cf. Oxford Bunyan, i. xxviii–xxix.

p. 238, l. 12. *essay*: try.

p. 240, l. 30. *Import*: meaning, purport, consequence. See *O.E.D.*

p. 242, marg. *Acts 15. 1, 2*. 'And certain men which came down from Judaea taught the brethren, and said, Except ye be circumcised after the manner of Moses, ye cannot be saved. When therefore Paul and Barnabas had no small dissension and disputation with them, they determined that Paul and Barnabas, and certain other of them, should go up to Jerusalem unto the apostles and elders about this question.'

p. 242, marg. *Gal. 5. 1, 2, 3, 4*. 'Stand fast therefore in the liberty wherewith Christ hath made us free, and be not entangled again with the yoke of bondage. Behold, I Paul say unto you, that if ye be circumcised, Christ shall profit you nothing. For I testify again to every man that is circumcised, that he is a debtor to do the whole law. Christ is become of no effect unto you, whosoever of you are justified by the law: ye are fallen from grace.'

p. 242, marg. *Rom. 2. 28. 29.* 'For he is not a Jew, which is one outwardly: neither is that circumcision, which is outward in the flesh: But he is a Jew, which is one inwardly; and circumcision is that of the heart, in the spirit, and not in the letter; whose praise is not of men, but of God.'

p. 242, marg. *Phil. 3. 3.* 'For we are the circumcision, which worship God in the spirit, and rejoice in Christ Jesus, and have no confidence in the flesh.'

p. 244, l. 36. *Acts 11. 19.* 'Now they which were scattered abroad upon the persecution that arose about Stephen travelled as far as Phenice, and Cyprus, and Antioch, preaching the word to none but unto the Jews only.'

p. 246, marg. *Eph. 1. 7, 8, 11.* 'In whom we have redemption through his blood, the forgiveness of sins, according to the riches of his grace: Wherein he hath abounded toward us in all wisdom and prudence.' 'In whom also we have obtained an inheritance, being predestined according to the purpose of him who worketh all things after the counsel of his own will.'

p. 249, l. 27. *like Quakers, stand with their Hats on their heads*: Quakers refused to show respect to their social superiors by removing their hats. See Oxford Bunyan, i. xx.

p. 249, marg. *Rom. 16. 17, 18.* 'Now I beseech you, brethren, mark them which cause divisions and offences contrary to the doctrine which ye have learned: and avoid them. For they that are such serve not our Lord Jesus Christ, but their own belly: and by good words and fair speeches deceive the hearts of the simple.'

p. 254, ll. 19–20. *They hold up Jewish observations*: This argument is especially notable since Jessey adopted the seventh day Sabbath. See above, p. xlviii, n. 1.

p. 258, l. 5. *corrival*: rival; see *O.E.D.*

p. 260, l. 38. *See Ainsworth*: Henry Ainsworth (1571–1622 or 1623), leader of a separatist congregation in Amsterdam, wrote annotations on several Old Testament books which were published in various combinations and editions (*D.N.B.*, s.v.). For Jessey's reference see *Annotations Upon the Seconde Booke of Moses, Called Exodus* in *Annotations Upon the Five Bookes of Moses, the Booke of the Psalmes, and the Song of Songs, or, Canticles* (1639), ii. 115–16.

NOTES TO *PEACEABLE PRINCIPLES AND TRUE*

p. 270, l. 23. *put case*: suppose, propose a hypothetical instance; see *O.E.D.*, 'case'.

p. 270, l. 26. *'Tis an ill Bird that bewrays his own Nest*. Cf. 'Tis a foul Bird that defiles his own nest.' (Tilley, B377.) *bewrays*: betrays.

p. 272, l. 6. *Dr. Owen*: John Owen; see, above, pp. xix–xx, xxxiii.

p. 272, l. 12. *Armour-bearer*: cf. 1 Sam. 16: 21.

p. 273, l. 6. *Mr. Danvers*: Henry Danvers; see above, p. xxxiv.

p. 273, l. 9. *Mr Denne*: John Denne; see above, p. xxx.

p. 274, marg. *Act. 8. 37 & 19. 17. & 16. 33*. 'And Philip said [to the Ethiopian], If thou believest with all thine heart, thou mayest. And he answered and said, I believe that Jesus Christ is the Son of God.' 'And this [miracle] was known to all the Jews and Greeks also dwelling at Ephesus: and fear fell on them all and the name of the Lord Jesus was magnified.' 'And he [the Philippian jailor] took them the same hour of the night, and washed their stripes; and was baptized, he and all his, straightway.'

p. 276, marg. *Gen. 3*. See v. 6.

p. 276, marg. *Mat. 7. 17*. 'Even so every good tree bringeth forth good fruit; but a corrupt tree bringeth forth evil fruit.' Cf. Bunyan's *The Barren Fig-Tree*, Oxford Bunyan, v.

p. 276, marg. *Luke 6. 43. 44*. 'For a good tree bringeth not forth corrupt fruit; neither doth a corrupt tree bring forth good fruit. For every tree is known by his own fruit. For of thorns men do not gather figs, nor of a bramble bush gather they grapes.' See preceding note.

p. 277, l. 4. *without the Lids of the Bible*: outside the covers of the Bible. See *O.E.D.*, 'lid'.

p. 277, l. 10. *Eph. 4*. See v. 5.

p. 277, l. 10. *1 Cor. 12*. See v. 13.

p. 277, marg. *Gen. 17*. See vv. 11–12.

p. 277, marg. *Ex. 12*. See v. 48.

p. 278, marg. *Josh. 5. Ch. 12*. See 5: 1–7.

p. 279, l. 8. *Rev. 12*. See vv. 5–6.

p. 279, marg. *Mat. 12. 3, 4*. 'But he said unto them, Have ye not read what

David did, when he was an hungred, and they that were with him; How he entered'into the house of God, and did eat the shewbread, which was not for him to eat, neither for them which were with him, but only for the priests?'

p. 282, ll. 28–29. *Ephraim-like are joyned to an Idol*: cf. Hos. 4: 17.

p. 283, l. 9. *Garland*: crown awarded to the victor.

p. 284, l. 18. *Mr. Baxter*: Richard Baxter; see above, p. xxxiv n. 51.

p. 285, marg. *Exod. 2*. See vv. 13–14.

p. 285, marg. *Acts 7*. See vv. 25–8.

p. 286, l. 22. *Mr. Thomas Paul*: See above, pp. xxx–xxxi.

p. 287, marg. *Ro. 15*. See v. 7.

p. 288, l. 4. *Mr. Lamb*: The reference is to Thomas Lamb's *Truth Prevailing* (1655). Lamb (d. 1686) was a General Baptist leader of a congregation at Lothbury (*B.D.B.R.*, s.v.). But by 1659 he had changed his religious views, his congregation was soon dissolved, and he subsequently joined with the Church of England. Disputes over paedobaptism, which in the 1650's involved Lamb, Richard Baxter, John Tombes (*D.N.B.*, s.v.), Henry Denne, and numerous others, erupted again in the 1670s, and Danvers (p. 53) employed Lamb's contribution from the earlier period in spite of his defection. Among the sections of Lamb's book most pertinent to Bunyan's arguments are pp. 32–5, 49–51, and 57–60.

p. 288, l. 19. *Mr. Dan*: perhaps Henry Danvers. See p. 404 above, note on: p. 273 , l. 6.

NOTES TO *A CASE OF CONSCIENCE RESOLVED*

p. 296, ll. 6–7. *run the Gantlet*: run between two rows of men (Gantlope) who strike the runner as punishment. See *O.E.D.*

p. 296, l. 16. *Mr. K*. Possibly William Kiffin; see above, pp. xxx–xxxvi, xlii–xliv.

p. 296, l. 21. *Lists*: wishes, desires, choices.

p. 297, l. 3. *meddling*: See above, p. liv.

p. 297, ll. 29–30. *S.B. S.F.* Bunyan's statement (p. 300) that 'his Women in their Letter told me that Mr. K. expects my Answer,' suggests that S.F. and S.B. were not members of Bunyan's congregation. It should be noted, however, that Sister Fenn (d. 9. May 1684), widow of the church elder Samuel Fenn (d. 12 Nov. 1681), is mentioned in the *Minutes* as are Susan Bromwell (d. 22 Dec. 1685) and Sarah Bishop. See *Minutes*, s.vv., and Oxford Bunyan, i. xxiv–xxvii.

p. 300, ll. 9–10. *I neither know the Mode nor Figure of a Sylogism*: Bunyan's perception of the enmity between grace and learning is further illustrated in his preface to *The Holy City*, Oxford Bunyan, iii. 69–73. The perception, common among mechanick preachers, included a disdain for vain heathenish philosophy. See p. 395 above, note to p. 68 l. 16; Oxford Bunyan, i. xxxviii–xli; Tindall, pp. 79–90.

p. 304, ll. 11–12. *Acts 12. 12.* 'And when he [Peter] had considered the thing, he came to the house of Mary the mother of John, whose surname was Mark; where many were gathered together praying.'

p. 305, ll. 20–21. *a Ranter or a Quaker*: Bunyan recognizes the expanded role women played in these two groups. See Introduction, above; A. L. Morton, *The World of the Ranters* (1970); J. C. Davis, *Fear, Myth and History: The Ranters and the Historians* (Cambridge, 1986).

p. 307, l. 17. *1 Tim. 2. 15, 16*. Bunyan quotes vv. 13, 14. there is no v. 16.

p. 307, l. 34. *Nadab and Abihu*: cf. Num. 3: 4.

p. 310, l. 11. *Cant. 1.* See S. of S. 1: 9.

p. 313, l. 28. *Song. 6. 12.* S of S. 6: 12.

p. 315, l. 39. *popt in*: popped in.

p. 317, l. 23. *any thing to save a drowning man*: cf. 'A drowning Man will catch at a twig.' (Tilley, M92.)

p. 327, l. 21. *fond*: foolish.

NOTES TO *QUESTIONS ABOUT THE NATURE AND PERPETUITY OF THE SEVENTH-DAY-SABBATH*

p. 335, l. 12. *short Memories, and but little Time to spare*: Bunyan reveals some of the assumptions lying behind his style of preaching and writing. See Tindall, ch. 8.

p. 337, l. 22. *Rom. 2*. See v. 14.

p. 337, l. 23. *stints*: ends, limits.

p. 338, l. 18. *here the Quakers and others split themselves*: cf. Oxford Bunyan, i. 54–64, 162–76.

p. 342, l. 30. *in ward*: in custody.

p. 343, l. 7. *stinted*: limited, restricted.

p. 345, ll. 26–28. *The Seventh-day-sabbath therefore was not from Paradise . . . but . . . from Sinai*. Here Bunyan differs from Baxter and Owen. See above, p. liii.

p. 346, l. 16. *a signe and token*: cf. p. 392 above, note to p. 33 l. 18.

p. 348, l. 11. *a Figure and Pledge*: cf. note to p. 346 l. 16 above.

p. 348, ll. 13–14. *a shadow or type*: cf. note to p. 346 l. 16 above.

p. 348, l. 35. *shadowish and figurative*: cf. Bunyan's arguments concerning water baptism in the open membership controversy.

p. 249, ll. 7–8. *two Tables*: cf. p. 397 above, note to p. 116 l. 21.

p. 349, l. 10. *concreate with him*: created together.

p. 350, l. 5. *Covenant of Grace*: cf. above, pp. xxii–xxiii, and Greaves, *John Bunyan*, pp. 104–18.

p. 350, l. 37. *time must be set apart*: Here Bunyan differs from Baxter and Owen. See above, liii.

p. 355, l. 23. *a type*: cf. p. 392 above, note to p. 33 l. 18.

p. 360, l. 30. *Peter saith*: See 1 Pet. 2: 7.

p. 360, l. 40. *This is the day*: See Ps. 118: 24.

p. 361, l. 16. *another Psalm*: Ps. 16: 10.

p. 362, l. 12. *This day*: The repetition of the phrase has a homiletical ring.

p. 365, l. 34. *let*: hindrance

p. 366, l. 30. *thorough*: through.

p. 371, l. 29. *The better Day, the better Deed*: see Tilley, D60.

p. 372, l. 3. *scrupleth*: has scruples.

p. 373, l. 30. *while the Iron is hot*: cf. 'It is good to strike while the Iron is hot.' (Tilley, I94.)

p. 380, l. 3. *Luther*: Bunyan had read Martin Luther's commentary on Galatians which, except for the Bible, he preferred 'before all the books that ever I have seen, as most fit for a wounded Conscience'. (*G.A.*, para. 129–30, pp. 40–1) Passages bearing on Bunyan's reference may be found on pp. 10ᵛ (Gal. 1: 4) and 42ᵛ–43ʳ (Gal. 2: 1) in *A Commentarie of Master Doctor Martin Luther Upon the Epistle of S. Paul to the Galathians* (1635).

p. 382, l. 33. *Market-day*: See above, pp. xlv–xlvi.

p. 386, l. 29. *proceeded to Circumcision, to many Wives*: See above, p. xlviii.

p. 386, ll. 32–33. *Jewish Sacrifices must up again*: See above, p. xlviii.

p. 386, l. 38. *to put stop*: to put a stop.

p. 388, ll. 25–27. *the Jews, Christs deadliest Enemies . . . the Believers, his best Friends*: Passages referring to the Jews, 'who killed all the prophets, yea even Christ Himselfe the Sonne of God their promised Messias,' and supporting Bunyan's Jewish-Christian dichotomy (see Introduction, above) may be found in Luther's *A Commentarie of Master Doctor Martin Luther Upon the Epistle of S. Paul to the Galathians* (1635), pp. 1ᵛ (preface, quoted), 101ᵛ (Gal. 3: 2), 143ʳ (Gal. 3: 14), 176ᵛ (Gal. 3: 28). For Bunyan's use of Luther on Galatians, see p. 408, above note to p. 380 l. 3.